PRAISE FOR *BLACK APRIL*

"*Black April* illuminates the last, dark days of a doomed war, spotlighting the courageous and indomitable Vietnamese nationalist soldiers who fought on despite shortages of the most basic resources and a host of challenges to their morale. In this book, George J. Veith provides a deeper understanding of the Vietnam War as a life-or-death struggle between the Free World and Communist repression."
— Major General Tran Ba Di, ARVN 9th Division Commander,
1968–1973; Deputy Commander, IV Corps, 1973–1974;
Commander, Quang Trung Training Center, 1974–April 1975

"Veith's exhaustive account of the undoing of South Vietnam is rich in detail mined from Southern and Northern participants. Faced with a faltering American ally and a formidably armed North Vietnamese foe, the South was forced to fight what Hanoi called 'a poor man's war.' *Black April* artfully dissects that war, unmasking Hanoi's calculations while shedding new light on the courage of the South Vietnamese military. Reading Veith's gripping narrative, this reader felt like he was back in Saigon, watching the map turn red as the North Vietnamese marched south."
—Colonel (ret.) Stuart A. Herrington, author of *Peace with Honor? An American Reports on Vietnam, 1973–1975* and *Stalking the Vietcong: Inside Operation Phoenix*

"In his prodigiously researched account of the last two years of the Vietnam War, after all American troops were withdrawn, George Veith makes a unique contribution to setting the record straight. Abandoned by the United States in a shameful failure to insist that the Communist leaders in Hanoi observe the agreements they had signed, with Congress refusing to provide the military assistance promised in those agreements, the South Vietnamese armed forces fought tenaciously, in often hopeless situations, against the military juggernaut converging on Saigon in April 1975."
—Wolfgang Lehmann, Deputy Ambassador to the Republic of Vietnam, 1974–1975

"This will appeal to readers who want military details of the conclusion of the Vietnam War, as well as those who share Veith's anticommunism."
—*Publishers Weekly*

"This is an excellent study. With its significant military lessons for the present, *Black April* deserves a wide reading."
— Spencer C. Tucker, *US Naval Institute Magazine*

"George J. Veith's *Black April* fills the gaping historical void, and in extraordinary fashion. Mr. Veith has tapped deeply into previously neglected Vietnamese sources, including North Vietnamese histories, and he has interviewed commanders of numerous South Vietnamese units. In a blow-by-blow account, he presents mountains of new details that enable him to answer the principal historical questions."
—*The Wall Street Journal*

"The book is nonetheless a service to military history, for no one has produced nearly as thorough an account of these events."
— Lawrence D. Freedman, *Foreign Affairs*

"Mr. Veith has done a remarkable job, gathering a wealth of information and presenting it in a style that can only be called riveting. It will not disappoint."
—Roger Soiset

BLACK APRIL

THE FALL OF SOUTH VIETNAM
1973–1975

GEORGE J. VEITH

Encounter Books NEW YORK • LONDON

Photo used on cover, title page, and chapter openers:

North Vietnamese T-54 tank destroyed on 11 April 1975 by forces from the South Vietnamese 18th Division during the battle for Xuan Loc. South Vietnamese soldiers were given a monetary reward for destroying North Vietnamese tanks, but they had to prove it; hence the painting on the destroyed tank.

The painting on the tank's hull says:
Su Doan, 18, LK 11-4 (*18th Division, Long Khanh, 11 April*)

The painting on the front slope of the tank's hull says:
Chi Doan, 1/5 CXA, Ban Ha Ngay, 11/4/75, Chi Doi 2 – Xa Doi [32 or 52] (*1st Tank Troop/5th Squadron. Destroyed 11 April 1975. 2nd Platoon/Tank Crew [32 or 52]*)

First American edition published in 2012 by Encounter Books, an activity of Encounter for Culture and Education, Inc., a nonprofit, tax exempt corporation. Encounter Books website address: www.encounterbooks.com

Manufactured in the United States and printed on acid-free paper. The paper used in this publication meets the minimum requirements of ANSI/NISO Z39.48 1992 (R 1997) (*Permanence of Paper*).

First paperback edition published in 2013.
Paperback edition ISBN: 978-1-59403-704-7

THE LIBRARY OF CONGRESS HAS CATALOGUED THE HARDCOVER EDITION AS FOLLOWS:
Veith, George J., 1957–
Black April: the fall of South Vietnam, 1973–1975/by George J. Veith.
p. cm.
Includes bibliographical references and index.
ISBN-13: 978-1-59403-572-2 (hardcover: alk. paper)
ISBN-10: 1-59403-572-5 (hardcover: alk. paper) 1. Vietnam War, 1961–1975.
2. Vietnam War, 1961–1975—United States. I. Title.
DS557.7.V45 2011
959.704'3—dc22
2011005905

10 9 8 7 6 5 4 3 2 1

Dedicated to the men and women,
soldiers, sailors, airmen, and Marines,
of the Republic of Vietnam Armed Forces,
1955–1975,
who stood and fought

And to the men and women,
U.S. Mission, Vietnam,
1973–1975,
who so valiantly tried to uphold America's honor

CONTENTS

Maps   *ix*
Acknowledgments   *xi*
List of Abbreviations   *xv*
List of Persons   *xvii*
Military Forces   *xxi*
Introduction   *1*

CHAPTER 1
"The U.S. will react vigorously": Signing the Paris Peace Accords   17

CHAPTER 2
"South Vietnam will have both peace and war":
The Collapse of the Accords   35

CHAPTER 3
"Enough to make the angels weep": Trading Blood for Ammunition   53

CHAPTER 4
"A rainy season like no other": The War Resumes   71

CHAPTER 5
"Even the gods weep for Phuoc Long": The Beginning of the End   91

CHAPTER 6
"How can the free world abandon us?":
Preparing for the Strategic Blow   115

CHAPTER 7
"Goodbye for now, Ban Me Thuot":
Beginning the "Great Spring Offensive"   141

CHAPTER 8
"Light at the top, heavy at the bottom":
Decisions That Destroyed a Nation   171

CHAPTER 9
"The Road of Blood and Tears": The Retreat from the Highlands   203

CHAPTER 10
"Chaos and disintegration": Surrounding Saigon   235

CHAPTER 11
"How could I abandon this rocky soil?": Fighting to Save Hue   263

CHAPTER 12
"The hours of hell": The Collapse of I Corps   299

CHAPTER 13
"The sea is our only hope": The Battle for the Coastal Cities   331

CHAPTER 14
"Lightning speed, daring, surprise, certain victory":
PAVN Surrounds Saigon   357

CHAPTER 15
"Hold fast the remaining land": The South Vietnamese Fight Back   383

CHAPTER 16
"No matter what happens, do not stop your attack":
Capturing Phan Rang   415

CHAPTER 17
"I will knock them down!": ARVN Holds at Xuan Loc   435

CHAPTER 18
"Do not come home until victory is won": The Fall of Saigon   463

Notes   501
Selected Bibliography   541
Index   557

MAPS

South Vietnam: Administrative Divisions and Military Regions,
    June 1967   xxvi

Communist Military Fronts in South Vietnam, 1975   16

The Battle for Phuoc Long, 13 December 1974–6 March 1975   105

PAVN Attacks and ARVN Reactions in II Corps, 5–11 March 1975   149

The Battle for Ban Me Thuot, 10–16 March 1975   157

PAVN Capture of II Corps, 12 March–3 April 1975   187

PAVN B-2 Front Attacks in III Corps, 10–31 March 1975   245

Initial PAVN Attack in I Corps, 6–12 March 1975   267

PAVN Attacks South of Hue, 8–25 March 1975   293

PAVN Captures Hue, 20–26 March 1975   301

The Fall of I Corps, 25–29 March 1975   321

The Battle for Phan Rang, 1–16 April 1975   385

The Battle for Xuan Loc, 9–22 April   439

The Fall of Saigon, 26–30 April 1975   465

ACKNOWLEDGMENTS

For me, writing a book while raising a family is a Faustian bargain. Every minute one spends toiling over prose is a minute stolen from one's wife and children. Thus, my deepest appreciation goes to my remarkably tolerant wife, Gina, and to our beautiful children, Analiese, Austin, Allegra, and Adia. For them, piles of documents and long hours spent by me staring at a computer are now synonymous with "Daddy's working on his book." I am also indebted to my parents, George C. and Joan A. Veith, who patiently supported my seemingly endless quest to complete this work.

The inspiration and hard work of two great Americans made this book possible. The first is Merle L. Pribbenow, whose skill at translating Vietnamese texts gave *Black April* its documentary heart. When I struggled with the intricacies of the North and South Vietnamese governments' decision-making, his insight, formed by more than thirty years of close interaction with Vietnam and its people, instantly cut through my confusion. His incredible knowledge of the war and boundless generosity in translating so many publications and documents enabled me to explore both sides' policies and motivations, which until now have remained hidden behind barriers of language and access. To Merle, I owe undying gratitude, not only for his knowledge, but also for his kindness and steady hand.

The other American to whom I am deeply beholden is Colonel William Le Gro, who served as Intelligence Chief, Defense Attaché Office, Saigon. Early on, he encouraged me to write the full story of the final years of the war. He poignantly insisted that the truth regarding the fall of South Vietnam remained untold, despite his own outstanding contribution to the field in *Vietnam from Cease-Fire to Capitulation*. His encyclopedic memory and collection of critical primary documents from that time provided the initial basis for my research, and his relentless efforts to improve my recounting of the last days proved crucial.

Among the many South Vietnamese to whom I am extremely grateful, Major General Le Minh Dao, the last commander of the 18th Division, stands foremost. Merle and I had just finished an article on the 18th Division's heroic struggle in April 1975 to defend Xuan Loc, a town about forty miles northeast of Saigon. After Dao read our account of the terrible fighting at Xuan Loc, he begged me to expand the article into a full-length book on the fall of his country. Too many Americans, he said, falsely viewed the Army of the Republic of Vietnam (ARVN) as weak, cowardly, and corrupt. He insisted it was past time to balance the ledger by also depicting South Vietnamese victories and successes, particularly in the last two years, long after most of the Americans had left.

Over time, many other former officers of the Republic of Vietnam Armed Forces (RVNAF) also opened their hearts to me, a process that for them was often sorrowful and always painful. I am particularly grateful to General Cao Van Vien (deceased); Lieutenant Generals Nguyen Van Toan (deceased) and Lam Quang Thi; Major General Nguyen Duy Hinh; Brigadier Generals Tran Van Nhut, Tran Quang Khoi, and Pham Duy Tat; Navy Captain Kiem Do; Air Force Colonel Le Van Thao; Marine Colonel Nguyen Thanh Tri; and many regimental and battalion commanders.

Two other gentlemen provided extraordinary, indeed vital, assistance. To Nguyen Ky Phong, author and historian, goes a tremendous sense of gratitude. If there was a typo, Phong would find it; if I garbled a Vietnamese name, he would correct it. To Doan Huu Dinh, profound thanks for helping me navigate the Vietnamese community.

I am also indebted to the superb staff at the National Archives and Records Administration (NARA), including archivist Richard Boylan, David A. Langbart in the Textual Archives Services Division, Jeffery Hartley in NARA's library, and Don McIlwain in Declassification, all of whom cheerfully processed my constant demands. Others who significantly shaped the book through editing, discovering documents, or discussing themes with me include Major General John Murray (deceased), Dr. Christopher Goscha, Dr. Stuart Rochester (deceased), Dr. Martin Loicano, Dr. Larry Engelmann, Don Price, and Dale Andrade. I am also grateful to Steve Sherman for his map software. Lastly, hearty thanks go to Dr. Henry Kissinger and to Roger Kimball at Encounter Books for their deep interest in this project.

Lastly, I cannot adequately thank all the Vietnamese who befriended me and fed me wonderful dishes while telling me their stories. As one Vietnamese friend remarked, I had now become "Vietnamese in the stomach." Whether that was true or not, understanding their long-neglected perspective on the war was a journey into a different dimension, one that I have tried to portray as accurately as possible. Only they can truly judge my efforts.

George J. Veith
13 July 2011

LIST OF ABBREVIATIONS

AAA—Anti-Aircraft Artillery
ARVN—Army of the Republic of Vietnam
CIA—Central Intelligence Agency
COSVN—Central Office for South Vietnam
DAO—Defense Attaché Office
DAV—Defense Assistance Vietnam
DIA—Defense Intelligence Agency
DMZ—Demilitarized Zone
DRV—Democratic Republic of Vietnam (North Vietnam)
FY—Fiscal Year
GVN—Government of Vietnam (South Vietnam)
JGS—Joint General Staff
LST—Landing Ship, Tank
MISTA—Monthly Intelligence Survey and Threat Analysis
MR—Military Region
MSC—Military Sealift Command
NCNRC—National Council of National Reconciliation and Concord
NIE—National Intelligence Estimate
NLF—National Liberation Front
NSC—National Security Council
NSSM—National Security Study Memorandum
PACM—People's Anti-Corruption Movement
PAVN—People's Army of Vietnam
PF—Popular Forces
PRG—Provisional Revolutionary Government
RF—Regional Forces

RVNAF—Republic of Vietnam Armed Forces (Army, Navy, Air Force, Marines)

SIGINT—Signals Intelligence

SNIE—Special National Intelligence Estimate

TF—Task Force

USA—U.S. Army

VNAF—Vietnamese Air Force (South Vietnam)

VNN—Vietnamese Navy (South Vietnam)

WSAG—Washington Special Actions Group

LIST OF PERSONS

Bui Diem, former South Vietnamese Ambassador to the United States

Cao Van Vien, General, ARVN; Chief, Joint General Staff

Dang Van Quang, Lieutenant General, ARVN; Military Assistant to President Thieu

Dang Vu Hiep, Senior Colonel, PAVN; Political Officer, B-3 Front

Dong Van Khuyen, Lieutenant General, ARVN; Chief of Staff, Joint General Staff

Duong Van Minh (Big Minh), retired General, ARVN; last President of South Vietnam

Ford, Gerald, Vice President, later President, of the United States

Hoang Cam, Major General, PAVN; Commander 4th Corps

Hoang Dan, Major General, PAVN; Deputy Commander 2nd Corps

Hoang Minh Thao, Lieutenant General, PAVN; commander of Ban Me Thuot campaign

Hoang Van Thai, Lieutenant General, PAVN; Deputy Chief of Staff

Kissinger, Henry, U.S. Assistant for National Security Affairs, and later Secretary of State

Lam Quang Thi, Lieutenant General, ARVN; Commander I Corps Forward

Le Duan, General Secretary of the Vietnamese Communist Party

Le Duc Anh, Senior Colonel, later Lieutenant General, PAVN; Deputy Commander B-2 Front

Le Duc Tho, Politburo member and head of the North Vietnamese delegation to the Paris Peace Talks

Le Gro, William, Colonel, USA; Intelligence Chief, Defense Attaché Office

Lehmann, Wolfgang, Deputy U.S. Ambassador to South Vietnam

Le Khac Ly, Colonel, ARVN; Chief of Staff II Corps

Le Minh Dao, Brigadier General, later Major General, ARVN; Commander 18th Division

Le Ngoc Hien, Major General, PAVN; Chief of Operations, General Staff

Le Trong Tan, Lieutenant General, PAVN; Deputy Chief of Staff

Le Van Thao, Colonel, VNAF; Commander 92nd Air Wing

Martin, Graham, U.S. Ambassador to South Vietnam

Murray, John, Major General, USA; Commander DAO, April 1973–August 1974

Ngo Quang Truong, Lieutenant General, ARVN; Commander I Corps

Nguyen Cao Ky, former Vice President, Republic of Vietnam

Nguyen Duy Hinh, Brigadier General, later Major General, ARVN; Commander 3rd Division

Nguyen Huu An, Senior Colonel, later Major General, PAVN; Commander 2nd Corps

Nguyen Thanh Tri, Colonel, ARVN; Deputy Commander Marine Division

Nguyen Thu Luong, Colonel, ARVN; Commander 2nd Airborne Brigade

Nguyen Trong Luat, Colonel, ARVN; Darlac Province Chief

Nguyen Van Dong, Colonel, ARVN; Commander 2nd Armor Brigade

Nguyen Van Thieu, President of the Republic of Vietnam (South Vietnam)

Nguyen Van Toan, Lieutenant General, ARVN; Commander III Corps

Nguyen Vinh Nghi, Lieutenant General, ARVN; Commander IV Corps

Nguyen Tu, journalist for Saigon-based newspaper *Chinh Luan*

Nixon, Richard, President of the United States

Pham Dinh Niem, Brigadier General, later Major General, ARVN; Commander 22nd Division

Pham Duy Tat, Colonel, later Brigadier General, ARVN; Commander Rangers in II Corps

Pham Hung, head of COSVN

Pham Ngoc Sang, Brigadier General, VNAF; Commander 6th Air Division

Pham Van Dong, Prime Minister of North Vietnam

Phan Van Huan, Colonel, ARVN; Commander 81st Airborne Rangers

Pham Van Phu, Major General, ARVN; Commander II Corps

Polgar, Thomas, Chief of Station Saigon, U.S. Central Intelligence Agency

Smith, Homer, Major General, USA; Commander DAO, September 1974–May 1975

Stennis, John, Democratic Senator, Mississippi; Chairman, Senate Committee on Armed Services

Tran Quang Khoi, Brigadier General, ARVN; Commander 3rd Armored Cavalry Brigade

Tran Quoc Buu, head of the South Vietnamese Labor Federation

Tran Thien Khiem, Prime Minister of the Republic of Vietnam (South Vietnam)

Tran Van Huong, Vice President, later President, of the Republic of Vietnam (South Vietnam)

Tran Van Lam, Foreign Minister, South Vietnam, until July 1973; then Chairman of the Senate

Tran Van Nhut, Brigadier General, ARVN; Commander 2nd Division

Tran Van Tra, Colonel General, PAVN; Commander B-2 Front

Truong Chinh, Politburo member, North Vietnam

Van Tien Dung, General, PAVN; Commander of Communist forces in South Vietnam

Vo Nguyen Giap, General, PAVN; Defense Minister, North Vietnam

MILITARY FORCES

SOUTH VIETNAM

Each regular infantry division had three regiments, except the 1st and 22nd Divisions, which had four. Each regiment had three battalions, numbered 1st, 2nd, and 3rd. In addition, any military unit includes numerous non-combat support personnel who make up the total unit strength.

The Airborne and Marine Divisions had three brigades, and each brigade had three battalions, but the battalion numbering differed from the Army standard. The Airborne Division retained the normal brigade designations of 1st through 3rd, but the battalions were numbered 1st through 11th (however, there was no 4th or 10th Battalion). The Marine Division battalion numbering was consecutive—1st through 9th Battalions—but it was not sequential. Instead, it matched the brigade numerical designation. For example, the 147th Brigade had the 1st, 4th, and 7th Battalions assigned to it. In early 1975, both the Airborne and the Marines formed a fourth brigade The battalion designations in the fourth brigade began with the 12th for the Airborne and 14th for the Marines, but they were not numbered consecutively.

Efforts to standardize Ranger and Regional Force units were undertaken in December 1973, but by March 1975, the process had not been completed. Each Ranger Group had three battalions, but the battalions retained their original numerical designation from when they were independent entities. Regional Force groups and battalions were structurally similar to the Rangers.

The 1st, 2nd, and 3rd Armor Brigades each had two armored cavalry and one M-48 tank squadrons. The 4th Armor Brigade had only two M-113 armored-personnel-carrier squadrons.

There were six Air Force divisions, 1st through 6th. II and III Corps had two each. In II Corps, Phu Cat and Pleiku had the 2nd and 6th Air Divisions respectively, while III Corps had the 3rd Air Division at Bien Hoa and the 5th at Tan Son Nhut. Each division had three wings, and each wing had three squadrons; some had three airplane squadrons, while others had two airplane and one helicopter.

The Navy had five Coastal Zone commands. The 1st, 2nd, and 3rd Coastal Zones worked with the respective ARVN Corps commands, while the 4th and 5th Coastal Zones were in the Mekong Delta and worked with IV Corps. The Navy also had Fleet, Sea Operations, and Riverine Commands.

The numbers given in the chart that follows reflect unit full strength circa early 1975. RVNAF unit strengths changed over time, and the chart reflects the last modification.

	Battalion, or Squadron for Armor and Air Force	Regiment/ Brigade/Group, or Wing for Air Force	Division
Army (Standard)	665	3,302	14,179
1st and 22nd Divisions (Heavy)	665	3,302	17,102
Airborne	865	3,596	16,609
Marines	875	3,474	20,353
Rangers*	683	2,324	
Regional Forces	570	1,947	
Armor**	708	2,336	
Air Force***	500	2,000	8,000

The figures for the divisions are from the Defense Attaché Office's (DAO) First Quarter 1975 report. The remainder of the force-structure listing is from the DAO files at the National Archives. See RG 472, U.S Forces in Southeast Asia, 1950–1975, DAO Saigon, Summary of Table of Organization, Box 5. The author also discussed these numbers with former RVNAF officers.

At the start of the offensive in March 1975, all RVNAF units (except the Airborne, Marines, and Air Force) were badly under-strength, averaging between 80 and 83 percent of their authorized manpower. The infantry battalions within the ARVN, Ranger, and RF units were generally much worse.

Naval strengths are not listed because of the complexity of the various divisions and groups.

* Ranger Group unit strength (general reserve, converted Border Ranger, or those previously part of each corps) varied slightly. The Border Ranger groups did not have a TOW (anti-tank) section. Most groups had been equipped with a 105-mm artillery battery by March 1975, but not all. The group number listed represents a general-reserve Ranger group with both a TOW section and an artillery battery.

** Armor strengths are averages because of variances in type (equipment and structure). The numbers represent the corps-level armor brigades, not the armored cavalry squadrons assigned to a regular infantry division. The 4th Armor Brigade only had two squadrons and was around 1,700 men.

*** Air Force numbers are approximations, since assigned strengths varied depending on location and mix of units.

I Corps

1st, 2nd, and 3rd Divisions
11th, 12th, 14th, and 15th Ranger Groups
1st Armor Brigade
Air Force—1st Air Division
Navy—1st Coastal Zone

II Corps

22nd and 23rd Divisions
21st, 22nd, 23rd, 24th, and 25th Ranger Groups
2nd Armor Brigade
Air Force—2nd and 6th Air Divisions
Navy—2nd Coastal Zone

III Corps

5th, 18th, and 25th Divisions
31st, 32nd, and 33rd Ranger Groups
3rd Armored Cavalry Brigade
Air Force—3rd and 5th Air Divisions
Navy—3rd Coastal Zone

IV Corps

7th, 9th, and 21st Divisions
4th Armor Brigade
Air Force—4th Air Division
Navy—4th and 5th Coastal Zones

General Reserve

Airborne Division—assigned to I Corps
Marine Division—assigned to I Corps

4th and 6th Ranger Groups—assigned to II Corps

7th Ranger Group—assigned to III Corps

8th and 9th Ranger Groups—Reserve (formed in 1975)

81st Airborne Ranger Group—assigned to III Corps

NORTH VIETNAM

Each division had three regiments, which retained their original designations from when they were independent entities. Each regiment had three battalions, and the numbering was consecutive for the whole division, with the battalions numbered 1st through 9th.

The full strength of a PAVN battalion was close to 500. A regiment was roughly 2,400 soldiers. An infantry division was approximately 9,600. Sapper battalions were much smaller than regular infantry battalions, roughly between 150 and 200 men. Tank regiments were also much smaller, generally less than 500 men. The independent infantry regiments were similar in structure to the ones assigned to a division. The 52nd Brigade was an ad-hoc unit cobbled together from various units in the B-1 Front area.

During the 1975 offensive, unit strengths varied widely, mainly on whether the unit had recently been engaged in combat. Some units, like the 316th Division from North Vietnam, were at full strength. Others, like the 304th Division, were terribly depleted from heavy fighting. Local forces—those assigned to province or below—were badly under-strength. This list includes only main-force units (regular army).

UNITS ASSIGNED TO VARIOUS CORPS

1st Corps (part of Strategic Reserve in North Vietnam)
     308th, 312th, and 320B Divisions
     202nd Tank Brigade

2nd Corps (northern I Corps)
     304th, 324th, and 325th Divisions
     203rd Tank Brigade

3rd Corps (Central Highlands, not formed until late March 1975)
     10th, 316th, and 320th Divisions
     273rd Tank Regiment
     198th Sapper Regiment

4th Corps (assigned to B-2 Front)
    7th and 9th Divisions
Group 232 (assigned to B-2 Front)
    5th and 303rd Divisions

UNITS ASSIGNED TO VARIOUS FRONT COMMANDS

B-1 Front (along the coast of central Vietnam)
    2nd and 3rd Divisions
    52nd Brigade
    573rd Tank Regiment
B-2 Front (southern half of South Vietnam)
    MR-6—812th Regiment
    MR-7—6th Division
    MR-8—8th Division, 24th and 88th Regiments
    MR-9—4th Division
    316th Sapper Brigade
    26th Tank Regiment
    16th and 271B Infantry Regiments
B-3 Front (Central Highlands)
    25th and 95A Infantry Regiments
B-4 Front (Thua Thien province and southern portion of Quang Tri province)
    4th, 6th, and 271st Regiments
Strategic Reserve
    46th Regiment
    341st Division
    968th Division (in Laos)

SOUTH VIETNAM

**ADMINISTRATIVE DIVISIONS
AND MILITARY REGIONS**
JUNE 1967

International boundary
Province boundary
Military corps boundary
National capital
Province capital
DA LAT   Autonomous municipality

INTRODUCTION

8 A.M., 11 MARCH 1975, BAN ME THUOT

The heavily armored Soviet-built T-54 tank maneuvered warily toward the front gate of the large South Vietnamese base in the heart of Ban Me Thuot, the capital city of Darlac province in South Vietnam's Central Highlands. Bright red stars adorned each side of the dark green turret. Inside, the gunner peered through the gun sight, hunting for concealed predators. As he swung the turret and the barrel of its 100-mm gun back and forth, the sounds of the tank's rumbling engine and clanking steel treads amplified its terrifying presence. Dozens of North Vietnamese assault troops crouched twenty yards behind it, automatic rifles pointed forward, poised to seize the base. When the gunner's search revealed no foes, with a roar from its engine, the tank surged forward.

The tank's dented fenders and mud-caked body gave ample proof of its difficult journey through the deep forest to reach the city. A surprise onslaught the day before by over sixty armored vehicles and thousands of soldiers had rapidly overwhelmed Ban Me Thuot's few defenders. Now the attackers were charging the last South Vietnamese position in the city, the rear headquarters of the Army of the Republic of Vietnam's (ARVN) 23rd Division. If it fell, the city would fall. If the city fell, the Central Highlands were in great danger, as was the rest of South Vietnam. Both sides had long believed that whoever won the battle for the Central Highlands would win the war.

Hidden inside the base, South Vietnamese Colonel Nguyen Trong Luat sat atop an M-113 armored personnel carrier, watching the approaching tank. Luat was the chief of Darlac province and a veteran armor officer. Awakened early the previous morning by the North Vietnamese artillery bombardment, Luat had retreated to the 23rd Division's headquarters to prepare for a final stand. Inside the M-113, a sergeant crouched next to him, ready to destroy the approaching tank with a high-explosive shell from a 106-mm recoilless rifle mounted on the vehicle. This was a key moment in the battle. If Luat could destroy the T-54 as it entered the gate, the North Vietnamese would then have to use infantry to capture the camp, and that would take time—enough time for South Vietnamese reinforcements to arrive and possibly save the city.

As the T-54 penetrated the front gate and lumbered into full view, Luat yelled at the sergeant: "Fire!" The sergeant pulled the trigger. Click. "Misfire!" the sergeant screamed. He pulled apart the breech and discovered the problem: a broken firing pin. And he had no replacement. Luat jumped off the M-113 to rally his troops to stop the advancing enemy.

Rarely in the history of nations can one point with such precision to the beginning of a country's demise. While scholars might argue that other notable events had heralded the war's denouement, the capture of the ARVN 23rd Division headquarters completed the seizure of Ban Me Thuot, which caused the chain reaction that led directly to the fall of South Vietnam.

America's Vietnamese allies call the loss of their country Black April (*Thang Tu Den*). That phrase captured for them, in semi-poetic terms, the events that led to a modern-day Diaspora of nearly a million Vietnamese from their native land. The fall also sent several hundred thousand to prison, and condemned the remainder—some eighteen million people—to a life of poverty and a loss of freedom. The Communists, not surprisingly, simply called it the Liberation of South Vietnam (*Giai Phong Mien Nam*).

The United States had spent billions of dollars and lost over 58,000 men defending South Vietnam, but ultimately failed. The defeat of South Vietnam was one of America's worst foreign-policy disasters of the twentieth century, yet a complete understanding of the end-game—from the signing of the Paris Peace Accords on 27 January 1973 to South Vietnam's surrender on 30 April 1975—has eluded us.

That absence of a comprehensive analysis of the finale of America's first lost war represents an enormous gap in our understanding of recent American history. This work attempts to address that deficit, and is the first of two volumes dealing with the final two years of the Vietnam War. Although multiple books explaining the fall were published in the 1980s, offering diverse commentary from senior policy-makers, military commanders, and journalists, nothing of consequence has been published since. Moreover, none of those authors had access to high-level internal documents from the North Vietnamese and American governments dealing with those final years.[1] Such primary source material is essential for scholars and others who wish to comprehend the complexities of that time.

Yet the need for a systematic review of the war's end goes beyond the imperative for accurate historical analysis. The traumatic fall of South Vietnam provides potential guideposts for devising current and future military policy for any war involving sizable U.S. combat forces. While this book does not compare South Vietnam with Iraq and Afghanistan, the lessons learned from how America exits a war are often as important as those drawn from how we enter one.

This first volume covers the military aspects of South Vietnam's defeat, and addresses five critical questions: (1) After the Paris Peace Accords, when did the North Vietnamese decide to return to war? (2) How did they disguise their decision and construct the successful surprise assault on Ban Me Thuot? (3) Why did President Nguyen Van Thieu withdraw his regular military forces from the Central Highlands, setting off the debacle that led to the fall? (4) What ensued militarily on the ground to trigger South Vietnam's fall in fifty-five days? (5) Was the South Vietnamese military as inept as it has been depicted in the American press and academia?

Volume 2 will discuss the political and diplomatic efforts to implement the Paris Peace Accords, including many of the social and economic events that had such a profound impact on the war. It will also deeply probe the various efforts to arrange a ceasefire in April 1975. Each volume will present significant new evidence that will provide a complete picture of which decisions made in Hanoi, Saigon, and Washington caused South Vietnam's defeat.

In addition to expanding our historical knowledge and gleaning lessons for future conflicts, there exists a third pressing reason for re-examining South Vietnam's fall. For most Americans, the destruction of South Vietnam during those traumatic fifty-five days in March and April 1975 validated the judgment that the war was a terrible mistake. Many Americans had come to believe that our South Vietnamese allies were corrupt and oppressive Saigon elites who opposed the desire of the vast majority of Vietnamese for a united country. The American Left, from college campuses to major media institutions, along with foreign anti-war elements, fed that belief. They painted the South Vietnamese government as a dicta-torial regime propped up by a crooked, poorly led military that was entirely dependent on U.S. aid, advice, and airpower to hold the Communist forces at bay. This portrayal of an inept South Vietnamese military was seemingly confirmed in late March 1975 during the chaotic fall of Danang, the capital of South Vietnam's most heavily defended military region, when scenes were televised of rampaging soldiers fighting helpless civilians for airplane seats.

The anti-war groups further eroded support among free-world and non-aligned countries for the elected Government of South Vietnam (GVN) by insisting on two conditions for ending the war. First, they claimed that a coalition government was the sole means to stop the fighting, a position that ignored past Communist transgressions in such political marriages. Second, they demanded that the U.S. cease all material support for South Vietnam in order to achieve the first goal. Since the Vietnamese Commu-nists stipulated the removal of the Saigon government before agreeing to join a coalition, the South Vietnamese and Americans rejected what would have been essentially a disguised surrender.

To eliminate American support for South Vietnam, the Left used a sim-ple argument: The Saigon government was a dictatorial regime refusing to share power and suppressing the will of the people; the South Vietnamese were militarily ineffectual because of the regime's lack of legitimacy; and hence the war was unwinnable. These conclusions endure in the public mind, often bolstered by those who view America's involvement as wrong, if not immoral.

As I will argue, that representation of South Vietnam's government and military is wrong. For example, the searing images from the collapse of Danang portray only a snapshot in time. To be sure, the images were grim, but they do not reflect the totality of events leading to that tragic moment. The chaos was not due to South Vietnamese incompetence or coward-ice, as the breakdown in discipline occurred only in the final days before Danang's capture. Few know that Republic of Vietnam Armed Forces (RVNAF) in this region fought well until news of the bungled retreat from Pleiku reached them. This shocking news, in combination with widely believed rumors of an imminent and secretly negotiated division of the country—compounded by a million panicky civilians fearful of Commu-nist atrocities—led many soldiers and officers to abandon their posts in order to rescue their families.

Although this book offers a counterweight to the prevailing portrayal of the South Vietnamese armed forces, it does not whitewash their mistakes or disregard their faults. The South Vietnamese have much to answer for, including debilitating factionalism and extensive corruption. Certainly large-scale corruption existed, and, occasionally, venal officers sold goods to their sworn enemy. But only through an extensive investigation—one that had to overcome significant cultural barriers, including an overarching suspicion among the Vietnamese of American writers—was I able to discover a long-ignored martial spirit in the South Vietnamese armed forces. Like any military, the RVNAF had both good and poor units, excellent and lackluster leaders, but only rarely are the good units and leaders depicted in the existing Western histories. As one South Vietnamese battalion commander said, commenting on the chaos in Danang and on the bungled retreat from the Central Highlands: "We are ashamed of these things, but they do not define us."[2] By that he meant that the South Vietnamese military, particularly in the 1973–75 period, had performed far better than anyone has realized.

Official American sources, and occasionally (and surprisingly) Communist histories, support this conclusion. For instance, many have asserted that the short, four-day final battle for Saigon that ended the war typified the overall ease of the North Vietnamese victory. Yet the North Vietnamese make no such claim. Writing after the war, Politburo member Le Duc Tho, probably number four in the hierarchy, stated: "The amount of blood shed during these four days was in no way small. . . . The battle at the belt of Saigon was fierce and marked many examples of noble sacrifices. Thousands of sons and daughters . . . [fell] on the outskirts of the city when peace was only 24 hours away."[3] Since North Vietnamese Communists typically denigrate their Southern opponents, for someone of Le Duc Tho's stature to concede even grudgingly the stiff resistance by the RVNAF until the end is a telling admission.

There were two reasons for this improvement in the South Vietnamese armed forces. First, Vietnamization—the process of transferring responsibility and control from the Americans to our allies—while still incomplete, had worked. Second, the 1972 Easter Offensive forced senior South Vietnamese officers to sweep out many incompetent commanders, replacing them with younger, combat-hardened, U.S.-trained leaders. For example, during the 1972 attacks the ARVN 3rd and 22nd Divisions were virtually annihilated. However, under the new leadership of then Brigadier Generals

Nguyen Duy Hinh and Phan Dinh Niem, the divisions were rapidly rebuilt and operated exceedingly well in the 1973–75 period. Unfortunately, American military advisors, who also sometimes had a poor opinion of their counterparts, were no longer around to see the fruits of their labor.

As this book depicts, South Vietnam was defeated not because of military incompetence or an unjust dictatorship, but because of six overriding facts: complete abrogation of the Paris Peace Accords by the North Vietnamese; dire South Vietnamese economic straits; lack of U.S. firepower to stem a massive assault; the vast reduction of U.S. aid; and President Thieu's military blunders in the face of a large-scale Communist offensive. In combination, these five facts created a sixth: devastated South Vietnamese morale, which led to the swift collapse.

Strategically, the main failure in 1975 was not RVNAF cowardice, but Thieu's aversion to a strong, centralized military command system. His structure of four corps commanders exercising complete control over their fiefdoms proved more devastating than anyone would have imagined. Faced with a nationwide offensive in 1975, and bereft of American fire support to counter the North Vietnamese army's ability to mass, ARVN corps commanders were left isolated against a powerful and centrally controlled enemy.

The Communist offensive, of course, remains the primary reason for South Vietnam's demise. Why did Hanoi succeed in 1975 when it had failed in 1972? Beyond the obvious impact of U.S. aid cuts on the South Vietnamese, the lack of U.S. firepower, and the massive infiltration of men and equipment, there were three significant improvements in the People's Army of Vietnam (PAVN) between 1972 and 1975 that helped Hanoi win.

First was the enhancement in North Vietnamese command and control, to include successfully using combined-arms formations, particularly armor. Soviet training assisted this development, but so did hard-won experience. Second, sophisticated logistics planning, improved engineering abilities, and detailed military and political analysis, even if heavily colored by Communist dogma, were all hallmarks of the 1975 campaign. In these fundamental aspects, the People's Army in 1975 was far superior to any previous incarnation, even though it had fewer heavy weapons than the 1972 version.

The third factor was Communist spies who provided Hanoi critical intelligence into Saigon's most closely guarded secrets. This advantage enabled PAVN to draft combat plans with almost real-time insight into

RVNAF designs for counterattacks, withdrawals, and other maneuvers. Without such intelligence coups, it is doubtful that the North Vietnamese could have conducted its war-planning with such precision. Moreover, several agents acted as provocateurs, including one who visited President Gerald Ford with a South Vietnamese delegation in late March 1975. Another convinced an entire ARVN battalion to surrender on 28 April 1975.

Three physical factors also played pivotal roles in the war: weather, infrastructure, and geography. Vietnam has a distinct rainy season and dry season, and they dictated the war's tempo. Since South Vietnam has few roads, the Communist tactic of using large units to grab and hold important sections of road, such as mountain passes and critical junctions, was essential in defeating the RVNAF. During the days of vast American-supplied helicopter mobility, cutting the roads was a nuisance. In 1975, with limited fuel supplies and few spare parts for South Vietnamese helicopters, it was a mortal blow.

Most important, South Vietnam's geography made defending the country against an invader extraordinarily difficult. South Vietnam is a long, narrow country, especially in the central and northern portions. This geographical fact meant the RVNAF had to protect an 800-mile western flank, most of which consisted of sparsely populated rugged mountain terrain covered with thick jungle vegetation. The difficult landscape provided plenty of concealment for enemy forces, enabling them to mass undetected at key points. Worse, there was little room between the mountains and the coast to absorb an assault. Armored columns could easily penetrate to the sea and cut the country in two, which is precisely what occurred in the Central Highlands in 1975. In perhaps the strangest twist of the war, in a conflict exemplified by the guerrilla on one side and the helicopter on the other, it was armor, the war's least-used weapon system, which was the key to victory. This shocking development began at Ban Me Thuot, and continued until North Vietnamese tanks burst onto the grounds of Independence Palace in Saigon.

These key features, from an improved PAVN to the geography, made having reserves, firepower, mobility, and supplies fundamental ingredients in defending South Vietnam. No senior American or South Vietnamese military or political figure expected South Vietnam to defeat a major attack without adequate U.S. military firepower. Thus, for the remaining American personnel in South Vietnam, the U.S. Congress's aid cutbacks and legislation denying fire support were the main culprits in South Vietnam's demise. This combination essentially gutted the RVNAF while enticing the Politburo into militarily re-escalating the war.

Historical records prove this perspective to be correct, as there is no doubt that congressional aid reductions were imposed in perverse synchronicity with increased Communist aggression. Communist accounts written after the war trumpet the fact that aid cuts progressively weakened the RVNAF, while North Vietnam's military strength concurrently recovered from the debacle of the 1972 offensive. In this volume, I discuss only briefly the anti-war groups' efforts to convince Congress to reduce aid, but it should surprise no one that Hanoi closely monitored the ongoing discussion, attempted to influence it, and calculated its own opportunities accordingly.

Yet Hanoi's decision to return to war was not based solely on American actions. Just as important was the North Vietnamese leaders' judgment that the circumstances of 1973–75 presented them with the best window for achieving victory. They viewed the burgeoning economic problems of both South Vietnam and the United States, along with American domestic dissent and occasional South Vietnamese street protests, as proof that "internal contradictions" (*mau thuan noi bo*) had badly weakened both countries. Eventually, the Politburo reasoned, both would recover from their economic and political frailty. Moreover, China and Japan would establish stronger ties with South Vietnam. The North Vietnamese judged that if they did not act soon, it would be nearly impossible to unify the country under their domination.

To achieve their long-sought goal of unification, and unknown to everyone else at the time, in May 1973 the Communist leaders in North Vietnam decided to resume full-scale warfare in the South. To justify their decision, they blamed the failure of the accords on "massive" South Vietnamese and U.S. violations. The Politburo then hid its decision behind a public façade that its priority was economic reconstruction.

While the record on that decision leaves little room for misinterpretation, the evidence remains thin on precisely how the decision was reached. The debate among Politburo members over returning to war was probably more intense than has been revealed. Undoubtedly, the Party suppressed evidence of internal dissent in favor of a glorious tale of a unified Politburo determined to "liberate" the South. Still, the suppression of such evidence does not alter the fact that less than four months after the signing of the

Paris Accords, the Party leadership in Hanoi secretly made a formal decision to return to war.

Ultimately, whatever errors were committed on the American and South Vietnamese side, the simple fact remains that a North Vietnamese military invasion conquered the country in direct violation of the Politburo's solemn written pledges against such an action. Hanoi's momentous choice to destroy the Paris Peace Accords and forcibly unify the country sent a generation of South Vietnamese into exile, and exacerbated a societal trauma in America over our long Vietnam involvement that reverberates to this day. How that transpired deserves deeper scrutiny.

RESEARCH, TERMINOLOGY, AND GEOGRAPHY

This book is the culmination of exhaustive research in three distinct areas: primary source documents from American archives, North Vietnamese publications containing primary and secondary source material, and dozens of articles and numerous interviews with key South Vietnamese participants. This work is mainly the voice of the Vietnamese—their stories, their view of what happened during the final days. It represents one of the largest Vietnamese translation projects ever accomplished, including almost one hundred North Vietnamese unit histories, battle studies, and memoirs. Most important, to celebrate the thirtieth anniversary of the conquest of South Vietnam, the leaders in Hanoi released several compendia of formerly highly classified cables and memoranda between the Politburo and its military commanders in the South. Using this treasure trove of primary source materials, along with unit histories and memoirs of senior officers, this work provides the most complete account of North Vietnamese decision-making in a particular era ever compiled. While official South Vietnamese documentation remains scarce, enough material exists to provide a decent overview.

All of these Vietnamese publications have been wonderfully translated by Merle L. Pribbenow. He is undoubtedly one of the best, if not *the* best, translators from Vietnamese to English in the United States. Mr. Pribbenow translated the official North Vietnamese book *History of the People's Army: 1945–1975*, published in English in 2002 as *Victory in Vietnam* by the University of Kansas Press. He served from April 1970 to April 1975 in the U.S. Embassy in Saigon. Not only does he possess an incredible fluency in both North and South Vietnamese military and political terminology, he is also familiar with such arcane subjects as ARVN slang.

Uncovering North Vietnamese decision-making during the last two years of the war was critical. What little had been revealed about Hanoi's strategy came mostly from Senior General Van Tien Dung's book, published a year after the war's end and translated into English as *Our Great Spring Victory*. Dung, a Politburo member and second-in-command of the PAVN, was Hanoi's overall commander in South Vietnam during the final offensive. Consequently, the bulk of his account focuses on late 1974 through April 1975, virtually ignoring the 1973 to mid-1974 time frame. Although three other books by senior North Vietnamese officers that provide inside accounts were published after Dung's and were translated into English, none had a similar impact. Since his version of events went largely uncontested in the West, Dung received the lion's share of the credit for North Vietnam's victory among Western authors.[4]

As with the Western perceptions of the South Vietnamese, the acclaim for Dung is also incorrect. The true architect of Hanoi's victory was Senior General Vo Nguyen Giap, who pressed hard within the Politburo after the signing of the Paris Accords to resume offensive operations. It was his vision that enabled the North Vietnamese to seize an unexpected "strategic opportunity" (*thoi co chien luoc*), and turn South Vietnam's worst strategic mistake into a rout that destroyed the country. This discovery came as a surprise, as most Western analysts at the time thought Giap was either absent during the last offensive because of illness, or sidelined owing to previous failures. It was even more shocking to learn that Giap had opposed major elements of the North's previous two large-scale offensives, in 1968 and 1972. Where Dung deserves recognition is for his decision-making after the Ban Me Thuot attack. As will be seen, it is Dung who correctly analyzed the situation, at first in the II Corps area and then as the offensive progressed, and who fought to modify the Politburo's overly ambitious plans.

While reviewing Communist publications was crucial to comprehending the policies that led to victory, accepting their claims at face value would have been a sure road to ruin. The Vietnamese have an old saying, one that resonates in any culture: "Losers are pirates, winners are kings." (*Duoc lam vua, thua lam giac.*) One must wade through massive propaganda distortions to find verifiable truths. North Vietnamese publications are fraught with misleading statistics, they ignore or gloss over defeats, and they are dramatically uneven in terms of factuality. PAVN's unit histories are designed to provide an uplifting story rather a "warts and all" review. Former Communist soldiers now blogging about the war often deride official publications as "political histories."

Regardless, once one moves beyond the turgid prose and exaggerated claims, North Vietnamese publications usually provide a detailed overview of the planning, execution, and aftermath of battles and campaigns. While it was vital to cross-check numerous Communist publications in order to confirm events, a process that was especially laborious since the authors often simply copied approved text about particular incidents from earlier books, eventually a solid framework emerged. Much of the strict Communist wartime secrecy has evaporated, even in security and intelligence matters, replaced by an acknowledgment that the lessons and episodes of the war needed to be studied and debated. Although Vietnam has nothing like Western transparency, given the vast range of Communist publications, we can now ascertain the Politburo's motivation and actions to a fair degree.

To balance the Communist version of events, I made broad use of South Vietnamese post-war journals published by the RVNAF military associations. Few American authors have made use of these magazines, which contain articles about various battles written by the participants. I used these materials in combination with scores of Vietnamese-language books by former military officers. Additionally, I incorporated my own extensive oral-history interviews plus interviews conducted by official American researchers in 1975. While generally more accurate in their depiction of battles, the South Vietnamese often succumb to the same temptations as their Northern brethren. A similar warning applies to use of this information.

The U.S. government's documentation regarding Vietnam in the final years is wide-ranging and detailed on both the military action and the internal deliberations in Washington. These sources provide a comprehensive discussion of the growing frustration, first in the Nixon and then in the Ford administration, over congressional restrictions that made it increasingly difficult to assist South Vietnam in its ongoing fight. I also conducted wide-ranging research at the Library of Congress to develop a thorough listing of scholarly articles on the final two years of the war. The result is a lengthy bibliography that I have placed online at www.blackapril75.com so that future scholars can avail themselves of these resources. By integrating all these sources, and constantly cross-checking claims, I was able to deduce what transpired on long-ago battlefields and in the chambers of government in Hanoi, Saigon, and Washington.

Although previous authors did not have the rich primary sources now available, I owe a debt of gratitude to earlier scribes. Foremost among their works are William Le Gro's *Vietnam from Cease-Fire to Capitulation*, Frank Snepp's *Decent Interval*, and Dr. Henry Kissinger's *Ending the Vietnam War*. Books by journalists who covered Vietnam include Arnold Isaacs's *Without Honor*, David Butler's *The Fall of Saigon*, and Olivier Todd's *Cruel April*. Providing the South Vietnamese perspective are Cao Van Vien's *The Final Collapse*, Pham Huan's *The Withdrawal from the Central Highlands*, Stephen Hosmer's *The Fall of South Vietnam*, and Nguyen Tien Hung's *The Palace File*. For the North Vietnamese, Van Tien Dung's *Our Great Spring Victory*, Tran Van Tra's *History of the Bulwark B-2 Theatre*, Hoang Van Thai's *The Decisive Years*, and Vo Nguyen Giap's *The General Headquarters* give the military perspective.

To ease the American reader's journey, I have taken several liberties. I refer to our allies as the South Vietnamese, and to their opponents as either the North Vietnamese or the Communists. I converted kilometers and meters to miles and yards. Directions in the text (north, south, east, and west) refer to map direction, not compass direction, although they are often the same. For dates I used the conventional military format of day-month-year (19 May 1973, for example), but used standard time as opposed to military time. I eliminated diacritical marks in the Vietnamese words in the text and notes. Also, although Vietnamese is a monosyllabic language (Hanoi and Danang, for example, should be written as Ha Noi and Da Nang), I used the combined form more familiar to Western readers. Since official Communist publications, such as division and corps histories, are usually written by committee, with multiple authors engaged in revisions at various levels, I have not included an author. Only for memoirs did I add the author's name. Moreover, in referring to a Vietnamese publication, I used the translated English title instead of the Vietnamese title. In addition to a list of acronyms, I have also included a register of prominent persons and their positions to help the reader keep track of the mostly Vietnamese personalities. I also included a directory of military units from both sides to help the reader keep straight the often bewildering array of units. As a refresher, Army and Marine units, from largest to smallest, are: corps, division, regiment (or brigade, or group), and battalion (or squadron for armor). For Air Force units, it is division, wing, and then squadron.

To simplify the war jargon, I have used the following conventions: South Vietnam had four corps areas, running north to south, and numbered I through IV. All South Vietnamese corps areas were also known as military regions. Hence, I Corps was in MR-1, and so forth. To prevent confusion, I have used roman numerals for the South Vietnamese (II Corps, for example), Arabic for PAVN (1st Corps), and either Front or Military Region (MR) for the North Vietnamese commands across the country. Lastly, maps depicting the terrain and flow of battles are included at various points in the text.

So as not to perpetuate the myth of a mainly Southern-based insurgency fighting against the Saigon government, I will not use the terms Viet Cong (VC) or People's Liberation Armed Forces (PLAF) to describe the Southern-based Communist military forces.[5] I believe that using this terminology inhibits our ability to understand the Communist movement in Vietnam and the history of the war. Scholars have argued passionately for decades about the correct use and meaning of the term Viet Cong. It is an abbreviation of *Cong San Viet Nam*, which simply means Vietnamese Communist. The South Vietnamese government coined the term sometime in the mid-1950s to describe the Communist movement that was seeking to overthrow it and unify the country under Party control. As originally used, the term applied to all Vietnamese Communists and did not connote a distinction between Northerners and Southerners. American military commanders, analysts, and journalists adopted the term to distinguish between the Southern components of the Communist movement—the shadowy guerrillas hiding among the villagers—and the Northern component, often called the NVA, or North Vietnamese Army. During 1973–75, Southerners represented only a small percentage of Communist military strength.

The Communists' title for their Southern-based forces was *Quan Giai Phong Mien Nam Viet Nam* (South Vietnam Liberation Army—SVNLA), often shortened to *Quan Giai Phong* (Liberation Army). The SVNLA was popularly called the Viet Cong by the American and South Vietnamese military. It is often depicted by the Western media and entertainment industry as the National Liberation Front's (NLF) "guerrilla army" of native Southerners. Popular misperceptions notwithstanding, the SVNLA, the National Liberation Front, and the NLF's replacement, the Provisional Revolutionary Government (PRG), were not independent entities. The Politburo and the Ministry of Defense in Hanoi created the SVNLA with the intention that it function as a Southern-based element of PAVN. In January 1961 the

Central Military Affairs Committee in Hanoi clearly established that the "Liberation Army of South Vietnam is a component of the People's Army of Vietnam, established, built, educated, and led by the Party."[6]

In every aspect, the SVNLA was under the unified leadership of the Vietnam Communist Party and the High Command in Hanoi. No independent Southern Viet Cong military force ever existed, nor was there a split chain of command or separate logistics systems. The Southern-based Communist forces either were forward-deployed elements of the People's Army, or locally raised units that recruited or kidnapped Southern youths into their ranks. Further, separating the People's Army and its Southern component does not address the third element of the PAVN wartime organization, the Vietnamese "Volunteer Army" forces in Laos and Cambodia. Would they be considered separate elements as well? The answer is no, and neither should the Communist forces in South Vietnam. Hence, I will use the term PAVN for all Communist military units. The only distinction will be between two key components of the People's Army in the South. They are main forces (regular military, consisting almost exclusively of Northern soldiers) and local forces (less well-armed and well-trained militias, usually Southerners infused with a healthy dose of Northerners), which are based at province level and below.

Politically also there was no division between the Communist Party in the North and the South. The Central Office for South Vietnam (COSVN, *Trung Uong Cuc Mien Nam*) and its Military Affairs Committee functioned as a branch office of the Politburo and a forward headquarters for the PAVN High Command. COSVN and its Military Affairs Committee controlled only those units operating in southern South Vietnam (*Nam Bo*) during 1951–54 and 1961–75. PAVN designated this region as the B-2 Front (*Mat tran B-2*). This was one of five military-front commands PAVN established in the Republic of Vietnam. Units based along the coast from Danang to Nha Trang, in the Central Highlands, and in the Thua Thien–Hue region operated under the control of separate Military Regions/Fronts—the B-1 Front, B-3 Front, and B-4 Front, respectively. These commands all reported directly to Hanoi. The old B-5 Front in Quang Tri was converted to the 2nd Corps in 1974. For a more detailed description of each PAVN command and region, see Appendix I at www.blackapril75.com.

To what extent, then, should history acknowledge the NLF/PRG and the PLAF? That the NLF and PLAF were simply front organizations is undeniable, but to ignore the Communist policies that spawned them is a mistake.

To allow future generations to forget how Hanoi skillfully and deceitfully created the elaborate political and military fronts with which it waged war against the GVN and the U.S. would be to deny those generations the tools with which to understand similar regimes. Although the NLF/PRG was undeniably a Communist front, some of its constituents believed it to be a mechanism to unite all classes and political parties to create a coalition government in the South. This, of course, was a fantasy, deftly manufactured by the Communist Party in Hanoi. It is also undeniable that many in both Vietnam and the West accepted this fantasy, but that is beyond the scope of this work.

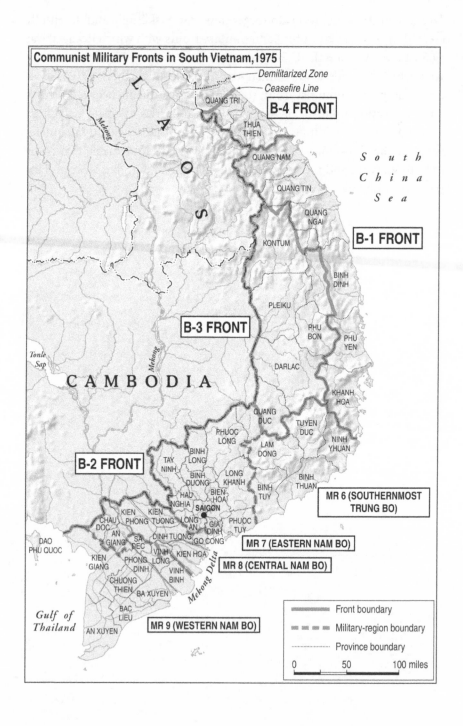

Communist Military Fronts in South Vietnam, 1975

1

"THE U.S. WILL REACT VIGOROUSLY"

SIGNING THE PARIS PEACE ACCORDS

The signing of the Paris Peace Accords on 27 January 1973 did not bring the respite from war so desperately desired by millions of Vietnamese and Americans. The great hope that the agreement would forge a lasting peace within Indochina was swiftly shattered by those in the North Vietnamese Politburo who advocated conquering the South by force. Perhaps ending the conflict was beyond negotiation: too much blood, too much hatred, too many long years of terrible war. Conceivably, a vigorous American military response to violations of the Paris Accords might have restrained Hanoi, but it might also have floundered like so many previous U.S. efforts to end the fighting. What is certain, however, is that the Paris Accords would be dead within four months of their signing, but only Hanoi would know it.

For the South Vietnamese government, the accords brought more fear than relief. President Nguyen Van Thieu viewed the draft accords as deeply flawed and a dangerous threat to his country's survival. In October 1972, Thieu balked at signing the agreement when presented with the final version by National Security Advisor Henry A. Kissinger. Thieu requested dozens of changes, but in his mind, three issues were crucial. They were the removal of North Vietnamese soldiers from South Vietnam, recognition of the Demilitarized Zone (DMZ) as the national boundary between the two countries, and guarantees that the formation of the National Council of National Reconciliation and Concord (NCNRC), a post-ceasefire body designed to oversee elections for a new government in South Vietnam, would not lead to a coalition government with the Communists. Since the agreement contained none of these, bitter wrangling quickly arose between the two allies. To appease Thieu, President Richard M. Nixon sent Kissinger back to Paris to amend the accords. Nixon also sought in a series of highly classified letters to allay Thieu's fears, particularly regarding the all-important presence of North Vietnamese troops on South Vietnamese soil. Nixon promised to "react vigorously" to any ceasefire violations, which the Americans and the South Vietnamese understood to mean that U.S. aircraft would bomb the Communists if they violated the ceasefire agreement. Nixon also promised to continue large-scale military and economic aid to ensure the survival of the South Vietnamese government.

Unfortunately, for Thieu and Nixon, with no acceptable military option to force Hanoi to withdraw its troops, negotiating their removal was impossible. Le Duc Tho, a Politburo member and Hanoi's chief negotiator in Paris, would not permit the U.S. to obtain at the negotiating table what it had been unable to achieve on the battlefield. Hanoi's most fundamental principle was that its troops would remain, while America's must leave. After increasingly acrimonious negotiations between Kissinger and Tho, in mid-December the North Vietnamese rebuffed any further substantive changes, and the talks broke down. To force Hanoi back to the negotiating table, on 18 December 1972 Nixon sent waves of bombers to pound the North Vietnamese capital. The so-called "Christmas bombing" generated worldwide outrage, with many demands from Congress, the U.S. media, and foreign governments to cease the attacks immediately. Yet Nixon held firm, and by the end of December, North Vietnam had agreed to resume negotiations. By mid-January, the Politburo was prepared to sign the new accords, but its bedrock strategy—refusal to remove its forces from South Vietnam—remained unchanged.

After Nixon repeatedly threatened to cut off all U.S. aid if Thieu did not sign, Thieu also finally agreed to ratify the agreement. Thieu told his senior officials that while he had failed to get the agreement modified in the key areas of North Vietnamese troops and the DMZ as a national boundary, the NCNRC would not become a coalition government. Moreover, he had firm commitments from Nixon on several major points. Economic and military aid would continue, the accords did not legally permit North Vietnamese troops to stay on South Vietnamese soil, and the Americans would "react vigorously" in case of ceasefire violations.

Nixon immediately sent another letter to Thieu, thanking him for signing but emphasizing that public unity between the two governments was now essential to ensure that Congress would continue to grant aid to South Vietnam. He also informed Thieu of the contents of the speech he planned to give announcing the signing of the Paris Peace Accords. Thieu, mindful of his own domestic audience, asked that Nixon include the statement that the accords also met Saigon's goals.

Nixon announced the accords to America on the night of 23 January. "The United States," the president said, "will continue to recognize the Government of the Republic of Vietnam as the sole legitimate government of South Vietnam. We shall continue to aid South Vietnam within the terms of the agreement and we shall support efforts by the people of South Vietnam to settle their problems peacefully among themselves."[1] On the matter of the U.S. response to violations, his tone was muted: "We shall do everything the agreement requires of us and we shall expect the other parties to do everything it requires of them." Dangling the carrot to Hanoi, he offered the prospect of aid to the war-ravaged Communists: "To the leaders of North Vietnam: As we have ended the war through negotiations, let us now build a peace of reconciliation. For our part, we are prepared to make a major effort to help achieve that goal. But just as reciprocity was needed to end the war, so too will it be needed to build . . . the peace."

Although the accords mandated a halt to warfare in the South and an end to further infiltration, and committed Hanoi to withdraw from Laos and Cambodia and account for Americans still missing in action, none of these occurred. Hanoi instead responded to Nixon's olive branch with stepped-up infiltration of men and equipment into South Vietnam, along with numerous attacks attempting to grab land and population. Counter-attacking swiftly and effectively, the South Vietnamese drove the Communists out of the hamlets they had occupied.

With North Vietnam already committing serious violation, Kissinger traveled to Hanoi in mid-February 1973 to discuss the agreement. Kissinger's main goals for the trip were to determine if Hanoi intended to keep its written pledges, and to see if a more positive relationship between the United States and North Vietnam could develop. What the principal architect of the accords wanted to learn was whether Hanoi would be "content to rest on the frenzied exertions of a lifetime of struggle and begin meeting the needs of its people? That was what Le Duc Tho had been saying. . . . Could Hanoi adjust its values to give building its economy a higher priority than it had in previous periods in its history?"[2]

Kissinger found the Politburo keen to discuss aid. The North Vietnamese leaders wanted American reconstruction money to rebuild the damages inflicted by the long aerial and naval campaign against their country, but they wanted the money without any strings attached. War reparations were always an integral part of Hanoi's conditions for a peace agreement, and the Politburo viewed Nixon's promise of post-war aid as a fig-leaf to cover its demand. Its interest was piqued by a 1 February 1973 letter from Nixon to Pham Van Dong, a Politburo member and the premier of North Vietnam. The letter outlined an aid program of $3.5 billion after the formation of a Joint Economic Commission to review the particular needs of each country in the region. Nixon, however, saw aid not as reparations, but as a "powerful incentive for Hanoi to keep the peace."[3] He would provide aid only if Hanoi fully abided by the accords. There was, Nixon told Kissinger, an unavoidable link between aid and Hanoi's performance on the accords.

In North Vietnam, Kissinger met with both Pham Van Dong and Le Duc Tho. Although the Politburo was a collective leadership in theory, in reality most policy was driven by three men. After the death of Ho Chi Minh in 1969, first among "equals" in the Politburo was Le Duan, the Party's general secretary. Number two was Truong Chinh, the Party's leading theoretician and a doctrinaire fanatic, even by Communist standards. Third was Pham Van Dong, the most urbane—although Kissinger found him dour—of the senior North Vietnamese leaders. Dong had been the foreign minister of the Democratic Republic of Vietnam (DRV) and the head of its delegation at the 1954 Geneva talks, and in September 1955, he had become prime minister. Although Dong was usually characterized as a moderate, he was not. He had worked with Ho Chi Minh since the 1920s as a dedicated revolutionary.

Meeting with Kissinger, Dong claimed that North Vietnam wanted to establish a long-term relationship with the United States, was serious about implementing the agreement, and desired to receive American aid. Following Nixon's instructions, Kissinger refused to discuss aid until the two sides finalized a timetable for the withdrawal of North Vietnamese troops from Laos and Cambodia. When aid was finally discussed, Kissinger spent considerable time outlining the congressional process for granting aid. He noted that it was often difficult to obtain money for America's friends, let alone a country the U.S. had just recently fought. His legislative lessons fell on unsympathetic ears, as Dong was extremely suspicious of Kissinger's explanation regarding the intricacies of obtaining aid from a recalcitrant U.S. Congress.

Regarding Laos and Cambodia, while Dong agreed to a ceasefire in Laos and a specific timetable for withdrawal of North Vietnamese forces, on Cambodia he was far less amenable. In Laos, Dong explained, the North Vietnamese could fulfill their obligations, but in Cambodia, they could not persuade the Khmer Rouge, the fanatical Communist faction in that beleaguered land, to agree to a ceasefire or a coalition government. How much Hanoi pressed the Khmer Rouge is open to debate, as Hanoi did not want to withdraw PAVN forces from their strategic locations in Cambodia alongside the South Vietnamese border. Consequently, no agreement on Cambodia was reached.

Nor was Dong forthcoming on eighty missing American military personnel who were believed captured, but for whom no information had been provided. Kissinger was further disappointed when Dong denied any ceasefire violations, blamed Saigon for all breaches, and demanded that U.S. assistance be unconditional. More menacingly, Kissinger recalled later, "less than two weeks after . . . the Paris Accords, [Dong] dropped an ominous hint of renewed warfare. If a new relationship did not develop . . . the just signed Paris accords would be 'only a temporary stabilization of the situation, only a respite.'"[4] Kissinger left Hanoi determined to make the Politburo choose between renewed warfare and honoring the accords.

THE FIRST TEST

While Nixon intended to defend South Vietnam if it was mortally threatened, he felt the Vietnamese needed to sort out their own political future with minimal American involvement. The strategy was simple: end the military conflict, continue to support the Saigon government, but let the Vietnamese resolve the political issues themselves. Supporting South Vietnam was important, Kissinger said, because the "impact on international stability and on America's readiness to defend free peoples would be catastrophic if a solemn agreement were treated as an unconditional surrender."[5] Both Nixon and Kissinger continually cited this potential blow to American credibility as a major factor in their resolve to enforce the agreement. In February 1973 Nixon told several senior Cabinet officials exactly that: "Vietnam was important not for itself but because of what it demonstrated in terms of support for our friends and allies and in terms of showing our will to our enemies. I could have 'bugged out' free in Vietnam after the 1968 elections, but we had to see it through."[6]

Still, there were competing forces shaping Nixon's Vietnam policy. While Nixon long claimed he achieved "peace with honor," there is no doubt he wanted to remove the conflict as a focal point of U.S. affairs. He was "acutely aware of all the things we had postponed or put off because of the war."[7] Nixon's second-term policy goals for America were ambitious: to reunite America after the angry discord over the war, and to refocus U.S. diplomacy on more pressing issues. In his second term, Nixon sought a "New American Revolution" in line with conservative values. He wanted to reduce the deficit and reform the massive federal bureaucracy. He could accomplish none of these objectives while consumed by Vietnam. Consequently, he bludgeoned Thieu into signing the accords, using a combination of threats and promises of the continuation of aid and the introduction of airpower to punish ceasefire violations. Yet the second crucial promise never materialized. Why?

Kissinger believed that a test of America's resolve to enforce the agreements was inevitable, given Hanoi's determination to unify the country under the Communist banner. The test soon came, with a major infiltration of men and equipment down the Ho Chi Minh Trail. Truck columns over two hundred vehicles long, impossible when the U.S. Air Force patrolled the skies, now brazenly drove the trail in daylight. Kissinger and Nixon were well aware of the ongoing infiltration. When the Politburo failed to respond to American warnings transmitted by letter via the North Vietnamese delegation in Paris, both Nixon and Kissinger instantly recognized the growing threat. Kissinger recommended bombing, the sole measure he believed Hanoi respected. Nixon, however, despite his earlier promises to Thieu, was suddenly reluctant to act. Kissinger notes that Nixon ordered a bombing attack against the trail on 6 March, but canceled it the next day. On 14 March, Kissinger again recommended bombing the infiltration columns, a threat which Nixon alluded to in a 15 March speech. Nixon stated that he hoped the problems of Indochina could be "solved at the conference table," but "we have warned Hanoi, privately and publicly, that we will not tolerate violations of the Agreement."[8]

The main reason Nixon refrained was bombing was that the growing Watergate affair was now absorbing most of his attention. In mid-April, Kissinger told his staff that, "In these circumstances, it would be reckless to urge Nixon to put his diminishing prestige behind a bombing campaign . . . that he was clearly reluctant to undertake. I therefore suggested . . . that we wait for an unambiguous direct challenge. . . . Up to then our strategy had been to prevent a major challenge rather than wait for it to occur. The decision meant we were postponing a preemptive strike indefinitely. Thus, sooner or later, South Vietnam would have to cope with the full fury of the unimpeded North Vietnamese buildup."[9]

Given Nixon's demonstrated ability to take harsh military measures, Kissinger's plan to "prevent a major challenge" rather than reacting to one was a sound policy, but the Watergate scandal and the anti-war mood in Congress destroyed that policy. The growing political crisis and congressional constraints, however, were not the only restraining factors. Nixon was also well aware that American public opinion had soured on South Vietnam. The "Christmas bombing" had spent what little political capital Nixon had left to prosecute the war militarily. Bombing North Vietnam to bring the Communists back to the conference table, a decision he called the "loneliest of his presidency," had worked, but it had emptied his hand for when he needed military force to enforce the accords.

With the bombing option withering fast, Kissinger hoped to leverage economic aid and a gradual normalization process to restrain the Politburo's adventurism. Kissinger's carrot soon became useless, however, when Congress, upon learning that American POWs had been brutally tortured, passed an amendment in early April 1973 barring any aid to North Vietnam. With military action and economic aid both out of the question, whatever influence the U.S. government had possessed disappeared. Since all of Hanoi's post-war writings have cleaved to the Party line that it was Saigon's and Washington's "massive violations" of the ceasefire that caused North Vietnam to resume the offensive, it is impossible at this point to ascertain whether either option would have worked. Still, given the Politburo's nervous watching of American military moves, an obsession that went well beyond a prudent respect, the suspicion remains that a forceful and early bombing of the infiltration columns would have prompted a more serious effort to adhere to the ceasefire.

THE SOUTH VIETNAMESE STAND ALONE

The last American troops left Vietnam on 29 March 1973. The next day, Thieu flew to the United States to meet Nixon at the Western White House in San Clemente, California. The visit was the fulfillment of another promise made by Nixon as an enticement to sign the accords. While Thieu remained deeply dependent on U.S. largesse, namely aid and firepower, and despite the looming threats from the ongoing infiltration, in the spring of 1973, he was at the pinnacle of his power. His base was the army, the police, and the Catholic minority; his mandate was that he was the man the all-powerful Americans wanted in power.

Nguyen Van Thieu was born on 5 April 1923 in a small hamlet near Phan Rang, a city on Vietnam's coast northeast of Saigon. He had a hard-scrabble childhood, but he attended a French high school in Saigon. In the late 1940s, after a year-long fling with the Viet Minh, he came to abhor Communist doctrine. Like many Nationalists—as the non-Communist South Vietnamese called themselves—he disliked the French, but he hated Communism. To him it was a choice of the lesser of two evils.

In December 1948, he joined an officer training class of the fledging Vietnamese National Army. His record was excellent, and over time, he held a variety of military positions. By 1963, he commanded the 5th Division near Saigon, which he used to participate in the overthrow of President Ngo Dinh Diem. Witnessing the bloody corpses of Diem and his brother, Ngo Dinh Nhu, instilled in him a permanent fear of a coup. After Vietnam had endured a series of inept military governments, in 1967 he was elected president. Air Force General Nguyen Cao Ky was his running-mate. In 1971, he ran without Ky and won in a controversial and uncontested election.

For most Americans, Thieu remains the archetypal tyrant—dictatorial, corrupt, and incompetent. That is a caricature. He was an extraordinarily complicated man, nothing like the one-dimensional despot portrayed by his implacable critics. The charge that he was dictatorial stems from his retention of all decision-making authority, although few realized that by historical precedent and constitutional authority the Executive Branch wielded vastly greater power than any other arm of the South Vietnamese government. The accusation of incompetence came from Thieu's penchant for moving glacially. Before committing himself, he subjected problems to long, slow study. He rarely let people other than his closest aides know his position on various issues. The Vietnamese people called him "the old fox" (cao gia), indicating a willingness to wait and watch, a sense of keeping one's counsel while others moved prematurely. Yet Thieu was cognizant that his deliberate pace and retention of power enabled a sluggish bureaucracy that was generally unresponsive to the people's needs. On 10 July 1973, he announced on TV and radio an "Administrative Revolution" designed to shake up the stubborn civil service. The goal was to provide more efficient and streamlined services to the mostly rural population. According to his second cousin and close adviser Hoang Duc Nha, Thieu hoped to foster an American-style management philosophy within his administration. This meant moving away from the French-era mentality of shifting the responsibility by forcing civil servants to assume more responsibility.[10]

Thieu's Vietnamese detractors criticized him for cronyism, tolerance of corruption, and over-reliance on the Americans. They also decried his "old fox" nature as overly suspicious and abnormally cautious. Thieu's closest military aide for six years was Captain Nguyen Xuan Tam. He describes Thieu's suspicious disposition as part character, part calculation. According to Tam, "Thieu listened carefully to proposals to see if people were trying to manipulate him or take advantage of a policy for their own benefit. He would examine a problem for a long time to ensure someone's true motivations were for the good of the country, and not themselves."[11] It was Thieu's chief survival mechanism in the internecine warfare that characterized South Vietnamese politics.

Thieu had few close friends, and his personal circle was small. Despite charges that he remained aloof from his political opposition, he did not isolate himself. He often met with foreigners and Vietnamese outside his circle to gain perspective. As president, he demanded complete loyalty from his ministers and generals, and he moved patiently over time to neutralize those officers and politicians who threatened his position. Although the military remained the key arbiter of power, by 1973 he had successfully clipped the military's wings when it came to overt involvement in political affairs. While Thieu remained fearful of a coup, by careful balancing of military assignments and patient deal-making, he virtually eliminated most plotting. He also succumbed to the Vietnamese predilection for astrology and superstition. It was widely rumored by both American and Vietnamese intimates that Thieu timed major decisions to coincide with favorable heavenly signs.[12]

Thieu's supreme talent was political maneuvering in a culture of endless intrigue and innumerable factions. He had little choice; he sat at the head of a fractious country held together by the sheer force of his will and the careful balancing of religious groups, political factions, business interests, and the ever-present national-security demands. That few outsiders understood the inner workings of his administration was not only deliberate policy, but typical Vietnamese clandestinism. Unfortunately, the lack of transparency resulted in numerous theories and large-scale gossip, which only fed the dictatorial image.

Initially his style was the antithesis of the jovial, back-slapping Western politician, but during his years in power he acquired a few barnstorming skills, which he employed in his travels around the country. By 1973, Thieu's standing among the vast majority of pro-government South Vietnamese ranged from barely tolerated to fairly well-regarded. He was generally accepted by the peasants in the countryside, who benefited from his program of transferring title from wealthy landowners to farmers. Among the Saigon intelligentsia, he was despised, a reflection of their own desire for power and their fury at his refusal to consult them on any issue. The truest test was that the Communists continually clamored for his removal. They clearly recognized that he was the glue holding together the South Vietnamese government and, by extension, the country.

American views of him ranged from supportive to disdainful. Kissinger, reflecting the prevailing opinion of the Nixon administration, described Thieu as "unquestionably the most formidable of the military leaders of South Vietnam [and] probably the ablest of the political personalities."[13] Arnold Isaacs, an American journalist with extensive experience in Southeast Asia, recounts a more widespread perception among those outside the administration: "Thieu's talents as a leader were manipulative, not inspirational. . . . The war served as Thieu's ally in stifling most normal political activity. His non-Communist opponents were paralyzed by the risk that in challenging him, they might also undermine the war. Many South Vietnamese disliked the inefficiency, corruption, and authoritarianism of their regime but feared a Viet Cong victory even more. Never in his years in power did he seek associates with a different perspective from his own, who might have given his regime and the nation a stronger sense of purpose."[14]

The odd reality is that both perceptions are correct, but unfortunately for South Vietnam the world's view of Thieu as a repressive dictator precluded political support or economic assistance after the ceasefire from all but a few countries. Much of this animosity coalesced from the one-man presidential campaign in 1971. After Thieu had blatantly suppressed his opposition, the election seemed farcical.

Thieu's stature in the world took another sharp fall when, during the darkest days of the 1972 offensive, he imposed martial law and declared the power to rule by decree. His opponents were outraged, but Thieu claimed this was the only way to deal with a murderous enemy bent on military conquest. His worst move was promulgating regulations restraining the freewheeling South Vietnamese media. Western journalists decried this as a curtailment of free speech, one of the bedrocks of democracy. Press reports in Europe and America quickly reflected their antipathy; yet in Thieu's mind, the newspapers recklessly printed every unsavory rumor picked up in Saigon's streets. He wanted them to show support instead of castigating him for every military or political setback, thereby lowering morale and playing into the enemy's hands.

In late December 1972, he further inflamed his opponents by curtailing the number of political parties. By forcing them to demonstrate a certain level of support in a majority of provinces, the law appeared designed to protect Thieu's political dominance, since few parties other than his Democracy Party could meet the law's requirement. Thieu quickly followed the decree with a formidable build-up of the Democracy Party, staffed mostly by military officers and government bureaucrats. While the criticism was partially accurate, his main intention was to force the twenty-some fragile, mostly regionally based political or religious parties to unite instead of remaining fractured. He hoped to create a strong base to compete with the Communists, whose organizational techniques included dealing with serious opposition by killing it. Corruption was the other issue, and while his enemies were on firmer ground here, corruption, black marketing, and pilfering were just as rampant in North Vietnam.[15] This was an inconvenient fact that many of Thieu's critics blithely ignored.

Another major accusation was that the government jailed thousands for simple political opposition. The reality was that South Vietnamese jails held mostly common criminals, along with some Communist cadre. The Left in the U.S., parroting a Hanoi accusation, claimed there were 200,000 political prisoners, an absurd figure given South Vietnam's prison capacity of roughly 35,000. Equally ridiculous was the U.S. Embassy's declaration that it could find no political prisoners in Saigon's dungeons. The actual number depended on the definition, and on this, the two sides could not agree. Still, the political-prisoner issue would burn brightly as long as Thieu was in power, and it was undoubtedly the most damning indictment used by American anti-war groups against his government. Yet despite these claims of jails filled with tortured souls, by 1 May 1973, Thieu had released 27,000 healthy North Vietnamese POWs. The Hanoi authorities promptly sent these men for re-education and then used them as replacement troops. The Communists released fewer than 5,000 prisoners, a mere fraction of the South Vietnamese missing. All those who returned were in poor physical condition.

Thieu's main principle was strident anti-Communism, which made him seem fanatical rather than statesmanlike in an era of détente. His post-war policies remained the same uncompromising formula of the "Four No's": no political recognition of the Communists, no neutralization of South Vietnam, no coalition government, and no surrender of territory. These policies were a final refinement of the rigid anti-Communist stance he had held for years. Paramount for Thieu was no coalition government, as the presence of North Vietnamese troops on South Vietnamese soil would make any compromise tantamount to surrender. This was the crux of the issue. Many outsiders and some South Vietnamese had strongly advocated a coalition government—known as the "political solution"—as the only possible resolution to the long war.

Thieu knew better. The Vietnamese Communists had a long history of ruthless elimination of opponents. From the earliest days of the Communist movement, most Nationalists who tried to work with the Marxists were soon betrayed or assassinated. As China's Mao Zedong once told a senior Laotian Communist leader, "The purpose of organizing a coalition government is to destroy the coalition government."[16] Hanoi felt no differently.

Thieu, however, was not the inflexible hard-liner often portrayed. In fact, he had stated at a press conference in September 1971 that he was not against the National Liberation Front participating in elections. The only stipulation was that it could not carry out Communist activities, which were banned by the Constitution. He also informed U.S. officials in late January 1973 that if elections were held, he expected the NLF to win a few seats. Despite his earlier disavowal of Kissinger's agreement, he now told U.S. visitors that he strongly favored the political solution envisioned by the Paris Accords. He believed the accords worked in his favor, since in his opinion the Communists had little political support in the country. Ultimately, Thieu's policies stemmed from his unyielding belief that the Communists would not negotiate on the political issues until they had concluded that a military victory was unachievable.

While his faults were well known—and often magnified—Thieu receives little credit for his positive attributes. Tough and hard-working, he molded grand ambition with intelligence, courage, and cunning to govern a fractious country facing an implacable foe. These were the qualities that, while not endearing him to most American officials, generally earned their support. He realized that the departure of U.S. troops offered high risks coupled with a chance to craft his country's destiny, and he was appropriately sobered by the enormous tasks he faced in rebuilding a country that had been devastated by war. Facing abundant problems in the economic, diplomatic, and security arenas, he tossed aside his instinctive caution and set an aggressive agenda.

Thieu's economic hopes for his country were high, and he displayed the flexibility to achieve his goal. On 20 May 1973, he announced an "Eight-Year Reconstruction and Development Plan" to resettle the remaining refugees from the 1972 fighting, increase rice production, and finance new development projects. His program dangled some of the most liberal investment incentives in the world to foreign investors. Moreover, he sought out new sources of aid, primarily from the French, West Germans, and Japanese. To demonstrate frugality in a time of contracting economic conditions, he ordered air-conditioners turned off in government buildings to conserve electricity.

As his jet crossed the broad Pacific for his meeting with Nixon, Thieu's main goals were to gain massive economic aid until South Vietnam could achieve self-sufficiency, and to find a solution to the vexing problem of the steadily infiltrating enemy forces. He knew his government faced stern tests in the months ahead, as the Communist build-up could only portend a new offensive. He eagerly looked forward to meeting Nixon and discussing the realities in South Vietnam since the signing of the accords. Given the lack of a specific U.S. public declaration concerning renewed bombing, Thieu sought a forthright avowal of U.S. military intentions. He arrived in Los Angeles on 1 April for two days of talks.

Thieu brought a detailed proposal regarding aid. South Vietnam, he told Nixon, "faced pressing emergency problems," including "resettling one million refugees, rebuilding large areas destroyed by war . . . [the need to] generate enough jobs . . . and to curb inflation. We have to solve these problems in order to ensure political and social stability. . . . On a longer term basis, our goal is to achieve self-sustained growth . . . in the shortest time [to reduce] the present excessive dependence . . . on external assistance."[17] Presenting his eight-year plan, Thieu wanted over $1.5 billion in economic aid a year for the next three years, with reduced amounts in succeeding years. By creating an economic program for South Vietnam similar to what the Marshall Plan did for Europe, he hoped to achieve what one aide called "takeoff." This meant that the vast infusion of aid would create a rapid expansion of the South Vietnamese economy, enabling it to grow faster than South Korea's economy did after the Korean War.

Regarding the military question, Thieu asked Nixon for a public pledge that the U.S. would "react vigorously" in case of grave violations by North Vietnam. Intelligence indicated that Hanoi had shipped south thousands of troops, hundreds of tanks and artillery pieces, and tons of supplies along the Ho Chi Minh Trail. Large construction projects had extended an oil and gas pipeline deep into South Vietnam, and upgraded numerous roads, including a major new artery of the Trail that ran inside South Vietnam. Thieu opined that, given the size of the ongoing infiltration, the Communists might launch a large attack in late April or May. One can only guess whether he believed his own warning. No doubt, he was sorely tempted to sound the trumpets in order to test Nixon's promises.

In response, Nixon agreed to Thieu's aid request, but only as a goal, not a commitment. Nixon said that his administration would continue, in conjunction with Congress, to supply South Vietnam, but he warned Thieu that the sums of money he was requesting were simply unrealistic. He did not want to present Congress and the American people with a large aid request "as Congress is presently bearish on foreign aid."[18] He recommended that Thieu stress to Congress that the GVN needed the aid to overcome the effects of the war, to achieve "takeoff," and that America "will not be involved in a permanent aid program." Nixon repeated the unity message again, stressing that cooperation was essential to the GVN's survival, not only to gain congressional approval for aid but to convince Hanoi, Peking, and Moscow that they should adhere to the accords.

While downplaying the need for a public utterance on a military riposte to Hanoi's breaches of the accords, Nixon privately left no doubts concerning his intentions. He assured Thieu that he would react harshly to violations. He then outlined for Thieu his strategic assessment of the situation: "We conditioned our better relations with the Chinese and Russians on the scale of their arms deliveries to North Vietnam. The Russians responded and promised that there would be no further military supplies to Hanoi. The price of what we were doing for them was military cooperation in Indochina. Before the January ceasefire . . . [Nixon had given] Thieu the firmest assurance of our desire to support him in the new conditions of peace. He wanted to repeat this assurance now and to make three points: 1) Thieu should do all he could to keep the Communists on the political defensive. 2) Our common enemies wanted Thieu to say that the U.S. would have to come back in. 3) In the event of a massive Communist offensive the American reaction would be sharp and tough."[19]

While Thieu did not receive the public declaration of renewed American bombing that he had been promised since January, his aides claim he was happy with the results of the conference. Thieu then flew to Washington to meet congressional leaders, and to hold a press conference. Meeting with a group of journalists at the National Press Club, Thieu followed Nixon's script. When asked, he said his government could defend itself against an attack, and that he would "never ask American military troops to come back to Vietnam."[20] In Thieu's mind, if Communist forces in South Vietnam remained at their current levels, ARVN could handle them. If they launched a major offensive, then Thieu expected Nixon to keep his promises. The bombers, after all, were only as far away as Thailand.

Thieu returned to Saigon on 14 April, where he was greeted by a large throng of people. He gave a short speech, in which he announced that the U.S. would continue economic aid through 1973, after which time the U.S. Congress would then consider any future amounts. Notwithstanding Nixon's warning, Thieu hinted that Nixon had guaranteed American military strikes if the ceasefire violations continued.

Despite the apparent success of Thieu's trip, events soon moved against him. Negotiations between the two Vietnamese sides that had begun in Paris in early 1973—to set up the National Council specified in the Paris Accords to arrange for post-ceasefire elections—had quickly stalemated. Among many issues, the two sides could not agree over who would constitute the supposedly neutral "Third Force." The Third Force consisted of the circle around retired General Duong Van Minh (Big Minh), various unaffiliated intellectuals, the An Quang Buddhists, several minor opposition parties, and some Vietnamese who lived in Paris. Many Western commentators pushed the Third Force as a viable alternative to Thieu's government, but Thieu summarily dismissed them as Communist sympathizers. He was mostly correct; after the war, many in General Minh's clique would be revealed as Communist agents. Minh was not the only one deceived. One U.S. journalist and aid worker who was sympathetic to the Provisional Revolutionary Government (PRG—the supposed Communist government in the South), and who remained in Vietnam after the fall of Saigon, revealed that infiltration. "Many foreign observers," he wrote, "had portrayed the third force as a neutralist coalition leaning neither towards Communism nor the U.S. From my conversations, however, they merged [sic] as a radical nationalist grouping which had frequent contacts with the NLF, and was aware that many NLF cadres were active in third force movements."[21]

Earlier the Communists had rebuffed a GVN proposal to hold national elections. On 25 April Thieu again publicly called for a national vote, and the Communists again refused. With political negotiations deadlocked, fighting soon flared in several regions, and the accords appeared close to collapse. To repair the deteriorating ceasefire, Kissinger and Le Duc Tho agreed to meet again in Paris in mid-May. Unfortunately for Kissinger—and in spite of the ceasefire's obvious failure—Congress turned away from a president increasingly tainted by the Watergate scandal. As Kissinger left Washington in May to meet Tho in Paris, Congress approved a devastating amendment. No funds in the Defense Supplemental Appropriations Bill could be used to support combat operations by American forces in Indochina. Although Nixon vetoed it, revelations that the U.S. Air Force had been conducting secret bombing raids in Cambodia so angered Congress that it passed the Case-Church amendment banning American air attacks in Cambodia effective 15 August. The amendment also specifically prohibited Nixon from using combat forces in Indochina without the express consent of Congress. That legislation would snowball into the War Powers Resolution, a bill passed by Congress on 7 November 1973 prohibiting the president from declaring war without congressional consent. It was the culmination of steps many anti-war congressional leaders had been pressing for since 1970.

Nixon and Kissinger maintain that these actions, "and not the legal terms of the agreement, ensured the collapse of Indochina."[22] Kissinger defends his and Nixon's failure to inform Congress of their private promises to Thieu by stating that it was "inconceivable that the U.S. should fight for ten years and lose over 55,000 men and then stand by while the peace treaty . . . was flagrantly violated. It was not a position the U.S. has ever taken."[23] While theoretically correct, both Nixon and Kissinger were well aware of public and congressional disapproval of re-entering the war. One can understand their reluctance to inform Congress of their plans; they were damned either way. If they had publicly acknowledged that they were willing to resume bombing, they would have been attacked for prolonging the war. By not openly admitting their private promises to Thieu, they provided Congress an excuse to cut off military support altogether. Regardless, the congressional edict banning the use of military power was a regime-threatening blow to Thieu. The main impediment to Hanoi's adventurism had now been swept away by Congress.

Thieu began to comprehend the effect Watergate was having on Nixon. In a speech on 29 May, Thieu publicly expressed his concern that the scandal was undermining U.S. policy toward South Vietnam. All that he had achieved during his visit—continued military and economic aid, plus Nixon's promise to "react vigorously" in case of a Communist attack—was in danger. Thieu tried desperately to make Congress understand that the Communists had signed the agreement only in order to get U.S. troops out of South Vietnam. The best way to keep South Vietnam free, he said, was for her to remain strong militarily and economically until the Communists realized they could not win. That would require large amounts of aid over the next several years, and American bombing of the Communists when they violated the agreement.

Deprived of the stick of bombing and the carrot of economic aid, Kissinger attempted to salvage the situation with diplomatic pressure. On 12 May he returned to Washington after a brief trip to the USSR and publicly announced that the Soviet Union recognized its responsibility not to supply arms to Hanoi or encourage violations of the truce. Kissinger saw improved trade and better relations with the Soviets, in exchange for restricting military aid to the North and prodding Hanoi to accept a diplomatic solution, as an inferior substitute for military pressure. U.S. planes in February and April had bombed North Vietnamese troops operating in Laos, and had also continued bombing in Cambodia throughout the spring. With that option soon to be cut off, Kissinger essentially hoped to bluff Hanoi into ceasing, or at least slowing, the infiltration.

But the talks in Paris quickly stalemated. Charges were hurled back and forth, and the meetings dragged on into June. Despite the wrangling, Kissinger and Tho slowly reached an agreement. Then the same problem that had dogged the original Paris Accords resurfaced: gaining Thieu's concurrence. Thieu wanted a definite timetable for national elections, and an acknowledgment that North Vietnamese troops remained in South Vietnam. As before, the U.S. side attempted to mollify Thieu, but eventually Nixon overrode Thieu's objections, and Kissinger signed the second agreement on 13 June.

The new ceasefire quickly took hold, and military action dropped sharply and stayed quiet for the rest of the summer, except in parts of II and IV Corps. For South Vietnam, however, it would mark a quickening decline, signaled by a contracting economy, increased corruption, and sinking morale. Kissinger would later claim that, "After the events of the summer of 1973, Vietnam disappeared as a policy issue."[24] For Kissinger this was especially true. He privately told the South Vietnamese that he was finished negotiating on their behalf. He wanted the Vietnamese to solve their own problems, no longer wishing to interact with such implacable adversaries and obstinate allies. Unknown to Kissinger, however, his June effort was wasted. Secretly, the Communists had made the historic decision to launch another offensive.

"SOUTH VIETNAM WILL HAVE BOTH PEACE AND WAR"

THE COLLAPSE OF THE ACCORDS

What did the Paris Accords mean to the Politburo in Hanoi? To answer that question, one needs a short primer on Vietnamese Communist doctrine. Their canon emphasized three forms of what it termed "struggle" to achieve victory: military struggle (large-scale offensive attacks), political struggle (local and international propaganda, along with guerrilla warfare and urban unrest), and diplomatic struggle (demanding that the U.S. withdraw, and pushing to form a coalition government). The three forms were a combined "fist" to strike the enemy. Military and political struggle were the two preferred methods, with diplomacy integrated within each scheme. The 1972 offensive was a manifestation of military struggle. Signing the accords indicated a shift to political struggle. How the shift occurred in 1972, who favored which method, and how the emphasis changed back to military struggle in 1973 are difficult questions to answer. But enough is known to sketch an outline.

In mid-October 1972 keen Politburo observers in the West had detected clues in Communist Party publications signaling a strategy change to political struggle and the imminent acceptance of a negotiated settlement. By signing the agreement, Hanoi abandoned its long-standing demand for the removal of Thieu and the formation of a coalition government. The men in the Politburo viewed the settlement as providing three advantages: withdrawal of U.S. forces, an in-place ceasefire that allowed their troops to remain in the South (which legitimized a Communist political presence in South Vietnam), and an opportunity to transform the accords into a political contest. In their minds, that did not mean elections, but a form of power-sharing that the U.S. would force on Thieu's government. Neither the U.S. nor the South Vietnamese accepted this last point; in fact, they had prolonged the war to prevent an imposed coalition.

In early 1973, signs that the political struggle members continued to hold sway appeared when the Party's theoretical journal, *Hoc Tap*, published articles stating that the leadership wanted to increase "socialist construction" on a large scale. Apparently, the 1973 accords had given rise to "rightist" tendencies, a desire for peace before victory. As General Vo Nguyen Giap notes: "Some people thought that the priority then was to preserve peace, achieve national concord, [and] create stability for about five or ten years."[1]

After the accords had been signed, Hanoi's public statements and internal policy documents trumpeted that the Paris treaty was a huge victory, since it compelled America to withdraw. By late March, however, Hanoi was confronted by a major propaganda problem. For years it had bandied the slogan "Americans out, puppets collapse." With the Americans now gone, and the South Vietnamese showing no signs of disintegration, what strategy should the Politburo adopt to achieve its goal of national reunification?

Hints that the Politburo had chosen to focus on the Northern economy resurrected the old "North versus South" debate among Western analysts. Hanoi watchers had long noted a factional split within the Politburo between those who favored pursuing economic growth in the North, and those who favored major military offensives in the South. At the third National Party Congress, held in September 1960, Ho Chi Minh had brought the debate into the open when he stressed that the nation's twin goals were to build socialism in the North while fighting for national reunification.

Some analysts attempted to boil down the "North versus South" schism into "hawks versus doves." That is a misreading of the dispute. It was not an either/or process, but a continuum. The Communists attempted to judge the most appropriate mix of agitation, guerrilla attacks, and main-force warfare for each specific time period. Moving from one method to another simply meant a shift in emphasis. The main argument was over the correct strategy to accomplish reunification at a particular time. All the evidence from Vietnamese post-war memoirs, which are prone to the same bellicose propaganda and vast overstatements typical of wartime Communist historical texts, indicates that the debate was between two groups: those who supported Party General Secretary Le Duan, and those who backed Truong Chinh, the number-two man. After the death of Ho Chi Minh in 1969, the two were often locked in strategy conflicts. Number-three man Pham Van Dong became the "swing" vote, switching between the two sides depending on the situation.

While the disagreement probably originated when Le Duan replaced Truong Chinh as General Secretary in the late 1950s, policy differences were at its heart. The two were far apart not only on military affairs, but on economic matters as well. Le Duan was willing to take risks to win fast (main-force warfare), while Truong Chinh supported a longer-term approach. Le Duan generally was an economic pragmatist, while Truong Chinh followed Marxist dogma and insisted on collectivizing agriculture and building heavy industry.

Chinh's real name was Dang Xuan Khu. Like many others, upon joining the Party he adopted a *nom de guerre*, both as a matter of security and reflecting his ascension as a new, socialist man. Chinh wanted to solve the North's economic problems first. He still wanted victory in the South, but he sought it through guerrilla warfare, political education, and economic persuasion. Hence, he was willing to settle for a slower method of achieving reunification rather than the major military campaigns favored by Le Duan.

Given the two factions, the Politburo pursued both goals—a "guns and butter" program. That was one reason for the continual aid requests by the North Vietnamese to their Communist brethren. To gain that aid, they played heavily on Marxist consciences around the globe by claiming that they alone were fighting imperialism and the capitalist giant. The failure of the "Easter Offensive" in 1972 allowed the faction that wanted a higher emphasis on political struggle and a priority on building the Northern economy to gather sufficient votes to force a policy change. Then, with the extreme damage caused by the "Christmas bombing" and Nixon's subsequent aid offer, enough Politburo members remained convinced to continue along that path.

Given that they soon changed back to "military struggle," which ultimately led to victory, it is not surprising that the Communists have written little about the Politburo's initial post-ceasefire strategy. Giap's sole insight into early Politburo planning indicates that Hanoi's immediate post-ceasefire policy goal was to demand the establishment of a new regime in the South—the long-sought coalition government with Communist and "Third Force" representatives—while undermining South Vietnam through propaganda. He also notes that the Politburo called for a rapid build-up of the liberated area, which required a major resupply effort. To achieve these aims, Giap's first post-ceasefire order was to build a second road inside South Vietnam paralleling the Ho Chi Minh Trail, which ran on the Laotian side of the mountains.

The political-struggle faction continued to hold sway into March 1973. According to Giap, a Central Military Affairs Committee meeting in early March decided that "we needed to closely combine our own military and political struggles with the legal provisions contained in the Paris Agreement. Gradually, we would take the offensive by political means and with the support of the armed forces, and thereby achieve a ceasefire, with peace restored, and advantage gained."[2]

Despite the sway of the political-struggle group, those like Le Duan who wanted to win via main-force warfare were not going away quietly. Le

Duan, whose true name was Le Van Nhuan, was born in 1907 to a peasant family in Quang Tri province in what would become South Vietnam. He was one of the first members of the Communist Party of Indochina. In late 1946 he was sent to COSVN, eventually rising to the position of Party Secretary. After the 1954 Geneva Agreement, he remained in the South, but in late 1957 he was ordered back to Hanoi. In 1960 he was elected First Secretary of the Party Central Committee. Only Ho Chi Minh ranked higher.

Le Duan's ascendancy in 1960 coincided with the Politburo's decision to resume armed conflict in the South. His entire career focused on military struggle for control of the South. He was also a die-hard Marxist, viewing the war in Indochina as the opening blow in a world-wide assault on colonialism that would topple capitalism. He fervently believed in two revolutionary stratagems to achieve his dream of reunification: proselytizing the population to join the revolution, and main-force warfare. Despite the enormous losses inflicted on his army in the failed 1972 offensive, he still judged North Vietnam stronger than its Southern adversary. He stated that the departure of the Americans was "an opportunity it has taken us twenty years to create," and he was determined not to allow this chance to slip away.

At other crucial junctures in the long war, the men in the Politburo had critically examined the balance of forces between their country and the enemy to determine the proper "struggle" method to achieve national reunification. This time was no different. On 27 March 1973 the Politburo held an expanded meeting (meaning that other high-ranking military and Party leaders were invited to attend), to review the first sixty days of the accords and develop policies toward both the U.S. and South Vietnam. Le Duan opened the session by inciting the other Politburo members, asserting "that the United States had withdrawn its troops but not ended its involvement; the puppets still obdurately tried to sabotage the Agreement."[3] More important, Le Duan pressed the argument that Saigon had refused to form a new government and was massively violating the accords by "nibbling" at Communist-held territory. If Hanoi did not resist, all its previous gains would be lost.

Le Duan's assertions were false. The accords did not stipulate that a new government would be formed, simply that a council would be created to hold elections for a new government. When the two sides could not agree on who would fulfill the "Third Force" role, Thieu called for direct elections, but the Communists refused to participate. As for the "nibbling" charge, South Vietnamese forces had spent considerable time clearing roadblocks and retaking territory lost when Communist forces launched assaults across the South a few days before the ceasefire. Allowing the North Vietnamese to keep those territorial gains would have badly damaged South Vietnam. Technically Thieu's forces had broken the ceasefire, but most of their violations stemmed from these counterattacks, although many of his generals continued to press forward after clearing out the initial incursions. To limit Hanoi's accusations, on 3 March Thieu instructed each of his four corps commanders to reduce air and artillery usage and halt offensive operations. He did permit his commanders to react forcefully to Communist incursions.

Still, for hardened revolutionaries, Le Duan's plea was hard to ignore, and it appears that this late-March Politburo meeting was the end for the political-struggle faction. Without access to contemporaneous documents it is difficult to determine whether the political-versus-military debate represented a real split in the Politburo, another in a series of strategy disagreements, or a change of tactics until a new direction could be determined. The memoirs of several high-ranking officers hint that a conflict existed, and subtle signs indicate that, to gain consensus, Le Duan may have promised the Chinh faction that rebuilding the Army would not detract from improving the economy. For example, the Central Military Affairs Committee soon added "economic construction" in the North to its portfolio.

In fact, though, the soldiers of the People's Army were receiving a message very different from "economic construction." The Communist leadership was desperately trying to rally its troops, as many believed that the war was over and that they could return to their Northern farms. Worse, in Giap's view, some had reacted passively to ARVN efforts to push into contested areas. To rectify that situation, Giap and several other Central Committee members went on inspection trips to improve spirits. They hewed to the Party line that the Communists were strictly observing the ceasefire, and they castigated the "massive violations" of the South Vietnamese. They had little choice. To justify maintaining a standing army in the South to their own people, and to defend their military actions to the international community, they had to rationalize the failure of the ceasefire. They did it by blaming the South Vietnamese and the Americans. The strategy proved wildly successful.

Hidden behind the protestations that Hanoi was strictly observing the ceasefire was the commencement of military planning to conquer South

Vietnam. Like Le Duan, Giap also wanted to return to main-force warfare. He refused to accept that the South Vietnamese, even given their large military, were stronger than his Northern army. After almost thirty years of warfare, all "foreign aggressors" had departed, and for Giap, this now was the "final stage" of the war.

In April 1973 he summoned his top lieutenants to his residence. He formed a top-secret team, named the "Central Cell," to prepare for another offensive. Given the timing, the formation of the Central Cell was probably approved at the 27 March Politburo meeting. Its purpose was simple: devise a plan to conquer South Vietnam within a two-year period, 1975 –76. As one senior general within the cell noted: "From mid-1973 to early 1975, the General Staff concentrated its efforts on three major tasks: (1) Developing a strategic plan and systematically updating and perfecting a basic strategy to completely liberate South Vietnam. (2) Directing combat operations to block, push back, and gradually defeat the enemy's territorial encroachment and pacification plan. (3) Provide guidance and direction for combat operations to create the necessary battlefield posture, for the preparation of the battlefield, for building forces, for conducting military training, and for sending steadily greater support and supplies to South Vietnam in order to create the necessary strength."[4]

Another expanded Politburo meeting was scheduled for late May, and Giap began to prepare. To gain clarity regarding the battlefield situation, between early April and mid-May he held working sessions in Hanoi with his staff and the commanders based in the South. Giap's key staff officer, Lieutenant General Hoang Van Thai, coordinated many of these sessions. Thai was one of the original thirty-four members of PAVN, and he commanded its first armed propaganda team. From late 1967 to early 1973 he fought in the South as the commander of the B-2 Front, the military region comprising the southern half of South Vietnam. Shortly after the ceasefire, he was recalled to Hanoi. He was the third most powerful officer in the Army, after Giap and General Van Tien Dung, who was a Politburo member and PAVN's chief of staff.

In preparation for briefing Giap, Thai collected information from PAVN commanders regarding a major victory in the lower Mekong Delta in which they claimed to have stymied an ARVN attempt to conquer Communist-controlled areas in Chuong Thien province. Because of its central location, Chuong Thien, known as the "hub of the Delta," was the second-most-important province in IV Corps. The main PAVN infiltration route to the lower Delta ran through Chuong Thien. Communist accounts, including the history of Military Region 9 (MR-9, the lower Delta), claim that in early March 1973, PAVN's intelligence services learned of a secret ARVN operational plan to recapture lost territory in Chuong Thien.[5] To stop the South Vietnamese, the Communists moved four regiments into the province. In mid-March the ARVN 21st Division pressed into Chuong Thien, but North Vietnamese stopped them. On 4 April PAVN commanders in the lower Delta reported to Thai in Hanoi that the South Vietnamese had launched a large number of operations. According to these accounts, PAVN forces easily contained the thrusts.

At Giap's first meeting with his senior commanders, Hoang Van Thai briefed them on these engagements in Chuong Thien. Giap claimed this was proof that PAVN was equal to ARVN. Others were not so sure; they believed the South Vietnamese remained stronger. Colonel General Tran Van Tra, who had replaced Thai as B-2 Front commander, claims that the meetings were contentious, and that the "matter that was discussed most . . . was the question of who was stronger, we or the enemy."[6] Tra states that during the sessions those who believed PAVN were the equal of ARVN succeeded in imposing their viewpoint on those who did not. Thus, as the Politburo gathered on 24 May to review the situation and determine the next steps, Giap entered the meeting determined to push his agenda of militarily conquering the South.

As was customary, Le Duan made the opening speech. Again he claimed that the South Vietnamese, with the full backing of the Americans, were massively violating the Paris Accords. While he continued to call the accords a "great victory," he insisted that "The revolution must march forward through the path of violence. By doing so, we are sure to win victory."[7] According to Giap's account, some opposition arose during the meeting. While not disagreeing with Le Duan, Truong Chinh noted that earlier offensives suffered from what he called "limitations" (meaning failure). Moreover, Pham Van Dong stated that while it was correct to "wage parallel military and political struggles, at this time, the military struggle must be the pillar and a support to the political struggle." After further discussion, Giap provided an overview of the military state of affairs, outlining the situations in the various regions. Since he needed to provide a compelling example to demonstrate PAVN's superiority, he boasted about its success in Chuong Thien in resisting ARVN efforts. He postulated that the primary reason for the South Vietnamese success in seizing territory was PAVN's refusal to fight back. In conclusion, Giap offered the following sharp assessment: "If things continue like this, the situation will leave us at a tremendous disadvantage."[8]

Despite the apparent doubts by Pham Van Dong and Truong Chinh, under continual prodding from Le Duan and Giap, the Politburo agreed to return to war. Dong and others might have preferred to maintain the current strategy, but they were soon squelched, even though public speeches continued to declare that Hanoi's priority was economic reconstruction. Moreover, it is well to remember that while the North Vietnamese had secretly decided to launch another offensive, Le Duc Tho was in Paris debating Kissinger on new measures to implement the ceasefire. The Paris Peace Accords were dead, but only the Politburo knew it.

Given the Communist commanders' claims that they defeated an ARVN offensive to retake Chuong Thien, and Giap's use of this example to persuade the wavering Politburo members to return to the military struggle, the events in Chuong Thien have profound implications. Did ARVN launch an offensive to retake Communist controlled areas in this province, thus "massively violating" the accords?

The answer is no. The U.S. Consulate in Can Tho claimed it was the Communists who had pushed heavily into Chuong Thien, driving deep into GVN territory. In fact, the ARVN 21st Division was almost stationary in March, conducting few offensive operations. Not until early May did the ARVN IV Corps commander, Lieutenant General Nguyen Vinh Nghi, move two regiments from the 21st Division into Chuong Thien to halt Communist gains. He also began visiting the province daily, and he assigned a new province chief, Colonel Ho Ngoc Can, who had been named ARVN's "Soldier of the Year" in 1972. In June he replaced the 21st Division's commander with Brigadier General Le Van Hung. Hung had led the ARVN 5th Division at An Loc during the tough days of 1972. While Hung's American advisers thought he was a poor officer, he had a good reputation within ARVN. He had served previously with the 21st Division under Nghi and knew the area. Nghi's last move was to assign an additional eleven Regional Force (RF) battalions from outside the province to help guard Chuong Thien.[9]

Corroborating the American account, after the war the PAVN commander of MR-9, Senior Colonel (equivalent in rank to brigadier general) Le Duc Anh, admitted that he had flouted orders regarding the ceasefire and continued fighting. Anh wrote that shortly after the accords were signed, he was ordered to de-escalate the fighting. In an unusual departure for the reputedly highly disciplined Communists, he refused. Two months later, he was directed a second time to retreat. He again refused. He believed that the war would persist regardless of the accords, and that following higher-level orders to remain passive would lead to his destruction. When he continued to disobey, COSVN instructed him once more to refrain from aggressive actions and withdraw back to his bases in the impenetrable U Minh Forest for retraining. When Anh did not, he immediately came under heavy criticism. He later wrote: "COSVN sent two more cables demanding that [Military Region 9] recognize the new situation and that we employ new methods. COSVN Military Headquarters sent out a cable criticizing [us] for not implementing COSVN's policy orders and sent information copies of this cable to all areas of South Vietnam. At that time the general opinion was that we in the lower Mekong Delta were 'ripping up the Paris Agreement.' In late May 1973 a conference was held at COSVN Headquarters to review political struggle and military proselytizing operations. The cadre group from the Center [Hanoi] and from COSVN participating in the review loudly criticized Region 9 for not following policy directives issued by higher authority."[10]

Not surprisingly, Anh's unprecedented disobedience threatened his job. Anh writes that one of his subordinates, returning from the May conference at COSVN, reported that "some people have recommended that you be prosecuted because you have not implemented and have sabotaged the Agreement!"[11] Yet Anh not only survived, he was eventually promoted. In Giap's view, Anh's actions were correct. Anh's boss, Tran Van Tra, later grudgingly lauded him for engaging in "specific acts [that] were completely contrary to a whole series of policies at that time . . . [his actions were] an incorrect understanding of the Paris Agreement and the new strategic phase. . . . Luckily, that was a distant battlefield, so upper-echelon policies were often slow in reaching it, and the rectification of mistakes was often not prompt."[12]

If ARVN's actions in Chuong Thien as reported by Giap to the Politburo never happened, did Giap deliberately falsify his account to convince the Politburo to change strategy? Or was Anh lying about South Vietnamese efforts in Chuong Thien to justify his disobedience? Either way, the return to war was based on a lie.

Regardless, the Politburo decision to return to war was precisely what Giap sought: "Nobody thought any longer in terms of respites. . . . The combat, we realized, would drag on. Because the enemy carried on with its . . . peace-sabotaging attempts, we had no choice but to defend our revolutionary gains, which we had earned at a great cost of blood." It was, he felt, "not possible to stop in mid-journey," and thus, "the situation would pass through a period of instability, and South Vietnam would have both peace and war."[13]

To formalize the return to military struggle, Le Duan sought the backing of the Central Committee. The 21st Plenum of the Central Committee was set for late June and would determine Communist strategy in Giap's "final stage of the war." Giap again prepared a major presentation. He wanted to impress upon the Central Committee members his belief that because U.S. forces had pulled out, by default PAVN was in its strongest position of the war. Giap invited leaders from the B-2 Front to discuss the defeat of ARVN's efforts in Chuong Thien. Since the GVN was "massively violating" the ceasefire, Giap wanted to highlight this battle so he could then ascribe PAVN failures in other regions to a lack of resolve, rather than admitting that the enemy was stronger.

As the Plenum began, Le Duan's opening speech made the same point as before: The South Vietnamese were blatantly violating the Paris Accords. Therefore, "military issues must be raised to the highest level possible. Political strategy must be combined with military strategy."[14] It was his way of telling the Committee members that North Vietnam must return to main-force warfare if it wanted to achieve victory.

Giap and other members of the Central Military Affairs Committee also gave speeches. While Giap was blunt about the various problems still confronting the military, he was resolute in his belief that the South Vietnamese were not invincible. Tra in particular recalls a lengthy discussion over how the PAVN commanders in the northern I Corps area had pulled their forces back to defined zones so their units could be refitted. Tra and the other B-2 Front commanders were adamantly against this, believing that the so-called "leopard spots," wherein the B-2 Front troops were mixed in among the South Vietnamese, provided them a tremendous advantage.

On 6 July the Central Committee rubber-stamped Le Duan's proposal that the path in the South was one of "revolutionary violence." The decision meant that the work of rebuilding PAVN, defending the areas that had been captured in 1972, expanding the Ho Chi Minh Trail, and isolating Saigon diplomatically, while creating unrest among the South Vietnamese military and people, would begin in earnest.

Now Giap had to implement the new strategy, but another internal roadblock surfaced. Le Duan, who was enamored of his own revolutionary military strategy and disdainful of Giap's generalship, wanted a broad offensive primarily focused on revolutionary uprisings in the cities to liberate the South. Namely, he sought a repeat of the 1968 Tet Offensive. Giap, however, was not going down that path again. He had strongly disagreed with Le Duan about launching the Tet Offensive, and when he lost that battle, he left the country on "medical leave." When the Central Cell revamped the Strategic Plan to reflect Le Duan's ideas, Giap quietly asked it to review the final stages of a number of wars, including the Soviet defeat of Nazi Germany and the Chinese Communists' victory in 1949. The historical appraisals provided Giap the ammunition he needed: "I believed that we could not make a general insurrection our first priority. Instead, the essential task was to conduct large attacks to destroy an important segment of the enemy's army first in order to create conditions that would allow us to attack the cities, the enemy's primary lairs . . . to secure total victory. I discussed this subject on many occasions with the Party First Secretary. In the end, he agreed."[15]

Giap needed new tactics designed to destroy major ARVN units, and he wanted his senior officers to learn the essentials for coordinating and sustaining combined-arms operations: command and control, staff planning, and logistics. These had been the great weaknesses of the 1972 offensive. PAVN needed to become a modern army, and only the Soviets could train it in this type of warfare. After the 21st Plenum, a group of North Vietnamese officers, led by then Senior Colonel Nguyen Huu An, who had commanded the two PAVN regiments at the famous battle of Ia Drang in 1965, traveled to Russia to attend a course on combined-arms operations. It would pay huge dividends during the 1975 fighting.

On 4 October, the Central Committee formally approved the Resolution of the 21st Plenum, more commonly referred to as Resolution 21. This resolution codified the Politburo's decision regarding a military conquest of the South. The ramifications were immediate. On 20 October, the Provisional Revolutionary Government in the South announced a decision to "fight back . . . in order to defend the liberated zone."[16] In mid-November, Le Duan sent a letter to the Party committees of the Southern military regions providing his personal guidance regarding the meaning of Resolution 21. He wrote: "The situation will develop depending on our actual strength and the manner in which we cope. The first thing we must decide upon is that we can only achieve victory in the South through incessant revolutionary warfare, by violence, while relying on political strength and the armed strength of the people to apply and develop a new factor, a new opportunity, presented by the Paris Agreement. This is the basic spirit of Resolution 21. . . . Almost 20 years of war and the Paris Peace Agreement have presented us with the best opportunity thus far for carrying out the revolution in the entire country, especially regarding the revolution in the South. We must not underestimate the enemy but our position of strength and our victory cannot be reversed."[17]

PREPARING FOR RENEWED WAR

For the few American officials remaining in South Vietnam, watching the growing distancing from Vietnam in Congress and in America at large was heart wrenching. Once the U.S. prisoners had returned home, most Americans were very eager to forget the war. The Gallup organization reported in March 1973 that Vietnam was quickly receding as a national issue.

The major remaining American presence in Vietnam was the U.S. Embassy, which soon had a new ambassador. On 17 July 1973, Graham Martin arrived to replace the highly esteemed Ellsworth Bunker. When tapped to be ambassador, Martin only reluctantly agreed. At age sixty, he was contemplating retirement. Born on 22 September 1912 in North Carolina, he had worked for various newspapers before joining the Social Security Board in 1933. In 1941 he entered the Army Air Corps and rose to the rank of colonel. In 1947 he joined the Foreign Service and was posted to Paris for eight years. After Paris, he worked in a series of government positions until chosen in May 1963 as ambassador to Thailand, where he spent four years. Upon his departure from Thailand he was given the State Department's Distinguished Honor award. In 1969 he was named ambassador to Italy. He expected to retire there, and bought a small Tuscan farm to enjoy his golden years.

Martin was a tough, hard-line anti-Communist. He ran a tight ship, tolerating little dissent, the very qualities that Nixon found so attractive. He was adamant about maintaining the president's commitments to South Vietnam, and he saw the GVN's continued existence as a key component of a robust American foreign policy. Before Martin left for his new post, he was summoned to the White House for an audience with Nixon and Kissinger and given his marching orders: "Your primary mission will be to ensure the survival of the GVN. I know you recognize how much is at stake for this country, and I do not underestimate the difficulty of the assignment I am giving you. The ultimate success or failure of our sacrifices for Vietnam will depend in large measure on your skill in dealing with the complex period ahead. There is no more important post and that is why you have been selected. . . . Please convey my best wishes to President Thieu and my solemn assurances of continued U.S. support. We will stand by the commitments made to him in April in San Clemente. . . . We will do all we can to support the GVN during this difficult period. To enhance our chances of Congressional support for adequate economic aid, you should repeat to Thieu the critical importance of maintaining a favorable image in the U.S. and of making every effort to comply with the Agreement."[18]

Martin did exactly that, and he fought valiantly for South Vietnam, long after everyone else wanted to forget the war. Even though he claimed to have had an epiphany in December 1974 that South Vietnam would not survive, he stayed and wrestled for more support, not only with the U.S. government bureaucracy but also from other countries. He secretly asked to become Kissinger's deputy in January 1975, but when he was rejected, he did not resign but stayed and continued to battle.

The South Vietnamese also did not sit idle. South Vietnamese military successes during the 1972 campaign had instilled in the RVNAF a new-found confidence. According to General Cao Van Vien, the commander of all South Vietnamese military forces, "morale in the military was high, and we believed we could defeat any North Vietnamese attack. But we needed U.S. weapons, ammunition, fuel and other supplies. We could not manufacture them ourselves, and without them, we could not survive."[19] Vien added that he believed the South Vietnamese could handle local offensives, but U.S. airpower "was critical in halting any major offensive."

In early 1973, the RVNAF was given four goals: recover any territory lost during the Communists' post-ceasefire incursions, finish rebuilding troop units that had suffered high casualties during the 1972 fighting, complete all military modernization projects, and assist the government's pacification and rural-development plans. The last priority meant fortifying GVN holdings while concurrently pushing into contested areas, a program Saigon called "flooding the territory." Hanoi described this as "nibbling," charging that it was a ceasefire violation, which sometimes it was.

The Joint General Staff (JGS) faced a formidable challenge in accomplishing these tasks. All allied troops and U.S. airpower had withdrawn, resulting in the need to defend the country with less than half the previous forces and a fraction of the firepower. Additionally, the 1972 offensive had left Communist units much closer to the major cities than ever before. In II Corps, Kontum was threatened from both the north and the west, while the defensive belt around Saigon had shrunk to thirty miles in some places. The situation was worse in I Corps, with the North Vietnamese for the first time poised near the plains instead of far back in the mountains.

To compensate, during the first half of 1973, the South Vietnamese increased the number of RF battalions from 189 to 339, mainly by merging existing units. The Popular Forces (PF) and local police, which defended the hamlets, were also expanded. A major governmental program began relocating the one million refugees from the 1972 fighting onto abandoned land. With these efforts, control in the provinces increased, at least initially. Many had predicted that Thieu's government would collapse after the U.S. withdrawal. Instead, after some initial nervousness among GVN officials, the government found an inner strength. Growing in confidence and now out from under the American umbrella—yet still requiring U.S. aid to survive—the South Vietnamese were finally taking control of their own destiny.

Thieu knew his most pressing needs were to jump-start the economy and provide security for the people. The economy had not recovered from the devastating 1972 offensive and the impact of the great reduction in the U.S presence. The country was staggering under the twin blows of serious inflation and increasing unemployment. June 1973 had seen a 19 percent jump in prices, and the price of rice had risen 25 percent since January. Since South Vietnam's economy was tied to the dollar, it had been particularly hard hit by the dollar's depreciation and higher world prices. Now it was on the precipice of a depression. Public discontent over the economy was the highest in years, and rising social evils, including alcoholism and drug use, crime, and increased corruption, were attributed to the worsening economy.

Thieu's hopes for post-war economic growth revolved largely around agriculture, although the discovery of offshore oil deposits would soon dangle the prospect of a much-needed alternative economic engine. Since the Mekong Delta was the country's breadbasket, the government turned its main attention to expanding rice production and extending control across the Delta. The fertile lowlands became even more critical when rice shortages appeared in South Vietnam in mid-1973. On top of every other

economic ill, a combination of rapidly rising prices and unexpected shortages of the country's most important food staple was a significant threat to
South Vietnam's government and society, second only to the Communists.

Typically a backwater of the war, the Delta suddenly became the military focal point in the summer of 1973 when heavy fighting erupted over
the country's main crop. The northern provinces of South Vietnam had
just suffered a horrendous drought that had badly damaged the summer
harvest, and the area was desperate to import rice. Contributing to the
area's rice shortage were heavy purchases by Communist supply agents.
By paying much higher prices, they bought rice and other commodities
to support their military forces. If local farmers refused to sell, they levied
a "tax" on them, essentially stealing their food. In the area around Saigon,
the North Vietnamese army acquired most of its rice from either the Delta
or Cambodia. Given that the Khmer Rouge had ordered no further sales of
rice to the North Vietnamese, Delta rice suddenly became hotly contested.

Though the Delta was a difficult command because of its size, high population density, and swampy terrain, ARVN Lieutenant General Nguyen Vinh
Nghi ruled a potent military apparatus. Nghi had three divisions: the highly
effective 7th Division, which operated in critical Dinh Tuong province in
the upper Delta; the efficient 9th Division in the eastern provinces; and the
poorly rated 21st Division, which maneuvered from the middle of the Delta
to Vietnam's southern tip. Nghi also had nine Ranger battalions, the 4th
Armor Brigade equipped with M-113 armored personnel carriers, and the
largest number of Regional and Popular Forces in the country. The Vietnamese Air Force provided air cover from a large jet-capable airport at Can Tho,
while the Navy's riverine force patrolled the myriad rivers and canals.

Nghi was born in October 1932 near Saigon. He graduated in 1952 from
the Dalat Military Academy, South Vietnam's West Point. Highly intelligent
and a firm anti-Communist, he had well-known friendships with both
Thieu and Prime Minister Tran Thien Khiem. He was a better staff officer
than combat leader, and in the first part of his career he served mainly on
divisional staffs. Despite long-standing and justified accusations of corruption, in June 1968 Nghi was promoted to brigadier general and given
command of the 21st Division. Under Nghi's leadership, the 21st Division's combat effectiveness slowly sank, but his connections with Thieu
and Khiem remained intact. On 3 May 1972 he was given command of IV
Corps.

Because of continued PAVN post-ceasefire attacks, including a major assault on the river port of Hong Ngu in early April 1973, Nghi moved to eliminate enemy base areas inside IV Corps. His first target was a key Communist hideout known as the Seven Mountains. Situated along the Cambodian border, the Seven Mountains are a chain of rugged peaks pockmarked with caves that rise out of the flat Delta terrain. Nghi, using both the Rangers and Regional Forces, began a methodical drive to clean out the base. Over a period of several months, the campaign so badly decimated the PAVN 1st Division that the unit was disbanded.

Yet despite this and several other victories, the U.S. Defense Attaché Office (DAO), the residual American military presence in South Vietnam, was growing increasingly concerned. Beginning in April 1973 and continuing until the end, the DAO intelligence chief, Colonel William Le Gro, wrote a monthly summary for U.S. government and military policymakers. Each report described the previous month's military events in South Vietnam, and analyzed trends and gave predictions for the future. In September 1973, Le Gro provided his first overall assessment. He bluntly informed Washington: "Hanoi has developed its strongest military position in the history of the war. The objective remains the complete takeover of South Vietnam."[20] Examining Hanoi's options, he surmised that Soviet and Chinese aid, which seemed more oriented toward economic support than weapons, would be a decisive factor in any major offensive. Even if the North did not receive any new military hardware, Hanoi was lacking only the manpower, especially in III Corps, before it could launch an all-out attack.

More important, according to Le Gro, the constant combat was draining ARVN morale. Like their Northern brethren, many South Vietnamese troops hoped the long war had ended and they could return to their villages. Instead, the fighting dragged on, the economy grew worse, and inflation sapped their meager earnings. Consequently, discipline eroded, looting increased, corruption expanded, and drug addiction climbed. News began to filter into Saigon about RF/PF units reaching accommodations with the Communists, as in, We will stay out of your area if you stay out of ours. Some civilians and soldiers were desperate to earn money and secretly traded with the enemy. Moreover, PAVN had scored a few victories in III and IV Corps, mauling several ARVN battalions in well-planned ambushes.

Although Thieu was aware of the despondency in his lower ranks, the growing military threat precluded any efforts to relieve the stress on his troops. On 31 October he announced on television and radio that he believed the Communists were preparing for another offensive. Within days his prediction was partially borne out when PAVN launched a major attack in Quang Duc province in II Corps. To back up his firm stance, Thieu began relieving commanders. The III Corps commander, Lieutenant General Nguyen Van Minh, was transferred on 27 October to become the commander of the Capital Military District, the area around Saigon. Within days, the commanders of two divisions in III Corps, the 5th and the 25th, were relieved for corruption. Thieu also replaced five province chiefs and several other division commanders. By early November, he had also relieved the Quang Duc province chief and the 23rd Division commander for their failure to retake two Montagnard villages lost during the Quang Duc fighting.

By the end of 1973, Thieu's tolerance for the Communist attacks and continued infiltration had reached its limit. Speaking in Can Tho on 4 January 1974, Thieu stated: "We cannot sit by idly. We must take appropriate actions to punish the Communist aggressive actions. We will not allow the Communists to enjoy stable security in their staging areas from which they will harass us, attack our posts, destroy our infrastructure, and steal our rice. We must take these actions not only in our zone of control, but also right in the areas where the North Vietnamese troops are still stationed. . . . Only when the Communists . . . have the good will to hold elections, will we stop these actions at precisely the moment the Communist actions are stopped. . . . We must not heed groundless comments and criticism—no matter where it comes from."[21]

It was a challenge to his enemies, and to the Americans. He could not watch the war, and his country, slip away. For Thieu, the ceasefire was dead. Looking out at the crowd, he spoke from his gut. "The war," he declared, "has begun again."

3

"ENOUGH TO MAKE THE ANGELS WEEP"

TRADING BLOOD FOR AMMUNITION

When his call to strike at the Communist strongholds was met with American dismay, Thieu realized he needed to mend fences with his benefactors. He moved swiftly to mollify them by taking steps that he felt would not only help his country but curry favor with the mercurial members of Congress. On 18 January 1974 he called a third time for the Communists to participate in national elections. A week later, the South Vietnamese foreign minister publicly declared a willingness to meet with the Communists to negotiate the normalization of relations between the two countries. As usual, both offers were rejected by Hanoi.

With the continuing poor performance of the economy, Thieu undertook another major shake-up of his Cabinet. In October 1973, Thieu had replaced his economic team, trying to find new formulas to improve the economy. On 16 February 1974, the Cabinet resigned, and Thieu asked Prime Minister Tran Thien Khiem to form a new government. The announced rationale for this second change was to improve government efficiency. Although some ministries were eliminated, however, most Cabinet ministers retained their original positions.

Khiem was Thieu's right-hand man. As ARVN's senior general (one of only two four-star generals in the South Vietnamese military), Khiem secured the Army's support for Thieu. Khiem had also participated in the coup against President Diem in 1963, but a falling-out with his co-conspirators forced him abroad as an ambassador, first to the United States and then to Taiwan. Thieu had brought him back in May 1968, and promoted him to Prime Minister in August 1969. Many outsiders searched for signs of a rivalry between the two men, but they usually were on good terms.

In various speeches, Thieu continued his emphasis on the need for the country to move toward self-sufficiency. He once more implored his people to work hard to develop the nation's resources, and to "tighten belts" (*that lung buoc bung*), a course of action he had called for since 1973. Thieu's call to "tighten belts" was not just rhetoric; it was a demand that struck to the very core of daily existence. Despite his efforts, the South Vietnamese economy continued to contract. The ranks of the unemployed swelled dramatically, followed by the repeated devaluation of the piaster. The worst economic shock, however, was the Arab oil embargo, which caused a massive hike in gas prices. The resultant surge, 67 percent in 1973, devastated the already slim wages of the lower-ranking soldiers. A survey of soldiers in the ARVN 3rd Division conducted in 1973 revealed that 90 percent of the families of enlisted men had not eaten meat for over a month, and 50 percent had eaten fish or shrimp only a few times. That the average soldier continued to fight was truly amazing.

Despite the poor economic conditions and worsening security, in the first quarter of 1974 Thieu's government completed the relocation of the final refugees from the 1972 offensive—one of its great but unheralded achievements. These citizens, some four hundred thousand people, were sent to areas recaptured from the Communists. The new villages drew immediate sniper fire, mortar barrages, and road mining. Worse were the terrorist threats: the people were told that they must either join the Communist side, or face poisoned wells and destruction of their livestock. To assist the refugees, on 26 March 1974, the fourth anniversary of the "Land to the Tiller" program, Thieu declared an accelerated plan of distributing land to farmers. The JGS also began reducing the size of the armed forces, hoping to shift the manpower into building the economy. In April, over four thousand officers and men who had reached service limits were discharged, with plans to release more. After Communist attacks increased in mid-1974, however, the idea was abandoned.

South Vietnam desperately needed aid, but its American benefactors had their own budgetary woes. The first rumblings of a possible cutback had come on 27 June 1973. Deputy Secretary of Defense Warren Clements testified during hearings for the 1974 budget that the new ceasefire agreement would permit a decrease of $500 million in military aid to South Vietnam and Laos, and that the aid ceiling could be shrunk from $2.1 billion to $1.2 billion. The Senate Armed Services Committee accepted Clements's recommendations and voted to reduce military aid to South Vietnam and Laos. Shortly thereafter, both houses of Congress agreed to cut funding to the recommended $1.2 billion level. With the revised ceiling, the budget hammer fell on South Vietnam in mid-December 1973, when the U.S. Army unexpectedly cut off all operational and maintenance funding for the rest of Fiscal Year (FY) 1974, which ran from July 1973 to June 1974.

Major General John E. Murray, who headed the Defense Attaché Office in Saigon, was the American official responsible for managing military aid to war-torn South Vietnam. A slim Irishman with a quick wit and a slashing writing style, Murray began his Army career in World War II as a private. He later became a lawyer and joined the Judge Advocate General Corps. After the Korean conflict, he switched careers again and eventually became one of the Army's top logisticians. He served tours in Vietnam as port commander at Cam Ranh Bay, and later as commander of the Saigon Support

Command. He returned in mid-1972 as the last American chief logistics officer, and then was ordered in January 1973 to head the DAO. Limited by the Paris Accords to fifty military men, the DAO was augmented by over a thousand civilians working on various projects, from maintenance to logistics. Overall, Murray was tasked with managing a billion-dollar-plus business while, as he put it, being "fine-tuned by a 12,000-mile Washington screwdriver."

When the Army cut off funds in mid-December, Murray immediately sought permission from Ambassador Graham Martin to inform the JGS. Martin denied his request, hoping the Nixon administration could restore the funding level. Murray then sought clarification from the Pentagon on precisely how much money remained for South Vietnam, particularly since the vast majority of FY74 cash had already been either spent or allocated. He was stunned when the Army was unable to provide an accurate audit of monies spent or remaining. Worse, the dramatic increase in worldwide inflation caused by the oil embargo, plus the inexplicable shifting by the Army of some FY73 costs onto the 1974 budget, further sapped the limited resources. As Murray later wrote: "December '73—that's the fatal date that the GVN started precipitously down the slippery slope . . . the Army in its . . . inept handling of Vietnam money suddenly and without warning cut off [all funds], and the terrible following troubles were accentuated by the Ambassador's unmoving insistence that the South Vietnamese not be informed. I pleaded with him . . . in vain. The RVNAF in their ignorance kept requisitioning and using up supplies at their usual rates. They were bleeding to death and I wanted to apply the tourniquet."[1]

Murray tried to impress upon Martin that it took 120 days for parts ordered from the United States to be packed and shipped to Vietnam. Hence, if ARVN did not quickly institute conservation measures, shortages would appear in six months. Martin remained unmoved. For Murray, "ARVN was euchred out of its right to fight by DOD [Department of Defense] fiscal witlessness, [and] mystifying Ambassadorial edicts."[2] While the majority of the blame for the aid debacle has been laid on Congress's doorstep, it was compounded by both the Pentagon's "fiscal witlessness" and the fact that its supply depots and funds had been sucked dry by the massive resupply effort to Israel during the October 1973 "Yom Kippur War." Martin certainly had been warned that the odds of gaining new monies for South Vietnam were long. National Security Advisor Brent Scowcroft summed up the situation to Martin at the end of December:

"The hard facts are that our options are very limited—commitments to Israel have . . . drawn down active force stocks and reserve inventories, and there is no money or legislative authority to procure a major package for Vietnam. There are terribly hard decisions to be made on the allocations of severely constrained fiscal and material resources between many competing requirements."[3]

In early January 1974 Murray met with General Cao Van Vien, head of the South Vietnamese military, to impress upon him the need to conserve ammunition. Vien was born to Vietnamese parents in Vientiane, Laos, in December 1921. He joined the Army in 1949, and he and President Thieu and Prime Minister Khiem served together in North Vietnam during the French war, which created a long-standing bond among the three. Vien was a very loyal supporter of President Diem, and after the failed 1960 coup by the Airborne Brigade, he was given command of that elite unit. When General Duong Van Minh launched the November 1963 coup against Diem, Vien was brought before Minh and ordered to assist in the coup. At the time, there was a carbine pressed into his back. Vien refused. He was not executed, but was instead tossed into jail. However, the coup and the carbine incident fostered in Vien a nasty grudge against Minh, and the events of November 1963 would later rebound in April 1975.

Despite Vien's refusal to take part in the coup, he was released and was reinstated as commander of the Airborne Brigade. In 1964 he was badly wounded in the shoulder while commanding his troops in an operation in the upper Delta. He was hit, he later told the author, because as an Airborne officer he was expected to display his courage by walking upright around the battlefield. In October 1965 Vien became head of the military. Eventually he became the second-highest-ranking officer in the Army, and the only other four-star general besides Prime Minister Khiem. A quiet, introspective man, he was not an overtly political officer, as were many of his counterparts. This was a key reason Thieu did not replace him, although rumors that he was considering doing so had floated since 1971. The problem, as was so often the case in Vietnamese society, was finding someone not only more talented, but also from an earlier military-academy class than the other senior generals. Lieutenant General Ngo Quang Truong was the obvious choice, but Truong was junior to many other generals, who would have balked at his elevation.

After meeting with Murray, Vien and his chief logistician, Lieutenant General Dong Van Khuyen, immediately cut the ammunition supply for each unit. Fuel was also restricted, resulting in the immediate curtailment of flying hours and vehicle movement. A military that depended heavily on firepower and mobility to offset the Communist propensity to mass forces suddenly had its two most important advantages sharply curtailed.

The Senate Armed Services Committee began hearings for FY75 on 12 March 1974. The Nixon administration pressed for restoration of its original $1.6 billion military-aid request. Pro-Hanoi groups like the Indochina Resource Center expended great efforts fighting the request, claiming that Saigon was the main culprit in violating the ceasefire. They insisted that cutting aid was the best method to force Thieu to form a coalition government. Many current and former government officials also subscribed to that theory. Clark Clifford, former advisor to President Lyndon Johnson and a powerful figure in the Democratic Party, spoke for most anti-war officials when he stated that Thieu was the main obstacle to peace. Cutting off aid, Clifford felt, would force Thieu to step down. Then, "a truly neutral and representative government would be formed in Saigon which would negotiate in good faith with the other side."[4]

On 3 April 1974, the House and the Senate separately voted down the $1.6 billion funding request for South Vietnam and Laos. The next day, a supplemental-aid request was also voted down. On 22 May, a joint House-Senate committee agreed to slash the Nixon administration's FY74 request for aid to Vietnam to a ceiling of $1.126 billion. A new low mark had been set, and with the final 1975 budget votes looming, it was an ill omen.

One must grant that most members of Congress felt antipathy to providing aid to a regime many believed restricted press freedoms, locked up political prisoners, and had grossly violated the ceasefire. Congress had also grown weary of the U.S. military's fiscal legerdemain in supporting Vietnam. For years, aid was supplied to Saigon by each military service, meaning that money for Vietnam programs was intermingled with the funding for that service. However, the Pentagon's byzantine bookkeeping prevented it from determining exactly what the South Vietnamese had received. Now, a hostile Congress viewed the confusion as an effort to sidestep the funding limitations. The specter of vast corruption involving U.S. aid also weighed heavily on congressional minds.

Moreover, while the congressional votes were partly a response to a worsening U.S. economy, they were also pursued with a view to restoring Congress's prerogatives over foreign aid. Cutbacks were not directed solely at the South Vietnamese; in December 1974, military aid to South Korea was cut by $20 million until the president could certify that the Koreans were loosening their own authoritarian grip. Turkey, after its military invasion of Cyprus, also felt the congressional wrath. But the overarching reality was that the anti-war lobby was determined to eliminate U.S. support for Thieu and force a political coalition with the Communists.

After Congress finalized the 1974 budget, on 1 June Murray sent a lengthy cable to the Pentagon outlining the harsh realities on the ground created by the cuts. Detailing the likely effects of the congressional action, Murray laid out four scenarios. In particular, he made an analogy that, while unforeseen then, would have far-reaching consequences. "In the final analysis," he wrote, "you can roughly equate cuts in support to loss of real estate."[5] Murray created briefing charts displaying that as aid dropped, Thieu would be forced to retreat to a truncated version of South Vietnam centered on Saigon and the Delta. While an aid level of $1.126 billion would enable the South to hang on, vehicles, ships, and aircraft lost in battle could not be replaced (the one-for-one replacement allowed by the accords), and without new equipment, the South Vietnamese military would slowly degrade. At $900 million, mobility and defensive capabilities in the third and fourth quarters of FY75 would be greatly reduced. At $750 million, ARVN would be hard pressed to stop a full-scale attack. At $600 million, Murray stated, the U.S. should "write off [South Vietnam] as a bad investment and a broken promise."

Murray briefed Thieu on these scenarios, but this was not the first time the president had been told that a reduction in territory might be necessary. When the JGS was finally informed in April that military aid was being cut, Vien sent Lieutenant General Khuyen to inform Thieu. Vien ordered Khuyen to use this opportunity to broach the concept of reducing South Vietnam's military forces and, consequently, the amount of territory to defend. Vien, however, instructed Khuyen to present the idea only orally. If nothing was in writing, Vien could not be accused of "defeatism."[6] When Thieu did not react to Khuyen's suggestion, the idea was shelved.

Murray designed his charts to convey a simple truth: that cutting aid was tantamount to destroying South Vietnam's territorial integrity because the military could not defend the entire country against the enemy's growing aggression. Unfortunately, the equation of loss of aid with loss of real estate would eventually become a fixation for Thieu, one that played into his fateful decisions in 1975.

Why did Murray not offer the South Vietnamese an alternative plan, something that they could do with the money they were receiving? For one simple reason: the Paris Accords prevented Murray from offering any military advice. Why did the U.S. Embassy not step in to provide options? Why did Thieu and his senior generals shrink from the tough decisions? Because Ambassador Martin, and the Nixon and Ford administrations, repeatedly told Thieu they would press Congress to restore the previous funding levels, and Thieu took the White House and Martin at their word.

Still, even if Thieu had heeded Vien's advice and sought to pull back to more defensible positions, logistically and politically it would have been an extraordinarily difficult proposition. After the many hoary orations by Thieu and others urging their people to defend every inch of the country, giving up land to the Communists would have been seen as a sign of great weakness. Hue, Danang, and other major cities would have had to be ceded to the Communists. A retreat to a Saigon-Delta redoubt would also have meant moving and resettling millions of people. Such a massive population relocation, even in peacetime, would have overwhelmed Saigon's resources. Imagine the situation if the North Vietnamese had attacked during the course of this effort.

Of all observers, Murray was the chief witness to the slow strangulation of South Vietnam. While ARVN expenditures on artillery ammunition had often been excessive, actions were instituted soon after the ceasefire to reduce the firing rate. Yet despite these measures, no one in the U.S. Army could provide the DAO a definitive accounting of how much ARVN had spent on ammunition. The variances between the different U.S. logistics centers were in the millions of dollars. Now, Congress was shrinking the aid program precisely at the moment the Communist threat was growing.

While Murray was watching the DAO's money like the proverbial green-eyeshaded accountant, he was not naïve about the South Vietnamese. He had railed loudly and often to ARVN logistics officers about local contractors' delivering poor-quality lumber or leaving expensive cement out in the open to harden. When he saw commercial vehicles in Saigon driving with military tires, and soldiers selling gas and batteries on the black market to make money, he pestered Lieutenant General Khuyen and his staff to develop better controls. Although they did, it was not enough. The ARVN supply system had simply never received the priority and training that other aspects of Vietnamization had.

After Murray's briefing, Thieu publicly protested the aid cuts and raised the specter of American abandonment of his country. In a speech on 6 June 1974, he again attempted to placate the U.S. by blasting corruption

and exhorting his people and the military to economize. He also reiterated his main point: a strong military would make Hanoi realize it could
not win. Only then, Thieu proclaimed, would the Communists seriously
negotiate. Moreover, this time he directly attacked the United States. He
contrasted the present treatment of his country to America's generosity
toward Europe after World War II and South Korea after the Korean conflict. Although he blamed most of the problem on American domestic
turmoil, he accused the U.S. of evading its responsibilities. When the Paris
Accords were signed, Thieu said, he was promised that if the Communists continued to infiltrate men into the South, the U.S. would "react
vigorously," and that North Vietnam's allies would restrain their "small
brother." However, all those promises "have been forgotten." Thieu again
stated he would not accept a coalition government, as that was a "sure
path to death."[7]

Reminding America of its commitments was useless, since Congress
was unaware of what Nixon had secretly promised. In late July, the joint
House-Senate conference again voted to reduce the amount of aid to Vietnam, this time from $1.126 billion to just $1 billion. More important, the
legislation concerning the new aid ceiling had other damaging provisions.
To solve the perennial accounting confusion regarding Vietnam, Senator
John Stennis (D., Miss.), the chairman of the Senate Armed Services Committee, decided to consolidate all money for Vietnam into one fund, called
the Defense Assistance Vietnam (DAV) program. The legislation was quite
specific as to what the military could and could not do with Vietnam aid
money. Everything was to be allocated to the DAV. All costs, including many
not previously charged for, such as the packing and crating of ammunition
and the DAO's operating costs, would henceforth be expensed to the DAV.
A rider also was attached stipulating a 10 percent cut in civilian contractors
in South Vietnam. Another one limited food money.

The grim aid situation grew progressively worse. In early August, the
House voted to appropriate only $700 million of the $1 billion authorized.
And since all costs were to be charged to the DAV, including the cost of the
DAO, the $700 million was in practical effect lowered to only $500 million.
This was below Murray's cut-off level at which the South Vietnamese could
sustain an adequate defense. With $500 million, Saigon could barely afford
ammunition and fuel, let alone other critical supplies. Worse, three price
increases for ammunition totaling 72 percent further reduced the number
of shells the South Vietnamese could purchase. The DAO predicted that by

the end of FY75 (30 June 1975), ARVN would be almost out of fuel and down to a thirty-day supply of ammunition.

Pentagon bookkeeping errors continued to make the situation even more untenable. Immediately after the start of the new fiscal year on 1 July 1974, Murray started receiving messages that large chunks of FY75 monies were being siphoned off. The main culprit was a $77 million charge for new F-5E aircraft, a luxury the VNAF could not afford. A line item had specifically been put into the budget at the request of Senator James B. Pearson (R., Kan.) to have the VNAF buy the new aircraft from their builder, Northrop. What was even more disheartening was that Murray had been told that the F-5Es were already paid for. Now the U.S. Air Force was reneging, and the South Vietnamese were paying the price.

Murray was outraged. He wrote a stinging cable to the Pacific Command outlining the impact of these decisions on the VNAF: "Since late June we have received directives for un-programmed expenditure of approx. $54.3m [the first payment of the F-5E cost plus others] in VNAF FY75 program.... If we are forced to pay these bills ... the VNAF will be virtually finished. At this time of intensifying enemy action and dire need for sustained high aircraft sortie rates, we should be pumping the pipeline full to overcome months of suppressed supply requisitioning caused by the sudden curtailment of FY74 funds. [Instead] we are receiving widespread cancellations ... even if these requisitions are reinstated, we have created another bubble in the pipeline while in the trough of previous cuts. Numbers of operational aircraft are declining as critical spares are consumed with scant replenishment and daily demand for sorties is up and up. Situation leaves VNAF with little recourse but cannibalization, which only digs the hole deeper.... Instead of getting a new start with the new DAV funding ... we're getting retroactively sandbagged."[8]

The U.S. Air Force was not the only service giving Murray fits. The Army's inability to track the amount of ammunition ordered continued to bedevil him. On 9 August, he received a message that $22 million worth of ammunition that had been paid for in 1974 had not been delivered, and now could not be sent because South Vietnam had exceeded the 1974 budget limitation.

Murray was now beyond anger; he was reduced to begging: "This is a super shock. In my twenty months here, I have been bewildered, baffled and dismayed by changing statistics.... I cannot imagine ... that anyone would let $22m worth of ammo be taken away from them.... You may not know that the $700m is really about $500m. . . . This does not leave enough even for ARVN ammo or fuel. And I can tell you plainly that the ARVN is compelled to trade off blood for ammo. That the casualties are going up as the ammo allocations go down. . . . So I plead with you—for them—not to let anyone cut the ARVN out of that $22m that is their due."[9]

The Pentagon denied his request. After his herculean efforts to keep the South Vietnamese afloat, Murray had seen enough. Given his long military career and his blistering arguments with DOD over funding, he asked to retire. He spent his last days in Saigon frantically helping the South Vietnamese program their limited funds. In late August, it was time to leave. After saying goodbye to the senior South Vietnamese officers that he had come to know so well, Murray paid his last respects to General Vien. Vien drove him to the airport. As they stood at the plane, Vien, as if desperately seeking some last messenger, told Murray of his growing fears about the course of the war. For the first time in years, Vien said, ARVN soldiers were losing more weapons to the enemy than they were capturing, a telling statistic on how the war was progressing. Cao Van Vien gripped Murray's hand tightly as he attempted to board the plane, and Vien's final statement rang in Murray's ears: "I am worried about the morale of the troops."

"Considering the tragic events we later lived through," Murray subsequently wrote about Vien's last words, "they are enough to make the angels weep."[10]

THE DIPLOMATIC FRONT

Given the growing debacle involving American aid, President Thieu was now belatedly looking for new sources of assistance and for diplomatic recognition from other countries. Starting in the winter of 1973–74, the GVN began an all-out effort to establish diplomatic relations with non-aligned countries, particularly those in the Arab world, Africa, and Latin America. Former Ambassador to the United States Bui Diem was sent to Japan, India, Indonesia, Malaysia, and other countries seeking aid and attempting to establish relations. The effort—designed to promote goodwill for South Vietnam while diversifying GVN relations so that the South Vietnamese were not seen as American stooges—was moderately successful. Saigon soon had improved contacts with Japan and Saudi Arabia, two significant potential donors.

The Communists also engaged in diplomatic maneuvers. In December 1973, Le Duc Tho and Henry Kissinger, newly promoted to the post of secretary of state, had met again in Paris to discuss the failing ceasefire. Tho seemed eager for a ceasefire and delineation of borders, but offered nothing concrete. On 20 December, after several hours of fruitless discussions, the meeting broke up with no result.

To break the impasse, the Politburo decided to launch a worldwide diplomatic and propaganda offensive. The "diplomatic struggle" consisted of four interlocking areas: the U.S., South Vietnam, the socialist bloc, and the remainder of the world. By exploiting the anti-war mood in the U.S., Hanoi hoped to convince Congress to vote against further aid. Analysis of a captured high-level document determined that the "Communist negotiating strategy is now designed simply to destroy public confidence in the GVN—particularly inside the U.S.—and thus to ward off the foreign trade and aid needed [by] South Vietnam."[11] Meanwhile, the Politburo would attempt to stir up resentment within South Vietnam against corruption in the government and the deteriorating economy, while continuing to appeal to its Communist brethren, especially the Soviets and Chinese, to provide badly needed support. Concurrently, North Vietnam sought to buttress its standing among the nations of the world as the aggrieved party. Behind the scenes, however, the Communists were secretly organizing to resume the war while publicly proclaiming that their main interest lay in rebuilding the Northern economy.

The opening salvo of Hanoi's diplomatic strategy came when it responded to Thieu's claim at Can Tho in January 1974 that the Communists were preparing another attack. In an interview in Paris to discuss the ceasefire anniversary, Foreign Minister and Politburo member Nguyen Duy Trinh strongly denied Thieu's accusation. According to Trinh, the priorities of the Democratic Republic of Vietnam (DRV) were to preserve the ceasefire, build socialism in the North, and move toward a peaceful reunification. He insisted that it was the Saigon regime and the Americans who were preparing new attacks.

Another Politburo member, Economic Minister Le Thanh Nghi, soon supplied more dramatic testimony regarding Hanoi's priorities. The "great victory" that was the signing of the Paris Accords had not brought a better life for the people of the North, and the Politburo intended to remedy that state of affairs—or so it claimed. If Hanoi's military might was growing, it was doing so upon a floundering economy. The DRV's economy was in even worse shape than South Vietnam's, and only Chinese and Russian aid was keeping it afloat. Production facilities were either closed, destroyed, or operating at a fraction of capacity. Transportation lines were in disrepair, and black marketeering was widespread. As in South Vietnam, agriculture was the economic foundation, but with too many unqualified cadres running the system, the Politburo was forced to employ military units to repair long-neglected dikes and irrigation systems. North Vietnam had never been self-sufficient in food, and the 1973 winter rice crop had been especially scanty, hampered by bad weather and poor management. Although North Vietnam had imported a record amount of food in 1973, by April 1974 rice shortages had appeared in certain areas. To improve production, the Politburo reorganized the governmental sections dealing with the economy, especially after a state inventory uncovered large-scale corruption and pilfering.

To address these problems, on 4 February 1974, Nghi gave the keynote speech to the National Assembly, the DRV's Congress. His report was a comprehensive discussion of new plans to improve North Vietnam's wallowing economy. He announced a large-scale two-year (1974–75) reconstruction program to rebuild the infrastructure destroyed by the U.S. bombing, plus an ambitious five-year plan (1976–80) for developing the economy. As Nghi stated, "Now that peace has been restored the need to improve the people's living conditions is a large and urgent one." He then listed the North's seven economic priorities. The first was to "heal the wounds of war." Notably, the last was to "fulfill the duty to the heroic South." In an interview in mid-March he amplified his comments: "We should not be too bent on maintaining vigilance and making preparations for war and thus become unsteady in . . . mobilizing all forces and latent capabilities to intensively perform the task of economic restoration and development."[12]

Nghi's comments caught the attention of many, who took his statement as a signal that North Vietnam was not preparing another massive offensive. To be successful, the economic plan would require a sustained commitment of cadre and materials that for years had been diverted to the war effort. The reality, however, was that the Central Committee had secretly held another plenum, this time to address the dismal economy. The 22nd Plenum, convened from late December to early January, produced Resolution 22. Entitled "Missions and Directions for the Resurrection and Development of North Vietnam's Economy during the Two-Year Period 1974–1975," it was approved and disseminated on 22 January 1974. Nghi's speech was merely a report to the National Assembly on the directives of the 22nd Plenum.

It is unknown whether Nghi's comments were a deliberate smoke-screen to the world, or instead reflected the views of the Politburo faction that wanted to improve the economy before conquering the South. Whatever his intent, the effect was immediate. Most commentators, discussing the one-year anniversary of the ceasefire, juxtaposed Nghi's declarations against Thieu's proclamation that the South Vietnamese would take aggressive action. Many accepted the drumbeat of statements from the DRV professing its deep commitment to peace and building the Northern economy, while concurrently condemning Thieu for his "warlike" stance. Coming just before another round of congressional scrutiny of the South Vietnamese aid programs, the contrasting announcements provided plenty of fodder for those who believed cutting aid was the surest method to force Saigon into reaching a political settlement to end the war.

The Politburo's diplomatic efforts to place Saigon on the defensive soon resumed. On 18 March Hanoi sent a letter to various Western and Eastern Bloc countries. The note vehemently protested U.S. arms and ammunitions shipments to South Vietnam, particularly the impending sale of the F-5E fighter jets to replace older-model F-5As. Le Duc Tho immediately followed up with a letter to Kissinger on 20 March complaining about the F-5Es, and claiming that the U.S. had military advisors disguised as civilians in South Vietnam. Both actions, according to Tho, flagrantly violated the accords.

It was political theater. With Kissinger consumed by the Middle East, the Soviet Union, and other diplomatic issues, Le Duc Tho publicly began re-interpreting provisions in the accords to Hanoi's advantage. He also pushed the boundaries on issues that had been deliberately left vague, attempting to paint Saigon and Washington as the culprits for the ceasefire's failure. North Vietnam's violations, such as continuing infiltration, rebuffing U.S. requests to account for MIAs, and refusal to remove its troops from Laos and Cambodia, were blamed on the American failure to supply economic aid.

Hanoi immediately followed its 18 March letter with a major new diplomatic proposal. On 22 March the Communist delegation in Paris offered a six-point plan that included provisions for a ceasefire and the holding of general elections in South Vietnam. It was the most concrete response by the Communists to the various offers put forth by Saigon after the accords were signed. The plan called for an immediate ceasefire, release of all captured personnel, formation of the National Council of National Reconciliation and Concord, the holding of elections, reduction of the two armies in South Vietnam, and a guarantee of "democratic liberties," such as freedom of the press and freedom of assembly. The last provision was a deliberate shot at one of Thieu's perceived weak points, his restrictions on the press. Believing the Communists were not serious, Thieu rejected the offer.

The North Vietnamese diplomatic offensive—claiming that economic reconstruction was the DRV's priority, and that it was Saigon that was breaking the ceasefire and was not sincere about finding a peaceful political solution—was timed to influence congressional votes on aid for 1974. Hanoi and its Western acolytes had cleverly laid the onus for the protracted warfare on Saigon's doorstep at the same time Congress was debating Nixon's aid request.

Yet behind the diplomatic disguise, the Politburo was preparing for renewed attacks. For the Politburo, 1974 brought a sense of growing military strength, but also the knowledge that Hanoi's armed forces were not ready to strike the final blow. Its assessment of ARVN ranged from respectful (firepower, equipment), to contemptuous (morale, tactics). Hanoi also recognized that Saigon's political control in the villages—the Communists it called repression—had increased.

At the end of January 1974, the Politburo held an expanded meeting to discuss escalating the North Vietnamese efforts in the South. Giap advocated a program of intense but limited combat until 1975, which the Politburo accepted. Pham Van Dong was now committed to the same course of action, recommending that Northern forces attack "critical points" to bring about a rapid collapse. At a Foreign Ministry conference in late December 1973, he commented to his audience on the similarities between the 1954 Geneva talks, in which he had led the Vietnamese Communists' delegation, and the 1972–73 Paris negotiations: "To the U.S., the Geneva Conference was just [a delaying action]. If we had known, right from the start, that this was a delaying action, we could have trumped their game with one of our own, as we are doing now with the Paris Agreement, and the situation might have turned out differently. If we had viewed the Geneva Agreement as we now view the Paris Agreement, as preparation to enable us to secure more victories in the future . . . we would have grown strong sooner."[13] His remarks, of course, were kept secret at the time.

Shortly after the January Politburo meeting, Giap became quite ill and was flown to the Soviet Union for emergency gall-bladder surgery. If he had died, what would have been the impact on Hanoi's war effort? His demise would have certainly removed one of the leading proponents of main-force warfare, but would it have enabled the "political struggle" faction to wrestle back control? Probably not. The Politburo had based its decision on a number of factors, including the survival of its forces in the South and the apparent short-term weakness of both the GVN and the U.S. Instead, the impact would have been felt in the conduct of the war, in the strategic military guidance emanating from Hanoi. Regardless, Giap's absence from several important public functions was noticed, and over the next months it led to much speculation regarding his health and his position in the hierarchy. General Van Tien Dung, the deputy commander of PAVN, was also ill and was on extended leave. Fortunately for the People's Army, Hoang Van Thai had returned from his own sick leave in East Germany and assumed command.

In March, the Central Military Affairs Committee held an important conference to draft policies to implement Resolution 21. The meeting would determine the military's main priorities for 1974, and provide operational guidance to each regional command. During the gathering, the members concluded that PAVN had regained the initiative in the South for the first time since 1972. To continue that trend, they laid out four tasks for the Army. They were: defeat the South Vietnamese "land-grabbing" efforts, step up attacks to wear down ARVN, expand the base areas and transportation corridors in and to the South—called "simultaneously fighting and building"—and improve the local forces and the urban political movement, which were vastly under-strength. As Giap later wrote: "All of this was designed to modify the all-around balance of forces to our advantage . . . to bring about by surprise a sudden change in the balance of power, [so as] to win absolute victory."[14] To accomplish these tasks, Giap intended to build main-force divisions and corps capable of fighting as combined-arms units.[15] All of this had one purpose: "when the comparison of forces between ourselves and the enemy underwent a fundamental change, when the U.S. was encountering many difficulties at home and abroad, when our preparations had been completed, we would . . . win victory."[16]

The Politburo quickly approved the committee's recommendations. The General Staff immediately held a second conference in April with many of the southern regional commanders. The purpose of the second conference was to ensure that the commanders in the South clearly understood the Politburo's intentions. With Giap undergoing surgery in the Soviet Union, it fell upon Thai to oversee the progress toward Hanoi's goals. His management was excellent, and by mid-summer 1974 Thai noted that "a new status and a new strength had clearly begun to take form" for the Army. The development of the "strategic transportation routes [the Ho Chi Minh Trail] . . . [was] pursued at an urgent pace . . . along the lines of preparing for large-scale combat."[17] With the Trail complex no longer subject to U.S. air attack, PAVN greatly expanded its logistics lifeline, erecting a series of supply depots and repair facilities. An oil pipeline was also extended deep into South Vietnam, the most important logistic improvement in the war for the Communist troops. In early July 1974, an ARVN reconnaissance team in II Corps found and examined a section of the oil pipeline. The team reported that it was eight inches in diameter and of Chinese manufacture, instead of four inches and of Soviet design as previously believed. Fuel shortages, Saigon now realized, would no longer constrain PAVN actions.

Not just supplies poured down the Trail. Large numbers of soldiers also moved south, and for the most part, they rode instead of walking. Without having to walk hundreds of miles across treacherous terrain, they arrived in record time and in better health than in any previous year. Replacement soldiers and supplies could now quickly replenish weary units, thus allowing PAVN to maintain a higher combat tempo. According to Thai, one hundred thousand fresh troops advanced southward in 1973, and another eighty thousand were headed to the battlefields during the first half of 1974. Within North Vietnam, the strategic reserves were expanded, and the armor, artillery, and anti-aircraft units were trained to fight in Soviet-style combined-arms formations. Just as important, the staffs responsible for controlling these units, the biggest PAVN had ever developed, had also made "new advances."[18]

Furthermore, in May the Central Cell completed the study it had begun in April 1973. Titled "Outline Study of a Plan to Win the War in the South," it was forwarded to Giap for his review. Giap returned from Russia in the summer of 1974, and after carefully evaluating the outline, on 18 July he issued orders to prepare a full-fledged campaign plan aimed at securing total victory by 1976. The plan would be presented to the Politburo in October. The overall concept was for a two-stage offensive, with a main blow supported by secondary attacks in other sectors. Most American intelligence analysts assumed, based on history, geography, and PAVN's overall combat strength, that the first area attacked would be I Corps. This was logical, but wrong. Giap told his staff to pick either the Central Highlands in II Corps, or the III Corps area. Giap had learned his lesson from 1972. Instead of attacking three areas concurrently with equal forces, he would mass and strike one very hard while the other regions "supported" the main assault by tying down ARVN forces. After a great deal of internal discussion, it was decided that Phase One would commence in the Central Highlands, followed by an attack against Saigon, which Giap considered the "decisive area." Phase Two would be Communist doctrine's much-vaunted "general offensive and general uprising," leading to complete victory. In the meantime, PAVN units would fight on a moderate scale during 1974 while concurrently increasing their strength and building logistics bases.

Shortly after Giap issued this order, Le Duan, who was vacationing at the beach resort of Do Son outside of Haiphong, asked to see Thai and Giap's other main deputy, Le Trong Tan. Le Duan wanted to discuss the new strategic plan. On 21 July 1974, Thai and Tan arrived at Do Son to brief Le Duan. The hour of decision was drawing near.

4

"A RAINY SEASON LIKE NO OTHER"

THE WAR RESUMES

For many years, the pendulum of war had swung in concert with the dry and wet seasons. Heavy combat raged in III Corps during the dry period—roughly from October to May—with reduced fighting during the monsoon. But 1974 was different. This time when the rains came, Colonel General Tran Van Tra's B-2 Front continued to attack in III Corps and in IV Corps, the southern part of South Vietnam. Tra's aim was to gut ARVN combat effectiveness while simultaneously improving his own strategic posture in preparation for striking even heavier blows in 1975.

Tra, unimposing and slight of build, typically wore a rumpled uniform, often minus any insignia or rank. Without the supplies and equipment of his peers closer to the great rear area of North Vietnam, he saw himself as a chess master, making subtle moves to achieve victory. His real name was Nguyen Chan, and he was born in 1919 in Quang Ngai province. He joined the revolution in 1936, and became a Party member in 1938. He fought near Saigon during the war against the French, and then departed for Hanoi after the Geneva Accords. He returned to the B-2 Front area in late 1962, and served as either commander or deputy commander until the end of the war. Few PAVN generals served in one location as long as Tra, a longevity which only buttressed his confidence regarding his own military acumen. The General Staff, on the other hand, viewed him with disdain.

In December 1973, COSVN issued its strategic guidance for 1974. Derived from the Politburo's Resolution 21, Tra decided to launch "strategic raids" beginning in March. Each raid would be a large attack against a specific target to achieve a particular and limited purpose. He wanted to accomplish four distinct goals in the III Corps area. His first objective was to prevent the South Vietnamese from strengthening Saigon's defenses. He would accomplish that by seizing territory in close proximity to critical locations. The North Vietnamese referred to this strategy as "fighting within the Paris Agreement," as if some new clause had been discovered that permitted the Communists to attack without violating the ceasefire. Tra's second objective was to expand the "liberated" zones by eliminating isolated ARVN outposts inside Communist-held territory—and to prevent the "encroachment" of new settlers through terror tactics—so that his units would have easy movement corridors. Third, by keeping ARVN on the defensive, he would prevent an attack against Loc Ninh, the small district down in Binh Duong province that was Tra's sole conquest from the bloody 1972 offensive. Lastly, Tra wanted to rebuild the very weak urban political movement so that it could foment unrest in the cities. This would assist the offensive by creating chaos and thereby undermining South Vietnamese morale.

To defend themselves, the South Vietnamese had significant forces in III Corps. They had three Army divisions—the 5th, the 18th, and the 25th—the 3rd Armored Cavalry Brigade, two VNAF air divisions, three Ranger Groups, dozens of Regional Forces (RF) battalions, and the elite 81st Airborne Ranger Group, a highly trained three-thousand-man reconnaissance element. However, all three Army divisions had been long regarded as among ARVN's worst units, although the 5th had overcome part of that reputation with its stubborn defense of An Loc in 1972. The 5th Division covered the northern approaches to Saigon, the 25th guarded the capital's western flank, and the 18th defended its eastern side.

Tra's first strategic raid came at the end of March 1974, when elements of the PAVN 5th Division attacked the district seat of Duc Hue in Hau Nghia province west of Saigon. His intent was to drive all South Vietnamese forces away from the Cambodian border and across to the Saigon side of the Vam Co Dong River. His troops could then use this area as a logistics base.

On 27 March the Communists infiltrated a small sapper unit into Duc Hue, held by the 83rd Border Ranger Battalion. After the Rangers repulsed them, a large infantry attack quickly followed. The Rangers defeated the second assault, and when an ARVN relief column was stopped short of the town, PAVN settled into a blockade. The 83rd Rangers, with their families in the camp, began to endure daily bombardments and infantry probes. A second rescue attempt by an ARVN 25th Division task force, combined with VNAF air strikes, failed to break the North Vietnamese encirclement. The two sides had now reached a stalemate.

At the end of April, ARVN decided to crack the cordon around Duc Hue. The III Corps headquarters coordinated a large-scale assault combining several battalions from the ARVN 25th Division, the 7th Ranger Group, and local Regional Forces, all under the overall direction of the 3rd Armored Cavalry Brigade. Commanded by Brigadier General Tran Quang Khoi, the brigade was a unique outfit in the South Vietnamese Army, more akin to an American cavalry unit than pure armor. Khoi, extremely intelligent and decisive, was considered by his former American advisors to be ARVN's best armor officer. He possessed an innate ability to adapt conventional armor tactics to Vietnam's distinctive geography. His brigade consisted of three subordinate units: Task Forces (TF) 315, 318, and 322. Each task force was a composite unit comprising a Ranger battalion from the 33rd Ranger Group, an artillery battery, and an armor squadron.[1]

The plan called for the Regional Forces and other ARVN units to attack and prevent the retreat of the Communist elements surrounding Duc Hue. Once that was accomplished, Khoi's armor columns would move north of Duc Hue into the region across the Cambodian border called the Parrot's Beak. Khoi's brigade would then execute a right hook deep behind the Communist lines and strike into the PAVN rear. On 27 April, VNAF fighters launched the first blows of the operation, striking targets around Duc Hue. ARVN units quickly blocked the North Vietnamese escape routes north and south of the village. During the night, Khoi's tankers and Rangers, using boats to float their armor across the Vam Co Dong River, struck west and blasted into Cambodia. Soon they turned south, where they encountered enemy logistics areas. With little room to run, the Communists were quickly routed, and many supply depots were discovered. ARVN casualties were light, while PAVN losses were very high.

The attack was a remarkable combined-arms operation, but it was ARVN's last true offensive operation of the war. On the North Vietnamese side, Tra's initial "strategic raid" had failed, and his losses in the 5th Division were high. Yet only one of his main-force units had fought, allowing his other divisions to prepare for new thrusts. Tra could attack different areas at different times, keeping ARVN off balance and bleeding it of supplies when it could ill afford to use them. It was Tra's best military option.

After the 1973–74 dry season, PAVN's B-2 Front commanders met to assess the results. Despite the heavy losses, Tra and his boss, Pham Hung, a Politburo member and the COSVN Party secretary, believed the dry season had been a success. In IV Corps, ARVN had been prevented from "stealing" all the rice in the Delta, and many outposts had been overrun. In III Corps, not only had they defeated what they thought was Thieu's plan to retake the lands seized in the 1972 offensive, but Loc Ninh was never threatened, and ARVN was unable to strengthen its defensive lines around Saigon. Strategically, Tra believed Thieu's "insane" plan to defend "everywhere" had forced the South Vietnamese into a passive defensive posture, making them unable to respond to concurrent attacks. In his mind, the fighting quality of the ARVN troops had declined; desertions were up and conscription was down. Because of the aid cuts, many aircraft and vehicles were in storage or needed major repairs. At the same time, given the large-scale infiltration of men and material, the fighting strength of Tra's forces had markedly improved.

That is why Pham Hung concluded it was time to change the normal rhythm of the war. For the first time, he would mount major attacks during the bad-weather period. It would be, he boasted, "a rainy season like no other." Speaking to the B-2 Front commanders, Hung noted: "In this year's dry season a new factor had appeared. We are winning victory and ascending while the enemy is weakening and descending. During this year's rainy season we have many advantages . . . [and] regardless of the weather and the difficulties, we must step up our activities . . . [so that] during the 1975 dry season, we will be capable of creating a new turning point, one of decisive importance. . . . The winning of a decisive victory in 1975–76 . . . is within the purview of Resolution 21. The basis of our decisions was the situation during the recent period, especially during the past four months."[2] It is no coincidence that the last successful South Vietnamese counteroffensive and the time frame Pham Hung identified as the beginning of ARVN's rapid decline is the same. It was the exact period Murray had forewarned about: the point where the effects of the supply cut-off would hit.

The program for the 1974 rainy season was little changed from the dry-season plan: strategic raids that would target specific locations, along with upgrading the urban movement and the local forces. Tra's most important task, however, was to strengthen his main-force units to fulfill the 1974–75 dry-season missions. To accomplish that goal, he turned to the General Staff for reinforcements. He had long believed B-2 was the most important theatre in the war, and he had repeatedly clamored for more troops and equipment, to the point where he had developed a reputation at the General Staff for constant carping. As usual the General Staff denied his request for several strategic-reserve divisions.

To compensate, Tra "decided to form one light division for each of our military regions by combining the independent regiments, providing them with additional combat support elements, and organizing a division headquarters staff. . . . MR-7 [the area encompassing most of III Corps] had only two independent regiments . . . which were combined to form the 6th Division (minus)."[3] Similar but full strength divisions—the 8th and 4th—were created in MR-8 and MR-9. Tra also decided to combine the 7th and 9th Divisions, his two best units, into the 4th Corps. Initially called Group 301, it was commanded by Major General Hoang Cam.[4]

Tra began his rainy-season attacks on 16 May with an assault by the 9th Division. This thrust was as difficult a battle as any during the war. The 9th, behind a large artillery barrage, attacked villages in the infamous "Iron Triangle," a long-fought-over piece of territory. Almost all of the fighting occurred along Route 7, the main road that crossed the northern side of the triangle. The Saigon and Thi Thinh Rivers formed the borders for the west and east sides respectively. Route 7 ran from the village of Rach Bap on the western side to the village of Ben Cat. The key to Ben Cat was the bridge on Route 7 over the Thi Thinh River.

Two infantry regiments of the 9th Division, backed by armor and artillery fire, attacked on the morning of 16 May. One regiment quickly took Rach Bap, and continued east along Route 7 to the next village, An Dien, where ARVN Regional Forces held out for thirty-six hours before retreating to Ben Cat. The North Vietnamese followed quickly, but the RF held Ben Cat and the critical bridge, preventing PAVN from seizing the crossing. Since the days of large-scale helicopter insertions were gone, without the bridge ARVN would have no easy route back in to recapture the lost ground. Realizing the situation, ARVN hurriedly sent some Rangers and engineers to secure the bridge. But instead of continuing to attack, the 9th halted its advance and dug in at An Dien. It brought in dozens of anti-aircraft and artillery guns, built bunkers and minefields, and dared ARVN to come push it out.

Rising to the challenge, the ARVN III Corps commander ordered the 18th Division, under Brigadier General Le Minh Dao, to kick PAVN out of the Iron Triangle. Le Minh Dao had been given command of the 18th Division in March 1972. In November 1972 he was promoted to brigadier general, and he remained in charge of the division until the end. Dao was a fiery leader, a man bristling with energy. Unlike many senior ARVN officers who stayed in their command posts and issued orders on the radio, Dao moved among his men during battle. He believed that the trust of his men must be earned, and he asked his officers to maintain contact with their subordinates at least "two levels down," and to "ask them their problems."[5] This was a radical approach for the status-conscious South Vietnamese officer corps, but as a result, Dao's soldiers rewarded him with their loyalty and admiration. Dao's effort to create a bond between his troops and his officers was so successful that the 18th quickly became, according to Le Gro, "the most effective ARVN unit" in III Corps.[6]

Dao launched the assault to recapture An Dien on 1 June with two regiments. Both quickly ran into well-entrenched Communist forces that refused to retreat. Artillery rained down on his advancing soldiers, who had to clear extensive bunkers and minefields. The PAVN 9th Division counterattacked with infantry and ten tanks. ARVN forces knocked out four of them, and threw back the infantry in hand-to-hand combat. After the attack, Dao's combat engineers, working at night with flashlights, removed forty anti-tank mines from Route 7.

The battle raged on for two more days. Finally, Dao committed his last regiment, and the Communists slowly began to give ground. By 5 June, he was in control of An Dien, but casualties had been high on both sides. Captured prisoners from the PAVN regiment holding An Dien reported that whole companies in some battalions had been wiped out.

With An Dien now secure, Dao could concentrate on taking the next objective on Route 7, an RF outpost called Base 82. Dao brought in the 3rd Armored Cavalry, and planned to attack from several directions. The North Vietnamese, however, were not retreating. The thick brush and rough terrain around Base 82 gave the defenders a distinct advantage, and the 9th Division intended to hold it. Gathering the remnants of the units that had fought at An Dien, the 9th resupplied them with troops newly arrived from North Vietnam and committed its third regiment. Engineers laid more mines, ammunition was stockpiled, and the artillery registered kill zones. After completing their preparations, the PAVN forces waited in their bunkers to avenge their losses at An Dien.

Khoi attacked on 7 June, but the assault stalled when his tankers ran into the teeth of the defenses. The interlocking bunkers, the minefields, the heavy anti-tank fire, and the difficult terrain prevented Khoi from making much headway. Dao was forced to commit his unit's men, who were worn down from the earlier fighting. With mortar ammunition and hand grenades tightly rationed, the 18th Division soldiers had to push the enemy out of prepared defensive positions the hard way, using carefully timed small-unit maneuvers that often resulted in hand-to-hand combat. Despite their excellent close-quarter combat drills, the 18th's attacks were resulting in heavy casualties. Dao's units suffered 275 men killed and one thousand wounded, which amounted to a 25 percent loss for his infantry battalions, a high ratio for any battle.

Meanwhile, the heavy anti-aircraft artillery and bad weather made air strikes ineffective, forcing III Corps to use thousands of artillery shells. But with the aid cuts, the South Vietnamese could not afford to use ammunition at that rate, a situation U.S. forces in South Vietnam had never faced.

With the Iron Triangle battle draining III Corps ammunition stocks, and given the aid reductions plus the dramatic price increase for artillery shells, General Vien realized he had no choice. He ordered an immediate cut in artillery fire. The III Corps commander, Lieutenant General Pham Quoc Thuan, promptly visited Generals Vien and Khuyen to beg for more artillery ammunition. Thuan asked for 150,000 more shells. He was given 45,000. Here was Murray's "trading blood for ammo." PAVN artillery, on the other hand, continued to blast away. When ARVN troops observed enemy trucks bringing in supplies directly to the front lines, an event that would have been unheard of even in 1973, morale in the 18th Division sagged. With the attack bogged down, the troops exhausted by a month of fighting in bad weather, and newly rationed artillery and limited air support, the III Corps commander ordered a halt to retaking Base 82. Dao's troops were pulled out and replaced by the ARVN 5th Division.

The situation remained quiet for the rest of the summer, but in early September the ARVN 5th Division resumed the attack and retook Base 82. By November, the rest of the Iron Triangle was back in South Vietnamese hands. By committing the fresh division, the South Vietnamese were able to nullify all of Tra's gains, and the PAVN 9th Division was badly mauled. As a fighting unit, it would not see action again until March 1975. Le Duan reacted with dismay upon learning of the setback, and the losses directly affected the General Staff's 1975 plan for the B-2 Front.

Yet despite the failure to conquer any territory and the heavy losses in the 9th Division, both Pham Hung and Tra believed that their rainy-season offensive had been successful. The combination of heavy attacks and aid cuts had worn down the South Vietnamese military, making them increasingly unable to respond to multiple attacks. South Vietnamese firepower had diminished, and the territorial forces seemed feebler than before. Tra and Hung's conclusion was that it was time to go for the kill. They would launch an even larger offensive in the dry season, but this time with bigger forces simultaneously attacking multiple objectives against a rapidly weakening Republic of Vietnam.

HANOI'S VIEW

The aid cuts were only one reason for the Communists' conclusion that the time to strike had come. Nixon's resignation in early August 1974 removed a major restraint on Communist strategy. Nixon, with his unpredictable penchant for releasing the bombers, was perhaps the only Western leader feared by the Communists. The Politburo welcomed his resignation with undisguised delight. In its *Weltanschauung*, Nixon's fall was a direct result of America's defeat in Vietnam, which was feeding a growing revolutionary movement around the world against the United States. Both Le Duan and Truong Chinh viewed the Vietnam conflict within a "big-power" international context, and their analysis was highly slanted by Marxist-Leninist ideology. Le Duan fervently believed his country was the vanguard in a worldwide struggle for national liberation, and he ascribed to Vietnam an importance far beyond its nominal weight in the world.

Shortly after Nixon's resignation, Truong Chinh analyzed the situation in precisely that framework: "Nixon's resignation . . . is an important political event that signals the weakness and defeat of American imperialists. . . . Nixon was not forced to resign . . . solely because of the crimes committed in the Watergate affair. . . . Watergate . . . set off an explosion of the U.S.'s social contradictions and the internal contradictions within the American monopoly capitalist class. In fact, the primary cause of these contradictions is the U.S. war of aggression in Vietnam. . . . For that reason, we can see that the deep, real reason for Nixon's forced resignation was the heavy defeat the U.S. suffered in Vietnam, while the direct, ulterior reason was Watergate. In order to exacerbate the contradictions, to add to the difficulties of the Americans, and to win victory for our people, we must implement the following measures: We must launch a continuous and wide-ranging propaganda campaign aimed at both domestic [Vietnamese] and world opinion. . . . We must link the corruption, the rottenness, the failures, and the stagnation of the Nixon government to [the] Thieu government. We need to form a broad-based front against Thieu, a front that demands that Thieu be thrown out, that supports . . . the Paris Agreement, that frees the political prisoners, and that implements peace and national reconciliation."[7]

As if reading Truong Chinh's mind, on the exact same day, the U.S. Embassy in Saigon sent a rocket of a cable to Kissinger, bitterly denouncing the FY75 congressional aid reductions. Predicting that the reduction of military aid would not bring peace, but would only encourage the Communists, Deputy Ambassador Wolfgang Lehmann (Martin was in the U.S.) wrote:

> Apart from the practical effects [of the aid cutback] the worst damage of a reduction in military assistance . . . by the House vote would be the political

and psychological. We are at a crucial point in the long drawn out process of decision-making in Hanoi. It is evident that Hanoi has been disappointed [that] after the withdrawal of American forces and advisers South Vietnam [did not] fall into its hands. After all, in Hanoi's view it was a colonialist war ... therefore, Hanoi has been in a dilemma. Faced not only with disappointment of their hopes in the South but with serious economic problems at home and limitation on their ability to obtain support from China and the Soviet Union, they obviously had problems in deciding what to do next [and] the balance between the two priorities of reunification and reconstruction remains extremely delicate. According to recent intelligence, should the North Vietnamese conclude that the U.S. is disengaging politically from the South, they would suspend serious economic planning [and move] militarily against South Vietnam at some opportune moment. Some intelligence sources indicate that the Communists are anticipating a 'decisive' political or military breakthrough as early as the spring of 1975 when the GVN's equipment and material shortages could be most severe if there is no additional US assistance. Hanoi's long and short-term intentions thus hinge critically on its current estimates ... of U.S. commitments.... We believe that a reduction ... by over 50 percent of the [aid] request will tip the balance in Hanoi irrevocably in favor of a decision for the military option. There is no doubt the South Vietnamese will not quit but will fight ... the result will be more war rather than less, more suffering rather than less, and further postponement of an acceptable political solution rather than the reverse.[8]

As prophecy, it was near perfect, but like most predictions, it was ignored. There was no response to Lehmann's cable.

A NEW PRESIDENT

On 9 August 1974, Gerald R. Ford took the presidential oath, stepping in for the disgraced Richard Nixon. Ford had replaced Spiro Agnew as vice president on 6 December 1973, after Agnew resigned following charges of tax evasion. Although Ford had been a member of the House of Representatives since 1949, he was essentially an unknown quantity to most Americans. Having achieved the pinnacle of American power under extraordinary circumstances, he entered the Oval Office at a time when his countrymen were profoundly disillusioned by the Watergate scandal and distressed over seemingly intractable economic issues. During his inaugural address to the nation, he tried to set a tone of reconciliation and hope, telling Americans that "our long national nightmare is over." In September, Ford pardoned Nixon, hoping to move beyond the rancor. His action, seen through Watergate-tinged eyes as politically motivated, unfortunately punctured the public's initial goodwill toward him.

Ford remained committed to Nixon's "Peace with Honor" program in Vietnam, but he knew he possessed limited ability to influence events in that country. Ford faced a recalcitrant Congress and a stagnant economy. Inflation hit almost 11 percent in September 1974, exacerbated by the OPEC oil embargo. Higher oil costs had an acute effect on U.S. markets, contributing not only to soaring prices but also to burgeoning unemployment. Most Americans were deeply concerned about the economy, and events in faraway Vietnam were viewed with a collective hope that they would quietly disappear. If it took political courage to pardon Nixon, it would take even more to tackle Vietnam. Yet Ford did not shy away from the challenge. He was determined to defend America's long-time ally, and he quickly confirmed U.S. backing for South Vietnam as a priority for his new administration.

On 10 August, Ford sent a letter to Thieu: "the existing commitments this nation has made in the past are still valid and will be fully honored in my administration."[9] Ford also lauded Thieu for his efforts to utilize U.S. aid properly. Lastly, he told him that while "our legislative process is . . . not yet completed . . . I do want to reassure you . . . that in the end our support will be adequate." He reinforced those comments in an address to a joint session of Congress on 12 August, pledging to support American allies in Indochina while demanding the observance of the ceasefire in South Vietnam.

While the letter to Thieu was one of several Ford signed that day reassuring allies, for an embattled Nguyen Van Thieu, these were magical words. Because of the aid cuts, Thieu had begun toying with the idea of reducing the territory held by the GVN to an area encompassing III and IV Corps. Major General Murray's charts and Khuyen's visit had unsettled him, and in the early summer he had asked his economic team to draft a study on the impact of retrenchment. It could be accomplished, his team advised him, but the problems would be enormous: resettling several million refugees, not to mention the tremendous loss of political face resulting from a retreat from Hue and Danang. Given those difficulties, with Ford's letter and assurances that the $300 million would be restored, Thieu shelved the idea.

When Murray reached Honolulu after departing Vietnam, he met with Admiral Noel Gayler, commander of U.S. forces in the Pacific, for an end-of-tour debriefing. In discussing Ford's letter, Gayler claimed it did not promise anything specific. Murray disagreed, pointing out that it was being "interpreted for the Vietnamese by our Embassy in Saigon as a promise of support for what they needed. . . . But the statement was wrong, what they were getting was inadequate—a starvation diet."[10] Once more Murray was confronted "with a basic contradiction between the guidance the Embassy was giving the Saigon government and what I was getting from [Secretary of Defense James R. Schlesinger] to give to the RVNAF. The Embassy was saying the support was going to be in accordance with Ford's letter . . . and [Schlesinger] was telling me that we must prepare for the $700 million ceiling." This amount would cover only 45 percent of South Vietnam's overall needs, needs calculated on the assumption that there would not be another major offensive, let alone the necessity of replacing equipment. The end result was that Thieu was being lured into a false complacency regarding more aid. Ultimately, Murray warned, "without proper support, the RVNAF are going to lose, maybe not next week, or next month, but after the year they are going to."

Into this quagmire stepped Murray's replacement. On 5 September Major General Homer D. Smith, U.S. Army, arrived in Saigon. A career ordnance officer, Smith was a highly regarded logistician. He cut short his honeymoon to arrive in South Vietnam early, knowing he was walking into a maelstrom. Before Murray left, the DAO staff had worked closely with the JGS to apportion the $1 billion in aid they believed the RVNAF was going to receive. Following normal financial procedure, DAO had broken out one-fourth of the money for each quarter. The $250 million for Q1 was quickly spent to fund contractors and purchase long-lead-time items like fuel and ammunition, leaving little for other important items like bandages. But when the $700 million figure was announced, the Q2 monies were reduced to $119 million. Given the continuing high demand for ammunition, little was left from the $119 million for spare parts or other necessities.

The impact was severe. In mid-October 1974, General Vien restricted major army operations to only two at a time for no more than ten days apiece each month. Thus each corps could carry out only one ten-day operation per month. The limiting factors, according to Vien, were "air support and artillery ammunition."[11] The Navy was forced to demobilize over a dozen riverine units, greatly weakening security in the Delta. The Air Force fared no better. Although the VNAF had managed to keep its "Operational Ready" rate fairly stable until mid-October 1974, it had achieved this by drawing down stocks and putting hundreds of older planes into storage. The DAO hoped to return some of the older aircraft for credit, with the funds then being re-programmed to buy parts and fuel. However, the new Defense Authorization Vietnam bill precluded any credits. It also placed an absolute ceiling on all security assistance to the GVN and barred any other funds from supporting Saigon. In summary, as Smith later wrote, "crippling limitations were imposed on . . . firepower and mobility. . . . All of this had a debilitating effect on morale and gave strong encouragement to the enemy."[12]

The JGS analysis of the $700 million aid level was also exceedingly grim. General Vien reported to President Thieu that "only 40% of the RVNAF operational and maintenance requirements [will be] filled. The RVNAF *will not be able to defend* against the Communists, who are better equipped and better supplied since the Paris Agreement. The Communists are ready, they only wait for the suitable opportunity. *There will be additional loss of land and population.*"[13] (Emphasis in the original.) Badly shaken, Thieu immediately replied to Ford's letter. When he received no response, in mid-September he wrote a second letter and dispatched Foreign Minister Vuong Van Bac to Washington to deliver it personally.

Thieu's new letter was pleading in tone. Peace prospects, he told Ford, were "bleaker than ever," and the "main cause" for the increasing Communist threat was the "utterly inadequate amount of military and economic aid." Thieu reminded Ford that he "had signed the Paris Agreement in good faith, under the double assurances that . . . Russia and China will exercise a restraining influence upon Hanoi and . . . all necessary military equipment and economic assistance will be provided by the United States to [enable the GVN] to maintain its self-defense and to develop its economy. The first assumption turned out to be an empty promise. . . . But I am convinced that thanks to your generous efforts, the second assumption will be borne out."[14] Thieu ended by asking for a meeting with Ford and a public statement "restating our common goals."

While Ford declined a meeting with Thieu, behind the scenes the administration was already lobbying key senators to approve a supplemental-aid request for the missing $300 million. Often, administration budget requests are cut by congressional committees, which siphon off the funds for their own programs. To compensate, later in the year a supplemental funding request is put forward to restore the administration's original budget. Congress grants the supplemental, and the complete funding is restored. Ford, having served in Congress for many years, was well aware of how the game was played.

On 12 September, in a private meeting with senior congressional leaders and Kissinger, Ford noted the U.S. faced "a number of difficult problems" around the world. Ford wanted Congress to refrain from passing restrictive legislation, particularly on Indochina. "We must assure," Ford said, that "Vietnam is not destroyed through lack of funding." Kissinger then outlined the various world crises, and said of Vietnam: "If we bug out, it would affect our whole foreign policy and the reliance countries place on us."[15]

Unfortunately, with congressional elections coming up in November, re-opening the funding debate now was impossible. One senator at the meeting commented that "I have never seen the Vietnam aid debate more acrimonious. This is an election year. . . . To talk two months before elections about more aid . . . is dreaming. Try to hold the line and come back after the elections," which meant delaying a discussion until the new Congress convened in January 1975. While some senators agreed that Ford should get other supplemental funding he had requested, particularly for the Middle East and the Greece-Turkey dispute over Cyprus, these were draining foreign-aid funds that otherwise might have supported Indochina. With a bad economy, Congress was reluctant to spend money on overseas problems.

On 13 September, Ford and Kissinger met with Ambassador Martin to discuss the previous day's congressional meeting. Kissinger remarked that "It is inconceivable we can spend $1 billion in Israel and not in Vietnam where so many Americans have died. . . . Vietnam is enormously important in the international perception of the United States."[16] Martin, who was preparing to return to South Vietnam, told the president that the current amount of $700 million in military aid would only enable Saigon to hold out through the winter. It would need the other $300 million before the end of the fiscal year on 30 June 1975. But Martin did not feel the situation was doomed: "If I thought [it] was hopeless, I would tell you. We can make it. But if North Vietnam sees the loosening of support it will change their perceptions." Ford directed Martin to tell Thieu of his admiration, and that he would fight for the additional money.

Martin returned to Vietnam and conveyed exactly that message, but just as Murray had predicted, Thieu could only wait helplessly for the Americans to supply the aid he so desperately needed for his country's survival.

LE DUAN DECIDES ON WAR

Sitting in the house at the beach resort of Do Son on 21 July, as the late afternoon sun filled the room, Generals Hoang Van Thai and Le Trong Tan briefed Le Duan. Tan outlined the improvements in PAVN since the beginning of the year, while Thai told Le Duan that PAVN forces had regained the initiative on the Southern battlefield. They had, Thai said, "won victories and were developing in an upward direction, while the enemy . . . was on a downward slide."[17]

Le Duan agreed that the South Vietnamese were very weak, and, just as important, he thought that the U.S. was also in serious political and economic disarray. He further asserted that the U.S. was now "colluding" with China, permitting China to gain influence in Southeast Asia in exchange for Chinese pressure on Hanoi to halt its attacks. Le Duan added that China and Japan would soon begin to "interfere" in Southeast Asian matters, citing the Chinese invasion of the Paracels Islands as a prime example. However, since America and South Vietnam were currently weak, and China and Japan were not yet ready to act, Hanoi had a small window of opportunity to win the war. It must act immediately to take advantage of this situation, or the Politburo's goal of unification would become extremely difficult to achieve.

The Politburo's own internal study of the war (completed in 1995) supports Le Duan's theories: "If we had waited and taken action later, the situation might have become very complicated and dangerous, in ways that no one could fully foresee. We quickly took the initiative and actively made strategic preparations, both in terms of our posture and of our forces and in both North and South Vietnam beginning in early 1973, and we skillfully coordinated our preparations with diplomatic offensives designed to win over world public opinion and to deceive and trick the enemy, thereby creating the greatest possible force and the most advantageous posture possible for our entire army and our entire population as we began the final decisive strategic battle."[18]

In essence, Le Duan's analysis represented a combination of Hanoi's rationales for launching its 1968 and 1972 offensives. In 1968, the Politburo decided to unleash a massive surprise attack because the war was not going well, and it needed to do something drastic to change the situation. In 1972, part of the motivation for Hanoi's attack was that it saw ARVN as very weak because of the U.S. troop withdrawal. Both these lines of reasoning surfaced again in Le Duan's thinking: the need to do something drastic combined with a badly weakened enemy.

Consequently, Le Duan ordered Thai to draft a "strategic plan in such a way as to create a strategic opportunity, and be prepared to immediately exploit that strategic opportunity."[19] For Le Duan, the strategic opportunity would be a sudden turn of events where Hanoi might "win victory earlier, before those countries were prepared to intervene. . . . China feared that if we won and became stronger it would impede its advance into Southeast Asia. . . . Therefore, when those countries were not yet able to carry out their ugly designs, the matter of creating, and taking advantage of, an opportunity to win complete victory was becoming increasingly urgent. When the South was liberated, and our fifty million people were united, those countries would no longer be capable of carrying out their designs on Indochina."

Le Duan's instructions to Thai were direct. In 1975, PAVN had to eliminate large numbers of ARVN troops to prepare for an offensive in 1976 that would achieve victory. The initial attack had to surprise the South Vietnamese, stunning them and causing a collapse so the North could win the war in the next two years.

Energized by Le Duan's command, on 26 August the Central Cell completed the seventh draft of the plan to conquer South Vietnam. The plan would have two stages: 1975 would be Stage One, a surprise attack to weaken the enemy, followed by Stage Two in 1976, when total victory would be achieved. The Cell members realized that PAVN did not have the resources to mount the kind of massive attacks they had employed in 1972, nor did Giap want a frontal assault on the cities similar to Tet '68. By necessity, their plan would have to be a compromise. Communist local units and the urban political base remained very weak, and PAVN faced significant shortages of heavy-artillery ammunition and armor.

Phase One of Stage One was a limited offensive in the B-2 Front that would last from December 1974 to February 1975. Phase Two, the heart of the 1975 campaign, would begin in March. A multi-divisional assault would target the village of Duc Lap in Quang Duc province in the southern portion of the Central Highlands.

Why the Central Highlands? Quite simply, it was the weakest point in South Vietnam's defenses. I Corps in the north and III Corps around Saigon were heavily defended, the GVN strategy called "strong at two ends." In the vast forests and mountains of the interior, ARVN forces were concentrated around the northern section, defending the main cities of Kontum and Pleiku. Moreover, capturing the southern part of the Highlands would enable PAVN to connect the B-3 Front (western Central Highlands) with the B-2 Front, providing easier supply lines and linking up the "liberated" areas. Phase Two would be supported by diversionary operations in III Corps, the lowlands of central Vietnam, and the northern portion of I Corps. Phase Three, August–October 1975, would consist of further attacks in central Vietnam and I Corps.

It was, in essence, a larger version of the 1973–74 dry-season attacks, and it was a countrywide offensive—just not a *complete* offensive. The goals for 1975 were: "destroy a significant portion of ARVN's total troop strength; defeat the pacification program; extend PAVN's logistics and supply network from Route 14 all the way to the Mekong Delta; cripple the South Vietnamese economy; and incite political opposition to the South Vietnamese government. These goals had the same purpose: wear down South Vietnamese resistance and create conditions for the appearance of a 'strategic opportunity.'"[20]

Giap viewed the future showdown as inexorably leading to one of two results: a triumph either from military success, or from a coalition government. A political arrangement would entail overthrowing Thieu to form a short-lived, three-component transitional government. Despite the persistent calls from the anti-war advocates in the U.S. and elsewhere to "give peace a chance," the North Vietnamese held no illusions regarding a coalition government including the so-called Third Force. It was merely a stepping-stone to victory.

The Politburo met on 30 September to hear the latest strategic plan. Maps and charts covered the walls of the conference room as Hoang Van Thai and Le Trong Tan briefed the Politburo. Thai provided a balanced overview. He reported that opposition to Thieu had recently risen, that South Vietnam's economic difficulties were clearly affecting troop morale, and that the RVNAF was badly weakened by the aid cuts. Despite those factors, the South Vietnamese military remained powerful, and its governing apparatus dominated the areas it held. Moreover, while PAVN forces had grown remarkably, they still had many problems to overcome. Those included a lack of artillery ammunition, inability to fight effectively in combined-arms operations, and too few local troops or urban cells. Regarding Le Duan's strategic opportunity, Thai anticipated that one might arise during Phase Two or Three of the first stage.

While the members of the Politburo agreed on the overall attack concept, including launching the main blow against Duc Lap, the major unanswered question was simple: Would the Americans send troops back in if Saigon was in danger of falling? They agreed the U.S. would not, but air and naval bombardment was still a danger. The group remained wary and deeply fearful of the American bombers. Before making a final decision, they wanted additional time to study the plan. The Politburo decided to hold an expanded meeting in December that would include the commanders from the Southern battlefields. Regardless, orders went out to the various fronts in South Vietnam to start preparing on the basis of the new plan.

Le Duan ended the conference with a speech summarizing the Politburo's thinking:

> Our Politburo is unanimously determined to achieve the people's democratic revolution in the South. [Even though] the Americans had to pull out because they were defeated, we knew that the U.S. still had . . . many wicked schemes. . . . The collusion between the U.S. and China has rendered our war of resistance more complicated. . . . For us, the importance of the Paris Agreement does not lie in the admission that there are two . . . areas of control [or] the formation of a three-faction government, but in the fact that the U.S. troops have to pull out while our forces can stay on. . . . *Our intention was to maintain the status quo of our strength and position in the South and later proceed to attack the enemy. . . . Now the opportune moment is coming.* Before taking this strategic decision, the crucial point we considered was whether the Americans would return to South Vietnam . . . we guessed that the Americans were not in a position to come back. But . . . even if the Americans interfered again . . . they could not turn the tables and we would win. The matter that gave us food for thought was how to fight and win in the best way. . . . [After the Paris Agreements] the puppets gained the initiative on the battlefields. This was due to our mistakes [but] wherever we . . . made appropriate attacks, not only did we remain strong, but our position and strength doubled. . . . Our main task now is to topple the

[Thieu] regime. . . . From now on preparations should be made with a sense of urgency, thus creating the basis for a powerful offensive to win complete victory in 1975 and 1976.[21] [Emphasis in the original.]

The effects were immediate. On 8 October, Hanoi broadcast a statement that the Provisional Revolutionary Government would no longer negotiate with Nguyen Van Thieu. It called on all elements to work in concert to overthrow Thieu and "implement the Paris Agreement," the code-phrase for a coalition government. It was a dramatic political offer: a solution to the South Vietnam problem through negotiations, but only if Thieu was removed.

Le Duan's July meeting, followed by the October conference, was a major turning point in the war. Nixon's resignation, the deep aid cuts, the sense that America was consumed with internal woes and that Hanoi's own strength had considerably grown—all these had coalesced at precisely the wrong time for South Vietnam. While the North Vietnamese had always viewed U.S./GVN strengths and weaknesses through a prism of ideology and wishful thinking, this time they were right. South Vietnam was exhausted, Thieu was facing opposition to his rule, the economy was crumbling, food production had dropped sharply because of the fighting, the piaster was nearly worthless, and morale was low. The slide down Murray's "slippery slope" was gathering speed.

"EVEN THE GODS WEEP FOR PHUOC LONG"

THE BEGINNING OF THE END

While battles had raged in III Corps in the spring of 1974, the war had mostly spared the northern military region of South Vietnam, called I Corps. The opposing forces were encamped in fairly well-defined positions: a GVN-controlled enclave in the foothills and coastal lowlands, and a Communist redoubt in the mountainous terrain to the west. Although occasional fighting flared, the situation was generally quiet. The corps consisted of five provinces running north-south. The northern-most was Quang Tri on the Demilitarized Zone (DMZ); the next province south was Thua Thien, housing the old imperial capital of Hue. Next was Quang Nam, home to Danang, South Vietnam's second-largest city. Last were Quang Tin and Quang Ngai.

Lieutenant General Ngo Quang Truong had assumed command of I Corps on 3 May 1972. He was born in December 1929 in Kien Hoa province in the Mekong Delta, and attended a French school in My Tho. After school, Truong joined the Army, and he graduated in 1954 from the Thu Duc Reserve Officers' School. He then went to Airborne training, and was assigned to help rebuild the 5th Airborne Battalion after it was decimated at Dien Bien Phu in 1954. By 1963 he led the unit, and he eventually went on to command the Airborne Brigade. In April 1966 he took over the ARVN 1st Division. He personally directed the ARVN effort to retake Hue during the 1968 Tet Offensive, and his strong campaigning afterwards significantly enlarged the GVN's control of northern I Corps. In 1970 he was rewarded with command of IV Corps after the death of Major General Nguyen Viet Thanh. He proved an excellent choice, and by 1971 he was routinely praised by both Vietnamese and Americans as ARVN's top commander. At the height of the 1972 offensive, he was tasked with preventing the disaster looming in I Corps. His brilliant leadership swiftly turned around the desperate situation and probably saved the country.

Truong was the least colorful but most capable of South Vietnam's senior officers. Despite his notorious reticence, he possessed both tactical brilliance and an uncanny ability to motivate his troops. His rapid advance was achieved on merit rather than because he was someone's protégé, a rare feat in Thieu's armed forces. Moreover, he was both non-political and incorruptible. Despite pressure from Thieu, he refrained from taking sides in the 1971 presidential election, and after the ceasefire, he resisted pressure to enroll in Thieu's Democracy Party. Neither action endeared him to Thieu. Given Truong's sterling combat record, the president kept a watchful eye trained on him for any signs of nascent political interests, despite

Truong's frequently expressed desire for the Army to remain aloof from politics.

Truong commanded five divisions in I Corps—three north of the Hai Van Pass, the major chokepoint on Route 1 between Hue and Danang, and two south of the pass. The pass also served as the border between Thua Thien and Quang Nam provinces. Because of the geographic isolation of Quang Tri and Thua Thien provinces and their proximity to North Vietnam, an ARVN command subordinate to I Corps, called I Corps Forward, was created for them. I Corps Forward was led by Lieutenant General Lam Quang Thi, who was concurrently Truong's deputy. Thi commanded South Vietnam's three finest divisions: the 1st Division, long considered the best regular ARVN unit, and the two elite general-reserve units, the Airborne and Marine Divisions.

Thi was from a land-owning family in the Mekong Delta. He was born on 7 May 1932 and joined the Vietnamese National Army in October 1950. He served as an artillery officer with the French in North Vietnam. In later years he commanded the ARVN 9th Division in the Delta during the Tet Offensive. His next assignment was as commandant of the Dalat Military School, which he transformed into a four-year institution modeled after West Point. He joined I Corps in April 1972, during the Easter Offensive, and remained there until the collapse.

South of the Hai Van Pass were the ARVN 2nd and 3rd Divisions. The 3rd Division was stationed west and south of Danang. Formed in 1971, the unit had been shattered during the opening campaign of the Easter Offensive, and was pulled back to Danang in late May 1972 for refitting. In mid-1972, Brigadier General Nguyen Duy Hinh was given command of the outfit, and he rapidly rebuilt it. In October 1972 the 3rd Division was given a new mission: create a security zone around Danang. So successful were Hinh's efforts that after the ceasefire, the 3rd's territorial duties were increased to include all of Quang Nam and the northern half of Quang Tin. Hinh's masterful turnaround of the badly battered unit earned him a second star; he was the only division commander promoted in 1973.

South of the 3rd was the ARVN 2nd Division, which was commanded by Brigadier General Tran Van Nhut. His courageous efforts leading the Binh Long provincial forces at An Loc in 1972 had earned Nhut a general's star and command of the 2nd Division. The 2nd also held a wide swath of territory: from the middle of Quang Tin to the southern border of Quang Ngai. In addition to the five divisions, I Corps also had the 1st Armor Brigade, the

1st VNAF Air Division, four Ranger groups (the 11th, 12th, 14th, and 15th), fifty Regional Force battalions, and naval assets.

I Corps's proximity to North Vietnam had made it the scene of the heaviest combat during the 1965–72 period, and the mountainous terrain along the western flank and the thin coastal plain also made it the most difficult to defend. Truong's corps was essentially a long, narrow rectangle. At the top of the box sat the Demilitarized Zone and North Vietnam. The major road through the area is Route 1, which snakes along the coast to Danang. Continuing north, the road meanders through the Hai Van Pass, where it enters Hue and the tiny lowlands of Thua Thien and Quang Tri, an area the Vietnamese call "the narrow strip of land" (*Mieng Dat Hep*). During the war against the French, Route 1 north of Hue was nicknamed "The Street without Joy" for the bloody ambushes that often erupted along its flanks. Later, during the 1972 offensive, it became known as "The Highway of Death" when Communist artillery shelled the refugee-clogged road, killing thousands of innocent civilians fleeing the advancing Northerners.

Since the Hai Van Pass was heavily defended, PAVN commanders sought another area to out-flank ARVN defenders north of the pass. Severing Route 1 would cut off Hue and South Vietnam's three best divisions. Of particular concern to Truong was the hill country between Hue and the pass. A series of hills overlooking Route 1 begins approximately ten miles southeast of Hue and the Phu Bai airbase, the only airfield serving the former imperial city. It was impossible to garrison every hill, and in the steep defiles and rolling ridges the North Vietnamese could pierce the ARVN defensive lines in any number of places.

Recognizing the precarious situation, in late December 1973 Major General Murray had requested additional cargo ships (specifically LSTs), which could rescue or resupply thousands of trapped soldiers. In perhaps his most prophetic vision, Murray noted that if PAVN managed to cut Route 1 between Hue and the Hai Van Pass, Truong, "brave, fierce, battle hardened as he is, would face Dunkirk without ships." The South Vietnamese Navy currently had nine LSTs, but Murray wanted six more. He also wanted to dredge the channel from the Thuan An Inlet on the coast to the small harbor of Tan My, located east of Hue at the mouth of the Perfume River. The harbor was currently silted up, and LSTs could not enter. Pentagon lawyers nixed Murray's LST request, claiming that adding even unarmed ships might violate the accords. In October 1974, Ambassador Martin again raised the issue, but the State Department's chief legal officer also denied it. While the LST denial was a small detail in the larger picture, it would have great repercussions during the 1975 debacle.

Luckily for Truong, PAVN commanders in I Corps had withdrawn their forces into more defined positions rather than remaining interspersed with South Vietnamese forces as in III and IV Corps. Several badly battered divisions had rotated back to North Vietnam in 1973 for refitting, leaving the remaining troops to quietly rebuild their strength. But after Le Duc Anh's insubordination in the lower Delta was trumpeted as a North Vietnamese victory, Giap considered the passive response of PAVN commanders in northern South Vietnam a major mistake. His orders to begin limited but strong attacks in 1974 were directed particularly at this area, as he wanted to alter the existing balance of forces dramatically. Thus, in the spring of 1974, Giap began a series of campaigns throughout the region that tested ARVN to the limit and caused severe casualties on both sides. What few know is that Truong, widely praised for reversing the tide of defeat in I Corps in 1972, performed a second such miracle in 1974. By swiftly redeploying his units and accepting significant risks in one area to stem attacks in another, Truong again saved I Corps. The cost, however, was 15,000 South Vietnamese casualties.

In May 1974, PAVN launched its first major attack in I Corps in a year. The target of the initial assault was the district seat of Tien Phuoc, located about twenty-five miles west of Tam Ky, the provincial capital of Quang Tin. Tien Phuoc was a key Regional Force base in the outpost shield protecting both Route 1 and Tam Ky. Given the heavy pressure on Tien Phuoc, Brigadier General Nhut was forced to move most of his division from Quang Ngai in order to defend Quang Tin. While he held the North Vietnamese at bay, Communist forces immediately attacked the Quang Ngai coastal plains. Truong then assigned two of his Ranger groups, which he had hoped to use as a corps reserve, to defend that province. Although ARVN held its ground, losses on both sides were high.

After the fighting in southern I Corps ended, PAVN forces mounted a major operation in central I Corps. The attack began on 18 July, and after two weeks of fierce fighting, a regiment of the PAVN 324th Division overran South Vietnam's only coal mine and a district town deep in the mountains.[1] The regiment continued east and assaulted Thuong Duc, a small district town that sits at the head of a valley leading directly to Danang. Anticipating the attack on Thuong Duc, Truong had transferred a Ranger battalion from Quang Ngai to guard the town. When the Rangers held out against repeated attacks, PAVN troops employed a new tactic. They dismantled their 37-mm anti-aircraft guns and hauled them through the mountains to the front lines to use as direct-fire weapons.

In early August the Northerners again attacked Thuong Duc. The direct fire from the anti-aircraft guns smashed the Ranger bunkers, forcing them to retreat. Truong quickly sent a Ranger group and a regiment from the 1st Division from I Corps Forward to stabilize the situation, but PAVN poured another regiment into the breach. Under Major General Hinh's command, the 3rd Division and the reinforcements halted the offensive and then counterattacked, but Communist units that had dug in on the nearby hills stopped Hinh's advance two miles from the town.

Overall, the fighting had been ferocious; more than 4,700 South Vietnamese soldiers had been killed or wounded since mid-July. The 3rd Division alone had taken 3,500 casualties, about 25 percent of the division, mostly in the infantry units. According to Hinh, "The losses were not replaced in full. . . . Combat effectiveness of units, as a result, decreased markedly for lack of adequate replacements."[2] Ammunition cuts played a large role in Hinh's failure to retake Thuong Duc. Hinh was limited to only six rounds of 105-mm and four rounds of 175-mm artillery shells per gun per day. That meant his artillery could fire less than five hundred rounds a day both to support a major attack and to conduct outpost defense within his one and a half provinces. Fuel was so scarce that Hinh could not commit his armored cavalry unit to support the counterattack. Even his command helicopter was limited to four hours of flight time per week. Meanwhile, in the eyes of increasingly demoralized ARVN troops, PAVN supplies appeared plentiful.

With all of Truong's reserve now committed, PAVN began concentrating troops in the hill area between Hue and the Hai Van Pass. With the situation stabilized, Truong shifted the 1st Division regiment and the Ranger group back to I Corps Forward. But when those forces withdrew from Thuong Duc, PAVN quickly pushed forward, seizing a dominating hilltop, known as Hill 1062, three miles northeast of Thuong Duc. Enemy 130-mm artillery was now in range of Danang. Truong immediately pulled the 1st and 3rd Airborne Brigades out of Thua Thien, and ordered the highly regarded Airborne Division commander, Brigadier General Le Quang Luong, to retake Hill 1062.

The appearance of the elite "Red Berets" (the Airborne Division's nickname) grabbed Hanoi's attention. General Van Tien Dung, the chief of the

General Staff, had just returned from a lengthy overseas medical leave. He recalled the 2nd Corps commander to Hanoi to give him orders personally. Dung emphasized that the defense of Thuong Duc was paramount; he said, "You must hold them there as long as possible, all the way through the spring of 1975, in order to enable our other areas to conduct their operations. You will receive ample supplies and ammunition and plenty of new recruits as replacements."[3]

Despite Dung's admonitions, the Red Berets methodically pushed forward. On 18 September, they retook Hill 1062, but a counterattack the next day drove them off. PAVN casualties were high, so the regiment from the 324th Division was swapped with a regiment from the 304th Division. After switching places, the 304th's troops dug in and grimly waited for the Red Berets to return to fight for Hill 1062.

After lengthy planning, Luong launched a surprise attack on 2 October that drove PAVN from the hill, killing four hundred North Vietnamese soldiers. Undeterred, the People's Army counterattacked, this time with a second regiment from the 304th. Hundreds of Communist soldiers were mowed down, but the 304th relentlessly pressed forward. For the next two weeks, the Red Berets fought off repeated attempts to regain the hill. Dung was furious at the failure. Feeling the whip, the 2nd Corps commander sent his deputy, Major General Hoang Dan, to take personal command of the battle. He brought with him the third 304th regiment, plus two battalions of engineers and four thousand rounds of artillery and mortar ammunition.[4]

Rallying the Communist troops, and using a two-day artillery barrage to keep the Airborne pinned down, Hoang Dan launched another assault on 1 November. The new regiment drove the airborne off Hill 1062. Determined to hold the position, Hoang Dan used the engineers to build extensive fortifications to defend his hard-won gains, knowing the airborne would return. True to form, several days later, Luong counterattacked. VNAF fighters bore in, pounding the 304th troops. Despite the new fortifications, within two days the Airborne had recaptured the hill. It was the final battle for Hill 1062. Both sides were too exhausted to move any further. In six weeks of fighting, the Airborne had lost five hundred dead and almost two thousand wounded, while claiming that PAVN casualties approached seven thousand. Although the threat to Danang had been halted, Thuong Duc remained in enemy hands.

Meanwhile, the removal of the two Airborne brigades from the defense of Hue had left it badly exposed. Truong moved the Marine Division from

Quang Tri province south to Thua Thien to cover Hue, and assigned the 15th Ranger Group and 1st Armor Brigade to take over the Marine positions. It was a move that he would partially duplicate in March 1975. While this time it worked, it would prove disastrous in 1975.

Between April and June 1974, PAVN units of the B-4 Front, the area north of the pass, had probed the most important section of the hill country between Hue and the pass, the Bong Mountain/Mo Tau Hill complex. Communist troops initially captured several of the almost two dozen hills running along Route 1, only to be pushed off by the 1st Division. The sector was then quiet for most of the summer, but as September approached that was about to change.

Taking advantage of the badly extended ARVN forces in I Corps Forward, on the morning of 28 August, artillery fire suddenly rained down on the troops of the ARVN 3rd Regiment, 1st Division, defending Mo Tau and Hill 350, another significant high point in the area. Striking swiftly, PAVN soldiers attacked and captured the hills. The 1st Division commander, Brigadier General Nguyen Van Diem, rushed his reserve regiment into the line to recapture the hills. Enemy artillery soon started shelling Phu Bai and Route 1, forcing the airport's closure and badly disrupting road traffic. Intense fighting raged for several weeks as the ARVN soldiers fought to reclaim the high ground, but they failed. Truong pulled Hinh's reinforcements, which were then engaged on the Quang Nam front, back to the area to reinforce the 1st Division. It was this move that allowed PAVN to capture Hill 1062.

Given the dangerous situation, Lieutenant General Lam Quang Thi at I Corps Forward took command of the counterattack to regain Mo Tau and Hill 350. He added an Airborne battalion and an RF unit to the newly arrived regiment and Rangers. Launching the attack in late October, ARVN made steady headway, but poor weather grounded all VNAF flights. In a desperate move, Thi pulled the 15th Ranger Group and more RF units from Quang Tri, leaving only the 1st Armor Brigade and RF/PF troops to defend the province and the ceasefire line. When the weather cleared, Thi focused on retaking Mo Tau and Hill 350. By mid-December, he was back in control of the hills, and air and ground traffic in the area returned to normal.

While PAVN had not seized much territory in the fighting, the initiative now clearly lay with the North Vietnamese. They had severely tested I Corps, although by attacking sequentially rather than concurrently (Giap's design for limited but strong attacks), they had achieved no major victory.

Regardless, Truong had been forced to redeploy existing units constantly to prevent breakthroughs, all the time hoping that a full-scale offensive would not occur, let alone the commitment of any of the reserve divisions in North Vietnam. More important, the Thuong Duc/Hill 1062 battle had serious strategic overtones. As Hoang Van Thai, North Vietnam's deputy chief of staff, stated, "After the Thuong Duc battle we noted that the enemy troops were becoming increasingly weak, their air and artillery support had declined, and the mobile troops had to be dispatched on a patch-work basis, and moved primarily by road. Thus they responded slowly and the morale of both the main-force and local troops had declined. . . . In sum, after the . . . Thuong Duc battles we could conclude that our mobile main-force troops had become superior to the enemy's mobile main-force units. That conclusion had a close relationship to our strategic intentions."[5] Still, Thai was not oblivious to PAVN losses, and he told the Politburo that "we attacked a district seat with many strong fortifications [Thuong Duc] and although we annihilated the enemy on a rather large scale we did not do so very effectively."

Although Truong's generalship and the fighting ability of his troops and subordinates had stymied the PAVN attacks, ultimately, in Truong's opinion, it was the Airborne that "had saved Danang," and the people knew it. This would have repercussions in March 1975: when the Red Berets were withdrawn from I Corps and sent south, the population panicked. From Truong's perspective, the 1974 summer-fall campaign "revealed that the PAVN were well equipped and had increased fire power significantly since the ceasefire."[6] While his troops had demonstrated excellent "combat effectiveness, strong spirit, and supply discipline," the lack of U.S. intelligence proved onerous. As Truong later wrote: "The most frustrating problem plaguing [me] was a severe lack of enemy intelligence . . . protected by the triple canopy jungle in the western part of the region . . . the deployment of the 304th Division . . . to Quang Nam was unknown until the 3rd Division had captured a number of prisoners."

The severe fighting throughout the region, which lasted from April to December 1974, while not as intense as the 1968 or 1972 offensives, was the next closest thing. ARVN casualties for the year were the second highest on record. Although Thieu's armed forces fought well, by the end of 1974 their morale was sinking fast. According to one American observer, the RVNAF was "a tired, dispirited, and frightened force, lacking confidence in its leaders, its future, and itself."[7]

TAKING PHUOC LONG

Meanwhile, Hanoi's plans for new military attacks continued to evolve. While Le Duan's Politburo comrades remained uneasy about Giap's strategic plan for 1975, the summer and fall battles convinced Giap that his main forces were now stronger than ARVN's. His assessment was wholly supported by Tran Van Tra and Pham Hung, who had just reported a similar analysis to the Politburo. After a COSVN conference in early August to evaluate the first half of 1974, Hung told the Politburo that "our movement . . . has been transformed and has scored many successes."[8] Good results had been achieved "in terms of enemy troops annihilated and enemy outposts eliminated; great progress had been made in comparison with the results during 1973." In the first six months of 1974, "throughout the entire COSVN area we had now recovered . . . back to the posture and the strength that we had possessed prior to 28 January 1973." Hung concluded that "we were on the road to victory and the enemy was weakening and was encountering difficulties [and] was on the defensive on the military front and was more politically isolated than ever before." Despite PAVN's heavy losses in 1974, both Tra and Hung believed that the South Vietnamese had dramatically weakened and that major attacks could bring victory.

In October, Hung and Tra finalized their 1974–75 dry-season plan. Since Tra recognized that his forces remained too weak to capture Saigon, he again fervently pleaded with Hanoi to provide him with additional divisions and new supplies of artillery ammunition. Just as before, the General Staff refused.

Tra's dry-season plan was bold. In Phase One, lasting from December 1974 to February 1975, his forces would attack to achieve three territorial goals. First, cut major transportation arteries in the northern Delta, especially Route 4, the main road from the Delta to Saigon. Second, capture the portion of Route 14 running north from the remote province of Phuoc Long on the Cambodian border to Quang Duc province. This would connect the B-2 Front's rear area with the Central Highlands. Third, seize two rich rice-growing districts in Binh Tuy province northeast of Saigon. Phase Two, beginning in March and going on until the end of May 1975, aimed for a large section of Tay Ninh and Binh Long provinces northwest of Saigon. Phase Three would continue attacks during the rainy season.

Tra chose these areas as "springboard" positions for his ultimate goal: attacking Saigon. In 1964 Tra had devised a five-column attack plan to seize the capital, and he still passionately believed in the concept. Just as he had done in the 1974 rainy season, Tra planned his new attacks to weaken Saigon's defensive ring in preparation for a future offensive against the capital. According to Tra, the dry-season plan "was in essence continuing to attack the enemy to accelerate their decline, changing the balance of forces . . . even more in our favor, and creating the opportunity for winning a decisive victory [that would] create conditions for the assault on the enemy's final lair [Saigon]."[9]

Phuoc Long was the primary target in Phase One, and the district seat of Dong Xoai was the key to capturing the province. Dong Xoai had long been a Communist objective, as the town controls an important road junction where Route 14 ends. Northward, the highway connects Phuoc Long to Quang Duc and goes on to Ban Me Thuot, the capital of Darlac province in the southern portion of the Central Highlands. Taking Dong Xoai would isolate Phuoc Binh, the provincial capital of Phuoc Long, and open Route 14 for the requested additional divisions to reinforce the B-2 Front. Tra committed elements of two divisions and his remaining armor and heavy artillery to capture Dong Xoai.

Phuoc Long was an easy mark. It was lightly populated by Montagnards, and only four RF battalions and several dozen PF platoons defended the large, mountainous province. For the South Vietnamese, supplying the province was even harder than defending it. The roads into Phuoc Long had been cut by PAVN troops shortly after the ceasefire, and resupply depended on C-130 cargo planes. In November, after repeated intelligence warnings by the JGS that Tra's B-2 Front planned to attack Phuoc Long, III Corps flew in the reconnaissance companies of the 5th, 18th, and 25th Divisions to provide reinforcements.

While preparing for the dry-season offensive, Tra and Hung received a message at the end of October telling them to attend a Politburo meeting scheduled for 18 December. They arrived in Hanoi from their jungle headquarters in Tay Ninh province in late November. In the course of briefing the General Staff on their offensive, both were shocked to learn that during their journey to Hanoi, Giap had canceled their dry-season plan. The General Staff had ordered B-2 to refrain from attacking Dong Xoai, and had forbidden it to use its tanks or heavy artillery. Instead, B-2 was ordered to seize two small villages on Route 14 north of Dong Xoai— Bu Dang and Bu Na—in preparation for a Phase Two attack toward Duc Lap. This thrust would support the main offensive in the southern Central

Highlands. Otherwise, B-2 should concentrate on the Mekong Delta and husband its forces for 1976.

Giap, and to some extent Van Tien Dung, reined in Tra because they did not want major attacks in other sectors tipping off the South Vietnamese to the overall strategy. Giap's Phase One was limited in scope, mostly for the purposes of surprise and diversion. Giap also needed to economize on the expenditure of equipment and ammunition for the main Phase Two attack. As Giap later wrote, he explained to Tra "that we must keep our strategic intentions, which had been approved by the Politburo and the Central Military Affairs Committee, a secret. It was not yet time for our tanks and heavy artillery to make their appearance in [his area], because we wanted to take maximum advantage of the element of surprise. If such weapons were to be used, Tra would first need approval from the General Staff. In addition, we needed to economize on our use of artillery and tanks, because after the signing of the Paris Peace Agreement, both the Soviet Union and China had stopped supplying us with these types of weapons."[10]

Tra, of course, strongly disagreed. He believed that ARVN was on the ropes, and that the North Vietnamese should commence strong assaults across South Vietnam. Such attacks would "win a great victory and create a new opportunity for the decisive phase of the war. The B-2 plan had been based on that spirit . . . and we had recommended the Politburo draft [such] a plan."[11] For his strategy to succeed, Tra needed to launch concurrent strikes across his region to keep ARVN pinned down. Just as important, Tra wanted to use Thieu's sensitivity toward Tay Ninh, the critical city west of Saigon, to fool the South Vietnamese. According to Tra, "The plan was based on the enemy's assumption that we would attack to liberate Tay Ninh province so that we could make Tay Ninh City the capital of the PRG. We would use feints to tie down his forces [in this area]." Instead, Tra would attack toward Dong Xoai. For Tra, Dong Xoai was the linchpin of the entire campaign, and capturing it would enable him to conquer the rest of Phuoc Long.

Hidden beneath Giap's explanation lay the real reason for his skepticism about Tra's plans: Tra's rainy-season attack in the Iron Triangle, supported by tanks and heavy artillery, had badly failed. The 9th Division had incurred very heavy casualties, and Tra had drained his stores of artillery rounds. Giap was afraid that if Tra attacked Dong Xoai, which seemed a more difficult target than Rach Bap in the Iron Triangle, Tra would again fail and expend even more precious artillery rounds. In addition, ammunition supplies were even scarcer in the northern part of South Vietnam—the battle for Thuong Duc had bled PAVN coffers in that region—making Tra's supply requests sound not only parochial but ludicrous. Moreover, the General Staff—led by Hoang Van Thai, who knew him well—were disdainful of Tra's military stratagems. The disaster of the 1968 Tet Offensive had soured the General Staff on Tra's advice, and his failure in 1972 to seize An Loc had hardened that attitude. Furthermore, it was difficult to reconcile Tra's claim that ARVN had dramatically weakened with the fact that his forces had taken heavy casualties in the Iron Triangle while seizing little terrain.

Despite the General Staff's attitude, Tra was not without influential supporters. Le Duan and Le Duc Tho, who had worked closely with Tra in the South during the 1940s and '50s, had previously supported his plans over the objections of his military superiors. This time, though, Tra found little backing. Even Le Duc Tho disagreed with him. He informed Tra that "The tendency [the fall of South Vietnam] is very clear and cannot be reversed. [But] our material stockpiles are still very deficient, especially with regards to weapons and ammunition. The situation in our country and the situation abroad are very complicated and it will be difficult to augment our strategic reserves. Therefore, we must limit the fighting in 1975 in order to save our strength for 1976, when we will launch large-scale attacks and win a decisive victory. . . . We should not and cannot prolong the war indefinitely."[12]

Regardless, Tra pressed his vision with the senior leadership. On 3 December, Tra and Pham Hung tried to convince the General Staff to let them attack Dong Xoai, but the General Staff refused. Hung then decided to go over their heads. Two nights later, he and Tra met Le Duan for dinner. After discussing the situation in his theater, Tra came right to the point: "Why did you instruct us not to attack Dong Xoai?" Le Duan said that the General Staff had told him that Tra was going to use his main-force units at the beginning of the offensive. "To attack Dong Xoai," Le Duan stated, "and then fight a whole series of other large battles, would not be appropriate. We must fight in such a way as to conserve our strength."[13] Hung and Tra argued that was not the case, and again laid out their plan.

Many analysts have claimed that Phuoc Long was a planned "test" by Hanoi of American will to respond to Communist attacks. That is only partially true. It was also an aggressive general, Tran Van Tra, pushing the envelope. Yet Le Duan needed little prodding to accept a plan that pressed hard against the South Vietnamese. In a key turning point of the war, he agreed to Tra's plan, but he also issued a stern warning; "You must be certain of victory and not use large forces!"

Tra was ecstatic. He fired off a cable to his headquarters ordering his officers to attack Dong Xoai. However, he soon discovered that was impossible. The units that were originally assigned to attack Dong Xoai had been dispersed. The tanks had returned to their base camp, and the infantry and sappers were maneuvering toward Bu Dang and Bu Na, as the General Staff had ordered while Tra and Hung were traveling to Hanoi. Because of the change to Tra's original plan, while the rest of the B-2 forces would launch their initial attack in Tay Ninh province on 6 December, the assault against the two villages had been delayed until 13 December. Dong Xoai would have to wait until after the villages had been captured.

On 6 December Communist forces opened fire. Elements of the newly formed 303rd Division attacked in Tay Ninh. ARVN forces stymied most PAVN's efforts in the province, but they were unable to lift the siege of Ba Den, a mountain rising out of the plains near Tay Ninh City where an important RVNAF communications outpost was located. Still, the feint succeeded admirably; both U.S. and ARVN intelligence firmly believed Tay Ninh was the major target.

On the eastern side of Saigon, another newly formed unit, MR-6's 812th Regiment, struck the district capitals of Tanh Linh and Hoai Duc in Binh Tuy province. Although local RF forces fought back, they slowly gave ground. On Christmas Day, PAVN captured Tanh Linh. Lieutenant General Du Quoc Dong, ARVN's new III Corps commander, rushed elements of the 18th Division and the 7th Ranger Group to protect Hoai Duc. They held despite heavy fighting.

In the Mekong Delta, the PAVN 5th Division and forces belonging to MR-8 and MR-9 launched the strongest probes in IV Corps since the ceasefire. Fighting raged across the breadth of IV Corps, but ARVN forces were able to stem the Communist advance. PAVN losses were high. The 5th Division alone took almost one thousand casualties.

On 13 December Tra's forces in Phuoc Long—consisting of two infantry regiments, one each from the 303rd and 7th Divisions, plus sappers, artillery, and engineers—made a surprise attack on Bu Dang. Concurrently, a PAVN battalion made a supporting attack against another town, the district seat of Bu Dop, an important defensive position guarding the approach to

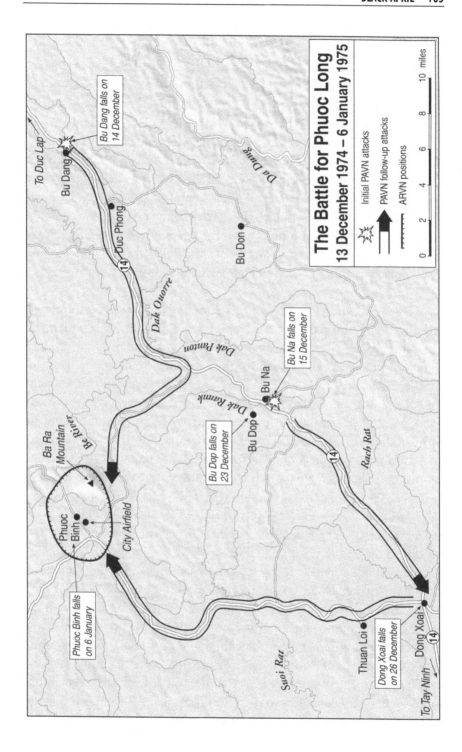

The Battle for Phuoc Long
13 December 1974 – 6 January 1975

Initial PAVN attacks
PAVN follow-up attacks
ARVN positions

0 2 4 6 8 10 miles

To Duc Lap

Bu Dang falls on 14 December

Bu Dang

Duc Phong

Da Dung

14

Bu Don

Dak Quorre

Dak Punton

Bu Na falls on 15 December

Bu Na

Dak Ramh

Bu Dop falls on 23 December

Bu Dop

Ba Ra Mountain

Be River

City Airfield

Phuoc Binh

Phuoc Binh falls on 6 January

Rach Rat

14

Suoi Rat

Thuan Loi

Dong Xoai falls on 26 December

Dong Xoai

14

To Tay Ninh

the provincial capital, Phuoc Binh. Another battalion was hurriedly sent to Dong Xoai to probe its defenses.

All the initial attacks were repulsed, but after a day of fighting against the outmatched RF, Tra's soldiers captured Bu Dang. A day later, Communist forces seized Bu Na. Like a wave, North Vietnamese troops began sweeping away RF outposts on Route 14 and closed in on Dong Xoai, where the RF continued to hold out. By 17 December over fifty miles of Route 14 was captured. Fortune then smiled upon Tran Van Tra. While searching the destroyed fortifications at Bu Na, the PAVN troops made a shocking discovery: the fleeing RF had abandoned their ammunition stores, leaving 6,400 rounds of 105-mm ammunition and two intact 105-mm cannons. In an instant, Tra's heavy-ammunition problem was solved. Given the ease of the victory and the impressive war booty, the Politburo voted to allow Le Duc Anh, commanding B-2's forces in Tra's absence, to continue the attack toward Dong Xoai.

Le Duc Anh quickly prepared to take both Dong Xoai and Bu Dop. He sent another infantry regiment and sappers to attack the RF battalion and the three divisional reconnaissance companies defending Bu Dop. Five battalions were assigned to assault Dong Xoai itself.

Striking first at Bu Dop, on 23 December PAVN regulars quickly penetrated the outposts around the town and threatened to overrun it. By noon, ARVN's III Corps recognized the serious situation and flew in the 2nd Battalion, 7th Regiment, to replace the three reconnaissance companies. Landing at the Phuoc Binh airfield, the 2nd Battalion assumed blocking positions between Phuoc Binh and Bu Dop but did not advance to the town. VNAF fighters flew bombing missions, but these were ineffective because of heavy anti-aircraft fire and SA-7 missiles. By nightfall on 23 December, Bu Dop had fallen. The next day, PAVN troops halted their advance at the 2nd Battalion's bunkers.

With ARVN's attention focused on the noose tightening around Phuoc Binh, PAVN struck Dong Xoai. Attacking on the morning of 26 December, Communist forces quickly breached the town's fortifications. Although the RF had earlier mounted a staunch defense, it crumbled under the larger attack. PAVN captured another three thousand rounds of artillery ammunition. With much of Phuoc Long province now under Communist control, Tra personally sought out Le Duan. He explained that the remaining South Vietnamese defenders were isolated, and that ARVN was incapable of dispatching strong reinforcements to lift the siege of Phuoc Binh. Tra asked permission to seize the city. Le Duan agreed. To ensure victory, Tra requested the use of a tank battalion and 130-mm artillery to capture the provincial capital. His second request was also granted.

For the defenders, although they were compressed into a tight defensive position, the terrain was advantageous. On the eastern and northern sides of Phuoc Binh flows the Be River. Dominating the city's southern side is Ba Ra Mountain. Remnants of three RF battalions held defensive positions around the city. Five artillery platoons provided immediate fire support, while police and PF soldiers helped patrol the city. The 2nd Battalion of the 7th Division was placed in reserve.

Arrayed against the defenders were five regiments of PAVN regulars, five anti-aircraft battalions, sapper and engineer units, three battalions of artillery, and twenty tanks. Studying the terrain, PAVN commander Le Duc Anh quickly determined that the key to seizing Phuoc Binh was to capture Ba Ra Mountain, which overlooked the city. Anh's plan was to send the sappers to capture the mountain, while concurrently striking Phuoc Binh by throwing a regiment each along two roads into the city. He would punch a hole in the ARVN lines with his infantry and then drive his armor into the city to capture the provincial headquarters. North of the capital, two regiments would block any attempt to retreat across the river. The last regiment would be held in reserve.

Attacking on the morning of 30 December, Anh's forces ran into difficulty. The regiments assaulting the roads stalled under withering fire from the RF, and the sappers were unable to take Ba Ra from its defenders. In response, Anh increased his artillery fire, and continued to press his infantry against the undermanned RF. In mid-afternoon on 31 December, Anh's infantry finally broke through. On 1 January, the sappers took Ba Ra. By the end of the day, South Vietnamese forces had fallen back to a two-mile perimeter around Phuoc Binh.

On 2 January Thieu called an emergency meeting of his Cabinet to discuss Phuoc Long. Thieu and the JGS were uncertain as to the true situation on the ground, mainly because, as General Vien later claimed, the province chief's reports were overly optimistic. To re-capture the province, Lieutenant General Du Quoc Dong, the commander of III Corps, requested immediate reinforcements, specifically asking for his old unit, the Airborne Division. Given the distance it would have to travel from I Corps and the difficulty of penetrating the enemy's air defenses, Thieu rejected Dong's request. He informed Dong that he must use his own forces to recapture

Phuoc Long. When Dong protested, a compromise was reached: the 81st Airborne Ranger Group would be sent. The 81st was an all-volunteer, three-thousand-man commando unit, highly trained in reconnaissance and small-unit tactics. It was not, however, designed for regular infantry use, although it had performed magnificently in a similar situation defending An Loc in 1972.

At the time of the emergency Cabinet meeting, the 81st was attempting to break the PAVN siege of Ba Den Mountain in Tay Ninh province. Only two companies totaling three hundred men were not currently on missions. The two companies would go in first, secure Phuoc Binh, and await the arrival of the remainder of the 81st Airborne. The VNAF was ordered to divert aircraft from II and IV Corps to provide firepower for the embattled provincial forces.

On the morning of 3 January, ARVN Colonel Phan Van Huan, commander of the 81st Airborne, flew a reconnaissance mission to Phuoc Binh and picked out a landing zone north of the city for his troops. Assembling his men at Bien Hoa Airbase, he organized two flights to land his soldiers. However, the first flight did not lift off until the afternoon because of VNAF mismanagement. Further screwing things up, the planes assigned to bomb the landing zone before the first flight arrived did not appear. With artillery exploding on the ground and heavy anti-aircraft fire, Huan called off the mission.

The next morning, rain and foggy conditions at Phuoc Binh delayed Huan's second attempt, but eventually the pilots lifted off. Following the twisting Be River, they arrived in mid-morning. This time, VNAF bombers flew sixty air strikes and cleared the landing zone of anti-aircraft fire. Lieutenant Colonel Vu Xuan Thong, commander of the initial task force, landed with his men and quickly linked up with the embattled defenders. The men in the second wave, however, were not so lucky. As their helicopters landed, hundreds of rockets pounded the area, causing moderate casualties.

Seeing the reinforcements, Le Duc Anh sent in his armor. The 81st Airborne hit the tanks with M-72 anti-tank rockets, but the North Vietnamese had learned the lesson of An Loc. The Communists had welded steel plates to the hulls and turrets of their old Soviet T-54s, and they had sappers riding on the tanks to provide infantry support. A tank hit by a rocket would shudder to a stop, but would soon resume its advance. Only direct hits from recoilless rifles, or shots in the rear, would stop the T-54s. Despite the onslaught, the 81st soldiers foiled the attack, but the defenders faced impossible odds. ARVN had one thousand defenders against more than ten thousand PAVN troops backed by tanks and heavy artillery and covered by an effective anti-aircraft umbrella. Even worse, Lieutenant Colonel Thong radioed Colonel Huan that the enemy artillery was heavier than what he had experienced at An Loc in 1972.

One 81st Airborne medical officer described the final days:

Late in the afternoon of 4 January, the enemy launched another ground attack directly at the headquarters of the defensive forces. The 81st engaged in hand-to-hand combat; Lieutenant Colonel Thong fought against them with hand grenades and killed an enemy group when they penetrated his defensive line. We also destroyed one of their four T-54 tanks. Once again, we succeeded in pushing them back, but we sustained heavy casualties. All of the M-72 anti-tank weapons were used up. Medical supplies that were supposed to last for ten days were quickly running out. The medics had to even use telephone wire to sew up the soldiers' wounds. Within a few hours of landing in Phuoc Long, the 81st had been under heavy attack twice. Wounded soldiers and injured civilians filled a small medical bunker; many of them were bleeding to death for lack of urgent medical supplies.

On 5 January, the enemy launched another wave of nonstop artillery attacks. All day long rockets landed in the dead zone of the city, but there was no tank or ground attack. At dawn 6 January, the enemy bombarded the city again for a few hours. Then, the grinding noise of the tanks could be heard. Everybody readied themselves. The carnage started again as the tanks approached: there were explosions everywhere, soldiers and civilians falling to the ground as shells and bullets ripped through them; it was a horrific scene. Captain Thu appeared at the entrance of the medical bunker and yelled for retreat. Walking wounded helped carry the seriously wounded soldiers on stretchers. This group withdrew along a different route than the rest of the 81st. After pulling out from the city, Lieutenant Colonel Thong tried to regroup in an attempt to retake the city. He did not succeed. The enemy immediately surrounded the 81st. With less than a few hundred men, Lt. Colonel Thong led his men to break through the enemy line in a bloody battle at the river. Enemy machine guns and rockets rapidly fired at them from the other side of the river cut them down one by one, turning the river red. Still, the 81st managed to break through and disappeared into the Phuoc Long jungle.[14]

With T-54s approaching his compound, the province chief and the remaining troops and staff also attempted to escape across the river. The province chief was not seen again, but Colonel Huan flew many rescue missions and managed to find about one hundred of his men. Phuoc Long had fallen.

While the province did not have a high military value, its loss devastated the South Vietnamese. Thieu declared three days of mourning for Phuoc Long, and Lieutenant General Dong resigned. Behind the scenes, Thieu ordered an investigation into the VNAF failure to properly coordinate with the 81st Airborne Rangers on the initial helicopter assault. Despite having little to show for the day's efforts—because of that sloppy operation and generally poor bombing results due to the heavy air defenses—the Air Force had lost almost twenty aircraft—including two irreplaceable C-130s—defending the province. At the same time, heavy rains swept Saigon, unusual for January. Colonel Le Gro later wrote that his Vietnamese driver, eyeing the pouring rain, turned to him and sadly remarked: "Even the gods weep for Phuoc Long."[15]

PRESIDENT FORD RESPONDS

After the loss of Phuoc Long province, Ambassador Martin immediately cabled Kissinger to demand action: "We have arrived at a turning point in the history of the Paris Agreement. . . . North Vietnam . . . is determined to use whatever military force is required to gain its objective of conquering South Vietnam. The U.S. reaction to the North Vietnamese conquest is thus of critical importance for the success or failure of our policy in Indochina."[16] It was past time, Martin believed, to launch a public-relations offensive to "get the truth out." He felt groups like the Indochina Resource Center were promulgating lies about the situation in South Vietnam.

Reacting to the overall Indochina situation (Cambodia was also in dire straits), on 7 January 1975 Kissinger called a meeting of the Washington Special Actions Group (WSAG), a National Security Council committee designed to handle serious crises and make policies and contingency plans.[17] The meeting was to determine the Ford administration's next steps regarding Southeast Asia. Kissinger reported at the meeting that President Ford had earlier told him he wanted "to take a forward-leaning position consistent with legislative considerations. The President wants to do as much as possible to restore the situation in South Vietnam and Cambodia. He is very positive about that."[18]

The discussion centered on gaining congressional approval for the $300 million in military aid approved for South Vietnam but not appropriated. Ambassador Martin had been pushing for a $700 million military package, but he also wanted greater economic funding. To counter congressional arguments that it made no sense to send a seemingly endless stream of money to prop up a dictator when America was suffering a recession and high unemployment, Martin instead proposed a three-year aid deal. Resurrecting Thieu's idea that sufficient aid would enable South Vietnam's economy to "take off," Martin urged Kissinger to press Ford to tie the complete aid package into one three-year agreement. He pointed to a December DAO study that found deteriorating South Vietnamese morale, particularly in the infantry units, because of a lack of support. It stated: "The conclusion of senior RVNAF commanders, supported by our own observations, is that the provision of adequate resources (ammunition, fuel, and pay and allowances) would dramatically reverse this trend. The economic conditions of the serviceman are such that he is unable to sustain himself and his family on his salary. DAO surveyed one-half of one percent of the assigned strength of each service/branch in each military region. Ninety-two percent of respondents stated that pay/allowances were insufficient to meet basic food/clothing/shelter needs. Over half of all respondents (officer and enlisted), declared monthly expenditures of from 100 to 200 percent of their military income. . . . Morale problems have a solution: provision of adequate compensation for the soldier's sacrifice and adequate support for his combat operations."[19]

The WSAG meeting also considered U.S. military options to block the Communist offensive that everyone acknowledged was forthcoming. Kissinger gloomily observed: "If North Vietnam makes the judgment that they can take South Vietnam there is nothing much we can do. We have to scare North Vietnam out of that judgment." Several military recommendations to "scare" North Vietnam were made to President Ford, including sending new reconnaissance flights over North Vietnam, placing a Marine unit on alert at Okinawa, and steaming carriers close to North Vietnam's shore.

Despite Martin's strong recommendations, the Defense Department decided to ask for only the $300 million. The State Department declined to make any additional economic requests, fearing that to do so might detract from military-assistance funds. And on 14 January Ford also chose to request only the $300 million. Moreover, Ford did not want to antagonize Congress, and so he turned down several of the WSAG recommendations regarding military bluffs. His assessment of Congress's mood was correct. When Kissinger leaked that the U.S.S. *Enterprise* had been ordered to divert toward Vietnam—an order the Navy never received—Representative Bella Abzug (D., N.Y.), the flamboyant liberal and extreme anti-war congresswoman, fired off a letter to the president denouncing the maneuver. Hanoi once again demonstrated its sensitivity to possible American re-involvement in the war. It vehemently protested the press reports on the *Enterprise*'s movement while secretly querying its ambassador in Paris to determine if the news was true.

Ford was boxed in not only by the congressional prohibition on further U.S. military force in Indochina, but also by public opinion against re-entering the war. Although the State Department sent protest notes to various countries in mid-January charging that North Vietnam had "flagrantly violated" the ceasefire, Ford put the final dagger into any notion that U.S. forces might intervene. In a TV news conference on 21 January, he admitted he could not foresee any circumstances in which American forces might return. However, he proclaimed his intention of asking for more military aid, adding that it was essential to boost Saigon's confidence.

Ford knew the aid request had little chance of success, but he would not abandon the fight. On 28 January he sent a letter to Congress requesting $300 million in new aid for South Vietnam and $222 million for Cambodia. To improve his chances, Ford held a meeting with key congressional figures to discuss his supplemental request. The meeting was not only to sound out the senior congressional leaders on the prospects for the aid bill; it was also old-fashioned arm-twisting. While Ford hoped that additional aid would lead to a stalemate and force new negotiations, his main short-term goal was simply to shore up South Vietnam and Cambodia. He laid out his reasoning: "The [Paris] agreements were predicated on certain assumptions, and now we are faced with developments that were not foreseen. Last year, we asked for $1.4 billion. That was cut in half, and as a result, we can't even supply them with the ammunition they need. The Vietnamese are fighting valiantly, they're not asking for troops, and they deserve our support.... Today I am signing a [request] for military assistance for South Vietnam. . . . I know it is unpopular and will meet with resistance. But I do not think we should let these countries sink slowly because we are not prepared to give them support. I feel very strongly about this."[20]

After listening to Ford's pleas and arguments, Senator Strom Thurmond (R., S.C.) offered support for the president's plan: "I just returned from a visit there. I am convinced they can make it if we help them. Martin says we won't have to help them forever—maybe three years. They are finding oil there. The rest of Asia is watching what we do in Vietnam."

Stennis spoke next: "I said last fall I would support additional aid if there was proof of dire need. I will redeem my promise, but I've got to see proof. You will have a hard time with this, and then there will be the 1976 bill." Other lawmakers were even less enthusiastic. Senator Mike Mansfield (D., Mont.), the Senate majority leader and a long-time critic of the war, was adamantly against further aid. The Speaker of the House, Carl Albert (D., Okla.), also appeared reluctant, remarking: "Mr. President, I want to cooperate on matters of foreign policy. But I can't help but say I want to reserve judgment on this. But my feeling is it will be almost impossible to get this through the House. I won't say what I will do, but when all your fellows are against you, what can you do?"

Congressional hearings on Ford's request were held on 30 January. While administration spokesmen provided detailed information, few congressmen changed their position. Ford was soon desperately searching for any measure that might salvage his request, which by now was on life support. He decided that a congressional "fact-finding" trip held the best chance for success. On 3 February Ford met again with congressional leaders and asked for a bi-partisan group to travel to South Vietnam and provide testimony to the various committees. Ford, however, was playing from a weak hand. His approval ratings were low, the country remained in a recession, and most of the public was apathetic about Vietnam. Yet Ford pressed on. Martin was summoned back to Washington to discuss his three-year proposal, which Ford decided to launch as a trial balloon. In an exclusive interview with the *Chicago Tribune* on 9 February marking his six-month anniversary of taking office, Ford offered to limit aid to South Vietnam to a single three-year package, provided Congress granted an adequate amount. He declared that he felt "very strongly that it was important for South Vietnam and Cambodia to survive . . . if there should be a disaster [there], I think the credibility of the U.S. would be hurt very badly."[21]

His proposal was immediately rejected by a large group of members of Congress. In a letter to Ford, eighty-two legislators claimed they saw no "national interest" in continuing aid. That almost one-sixth of the membership of both houses voiced their opposition was an ominous sign. It was obvious that the multitude of new members elected in 1974 were determined to chart a new foreign-policy course.

For South Vietnam, meanwhile, even if Congress had granted Ford's request immediately, it was growing too late. Giap's army was secretly gathering in the Central Highlands.

6

"HOW CAN THE FREE WORLD ABANDON US?"

PREPARING FOR THE STRATEGIC BLOW

Claims that the South Vietnamese were not expecting Hanoi's 1974–75 dry-season offensive are wrong. U.S. and ARVN intelligence had both predicted large-scale Communist attacks. Captured documents, prisoners, and defectors alerted them to the Politburo's intentions. At the same time, signals intelligence (SIGINT) had detected the potential movement of three North Vietnamese strategic-reserve divisions toward South Vietnam, long considered the pre-eminent indicator of a new general offensive. As Major General John Murray, the departing defense attaché, told Admiral Noel Gayler during his end-of-tour debriefing in August 1974: "Watch those six enemy divisions in the North. Watch them like the flute player watches a cobra."[1]

Yet while Nguyen Van Thieu continued to loudly proclaim that Hanoi would soon launch a "general offensive," many U.S. intelligence analysts and most outside observers dismissed the possibility of such a large-scale attack, declaring they did not see the indicators. For example, one scholar writing in the January 1975 issue of *Foreign Affairs* stated that Hanoi had, "for the next two or three years, opted for a period of reconstruction in the North and a moderately intense war of attrition in the South that stops short of a general offensive."[2]

Hanoi had provided ample evidence for that conclusion, as the Politburo continued its stratagem of hiding its military preparations behind pronouncements that its priority was economic expansion. In mid-December Politburo members Le Thanh Nghi and Nguyen Duy Trinh addressed the DRV National Assembly. They again ranked building socialism above completing the revolution in the South. Following their presentations, in late December the North Vietnamese media broadcast new speeches honoring the thirtieth anniversary of the founding of the People's Army. The commentators proclaimed that Hanoi was more concerned with creating a socialist economy than with launching an offensive. PAVN Chief of Staff Van Tien Dung also published an important article that month, postulating that the military must devote its energies to developing the economy and defending the North.

The South Vietnamese were not fooled. To prepare for the looming dry-season attacks, on 9–10 December 1974 Thieu chaired a two-day meeting of his National Security Council to develop the 1975 National Defense Plan. Unlike Thieu, the JGS estimated that there would not be a coordinated countrywide offensive similar to the one in 1972. Instead, it briefed the NSC that only regional offensives, similar to the ones in 1974, would occur. These would probably begin in late March. General Cao Van Vien stated that if the Communists did not bring in any reserve divisions, the RVNAF could defeat them with only limited loss of territory. Strategically, he predicted that Hanoi's goal was to force out Thieu and create a coalition government. Tactically, he believed the North Vietnamese would strike II Corps first, "in an effort to drain our reserves," before making their main attacks in I and III Corps.[3] In I Corps, Vien believed, Hanoi would seek to occupy Quang Tri province and isolate Hue and Danang; if PAVN reinforced the northern front, Vien explained, Lieutenant General Truong would be forced into a defense concentrated around those two cities. In II Corps, the enemy would try to annex Kontum province, where ARVN forces controlled little more than the city and Route 14 into town, and would also attack northern Binh Dinh province. In III Corps, Tay Ninh province on the Cambodian border would be the main target, while IV Corps would be a diversionary theater.

Despite the meeting's purpose, Vien later wrote that Thieu provided only limited military guidance to the JGS. Vien's characterization of Thieu, however, is not totally accurate. In December 1974, Thieu had few answers to the country's deepening problems. His reserves were pinned down, the army had taken heavy losses, and the aid cuts had left the military desperately short of supplies. The economy was in a depression, and Thieu faced enormous pressure to seek a political accommodation with the Communists. Yet he did not sit completely idle. During the NSC meeting he demanded an inventory of all ammunition and equipment by region. He also wanted more accurate hamlet security evaluations. These would form the basis for a new pacification drive to be launched in the first three months of 1975. Led by Prime Minister Tran Thien Khiem, the effort was designed to prepare for the looming offensive by improving provincial forces, stiffening outpost defenses, and perhaps even recapturing some lost territory.

More important, Thieu also ordered the formation of new reserve units. The Marine and Airborne commanders were ordered to form one new brigade each. Because of the desperate need for more reserves, two new Ranger groups, the 8th and the 9th, were cobbled together from demobilized military-police battalions and former deserters. With equipment scraped together from a few remaining stores, the units were assigned to the defense of Saigon and made a part of the JGS general reserve. Vien planned to eventually send the new units to I Corps to replace the Airborne

Division. I Corps was also ordered to draft a plan to release the Red Berets within seventy-two hours if Saigon was attacked. An additional forty-five new RF groups were formed. The groups were designed to provide the province chiefs and corps commanders increased flexibility in shifting the RF to meet attacks.

In October 1974 both the DAO and the ARVN Central Logistics Command had begun planning for future fighting by adjusting the remaining aid funds to purchase more ammunition and fuel. American logisticians considered it essential to have in South Vietnam a stockpile of ammunition and fuel that could last through sixty-days of a high-intensity offensive. This provided a cushion until U.S. supplies could reach the country. Given the cutback in funds and high inflation, the DAO was only able to restore ARVN's artillery ammunition stores to a forty-five-day level. With no money remaining, this left bandages, boots, radio batteries, grenades, tires, spare parts, and many other items in very short supply.

Since the JGS expected the enemy to interdict the main roads in the Highlands, in late January 1975 it shipped large amounts of ammunition and food to Pleiku and Kontum. According to the chief of staff for RVNAF logistics, "The amount of supplies placed in storage was sufficient for 20,000 men to defend Pleiku and Kontum for a period of sixty days without requiring additional supplies. That was a precaution against the dangerous eventuality that no supplies could be delivered. When Phuoc Long was lost, Lieutenant General Khuyen estimated that the Communists would attack . . . the Highlands earlier than the JGS estimated they would."[4] Logistically at least, the RVNAF had done its best to position itself for the coming offensive.

POLITICS AGAIN

The second anniversary of the Paris Accords brought an introspective review by President Thieu. Philip McCombs of the *Washington Post*, one of the few American reporters remaining in Saigon, was summoned to Independence Palace in late January for a one-on-one meeting, the first interview Thieu had given to a Western reporter since July 1973. In the discussion, Thieu sounded familiar themes. McCombs wrote that Thieu "wanted to impress on the American people and Congress that we badly need their support to resist Communist aggression . . . he wanted to see free democratic elections carried out under the terms of the Paris agreement . . . and he is unconditionally ready to return to the negotiating table."[5] However, there would be no "further concessions to the Communists other than those provided for in the agreement." Politically, there would be no coalition government, unless one was achieved via free elections. Brushing aside the question of whether the U.S. was betraying him, Thieu instead responded that "the South Vietnamese people were beginning to feel the United States had let them down." Regarding economic aid, what he had requested was not open-ended, as his critics charged, but only enough to achieve "economic takeoff"; however, it would be needed until at least 1980. Militarily, while the Communists were preparing a massive offensive, U.S. aid cutbacks had "reduced the combat effectiveness of his army by almost two-thirds," and withholding the $300 million in new military aid would be "disastrous." Still, he said, "We will fight to the end." Finishing the interview, Thieu spoke from his heart: "We would like to be on the side of freedom. How can the free world abandon us?"

In addition to his military dealings, on the eve of the Tet holiday (the Vietnamese New Year, usually falling in late January or early February), Thieu took four other actions. First, he tasked Tran Van Lam, a former foreign minister and the president of the GVN Senate, with assembling a congressional delegation to visit the U.S., Britain, and France to appeal for support. Lam's group, visiting the U.S. at roughly the same time the U.S. congressional delegation was visiting South Vietnam, was politely received by congressional leaders, but it made little progress. Several senators, however, including Majority Leader Mansfield, Frank Church (D., Idaho), and Clifford Case (R., N.J.), refused to meet with them. To the congressional leaders who did meet with him, Lam says that he revealed Nixon's promise, made at the time of the Paris Accords, to "react vigorously" to Communist violations. He also told his American hosts that for the GVN, the political significance of receiving new aid was more important than the amount. While Congress ignored Lam's pleas for aid, several senators immediately jumped on Lam's revelations concerning secret commitments to Saigon that Congress had never been briefed on.

Second, Thieu composed a letter to Ford. He again pleaded for more aid and for political support. He described the difficulties resulting from the continued North Vietnamese build-up in defiance of the Paris Accords, the disastrous U.S. aid reductions, and the effects of the fall of Phuoc Long. His growing sense of desperation was obvious: "Two years ago we signed the Paris Agreement with the hope that the elaborate structure for global peace would work. We also signed with the great conviction that should the Communists resort to the use of force again we will be provided with adequate means to defend ourselves. Today I wish to appeal to you to take all necessary action to preserve the Paris Agreement. I am aware of and thankful for the numerous personal efforts and intervention you have made in our behalf since you took over."[6]

Third, Thieu again started to seriously consider pulling back his forces and population into more defensible positions. Retrenchment had been first raised in early 1974, but Thieu had rejected the idea as too difficult to implement. In late August 1974 Thieu reiterated that view to visiting Admiral Noel Gayler, commander of all U.S. forces in the Pacific, stating that "giving up any real estate creates psychological problems for the GVN."[7] Despite Thieu's aversion to the plan, at the December 1974 NSC meeting, General Vien, supported by Prime Minister Tran Thien Khiem, again raised the issue of ceding territory. When Thieu waffled, both generals turned to a former Australian officer, Brigadier Ted Serong, for help in convincing him. Serong had spent years in South Vietnam and had developed important connections among the senior GVN leadership. Serong sent Thieu a plan that advocated a withdrawal from I and II Corps to the more economically viable southern part of the country, especially since the potential oil deposits were located off the coast of this area.

Thieu considered Serong's plan, but after mulling it over, in January 1975 he rejected it. The old fears remained: such an action would shatter the currently fragile South Vietnamese psyche, let alone the enormous upheaval caused by relocating several million people. Further, he worried that a withdrawal would only make the thorny aid effort tougher. Additionally, Ford's request for supplemental aid had bolstered his resolve. For whatever reason—whether blind refusal to admit that the mood in Congress had hardened, or too many optimistic assurances—Thieu continued to believe the Americans would not betray him.

Still, Thieu wanted to prepare his people for the dangerous times ahead, and his fourth action was to speak bluntly to the nation. His Tet message to the South Vietnamese people was grim. The year ahead, he told them, would bring "even greater difficulties" than the previous year, yet he remained determined "not to let South Vietnam fall into the hands of the Communists." The president further stated that his three main goals for 1975 were: "Maximum support for the front line, maximum stabilization of the rear, and increase of production. In the rear, we cannot afford to let the Communist underground agents . . . influence our nationalist ranks to . . . promote solutions of surrender to the Communists."[8] On the eve of the U.S. congressional visit, he intended his remarks as a warning to his people that the most pressing issue remained the physical survival of the Republic of Vietnam.

"NO MATTER WHICH WAY I VOTE"

Unfortunately for Ford, his 3 February request to form a congressional delegation to visit South Vietnam had been badly delayed. Congress was more focused on Ford's proposal to solve the U.S. energy crisis, and then the members departed for their normal two-week break for Lincoln's birthday. Behind the scenes, some congressional leaders were against the trip, and the delay by the House leadership in forming the delegation was seen as an implicit rejection of Ford's request for a three-year aid package. It took over three weeks from the time Ford requested the delegation before the list of members was finalized. Since the trip's purpose was to report back regarding the necessity for further aid, the effect was to delay congressional action on the $300 million supplemental-aid request into March.

Despite the long odds against gaining new aid, while waiting for the return of the delegation, several senators decided to offer a compromise. In early March Senators Frank Church and James Pearson (R., Kan.) sought a meeting with Ford and Kissinger to solve the impasse. Church told the president he hoped to "work out a scheme for phasing out both Cambodia and Vietnam. Now you are faced with ceilings and there is a strong chance that Congress won't grant relief. I wanted to break the stalemate and see if there was some way out of this open-ended subsidy of an on-going war."[9] Ford was looking for $6 to $7 billion over three years, with two-thirds going to military aid. Church, a long-time critic of the war, wanted much less, only $2.5 billion. Pearson informed Ford that he doubted the aid bill would pass; but he added, "There is a gnawing conscience at work on the Hill—not really connected to current arguments or a 'commitment.'"

Ford responded that he felt "an obligation. We must make a last massive effort to negotiate. . . . Our people say that with the supplemental there is a chance to get through the dry season." Kissinger added that while he preferred to have the aid voted on each year, "this is an alternative. If the levels were adequate, this would be more bearable than for Congress to appear to be stabbing an ally in the back. If it is done over three years, our diplomacy and other countries could adjust to it." Ford supported Kissinger's view, adding: "If we can get a three-year program, adequately funded, it is the best way to save the American perception in the world, and the commitment to an ally." Church and Pearson promised to work with the administration to find a solution, but the senators and Ford remained far apart on the amount.

Despite Ford's best intentions, the U.S. congressional visit to South Vietnam from 25 February until 3 March was, for the most part, an abject failure. So much has been written about the disastrous congressional trip that the author will not cover it here. The level of buffoonery exhibited by Representative Bella Abzug surely was a new low in American diplomacy. The Ford administration had gone to considerable lengths to placate the members of the delegation, including sending along White House staff, pressing the embassy and the GVN to provide them access to any location or person, and having Ford personally phone and meet with them when they returned. On 5 March, they met with the president at the White House. True to form, Abzug was late to the meeting.

Representative John Flynt (D., Ga.)—the delegation chairman and a supporter of continued aid—opened by stating, "We were manifestly shaken and impressed by what we saw. Our task is to convince the public and the Congress . . . not to abruptly terminate sufficient military and economic aid which could become the most tragic mistake of a series of tragic mistakes. All of us have a difficult job of convincing the Congress and the people that we cannot drop the ball."[10] Others opined that Thieu should broaden his base of support to help his cause and score points with Congress. Representative Paul McCloskey (R., Calif.), a major critic of the war, was "surprised by the success [and] capability of the [South] Vietnamese army. Vietnamization has succeeded from a military standpoint. It is a superb fighting force." Regardless, McCloskey believed "the will to fight and the terrain favors the North," and that "the North Vietnamese are going to win."

Another major anti-war activist, Representative Donald Fraser (D., Minn.), thought the best option was a phase-out of the aid program, and then only if Saigon began moving toward "traditional" American values regarding political openness. He also advocated the immediate removal of Ambassador Martin, labeling him a "first-rate disaster. He is inflexible and a total spokesman for the Thieu regime," a position that Flynt and others agreed with.

Kissinger again provided commentary regarding a political solution. "It was my misfortune to negotiate with the North Vietnamese for four years. I wish I could agree to get a political solution along with a military solution. It was not possible to negotiate a political solution with them in a strong military situation. They are the most devoted, single-minded abrasive Communists I have ever seen.... As far as the three-year program is concerned ... it must be done right. We have to give enough to succeed rather than produce a lingering death. The domino theory is unpopular, but ... when other countries see the U.S. providing ... no help for Vietnam the impact will be strong."

Writing later, Kissinger again elucidated that Hanoi was most truculent when it felt the battlefield situation was advantageous to its forces. He was disdainful of those who thought otherwise. "The favorite theme of those who opposed the supplemental was the administration should seek political rather than military solutions. But the aging revolutionaries in Hanoi had nothing but contempt for the proposition that diplomacy was somehow separable from strategy.... If America could not influence the situation on the ground, it stood no chance of making any impact on Hanoi via diplomacy."[11]

The discussion went on for another hour, ending with Ford again appealing for his three-year program. Flynt tried to mollify the president by stating, "Most of us want to support you as much as we can." The anguish of many members, torn over the aid question, was reflected in the last statement by Representative Millicent Fenwick (R., N.J.). In response to Ford's question as to how she would vote, she said, "I'll regret my vote no matter which way I vote."

THE FINAL DECISION

While Congress dithered, the Politburo was completing its military plans for 1975–76. In October 1974, Le Duan had convened the Politburo to decide its strategy for the next two years. While a general outline was agreed upon, the Politburo had postponed a final decision. The purpose of the second meeting, starting on 18 December, was to review the political and diplomatic changes since then, and to finalize its designs. Le Duc Tho, confirming Kissinger's beliefs regarding mediation, commented on the potential for a negotiated settlement: "In 1975 diplomacy will not pose any major problems for us. If there was a resumption of negotiations right now, I am certain that the only purpose would be to prolong the talks and to try to expand them. If our posture is not strong, diplomacy will not be able to resolve anything."[12]

At the 18 December meeting, the Central Cell provided an overview of the eighth and newest draft plan to conquer South Vietnam. The plan was the subject of much discussion, but the southern Central Highlands remained the main focus. PAVN forces in the vast middle portion of South Vietnam were divided into two fronts. The B-3 Front in the Central Highlands ran north to south from Kontum province to Quang Duc province in the under-populated forest and mountain region that the Vietnamese call the Tay Nguyen (Western Highlands). Assigned to the front were two main-force units, the 10th and 320th Divisions, along with the recently formed 198th Sapper Regiment; two independent infantry regiments, the 95A operating near Kontum and the 25th in Darlac; and an assortment of armor, artillery, anti-aircraft, engineer, and signal units. The second command was called the B-1 Front (more commonly known as MR-5), which stretched from the seaside resort of Nha Trang north along the coast to Danang, ending at the southern end of the Hai Van Pass. The B-1 Front had the 3rd Division in Binh Dinh province, the 52nd Brigade in Quang Ngai province, and the 2nd Division in Quang Nam province, along with two artillery regiments and under-strength armor and anti-aircraft regiments.

As the Politburo began its deliberations, the North Vietnamese pulled off another major intelligence coup. One of Hanoi's top spies had sent the Politburo the JGS estimate of PAVN intentions from the National Security Council meeting in early December, plus the complete ARVN disposition of forces, including the precise count by military region of artillery, armor, and aircraft that Thieu had requested. Hanoi learned that the JGS expected an attack in the northern section of II Corps, and that ARVN troops were positioned accordingly. With the southern section thinly defended, the Politburo was now even more eager to attack that area.

Who was this agent providing the Politburo such critical material? CIA analyst Frank Snepp states that "Among those responsible for the ultimate North Vietnamese victory, the spy in Thieu's entourage clearly must rank high on the credit list."[13] Snepp is correct, for the Politburo was able to craft its 1975 plan with complete insight into Thieu's military deployments. Back in September 1974, PAVN Deputy Chief of Staff Hoang Van Thai had received a copy of Major General Murray's June 1974 briefing charts describing the deleterious effects of aid cutbacks. While Hanoi has never revealed the spy's identity, in 2005 an account was published detailing the exploits of "Warrior H3." This man is the most likely candidate. Surprisingly, he was not a member of Thieu's inner circle, nor was he a senior ARVN officer; in fact, he was a low-ranking sergeant in General Cao Van Vien's office.[14] His name was Nguyen Van Minh, and his job was to store and handle classified documents and official correspondence between Vien and the "various staff agencies of the Ministry of Defense, the Joint General Staff, and the various military regions . . . and units of the puppet armed forces. He even handled correspondence with the Office of the President and the U.S. Military Headquarters."[15]

He was the perfect spy in a perfect position. Low-ranking, trusted, and rarely scrutinized, this nondescript man worked clandestinely at night copying and then passing along Saigon's most closely guarded military secrets. According to this same post-war Vietnamese article, "In April 1974 he provided an update on the activities of the general reserve force units—the airborne, the Marines, the rangers, and the air force—and provided a summary report on the military plan for all of South Vietnam. The intelligence information he gathered helped the [Central] Military [Affairs] Committee resolve a series of important strategic issues at a key point in time [during the April meeting to implement Resolution 21]. . . . The information he provided helped our senior leaders maintain the initiative and make correct decisions so that we could organize combat forces to secure victories on the battlefield. . . . Minh's information when combined with information from other sources strengthened our resolve to attack to liberate all of South Vietnam."[16]

Even with this vital intelligence, the Politburo kept a suspicious eye trained on U.S. military moves. The debate was fierce at the December 1974 meeting on whether the U.S. would resume bombing if PAVN launched large-scale attacks. Ultimately the Politburo concluded the U.S. probably would not respond, but it remained worried. As one senior participant recalled, "That was a very difficult question on which there were many differing opinions. The discussion was animated, and the opinions were often heated, and people whispered their own private thoughts. The vast majority of opinions . . . held that the U.S. would not send in ground forces, and that in any case, even such an action could not save the puppets from collapse. This was . . . the majority opinion . . . held by those of us from the battlefields. . . . However, there were still a small number of people who, speaking during the intermissions in the conference, worried that the

U.S. would re-intervene in South Vietnam."[17] Even Ford's later statement of 21 January 1975 that the U.S. would not re-enter the war did not eliminate the Politburo's unease.

After several weeks of on-and-off deliberations, on 6 January, Le Duan closed the meeting with a blustery speech. His conclusion left no doubt as to his aims: "In the [October] meeting, the Politburo reached consensus on the strategic orientation aimed at taking . . . complete victory. All of us have reached full agreement . . . to achieve the . . . revolution in 1975–76. In 1974, while we were gaining in both strength and position, the enemy was declining in all fields. Our immediate task is to seize the historic opportunity [by] launching coordinated campaigns of our main forces."[18]

Le Duan then went on to describe the main goals for each front in South Vietnam. "The 1975 plan of action sets the tasks for each battlefield . . . namely advancing by the shortest way towards the decisive battle in the enemy's last stronghold [Saigon]." Both Le Duan and Giap wanted to first strike a major blow in the Highlands, and if the "strategic opportunity" arose, move immediately against Saigon. Tran Van Tra's troops would disrupt pacification in the Mekong Delta, encircle the main cities, and widen the liberated zone. Instead of attacking Duc Lap, as the Central Cell had proposed back in August, the B-3 Front would instead capture Ban Me Thuot, the capital of Darlac province and the main town in the southern Central Highlands. PAVN forces would also seize the stretch of Route 14 from Ban Me Thuot south to Phuoc Long, thus allowing PAVN main-force units easy access to staging areas near Saigon. If the strategic opportunity appeared, PAVN would send two corps to Tra's area to make a thrust at Saigon. In the northern portion of I Corps, just as General Vien had predicted, PAVN "should occupy the plain, control the area south of Hue, and cut off Hue from Danang." Finishing with a thunderous exhortation to the leadership, he proclaimed: "This strategic battle . . . will lead our people's struggle . . . to complete victory, thus contributing to changing the situation in Indochina . . . and will give rise to a new development in the revolutionary movement of the world's people." Le Duan's heart was Vietnamese, but his soul was that of a pure Leninist revolutionary.

CHOOSING BAN ME THUOT

Two days after the Politburo meeting, the Central Military Affairs Committee met to finalize the operational details. While the Politburo chose the strategy, the committee decided on the tactics. Shortly after the meeting began, Le Duc Tho unexpectedly joined it. His purpose was to emphasize that the Politburo wanted to attack Ban Me Thuot instead of Duc Lap. As Van Tien Dung wrote, "It was only in the course of this meeting that the idea of striking Ban Me Thuot really began to take shape. Everyone saw the significance of an attack on this town, but it would take practical investigations . . . before we could decide how to [achieve] a quick victory."[19]

Oddly, none of the available memoirs are clear as to precisely how and when the decision was made to change the objective from Duc Lap to Ban Me Thuot. It appears that as Tra's forces were on the verge of victory in Phuoc Long in late December, the Politburo realized that its initial objective of Duc Lap was too conservative and swapped targets. One startling admission concerning the debate was provided years later. In a speech at a military-history conference, Le Duc Tho described the decision to assault Ban Me Thuot. "When we got down to detailed discussions about where the key attack to open the campaign would be launched, the discussion became very tense and heated. . . . A number of our comrades did not yet agree with the plan to select Ban Me Thuot for the opening attack of the campaign. . . . In fact, however, after we had obtained unanimous agreement in the discussion, but before Van Tien Dung was sent down to the battlefront, there was a comrade who still did not agree with the decision to attack Ban Me Thuot. That was why, during a meeting of the Central Military Party Committee and the General Staff, we had to discuss this decision once again, and we again made a final and clear-cut decision to attack Ban Me Thuot. Because there was a comrade who still was uncertain and wavering about this decision, the Politburo decided to send Van Tien Dung down to the battlefield. This was because we believed that such a vital, key attack required a commander who had full authority and who was fully determined and committed to carrying out the strategic intentions of higher authorities."[20]

Who was the "comrade" who was "uncertain and wavering" about Ban Me Thuot? While Le Duc Tho is silent on his identity, one possible candidate is Truong Chinh. Another candidate is General Vo Nguyen Giap. After the death of General Nguyen Chi Thanh in June 1967, Dung succeeded Thanh as Le Duan's favorite general. Dung had never been part of Giap's clique. He took advantage of the Le Duan–Giap rivalry, which had begun in the late 1950s, to advance his own career by supporting Le Duan within the military against Giap. He took Le Duan's side in a heated dispute between

Le Duan and Giap over the plan for the 1968 Tet Offensive, an offensive that Giap was against.[21] Post Tet, Dung assumed increasing responsibility for the conduct of the war in the South, while Giap maintained responsibility for the North as well as for training, organization, and logistics support for the armed forces. After 1968, Dung was dispatched several times from the General Staff headquarters to directly supervise PAVN forces in major campaigns, notably the PAVN counteroffensive against the South Vietnamese incursion into Laos in February 1971 (Lam Son 719) and the Easter Offensive in Quang Tri and Thua Thien in April–May 1972. In return for his loyalty, Le Duan rewarded Dung with elevation to full membership in the Politburo in March 1972. While Giap never publicly disputed Le Duan's decisions to launch the Tet Offensive in 1968 and the Easter Offensive in 1972, he was against such high-risk assaults. After those decisions had been made, he had left the country for "medical leave." Thus he may have also quarreled over this assault, but his writings are mute regarding any such internal disagreements.

Another unanswered question is: Whose idea was it to attack Ban Me Thuot? The Communists have not singled out one individual, instead stating it was an idea that developed collectively. While several have claimed ownership of the Ban Me Thuot attack concept, Lieutenant General Hoang Minh Thao, who had served as commander of the B-3 Front from November 1966 until July 1974, is the most likely originator. In early December 1973 he had recommended attacking the city to both Van Tien Dung and Le Trong Tan. As Tran Van Tra would do with regard to Phuoc Long in 1974, he requested three strategic-reserve divisions to accomplish the task. Hanoi also denied Thao's request. In September 1974 Giap brought Thao to Hanoi to discuss the southern Central Highlands campaign. During the meeting, Thao reminded Giap that of the seven Highlands campaigns conducted since the beginning of the war, six had been aimed at the northern sector because of difficulties in supplying the southern sector. Yet Thao still recommended attacking Ban Me Thuot: "I had raised the idea that if we selected the Central Highlands as our strategic offensive sector, the first thing we should do is attack Ban Me Thuot, because it was a large city [in] a vital, sensitive area, because it was the place where the enemy's defenses were the most exposed and weakest, and because it would be easier for our forces to develop the attack down into the coastal lowlands from Ban Me Thuot than it would be from Kontum. I said that the difficulties that we would have to overcome . . . to launch an attack in this sector were the lack of roads for our troops to approach the target and the lack of water. . . . We would [also] liberate Duc Lap, hold the area firmly, and immediately connect [the Ho Chi Minh Trail] with Route 14 . . . thereby forming an uninterrupted North-South supply corridor that was entirely located on Vietnamese soil."[22] Given his passion for attacking the Montagnard capital, Dung's committee chose Thao to serve as "campaign commander" for the Ban Me Thuot operation. He reported directly to Dung.

To summarize Hanoi's military analysis of the reasons for choosing Ban Me Thuot, the two main east-to-west roads from the coast to the Central Highlands are Routes 19 and 21. Only one road, Route 14, runs north to south through the Central Highlands. (Route 1 runs along the coast.) Ban Me Thuot straddles the vital road junction of Route 14 and Route 21, just as Pleiku does for Routes 14 and 19. The Politburo chose Ban Me Thuot because it was surrounded by coffee plantations that provided good cover for attacking forces; it was lightly defended; and Route 21 to Nha Trang was wide open. Pleiku, on the other hand, was heavily defended, and its avenues of approach offered little concealment. If PAVN forces had taken Pleiku, they would then have had to fight the ARVN 22nd Division down Route 19 to the sea. Moreover, grabbing the Ban Me Thuot section of Route 14 and the section near Duc Lap, combined with the section recently captured in Phuoc Long, would provide Hanoi's reserve forces a motorized artery straight to Saigon. Plus, Ban Me Thuot held the major but lightly guarded ammunition dump, the Mai Hac De supply depot, an enticing target for the Communist logisticians. In hindsight, it appears the logical choice, but as Thao notes, Hanoi had chosen the northern section of the Central Highlands (Kontum and Pleiku) six out of seven times. The main reason was logistics: Kontum and Pleiku were hundreds of miles closer to the main PAVN supply coffers. Only during Tet '68 had PAVN attacked Ban Me Thuot, and then only for a few days before retreating.

During two weeks in January, the Central Military Affairs Committee completed the 1975 campaign plans, including how the other theaters would coordinate their actions. The design was to pin down RVNAF forces countrywide—Thieu's long-predicted "general offensive"—to ensure that Saigon could not dispatch reinforcements to the Central Highlands. For the surprise attack against Ban Me Thuot to succeed, deception was critical. According to Giap: "With regard both to our combat strategy and [to] our deployment of forces, we must employ audacity [and] secrecy . . . to divert the South's attention to the northern [Central Highlands] and

Quang Tri–Thua Thien sectors."[23] To ensure secrecy, the new target of Ban Me Thuot was so tightly held that only a select few in the General Staff knew of the change. The B-3 Front commander was not informed until late January, and the division commanders and their staffs who would carry out the operation were not told until early February.

Preparations for the offensive began immediately after the end of the Central Military Affairs Committee meeting. The Politburo sent some of PAVN's most experienced officers to oversee the attack, including Major General Le Ngoc Hien, the General Staff's chief of operations, and Lieutenant General Dinh Duc Thien, head of the General Logistics Department.[24] This command group was given the code-name A-75. The attack was called Campaign 2-75.

On 21 January, Hien arrived at the B-3 Front headquarters, just across the Laotian border from Pleiku, to distribute the new instructions and begin drafting battle plans. The B-3 Front staff, which was preparing to attack Duc Lap, now had to scramble to adapt to Ban Me Thuot as the main target. According to Senior Colonel Dang Vu Hiep, the B-3 Front's political officer, the new orders were to "liberate all or most of the territory of Darlac, Phu Bon, and Quang Duc provinces, open a strategic corridor linking the Central Highlands and [the B-2 Front] and a corridor linking the Central Highlands with the provinces [along the coast]. . . . The focal point will be Darlac, and the primary target will be Ban Me Thuot. In the Pleiku and Kontum sector you will pin down, divert, and deceive the enemy. With regard to your use of forces, the General Staff grants you authority to use all the heavy, technical weapons [tanks and heavy artillery] at your disposal, without restriction."[25] It is an indication of the attack's strategic importance that, while Tra (and PAVN commanders in I Corps) were denied the employment of heavy artillery and armor, Giap had authorized their use for the assault against Ban Me Thuot.

Even before the Politburo's plans were final, Giap had begun pouring reinforcements into the Central Highlands. In late December, he shifted the 968th Division, based in Laos, across the border into South Vietnam. The 968th was a light division, with only two regiments. Later that month, Giap also ordered the 316th Division to depart for South Vietnam. In anticipation of renewed fighting in South Vietnam, the division had returned to North Vietnam from Laos a year earlier for refitting. Since the 316th had fought exclusively in Laos for many years, its appearance in South Vietnam was one of the great surprises of the Central Highlands campaign, if not the entire 1975 campaign. The 316th departed North Vietnam on 15 January 1975, leaving its radio transmitters behind to continue broadcasting reports in order to fool signals intelligence. Transported south in a convoy of eight hundred vehicles, the 316th Division arrived at an assembly area southwest of Ban Me Thuot on 3 February.

Apparently this ruse was not completely successful. ARVN SIGINT uncovered the 968th's move across the border, and also detected the potential movement south of the 316th. Since shifting the 316th from Laos to South Vietnam was a key indicator of a major future attack, CIA analysts, according to Frank Snepp, remarked on this new intelligence in the President's Daily Intelligence Briefing for 25 January. However, no further information on the 316th's movement was discovered, leaving allied intelligence uncertain of the division's intentions. Its presence was not confirmed until a prisoner was captured during the Ban Me Thuot attack.

Given the great significance of reserve divisions moving into South Vietnam, what intelligence was uncovered? What little is known is contained in Colonel Le Gro's diary. He notes that the 316th Division stopped internal communications on 18 January, and halted communications with PAVN Military Region 4 headquarters on 20 January. More important, South Vietnam was added to the 316th's postal codes. According to Le Gro, these signs indicated movement of the unit south. A further warning occurred when SIGINT intercepted a conversation in which one speaker remarked that "the division has gone far away."[26] Another intercepted message stated the speaker was "enroute to South Vietnam." After that, nothing concrete was received.

Besides these two divisions, in February, Giap sent the 341st Division to the B-2 Front. At the same time, Giap also directed the 27th Sapper Battalion to move from North Vietnam to the Highlands to reinforce the 198th Sapper Regiment, making the regiment, now with six battalions, the most powerful sapper unit in South Vietnam. Giap also sent the crack 95B Regiment, 325th Division, from PAVN forces in Quang Tri in I Corps to augment the forces attacking Ban Me Thuot. Lastly, he dispatched another anti-aircraft and engineer regiment to the Highlands, along with eight thousand new recruits to replace future combat losses. Logistically, the B-3 Front was also well provisioned: "By the end of February, Group 559 [the element commanding the Ho Chi Minh Trail complex] and its supporting elements had fulfilled 110 percent of the transportation plan for the campaign, ensuring . . . sufficient supplies to operate through the end of 1975."[27]

Thus, while retaining the powerful 1st Corps in North Vietnam to exploit any opportunity, Giap had dispatched half of his six-division strategic reserve—the 316th, 341st, and 968th—to strongly reinforce the Southern battlefield, particularly for the Central Highlands attack. This critical action is one that U.S. analysts should have been closely watching—as Major General Murray had reminded Admiral Gayler—since it was one of the main predictors of Hanoi's intentions. But now, in an era of congressionally mandated U.S. intelligence cutbacks in South Vietnam, our analysts could barely discern it.

Hoang Minh Thao arrived at the campaign headquarters in early February. His first mission was to get the right mix of units into the right position. He wanted to put ARVN in a situation such that its only choices would be "flee, surrender, or die." As Giap had said, "feints to deceive the enemy" were another key element of Thao's plan. His units "carried out a whole diversionary campaign [, and] during the final period . . . by which time the enemy had obtained some real evidence about our intentions [at] Ban Me Thuot, we even sought ways to neutralize that evidence to cause the enemy to believe that those moves were the feints. The Campaign Command was very concerned with, and directly commanded the diversionary tactical moves. We regarded them as ensuring the element of surprise, and surprise would ensure victory."[28]

In early February, Major General Vu Lang, the B-3 Front commander, gave each unit its mission orders. The 968th Division would conduct diversionary measures and pin down ARVN forces around Kontum and Pleiku. Afterwards, the first blow of the campaign would commence with the 320th Division cutting Route 14 near Thuan Man district, halfway between Pleiku and Ban Me Thuot. After blocking Route 14, the independent 95A Regiment and the B-1 Front's 3rd Division would strike Route 19 west and east of the An Khe Pass respectively. Simultaneously, the independent 25th Regiment would block Route 21 east of Ban Me Thuot. Once all these missions were accomplished, the 10th Division would overrun Duc Lap. At that point, the 316th Division, the 198th Sapper Regiment, the 24th Regiment, 10th Division, and the recently assigned 95B Regiment, 325th Division—along with artillery, anti-aircraft, armor, engineer, and signal units—would attack Ban Me Thuot. After capturing Duc Lap the 10th Division would move to Ban Me Thuot and join the battle if the initial assault was unsuccessful.

The 316th Division would carry the brunt of the attack against Ban Me Thuot. The division commander, Senior Colonel Dam Van Nguy, was ordered by the B-3 Front to first "peel away the outer defenses," then make a follow-up attack into the city against the ARVN 23rd Division head-quarters and the Darlac province chief's headquarters. Nguy, an ethnic T'ai from North Vietnam, had previously fought in the Central Highlands against U.S. forces at the bloody battle of Dak To in 1967. Upon examining Ban Me Thuot's defenses, Nguy began to question the wisdom of attack-ing the town in this manner. He later wrote: "If we tried to peel away the outer defenses first, the battle would naturally take a considerable length of time. . . . After each round of fighting we would have to stop to regroup and regain our combat strength, while at the same time responding to enemy counterattacks. If this kept up, the balance of forces would gradually turn against us, the division's attack power would gradually deteriorate, and we might have to halt or perhaps even fail to meet the goals of the cam-paign. The enemy would strengthen the defenses of his key installations, and powerful enemy counterattack forces, including tanks, artillery, and air support, would push us back away from Ban Me Thuot city."[29]

Moreover, Nguy believed that "If we fought in this manner under the existing conditions in 1975, when the enemy was armed to the teeth with the best weapons and technology, we would have to expend a great deal of time, strength, equipment, and blood. As for myself . . . during the entire course of my military career I had never fought a battle to 'peel away the outer defenses.'" Instead, Nguy proposed a different tactic: "use a powerful force to make a surprise attack penetrating deep into the enemy's head-quarters, his nerve center, to throw enemy troops into confusion and make them thrash around wildly like a snake whose skull has been crushed." After reviewing Nguy's plan, Major General Vu Lang turned him down.

Shortly after Van Tien Dung arrived at B-3 headquarters, he called for a meeting with Thao and the local commanders to receive a briefing on the attack preparations. Vu Lang was suddenly stricken with malaria and was unable to attend, and so Dang Vu Hiep led the briefing. As Dung listened to Hiep's report on the campaign battle plan, he became perplexed. Why was the 10th Division being used to attack Duc Lap rather than Ban Me Thuot? Dung thought the plan was for the 316th to attack Duc Lap, while the 10th would assault Ban Me Thuot. Hiep tried to explain, but the answers did not satisfy an increasingly angry Dung. As Hiep notes:

During a recess in the meeting, I hurried off to see Vu Lang. When I saw him his face was ashen, his lips were purple, and his body was shaking like a leaf, but he was still anxiously awaiting word about our discussions with Dung. I was concerned about him and felt the deepest affection for him. However, I described the situation to him and joked, "If you're going to die, you'll just have to wait to do it tomorrow, because right now you have to come and 'argue' for us about the use of 10th Division to attack Duc Lap!" At my rec-ommendation and in spite of the fact that his malarial fever had not yet bro-ken, Vu Lang came to the meeting and gave a detailed briefing on our plans for 10th Division. Vu Lang clearly spelled out [our] intentions. . . . It was precisely because 10th Division had experience in attacking heavily fortified enemy positions that we had to use 10th Division (minus 24th Regiment) to attack Duc Lap, because the Campaign Headquarters had specified that we must be certain of victory when we launched our attack on Duc Lap, and that the battle must not last more than one or two days. . . . In addition 10th Division had already been deployed to an assembly position in the Duc Lap sector. If we decided to move the division again it would not only cause us to lose more time, it would also create a lot of problems for us, especially with regards to maintaining the secrecy of our planned attack.[30]

Given that the 10th was already in position, Dung grudgingly approved the plan, but he was adamant that the division must capture Duc Lap and then quickly reinforce the Ban Me Thuot battlefield. This was the first time, but by no means the last, that the attack direction of the 10th Division would be controversial. During the rest of the 1975 offensive, the 10th Divi-sion would bounce like a pinball around South Vietnam, becoming one of the most heavily engaged divisions during the "Great Spring Offensive."

On 25 February, Dung called a final meeting to discuss campaign tactics. Again Nguy presented his plan for bypassing the outer defenses and strik-ing the headquarters. As he later wrote: "There was vigorous discussion of my plan as we stood over the sand table. There were several occasions when some of the generals got into heated, ferocious arguments over the plan, but in the end, everyone unanimously approved of my division's battle tactics. After concluding the discussion on the plan of attack . . . General Dung . . . gave us some words of encouragement: 'The tactic that Dam Van Nguy has just presented to us is called 'a flower blossoming behind enemy lines.' When I was commander of 320th Division, I organized a powerful, elite force to attack the center of Thai Binh City, leaving the enemy no time to react.'"[31]

While Dung has long been credited with using the "blooming lotus" technique for attacking Ban Me Thuot (penetrating the city first, and then moving from the inside to attack the outer defenses), it was the 316th Division commander who actually proposed it. While it is true that Dung had once used the tactic in a battle against the French in North Vietnam, it was Nguy who asked to fight in this manner at Ban Me Thuot. Why Dung omits this fact from his book is unknown.

Despite internal debate over tactics, PAVN's daring plan was swiftly taking shape. However, Dung now had another problem: ARVN was growing suspicious about Ban Me Thuot.

THE ARVN RESPONSE

Responsibility for the vast swath of South Vietnam known as the Central Highlands rested on the thin frame of Major General Pham Van Phu. Born in October 1928 in North Vietnam, Phu had compiled a storied twenty-four-year career in the Army when he was chosen to be II Corps commander. He twice won the French Croix de Guerre, earned the Vietnamese Cross of Gallantry seventeen times, and was wounded four times in combat. He began his career as an interpreter for the French army, and then was sent to Dalat to attend officer school. Graduating in July 1953, he was assigned to the 5th Airborne Battalion. The battalion fought at Dien Bien Phu, and there he gained a well-deserved reputation for bravery, as his unit fought practically until the last man. After the French surrender at the besieged outpost, he and seven thousand other POWs began a five-hundred-mile trek to a Communist prison camp, where he endured sixteen months of horrific captivity. There he contracted tuberculosis, and the terrible conditions induced in him a great fear of ever again suffering the draconian hospitality of the Communist prison system.

After returning to the South, he became one of the first Vietnamese Special Forces commanders. In 1969 he went to the Delta, where he earned his first star. He then went to I Corps. and was assigned as Truong's deputy commander for the 1st Division. When Truong went to the Delta as deputy commander of IV Corps, Phu became 1st Division commander. This was a prestigious assignment, as the 1st Division had long been considered

ARVN's best regular infantry outfit. During Lam Son 719 in February 1971 the division suffered heavy losses, but he retained command and was promoted to major general. During the 1972 offensive, he worked himself so hard his health collapsed. He was relieved in October 1972 and sent to a hospital to recuperate. For the last two years he had been commandant of the Quang Trung Training Center located outside of Saigon, the main instructional facility for enlisted soldiers. On 5 November 1974, he assumed command of II Corps after Vice President Tran Van Huong had doggedly insisted that Thieu replace the corrupt but effective Lieutenant General Nguyen Van Toan.

Phu was generally non-political and not particularly corrupt himself. But, like most senior officers, he turned a blind eye to his wife's extracurricular business activities. Because of Dien Bien Phu, the French had a particularly high regard for him, which caused Thieu to consider him one of his best generals. However, according to those who knew Phu, while he had a deserved reputation as a brave officer and a good division commander, he was not capable, for reasons of both health and education, of assuming the heavy demands of corps command.

Upon assuming command, Phu faced two simple but profoundly difficult questions: What locations in the vast expanse of II Corps would PAVN attack, and how should he deploy his troops to defend those locations? The vast majority of Phu's actions were in response to those two questions. In December 1974, both the JGS and Phu believed PAVN would first cut the three main highways providing access to the Highlands, Routes 14, 19, and 21, and then attack Kontum and northern Binh Dinh. Phu thought that another objective of the Communists was to take advantage of the new road they had built paralleling the Ho Chi Minh Trail—the so-called Eastern Annamite Road—by tying it into Route 14. He recognized that the new road detoured into Cambodia near Duc Lap, thereby adding 125 miles for the supply convoys headed for the B-2 Front. After the attacks against Phuoc Long, Phu, Vien, and Thieu all believed PAVN would attempt to march north and seize Route 14 in Quang Duc, as it had tried to do in late 1973, to shorten that supply line. It was a logical breakdown of Politburo plans, and Phu quickly dispatched the 24th Ranger Group to protect Quang Duc.

In January, however, Phu was forced to adjust his analysis of enemy intentions. In early January the ARVN 22nd Division captured a soldier in the western part of Binh Dinh province near the critical An Khe Pass. The

An Khe Pass and Mang Giang Pass are the two main chokepoints on Route 19 between the coast and Pleiku. Interrogators gleaned from the prisoner that the An Khe Pass was a major North Vietnamese target. The POW had accompanied the PAVN 3rd Division commander on a reconnaissance of the pass, and he was caught with a map showing the locations of the Communists' proposed blocking positions. Interdicting the road had been a Communist tactic since the days of the French war, and the secret plan called for the entire 3rd Division to assault the pass in conjunction with large-scale attacks against Pleiku.

This was a critical change in tactics. During the 1972 offensive the 3rd Division used only one regiment to cut the road at the An Khe Pass, and it had taken several months of hard fighting to remove them. If PAVN severed Route 19, Kontum and Pleiku would be isolated from their primary supply route. This new intelligence—combined with recent signal intercepts indicating that the PAVN 968th Division had slipped into South Vietnam from Laos—convinced Phu that Pleiku and not Kontum was now the Communists' main objective. Thus, in late January his priority changed from guarding Kontum to securing Route 19 and Pleiku.

The ARVN 22nd Division quickly assigned its 47th Regiment to hold the pass, but Phu also remained concerned about northern Binh Dinh along the coast, the area in the province most often contested.[32] He also possessed some spotty intelligence about an attack into Binh Dinh by the PAVN 52nd Brigade. Consequently, instead of assigning the entire 22nd Division to guard the pass area against the expected attack by the PAVN 3rd Division, he ordered the 22nd to hold two regiments in the north, leaving its fourth regiment in reserve.

In mid-February 1975, Phu was interviewed by Nguyen Tu, the highly influential chief correspondent for *Chinh Luan*, long regarded as the best newspaper in South Vietnam. Tu had graduated from the Son Tay Military Academy in North Vietnam. He was an institution among Vietnamese reporters, having worked for newspapers in Hanoi and Saigon. Instead of lounging in Saigon coffee shops trading or making up gossip, Tu spent his time in the field, talking to soldiers and reporting on their lives. He was the Vietnamese equivalent of Ernie Pyle, the famed American World War II war correspondent. In March, his series of articles on the withdrawal from Pleiku would devastate morale in Saigon.

Phu gave Tu his analysis of the coming campaign, and predicted that a "division-size force" would attempt to interdict Route 19.[33] Colonel Hoang

Ngoc Lung, the J-2 (intelligence officer) for the Joint General Staff, was aghast at the amount of information Phu revealed during the interview. Lung later wrote: "In a press interview in February 1975 . . . the commander of II Corps withheld nothing from what he knew about the enemy's goals and future actions in his MR and even outlined his operational plans in no uncertain terms."[34]

Phu's staff, however, only partially agreed with their commander's estimate. The II Corps intelligence officer, Colonel Trinh Tieu, judged that PAVN's main objective was not Pleiku, but Ban Me Thuot. Tieu had served as an intelligence officer in the Central Highlands for many years, including as the 23rd Division intelligence officer (G-2) during the Easter Offensive. Tieu based his analysis of Communist plans on old-fashioned human intelligence. In early January, ARVN had lost track of the PAVN 10th Division, which normally operated around Kontum. Soon thereafter, a report was received that a 10th Division reconnaissance team had been spotted in Quang Duc, 150 miles to the south. Tieu also learned that both the PAVN 10th and 320th Divisions had celebrated Tet early, and had then moved southward. A POW reported in late January that the 25th Regiment, an independent B-3 Front unit, had been ordered to move east of Ban Me Thuot to cut Route 21.

More important, on 4 February, a communications sergeant from the PAVN 320th Division deserted to ARVN. He confirmed that his unit had moved south from its position around Duc Co, a village west of Pleiku, leaving its broadcasting gear in place to send out misleading radio messages. He also provided the secret location of the 320th in Thuan Man district on the border between Darlac and Pleiku provinces, along with detailed information on North Vietnamese plans. He claimed the 320th intended to cut Route 14, the 10th was planning to strike Duc Lap, and PAVN would assault Ban Me Thuot with two divisions, reinforced with tanks, artillery, and sappers. However, he did not know when the attack would happen.

This was another ominous development for Phu. If the 320th cut Route 14 between Pleiku and Ban Me Thuot, and the 3rd Division simultaneously interdicted Route 19 while Route 21 was also blocked, the Central Highlands would be cut into two isolated chunks of real estate. With most of Phu's forces in the north, a major PAVN assault would easily capture Ban Me Thuot and the weakly defended southern section of the Highlands.

President Thieu was briefed on this new information during a stopover two days later at the defensive positions of the 44th Regiment, 23rd Division, about ten miles northwest of Pleiku. He made yearly visits to each corps right before the Tet holiday to bring gifts to the troops and receive a briefing about front-line conditions. During the meeting, he asked Phu his opinion of the rallier (the term commonly used for a defector) from the 320th Division. Phu responded that he felt the North Vietnamese were trying to deceive him into moving the 23rd Division to defend Ban Me Thuot, leaving Pleiku exposed. Thieu disagreed and ordered Phu to concentrate the 23rd Division around Ban Me Thuot, and to bolster it with a company of tanks. The 53rd Regiment, 23rd Division, was immediately dispatched from Pleiku, sending its headquarters and two battalions to Ban Me Thuot and one battalion to Quang Duc. A week later, however, Phu canceled moving the rest of the 23rd Division, apparently without Thieu's knowledge.[35] Phu had received new signals intelligence that the 320th Division was once again transmitting radio messages from its usual location at Duc Co. Now convinced the rallier was a plant, Phu terminated the move of the 23rd Division.

It was a huge mistake. Just as the defector had revealed, the radio messages were a massive ruse. In early February the 968th Division initiated Phase One of Thao's deception plan in the Highlands by establishing "a phony communications network to mislead the enemy." Near Pleiku, "19th Regiment's cryptographic team pretended to be the Central Highlands Campaign Headquarters, and the role of the 320th Division Headquarters was played by 4th Battalion, 19th Regiment. 29th Regiment organized a radio network playing the role of 10th Division."[36] Not only were false messages transmitted, but open preparations such as reconnaissance teams that were "discovered" and road building made it seem that PAVN was preparing to attack Pleiku.

Despite the details from the defector and the conclusions drawn by Phu's own staff, he disregarded their advice. He remained adamant that Pleiku was Hanoi's focus. Phu was convinced by the resumed chatter from the 320th radios, the "harder" intelligence on the 968th Division's entry into II Corps, and the captured map showing the 3rd Division's plan to cut Route 19. A month before the opening battle of the final campaign, ARVN in II Corps remained badly divided over Hanoi's military plans.

7

"GOODBYE FOR NOW, BAN ME THUOT"

BEGINNING THE "GREAT SPRING OFFENSIVE"

As of late February, the bulk of Major General Pham Van Phu's forces still protected Kontum and Pleiku. Kontum was defended by three Ranger groups, while a fourth group held Route 14 between the two cities. This force was led by Colonel Pham Duy Tat, the II Corps Ranger commander. Tat, a former Special Forces officer and protégé of Phu, was ecstatic that the Rangers had been given a specific mission under his command. He had come to II Corps in late 1972, and was well known in the Vietnamese military for his combat prowess and courage in battle. He had won several U.S. awards, including a Silver Star and several Bronze Stars. He had boldly pledged to Thieu at the early-February meeting at the 44th Regiment that he would hold Kontum at all costs. Hence he supported Phu's decision to maintain strong forces around the city, and resisted any efforts to parcel out his Rangers.

Brigadier General Le Trung Tuong, commander of the 23rd Division, led the Pleiku front. Tuong had spent much of the previous eight years on the II Corps staff, first as chief of staff and then as assistant commander for operations. On 20 November 1973, he was given command of the 23rd Division. The 25th Ranger Group and two regiments of his division—the 44th and 45th—guarded the approaches to Pleiku. The division's third regiment, the 53rd, had two battalions protecting Darlac province and one battalion in Quang Duc. Phu also had the 24th Ranger Group defending the vast province of Quang Duc. The 23rd's organic armor squadron, the 8th Cavalry, had one troop of M-113 armored personnel carriers at Ban Me Thuot, while its armor troop, equipped with vintage M-41 tanks, supported an RF battalion holding Duc Lap.[1] In reserve at Pleiku, Phu had the 4th Ranger Group and one tank squadron from the 2nd Armor Brigade, plus the other M-113 troop from the 8th Cavalry.

Despite Phu's insistence that Pleiku was the target, his intelligence officer, Colonel Trinh Tieu, remained convinced that PAVN intended to attack Ban Me Thuot. At a meeting on 19 February with Phu and the assembled II Corps commanders and staff, Tieu recounted the previous intelligence from various ralliers and briefed Phu on some new information. Scouts at the remote outpost of Ban Don on the Cambodian border twenty-two miles northwest of Ban Me Thuot had reported finding tank tracks and seeing large fleets of North Vietnamese trucks moving south. Previously, all of PAVN's armor in II Corps had been concentrated in the north. More recently, the Quang Duc province chief had informed Tieu that a large truck convoy had been spotted dropping off a PAVN regiment right across the Cambodian border from Duc Lap. Tieu believed both pieces of intelligence were clear signs that Ban Me Thuot was the objective.

Phu again insisted these were diversions. He stuck to his opinion that since Pleiku was the headquarters and nerve center of II Corps, it was the most likely target. Moreover, Phu had just returned from a meeting in Saigon on 18 February. Thieu, Vien, and the corps commanders had met to review the progress of the 1975 national-defense plan developed at the December 1974 NSC meeting. Regarding II Corps, Thieu had asserted that the main attacks would be directed at provincial capitals like Gia Nghia in Quang Duc and Pleiku.

Hanoi promptly learned of the Saigon meeting, as its spy in the JGS once again exposed the RVNAF's strategic thinking. According to Hoang Van Thai, "We learned that Thieu had held an emergency meeting with his generals in Saigon on 18 February. Two remarks by the enemy drew particular attention from us. First, they thought we would launch a spring-summer offensive in the near future aimed at neutralizing their pacification strategy and regaining lost territory and population on all battlefields, mostly in [II Corps]. Second, Thieu had asked to take precautions against an attack by us on [Duc Lap], Pleiku, and Kontum, which would be the main targets. As for Ban Me Thuot, this would be only a support target, if ever we chose to attack."[2] This intelligence confirmed for the Politburo that its true plans remained secret.

The major military issue for Phu was how to deploy his limited units in the vast Highlands. Given the enormous territory, the security of II Corps was heavily dependent on accurate intelligence on enemy intentions, and then the capability to rapidly reinforce threatened positions by airlift. Phu had neither. His main concern was whether the North Vietnamese 968th Division would combine with the 320th to attack Pleiku, or instead replace the 320th, allowing it to move south and attack Ban Me Thuot. Without intelligence confirming that the 320th had moved into Darlac to strike Ban Me Thuot, Phu felt he could not strip units from Pleiku and take the risk that both enemy divisions might assault the city. Phu thought that if Hanoi did attack Ban Me Thuot, he could rapidly airlift troops to the city. However, he vastly overestimated his airlift capabilities, still thinking as if it were the old days of American-supplied mobility. He did not understand that now he had even less than when Toan was in charge of II Corps.

Another reason PAVN achieved tactical surprise was that Phu, after the discovery of the map in January, remained in a defense-oriented stance instead of launching pre-emptive strikes to destroy the PAVN forces in their lair. After Thieu made his annual Tet visit to the troops, General Cao Van Vien sent another directive to conserve resources. Vien noted that foreign assistance had been reduced because of "internal difficulties in the allied countries," and that the world oil crisis had caused problems for the Vietnamese economy. The aid cuts had forced Vien to scale back his previous order of October 1974 limiting corps to only one ten-day operation per month. Now he requested the senior commanders to apply

> the following operational concepts in a manner suitable to each locality: With regards to tactics, large-scale engagements with joint service coordination demanding massive and costly amounts of equipment and support are no longer appropriate, in part because of reductions in the level of assistance provided to us, and in part because of the restrictions imposed by the Cease-Fire Agreement. For that reason we must [not overly rely] on air and artillery support. . . . With regards to transportation, human labor will be the primary method, with transportation equipment like trucks, helicopters . . . serving only a secondary role, or only using these resources in situations when it is absolutely necessary and human labor, human legs, cannot carry out the mission.
>
> As for unit operations from battalion size upward, we will only use such operations against large, confirmed, and evaluated targets. In this way we will be able to economize on our use of forces and will have a number of large reserve units on hand ready to send out to deal with the enemy when necessary. From the logistics standpoint, one of our greatest problems is that at present weapons, ammunition, and fuel are incredibly expensive, and continuing at our former rate of expenditure would be impossible for the national budget to sustain. The Joint General Staff has previously issued instructions to all units to economize on their expenditure of resources, but we have not yet reached the proper levels. In the future we will have even greater difficulties in this respect. For that reason, from this moment on we must conserve and economize on the use of each individual bullet, each drop of gasoline.[3]

This mid-February order restraining even battalion-size operations forced Phu into a defensive stance. Moreover, since the December 1974 NSC plan had ordered a nationwide pacification campaign for the first three months of 1975, Phu had concentrated on this campaign rather than large maneuvers. The aid cuts had done precisely what the anti-war groups sought: dramatically weakened the South Vietnamese military. And those cuts occurred precisely at the point when the Politburo was expanding the war. Hanoi then judged Saigon's diminished power not as a condition for achieving a favorable peaceful settlement, but as an invitation to strike.

Despite Phu's insistence that Pleiku was the main target, the new intelligence made him uneasy about Ban Me Thuot. To calm his own uncertainty, he dispatched the 45th Regiment, 23rd Division, from Pleiku to Thuan Man, a district seat about halfway between Pleiku and Ban Me Thuot. Its mission was to seek evidence that the 320th Division was hiding near Route 14. After the 45th Regiment had finished searching, Phu planned to send it to Ban Me Thuot. He also ordered a second battalion of the 53rd Regiment from Darlac to Quang Duc to bolster its defenses.

Van Tien Dung's headquarters soon learned of Phu's orders to transfer the 45th Regiment south. The worried PAVN commander realized that if Phu shifted troops to Ban Me Thuot, capturing the city would become very complicated. Although contingency plans had been drafted to strike Ban Me Thuot even if the city was reinforced and expecting an attack, Dung fervently hoped to assault an unsuspecting town. Otherwise the cost in blood and equipment would be high. For Dung, Phu's move was a dangerous new element that had the potential to upset Hanoi's grand strategic plan. If ARVN soldiers stumbled upon the 320th's hiding place, that would provide compelling proof of North Vietnamese intentions and eliminate the element of surprise Dung and his generals had so arduously worked for.

Dang Vu Hiep, the B-3 Front's political officer, later explained that to prevent Phu from discovering their plans, PAVN undertook "active deception measures in the Kontum and Pleiku sectors to lure 45th Regiment back to Pleiku. To implement this decision, the . . . staff ordered a false radio message to be transmitted to trick the enemy. The text of the message read, 'The enemy has fallen for our deception and believes we will attack Ban Me Thuot. That is why he has sent 45th Regiment south.'"[4]

Phu fell for the ploy. After reading the intercepted message, he canceled the 45th Regiment's onward movement to Ban Me Thuot. However, he left it at Thuan Man to continue searching. Concurrently, Hoang Minh Thao told the 320th to avoid any contact with ARVN troops and to pull its combat formations back from Route 14.

Much to Thao's chagrin, however, more mistakes occurred. On 28 February, Phu was handed another piece of the intelligence puzzle when a prisoner was captured six miles northwest of Ban Me Thuot. He was from the B-3 Front's artillery unit, and he informed his captors that he had left the Duc Co area in western Pleiku, the 320th's traditional base area, in early January and had arrived in Darlac on 26 January. He was scouting firing positions in preparation for an upcoming "joint campaign." This seemed to corroborate the earlier rallier's information that the 320th had moved south, but the prisoner had been severely wounded, and interrogators were unable to glean any further information from him. Thus the presence of his artillery unit confirmed nothing; one could not deduce whether it was preparing to engage in a major attack against the town, or a routine bombardment.

Still, given the 45th's movement and the newly captured soldier, Dung was taking no chances. On 1 March the 968th Division launched Phase Two of its deception plan (Phase One had been the fake radio messages), a series of attacks near Pleiku. The primary assault was against a battalion of the 25th Ranger Group holding positions west of the village of Thanh An. The village sat on the Route 19 extension southwest of Pleiku at the edge of ARVN-controlled territory. Under cover of an artillery barrage, 968th Division infantry—using 320th Division radio call signs—overran several Ranger positions and directly threatened Thanh An. Just as Dung hoped, when PAVN attacked the Rangers, Phu immediately shifted the 45th Regiment back to help defend Thanh An.

Seeing Phu's continued sensitivity to Pleiku, Dung ordered the 968th Division to create even greater turmoil in the area. He implored his forces to make "one man seem like ten!" The division promptly dispatched small teams to rocket targets near Pleiku, including the II Corps headquarters and the Cu Hanh airfield, home of the VNAF 6th Air Division. It worked: the shelling kept Phu fixated on Pleiku.

The 968th action's left the other PAVN units relatively free to continue their preparations, albeit still dodging South Vietnamese patrols. The 316th and 10th Divisions were preparing for the attacks on Ban Me Thuot and Duc Lap, while the 320th was organizing to cut Route 14 at Thuan Man. It also had a follow-on mission: seizing Cheo Reo, the capital of Phu Bon province. The division had sent a reconnaissance team in February to scout Cheo Reo. Afterwards, the division ordered its engineers "to secretly prepare a road toward Cheo Reo to ensure that troops and technical equipment could be moved to that area when necessary . . . the division sent one battalion (9th Battalion, 64th Regiment) to a base position four miles west of Cheo Reo city. The division's communications personnel overcame many difficulties to string a direct line of communications to 9th Battalion. This telephone line would later provide outstanding service enabling the division to provide directions directly to the battalion after the situation began to develop."[5] That was an understatement. The line, which ran thirteen miles to the 9th Battalion, would later pay a pivotal role in the defeat of II Corps.

On 1 March, Hoang Minh Thao took direct control of all troop movements from the B-3 Front headquarters. After the capture of the artilleryman, Thao's first order was for each unit to take extra precautions to prevent discovery. Despite his admonitions, small encounters were unavoidable. Between 28 February and 3 March, RF troops in Darlac province had six separate engagements with North Vietnamese units. Also, on 3 March an ARVN spy posing as a woodcutter spotted a PAVN battalion west of Ban Me Thuot in an area where no enemy troops had been seen for some time. Then the Communists suffered another potentially serious blunder—although, luckily for Thao, it happened in the midst of major attacks in other areas. While crossing Route 14 south of Ban Me Thuot on the night of 4 March, a young lieutenant with the 316th's southeastern assault column dropped his diary. A Darlac sector patrol discovered it the next day and gave it to the province intelligence section. The diary's owner had noted his departure from North Vietnam on 24 January and his arrival in Darlac on 4 February. An entry for 3 March said that his unit was to proceed to Ban Me Thuot and participate in an attack. The last entry read: "4 March: crossing Route 14 on the way to Ban Me Thuot."[6] However, fortune again smiled on Giap's army. The lieutenant did not identify his unit, leaving ARVN unsure who planned to attack the town, and when.

Given the growing human intelligence that Ban Me Thuot was the main target, Vien's top intelligence officer, Colonel Hoang Ngoc Lung, had come to the same conclusion as Colonel Tieu. Under prodding from Tieu, Lung flew to Nha Trang in early March in an attempt to convince Phu of his analysis. Phu declined to meet with him.

With all these signs, plus the pleadings of Tieu, Lung, and others regarding an attack against the southern Highlands, why did Phu remain obsessed with Pleiku? Many have speculated as to the factors that shaped his thinking. They include fear of capture and loss of prestige if he was defeated.

In his defense, the Central Highlands is a vast domain of trackless forests and steep mountains, and the draconian aid cuts had severely hampered intelligence efforts. Most ARVN observers believe that Phu's unfamiliarity with the area also greatly contributed to his decision. Phu had never served much time in II Corps. These observers contend that if Thieu had retained Lieutenant General Nguyen Van Toan as II Corps commander, Toan would have deciphered the Communists' intentions. In fact, Toan had planned to attack Duc Co in November 1974 to disrupt Hanoi's dry-season preparations, but he was relieved before he could implement his plan. A successful spoiling attack against the 320th might have forced Hanoi to alter its design. Toan's removal left only one person who could have overruled Phu: President Thieu. But although he had ordered Phu at the early February meeting to send a regiment from the 23rd Division to Ban Me Thuot, he also later seemed to discount Ban Me Thuot as a target.

U.S. intelligence also provided contradictory information. Frank Snepp writes that the CIA's base in Ban Me Thuot had recently closed, leaving the CIA dependent upon GVN intelligence sources, which were scarce in the thinly populated region. Snepp's boss, Thomas Polgar, the CIA Station Chief in Saigon, disagrees with that statement.[7] He claimed in numerous interviews that the CIA had human information that Ban Me Thuot was the target. Polgar indicates that this information came from captured documents and prisoners, which means he is probably referring to the same South Vietnamese intelligence reviewed above.

Polgar further states that the Defense Department would not accept the CIA's analysis without confirmation from signals intelligence, which he says the U.S. did not possess.[8] NSA historian Robert Hanyok's study of the U.S. National Security Agency in Vietnam agrees with Polgar on this point, stating that allied SIGINT before the Ban Me Thuot battle "did not do well in discovering what the communist troops were up to."[9] Since U.S. aerial photography and VNAF reconnaissance were severely crimped by the budget cuts, the North Vietnamese specifically targeted the allies' best remaining source of tactical intelligence, signals intercepts. That is why the main component of PAVN's deception plan was using the fake radio transmissions, while imposing strict radio silence upon its troops on the march. All accounts to date accept that Hanoi fooled allied SIGINT into believing that its soldiers remained in their usual operating areas.

Those accounts are incorrect. On 7 March the head of South Vietnamese signals intelligence, Brigadier General Pham Huu Nhon, and the American head of the National Security Agency in Vietnam, Tom Glenn, flew to see Phu. The purpose of their trip was to warn Phu that ARVN SIGINT ana-

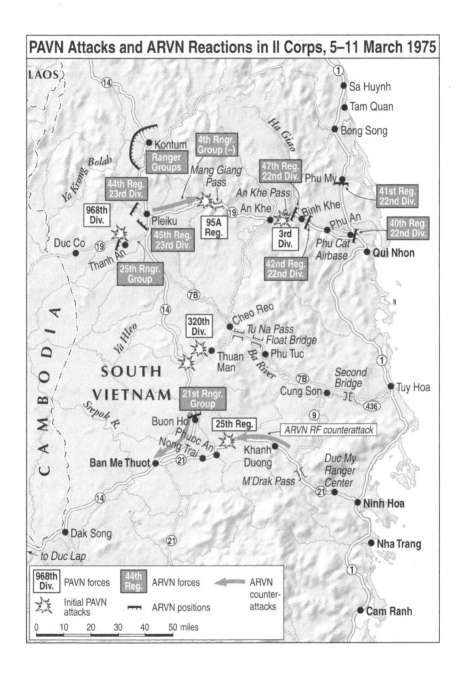

PAVN Attacks and ARVN Reactions in II Corps, 5–11 March 1975

LAOS

Sa Huynh
Tam Quan
Bong Song

Kontum

4th Rngr. Group (–)

Ranger Groups

Mang Giang Pass

47th Reg. 22nd Div.

Phu My

44th Reg. 23rd Div.

An Khe Pass

41st Reg. 22nd Div.

968th Div.

Pleiku

95A Reg.

An Khe

Binh Khe

Phu An

40th Reg. 22nd Div.

Duc Co

45th Reg. 23rd Div.

3rd Div.

Phu Cat Airbase

Qui Nhon

Thanh An

25th Rngr. Group

42nd Reg. 22nd Div.

Cheo Reo

320th Div.

Tu Na Pass
Float Bridge

Thuan Man

Phu Tuc

Second Bridge

Tuy Hoa

SOUTH

VIETNAM

21st Rngr. Group

Cung Son

Buon Ho

25th Reg.

ARVN RF counterattack

Phuoc An

Nong Trai

Khanh Duong

Duc My Ranger Center

Ban Me Thuot

M'Drak Pass

CAMBODIA

Dak Song

Ninh Hoa

to Duc Lap

Nha Trang

| 968th Div. | PAVN forces | 44th Reg. | ARVN forces | ⬅ ARVN counter-attacks |
| Initial PAVN attacks | | ARVN positions | |

0 10 20 30 40 50 miles

Cam Ranh

lysts had concluded that PAVN intended to attack Ban Me Thuot. According to Glenn, "We had previously warned the JGS that the PAVN were about to attack Phuoc Long. Nhon had now concluded that Ban Me Thuot was the next target. He based his conclusion on a combination of radio direction finding, message traffic analysis, and a few readable messages. We met Phu in Pleiku. Nhon treated Phu with great respect, but Phu did not believe Nhon's analysis or the SIGINT reports. Colonel Tieu was with us, but he was also unsuccessful."[10]

While hindsight is always 20/20, it appears there was a breakdown in intelligence coordination between South Vietnam and the U.S., or between American agencies. Unfortunately, there is no answer to the question why Nhon's analysts, who shared all the information they received with the U.S., had determined that Ban Me Thuot was the primary target while most of the Americans failed to reach the same conclusion.

Hanoi's deception plan was a significant element of the successful assault on Ban Me Thuot, but it was not the only reason victory was achieved. Overwhelming force and the use of armor in an urban environment were also noteworthy. Both rested upon avoiding discovery of PAVN's growing presence around the town, or the placement of the 320th and 10th Divisions in their respective hiding spots.

Yet how did the PAVN soldiers in the Central Highlands successfully evade the ARVN patrols? As mentioned, fuel cuts had limited the mobility of the reconnaissance teams and the amount of aerial reconnaissance. Most important, just as Hanoi's spy at JGS had provided crucial intelligence, the B-3 Front also had a critical agent in the South Vietnamese ranks. A warrant officer working at the communication center for the II Corps logistics agency stole the codebooks for ARVN forces in the Central Highlands.[11] His theft enabled the Communists to both monitor South Vietnamese radio frequencies and crack ARVN codes. This gave them advance knowledge of ARVN patrol routes, a point hinted at in the histories but never fully acknowledged. For example, Van Tien Dung notes that "By following enemy radio transmissions we knew that [ARVN] had ordered their reconnaissance units to find out where our 10th Division was located."[12]

Ultimately, the North Vietnamese deception and concealment efforts were extraordinarily successful. Some of it was luck, but much of it was thorough planning and execution. The outcome was a remarkable transfer of men and equipment that enabled the North Vietnamese to concentrate substantial combat power, which produced victory in one of the defining battles of the war. From North Vietnam came the 316th Division and Dung's campaign headquarters. From I Corps came the 95B Regiment, 325th Division. The two divisions that had been based in the northern part of the Central Highlands—the 10th and the 320th, along with artillery, sappers, and air-defense guns—marched over one hundred miles out of their normal operating areas near Kontum and Pleiku south to new locations. PAVN logisticians and engineers supported the effort by stockpiling large stores and building rough roads. Only the 968th Division was discovered, but its intentions remained unclear. This enormous strategic thrust was completed virtually undetected, and what little was discovered was not believed by the people who had final decision-making power.

THE CAMPAIGN BEGINS

ARVN Lieutenant Colonel Le Cau, commander of the 47th Regiment, 22nd Division, fell wearily onto his cot in his makeshift headquarters just east of the An Khe Pass on Route 19 in Binh Dinh province. It was late at night on 3 March. For ten hours he had climbed steep, rocky hills and walked among his troops, reviewing their defensive positions.[13] Since the capture in January of the prisoner with the map, his regiment had been defending the pass. After six weeks of constant patrolling and twenty-four-hour guard duty, Cau and his troops were exhausted.

Cau had been given this mission because of his familiarity with the terrain; he had fought there during the difficult days of the 1972 offensive. He knew that the 3rd Division would attempt to capture the pass, but he did not know the exact date or time. Despite the intelligence that the entire 3rd Division would attack the pass, both Cau and his division commander, Brigadier General Phan Dinh Niem, believed that the 3rd would follow its typical pattern: one regiment would seize the pass while the rest of the division would attack the coastal region in northern Binh Dinh. Given that the two sides had been locked in a bitter struggle in that area since December 1974, and because Phu was afraid of an attempt by the PAVN 52nd Brigade to capture the port of Sa Huynh, Niem had kept two of his regiments there, leaving one in reserve. The only unit he had available to reinforce Cau was a newly formed RF group.

This time, however, the 3rd had altered its traditional approach. The division had been regenerating in its base camps in northern Binh Dinh when new instructions arrived. As part of the Central Highlands Campaign, its mission was critical. It was, as the division history later put it, to destroy "a significant portion of the enemy's troop strength and . . . cut Route 19 for an extended period of time to create favorable conditions to allow the primary offensive in the Central Highlands to annihilate enemy forces and to create a vacuum in the east to support our local movement in Binh Dinh. The difference was that this time the scale of the battle, the length of time the road had to be cut, and the objectives of the campaign were all much greater than they had been during the 1972 offensive. In 1972 the division only cut the road . . . to help other units win a victory. . . . This time the division was ordered to annihilate enemy forces so that we could keep the road cut for an extended period of time."[14]

Blocking the road indefinitely would strangle Kontum and Pleiku, and prevent ARVN forces from retreating to the coast. Route 19, almost 125 miles long, is the chief lifeline of the Central Highlands. Supplies for Kontum and Pleiku travel by truck from the port at Qui Nhon, Binh Dinh's provincial capital and the fourth-largest city in South Vietnam. The road begins on Route 1 near Qui Nhon. It cuts through rice fields and foothills to the treacherous An Khe Pass and then continues to the famous Mang Giang Pass, where in 1954 French Mobile Group 100 had been ambushed and almost destroyed. The road then enters Pleiku province and continues west on the Route 19 extension, ending at Duc Co near Cambodia.

To keep Niem guessing, the 3rd Division also conducted a deception campaign. The 3rd's troops "spread the word that they were going to liberate northern Binh Dinh. At night many units sent forces up to the enemy's perimeter fences, and when they pulled back they intentionally left blatant signs of their presence behind. Tractors and bulldozers belonging to the province agriculture committee were ordered to drive north with their headlights burning and their engines revving loudly, leaving behind track-marks which resembled tank tracks. Right up until the final days the enemy was certain we would launch our attack in the north, even though the entire division and all its troops had quickly but quietly moved south."[15]

On 2 March, Phu flew in to review Cau's efforts. Phu emphasized to Cau that Route 19 between Pleiku and Qui Nhon must be kept open at all costs. Cau replied that holding every piece of this long road against an initial attack was impossible. There were too many bridges, the terrain was too difficult, and his troops were spread too thin. Aerial reconnaissance provided little help. The 22nd Division was limited to one plane for three hours a day. Still, Cau personally vowed to Phu that he would reopen the road if the Communists cut it.

Around 6:20 A.M. on 4 March, a thick cloud of fog and mist covered the ground, shrouding the mountain peaks from view. Suddenly a shattering explosion rocked Cau's headquarters. Bridge #13, a nearby culvert that was poorly guarded by a Popular Force platoon, had been destroyed by sappers. Phu's lifeline had been cut. At 6:35 A.M., as the morning fog lifted, two flares shot into the sky. Artillery shells immediately began bombarding RF and Cau's troops. The "Great Spring Offensive" had begun.

CLOSING THE TRAP

Concurrent with the 3rd's attack at An Khe, the 95A Regiment struck RF/PF positions on Route 19 on the western side of the Mang Giang Pass in Pleiku province. By late afternoon, it had captured a large stretch of the road. With most ARVN troops tied down protecting Kontum and Pleiku, Phu could only dispatch a battalion from his reserve, the 4th Rangers, along with limited armor support, to dislodge the 95A. He had to keep the rest of the 4th to await the next threat. Phu also ordered the 42nd Regiment, 22nd Division, to move from northern Binh Dinh to the small town of Binh Khe on Route 19 near the pass to defend it against an expected PAVN attack.

Although the diary found on 5 March was the clearest indicator yet that enemy forces were encircling Ban Me Thuot, apparently it was overlooked when the PAVN 25th Regiment attacked and cut Route 21 on the same day. Phu now had four brush fires going simultaneously: two on Route 19, a third one at Thanh An, and a fourth on Route 21. Phu organized a large task force to pry open Route 21 where it was blocked east of Ban Me Thuot near the Darlac–Khanh Hoa province border. Made up of "virtually every RF unit that could be spared from the coastal provinces," it was assigned the mission of reopening the road.[16] Commanded by the Khanh Hoa province chief, the counterattacks began on 7 March. Despite support from air, artillery, and armor, the RF failed to dislodge PAVN forces holding the high ground astride Route 21.

As for Phu, when the attacks came, he basically took up residence at corps headquarters, even eating and sleeping there. Ever the brave soldier, he raced to the scene of the fighting, managing each battle personally. It was the *esprit de corps* expected of a South Vietnamese Airborne officer. Yet while such action was required of a brigade or division commander, corps command was different. Courage alone was not enough. Phu's style might have worked in the past, but in 1975, the war was vastly different. PAVN had committed larger, more mobile forces, with superior firepower and logistics, all synchronized by superb planning and enhanced control by commanders who had war-gamed in advance Phu's every move. This situation required a leader who could simultaneously react and plan ahead.

Phu was good at reacting, but not at planning ahead. He countered the closure of Route 21 by ordering the 3rd Battalion, 53rd Regiment, to immediately leave Duc Lap and return to Ban Me Thuot. He also sent some artillery and the deputy commander of the 23rd Division, Colonel Vu The Quang, in a convoy to Ban Me Thuot to coordinate ARVN defenses in Quang Duc and Darlac. Colonel Quang was given complete authority over all forces in those two southern provinces. However, despite the injunction against revealing its presence, the 320th Division ambushed Quang's south-bound convoy, destroying ten vehicles. Although Quang escaped, a captured major from the convoy revealed that the 45th Regiment, 23rd Division, was returning a battalion to Thuan Man to search for the 320th. The PAVN division commander immediately asked permission to cut the road in order to prevent the 45th from traveling south.

With Routes 19 and 21 blocked, Van Tien Dung next intended to interdict Route 14 between Pleiku and Ban Me Thuot, but the timing was critical. He wanted to capture Thuan Man and cut Route 14 at that location, but if he did it too soon, Phu might recognize that Ban Me Thuot was the main objective and reinforce the town. If Dung did not cut the road, and the 45th Regiment went to Ban Me Thuot, the town would be considerably harder to capture. It was a tough decision, and the 320th's commander pressed him to make a choice. After reviewing Phu's moves, Dung concluded that Phu seemed focused on Route 19 and had not changed his troop concentrations. Consequently, Dung made a critical judgment: he told the 320th to "remain silent, avoid exchanging fire with spy patrols, [and] not fight on Route 14 without orders."[17] It was a tremendous risk, but it paid off when the 45th Regiment remained near Pleiku.

After two nervous days, Dung decided the opportunity had finally arrived to cut Route 14. On 7 March he sent a unit of the 320th Division to seize an RF base south of Thuan Man. His intention was to draw the newly arrived 3rd Battalion, 53rd Regiment, away from its patrols north of Ban Me Thuot. The ploy failed when the 48th Regiment, 320th Division, overran the RF position in forty minutes. However, even though the attack did not succeed in luring in the 3rd Battalion, the next day the 48th Regiment struck Thuan Man and a section of Route 14, and seized both in less than two hours. All three of the main roads in the Central Highlands had now been severed.

Meanwhile, the regiments that would assault Ban Me Thuot slid into position. Five separate columns would attack the town. Each was a combined-arms operation that would penetrate into the city to capture the command centers and major installations. In this way South Vietnamese control would be destroyed, and the outlying outposts would easily fall.

The initial assault into Ban Me Thuot would be led by the 198th Sapper Regiment. Its strike force comprised three sapper battalions. Two of the regiment's other battalions would harass Pleiku, while the last one would support the 10th Division at Duc Lap. The 198th made three reconnaissance forays into Ban Me Thuot to determine infiltration routes and observe the defenses of its objectives. The sappers would attack in conjunction with a two-hour artillery barrage to paralyze four main targets: the city airfield, the 53rd and 44th Regiment base camps, the Mai Hac De ammunition storage facility, and the larger Phung Duc airfield east of town. The airfields were chosen so as to prevent escape or reinforcements, and Mai Hac De to foil any resupply efforts.

After the 198th hit its targets, the five attack columns would advance on the town. Their objectives were to seize the main six-way intersection in the town center, the 23rd Division headquarters, the Darlac province headquarters, and the 8th Cavalry's base camp. The 316th Division would control three columns. One would hit from the northwest, another from the southeast, and a third from the southwest.[18] Each column was supported by an anti-aircraft battalion. The northwestern and southwestern columns had a powerful additional punch—eight tanks and eight armored personnel carriers each.

The 10th Division formed a light headquarters to command the fourth and fifth columns, and to coordinate the return of the division from Quang Duc. The fourth prong was the 95B Regiment, the crack unit that had held the Quang Tri citadel for many days in 1972 in some of the toughest fighting of the war. The fifth spearhead was a lone infantry battalion from the 24th Regiment, 10th Division. Both of these columns were also strengthened with anti-aircraft battalions and armor. The 95B would smash from the northeast to secure the main six-way intersection, the city airfield, and the province headquarters. The 10th's strike force would seize the 23rd

Division headquarters in combination with the southwestern column. Two artillery brigades would fire in support of the attackers.

Dung and Thao staked everything on the initial assault. In essence, the plan was to commit virtually their entire force to a mad dash into the city, gambling that they could overwhelm Ban Me Thuot in one massive wave. Only one battalion from the 10th Division remained in reserve. If ARVN survived the first onslaught, and Phu was able to reinforce the defenders, Dung's troops would be trapped in the open, cut off from any easy retreat.

The plan depended heavily on reaching the jump-off positions undetected. This was perhaps the most difficult aspect of the operation. The southeastern column marched for two days and nights, forded two rivers, and then crossed Route 14 undetected. The northern columns passed numerous settled areas and outposts. The armor units had a formidable task: depart from hiding spots some fifteen to twenty miles from the city without getting lost or stuck, cut through the thick forests, cross the wide and fast-flowing Srepok River on flotation devices, and then finally link up with their assigned attack columns. The artillery guns and the signal, engineer, and anti-aircraft units also had to maneuver into position undetected.

With Ban Me Thuot isolated, and Phu's attention drawn to Pleiku and Route 19, the next phase of the Central Highlands campaign began in Quang Duc. On the afternoon of 7 March, the 10th Division command group met in the jungle west of Duc Lap to make the final decisions about the attack. Duc Lap was considered a formidable target. It was viewed as the southern flank of Ban Me Thuot. To protect it, ARVN had built five fortified strong-points around the town, with fighting positions, underground bunkers, and minefields. Defenders included an RF battalion, three artillery batteries, and the M-41 tanks.

Like Dung and Thao, the 10th Division commander, Senior Colonel Ho De, also decided to gamble everything on one great assault. Cognizant of his orders to win fast and return immediately to Darlac, Ho De made a plan similar to the one for Ban Me Thuot: bypass the strong-points on the outer perimeter and strike at three chief targets. They were the main military base, a 23rd Division tactical headquarters, and the district headquarters inside the town. Two battalions would strike each target. Division artillery would provide fire support. ARVN's 24th Ranger Group in Quang Duc would be concurrently attacked by the B-2 Front's recently formed 271B Regiment. After the 10th captured Duc Lap, the 271B would seize the rest of the province.

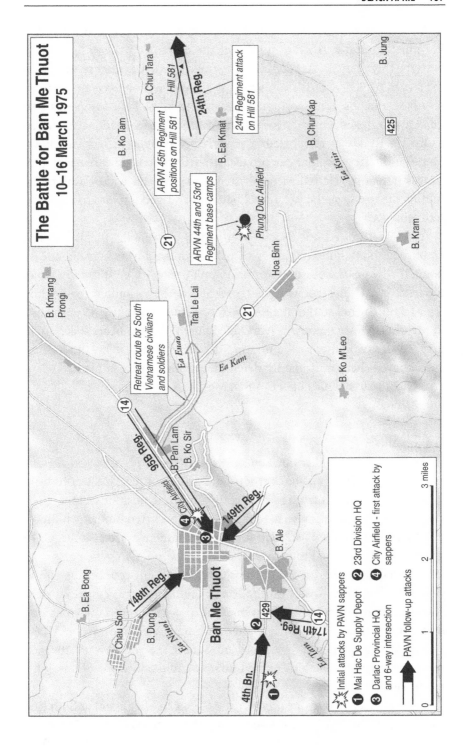

The Battle for Ban Me Thuot
10–16 March 1975

B. Jung

B. Chur Tara

Hill 581

24th Reg.

ARVN 45th Regiment positions on Hill 581

24th Regiment attack on Hill 581

B. Ko Tam

B. Ea Kmat

B. Chur Kap

425

Ea Knir

B. Kram

Phung Duc Airfield

ARVN 44th and 53rd Regiment base camps

Hoa Binh

B. Kmrang Prongi

Trai Le Lai

Retreat route for South Vietnamese civilians and soldiers

Ea Enao

Ea Kam

B. Ko M'Leo

95B Reg.

B. Pan Lam

B. Ko Sir

City Airfield

149th Reg.

B. Ale

B. Ea Bong

Chau Son

B. Dung

148th Reg.

Ban Me Thuot

429

174th Reg.

4th Bn.

Initial attacks by PAVN sappers
1 Mai Hac De Supply Depot 2 23rd Division HQ 4 City Airfield - first attack by sappers
3 Darlac Provincial HQ and 6-way intersection

PAVN follow-up attacks

0   1   2   3 miles

At 5:55 A.M. on 9 March, the 10th Division transmitted the attack order. For ninety minutes, the fifteen guns of the division's artillery fired shells onto the three targets. As soon as the barrage lifted, the infantry was given the signal. At 9:30 A.M. the soldiers of the 10th Division overran the military base and the 23rd's command post. The M-41 tank troop was also quickly eliminated. Only the assault against the district headquarters fared badly. The RF forces, supported by air strikes, fought back. Suddenly, however, the district commander broadcast an uncoded radio message that he was retreating. He requested air strikes to cover his withdrawal. Intercepting the message, the two PAVN battalions surged forward to catch the retreating RF.

It was a trap. As the North Vietnamese moved in, the RF troops ambushed them, inflicting heavy casualties on the advancing soldiers. By noon, the two battalions were forced to pull back and regroup for a strike the next day. The division engineers were ordered to build a road to the top of a nearby hill so that the PAVN troops could move two 85-mm guns to fire directly into the town. Working all night, the engineers successfully dragged the two guns to the hilltop. Attacking at first light, the 85-mm guns poured shells onto the RF defenses, crushing many bunkers. At 8:30 A.M. on 10 March, Duc Lap fell.[19] Ban Me Thuot stood alone.

INTO THE STORM

On Route 19, the soldiers of Le Cau's 47th Regiment withstood furious assaults by 3rd Division shock troops and artillery fire. Cau's troops were strung out holding platoon- and company-sized positions along both sides of the road near the pass. Savage fighting occurred on many hilltops. PAVN artillery would blast away, followed by human-wave assaults. Once a position fell, Cau had to counterattack to regain it. Often, he personally led his troops to reclaim the lost positions. While his courageous efforts were inflicting heavy losses on the North Vietnamese, his casualties were also high. Outnumbered three to one, the attackers were slowly pushing him out of his positions. By late afternoon on 5 March, only one ARVN strong-point remained at the eastern entrance to the pass. If it fell, the pass would belong to the People's Army. Cau now could only dig in and wait for reinforcements.

Using excellent close air support, the ARVN 42nd Regiment at Binh Khe had stymied the PAVN efforts to occupy the town. With the 47th Regiment unable to dislodge PAVN from the pass, Brigadier General Niem dispatched his 41st Regiment to replace the 42nd, sending that regiment to help Colonel Cau. That left Niem with only one regiment and RF/PF to cover hundreds of square miles along the heavily populated coast.

With the 41st Regiment occupying Binh Khe, on 7 March the 42nd Regiment moved to help Cau's men wrest back control of the lost ground. The 42nd attacked to clear the area north of the eastern entrance, but was soon bogged down in the tough terrain. Fearful of the 22nd Division's new efforts, on 8 March the 3rd Division attacked to destroy Cau's remaining position. It changed hands several times, but after two days of ferocious fighting, Cau's troops remained in control.

Despite heavy losses, the North Vietnamese would not relent. On 10 March, under orders from Dung to intensify the fighting and tie up the 22nd Division, PAVN threw an entire regiment at Cau's forces. His 2nd Battalion was overrun and its commander killed. Brigadier General Niem had no choice; he pulled his 41st Regiment out of Binh Khe and raced it into the breach to replace the 47th Regiment. Cau's troops had sustained 40 percent casualties while holding the pass area against the 3rd Division. Niem sent the 47th to defend northern Binh Dinh and recuperate. Before departing, he promoted Cau to colonel.

Meanwhile, on the morning of 9 March, Phu flew into Ban Me Thuot to see Colonel Vu The Quang, the deputy commander of the 23rd Division, and Colonel Nguyen Trong Luat, the Darlac province chief, to discuss the city's defenses. Luat was a career armor officer, and one of Nguyen Van Toan's fair-haired boys. Luat had commanded the 2nd Division's armor unit when Toan was the division commander, and he led the 1st Armor Brigade's spearhead into Laos in February 1971 during the abortive Lam Son 719 incursion. Toan made him Darlac province chief shortly before Toan was relieved of command.

Luat met Phu at the airport, and took him to the 23rd Division headquarters in Ban Me Thuot. They were joined by Colonel Quang, Brigadier General Le Trung Tuong, and the Quang Duc province chief. The chief informed Phu that during the battle for Duc Lap, a document was captured identifying the 10th Division as the unit assaulting the town. After discussing the situation, Phu decided against attempting to recapture Duc Lap. He reviewed the defense plan for Ban Me Thuot, and ordered the city to be placed on 100 percent alert. Phu also sent the 21st Ranger Group (minus one battalion, which was supporting Thanh An) to reinforce the village of

Buon Ho in Darlac province, twenty-five miles north of Ban Me Thuot on Route 14. If Duc Lap was Ban Me Thuot's southern flank, Buon Ho was its northern flank. Phu expected it to be the next Communist target.

The 21st Rangers were led by Lieutenant Colonel Le Qui Dau, who had commanded one of the Ranger battalions that fought at An Loc in 1972. By late afternoon of 9 March, the Rangers had completed the helicopter lift into Buon Ho. From there they could move to recapture Thuan Man, or they could support Ban Me Thuot if needed. Additionally, Luat ordered one of his RF battalions at Ban Don to pull back to defend Ban Me Thuot. Despite the reinforcements, ARVN forces around the Darlac capital were thin. Regular Army units consisted of the 23rd Division Reconnaissance Company, the 1st and 3rd Battalions, 53rd Regiment, and one M-113 troop from the 8th Cavalry. The rest were rear-echelon soldiers. Darlac sector forces included two RF battalions and local police. VNAF personnel were stationed at the two airfields.

At the same time Phu was discussing the city's defenses, Dung was finalizing the last details of the attack. On the afternoon of 9 March, he sent a cable to Giap. In it he outlined the preparations for the Ban Me Thuot attack and reported the Duc Lap victory. In closing he noted that his troops and equipment were in good shape, and that the men's morale was high.

On the afternoon of 9 March, Dung's armor began to move to the Srepok River. The 316th Division engineers constructed wooden boats and bamboo rafts to cross the 250-yard-wide, crocodile-infested river. Cables were strung across the river to pull the rafts to the eastern bank. The armor was forbidden to cross the river until the artillery began firing, making the timetable very tight. At the same time, the sappers moved in close to town.

As the minutes ticked down to H-hour, Dung picked up the field telephone and called Thao at his campaign headquarters five miles west of Ban Me Thuot. The PAVN signal troops had just finished stringing the wire across the Srepok River. Dung asked for a status report. Thao replied that all columns reported they were ready. Dung told Thao to maintain close communications with him so that they could make decisions quickly and decisively. Finishing the call, Dung exclaimed, "I wish you victory!"[20]

"WE HAVE WON A GREAT VICTORY"

At 2:45 A.M. on 10 March, the sappers were in position. Three companies were right next to the barbed-wire fence at the city airfield on the northeastern side of Ban Me Thuot. Another company totaling thirty-eight men slipped close to the Mai Hac De supply depot located in the southwestern corner of the city.

At 3:00 A.M. all the months of planning and debate, and the sweat and labor of thousands of soldiers, were realized when an officer shouldered his AK-47 at the city airfield and shot out its main searchlight. Immediately, a wave of satchel charges, mortar rounds, and rocket-propelled grenades exploded onto various sections of the airfield. At a second signal, 122-mm rockets began to rain down on the province headquarters and the 23rd Division command post. Sappers then swarmed onto the airfield, firing at guard positions. The Air Force technicians and RF troops manning the base fought back, but by 6:00 A.M. the sappers had secured one part of the airfield from the outgunned South Vietnamese guards. Shortly thereafter, one sapper company set out for the adjacent city center to capture the important six-way intersection. Meeting little resistance, the sappers quickly surrounded the crossroads and hunkered down to wait for the arrival of the tanks and infantry of the 95B Regiment.

While the attack on the city airfield was going on, the small sapper company at the Mai Hac De supply depot opened fire on the depot's command center. The depot sat on a piece of land 1,300 yards long and 750 yards wide. Over sixty-four warehouses and open-air dumps holding ARVN's largest ammunition supply in the Highlands were contained within the barbed-wire fences. Local Route 429 ran from the city alongside the depot to the Srepok River. After a sharp firefight, by 6:00 A.M. the depot commander had been killed and the depot captured.

Colonel Luat sent an RF company to counterattack. When the sappers beat off the first assault, the RF regrouped for a second wave, this time from two separate directions. Thao ordered the sappers to blow up several open-air ammo dumps to block one of the RF assault prongs, enabling the sappers to concentrate their firepower against the second prong.

The tactic worked. After three hours of fighting, the Regional Forces had not succeeded in recapturing the depot. Fortunately for the exhausted sappers, a battalion from the 316th Division's southwest deep-penetration column arrived at that very moment to assist them. After several more hours spent cleaning out the remaining guards, the entire complex was theirs. Only eighteen of the thirty-eight sappers who began the attack were still alive.

Meanwhile, the main sapper thrust was directed at the Phung Duc airfield about five miles east of town. This military area also included the base camps of the ARVN 53rd and 44th Regiments. The 3rd Battalion, 53rd Regiment, was currently holding the regiment's well-fortified base, while the 44th's was manned only by support troops. Two PAVN sapper battalions, one of them the powerful 27th Battalion, which Giap had personally sent from North Vietnam, would attack this critical area. The 27th Sappers would attack the 44th Regiment camp and the airfield command center while a battalion from the 198th would strike the 53rd Regiment camp. Because of the importance of this assault, the 198th Regiment's commander personally accompanied the attackers.

The two sapper battalions opened fire at 3:20 A.M. By 7:00 A.M. they had overwhelmed the 44th Regiment base camp and the airbase command center. At the 53rd Regiment's camp, however, the sappers faced a sterner test. No longer fighting guards or rear-service troops, the sappers ran into trouble when the regulars of the 3rd Battalion reacted quickly to the initial attack. Steadied by the 53rd Regiment commander, Lieutenant Colonel Vo An, the ARVN troops retook the initial breach point. As dawn broke, ARVN artillery poured fire onto the advancing sappers. The sapper battalion's assault soon collapsed. The 27th Sappers were ordered to join the assault in order to assist their pinned-down brothers. Although they threw themselves against the base defenses, they also bogged down under the withering fire. To rally his troops, the 27th's commander personally moved up to the barbed-wire fence to direct the attack. He paid for his courage with his life. With the 27th's chief killed, artillery fire battering his exposed troops, and wounded and dead sappers littering the ground, the 198th's commander broke off the attack.

Despite the setback at the 53rd's base camp, the 198th had achieved its main objectives, but at a high cost. During the opening attacks and the ensuing six days of the Ban Me Thuot campaign, the 198th lost almost 150 dead and wounded, close to one-third of its troops assigned to the initial assault. According to the regiment's official history, "This was many times less than the enemy's casualties, but for sapper troops these were very heavy losses."[21]

For the defenders of the 53rd base camp, their victory was ephemeral. While well protected by their extensive fortifications, they were surrounded and unable to move beyond their own perimeter. In the days to come, however, and almost completely unknown to the outside world, the continuing stalwart defense by the 3rd Battalion, 53rd Regiment, provided ARVN with one of its few moments of glory in II Corps.

At 6:30 A.M. the rocket attacks against Ban Me Thuot were halted, and the deep-penetration columns began moving. From the north, the 95B Regiment and armor raced into town along Route 14. One column advanced to the city airfield while another occupied the six-way intersection. After defeating RF counterattacks at both locations, the column at the intersection headed for the nearby province headquarters. Montagnard guards and troops of the 23rd Division Reconnaissance Company fought back fiercely. To defend against an armor assault, Colonel Luat had trained his troops in the use of the M-72 anti-tank rocket, and now it was paying dividends. Several T-54s were soon burning around the province headquarters, and after four hours of heavy fighting, the headquarters still held.

The PAVN forces, however, were too strong. In the Highlands, a cool mist often hangs near the ground in the morning, making visibility poor. Once the sun had burned off the haze, and the forward observers could see their targets and adjust fire, Thao directed an intense artillery barrage to support the 95B column. Darlac sector's ability to coordinate the RF defenses crumbled when one round finally found its mark, hitting and destroying the province headquarters' main radio transmitter. PAVN soldiers soon breached the compound. Although the South Vietnamese retreated into nearby buildings to fight back, it was useless. Badly outnumbered by the experienced troopers of the 95B Regiment, the last remaining pockets of resistance were cleaned out by nightfall.

In the west, the PAVN 4th Battalion, 24th Regiment, 10th Division, reinforced by eight T-54 tanks and eight K-63 armored personnel carriers, poured out of the jungle, crossed the Srepok River, and sped down Local Route 429. They motored past the Mai Hac De depot and penetrated through the housing compound for enlisted families and into an area near the 23rd Division headquarters. The 10th's column quickly reported its success to Thao, stating that it had taken the 23rd's headquarters. However, Thao's military-intelligence staff disagreed, insisting it was still monitoring transmissions from the command post. Thao then recalled a comparable incident during the battle for Kontum in 1972. An attack column claimed to have captured an important position. His intelligence staff back then had also disagreed, and it was soon proven correct. The column in Kontum had confused a similar-looking building with the headquarters. Thao immediately ordered a senior officer to drive out to inspect the situation. Sure enough, the 10th had mistaken the medical and communications compound for the 23rd's headquarters.

At 7:30 A.M. VNAF bombers appeared in the sky and began pummeling the exposed 10th Division formation. Supported by the air strikes, RF troops attempted to retake the compound. PAVN casualties began to mount, and several tanks were destroyed. According to the 10th Division's history: "After one day of continuous combat, [the] combined-arms deep-penetration force had managed to capture a number of targets, but our forces had also suffered heavy losses. The battalion commander was killed and the deputy battalion commander was wounded. Eight platoon- and company-level cadre were killed or wounded, we were out of virtually all types of ammunition, and if a night assault was ordered . . . the attack would run into difficulties."[22]

On the other side of town, the 316th Division's deep-penetration columns faced their own problems. The northwestern infantry column was in position by 6:30 A.M., but the armor and anti-aircraft guns had gotten lost. As dawn broke, PAVN commanders attempted to hide the regiment in a cemetery near the 8th Cavalry compound, but lookouts spotted them. Artillery and machine-gun fire began killing exposed North Vietnamese soldiers. Several times the Communist troops pressed forward, but they could not advance. Miraculously for them, the missing tanks suddenly arrived. The tanks' main guns began blasting away at ARVN bunkers and defensive positions. Despite continued heavy resistance, by noon the 316th had taken the 8th Cavalry's compound. Moving into the city, it linked up with the 95B at the six-way intersection, and the two units combined to attack the province headquarters.

The armor and artillery assigned to the southwestern column also failed to arrive on time. The original plan had called for the tanks to cross the Srepok River first, followed by the anti-aircraft guns. The engineers at the river, however, reversed the order. Then the trucks towing the guns got stuck in the middle of the river. It took several hours before the traffic jam was finally cleared. Despite the lack of support, the infantry captured a ridge line near the Mai Hac De depot to ensure that the 10th Division's armor had unimpeded access along Local Route 429. By mid-morning, the column's assigned armor finally caught up. Pushing up Route 14 from the south, the rest of the regiment and the armor advanced into the city under a cloud of VNAF air strikes, eventually linking up with the 10th Division's column at the medical compound. They remained there the rest of the day.

The 316th's southeastern column was two miles from the city when its artillery opened fire. With no heavy weapons to impede them, by alternately running and walking, the troops reached the city's outskirts at first light. The column fought its way into the city, sending one battalion up to the gate of the 23rd Division camp, but failed to break into the base.

By the end of 10 March, the Communist troops had captured the city center and overcome many strong-points inside the city. While Murphy's Law often hampered the North Vietnamese effort, overall the first day had gone exceedingly well for them. Analyzing the triumph, the campaign command noted: "In the first day of the attack on the city we have gained a great victory. We captured two important targets, the city airfield and the province headquarters, and have paralyzed the Phung Duc airfield. All spearheads fought well, although the southern spearhead had problems, and its successes are not commensurate with the number of casualties suffered by its troops. In spite of ferocious counterattacks by local enemy forces [the oft-maligned Montagnards had fought hard in many cases] supported by air strikes, the enemy has not been able to expel our forces from the city, and the puppet officers and soldiers are extremely frightened. However, the enemy leaders are still resisting stubbornly. Campaign Headquarters has decided to concentrate a powerful force to quickly destroy and overrun the headquarters of the 23rd Division and the other remaining targets."[23]

The next day would bring no respite for the battered ARVN in Ban Me Thuot.

"GOODBYE FOR NOW, BAN ME THUOT"

Shortly after the shelling began on 10 March, Colonel Luat left for the 23rd Division headquarters to coordinate the city's defenses with Colonel Vu The Quang. That morning, Quang radioed Brigadier General Tuong requesting relief forces, but Tuong denied the request. Tuong passed along a message from Phu asking Quang to try to hold the city for a few days. Phu thought the Communists would follow their 1968 pattern: attack Ban Me Thuot for three or four days, and then retreat. His belief was buttressed when Lieutenant Colonel Vo An at Phung Duc informed him of the defeat of the attack against the 53rd Regiment base camp. An reported his troops had killed over one hundred enemy soldiers. Convinced the assault against Ban Me Thuot was being conducted by the 320th Division and local forces, Phu stubbornly clung to his belief that the attack was a diversion for an assault against Gia Nghia in Quang Duc, followed by the main thrust against Pleiku. Moreover, given the incorrect identification of the PAVN units attacking Ban Me Thuot, along with Lieutenant Colonel An's stellar defense of the 53rd base, Phu was convinced that the city could hold and that the enemy would soon retreat.

Sadly for the South Vietnamese, these were deadly misjudgments. One can only surmise that had Phu known from the start that the 316th Division and the 95B Regiment were on the battlefield, he would have reacted differently. Not only did the lack of reinforcements doom Ban Me Thuot, but it fed Dung's and Thao's perceptions that ARVN defenses were weak, spurring them to press even harder.

President Thieu called Phu at 9:00 A.M. on 10 March for an update on the situation.[24] Phu stated that while VNAF bombers had flown over eighty sorties and had destroyed many tanks, intense anti-aircraft fire had prevented them from completely destroying the attackers. Phu had also ordered ARVN counter-battery artillery fire to refrain from shelling the city in order to prevent civilian casualties. Never having been subjected to artillery fire, the city's residents had no bunker system.

Thieu told Phu to recapture Ban Me Thuot. Phu immediately ordered the 21st Ranger Group to depart Buon Ho and retake the lost positions in the city. The Rangers arrived by nightfall but were unable to break through enemy lines, and they retreated to the western outskirts of town. Phu ordered Lieutenant Colonel Dau to launch an attack the next morning to recapture the province headquarters and support the 23rd Division headquarters. Additionally, the 45th Regiment at Pleiku was restricted to base and ordered to prepare to fly by helicopter to Ban Me Thuot. Thieu also wanted Phu to identify precisely which PAVN divisions were engaged in the attack, a key element in determining Hanoi's intentions.

Phu was about to discover the Politburo's plans the hard way. Following their first-day analysis of the battle, and after all-night preparations, on 11 March the Communists launched a massive assault against the 23rd Division's command post. Artillery began pounding the complex at 5:30 A.M. Hoang Minh Thao sent the 10th Division's deep-penetration column plus four battalions from the 316th and a battalion from the 95B—essentially two infantry regiments supported by armor, artillery, and anti-aircraft guns—against a rear headquarters defended by ARVN support personnel and elements of the 1st Battalion, 53rd Regiment. It was no match.

As the artillery fire lifted at 7:00 A.M., the tank-led infantry attempted to break into the compound. Once again PAVN armor tipped the scales. As tanks reached the base, Colonel Luat lay in wait on an M-113 armored personnel carrier equipped with a 106-mm recoilless rifle. As the first tank closed in, Luat gave the order to fire—but the recoilless rifle malfunctioned (see Introduction, p. 2). Realizing the great danger, Luat radioed to the circling A-37 pilots to provide close air support. Diving in, the planes missed their target and instead hit the 23rd command post, destroying the transmitter and wounding and killing many soldiers. Despite the loss of communications, the ARVN troops fought on, but their valiant efforts went for naught. By 11:00 A.M. the entire complex had been captured.

Both Luat and Quang escaped, but in different directions. Quang was quickly captured, but Luat eluded the North Vietnamese. Leading a group of about one hundred soldiers out a side gate, he headed for the dense brush of a nearby coffee plantation. He planned to hide there overnight and then head for Nha Trang. As he led the group toward the plantation, they began traversing a clearing. Machine-gun fire suddenly ripped through the men, killing and wounding many. In an open field, pinned down by heavy fire, with no hope of rescue, Luat ordered his assistant to wave a white flag of surrender. North Vietnamese troops soon appeared from their hidden positions. Luat was forced to identify himself. As he sat on the ground handcuffed, stripped to his underwear, his mood bitter and sad, he thought: "Goodbye for now, Ban Me Thuot; we promise to return somehow, someday."[25] The main battle for the city was over.

After capturing the 23rd Division headquarters, Thao followed the original "blooming lotus" plan. He ordered his units to eliminate the remaining bases on the outer perimeter: the Phung Duc airfield, the two remaining regimental base camps, the local training compound, and almost a dozen village strong-points surrounding the city. Much of the city was still untouched by the North Vietnamese, who were concentrated mainly in the city center and the southern portion. Over the course of the day, the 316th Division mopped up most of the local village positions surrounding the city. The division then sent its 149th Regiment to attack the ARVN 53rd Regiment base camp.

When the fighting began at the 23rd headquarters, Lieutenant Colonel Dau's 21st Rangers launched their counterattack. After bypassing enemy positions, by 10:30 A.M. on 11 March he had reached the edge of the headquarters complex. Thao's military-intelligence unit then intercepted a radio message from Dau reporting that the Darlac province headquarters and 23rd Division headquarters had both fallen, and that many enemy tanks were in the area. Dau said his two battalions, with limited fire support, could not rescue the besieged base. He was ordered to hold his position and assist any Darlac sector forces still fighting inside the town.

That night, Phu spoke with Thieu again. Phu indicated that while he now believed Ban Me Thuot was a major target, it was only one part of PAVN's effort to capture the Highlands. However, Thieu had now changed his mind. Given the loss of the 23rd headquarters, he told Phu to recapture the city at all costs.

Phu quickly designed a counterattack to retake the city. He would send an M-113 troop along with the 40th Regiment, 22nd Division, to assist in opening Route 21. He would employ the 21st Ranger Group in coordination with the battalion of the 53rd Regiment at its base camp to form one counterattack group. The 23rd Division would then mass its other two regiments east of Ban Me Thuot to form a second attack group. These two groups would launch a direct assault on the city with maximum air support. Brigadier General Tuong would command the counterattack. Phu requested that the 7th Ranger Group be shifted from Saigon to replace the units of the 23rd Division that were still based at Pleiku, 115 miles away from Ban Me Thuot.

Thieu approved Phu's plan, but Thao had no intention of allowing any counterattack. For Thao, defeating the ARVN response was the key to securing victory. He had carefully prepared for this response and calculated where Phu would land his reinforcements after Ban Me Thuot was attacked. He realized that with Route 14 blocked to the north and south, Phu could only land reinforcements east of the city. And the further away from the city Phu had to begin his attack, the more difficult it would be for him. More important, with the roads cut, Phu could not bring in armor or artillery to assist the counterattack, leaving the unsupported infantry easy prey for a tank-led assault. This preparation for Phu's expected counterattack is the least appreciated aspect of Thao's design, yet one with far-reaching consequences.

To prevent Phu from using footholds near the city, on the night of 11 March, Thao rapidly issued new orders. He told the 10th Division to attack and capture the remaining ARVN positions on the eastern side of the city, particularly the 45th Regiment base camp. The two regiments of the 10th Division still in Quang Duc were told to immediately depart, leaving the 271B Regiment to finish PAVN's mission there. He also ordered the 316th Division to attack the 53rd Regiment base. Additionally, Thao ordered the capture of other towns defending the approaches to Ban Me Thuot—Buon Ho to the north, and Ban Don to the west.

After moving into position during the night, at 5:00 A.M. on 12 March one battalion from the 24th Regiment, 10th Division, accompanied by tanks and supported by division artillery, struck directly at the 45th Regiment base. By 9:30 A.M. the battalion had secured complete control of the position, capturing almost five hundred soldiers along with twelve howitzers, five thousand rounds of artillery ammunition, and thousands of liters of fuel. At the same time, the 9th Regiment, 320th Division, attacked and captured Buon Ho, securing the last section of Route 14 within Darlac province. PAVN now had unimpeded use of Route 14 from the Darlac–Pleiku border through Quang Duc to Phuoc Long. Within Ban Me Thuot, PAVN troops began a house-to-house search. Civilians soon began to stream out of the city onto Route 21, headed for Nha Trang. Others holed up in nearby villages.

That same morning, Phu ordered the 45th Regiment, 23rd Division, to board helicopters and fly from Pleiku to a landing zone near Ban Me Thuot. Just as Thao had predicted, the ARVN troops landed east of the city. They landed at Hill 581, the main high ground between Route 21 and the Phung Duc airfield. The hill, one mile east of their surrounded comrades at the 53rd base camp, provided a dominating position from which to launch a counterattack. According to journalist Pham Huan, the 45th Regiment "volunteered to the last man" to return to Ban Me Thuot; their morale was high, and "they were determined to get back into Ban Me Thuot at any price to rescue their families."[26]

However, because of maintenance problems with the heavy-lift Chinook helicopters, the entire lift was not completed until late afternoon the next day, 13 March. It had taken almost two days for the 45th Regiment to fly from Pleiku and assemble east of Ban Me Thuot to link up with the 21st Rangers. Under orders from Brigadier General Tuong, the Rangers had pulled back on the afternoon of 12 March to secure the training center east of town. Tuong then sent in a helicopter to rescue his family hiding at the center. With the Rangers pulled out of the city, at 6:00 P.M. on 12 March Phu reported to Saigon that all organized resistance in the city had ceased.

Meanwhile, the 7th Rangers boarded planes in Saigon on the morning of 13 March and landed in Pleiku that afternoon. The helicopter lift from Pleiku resumed on the morning of 14 March, carrying one battalion of the

44th Regiment, regimental support elements, and the tactical headquarters of the 23rd Division to Phuoc An, a town farther to the east of Ban Me Thuot.

Phu's plan, however, was already known. Using the broken codes, Thao's signals-intelligence unit had intercepted a critical message. On 12 March, it picked up a conversation between Tuong and Lieutenant Colonel Vo An at the 53rd base camp. Tuong told An that reinforcements were arriving, and that "there would be a counterattack to recapture Ban Me Thuot. Under this plan . . . they would use the [53rd base camp] and Hill 581 as a springboard area, remnants from Ban Me Thuot would regroup there, and coordinate with the relief force in a two-prong counterattack to the east and southeast of Ban Me Thuot."[27] Once again, PAVN intelligence provided total insight into South Vietnamese operational plans.

Meanwhile, the Chinooks' mechanical breakdowns had given Thao precious breathing room to prepare for the next round. Worse yet, as the 45th Regiment landed on Hill 581, the men saw a mass of refugees streaming from Ban Me Thuot. Despite having sworn to recapture the city, soldiers soon began sneaking away to find their loved ones in the wave of humanity moving along the road. This was the first manifestation of the "family syndrome," wherein ARVN soldiers and officers deserted their posts to find their families. The world would famously see this syndrome reoccur on a grander scale during the disastrous collapse of Danang.

On 13 March, Phu received a telephone call from Thieu's chief of staff. Phu was to meet Thieu at Cam Ranh Bay the next morning. It would be the most important meeting of the war.

8

"LIGHT AT THE TOP, HEAVY AT THE BOTTOM"

DECISIONS THAT DESTROYED A NATION

The loss of Ban Me Thuot set in motion a series of decisions that triggered the spectacular collapse of the Republic of Vietnam. Over a five-day period, choices made independently in Hanoi, Saigon, and Washington unraveled two decades of grand strategy crafted by generals and politicians on both sides. The quagmire had suddenly morphed into a runaway train.

General Cao Van Vien, the head of the South Vietnamese military, later said he believed the Communists' successful assault on Ban Me Thuot acted "like a catalyst on the mind" of President Thieu. It was more than just the city's loss, however. The countrywide attacks, the American failure to respond militarily, and the U.S. Congress's likely refusal of further aid all spurred the president to make rash changes to his fundamental strategy. Since 1973, Thieu had fought the war based on Nixon's twin pledges of vigorous reaction and plentiful aid. Since neither pledge had been honored, Thieu decided to abandon his policy of no territorial concessions. Holding every inch of soil had been a political, not a military, stratagem. Thieu hoped that when the North Vietnamese attacked his outposts, the world would acknowledge that the Communists had destroyed the accords.

His plan failed because the North Vietnamese had succeeded in painting the U.S. and South Vietnam as serial violators solely responsible for the current situation. Although Thieu's forces *had* violated the ceasefire on occasion, and he had balked at implementing certain provisions, in comparison the Communists had broken virtually every clause in the Paris Peace Accords. Now, with Giap's armies pouring down the Ho Chi Minh Trail, and the world deserting South Vietnam, Thieu believed he had no option but to take an extraordinarily perilous step to save his country.

On the morning of 11 March, Thieu convened his top three military advisors at Independence Palace for a working breakfast. Attending were General Vien, Prime Minister Tran Thien Khiem, and Lieutenant General Dang Van Quang, Thieu's long-time aide for National Security Affairs. Khiem was the most senior officer in the Army, but had long remained in Thieu's shadow. Many Vietnamese referred to Quang, often accused of being the most corrupt officer in South Vietnam, as "Fat Quang" because of his corpulence. These four men would decide South Vietnam's fate.

After waiters cleared the plates, Thieu pulled a small map of the country from his pocket. Looking at his senior officers, he outlined the situation. In his view, South Vietnam could no longer defend all its territory. With little hope for the reintroduction of American military power, a drastic consolidation of units and supplies seemed the best chance for survival. It would also buy additional time to prepare for what everyone knew would be the North Vietnamese attempt at a coup de grâce in 1976. Protesting the obvious current North Vietnamese offensive would be an empty gesture: the other countries of the world were preoccupied with the energy crisis and their own economic problems.

Thieu now believed the South Vietnamese government needed to redeploy its military forces to defend the most populous and economically significant parts of the country. Those areas were the heartland of South Vietnam, from the southern portion of II Corps—a line stretching across the country from Ban Me Thuot to Tuy Hoa on the coast—to the southernmost tip of the Mekong Delta. This was a larger version of the old Cochin China section of the country, that part considered truly "southern" by the people of Vietnam. There was a longstanding and distinct cultural identity among the people of this region, and Thieu hoped to use it to rally them against the northern invaders. Most of South Vietnam's natural resources, including the all-important oil deposits and the majority of the agricultural base, lay within this area. Thieu would abandon much of I Corps, although he wanted to hold Danang as an enclave for a future counterattack to regain lost territory. He also wanted to defend Hue if possible, but he felt it would be difficult to hold against a determined thrust.

Accordingly, it was imperative to recapture Ban Me Thuot, which anchored the northwestern end of Thieu's bisected South Vietnam. If the Communists held the town, they could threaten Saigon from three directions: from Dalat in the north, Nha Trang in the east, and Tay Ninh in the west. Thieu had absorbed this lesson from the French, who had used the Montagnard capital as their main stronghold in the Highlands. Moreover, Thieu wanted to destroy the 320th Division, which he thought had taken the city. Lastly, he wanted to retrieve his troops from isolated and vulnerable positions in the Highlands. Otherwise, "they would be decimated because of a lack of reserves to support them and the inability of the air force to resupply them."[1] After retaking the city, Thieu could then move against Pleiku or Kontum. Thieu named his new strategy "Light at the top, heavy at the bottom." Since he was fearful of leaks and spies, only a select few were informed of his decisions. That did not include the Americans.

Thieu's choice to abandon a large chunk of the country was the first major strategic decision made strictly by the South Vietnamese in nearly a decade of war. Many have theorized as to why Thieu abruptly chose this course of action.[2] Previously, he had opposed it because of the overwhelming logistical complexities and the probable damage to South Vietnamese morale. Thieu had also feared that a retrenchment would negatively influence American congressional and public opinion at a time when he could ill afford it.

Ambassador Martin and other senior U.S. officials soon claimed that Thieu's decision stemmed solely from a lack of hope for any future aid. Martin told Kissinger and others that the unsympathetic reception given the GVN Senate delegation in February, plus the visit of the recently departed and mostly hostile U.S. congressional delegation, had finally convinced the president there would be no further aid. Martin's analysis, however, was only partially correct. Although the results of Lam's trip and the congressional visit had disheartened Thieu, he continued to seek aid until the very end. Thus, lack of aid was not the sole rationale for Thieu's decision. In fact, Thieu had faced a similar military crisis during the 1972 offensive, but had decided to stand and fight instead of retreat. Indeed, the military situation at that time was far worse; An Loc was surrounded, Kontum was cut off, and Quang Tri was already captured. Yet Thieu ordered those cities held at all costs or recaptured. Why then and not now?

According to General Vien, while Thieu's decision in 1972 to defend those cities was a poor "tactical judgment," the president had ordered the Army "to hold at these places because the political and psychological repercussions of losing them would have destroyed South Vietnam. . . . To have abandoned these positions would have been to cause a political collapse. That was Thieu's clear judgment."[3] Vien further stated that if ARVN had abandoned Kontum in 1972, "the whole Central Highlands and Binh Dinh would have been lost . . . further defense would have been impossible because the blow to morale . . . would have caused a complete loss of nerve. . . . South Vietnam would have been cut in two," leading to "the eventual doom of the country."

If Thieu had decided against moving the regular forces out of the northern Highlands in 1972 because doing so would have risked "political collapse" (and had rejected this course again as recently as Serong's effort in January), why did Thieu believe it would have a different result now? The Speaker of the South Vietnamese House of Representatives, Nguyen Ba Can, offered this assessment: Thieu's decision, he said, "cannot be viewed as an inspiration of the moment, nor as a move by an exhausted man stunned by the loss of Ban Me Thuot. Rather it must be viewed as the result of his revised strategic assessment of the general situation of the country and mainly of the balance of forces that had become tipped in favor of North Vietnam."[4]

The difference, therefore, was not just the lack of aid, but also the absence of American military support. In 1972, Thieu had the U.S. Air Force and Navy supplying the necessary firepower and mobility to neutralize the North Vietnamese ability to hide and mass. He also had a seemingly endless flow of supplies from the United States. Now he had neither. With his troops outflanked and facing North Vietnam's battle-hardened army of twenty divisions alone, retrenching to a more defensible territory seemed the only viable solution.

Withdrawing from the northern Highlands was the riskiest of maneuvers. Thieu was attempting this retreat while strong enemy forces were nearby, and without American firepower to hold them off if they attacked. Yet in his mind, he was on the horns of an impossible dilemma: If he left the Pleiku and Kontum garrisons in their bunkers while Dung struck east to the sea, those ARVN units would slowly starve while doing the rest of the country absolutely no good. Pleiku was blockaded on three sides, and with Cu Hanh airfield under sporadic shelling, the city would soon feel the supply pinch despite the sixty days' worth of stocks that had been shipped in earlier. In Ban Me Thuot, the Communists had strong forces. On Route 21, there were only RF troops and the newly arrived units of the ARVN 23rd Division to block them. If those defenses were penetrated, PAVN troops and their tanks, artillery, and anti-aircraft guns could barrel straight down Route 21 to the coast, severing South Vietnam. PAVN could then move south on Route 1 to the very outskirts of Saigon.

Most of Thieu's senior officers disagreed with his decision. They believed it would have been better to stay in their bunkers and go down fighting rather than hazard such a perilous journey while under heavy pressure. Many of his generals also hoped the scenes of South Vietnamese soldiers defending their positions against massive North Vietnamese attacks might finally convince the U.S. Congress to loosen its purse-strings.

Thieu's decision, moreover, may not have been as sudden as has been long believed. The American consul general in Nha Trang, Moncrieff Spear, wrote in his review of the fall of II Corps that "in early 1975 I was advised in confidence that in the event of an all-out offensive in the Highlands, a top-level GVN decision had been made not to defend Kontum."[5] While Thieu had outwardly rejected the withdrawal plan, apparently he had kept the option open. Since he rarely communicated his inner thoughts, it is not shocking that he had secret contingency plans that he did not share with his senior military commanders.

Unfortunately for the South Vietnamese people, the new decision was executed with no preparation. Even though Thieu had kept the option open, he had not called for any comprehensive planning. Now that he had abruptly changed course, his three top generals quickly agreed with the new strategy, with hardly any dissent. Actually, Thieu had decided and his advisors meekly acquiesced. Now it was up to them to make it work, regardless of the difficulty. With no plans to draw upon, the withdrawal would become an improvisational ballet, requiring discipline and dedicated leadership, skills the war-weary South Vietnamese society had in short supply.

After the breakfast meeting, events were set in motion by an order from Thieu to withdraw the Airborne Division from I Corps. On 12 March—the day Phu reported to Saigon that all organized resistance in Ban Me Thuot had ceased—the JGS ordered Lieutenant General Ngo Quang Truong to return the Airborne Division to Saigon. Truong immediately requested an audience with Thieu. Upon Truong's arrival the next day, Thieu explained his concept of a retrenchment to a smaller, more easily defensible country. In I Corps, Truong was to hold Danang at all costs, but he could sacrifice everything else.

Truong was flabbergasted. He declared that removing the Airborne on the eve of a major attack might lead to a serious defeat. At best it would force him to relinquish key terrain as he shifted forces to cover the Airborne positions west of Danang. Faced with his general's impassioned pleas, Thieu partially relented, allowing Truong to stagger the withdrawal one brigade at a time. However, Thieu ordered the first Airborne brigade to depart by 17 March. As a replacement, Truong would receive the newly formed 468th Marine Brigade. Thieu had nothing else to give him. The two newly formed Ranger groups were not combat-ready, the 7th Rangers were going to II Corps, and the new 4th Airborne Brigade would remain near Saigon. That left only the 468th Marine Brigade. A deeply upset Truong flew back to I Corps to carry out his orders.

Meanwhile, after the meeting with Truong, the message went out to Major General Phu to meet Thieu on 14 March at Cam Ranh Bay.

On the morning of 14 March, Thieu, Khiem, Quang, and Vien flew to Cam Ranh Bay to inform Phu of the new plan. This was the second, more perilous adjustment in Thieu's new strategy. Abandoning whole regions was more dangerous than shifting forces between corps. While there is no transcript of what is undoubtedly the most critical meeting of the war, and only one participant (Vien) has provided a written summary, enough has surfaced from other sources to piece together a reasonable outline of what transpired.

Thieu began by asking Phu for his analysis of the situation. Painting a dismal picture, Phu noted that Route 19, the most important road in the Highlands, was cut in two places. The other main roads were blocked as well. He also informed Thieu that his forces had just captured a soldier from the 316th Division near Ban Me Thuot. Thieu grimly absorbed the news. He was well aware that the addition of a strategic-reserve division to the PAVN forces in the Highlands had decisively tipped the balance of forces against ARVN.

After Phu finished speaking, Thieu asked him if he could retake Ban Me Thuot with the forces currently deployed around the town. Phu said no, and he asked for reinforcements from the Airborne Division to retake the city. Thieu denied his request. Turning to Vien, Thieu asked if there were any other reserves. Vien stated that Phu had already received the last unit, the 7th Rangers. With no reserves available, Thieu ordered Phu to redeploy his regular units from Pleiku and Kontum and retake Ban Me Thuot. Most important, no one was to know about the plan, including the Americans. The Montagnard regional and popular forces and the local administrations in Pleiku and Kontum would remain and defend their areas as best they could.

Vien later accurately described this as "the most critical juncture of the entire war."[6] Much confusion remains, however, regarding precisely what Thieu ordered versus what Phu understood. Phu's aide and biographer, Pham Huan, was sitting outside the room and claims that Phu told him that Thieu had ordered him to withdraw. Huan provides snippets of Phu's version, but they are interspersed with made-up dialogue and his own analysis of the motives of the various personalities. Over the years, Vien has denied that Thieu ordered Phu to withdraw from Pleiku. In September 1975, Vien told an American interviewer, "somehow the impression was given that Thieu's order could be interpreted as tantamount to a withdrawal. But never did he give such an order. He just told Phu it was up to him to redeploy his forces to reoccupy Ban Me Thuot."[7] The CIA base chief in Nha Trang disagrees, and later wrote that Thieu "categorically ordered Phu to abandon Pleiku and Kontum."[8]

Both Quang and Khiem seem to be fence-sitting, as they later informed CIA Saigon Station Chief Thomas Polgar that they were unaware that Thieu intended to order Phu to withdraw. They also claimed the same thing at a GVN Cabinet meeting. Although Polgar accepts their version, it is difficult to believe, but the possibility cannot be dismissed. The reality seems to be that while Thieu did not explicitly say he was abandoning Pleiku, and in fact ordered the RF to remain and defend it, the practical effect was the same. Although Thieu was notorious for providing imprecise instructions, given the outcome, the various South Vietnamese accounts of these events seem to have been crafted for maximum spin.

Despite the difficulties involved in redeploying large numbers of troops while under attack, Phu apparently did not try very hard to change Thieu's mind. Perhaps one explanation for Phu's not arguing with Thieu or threatening to resign is that he did not have any reasonable alternative. In fairness to Phu, it is impossible to judge whether Thieu would have relented even if he had been presented with a different plan to recapture Ban Me Thuot. Truong's impassioned pleas to keep the Airborne Division had netted him only a small reprieve. One gets the sense that Thieu would not be dissuaded from the monumental decisions he had made. He was also furious at Phu for failing to follow his order in early February to reinforce Ban Me Thuot. This definitely colored Thieu's later decision-making and interaction with Phu. He was brooking no dissent, and Phu had little choice but to carry out Thieu's order or offer his resignation, which Thieu would probably have rejected.

Phu's senior aide, Lieutenant Colonel Nguyen Quang Vinh, who had traveled with Phu to Cam Ranh and was also sitting outside the meeting room, relates that upon departure, Thieu did not shake Phu's hand and ignored Phu's salute. Vinh had heard Thieu raising his voice inside the room, and pounding on a table. Vinh notes that on the flight back to Pleiku, Phu "sat silently, staring at the floor. After awhile, I asked him if he had been relieved of command. Phu looked up and burst into tears, saying that the country had no future, and that his career as a general was over. Thieu had ordered him to retreat in three days, and if he did not, he would face a military tribunal."[9]

With the decision made, how then would the retreat be accomplished? Airlift capability being limited, that option was discarded. Route 19 appeared too difficult to reopen. The PAVN 95A Regiment had made a surprise attack the day before and wiped out the M-113 troop assisting the

4th Rangers. In addition, as Vien warned Phu, attempts by the French army to withdraw down this road had met with destruction from well-planned Communist ambushes. As for Route 14, any movement south would be easily detected. Phu would then have to fight through the 320th Division just to get to Ban Me Thuot, where two more PAVN divisions awaited him. Route 21 was still blocked, but could be easily reopened with more troops.

Vien designed his remarks to force Phu to consider the difficulty of the task he was accepting. Contemptuous of Phu, particularly after he had disregarded the JGS's warnings about Ban Me Thuot, Vien hoped he would resign rather than carry out the withdrawal. Although Vien told his J-3 (operations officer) to monitor Phu's progress and provide any requested assistance, the commanding general of South Vietnam's armed forces was content to stand aside and let Phu succeed or fail on his own. With Thieu having given a direct order to the corps commander, Vien felt the operation was Phu's responsibility, not his. Underscoring Vien's attitude was his refusal even to summon his deputy, Lieutenant General Dong Van Khuyen—who had just taken his cancer-stricken father to Japan for treatment—to return and oversee the retreat. Despite a strategy transformation of this magnitude, Vien claims he saw "no reason" to recall Khuyen. While it is true that Thieu's policy of denying the JGS any oversight of the corps commanders prevented Vien from overruling any of Phu's decisions, given the importance of the operation, Vien's hands-off approach to Phu's planning is stunning.

Phu realized that a successful withdrawal would require surprise. He therefore proposed using Route 7B, the only highway out of the Highlands still open. This road branches off from Route 14 south of Pleiku, passes through Cheo Reo, the capital of Phu Bon province, then turns east and ends on the coast at Tuy Hoa, the capital of Phu Yen province. From there, Phu's soldiers would move south on Route 1 to Route 21, and then west along this road to Ban Me Thuot. The total distance from Pleiku to Tuy Hoa is 155 miles, and from Tuy Hoa to Ban Me Thuot another 147 miles. Phu's forces would have to march three hundred miles just to enter battle.

Moreover, only part of Route 7B was fully trafficable. Although excellent from Pleiku to Cheo Reo, after leaving the provincial capital it was eighty miles of narrow, rough, badly rutted road to the coast. Major stretches snake through mountains covered with thick forests that converged on the road. Washouts, steep passes, and ruined culverts over many small streams added more problems. There were seventeen bridges on the road from

Cheo Reo to Tuy Hoa. All were too weak—a maximum weight of twelve to twenty tons—to support armor. More significantly, the retreating column would have to cross the sizable Ba River twice. The first crossing was about ten miles southeast of Cheo Reo. The existing bridge would not support tanks, so a float bridge would have to be built to enable the armor to cross the fifty-yard-wide river. From there to the town of Cung Son in Phu Yen province was an additional fifty-five miles of bad road. The only town between Cheo Reo and Cung Son was the village of Phu Tuc. Here another large stream with a rickety bridge would have to be traversed.

And that was the easy part. The final stretch of road, some fifteen miles from Cung Son to Tuy Hoa, had been heavily mined years earlier by Korean forces. The only bypass around the mines—a bridge that branched off from Route 7B, crossed the Ba River and linked up with Local Route 436 to Tuy Hoa—had been destroyed long ago. To reach Tuy Hoa, Phu's troops would have to build a new bridge at Cung Son to cross the Ba River, which at this point was three hundred yards wide.

Phu, however, claimed the road was in better shape than was generally believed. Additionally, since it was nearing the end of the dry season, the water in many streams was low, so they could be easily forded. The biggest problem was the mines on the main road. Phu's troops would have to detour around them. However, since the river was low, he did not believe they would have to build a bridge at Cung Son. He declared that if they lined the river bottom with steel planks from local airfield runways, his vehicles could drive across the river on the steel planks and then link up with Local Route 436.

Thieu accepted Phu's proposal, and gave him three days to complete the withdrawal. The other senior generals voiced no dissent. Thieu added that if Phu succeeded in retaking Ban Me Thuot, he could then drive north to Pleiku and Kontum.

Phu did not ask for any assistance from the JGS other than river-crossing equipment, which Vien promptly granted. Closing the meeting, Phu made one final request, pleading for Colonel Pham Duy Tat, the II Corps Ranger commander, to be promoted to brigadier general. Thieu hesitated, but finally agreed. In a rare move, he also gave Phu permission to promote anyone else he felt deserved such a reward. Normally, only Thieu had the authority to promote officers to general. It was Thieu's way of giving Phu flexibility. Advancing a soldier or officer in rank or giving him monetary gifts was the ARVN method of rewarding those who performed a success-ful deed in combat.

In summary, Phu had only two choices for the retreat: open Route 19, or create a diversion and then personally lead his men out on Route 7B. A determined thrust against Route 19 would probably have opened that road. The PAVN 3rd Division was weaker than believed, and probably could not have withstood a large-scale assault. But even if he had opened Route 19, that would have added significantly to his forces' journey to Ban Me Thuot. As for a diversion, Phu might have sent an armored task force south on Route 14 to tie down the 320th Division, allowing the remainder of his units to retreat along Route 7B. Another possibility for a diversion was to attack toward Duc Co, threatening Dung's supply lines. Yet Phu never broached any other concept than the one he offered at the meeting. Embarrassed over the loss of Ban Me Thuot, he did not have the force of personality to con-vince the president that the idea of withdrawing from the northern High-lands was unworkable, even though Phu knew his forces would not make it without heavy losses. According to a South Vietnamese general with whom Phu discussed the meeting at Cam Ranh Bay, Phu claimed that if he got 50 percent of his men and vehicles to the southern Highlands, he would be "a hero." The officer responded that if Phu lost half his troops and equipment he would not be a hero; he would be relieved of his command.[10]

Thus, Phu had committed himself to moving thousands of troops and their equipment and supplies, while rebuilding bridges and repairing the road as he went, before the enemy could react. Oddly, it apparently never occurred to Phu that the North Vietnamese might have stationed recon-naissance troops on hilltops to monitor ARVN movements. In addition, he seems to have forgotten the horrific scenes of hordes of refugees following the retreating ARVN south along Route 1 from Quang Tri during the 1972 Easter Offensive. Why neither Phu nor Thieu considered the civilians in their planning is incomprehensible.

Ultimately, the horrendously mismanaged retreat directly caused the defeat of South Vietnam. Phu was to blame for his failure to properly plan and oversee the retreat. Phu, however, was far from the only one culpable. While Thieu's decision to withdraw from the northern Highlands was logi-cal, it was impractical. His orders to complete the retreat in three days and to leave the civilian population and local administrations to fend for them-selves were disastrous. Nor did any of Thieu's senior aides protest, voice concern, or demand that Phu provide a detailed withdrawal plan before initiating the retreat. These were the final mistakes in a series of critical military blunders in II Corps.

THE AID DEBATE RESUMES

For the Ford administration, the argument was simple: Without U.S. aid, South Vietnam could not survive. In new hearings before the House Foreign Affairs and Senate Foreign Relations Committees, administration spokesmen and the members of the congressional delegation to Indochina presented their viewpoints. Yet the delegation, while recognizing the seriousness of the situation, declined to recommend continued aid. The hearings, which President Ford had worked on since September 1974 to persuade Congress to grant more aid, had failed decisively. On the morning of 12 March, the House Democratic Caucus, spurred by Bella Abzug and three others, passed a resolution opposing any further aid to Vietnam and Cambodia in 1975. It was not even close. The vote was 189 to 49. The next day, the Senate Democrats voted 34 to 6 against further aid. While the caucus does not bind party members, its votes are made public. As one House committee staffer later wrote: "by revealing the striking absence of support in the dominant party for aid to Cambodia and South Vietnam, the caucus votes undoubtedly shaped the expectations of supporters and opponents of the president's request in both houses."[11]

To what extent this congressional action influenced Thieu is unknown, but Ambassador Martin certainly could count votes. On 12 March, he and Philip Habib from the State Department met with Senators Church and Pearson to discuss Martin's three-year aid proposal. Both Church and Pearson saw no possibility that Congress would agree to the sums Martin was seeking, but they sought some compromise. They felt combining economic and military aid into one package was the best option. The ambassador instead pressed his case for separate aid packages, explaining that "if clear American commitment given for three years he was confident Hanoi would return seriously to conference table . . . and put military action in south on back burner."[12] Martin further articulated his belief that Hanoi had made the decision to launch the current heavy fighting after learning Congress had cut the appropriations. Martin knew the American public would not indefinitely support aid to Saigon, but he was convinced that the South Vietnamese economy had bottomed out. He thought another infusion of aid would get it moving again, and if the oil deposits produced a steady revenue stream, he believed Hanoi would reluctantly conclude that a political compromise was its best choice. The Communists were striking now because this was their last chance to win. Apparently, Martin's and Le Duan's analyses were not that dissimilar.

The senators were unconvinced. The $6 billion Martin wanted for economic and military aid was simply not feasible during a recession. Church offered $1 billion for the first year, with that amount to be reduced by one-third each year. It was either that or return to annual requests. Habib indicated that Church's offer was not sufficient for Saigon's needs, and that the administration would take its chances on a yearly budget. Despite the failure to agree on an aid package, Pearson promised to sound out his colleagues on Martin's three-year plan.

For some reason, Martin believed the meeting had been positive. He immediately drafted a letter to bolster Thieu's morale, and he tasked his deputy, Wolfgang Lehmann, with presenting it in person. Arriving at Independence Palace on the morning of 15 March, Lehmann handed Thieu the letter. The note was supportive, but Martin could not disguise the increasingly gloomy chances for aid. He wrote: "Reading the recent news from Washington regarding Congressional action on Indochina aid must give you and your colleagues . . . a feeling of discouragement about the constancy of American policy."[13] The bad news from Cambodia was contributing "to a Congressional sense of hopelessness that future aid would [not] really change the course of events." Martin feared that Congress was drawing a parallel between Cambodia and Vietnam. Therefore, "To lessen this tendency . . . I do not want the $300 million supplemental to come to a vote in the near future." Congress would be taking its Easter recess from 21 March to 6 April, and Martin wanted the extra time to persuade recalcitrant congressmen to vote for the funding.

To help his efforts, Martin pressed Thieu to loosen General Vien's tight restrictions on munitions. While concerned that Thieu "may expend too much force in an immediate effort to retake Ban Me Thuot," Martin still expressed full confidence in Thieu's military decision-making. In closing, he stated: "It is going to be a tough time ahead on the battlefront in Vietnam. Very soon, the Defense Department will agree with your assessment that what you now confront is indeed a general offensive whose intensity may well exceed that of 1972. It is also going to be a tough time on the battlefront in Washington and I believe I may serve the common interests of

both our countries by staying here for a while. I can give you the most cate-
goric assurances that the President and the Secretaries of State and Defense
are determined that when the Washington battle is over you will have the
resources you need. With those I am certain the will and determination of
the Vietnamese people to remain free will prevail." Despite Martin's statement that he was remaining to fight the aid battle, he promptly had dental
surgery and traveled to his farm in North Carolina to recuperate. He was
out of touch for over ten days in March.

After reading Martin's letter, Thieu provided Lehmann a few insights
into his thinking. Thieu said that he intended to use the Ban Me Thuot
battlefield to destroy the 320th and 316th Divisions, which had been posi-
tively identified in the area. Lehmann then echoed Martin's concern as to
whether Thieu could concentrate sufficient forces at Ban Me Thuot without unduly exposing other areas. As Lehmann reported to Martin, Thieu
agreed that this was "a very difficult problem and that the defenses in the
northern part of the Highlands, especially around Kontum, would have to
be substantially thinned out."[14] Thieu expected "the Ban Me Thuot battle
to be hard and last for some time, perhaps two weeks." Phu would halt the
effort to reopen Route 19, while expanding the operation on Route 21.
The reasons for Thieu's decisions were simple: "the loss of southern Darlac
province . . . would jeopardize Dalat and Khanh Hoa [province], and that
he could not afford to let go." As to Martin's point about ammunition, he
had ordered Vien to remove any limitations. After the meeting, Lehmann
informed Martin that he expected Kontum would fall if attacked, but that
four Ranger groups would continue to defend Pleiku.

While Thieu had not lied to his ally, he had been less than forthright. In
an interview years later, Lehmann admitted that "Thieu did not directly
inform me of that decision, but he hinted that a major decision was in the
process of being made and that it had been a rather difficult one. I could
not draw him out on the details. However, what he did say set a slight alarm
bell ringing in my head as I left the palace." Lehmann added, "The question
is sometimes raised whether that was a proper way for a president to deal
with us and whether I was not considerably annoyed by the fact that he had
not directly and clearly conveyed this decision to me. My feeling about that
is . . . in light of the fact that we were letting the [other] side down, he had
a right to make his own decisions."[15]

In Saigon, many senior South Vietnamese political figures, including
those who were not part of Thieu's government, were deeply alarmed over

the Communist attacks. To survive the onslaught, they believed, Thieu needed to expand his government in order to help rally the people, before it was too late. Since Thieu had just asked former Ambassador Bui Diem to meet with him and discuss a mission to Washington to assist with the aid request, Diem decided to bring along two allies to force that very question: former Foreign Minister Dr. Tran Van Do, a highly respected member of Saigon's intelligentsia, and Tran Quoc Buu, the head of the labor federation. Soon after Lehmann left Independence Palace, they met with Thieu to discuss the political situation.

By no means were these men part of the Third Force. They viewed themselves as supporters of an independent South Vietnam, though not necessarily of Thieu. Nor was this the first time they had pressed Thieu to broaden and improve his government. All three had badgered him for years on the subject. In this particular meeting, however, they had come as mediators between the opposition and Thieu. They began by stating that a gulf existed between the government and the people, a gap deepened by corruption, military reverses, and a declining economy. Diem and Do pressured Thieu to form a government of national unity as the best hope of rallying the country. Thieu asked what they could do in this regard. The three agreed to begin a dialogue with the opposition, but insisted that new blood had to be brought into the government and given real authority. Thieu agreed to restructure the government, but cautioned that he could work with only about 50 percent of the opposition. A coalition government with the Communists remained out of the question.

Thieu's agreement did not fool Bui Diem, who had heard his promises too many times. He was correct. While Diem's mission to Washington was real, Thieu had an ulterior motive in sending him there. He wanted Diem and Tran Quoc Buu out of the country to prevent them from rallying the opposition and potentially overthrowing him. His ploy failed, however. As the military situation dramatically worsened, in early April Thieu would be forced to broaden his government anyway.

THE WITHDRAWAL BEGINS

Lieutenant Colonel Ngo Le Tinh, commander of II Corps's 20th Combat Engineer Group, was working in his office around 7:00 P.M. on 14 March when his phone rang. Tinh had taken command of the engineers in January 1975, having served previously on the staff of Brigadier General

Nguyen Van Chuc, chief of all military engineers. Tinh had been responsible for maintaining all the bridges and roads across South Vietnam, an unenviable job given the constant Communist sabotage, but one at which he had labored vigorously. His reward for his hard work was command of the 20th Engineers, a unit with over 2,500 men and millions of dollars in equipment.

The caller was Colonel Le Khac Ly, II Corps chief of staff. Ly wanted Tinh to immediately report to the II Corps command bunker to meet with Phu, and to bring his maps and a status report on all bridges and roads in II Corps. Tinh was astonished. He had spoken to Phu only twice since his arrival in II Corps, and he did not understand why the commander suddenly wanted to see him now. Picking up his maps, however, Tinh grabbed his helmet and left for the command bunker.

Phu had returned in the late afternoon from the meeting at Cam Ranh Bay. He immediately summoned Colonel Tat, Colonel Ly, Brigadier General Pham Ngoc Sang, commander of the VNAF 6th Air Division, and Brigadier General Tran Van Cam, Phu's deputy for operations. Phu began the meeting by announcing that Thieu had authorized him to promote Colonel Tat to brigadier general. After pinning the star on Tat's collar, Phu came to the heart of the meeting: the president had decided to withdraw all regular forces from the Central Highlands back to the coast. These forces would then conduct two missions: defend the coastal areas, and counterattack along Route 21 to retake Ban Me Thuot. Secrecy must be preserved at all costs. Phu would not inform the province chiefs, sector commanders, and their subordinates, as RF/PF units and others would stay and defend Kontum and Pleiku. Local governmental offices and organizations would also remain open. This order meant that over 100,000 Montagnard and Vietnamese civilians, including the families of the very same ARVN soldiers who would be retreating, would be left behind to face three PAVN regiments.

Phu ordered Colonel Ly to plan a corps-sized road march from Kontum and Pleiku along Route 7B to Nha Trang. The movement would occur between 16 and 19 March. The bulk of the corps headquarters would relocate via helicopter to Nha Trang, while the 6th Air Division would transfer from Pleiku to the Nha Trang and Phan Rang airbases. The engineers would repair the road and bridges. Ly would move in the convoy with a light corps headquarters.

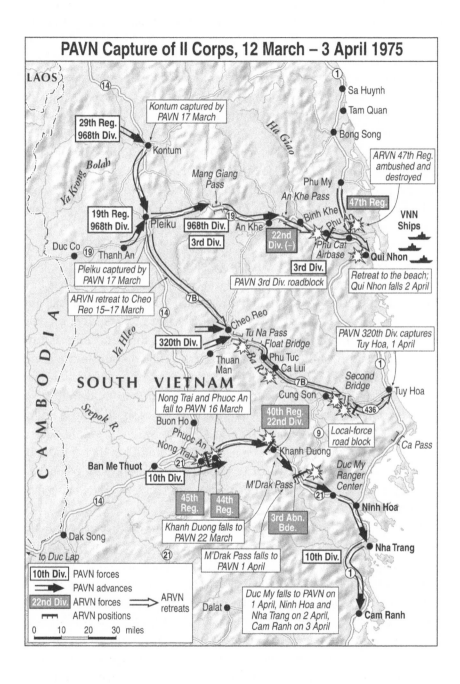

PAVN Capture of II Corps, 12 March – 3 April 1975

LAOS

Sa Huynh

Tam Quan

Bong Song

Kontum captured by PAVN 17 March

29th Reg. 968th Div.

Kontum

Ha Giao

Ya Krong Bolah

Mang Giang Pass

Phu My

An Khe Pass

ARVN 47th Reg. ambushed and destroyed

47th Reg.   VNN Ships

19th Reg. 968th Div.   Pleiku   **968th Div.**   An Khe   Binh Khe   Phu An

22nd Div. (−)

Phu Cat Airbase

Qui Nhon

Duc Co   Thanh An

3rd Div.

Pleiku captured by PAVN 17 March

3rd Div.

PAVN 3rd Div. roadblock

Retreat to the beach; Qui Nhon falls 2 April

ARVN retreat to Cheo Reo 15–17 March

Ya Hleo

Cheo Reo   Tu Na Pass

320th Div.   Float Bridge

PAVN 320th Div. captures Tuy Hoa, 1 April

Thuan Man

Ba Rai

Phu Tuc   Ca Lui

Second Bridge   Tuy Hoa

SOUTH   VIETNAM

CAMBODIA

Srepok R.

Nong Trai and Phuoc An fall to PAVN 16 March

Cung Son

Buon Ho

Phuoc An

40th Reg. 22nd Div.

Nong Trai

Local-force road block

Ca Pass

Ban Me Thuot

Khanh Duong

Duc My Ranger Center

10th Div.

M'Drak Pass

Ninh Hoa

45th Reg.   **44th Reg.**

3rd Abn. Bde.

Dak Song

Khanh Duong falls to PAVN 22 March

Nha Trang

to Duc Lap

M'Drak Pass falls to PAVN 1 April

10th Div.

10th Div.	PAVN forces
➡	PAVN advances
22nd Div.	ARVN forces
⌐	ARVN positions

ARVN retreats

Dalat

Duc My falls to PAVN on 1 April, Ninh Hoa and Nha Trang on 2 April, Cam Ranh on 3 April

Cam Ranh

0   10   20   30 miles

Ly was stunned. He begged Phu to give him more time. It was impossible, he exclaimed, to organize a movement of that scale in thirty-six hours. Phu denied his request, claiming the president's instructions were firm. Part of Phu's refusal was motivated by disdain for Ly. Phu had always been a field officer, with little training in or understanding of staff operations, while Ly had spent his entire career working at the staff level. It was one source of friction between the two, but not the only one. Ly had been chief of staff for I Corps Forward for two years. At the end of that tour, he was ordered to II Corps on 1 December 1974 to become Phu's chief of staff. Since he was not Phu's choice for the job, Phu harbored suspicions that Ly was spying on him for Vien and the JGS. He was not. Instead, Ly was, and had been for years, a CIA source, one of many the agency had among the South Vietnamese officer corps.[16]

As Ly set about planning the retreat, his first call was to Lieutenant Colonel Tinh. When Tinh arrived, Phu came right to the point. II Corps would conduct a withdrawal from Pleiku to Tuy Hoa along Route 7B, and Phu needed to know the status of the roads and bridges. Tinh said that the first obstacle was the bridge over the Ba River east of Cheo Reo. It could not support tanks and artillery. Since the river at this location was fifty yards wide, Tinh would have to build a float bridge to enable the heavy equipment to cross. A float bridge consists of decks of square, hollow aluminum sections lashed to pneumatic floats. Boats then hold the bridge in place against the current. Depending on the water speed, a float bridge can handle up to seventy tons. Phu asked Tinh how long it would take to build it. Forty-eight hours, Tinh replied. Phu granted Tinh that amount of time, but no more. Tinh immediately left the bunker and headed back to his compound to inform his best battalion commander that he had a new mission for him.[17]

Phu then made two decisions that helped doom the already problematic retreat. First, instead of directly supervising the retreat himself, he placed Brigadier General Tat in command of the evacuation. Brigadier General Cam was told to "supervise." This arrangement only exacerbated long-simmering personal conflicts among the upper-echelon officers. Second, after his engineer commander's request for forty-eight hours to construct the floating bridge, Phu did not delay the main group's departure until the 17th. Certainly he could have called Thieu and provided his rationale for delaying one day to allow for the bridge construction. This would have prevented the first part of the column from being stuck in

Cheo Reo for twenty-four hours and tipping off the North Vietnamese, as in fact it did.

Regardless, orders quickly went out. The initial part of Ly's plan called for the 20th Engineers to depart first and move to the Ba River to begin building the float bridge. The 23rd Ranger Group was ordered to move with the engineers and then stay and defend Cheo Reo. The 6th Ranger Group was ordered to depart Kontum the night of 15 March and link up with the engineers in Cheo Reo. The 6th Rangers and an armored cavalry element would move with the engineers along Route 7B and protect them. Local RF/PF units would be responsible for security along the road from Cheo Reo to Cung Son. The 22nd Ranger Group, also defending Kontum, was pulled back to defend the critical Chu Pao Pass on Route 14 between Kontum and Pleiku. The 25th Rangers at Thanh An were ordered to hold their positions, as were the 4th Rangers on Route 19. The 6th Air Division began preparing to move from Cu Hanh airfield to Nha Trang. How all this movement was to remain hidden from the Communists, not to mention the civilian population, apparently was never discussed.

ROUND TWO AT BAN ME THUOT

It was late on 12 March when the two lead battalions of the ARVN 45th Regiment landed outside of Ban Me Thuot and occupied Hill 581, just one mile from the beleaguered defenders at the 53rd Regiment base camp. PAVN Lieutenant General Hoang Minh Thao was instantly informed. This was precisely what he had predicted: Phu's only recourse to recapture Ban Me Thuot was to land reinforcements east of the city and storm it from that direction. When the 45th Regiment's reconnaissance company was spotted trying to link up with its sister regiment, Thao immediately ordered the two positions destroyed.

The 53rd Regiment base, about four miles from town, lay on flat, open ground sandwiched between Route 21 and another road leading south. To defend a perimeter over a half-mile long, the 53rd's commander could muster only around five hundred soldiers—the 3rd Battalion and the regimental headquarters company. Fortunately, previous commanders had prepared stiff defenses. The camp was surrounded by seven rings of barbed wire, then a deep anti-tank ditch, and, last, a massive dirt barricade with built-in bunkers fitted with machine guns. Several M-113s and mortar teams augmented the defenders. It was these stout defenses, and good leadership by

Lieutenant Colonel Vo An, that had enabled the ARVN troops to beat back the sappers on the morning of 10 March.

There had been another attack on 11 March, when the 149th Regiment, 316th Division, made its first assault against the 53rd camp. After an artillery barrage, the Communist troops attacked. Two hours later, dozens of PAVN casualties littered the battlefield. The men of the 53rd had held their ground a second time, but the longer they were surrounded, the more precarious their situation became. The wounded could not be evacuated, and supplies were dwindling. Some fresh supplies were reaching them via airdrop, but that link grew more tenuous each hour as the North Vietnamese pushed their air defenses closer to the base. The ARVN troops suffered daily artillery bombardment, followed by nighttime infantry probes. The news grew worse on 13 March when the 53rd captured a POW and discovered he was from the 316th.

The latest PAVN design to capture the base called for two columns, one to attack the camp and another to assault the nearby Phung Duc airfield. Like most ARVN bases, the 53rd's had a major weak point: no physical blockade of the main gate. Naturally, that is where the North Vietnamese chose to strike. Three tanks would spearhead each attack, closely followed by an infantry battalion. The Communists, however, did not adequately plan this new attack. In particular, there was no preparatory artillery fire against the ARVN fortifications. The North Vietnamese wrongly assumed that enemy morale had collapsed, and that a tank-led assault would lead to a quick surrender. Their newfound arrogance would cost them.

At dawn on 14 March, the 149th Regiment, accompanied by six tanks, attacked the 53rd's camp and the airfield. Launching the attacks, the airfield column quickly discovered that ARVN had abandoned the airfield. The column at the 53rd base, however, fared much worse. One tank got lost, and the other two mistakenly turned left at the main gate, exposing their flanks to the defenders. One tank was soon knocked out, and the accompanying infantry took heavy casualties. The other tank continued past the base and also got lost.

Despite their third failure, the attackers were undeterred. The 149th Regiment's commander requested reinforcements and time to plan a new attack. Thao denied his appeal. The 149th was ordered to take the base by nightfall, no matter the cost. Thao sent five more tanks to reinforce the four still operational from that morning. The new plan called for another attack against the base's main gate, along with a second spearhead from the southwest, while three tanks would provide direct fire support from the north. The attackers would strike again in the late afternoon.

The lack of time exposed PAVN's biggest weakness: poor flexibility. The North Vietnamese operated best when they had carefully studied the battlefield and rehearsed. When they had little time to prepare, Murphy's Law hit them hard. The infantry battalion that was to accompany the southwest column failed to arrive in time, as did other units. Watching in despair as the sun sank behind the hills, the PAVN regimental commander gave the order to attack.

The result was the same. The gate column quickly bogged down under withering fire from the ARVN defenders. Infantrymen riding on the tanks were swept off by accurate machine-gun fire. When night fell, the tanks became disoriented. One fell into the anti-tank ditch and was hit by a rocket. Another cracked its barrel against a tree trunk. A third became tangled up in the barbed wire and ground to a halt.

The other spearhead fared no better. The armor advanced, but one tank was hit and the others were unable to penetrate the base defenses. Although the infantry finally arrived, night had fallen. With no prior reconnaissance, the troops became confused and were pinned down by heavy fire. At midnight the PAVN commander ordered his troops to retreat. The 3rd Battalion had inflicted such heavy losses on the 149th Regiment that it was pulled back to regroup.

Jubilant over the stalwart defense, Phu promoted Lieutenant Colonel Vo An to colonel and told him to hang on, help was on the way. Aircraft soon dropped more supplies to the defenders, bombers pounded suspected Communist positions, and Phu ordered the RF task force on Route 21 to clear the roadblock at all costs.

While the men of the 53rd Regiment were repulsing the enemy attacks, Thao was planning an assault against the two battalions of the 45th Regiment organizing on Hill 581. The 45th was considered the best regiment in the 23rd Division, but here the results would be diametrically opposite to the 53rd's. The main reasons were the lack of prepared fortifications and the desertion of many enlisted men to find their families. The PAVN 24th Regiment, 10th Division, heavily supported by armor and an anti-aircraft battalion, had secretly moved into place on the night of 13 March. While C-119 gunships kept a steady air patrol over the 45th's location, dropping flares and firing at any suspected enemy concentrations, the PAVN troops managed to reach their planned jump-off positions.

At 7:00 A.M. on 14 March—as Phu was flying to Cam Ranh Bay to meet with Thieu—the North Vietnamese attacked. One ARVN battalion held the hill, while a second was getting organized about half a mile to the rear. Their only fire support was a nearby RF 105-mm howitzer battery and whatever air power could be mustered. Seeing the infantry and tanks charging straight up Hill 581, the ARVN troops scattered. Surging forward, the North Vietnamese infantry and tanks roared down the backside of the hill and into the second ARVN battalion. Direct fire from the lowered barrels of the anti-aircraft guns added to the firepower of the tank cannons blasting at the exposed ARVN troops. By 11:00 A.M., PAVN forces had crashed through the second battalion and poured onto Route 21.

They soon reached the first bridge east of Ban Me Thuot. If the bridge was taken, PAVN would have its first foothold in its drive to the coast. An RF company was guarding the bridge, but when its soldiers saw the approaching tanks, they destroyed the bridge and fled. The 10th Division engineers quickly built a ford to enable the tanks to continue the pursuit. As soon as the tanks and infantry got back on the road they spotted the RF artillery position about six hundred yards away. For a third time, the armor charged. The results were similar. The North Vietnamese captured four 105-mm howitzers and hundreds of rounds of ammunition.

The infantry and tanks continued on Route 21, where they attacked and dispersed an RF battalion defending a small town. By noon on 14 March, the 10th Division had scattered three battalions, killing two hundred soldiers and capturing many prisoners and hundreds of weapons. In one lightning blow, a second 23rd Division regiment was heavily damaged, and the main springboard of Phu's counterattack was destroyed. Phu's initial effort to recapture Ban Me Thuot had been soundly defeated.

Meanwhile, the 23rd Division commander, Brigadier General Tuong, ordered the fleeing elements of the 45th Regiment to link up with the 21st Ranger Group at the small village of Nong Trai on Route 21, located about twelve miles east of Ban Me Thuot. Unfortunately, Communist signals intelligence picked up Tuong's orders to regroup. Scouts were sent forward to monitor the ARVN efforts to form a defense around Nong Trai. About five miles further east was the district town of Phuoc An, where the 23rd Division had established its forward headquarters.

While Tuong tried to gather his scattered units, Phu's plan was again disrupted by the maintenance problems that bedeviled the large CH-47 Chinook helicopters; fewer and fewer were available each day. Phu's belief that he could conduct an American-style airlift of regimental size was now proven wrong. Despite additional helicopters from other corps, by late afternoon on 14 March, only the 45th Regiment and one battalion and the headquarters of the 44th Regiment had landed. The 44th was put down closer to Phuoc An. The rest of the regiment would not arrive until the next day.

Furthermore, since the enemy roadblock of Route 21 was located between Phuoc An and the coast, all supplies had to be flown in by helicopter. With the number of flights rapidly dwindling because of limited fuel and lack of spare parts, ARVN could not ferry in any armor or artillery. Bad weather and the constant threat from the SA-7 anti-aircraft missiles had badly reduced air power. The South Vietnamese were fighting against armor and artillery with little more than light infantry weapons.

After the defeat of the 45th Regiment, Phu realized that the situation around Ban Me Thuot had dramatically changed. With Thieu's new orders, Phu decided it was useless to try to retake Ban Me Thuot until he could clear the roadblock on Route 21. On 15 March, Phu ordered Tuong to abandon the counterattack. Instead, Tuong would punch through the blockade from the west, while the RF task force attempted to break through from the east. Phu also halted the helicopter flights lifting in the rest of the 44th Regiment. Instead, he diverted the helicopters to move his headquarters to Nha Trang. The 44th Regiment would retreat down Route 7B with the rest of II Corps.

Hoang Minh Thao, however, had no intention of letting Phu consolidate his forces. The last 10th Division regiment still at Duc Lap was ordered to move rapidly and arrive at Ban Me Thuot by the morning of 15 March. The division's other two regiments, the 24th and 66th, were ordered to sweep north and south of Route 21 and converge on Nong Trai. The two regiments had a difficult task. They would have to walk fifteen miles through the mountains at the end of the dry season to reach their positions. The combination of heat, difficult terrain, and lack of water would take a heavy toll on the young troops, but cutting through the woods would spare them from air strikes. The main assault would be one infantry battalion, bolstered by armor and an anti-aircraft battalion, which would strike straight down Route 21 into the ARVN formations at Nong Trai.

On the morning of 16 March, the 10th Division launched its attack. With a heavy cloud cover preventing the VNAF from supplying air support, the results were predictable. The armor raced down Route 21 and easily penetrated the 45th Regiment's positions. The two pincers swept into Nong Trai and captured it. ARVN stragglers were policed up, and then the armor proceeded toward Phuoc An. ARVN troops fled in disorder as the armor sped past them. Only when the clouds finally cleared did the VNAF manage to engage the armor, knocking out several vehicles. This halted the North Vietnamese advance long enough for the ARVN elements at Phuoc An to escape.

Later that day, while flying in his helicopter near the front, Brigadier General Tuong was slightly wounded in the face by an anti-aircraft round that hit his helicopter. Tuong immediately had himself flown to the hospital in Nha Trang. Phu was furious. He berated Tuong in his hospital bed for cowardice, and relieved him of command. Phu then departed for the collapsing ARVN front lines near Phuoc An. He appointed Colonel Le Huu Duc, his officer in charge of pacification, to assume command of the disintegrating 23rd Division. It made little difference. By the late afternoon of 16 March, the 10th Division was in complete control of Phuoc An.

As the elements of the 23rd Division, the Darlac RF, and the 21st Rangers were falling back, Phu again ordered the Khanh Hoa province chief to clear the roadblock on Route 21. His efforts were only partially successful. While he managed to clear the south side of the road, the main position at Chu Cuc remained in the hands of the PAVN 25th Regiment. The attack was no doubt hindered by the fact that a Communist penetration agent commanded one of the RF battalions engaged in the fighting.[18]

Colonel Duc had been assigned a near-impossible task. That night, five thousand refugees from Ban Me Thuot arrived at the ARVN front lines east of Phuoc An. As Duc made his rounds, he was stunned at the almost complete collapse of ARVN troop strength, either from enemy action or from desertion by men hoping to find their families. The 21st Rangers reported less than 240 men out of a normal strength of one thousand (the group was minus one battalion). The 45th Regiment had around two hundred men out of 2,500. Division headquarters had only forty-two men. Most of the specialized companies such as signals, transportation, and engineers had been wiped out. Only a lone battalion of the 44th Regiment had any cohesion left.

With the ARVN counterattack demolished, Thao moved to eliminate the 53rd Regiment base camp. He sent four more tanks and additional artillery, and he pulled the 66th Regiment, 10th Division, back from Nong

Trai to reinforce the attackers. The PAVN commander again divided his forces into two columns. The 66th would attack from the north and the 149th Regiment, 316th Division, from the south. A massive artillery barrage would commence first, and then engineers would blow holes through the barbed wire with explosives. The infantry would then charge the base.

At 3:00 P.M. on 16 March, the artillery opened fire. For ninety minutes, shells rained down on the ARVN defenders, destroying vehicles and setting the base on fire. At 4:30 P.M., the tanks began roaming around the exterior, firing at the bunkers in the wall. Soon, the engineers advanced into the barbed wire, blasting off charges to cut a path for the infantry.

Even with the ferocious bombardment, as soon as the engineers appeared, the South Vietnamese poured machine-gun fire and mortars into them. Both North Vietnamese columns took losses, and after making progress through the ARVN defenses, they ran out of explosives. The armor also became bogged down. An anti-tank rocket hit one tank, while another fell into the anti-tank ditch. After nine hours, neither column had been able to breach the perimeter wall. Yet despite the growing casualties, the PAVN forces grimly pressed forward.

As night fell, the PAVN commander sent his tanks closer to the dirt barricade. All night long they fired at ARVN positions, shooting at anything that moved or shot back. At the same time, North Vietnamese supply troops hurried forward with more explosive charges and ammunition. After completing a path through the barbed wire during the night, the engineers broke through the dirt wall at first light. Tanks quickly entered the base camp, followed by infantry. At 8:00 a.m., 17 March, Colonel Vo An led about a hundred soldiers out of the base and escaped toward Phuoc An. After a valiant defense, the base had fallen. Colonel An's men had held out for seven days against multiple tank-led assaults and artillery attacks. They had fought splendidly against tremendous odds, destroying five tanks and causing hundreds of Communist casualties. Their own losses were staggering, and in the end, An's small unit was no match for the attackers' superior firepower. On 24 March, he and thirty of his men made it into Nha Trang.

On Route 21, the 10th Division commander gathered his staff to plan the final destruction of the 23rd Division. ARVN's rapid collapse provided him an opportunity to destroy the division's last remaining unit, the 44th Regiment. The 10th Division's newly arrived 28th Regiment replaced the tired 24th. The PAVN commander saw no need to change what had been extremely successful tactics. He would send one infantry battalion supported by armor and anti-aircraft units barreling straight down Route 21. Two infantry battalions would swing behind the 44th Regiment and trap the retreating South Vietnamese.

Early in the morning of 17 March, the 28th Regiment launched its attack. While the 44th put up some resistance, the North Vietnamese burst through the ARVN lines and continued moving east. In desperation, Phu immediately moved the 40th Regiment, 22nd Division, currently in reserve in Binh Dinh, to the district town of Khanh Duong to create a new defensive position. Phu then called Thieu and begged for reinforcements. The 3rd Airborne Brigade, sailing south by ship from I Corps, was ordered to divert to Nha Trang and take up defensive positions at the M'Drak Pass, halfway between Khanh Duong and the coast. By noon on 18 March, the 10th Division had moved close to Khanh Duong and had captured over two thousand ARVN and RF soldiers. The 23rd Division had been destroyed as a fighting unit. It would never recover.

"CAN WE ACCELERATE THINGS EVEN MORE?"

On the morning of 11 March, the Politburo met to assess the first days of the March attacks. After listening to Hoang Van Thai's briefing on the victories in the Central Highlands and the "coordinating battlefields," everyone began to speculate on next steps. One possibility was capturing Hue and Danang. Some thought ARVN would dig in at Pleiku, while a few thought it might withdraw from the Highlands altogether.

After listening to the discussion, Le Duan posed an important question: "In the past, we drafted a strategy to liberate the South in two years. A short time ago it was Phuoc Long; now there is Ban Me Thuot. Can we accelerate things even more? Is Ban Me Thuot the beginning of a general strategic offensive?"[19] Essentially, he sought answers to two critical questions: Did their initial success portend the coming of the long-sought strategic opportunity? If so, was it time to turn south toward Saigon, as originally conceived at the December meeting?

Ever the aggressor, Le Duan wanted to launch a major military thrust at Saigon, but he quickly ran into a roadblock. The viewpoint of Van Tien Dung, the commander in the field, differed from that of the men sitting in Hanoi. Instead of favoring the bold gamble of wheeling south to attack Saigon, Dung sought incremental improvement. He wanted to speed up the initial timetable for capturing Darlac and Phu Bon provinces, and then strike north toward Pleiku and Kontum. Shortly after overrunning the 23rd Division's headquarters, Dung cabled Giap with an update and new proposals: "We have secured complete control of Ban Me Thuot. All major targets, including the 23rd Division headquarters, the Darlac province headquarters, the armored and artillery compounds, and the city airfield have been taken and are being occupied by our troops. We are now hunting down enemy remnants hiding inside the city. Preliminary figures indicate we have taken almost 1,000 enemy troops prisoner . . . and have captured a very large quantity of enemy equipment. . . . Based on the fact that enemy morale in the Tay Nguyen is collapsing and they are weakened and isolated, and considering that our forces are still strong . . . our preliminary intention is to: 1) both strengthen Ban Me Thuot to fight enemy counterattacks, and proceed to the outlying areas to take complete control of Darlac province, [and] 2) continue east to Cheo Reo (possibly wiping out or encircling it), then turn back up to surround and wipe out Pleiku, and isolate Kontum to take care of later. We can postpone moving toward the South."[20]

Dung's recommendation to postpone the move south was the first dust-up in what would become a sizable squabble between the Politburo and Dung during March 1975. The question was: Which direction should Dung's forces move after the victory at Ban Me Thuot? Since the earliest days of the Central Cell's planning, the main target had always been Saigon. Internally called "Plan One," the idea shared by Le Duan, Giap, and Tran Van Tra, the B-2 Front commander, was for Dung to use the newly captured stretch of Route 14 to shift immediately toward Saigon. With his three divisions added to Tra's forces, they would launch a massive attack to capture the South Vietnamese capital and end the war in one stroke.

Dung did not want to wheel toward Saigon. Why? Two reasons: First, he sought to clear everything behind him so that his rear would be safe. He did not want his supply lines open to interdiction by ARVN forces in Pleiku while he and Tra were banging at the gates of Saigon. Second, he felt that an attack against ARVN troops in III Corps who were prepared for a PAVN assault was a bad strategy. The fighting at the 53rd Regiment base camp provided plenty of support for that belief. Plus, he was certain that Phu would attempt to recapture Ban Me Thuot, and Dung believed he could easily defeat that effort. Then he would be in a position to mop up the rest of the Highlands.

Giap responded to Dung's cable on the night of 11 March:

I received your cable…and am very excited about the tremendous, clear victory our troops have won in the primary sector as well as in the supporting sector. This morning, before we received your cable, the Politburo and the Central Military Party Committee met to assess the situation. The following are the main points from that meeting:

The strategic and campaign plan that the Politburo and the Central Military Party Committee approved was precisely correct, our preparations for this attack were rather good, and we achieved surprise, and that is why we have been able to achieve such great victories in the very first days of the campaign. The victories at Ban Me Thuot and Duc Lap, along Route 19, and in other sectors demonstrate that we have the capability of winning a tremendous victory more quickly than we anticipated. … Because of this situation, during this current phase of operation, and even in our follow-up plan, we need to display a spirit of urgency and daring, because only by exploiting this opportunity in a timely fashion will we be able to win a great victory. …

I received your cable this afternoon. I believe that the policy you propose in your cable is completely consistent with the ideas discussed this morning in the meetings of the Politburo and the Central Military Party Committee. I have just discussed your cable with [Le Duan] and [Le Duc Tho]. We are all in complete agreement with the proposals you make in the cable.[21]

In agreeing to postpone the move against Saigon, the Politburo was bowing to its field commander's assessment. In the same message, Giap ordered Dung to annihilate all remaining ARVN units near Ban Me Thuot "while at the same time spreading out through the surrounding area and standing ready to attack any enemy relief force." Moreover, he agreed with Dung that he should "send forces … to immediately surround and besiege Cheo Reo in order to overrun it and at the same time annihilate enemy troops in the area." The next step was even more vital: "Immediately deploy your forces to surround Pleiku, block their avenues of supply, and prepare to advance toward overrunning and taking Pleiku. As for Kontum, you should isolate it and overrun it later." To support Dung, Giap ordered the 3rd Division and 95A Regiment to expand their control of Route 19 to isolate the Pleiku-Kontum area.

While Thieu had no way of knowing Hanoi's intentions, if Phu had remained in Pleiku, he would have been surrounded and would have faced a massive PAVN attack. Still, he would probably have fared much better than by attempting to retreat to the coast. The terrain around Pleiku was more open than the terrain around Ban Me Thuot, allowing for greater use of firepower, and the defensive positions at Pleiku were far superior.

At noon on 12 March, Giap sent a follow-up cable to Dung. Based on new information (Hanoi was now receiving almost real-time intelligence of the highest caliber, probably from the spy in Vien's office), Giap precisely outlined the plan that Phu had presented and Thieu had approved on the night of 10 March. "The enemy intends to utilize those forces that have not been destroyed and his surviving outposts on the outskirts of the city, together with reinforcements and air support, to conduct a counterattack to retake Ban Me Thuot. . . . For that reason it is vital that you quickly concentrate your forces to rapidly eliminate enemy units and bases around Ban Me Thuot and destroy the enemy reinforcements. The destruction of an important portion of the enemy's forces in the Ban Me Thuot area will have a decisive impact on the progress of this campaign."[22]

On the afternoon of 12 March, Dung was handed a decoded copy of Giap's response to his 11 March message. Scanning its contents, Dung became ecstatic. The Politburo had approved his recommendations. A few minutes later he received Giap's next message detailing Phu's initial plan. As Dung surveyed the battlefield, he realized that "another key battle in the Tay Nguyen was about to begin." With the rainy season only two months away, he knew that "a race with the enemy as well as the heavens began on the morning of 12 March."[23]

On 13 March Giap's staff analyzed Phu's potential courses of action. They surmised that if Dung's troops destroyed ARVN forces around Ban Me Thuot, if the city remained in North Vietnamese hands, and if Route 19 stayed blocked, Phu had only two options: either pull back into an enclave around Pleiku, or retreat from the Highlands. Giap's staff surmised that Phu would stand and fight. Giap immediately ordered Dung to ring Pleiku with "all kinds of firepower, including anti-aircraft guns, to cut off Southern supply routes, while simultaneously preparing to defeat the enemy with regard to each of these eventualities."[24]

Although only two days had passed since the taking of Ban Me Thuot, the ease of the victory convinced Dung that he should expand his vision. To Dung, his casualties had been low and his supplies barely dented. Earlier he had told Giap that he could achieve his goals sooner than planned. Now he was thinking on a grander scale. Replying to Giap on 14 March, he claimed he could "achieve the goals set by higher authority to shorten the timing and exceed the plan by achieving in a few months the planned goals for the entire year of 1975."[25] Given his superior strength, Dung believed that his forces were capable of more than just conquering the provinces of Darlac, Phu Bon, and Quang Duc. He might be able to capture not just the entire Highlands, but the coastal areas as well.

On 15 March, the PAVN intelligence department informed the General Staff that on 12 March, Thieu had ordered Phu to make an all-out effort to retake Ban Me Thuot using the positions around the city as a springboard. During the same briefing, it also informed Hoang Van Thai that the South Vietnamese had discovered the presence of the 316th Division in the Highlands, that ARVN now realized this area was PAVN's main thrust, and that the 3rd Airborne Brigade was being sent to reinforce a large-scale effort to reopen Route 21.

Giap immediately forwarded this information to Dung, and repeated his earlier instructions: "The first thing we must do is to concentrate our forces in Ban Me Thuot . . . to annihilate individual enemy columns, with the first one being the Phuoc An sector, and be prepared to annihilate enemy reinforcements and relief forces sent in by air and overland. . . . With regard to Pleiku, systematically, step by step, surround and besiege the city, step up operations to suppress the enemy's airfields and to destroy his supply warehouses. Carry out all necessary preparatory tasks on a truly urgent basis in order to do a truly good job on this target without giving the enemy time to react. . . . Just as I finished writing this cable I received your Cable No. 5. We are in complete agreement with your assessment that we will complete our mission much earlier than the time specified in the overall plan. We are currently studying this and making urgent preparations along that line. Early next week, after requesting further instructions from the Politburo, I will send you another cable."[26]

But as even Giap was assuring Dung that the Politburo accepted his recommendation that he not turn his troops toward Saigon, Le Duan was now having second thoughts. He decided to convene another Politburo meeting to re-evaluate the main direction of attack. Learning of the impending meeting, on 16 March Dung sent a summary report to Hanoi. He requested permission to continue cleaning out ARVN units around Ban Me Thuot, and then to move against Cheo Reo and Pleiku. Dung also recommended a change in the original plan: the B-2 Front should capture the rest of Quang Duc province, thus freeing his forces for an attack north toward Pleiku.

At the General Staff in Hanoi, Hoang Van Thai quickly copied the message and distributed it among his colleagues. The senior staff officers now believed that Thieu had changed strategy, and that he was forming enclaves around Danang, Cam Ranh Bay, and Saigon. Le Duan, therefore, felt PAVN needed to press hard against the faltering South Vietnamese. More important, had this new information overtaken the decision made several days earlier to not move against Saigon? If so, which direction should the offensive now take?

Meanwhile, Dung's intelligence teams noticed some strange enemy behavior. At noon on 16 March, they intercepted VNAF communications from numerous planes taking off from Pleiku and requesting permission to land at Nha Trang. Dung was puzzled by this, since his forces had not heavily shelled Pleiku airfield. At 3:00 P.M., Giap telephoned and informed Dung that II Corps headquarters had moved to Nha Trang. An hour later, a reconnaissance team reported a long convoy from Pleiku moving south on Route 14.

Dung immediately called a staff meeting, but no one could decipher the ARVN plans. Then at 9:00 P.M., new intelligence poured into Dung's headquarters. The Pleiku ammunition dumps were exploding, there were many fires in town, and the convoy that had left Pleiku had been spotted on Route 7B. ARVN was pulling out of Pleiku.

Dung was furious. He immediately picked up the field telephone and called the commander of the 320th Division, Senior Colonel Kim Tuan. Tuan had assured Dung two days earlier that Route 7B was unusable. Now the South Vietnamese were retreating along the very road that Dung had left unguarded, and there were no forces to block them. Dung read Tuan the riot act, telling him that "if the enemy escapes, it will be a big crime, and you will have to bear responsibility for it."[27]

Dung swiftly issued a flurry of instructions. The 320th Division was ordered to immediately move toward Cheo Reo and cut off the retreating ARVN troops. Since the division's units were currently scattered from Ban Me Thuot to the Darlac-Pleiku border area, the B-3 Front was instructed to mobilize anything with wheels and send it to the 320th. The 968th Division was ordered to leapfrog enemy positions and attack Pleiku. Local forces in Phu Yen province were instructed to close in on Tuy Hoa and block the retreat at that end of the road.

Then Dung realized he had a trump card. The 9th Battalion of the 320th Division, which had been secretly waiting to attack Cheo Reo since the beginning of the offensive, sat only a couple of ridgelines away from the town. At 10:30 P.M. on 16 March, the telephone line that had been cleverly strung thirteen miles to the 9th Battalion suddenly sprang to life. The voice on the other end of the phone was that of the division commander. His orders were brusque: Move out as soon as possible, cut Route 7B south of Cheo Reo, and block the withdrawal.

The 9th Battalion moved out within ten minutes, but the dark night and rugged terrain hampered its speed. By midnight, the battalion had covered only a short distance. Looking at his watch, the commander made a critical decision. If he was to cross the forest-covered mountains and reach Route 7B by dawn, his men would have to run. Running at night was dangerous, and they could easily stumble into an ARVN ambush. In addition, the heat and lack of water would seriously affect his troops. To attempt to accomplish his mission, he would have to risk the life of every soldier in his battalion. Turning to his deputy, he barked an order. Each soldier would light a torch made of either bamboo or a spare rubber sandal. It was now a race between Phu's column and the 9th Battalion. Who won would determine the fate of the Republic of Vietnam.

9

"THE ROAD OF BLOOD AND TEARS"

THE RETREAT FROM THE HIGHLANDS

Working throughout the night of 14 March and into the morning, Phu and Colonel Le Khac Ly developed a rudimentary plan for the redeployment to Nha Trang. Ly tried again to persuade Phu to use Route 19, but Phu refused, saying his orders from Thieu were unalterable. Phu's first decision was to send the bulk of the corps headquarters to Nha Trang. From there, it would commence planning for the counterattack against Ban Me Thuot and the movement back to Pleiku. He halted the deployment of the two remaining battalions of the 44th Regiment so that the helicopters could be used in the morning to shuttle his staff to Nha Trang. A light corps headquarters commanded by Colonel Ly would move with the retreating column. Phu's design was for his subordinates to handle the retreat, while he set up a forward headquarters near Phuoc An to oversee the clearing of Route 21 and the effort to retake Ban Me Thuot.

If the retreat was to succeed, Lieutenant Colonel Tinh's engineers had to perform several critical missions. First they had to build the float bridge on the Ba River about ten miles southeast of Cheo Reo. Tinh, though, had a serious problem. His specially trained float-bridge troops were in Nha Trang, which meant his regular engineers would have to construct the float bridge. Without the specialists, building it would take two full days. Tinh's second mission was to strengthen a weak bridge at the district town of Phu Tuc, about halfway between Cheo Reo and Cung Son. His third mission was to grade and repair the road between Phu Tuc and Cung Son. Then, he had to build a second, more important bridge across the Ba River near Cung Son. If he failed at any of these missions, the retreating II Corps forces would be caught out in the open, with no fortifications and few supplies. They would be the proverbial sitting ducks.

Remote and virtually unknown, the sleepy provincial capital of Cheo Reo was about to become one of the key battlegrounds in the final drama for South Vietnam. The town sits in a small, picturesque valley, bordered on the west by a number of high peaks that form the Chu Pa ridgeline, and on the east by the swift-flowing Ba River. The ramshackle settlement consisted mainly of one-story, tin-roofed houses around a small city center. From the local population of 20,000 Montagnards of the Jarai tribe, the South Vietnamese had raised three RF battalions to defend the area. One battalion was in the city, while the other two guarded the local countryside.

Le Khac Ly's rudimentary movement plan called for the corps to depart in three elements over three days, one element per day. The first priority was to get the engineers moving and to secure Cheo Reo. The lead battalion of the 20th Engineers left Pleiku on 15 March. Shortly after the engineers moved out, the 23rd Ranger Group set off to secure Cheo Reo. Once they arrived in town, one battalion occupied the Chu Pa ridgeline to screen against a possible attack. Then the First Element—made up of the 6th Ranger Group, a troop of M-113 personnel carriers, and the rest of the combat engineers—would depart Pleiku on the morning of 16 March and move to Cung Son. Security from Cheo Reo to Phu Tuc would be the responsibility of the Phu Bon regional forces. The 6th Rangers would secure the road from Phu Tuc to Cung Son, and guard the engineers fixing the road and building the second, bigger bridge at Cung Son. Phu Yen RF units would secure the road from the second bridge to Tuy Hoa.

The Second Element would depart early on 17 March. It consisted of Ly's light corps headquarters, the 4th Ranger Group, armor and artillery, the rest of the 44th Regiment, and the corps support units. The Third Element, comprising the 25th, 7th, and 22nd Ranger Groups, would set out on 18 March. To maintain secrecy, each unit would be informed only an hour in advance. The local administrations and RF/PF troops would remain and defend Kontum and Pleiku. Once everyone else passed through Cheo Reo, the 23rd Rangers would follow.[1]

After the 23rd Rangers departed Pleiku, Phu got into his plane and flew to Nha Trang. When Brigadier General Cam learned that Phu had left, he stormed out of the II Corps headquarters. Cam, whom Phu had directed to "supervise" the retreat, refused to work with a new general like Tat. Instead, he took off for Tuy Hoa, telling Ly he would shuttle via helicopter between Tuy Hoa and Cheo Reo to oversee the operation.

Ly was furious. He suspected that Cam was more concerned with "overseeing" his business interests in Tuy Hoa than in helping plan the corps movement. Since Tat was arranging transportation for the Rangers, and Phu had flown the senior staff to Nha Trang, Cam's departure left only Ly and several deputy staff officers to complete the planning for the movement of thousands of troops and vehicles. How an officer of Phu's experience could have believed that his muddled chain of command, the abandonment of the civilians, and his presence in the rear instead of personally leading the column would not lead to a massive disaster is beyond understanding. The only possible explanation is that he was fixated on following Thieu's order to retake Ban Me Thuot, thinking the retreat would be a fairly easy affair. If so, this again points up Phu's lack of formal military education, as retreats and large-scale troop movements are difficult maneuvers requiring precise planning.

After the usual morning staff meeting on 15 March, Ly violated Thieu's orders about informing the Americans. He covertly told the local CIA representative to gather his people and depart. After the CIA officer left, Phu and Ly pulled the American province representative for Pleiku, Earl Thieme, into Phu's office. Phu informed Thieme that he should immediately begin evacuating all U.S. and foreign nationals, although Phu did not tell him why.[2]

Shortly thereafter, the CIA officer informed Tom Polgar in Saigon that II Corps was retreating. At the same time, Thieme alerted his boss in Nha Trang, Consul General Moncrieff Spear. Polgar immediately called Lieutenant General Dang Van Quang at the palace to determine whether this information was true. Quang, following Thieu's stricture not to tell the Americans, denied it. Despite the denial, Polgar chose to believe his man on the scene and ordered all CIA personnel out of the Highlands. Deputy Ambassador Wolfgang Lehmann, after learning from both Spear and Polgar about the impending retreat, followed suit later that morning and ordered out all other U.S. staff. The first Americans were now heading for the exits.

Phu and Ly were not the only officers disobeying orders about keeping the retreat secret. After the afternoon meeting in Pleiku on 14 March in which Phu relayed Thieu's orders, Air Force Brigadier General Pham Ngoc Sang immediately called the VNAF commander, Lieutenant General Tran Van Minh, to ask what he should do about his people and equipment. Sang could not just depart on a moment's notice; he had tons of spare parts, engines, fuel, ammunition, disabled aircraft, and repair stands. Minh told him to follow Phu's orders, but he also adopted a prudent course. Early on 15 March, Minh sent several C-130s to Pleiku with the supposed mission of flying out equipment. In reality, the planes were ferrying out not just supplies, but VNAF personnel and their families.

With the arrival of the lumbering cargo planes and the movement of the Air Force families to the airfield, rumors began to swirl among the rest of the population. In South Vietnam, people who lived near large bases always closely watched the military's movements and would immediately flee whenever ARVN retreated. In this case, the roads had been cut for ten days, and the civilians and soldiers' families were particularly anxious. When they then learned that the price of a ticket on Air Vietnam from

Pleiku to Saigon had suddenly jumped, they rushed to the airfield. Chaos spread, and VNAF personnel and civilians fought with one another to get onto the planes. Sang tried to restore order, but panicked civilians interfered with his airmen's efforts to destroy equipment and material that could not be taken along. Although the Air Force did ferry out some equipment and records, including much of the highly classified Pleiku signals-intelligence station, large amounts were left behind. Later that afternoon, PAVN sappers shelled the airfield again, closing down the airlift. Some VNAF personnel and many unlucky civilians would now have to walk or ride down Route 7B with the Army.

That same morning, Brigadier General Tat flew out to the Rangers and tankers trying to break through the roadblock on Route 19.[3] He wanted to speak with Colonel Nguyen Van Dong, the commander of the 2nd Armor Brigade, who was leading the operation by the 4th Rangers to clear the road. Tat ordered Dong to halt the attack, and informed him of the plan to withdraw. Tat ordered Dong to fly to Cheo Reo and set up a command post there. The 6th and 23rd Ranger Groups would be attached to Dong's 2nd Brigade. Dong's mission was to secure Cheo Reo and hold Route 7B open with his armor and the Rangers so that the rest of II Corps could retreat.

Dong was flabbergasted. Despite the heavy loss of the M-113s the day before, the operation was slowly making progress against the Communists. Worse, retreat would mean abandoning the huge stockpiles of precious fuel and tank ammunition the JGS had sent into Pleiku and Kontum in January. Dong's brigade had so many extra supplies the engineers had had to build temporary field dumps to stockpile all the gas and ammunition.

Despite his frustration, Dong obeyed orders and flew by helicopter to Cheo Reo, arriving at noon on 15 March. He found the province chief at home enjoying his lunch break, unaware that II Corps was preparing to retreat through his town. The next morning, Dong and some of his staff made a reconnaissance of the road from Cheo Reo to Phu Tuc. Dong immediately realized that the Tu Na Pass, a steep mountain pass between Cheo Reo and where the float bridge on the Ba River would be constructed, should be occupied by the Rangers. It was the natural choke-point on the road, and the easiest place to create an ambush. He claims he radioed Brigadier General Tat with his recommendation, but Tat said, "No, wait for orders."[4] Tat denies Dong's story, saying Dong had full control of the Rangers in Cheo Reo and could have easily occupied the pass. It would be the first, but by no means the last, miscommunication between senior ARVN II Corps officers over who was responsible for which part of the operation.

That same morning of 16 March, Dong's 19th Armored Cavalry Squadron arrived at Pleiku from Kontum. A troop of M-113 APCs from the squadron was immediately placed under the command of the 6th Ranger Group. With the M-113s leading the way, the First Element departed Pleiku, with a long convoy of vehicles belonging to the Rangers, engineers, and other support units following behind. Arriving in Cheo Reo at 11:00 A.M., the squadron commander went to see Dong, who instructed him to proceed on Route 7B past Phu Tuc to the Ca Lui Regional Force outpost thirty-four miles southeast of Cheo Reo. The Rangers would guard the engineers strengthening the bridge at Phu Tuc, while the armor would protect Ca Lui. An hour later, the First Element set off.

As it turns out, Phu was right on two points. His estimate that using Route 7B would provide tactical surprise was correct. Two ARVN Ranger groups plus armor had shifted from Pleiku to Cheo Reo, and PAVN had not reacted. The North Vietnamese, while aware of the arrival of the Rangers at Cheo Reo, misinterpreted the ARVN movement. One of their histories states: "when the enemy began his evacuation, we thought that the enemy was moving forces into Cheo Reo as a precaution to prevent us from attacking and taking the city. We thought that these forces were . . . to prepare a springboard position for use when the situation permitted to launch an attack to recapture Ban Me Thuot."[5] It is an easy mistake to make; one often construes the enemy's actions as a reaction to one's own plans, rather than as possessing a separate motive.

Phu was also correct regarding the need to move fast, but just how fast is uncertain. While North Vietnamese accounts do not provide a precise date for the follow-up attacks against Cheo Reo and then Pleiku, Giap's instructions and Dung's intent were clear: the two towns were the next targets. In addition to the PAVN 9th Battalion hidden in the mountains several miles west of Cheo Reo, another infantry battalion was moving into position to help assault the town. In February, PAVN engineers had begun constructing a secret road from Route 14 toward Cheo Reo. The 2nd Battalion, 48th Regiment, was now completing that work and was less than ten miles away from the town. Further, on 14 March an artillery reconnaissance element had snuck inside the town and surveyed a number of targets. Given that secret mission, an attack against Cheo Reo was probably less than a week away.

Thus the question is: Did Phu have a chance of repairing the road and executing a withdrawal before PAVN could react? The answer is maybe, but only if he had more carefully planned the retreat. But Thieu's deadline of three days plus Phu's refusal to consider anything but an immediate withdrawal doomed the effort. His excuse that Thieu's orders were firm is thin at best. He certainly had no qualms in early February about disregarding the president's directive to send the 23rd Division to Ban Me Thuot. While Phu was unaware of the close proximity of Communist forces, from the morning of 15 March until the morning of 17 March, he had a free hand on 7B. Since the Communists had misread the Rangers' movement, if Phu or Ly had waited until the first float bridge was completed, and then sent the heavy equipment in one column, the armor would have probably escaped Cheo Reo. Granted, the critical bridges at Phu Tuc and Cung Son were not completed, but in the tight constraints of the Cheo Reo valley, everyone was easy prey for the PAVN gunners. If Phu had spent more time planning the retreat instead of delegating this unenviable task to his subordinates, he might have pulled it off.

The other problem was controlling the civilians. Rolling behind the First Element was the ruin of whatever chance Phu's troops had to escape: a fleet of trucks, buses, motorcycles, and small cars, packed with frightened civilians, mostly the families of officers and enlisted men who had learned of the pullout. Phu later claimed that the Air Force had sabotaged the retreat by flying out their families ahead of time, thus alerting the town to the impending retreat. While partially right, he was mainly looking for a scapegoat. After the previous day's bedlam at the airfield, Pleiku was on edge. Although the VNAF flights certainly tipped off the civilians, it was only a matter of time before a mass exodus began. Pleiku was swollen with people from Kontum and outlying areas who had fled to the city when the North Vietnamese first cut the roads. After BBC radio broadcasts announcing the redeployment of the II Corps headquarters to Nha Trang, the commencement of the destruction of supplies was the final signal. Thousands of civilians soon fled. Panic-stricken, few thought to bring food, fuel, or water, a tragic mistake that was compounded by vast overcrowding of wildly driven vehicles. It was this unruly mob of civilians that finally caught the Communists' attention.[6]

By mid-afternoon on 16 March, approximately nine hundred vehicles had crowded into Cheo Reo. Because of the steep grades at the Tu Na Pass, a major traffic jam soon clogged the road south of town. Yet by the early evening of 16 March, a large number of these vehicles had crossed the existing bridge over the river. The bulk of Phu's troops, however, including all the tanks and artillery, still remained in Pleiku.

Meanwhile, the PAVN 320th Division commander, Senior Colonel Kim Tuan, had set about implementing the orders he had received from General Dung. Tuan ordered his two battalions near Cheo Reo to move out. The 2nd Battalion, 48th Regiment, would attack from the Chu Pa ridgeline west of Cheo Reo, while the 9th Battalion, 64th Regiment, would swing south and block the road near the Tu Na Pass. All available vehicles would transport the other two battalions of the 48th Regiment from Route 14 to link up with the 2nd Battalion. The trucks would then return and pick up the remainder of the 64th Regiment. The last 320th Division regiment, the 9th, was on Route 14 at the Darlac–Pleiku province border. The regiment's new mission was to move north on Route 14 to the Route 7B turnoff and block any retreating units. It would then turn down Route 7B toward Cheo Reo. Thus, the 320th's plan had three elements converging on Cheo Reo: the 9th Regiment from the north, the 48th Regiment from the west, and the 64th Regiment blocking the Tu Na Pass south of town.

They all needed to hurry, as the ARVN movement was continuing. On the night of 16 March, the First Element reached Phu Tuc and Ca Lui. Here occurred the first of many failures to follow orders, whether through disobedience or misunderstanding. While the 6th Rangers left a battalion to guard the engineers improving the bridge at Phu Tuc, the rest of the Rangers and armor, instead of remaining at Ca Lui per Dong's orders, continued on to Cung Son. There they sat for several days, doing nothing.

As night fell on 16 March, thousands of hungry civilians and soldiers began searching Cheo Reo for food and shelter. The town quickly descended into anarchy when Vietnamese soldiers began breaking into stores and homes, robbing and shooting the mostly Montagnard locals.[7] Leaving the wrecked buildings, they set them on fire. Groups of leaderless soldiers began stealing vehicles from civilians, or selling rides in their own vehicles.[8] With gangs of unruly soldiers rampaging through town, the local Vietnamese police deserted and joined the pillage. Montagnard civilians fled their homes, while some Jarai RF troops fought gun battles with the rioters to protect their families.

Pleiku was also teetering on chaos. The previous day, the city had been heavily patrolled by police. At noon on 16 March, seeing the destruction of supplies and the departure of the First Element, the provincial security forces abandoned their posts to flee with their families. That afternoon, Ly called Brigadier General Tran Dinh Tho, the J-3 (operations officer), JGS, and reported that soldiers were roaming the streets, looting and raping, and that the anarchy was interfering with the planned withdrawal from the city. Tho immediately took Ly's report to General Cao Van Vien, who called Phu to demand that he take action to halt the mayhem. Phu denied Ly's account, claiming that Pleiku was still under his full control. But instead of flying back to assume command, Phu castigated Ly for calling the JGS. Relations between Ly and Phu then collapsed. From this point onwards, Ly was in almost open rebellion against Phu and, shortly, against his fellow senior II Corps officers. He refused to work cooperatively, making the convoy's command structure even more unstable at precisely the point when it needed superior leadership. Worse, it was not until the night of 16 March that Phu told Brigadier General Cam to inform the province chiefs of Kontum and Pleiku that they were to stay and defend their territory so that the regular military could withdraw. However, when the Montagnard RF/PF forces learned that the Vietnamese were retreating, they promptly deserted. They had no faith in Thieu's plan to return once Ban Me Thuot was recaptured.

Nguyen Tu, the highly influential *Chinh Luan* correspondent who had interviewed Phu in mid-February, had returned to Pleiku shortly after the Ban Me Thuot attack. He was in the city when the flight began, and he published a series of newspaper reports describing the horrors of the retreat. He was the only journalist who accompanied the column, and his dispatches provided the people of Saigon their first information on the botched withdrawal. The power of his pen would spur deep popular discontent with Thieu's government.

Tu noted that in the early hours of 16 March, with the beginning of the destruction of supplies, citizens flooded out into the streets. People "hastily and fearfully loaded goods, furniture, and personal belongings onto every type of vehicle imaginable—trucks, jeeps, garbage trucks, motorcycles, tractors, and even fire trucks.... After the vehicles were crammed full of possessions, people climbed up and sat on them. Every vehicle was so heavily loaded that its springs sagged almost to the ground."[9] The mass of people and vehicles then just sat there for hours, unsure of what to do next. Tu confirms that the first civilians departed at noon on 16 March, but the majority left around 8:00 P.M. A traffic jam a few miles outside of Pleiku halted the flow. It soon resumed, but it was constantly halted for various reasons, including many broken-down vehicles. The saddest part, however, was the thousands of people who were walking. Tu, fifty-six years old, was walking along with these forlorn refugees. He was especially worried about the "young and old, babies and toddlers carried by their parents, and pregnant women. They walk along," he wrote, "each carrying a few bamboo sleeping mats and bundles of clothing. Sad and worried, family after family walks along in a long line on one side of the road to avoid being run over. The headlights of the vehicles illuminate the bent backs of adults carrying heavy burdens and the smaller shadows of little children desperately holding onto the shirttails of their mothers or fathers."

All night the column proceeded toward Cheo Reo. As the sun rose, the heat began to take its toll. The elderly and the women and children "walk along the side of the road under the blazing sunlight with not a drop of water to drink." Tu was fearful that many of them would die of thirst. He had witnessed many evacuations, including the tragic retreat on Route 1 from Quang Tri in 1972 when the Communists shelled the road, earning it the nickname "The Highway of Death." Tu felt this was a far worse calamity.

Outside of Pleiku, three other Ranger groups struggled to execute the plan. The 25th Group began disengaging from Thanh An to join the column on Route 14, while the 4th Group retreated along Route 19 toward Pleiku. At Kontum, however, another problem arose: the 22nd Group had only enough trucks to move two battalions, stranding one battalion still defending the city. Since most of the unit was already halfway to Pleiku, Tat ordered the group commander to leave the last battalion, but the group commander refused. He sent his trucks back to pick up his men, telling Tat that he and his soldiers would either "leave together or die together."[10] They did both: being the last to withdraw, very few 22nd Rangers would reach the coast.

By the morning of 17 March, the idea of informing each unit one hour in advance was abandoned. Everyone knew about the retreat, and no one wanted to be left behind. One final, massive military convoy departed Pleiku. Shortly thereafter, telephone service with II Corps headquarters was cut. A few remaining engineers prepared demolitions to destroy the command bunkers. The 7th Ranger Group joined the rear of the column as it passed by on Route 14. The 4th Rangers fell in behind them. The 22nd Rangers acted as rear guard. They arrived at Pleiku around noon, but congestion forced them to bypass the town. Later in the day, air strikes attempted to destroy the remaining stores and disabled planes at the airfield. The first vehicles arrived in Cheo Reo around noon, with others not pulling in till the early evening.

The 25th Rangers, however, could not extricate themselves from Thanh An. After receiving Dung's orders to trap the Rangers there, the PAVN 968th Division snuck a battalion through the forest behind them to block their retreat. At first light on 17 March, the remainder of the regiment surged forward. With artillery fire crashing down, they struck just as the 25th Rangers were departing. Caught out in the open, the Rangers took heavy casualties. They attempted to pull back, but were pinned between the advancing North Vietnamese and the blocking force behind them. Alone at the II Corps headquarters, Tat desperately requested air support, but none was available. He ordered the Rangers to break into small groups and escape through the jungle, but only a few remnants made it out. Tat then left Pleiku and arrived in Cheo Reo around 3:00 P.M.

That same morning of 17 March, the other regiment from the 968th Division near Kontum cut Route 14 south of the city. The province chief and his staff were captured attempting to escape. North Vietnamese histories claim that by 11:30 A.M., the 95A Regiment and the 968th Division advanced into Pleiku, and that they took Kontum shortly thereafter. South Vietnamese accounts, however, indicate ongoing functions at the airfield and other places until 18 March. Regardless, the Communists took the two formerly heavily defended cities without firing a shot.

In Cheo Reo, the trap closed slowly on the bottlenecked South Vietnamese convoy. During the night of 16 March, the PAVN 2nd Battalion, 48th Regiment, moved up to the Chu Pa ridgeline on the western outskirts of Cheo Reo and tangled with some 23rd Ranger outposts. At dawn on 17 March, the rest of the 48th Regiment joined the 2nd Battalion west of town. The Rangers sent out a large force to push back the encroaching PAVN troops, but they fell into an ambush and took heavy losses. At 10:00 A.M., the 48th Regiment commander ordered his 1st Battalion to move through the woods and cut Route 7B north of the city. Two 105-mm howitzers soon joined the regiment, but it was dark before the guns were in position.

Meanwhile, after walking and running all night, by late morning of 17 March PAVN's 9th Battalion, 64th Regiment, had finally arrived at Route 7B. Comparing his location with the map, the commander quickly realized he was in the wrong position. Moving out again, he finally had one company in place near the Tu Na Pass by 4:00 P.M., with the rest of the battalion not far behind.

Although civilian and light military traffic continued to flow across the existing bridge on the Ba River, the previous night's chaos had created a tremendous traffic jam, preventing the orderly movement of troops and vehicles. But with the float bridge finally completed, by late afternoon on 17 March the first armor element left the town and headed for the pass.

Upon hearing the armor rumbling toward it, the lead company from the 9th Battalion quickly hid behind termite mounds and in the dense forest along both sides of the road. Armed with anti-tank rockets, the troops waited until the armor slowed as the heavy vehicles climbed the steep grade. When the tanks reached the ambush point, the Northerners opened fire. Numerous rounds hit the armor. Within a few minutes, over ten tanks and APCs were burning. The failure to secure the Tu Na Pass—whether Dong's fault or Tat's—had proven deadly.

After the attack at the pass, Colonel Dong realized he needed to escape Cheo Reo now. He decided on a night attack to punch through the blockade. His plan called for helicopters to shine searchlights along the road while planes circled overhead and dropped illumination flares. His armor would then drive at high speed through the enemy. Unfortunately for him, PAVN intercepted his communications. The North Vietnamese immediately laid mines and reinforced their positions. Around midnight, Dong tried to break through the enemy siege ring. With him personally commanding his best armor, the M-48 tanks, his units surged forward, machine guns blazing, while helicopter gunships poured fire along both sides of the road. The men of the 9th Battalion, however, refused to retreat. Without any ARVN infantry support to clear the road, and with little room to maneuver, the tanks were not terrifying steel monsters but simply large, inviting targets. As the armor entered the kill zone, the Communists again opened up with anti-tank rockets. Within five minutes, seven vehicles were burning. As Dong tried to maneuver his forces, civilians surged forward, interfering with his attack. To avoid running over the civilians, Dong ordered the tanks to turn on their headlights. When they did so, the results were predictable. Several more tanks were also hit. Realizing the futility of his efforts, Dong ordered his units to withdraw. Within the span of six hours, ARVN armor had suffered one of its heaviest losses of the entire war.

At 7:00 A.M. on 18 March, the remainder of the PAVN 64th Regiment arrived at Cheo Reo. The division artillery was also finalizing its positions and firing data. Shortly thereafter, the JGS relayed to Major General Phu in Nha Trang the information that intercepted radio transmissions had revealed that the 320th Division intended to attack and destroy the column at Cheo Reo. Phu immediately jumped into his plane and flew toward the town. He ordered Dong to use the 7th Ranger Group and armor to break through the roadblock at the pass.

Gathering together over twenty tanks and numerous trucks, Dong began the assault shortly before noon. The Rangers carefully maneuvered through the pass, with the armor following close behind in support. The infantry moving ahead to clear the road made all the difference, and this time the Rangers punched through easily. Disaster, however, struck again. When the lead Ranger battalion reached the top of the pass, VNAF fighters called in by Dong to support the assault mistakenly bombed the unit. Several tanks were knocked out, and the Ranger battalion commander was killed.

When the 320th Division commander learned that the 7th Rangers had broken through, he rushed the rest of the 64th Regiment to the pass. They were too late: the 7th Rangers and a portion of Dong's armor had escaped. However, the PAVN troops were able to close the road to further traffic.

While the Rangers fought for their lives at the pass, the PAVN artillery was finally ready. At noon on 18 March it began firing at Cheo Reo. With thousands of people and hundreds of vehicles confined to a small area, the artillery rounds created havoc. Many vehicles were hit and hundreds of South Vietnamese civilians and soldiers were killed or wounded. People fled in all directions to escape the barrage. Vehicles were abandoned or careened madly down the road to get away from the shelling, often running over women and children. Journalist Nguyen Tu described the carnage: "The roaring artillery, cracking small arms, screams of the dying and crying of children combined into a single voice from hell."[11]

At 5:00 P.M. on 18 March, the 1st and 2nd Battalions, 48th Regiment, launched their attacks on Cheo Reo. The 2nd Battalion assaulted the province headquarters, while the 1st Battalion swept down from the north to take the main RF camp. Despite resistance by small groups of desperate Rangers, by midnight the PAVN forces held complete control of Cheo Reo. Only the remainder of Dong's armor and some Rangers and support troops south of town remained free.

At the first ground attack, Phu immediately sent in helicopters to pick up Ly and Tat. Phu ordered Dong to stay behind and attempt to break out, no matter what the cost.[12] As Tat and Ly flew away in helicopters, an angry and bitter Dong immediately began gathering his remaining armor and whatever Rangers he could round up. Early in the morning of 19 March, he launched his final assault. His forces fought valiantly to penetrate the lines of the 64th Regiment, but after several failed attempts, Phu ordered him to abandon all heavy equipment and escape on foot. Some soldiers avoided the North Vietnamese search teams, but many others were killed or captured. By 1:00 P.M. on 19 March, the 64th Regiment had eliminated all remaining ARVN forces in the Cheo Reo valley. For the next two days, VNAF air strikes attempted to destroy the abandoned vehicles and equipment. Although Colonel Dong managed to get away, he was captured on 26 March in Phu Yen province. He spent twelve years in prison.

The 320th Division claims that after three days of fighting, it had killed 755 ARVN soldiers, while capturing 5,590, including 512 officers. Another 7,225 soldiers "turned themselves in voluntarily to our forces," for a total of 13,570.[13] According to Dang Vu Hiep, the B-3 Front political officer, some 20,000 civilians remaining in the Cheo Reo valley were fed and then sent back to Pleiku and Kontum.[14] Given the large numbers of civilians that were later reported at Cung Son, this would indicate that the vast majority of South Vietnamese civilians escaped the carnage at Cheo Reo, but that the bulk of II Corps soldiers did not. Only a third of Dong's vehicles escaped the pocket and made it to Cung Son, mainly after the 7th Rangers broke through. The defeat, therefore, was staggering. The 4th, 22nd, 23rd, and 25th Ranger Groups were destroyed, the 2nd Armor Brigade and II Corps artillery were rendered combat ineffective, and the II Corps support and maintenance units were decimated. It was the worst defeat of the war inflicted on ARVN up to this point.

"THE SITUATION IS DEVELOPING SO FAST!"

After carefully monitoring the evolving situation, Giap began contemplating each side's future moves. The same question remained. What should be PAVN's next objective: the destruction of II Corps, or a bold stroke at Saigon? At the Politburo meeting on 12 March, Le Duan and Giap had wanted to attack the capital, but Dung convinced them to pursue the II Corps forces instead. Subsequently, Giap's staff drew up two contingencies. Plan One called for developing the offensive in two directions. The main thrust would be toward Saigon. The B-3 Front units at Ban Me Thuot would move south on Route 14 and would assault Saigon in conjunction with Colonel General Tran Van Tra's B-2 Front. The 968th and 3rd Divisions would continue east along Route 19 into Binh Dinh province. Plan Two called for sending Dung's divisions first toward the coast, liberating Binh Dinh, Phu Yen, and Khanh Hoa provinces. Then they would drive south and attack Saigon from the east while Tra attacked from the west. As for the South Vietnamese, Giap and his lieutenants concluded that ARVN would retreat into enclaves around the coastal cities. The enclave concept was first put forth in 1966 by American Lieutenant General James M. Gavin, and was thus called the "Gavin Plan" by the Communists. For Giap, it was critical to prevent ARVN from withdrawing into enclaves, as it would prove costly to seize them.

On the morning of 17 March, Giap cabled Dung with an explanation of his thinking: "The enemy is now conducting a strategic withdrawal and regrouping earlier than we had anticipated. His plan is to mass his forces at Saigon, Cam Ranh, and possibly also Danang. This is a great opportunity. Expand your attacks in whichever sector you consider to be the primary sector. Send me your answer on the question of the development sector so that I have time to seek the opinions of the Politburo tomorrow morning."[15]

Shortly after Giap had given Dung free rein to choose in which direction to attack, PAVN's deputy chiefs of staff, Lieutenant Generals Hoang Van Thai and Le Trong Tan, learned that Le Duan still wanted to wheel toward Saigon. They immediately recommended that Giap implement Plan One. Since Giap also favored this move, he quickly rescinded his previous instructions. In a follow-up cable that same morning, he ordered Dung to implement Plan One.

On 18 March the Politburo gathered to assess the progress since their meeting a week earlier. Le Duan began by exclaiming, "The situation is developing so fast!"[16] He demanded that the North Vietnamese forces press hard against the South Vietnamese to prevent them from forming enclaves. While he recognized that taking Saigon would be difficult, he favored shifting Dung's units toward the capital.

The General Staff then made a report on the overall situation, although they admitted they lacked information on what was transpiring in the B-2 Front. They had received the front's plan to attack in coordination with Dung's assault on Ban Me Thuot, but they had been given few updates since then. Upon hearing this report, Le Duan became angry. The Politburo was already displeased with Pham Hung, the head of COSVN. In late February the Politburo had received his strategy for its Phase Two offensive, which outlined an aggressive plan calling on villages, districts, and provinces to "liberate" themselves through armed uprising. On 13 March Le Duc Tho replied, criticizing Hung for what he considered a flawed approach. Hung answered that while similar COSVN plans had failed in the past because of the enemy's superior strength, this plan would succeed because the enemy was much weaker.[17]

However, by the time Hung's message reached Hanoi, it was too late to decode it before the meeting. Thus, the Politburo became convinced that COSVN might need steadier leadership. If the North Vietnamese were to launch a risky attack against Saigon, it might be necessary to send Le Duc Tho himself to the B-2 Front to oversee operations. In the meantime, Tho and Le Trong Tan would go to the B-1 Front and provide a briefing to the leadership there on the Politburo's strategy. If needed, Tho could then continue south to COSVN.

Next it was Giap's turn to speak. Rising to his feet, the senior general of the People's Army laid out a case for increased action. In the course of ten days, he said, the South Vietnamese had weakened rapidly, and they were pulling back into enclaves. The U.S. had many internal difficulties and would not dare intervene again. The People's Army was at full strength, its forces were concentrated, and its morale was high. Giap recommended that PAVN should attack in three directions. One column would cut Hue off from Danang, the second would punch along Route 19 to the coast, and, lastly, Dung's units should move toward Saigon while Tra's troops cut Route 4 south of the city. More important, Giap said, it was time for Hanoi to re-adjust its goals, and liberate South Vietnam in 1975. The 1st Corps, PAVN's last reserve, should be committed to the Southern battlefield. Only one division would remain to protect the homeland, just in case the Americans invaded.

Le Duc Tho quickly agreed, stating that ARVN, no longer stiffened by U.S. firepower, was on the verge of collapse. He also believed the Americans would not interfere. The only obstacles to victory were internal. Giap's staff had to prevent the old PAVN failings from resurfacing: poor organization, clumsy logistics, and bad leadership. When Truong Chinh and Pham Van Dong also supported Giap's position, the decision was inevitable. A quick vote was taken, and it was unanimous. The previous two-year plan to conquer the South was tossed aside. The long-feared general offensive was about to crash down on South Vietnam.

After the meeting, Giap visited the 1st Corps's headquarters and ordered its commander to send half its forces to a staging area just north of the

DMZ. Soon a thousand vehicles were rolling south on Route 1. Giap also sent another cable to Dung outlining the Politburo's decision and reinforcing his previous order to Dung to turn his divisions toward Saigon. Giap also informed Dung that both Tho and Tan were being sent to the South to ensure that everyone understood the Politburo's intentions. Ending his cable, Giap noted another possible South Vietnamese strategy. He predicted that Thieu might be planning to hold out "for a political settlement or a solution that would divide up the territory of South Vietnam."[18] Giap had scored another intelligence coup, and he was now aware of Thieu's decision to truncate the country.

Dung, however, remained convinced that Giap's plan was wrong. After receiving Giap's initial 17 March message—the one giving him the choice of which direction to strike—Dung and his staff discussed Giap's request. They understood the grave dangers Thieu risked by retreating from the Central Highlands. They concluded that their "tremendous" victory in the Central Highlands had "badly weakened the Thieu administration" and that "more military defeats might lead to [its] collapse."[19] Everything from logistics to mobility to time was now in PAVN's favor. Dung understood the strategic question Giap had posed, but he believed that destroying II Corps would "stimulate further military disintegration and political collapse for Thieu." He was afraid that if "we stopped or attacked in a different direction, the enemy would regroup." Although there was "heated discussion" among Dung's staff, everyone eventually agreed that continuing east to the coast rather than turning south to Saigon was the better option.

Dung responded to Giap with a proposal to continue east, but because of the slow communications system, his response and Giap's second message crossed each other. No doubt Giap's second cable, stating that Le Duan also wanted to turn south, must have given Dung pause. While he could oppose Giap, he could not ignore Le Duan. Couching a second reply in more diplomatic language, Dung agreed with the overall "strategic direction," but pointed out that reorienting his troops to attack Saigon would require lengthy planning and reorganization. Moreover, such a move would consume precious time, eating into what was left of the dry season. Dung pleaded to be allowed to annihilate the rest of II Corps. Instead of sending his troops south, he proposed sending the 316th Division, currently guarding Ban Me Thuot, to the B-2 Front. He also rejected any meeting with Le Duc Tho. As a substitute, he recommended that the General Staff write brief messages and use couriers to bring them to the front.

Dung's plea was successful, and once again Giap and the Politburo deferred to their field commander. Dung soon issued new orders. "Continue a fighting advance down Routes 19, 7, and 21 to liberate Phu Yen, Khanh Hoa, and, in cooperation with 3rd Division, liberate Binh Dinh. Your primary objective is to . . . liberate Nha Trang and Cam Ranh."[20] After reading Dung's cables, Giap even sent a short message to allay Dung's fears about not following the Politburo's instructions. On 22 March he informed Dung that "after receiving your cable . . . I discussed the situation with Le Duc Tho and also asked Le Duan for his thoughts. Right now we are in complete agreement with the plan for development of the offensive and for the employment of forces outlined in your cable."[21] Dung had won round two, and Phu would get no respite.

"SEE THIEU AS SOON AS POSSIBLE"

As alarming messages poured in from Saigon, the U.S. government was desperately trying to understand the rapidly unfolding events. On 17 March, a National Intelligence Bulletin was published analyzing the impact of Thieu's recent decisions. Jointly written by the CIA, the Defense Intelligence Agency, and the State Department, the report was pessimistic; Thieu's change of strategy in I and II Corps, while probably necessary, "risks a psychological unraveling within ARVN that could seriously complicate an orderly consolidation of the GVN's military position." It was precisely the same fear that Thieu had expressed since 1972: giving up ground would devastate South Vietnamese morale. Even if the strategy was successful, substantial territory and population would come under Communist control, and the huge influx of new refugees would severely strain the South Vietnamese economy. The Politburo "will view Thieu's moves as a clear sign of weakness," and Hanoi might choose either a consolidation of its gains, or an immediate stab at Saigon. However, like most observers, the American intelligence community believed that "barring a psychological collapse . . . the GVN will survive the communist dry season campaign."[22]

That same day, Deputy Ambassador Lehmann (Ambassador Martin was still in North Carolina recuperating from his dental surgery) sent National Security Advisor Brent Scowcroft the latest information on South Vietnamese plans. He noted that the GVN leadership faced a difficult situation, "quite possibly calling for some very basic far-reaching decisions."[23] While his information was fragmentary, Lehmann had learned that "serious thought is being given to dramatic policy revisions which would call for abandoning major portions of the country in order to enable a truly workable defense of the remainder." Worse, many government and military officials were grumbling that the Americans could not be "counted upon," especially given recent congressional actions.

The American government could not make decisions based upon conjecture. Kissinger was still in the Middle East, but his deputy, Robert Ingersoll, ordered Lehmann to "see Thieu as soon as possible to obtain from him his rationale for the withdrawal of his forces. . . . You should tell him that we need a clear picture as to his intentions and strategy to deal with what is now clearly a general North Vietnamese offensive."[24] Ingersoll was particularly upset that "we have learned of what obviously are major decisions on his part only through the newspapers and informal contacts at staff levels." Since President Ford still sought congressional approval of the supplemental aid, administration efforts "in regard to the $300 million and future funding would be immensely strengthened if we can know his thinking first-hand."

At 9:00 A.M. on 20 March, Lehmann met with Thieu. Upon the delivery of Ingersoll's message, Thieu opened up. The loss of Ban Me Thuot, he told Lehmann, "had definitely been a blow."[25] Thieu claimed that he faced a strong enemy with an unending stream of reinforcements that could concentrate a sizable force at any point. Since Thieu's forces were spread out defending territory and population, his military was at a severe disadvantage. In this situation, he said, he "could no longer fight what from a military standpoint [had been] a stupid way to fight a war. He had to give up territory or face the prospect of having his forces defeated piece by piece." In the Highlands, opening the roads could only have been done at great cost. With the enemy's "strong local superiority," the defense of Pleiku was "a suicide mission." He had decided to pull out those forces, and because of the "close proximity of strong enemy forces he had considered speed and surprise to be essential. It had been a trade-off between losing some equipment and aircraft and perhaps at the expense of a carefully organized and very orderly withdrawal, or losing all of his forces because of inability to disengage themselves from imminent enemy attack."

After discussing the situation in I Corps, Thieu stated that the "current North Vietnamese offensive had ended any hope of fighting on the premises of the Paris Agreement. Therefore, consideration of what is militarily most effective in defending as much of the population as possible and maintaining the integrity of the armed forces" was now paramount. Finally, while he appreciated Ford's effort regarding the supplemental aid, the $300 million would not replace the items recently lost in combat, let alone provide for the one-for-one replacement called for in the accords. Lehmann ended the cable by stating that Thieu "had made a basic decision to trade major parts of territory . . . in order to provide for an effective defense of the remainder . . . It is, in my view, a courageous decision."

The senior RVNAF leadership did not share that view. Knowledge that the abandonment of the Highlands was going badly was already spreading within the South Vietnamese armed forces. Many generals bitterly denounced the botched planning and execution. They blamed Thieu, who in turn was already casting Phu as the scapegoat. Thieu told his staff that Phu had misunderstood his orders, particularly regarding timing— although Thieu's comments to Lehmann contradict that. The II Corps situation, moreover, was not Thieu's only problem. Lieutenant General Truong remained upset about the pullout of the Airborne from I Corps, and many JGS officers were describing the overall situation as hopeless. Some were even advocating Thieu's removal. Opinions that could only be whispered previously were now openly discussed.

For the badly demoralized JGS, the return of Lieutenant General Dong Van Khuyen from Japan on 19 March was the lone bright spot. As South Vietnam's second-in-command and its best staff officer, Khuyen had the knowledge and dedication to right the drifting ship. He immediately sent JGS teams to Tuy Hoa to begin re-organizing and re-arming the II Corps troops. He also quickly formulated plans to help Truong withdraw equipment and men from I Corps Forward. Khuyen, however, was well aware that without major assistance from the Americans, he was only delaying the inevitable. He asked Major General Homer Smith at the DAO to coordinate the replacement of ARVN material losses. Khuyen also persuaded Smith to request once again the long-discussed but never-delivered LST ships.

Smith did not need any prompting. Several days earlier, he had asked the Pentagon to make all South Vietnamese equipment requests currently awaiting fulfillment a top priority. Now, after talking to Khuyen, much like Major General John Murray before him, Smith was virtually begging. Smith wrote a cable on 23 March to Admiral Gayler at CINCPAC relaying Khuyen's concerns and requests: "The morale of the populace and particularly the armed forces, at all levels, is about as low as it can get. . . . Khuyen, with tears in his eyes, told me that something had to be done to at least stabilize RVNAF morale. He stressed that the RVNAF desperately needed some kind of assurance that the U.S. would continue to provide them with material support, and that they also needed B-52 support to help them buy time in order to solve the refugee problem and to get the material situation under control. I told him that I did not believe that reentry of the B-52 raids into the conflict was possible, but that I would ask for some indication of continued support on the material side."[26]

Smith asked Gayler to move beyond just prioritizing South Vietnamese equipment requests and, instead, to begin airlifting in all items apart from tanks. He promised Gayler that he would re-examine all remaining Defense Assistance Vietnam funding to provide the RVNAF "with those items necessary to fight." He pleaded with Gayler to "pull out all stops in moving material . . . even if it requires withdrawing it from U.S. forces." It was a bold, even career-threatening request, yet he staunchly defended it. "In my judgment, that will be necessary. Time has become most precious out here, and unless RVNAF can buy enough time to properly execute their retrograde plans . . . the situation will become desperate." Finishing, he noted again that what Khuyen needed was time. "I hope," Smith ended, "we can find a way to buy him some."

Within hours, Gayler had sent a message to the Chairman of the Joint Chiefs of Staff supporting Smith's requests. In particular, he recommended a presidential statement and the release of the six LSTs that had been delayed by legal wrangling over whether the ships constituted a violation of the Paris Accords. Gayler apparently was unaware that President Ford had just sent a letter to Thieu. Unfortunately, Ford's message to Thieu only contained additional encouragement and vague promises of support. Telling Thieu that "Hanoi's attack represents nothing less than an abrogation by force of the Paris Agreement," Ford stated that the attack was "no less critical" to the U.S. than to South Vietnam. He was "determined that America shall stand firmly behind the Republic of Vietnam at this crucial hour." Ford claimed he was paying "the closest attention and am consulting on an urgent basis with my advisers on actions which the situation may require and the law permit." Most important, "with regard to the provision of adequate military assistance to your armed forces, you can be sure that I shall bend every effort to meet your material needs on the battlefield."[27]

While Thieu still clung to a vain hope that the B-52s would return, aid remained his primary focus. He dispatched to Washington senior dignitaries with close American ties, along with official delegations, in the hope that they might persuade the U.S. Congress to provide money. With a growing number of press reports detailing South Vietnamese military failures, Thieu had to convince the American legislators that providing more aid was not throwing good money after bad. As usual, poor luck played a key role. In particular, there were the repercussions from the accidental killing of Agence France-Presse journalist Paul Leandri by the Saigon police on 18 March. Both Thieu and Vien were upset over reports that the Montagnard RF in Ban Me Thuot had deserted. When Leandri wrote an article claiming that Montagnards from the rebel group FULRO had led Communist troops through the jungle and into Ban Me Thuot, Thieu exploded. The police appeared at Leandri's office and demanded that he reveal his source. When he refused, the Bureau of Immigration told him to report to their office. The implication was that Leandri's visa was to be revoked. While at the bureau, he asked to speak to a superior officer, who was at that moment across the street at the National Police Headquarters. After waiting several hours without seeing anyone, an impatient Leandri jumped into his car and attempted to leave. A trigger-happy guard opened fire, hitting Leandri and killing him. Press reports were immediately filed using this as evidence of the repressive nature of the Thieu government. The news of this incident broke just as two GVN delegations reached Washington.

On 18 March Bui Diem departed for Washington to lobby for more aid. Close on his heels was the South Vietnamese labor leader Tran Quoc Buu. He would join a GVN parliamentary delegation that had left on 13 March. Thieu also sent his former vice prime minister, the former general Tran Van Don, to tour Africa to drum up support for the South Vietnamese. Like Bui Diem, Don had long pressed Thieu to open his government to other nationalists, although Don's definition of "nationalist" was far broader than Thieu's. While the delegations were a major initiative, Thieu was also getting potential opponents out of the way by sending them abroad.

Buu reached Washington first, as Bui Diem had initially stopped in Paris. Buu called on several senators, including Hubert Humphrey (D., Minn.), who promised to support increased aid to South Vietnam. Humphrey then promptly voted against any further aid. On 25 March, Buu met President Ford. Accompanying him were the current South Vietnamese Ambassador, Tran Kim Phuong, and several GVN parliamentary leaders, including Dinh Van De, a Lower House deputy. De was a former ARVN lieutenant colonel who had been the province chief in Tuyen Duc and later Binh Duong. He was elected to the Lower House in 1967, and was currently the chairman of its Defense Committee. In one of the truly bizarre twists of the Vietnam War, Dinh Van De was also a Communist spy. The U.S. Secret Service was completely unaware that the leader of the Free World was sitting across from a man who belonged to a political organization that America had been at war with for the past fifteen years. Fortunately, De's mission was subversion, not assassination. His mission was to describe "the situation in such a way that the U.S. would see that even if they provided mountains of money they still would not be able to rescue a regime that was falling apart."[28]

Phuong began the meeting by telling Ford that Thieu appreciated Ford's letter of 22 March and his efforts with Congress. The president responded that he was sending General Frederick C. Weyand to Vietnam to assess the situation and report back on precisely what military supplies the South Vietnamese needed. Ford also promised to "expedite the military and economic assistance and try to get Congress to make additional funds available."[29] Echoing Major General Smith, Buu concisely summed up South Vietnam's desperation: "Whatever you can do, do it quickly."

Thieu also searched for other means to convince the Americans to assist him. On 22 March, he met with Senate Chairman Tran Van Lam and Speaker of the House Nguyen Ba Can to discuss means to convince the U.S. to grant aid. Lam suggested that he and Can write joint letters to President Ford, Speaker of the House Carl Albert, and Vice President Nelson Rockefeller. Why Lam and Can thought that these letters would be received any differently from the ones they had written in January is unknown.[30] Regardless, Thieu agreed with their idea, and on 24 March, the first letter was sent to Ford. Lam's letter revisited the pledges Kissinger had personally given him at the time of the Paris Accords. He detailed Kissinger's promises that the Russians and Chinese would reduce aid to their ally, that the U.S. would undertake "vigorous and immediate reaction in case North Vietnam launched an offensive," and that the U.S. would "continue substantial military and economic aid."[31] Since none of those promises had been kept, the letter asked Ford to take action to deter the Communist attack while also providing aid.

Thieu also dictated another letter to Ford. The letter was blunt. Outlining the military situation as "very grave and growing worse by the hour," Thieu informed Ford that it "would be extremely difficult for us to contain the advance of the communist forces" without "prompt measures on your part."[32] After reiterating that "we trusted in America's solemn commitment to safeguard the peace in Vietnam," Thieu asked for "a brief but intensive B-52 air strike" against enemy concentrations, and requested that the U.S. "urgently provide us the necessary means to contain and repel the offensive." Ending his letter, Thieu appealed "to the conscience of America" so that "generations of South Vietnamese" will be "free from the horror of North Vietnamese domination." It was all in vain. Thieu and the ARVN troops fighting for their lives would not get the answer they so desperately needed.

THE PUSH TO THE COAST

Although PAVN had destroyed a significant portion of II Corps in the Cheo Reo valley, several Army units and some armor, the majority of the civilians, and a large number of disorganized troops escaped the pocket. The 320th Division's new mission was to hunt down and destroy these fleeing remnants. Working through the night to scrape together any vehicle that could roll, the first column departed Cheo Reo on the morning of 20 March heading east. When it reached the float bridge over the Ba River, A-37 aircraft repeatedly bombed the pursuers, knocking out numerous vehicles and forcing a halt. The VNAF soon destroyed the bridge, but not before the PAVN 64th Regiment, six K-63 APCs, and the 320th Division headquarters had made it across. Although the PAVN engineers worked feverishly to rebuild the destroyed bridge, the rest of the 320th remained stuck on the other side.

The fighting in Cheo Reo, however, was only part of the action roiling the Central Highlands. In Quang Duc, the 24th Ranger Group held firm after beating back a large assault on the district seat of Kien Duc, but the pressure was growing. In Binh Dinh, the ARVN 22nd Division commander had pushed the 41st Regiment against the now-weakened 3rd Division blocking Route 19. Commanded by Colonel Nguyen Thieu (no relation to the president), by 16 March the regiment had moved up to the eastern entrance to the An Khe Pass. However, since the withdrawal from the Highlands had just begun, the 41st and 42nd Regiments pulled back into defensive positions at Binh Khe on Route 19. Meanwhile, the ARVN 47th Regiment continued to secure Route 1 near the Quang Ngai border to prevent the PAVN 52nd Brigade from marching south. The 40th Regiment and Binh Dinh RF were holding the Phu Cat airbase and Route 1 north and south of the provincial capital. Believing that the 22nd Division had stabilized the situation on Route 19, Phu pulled out the 40th Regiment. He allowed Brigadier General Niem to keep one battalion, but Phu sent the rest of the regiment to defend the district town of Khanh Duong on Route 21.

On Route 21, once the PAVN 66th Regiment, 10th Division, had captured the 53rd Regiment base camp at Ban Me Thuot on 17 March, it was assigned thirteen armored vehicles and was ordered to continue east and seize Khanh Duong. The town lies in a flat valley surrounded by high mountains. It was the last blocking position before the critical M'Drak Pass, which is the gateway to the coast. ARVN was using Khanh Duong as a collection point for the many stragglers still streaming out of Ban Me Thuot. Several RF battalions guarded the town, along with multiple tubes of artillery. Normally it was a solid defensive position, but RF morale was shaky from the recent crushing defeats. The two battalions of the 40th Regiment reached Khanh Duong on 19 March. One battalion was deployed several miles northwest of the town, while the other battalion defended Route 21.

At the same time Phu was trying to impede the PAVN advance on Route 21, he was determined to hold two other lines: one at Binh Khe in Binh Dinh province, the other at Cung Son. Holding from Binh Khe through Cung Son to Khanh Duong would enable the South Vietnamese to build a thin but defensible buffer zone to protect the coast. To accomplish that, Phu needed reserves. He ordered all RF/PF soldiers who had escaped from Darlac to be integrated into Khanh Hoa province RF units. The 23rd Division was told to reorganize at an old Special Forces camp on Route 1 just north of Nha Trang. Thieu also ordered the 3rd Airborne Brigade, which was sailing from I Corps down to Saigon, to disembark at Cam Ranh Bay. The ships moored at 1:30 A.M. on 19 March. The Red Berets' mission was to hold the M'Drak Pass and provide a backstop for the 40th Regiment and RF defending Khanh Duong.

It was all that Thieu could give Phu. The VNAF was stretched to the limit. The 2nd Air Division at Phu Cat airbase was supporting the 22nd Division and trying to destroy the Air Force equipment and the mountains of supplies abandoned in the mad rush to leave Pleiku. The 6th Air Division, principally Colonel Le Van Thao's 92nd Wing at Phan Rang, was conducting strikes in various locations. It was supporting the retreating column on Route 7B and the defenders on Route 21, while also trying to destroy the armored vehicles left at Cheo Reo.

Time, however, was what Phu needed most. If he could cobble together even a rudimentary defensive line, Dung would have to leave his divisions in place, preventing them from turning toward Saigon as the Politburo desired. Dung was determined not to allow Phu any breathing room, and he pressed his commanders to advance irrespective of any logistical issues. On all three fronts—Binh Dinh, Route 7B, and Route 21—PAVN units surged forward to deny Phu the time to regroup.

Dung's renewed pressure soon worked. In eastern Binh Dinh, taking away the 40th Regiment created a vacuum for Communist local forces, newly organized into two regiments. They struck hard at RF/PF units on Route 1, and with South Vietnamese morale sagging because of the disasters on Route 7B and in I Corps, the RF crumbled. Within a week, Communist forces had swept away most positions north and south of Qui Nhon, and were threatening the capital itself. The 47th Regiment suddenly found its rear enveloped by enemy forces. The 3rd Division had also snuck a regiment behind the two ARVN regiments at Binh Khe, blocking their retreat and threatening Phu Cat airbase. The only hope now was for the 22nd Division to fight its way to Qui Nhon and set up a new defensive perimeter.

On Route 21, the PAVN 66th Regiment, 10th Division, organized its troops into two spearheads to assault Khanh Duong. One column, with six armored vehicles, positioned itself to strike from the northwest. Another column, with seven tanks, moved along the main highway. On 21 March, the northwestern column launched the first assault, but the 40th Regiment drove it off after VNAF air strikes knocked out several armored vehicles. Not giving up, at dawn on 22 March PAVN resumed the attack. The column from the northwest charged again, and once more lost several vehicles to air strikes. The column along Route 21 attacked, but it was halted by a blown-up bridge. The 66th Regiment commander ordered the northwest prong, now down to one tank and one personnel carrier plus infantry, to again press forward. This time it outflanked the ARVN regulars and drove straight into the city. The RF promptly collapsed. At noon, Phu ordered the 40th Regiment to retreat and defend the western approaches to Nha Trang. A second location on Phu's improvised defensive line had now fallen.

After the blown-up bridge had been fixed, the 10th Division commander, Senior Colonel Ho De, ordered the other spearhead to capture the M'Drak Pass. From its vantage point on the high ground, the 3rd Airborne spotted the Communist troops coming and prepared an artillery ambush. As the enemy column entered a flat area right before the pass, the Airborne opened fire. As shells rained down, several vehicles burst into flames, prompting a quick retreat. PAVN would have to wait until the 10th Division was completely re-assembled before trying again. Finally, an ARVN position on Route 21 had held.

In the meantime, the convoy on Route 7B was struggling onward. Different groups were strung out from the float bridge through Phu Tuc to Cung Son. The lead element—the 6th Rangers and a troop of APCs—had moved on ahead and reached Cung Son on 17 March. However, while they sat doing nothing, three Communist local-force battalions from Phu Yen province raced south from their traditional strongholds in the northern part of the province. Their orders were to block Route 7B, which ran along the northern side of the Ba River, and Local Route 436, which followed the southern side. While these battalions were badly under-strength (each was barely the size of one company), their mission was to block the roads at all costs. Moving quickly, on 17 March one unit seized an important bridge about ten miles west of Tuy Hoa on Route 7B and set up a second block closer to Cung Son. Another battalion dispersed into small units and used rifles, mortars, and rocket-propelled grenades to harass the traffic on Local Route 436. Phu Yen RF troops were ordered to clear the roads, but their efforts were desultory, and they failed.

As the escaping column continued moving east, the next town along the road from Cheo Reo was Phu Tuc. Two days behind the 6th Rangers were the 7th Rangers and the portion of Dong's armor that had escaped with them. Following them were thousands of forlorn civilians and a few small units of the 4th, 22nd, and 23rd Rangers who had cut through the mountains and jungle after the North Vietnamese captured Cheo Reo.

Striking out of nowhere, local guerrillas snuck into Phu Tuc and seized the district headquarters on the evening of 18 March. The 7th Rangers reached the town later that night. Attacking at dawn, the Rangers quickly drove the guerrillas out. However, another problem that should have been fixed earlier had not: the weak bridge at Phu Tuc had not been reinforced. Lieutenant Colonel Tinh's engineers did not have enough materials to improve the bridge, so they had concentrated their efforts instead on fixing the narrow, rutted road between Phu Tuc and Cung Son.

The 7th Rangers moved on, leaving the remaining units of the other three Ranger groups to guard the tanks stuck at Phu Tuc. The armor had no choice but to try to ford the small river. While the water was shallow, both banks were marshy. As the first tank drove down to the water, the steel treads churned up the swampy ground, and it got stuck. Radio calls soon went out for help. The previous day, Brigadier General Nguyen Van Chuc, the commander of the ARVN Engineers, had flown from Saigon to assist Tinh with his efforts. Upon learning of the stuck tank, Chuc ordered steel plates called PSP (pierced steel plating) picked up from the Cung Son airfield and laid across the muddy ground to enable the armor to cross. Two Chinook helicopters carried one thousand pieces of PSP to spread over the boggy stretches. By 20 March, the job was completed. The last elements of the convoy, composed of hundreds of military and civilian vehicles, made it across. According to Pham Huan, "the total number of armored vehicles . . . able to cross the river was six M-48 tanks, sixteen M-41 tanks, and thirteen M-113 armored personnel carriers."[33] If Huan's numbers are correct, then over 70 percent of II Corps's armor had been destroyed or abandoned at Cheo Reo.

The delay at Phu Tuc, meanwhile, enabled Dung's troops to catch up. On 21 March, the PAVN 64th Regiment captured the town. The next day it reached the Ca Lui River and engaged a combined Ranger/armor rear guard using the small river as a blocking position. VNAF fighters were called in, but errant bombing again hit several ARVN tanks and killed many Rangers, enabling the PAVN troops to overrun the rear guard. This was the third costly friendly-fire incident of the campaign—the hit on the 23rd Division command post in Ban Me Thuot, the strike on the 7th Rangers in the Tu Na Pass, and now this. The combination of enemy attack and friendly fire destroyed the last vestiges of the other Ranger groups. On 23 March, the 64th Regiment's lead elements reached Cung Son.

Lieutenant Colonel Tinh, meanwhile, had arrived at Cung Son on the afternoon of 18 March. Chuc and Tinh examined the river and picked a bridge site about six miles east of Cung Son, some three miles west of the original destroyed bridge. Although the engineers had to cut a fifty-yard path down a steep bank to the water, the river here was wide and the water was low with a slow-moving current. The area also had a large, flat, treeless section that could serve as a parking lot.

What Tinh did not realize was that the river bottom was very sandy. Vehicles attempting to drive across the river quickly bogged down. The next morning, while the engineers began erecting the bridge, a sergeant used a bulldozer and began towing vehicles across. By the afternoon of 20 March, about three hundred vehicles had traversed the river and arrived at a village near Local Route 436, where they were halted by the Communist roadblock further east.

Despite the pressing need for helicopters, maintenance issues with the few remaining Chinooks prevented Chuc from receiving more than ten sorties per day. Using the Chinooks to fix the ford at Phu Tuc also reduced the number of sorties to the Ba River. Because of the river's width, the bridge company ran out of floats. Although Phu's original plan was to use PSP plates to line the river bottom at Cung Son, nothing had been done. Chuc ordered the engineers to dismantle all the PSP plates from the Cung Son airfield and bring additional ones from storage facilities at Cam Ranh. With only a few operational Chinooks shuttling material, however, it took five precious days to build the bridge across the three-hundred-yard-wide river. Time, never on Phu's side, was perilously close to running out.

Journalist Nguyen Tu, who had been picked up by a helicopter near Cheo Reo, rejoined the column at Cung Son and continued to file reports on the evacuation. His description of the refugees' continuing misery was heartbreaking. "Sometimes one sees a few civilians walking down the road from Kontum, Pleiku, and the hell that is Cheo Reo. . . . These refugees, struggling down the road, now have nothing left but the dusty, sweat-soaked clothes on their backs. Their feet are swollen and their eyes are life-less and devoid of hope. Small children, from twelve years old down to four, struggle along behind, their feet swollen and cracked, and dust the only medicine covering the soles of their feet."[34] Based on Tu's reports, people in Saigon began to call the retreat "The Road of Blood and Tears."

While waiting for the second bridge to be built, an estimated one hundred thousand people and approximately three thousand military and civilian vehicles began bunching up at the Ba River. The people sat on the river bank, starving and thirsty. Families had become separated, and many people had died in traffic accidents—collisions, vehicle rollovers, and pedestrians hit by wild drivers. Others had died crossing streams or had gotten lost in the forest. Phu ordered the VNAF to send helicopters to begin shuttling food to the stranded refugees, and to airlift them to Tuy Hoa if possible. Although some pilots stopped to pick up women and children, the elderly, or the injured, others were not so caring. Fearful of the Communist gunners, they simply dropped the rations and flew away. By 22 March, although several thousand people had arrived in Tuy Hoa, either on foot or by helicopter, it was a drop in the bucket. Catholic priests in Tuy Hoa and Nha Trang worked feverishly to supplement the Army's resupply efforts, but there were too many mouths to feed. In particular, the lack of water caused many deaths among the children. The enormousness of the crisis simply overwhelmed GVN efforts to shelter and feed the population.

Despite the many difficulties, the bridge was finally completed at 9:30 A.M. on 23 March. As the first civilian vehicles madly raced to enter the slot cut into the steep river bank, so many vehicles jammed onto the floats that the bridge collapsed. Soon thereafter, Communist mortar rounds struck the crowd, killing and wounding almost one hundred civilians. That night, the weather turned cold and rainy, adding to the misery. The next morning, high water and a fast current halted further efforts to wade across. Despite these problems, by the end of the day, over one thousand vehicles, mostly military, had crossed. More traversed that night. By 10:00 A.M. on 24 March, the 6th Ranger commander reported that all military vehicles were across.

Now the column faced another problem. The Communists still blocked Local Route 436. Civilian vehicles crossing the bridge were halted until the block could be cleared. Since the enemy troops had seized old but well-built Korean fortifications, Phu ordered Colonel Thao's 92nd Wing to drop napalm to help clear the road. Brigadier General Cam begged one of the few II Corps units still maintaining integrity, the elite reconnaissance teams of the Vietnamese Special Forces known as the *Loi Ho*, or "Thunder Tigers," to help destroy the enemy positions. The *Loi Ho*, who had already bypassed the roadblock and were walking with their families, refused to leave their loved ones. A compromise was soon reached. VNAF helicopters ferried the *Loi Ho* families to Tuy Hoa, whereupon the elite soldiers turned around and, in conjunction with Thao's air strikes, quickly destroyed the roadblock.

Although the column soon began moving again, a third Communist unit blocked the road closer to Tuy Hoa. The 34th Ranger Battalion was pulled out of the bridge site to break the roadblock. It launched several assaults but failed. Phu personally flew in to help command the attack. He landed at Tuy Hoa and ordered the M-113 troop, which had accompanied the lead Rangers down Route 7B and had just arrived in the city by driving around the roadblocks, to turn back and attack from the opposite direction. The soldiers refused. To get them to return, Phu promoted all officers and men one rank. After several hours of fierce fighting, the combination of the Rangers pressing from one side and the M-113s from the other eliminated the last roadblock. The first vehicles from the convoy drove into Tuy Hoa on the afternoon of 25 March.

The delay in clearing the road had kept most of the civilians stuck on the other side. Late on 23 March, the PAVN 64th Regiment reached Cung Son and linked up with Phu Yen local forces. Since the PAVN engineers had not yet fixed the first float bridge, the 64th Regiment had only its own infantry weapons, two heavy 120-mm mortars, and six K-63 APCs for support. The Ranger rear guard was reinforced by tanks and a few artillery pieces. Consequently, PAVN Senior Colonel Kim Tuan determined that he could not make a successful attack until the remainder of his division arrived. Tuan would risk his men against the defenders only if it appeared that the ARVN troops were about to escape.

At about 4:00 P.M. on 24 March, the regiment's reconnaissance troops saw the Rangers and remaining armor leave their positions and line up on the road, apparently to move to the bridge site. The reconnaissance troops were correct. With most of the military vehicles across, the 6th Ranger commander ordered a portion of the rear guard to pull out and proceed to the crossing.

Senior Colonel Tuan instantly told the 64th Regiment and Phu Yen local forces to attack. Luckily for him, the first rounds from the 120-mm mortars landed in the middle of the road formation. Confusion reigned as the Rangers and their vehicles scattered in every direction. PAVN anti-tank teams crept in close to the armored vehicles. Firing at point-blank range, they knocked out five tanks. The remaining armor escaped to a small hill east of Cung Son. Unfortunately, it was right next to the Communist local-force position. The Communist commander sent his men with anti-tank rockets to attack. Within thirty minutes the few ARVN tanks and armored vehicles that had escaped the Cheo Reo pocket were either burning or captured. Concurrently, the Communist local forces hit the pontoon bridge with mortars and destroyed a number of trucks. Panicky civilians raced around to escape the enemy fire. By late afternoon on 24 March, the last pockets of resistance were eliminated. Disorganized Rangers fled down to the bridge site. Both soldiers and civilians attempted to wade across. When the water proved too deep, many tried to swim, but the strong current swept away hundreds.

Just as the disaster at Cheo Reo could have been prevented with better planning, the failure at Cung Son could also have been avoided. First, General Vien, aware of the impending retreat, should have re-directed the 7th Rangers from Pleiku to Tuy Hoa to secure the roads and the bridge site. Second, Phu should have immediately dispatched the bridge company in Nha Trang to the ford. Third, the lackluster performance of the Phu Yen RF in attempting to break through the Communist roadblocks badly delayed the vehicles that got across the river. The combination doomed significant numbers of those who had escaped Cheo Reo.

Oddly, the Communists' official histories neglect any discussion of their troops' actions at the bridge site. Despite the PAVN victory on 24 March, South Vietnamese vehicles and civilians continued to cross the bridge the next day. It is uncertain when PAVN troops secured the bridge site. The North Vietnamese accounts simply jump from the victory at Cung Son to the attack on Tuy Hoa on 1 April. It is a strange omission. ARVN officers interviewed for this book claim that the Communists shelled the bridge area on 25 March, killing hundreds of people. One U.S. Embassy report seems to corroborate that. On 26 March, the Embassy reported that the "river crossing was heavily shelled by communist mortar fire," leaving "over one thousand burning vehicles at the river crossing."[35] What happened at the bridge on 25 and 26 March remains shadowy.

By the end of the evacuation on 28 March, an estimated forty thousand civilians had reached Tuy Hoa, along with numerous vehicles. If one adds the twenty thousand civilians captured at Cheo Reo to the hundred thousand at the bridge site, then only one in three civilians made it to Tuy Hoa. How many civilians died along Route 7B is unknowable, but it was certainly thousands. Military casualties were also heavy. Most South Vietnamese accounts indicate that barely nine hundred Rangers out of approximately eleven thousand escaped. Colonel Ly estimated that five thousand out of twenty thousand ARVN support troops reached Tuy Hoa. Only portions of the 6th and 7th Ranger Groups would be reconstituted to fight again. All of the II Corps's armor was lost save the one troop of M-113s. Six artillery battalions were destroyed, with many of the guns falling into North Vietnamese hands. Several thousand vehicles were captured, plus tons of supplies and repair facilities. The North Vietnamese state they killed 755 ARVN troops and captured 13,570 at Cheo Reo. Roughly three hundred more ARVN troops were killed and a thousand captured along Route 7B. PAVN claims that another two thousand South Vietnamese soldiers out of roughly six thousand were either killed or captured at Cung Son. Thus, approximately eighteen thousand ARVN troops were killed or captured from Cheo Reo to Tuy Hoa, and about six thousand made it to friendly lines, or one in four. By any measure, it was the second worst South Vietnamese defeat of the war. Only the debacle in I Corps dwarfed the horror that was "The Road of Blood and Tears."[36]

10

"CHAOS AND DISINTEGRATION"

SURROUNDING SAIGON

While the South Vietnamese positions in the Central Highlands were collapsing, the Communists were attacking in other regions to support the main battlefield. The area around Saigon was especially critical, as the capital was the eventual target. After the long Politburo meeting ended on 6 January, Colonel General Tran Van Tra hurriedly returned to South Vietnam to revise Phase Two of his 1975 dry-season campaign. The Phase One attacks in December 1974–January 1975 had captured Phuoc Long and portions of the Delta. While individually the Communist gains in the early dry-season battles were relatively minor, taken as a whole they constituted a huge blow to the psychologically fragile South Vietnamese.

Another important victory in Tay Ninh soon followed. On 6 January, PAVN seized Ba Den Mountain, a three-thousand-foot conical peak rising from the plain near Tay Ninh City. The high ground dominates the city and provided the RVNAF with an important communication and observation station. Since Tay Ninh province was long considered the main invasion route to Saigon, the mountain's loss was a serious setback. Worse was the compromise of ARVN codes from the capture of the communication center. As with the stolen ARVN codes in II Corps, the North Vietnamese "were able to utilize the secret codes [cryptological material] we captured there in our battle against the enemy right up until the last day when we won complete victory."[1]

After many long years of war, Tra believed that his time had finally come. He thought that the South Vietnamese were weak, and that the Phuoc Long victory had exposed ARVN's inability to reinforce remote areas. Even if the South Vietnamese had the reserves to mount relief missions, they no longer had the airlift capacity to move them. RVNAF firepower was also dramatically reduced. Artillery shells were rationed, and PAVN's multi-layered air defenses were hampering the VNAF's ability to conduct air strikes. More important, the lack of a U.S response to the fall of Phuoc Long confirmed for the North Vietnamese planners that the American tiger was indeed toothless.

After the Phuoc Long victory, and to the surprise of no one on the PAVN General Staff, Tra once again pleaded for more troops to attack Saigon. For two years he had begged for more divisions, but the General Staff always refused. It did not want to risk the strategic reserves in a large-scale assault against the well-defended city. Tra and Pham Hung had lobbied hard at the October and December 1974 Politburo meetings for additional troops and supplies, but Van Tien Dung had resisted his southern colleagues' demands. Not surprisingly, he preferred to reinforce the Central High-lands attack. But Tra would not be swayed from his dream of leading his troops into Saigon and conquering the South on his own. He sarcastically responded that the assignment of such a large force to the Ban Me Thuot operation would "surely guarantee victory," impugning the General Staff's and Dung's allocation of troops. Overall, Tra believed that the Politburo's war strategy was too cautious, and that any plan that did not include a bold strike at Saigon was misguided. He believed he could take Saigon now, but he needed three or four more divisions to do it, if only the parsimonious General Staff would provide them.

Soon after the Ban Me Thuot attack plan was finalized, Giap moved to end the bickering between his two ambitious subordinates. While he dif-fered with Tra in terms of timing and the proper use of PAVN resources, he agreed that Saigon should be attacked sooner rather than later. As part of Giap's 1975 strategy, however, Tra's first missions were limited. He was to launch large-scale assaults in III Corps simultaneously with the Ban Me Thuot assault, tie down ARVN forces, and create secure base areas close to Saigon. Those bases would be used for an eventual thrust at the South Vietnamese capital.

To help him carry out these new tasks, Giap sent Tra one strategic-reserve unit, the 341st Division. Since this outfit was not earmarked for the Ban Me Thuot attack, Giap was able to appease Tra—and Tra's power-ful mentors, Le Duc Tho and Le Duan—while avoiding any conflict with Dung. On 20 January the 341st Division commander, Senior Colonel Tran Van Tran, received a cable directing him to report immediately to Giap in Hanoi. When Tran arrived on 25 January, Giap's instructions were simple: Cease training and prepare to move south; complete all arrangements to depart by 10 February; have the first unit moving by 15 February.[2]

After Phuoc Long fell on 6 January, Pham Hung and Tran Van Tra real-ized the victory made their earlier plans obsolete. Cabling COSVN from Hanoi, Hung told his staff that "through the progress of Phase One of the dry-season campaign we can see even more clearly the extent of the ene-my's decline on the military, political, and diplomatic fronts, and we can see that the level of victories we have achieved has in many places exceeded the goals that we had set. . . . With respect to the goals for the dry season, we need to readjust them . . . to the actual situation."[3]

Leaving Hanoi, Tra arrived back at his headquarters along the Cambo-dian border in Tay Ninh province on 3 February. He immediately called together his various staffs to modify the Phase Two plan. He devoted particular attention to creating an attack model that would prevent ARVN forces from withdrawing into defensive "enclaves" in the southern half of South Vietnam. In his memoir, Tra repeatedly refers to General Gavin's enclave design. It worried him and many other senior Communist leaders, since a retreat into well-defended redoubts would indefinitely prolong the war. To prevent this, Tra needed new tactics. He did not want his forces to make frontal assaults, because "it was necessary not to push the enemy back from one line of resistance to another."[4] For this reason, Tra took "steps to prevent the enemy from creating solid lines of defense and had gradually eliminated the possibility that they could form an enclave in Saigon . . . by isolating it from the surrounding areas so that [ARVN] forces could not be withdrawn into Saigon . . . [and] so that there could be no reinforcements or way out."

In essence, Tra wanted to cut Saigon off from the surrounding countryside by blocking the roads in all four directions on the capital's periphery— far enough away to avoid heavy combat yet still close enough to isolate the city. Although Tra had long planned a five-pronged assault against Saigon, he did not have the combat strength to launch a direct attack. So he had chosen a different path. Commencing in 1974, he sought to soften up Saigon's outer defenses through a series of battles and his own organizational restructurings. While at times the combat that year had been extremely heavy, his success was limited. He had refrained from committing his entire force to an all-out offensive, reined in by the General Staff, by the disparity of forces, and by his own supply situation. Now with ARVN weakening, Tra tossed away his original dry-season plans in favor of a series of concurrent attacks on the capital's periphery. If these attacks were successful, he believed, the real battle for Saigon could begin.

In creating his new campaign plan, he adopted the philosophy of the ancient Chinese strategist Sun Tzu. Tra fancied himself a Sun Tzu disciple, and he believed he could achieve his goals by copying Sun Tzu's tactic of the indirect approach. His main concept was to avoid heavy losses to his main-force units by attacking important district towns guarded by the less effective RF troops, rather than large cities or bases defended by regular ARVN soldiers. He wrote: "we had to flexibly maintain the initiative so that we would not get caught up in a tug of war between ourselves and the enemy," since he knew that ARVN would defend this area "to the end." His intent was "to take steps and carry out schemes to disperse the enemy, deceive the enemy and prevent it from discerning our intentions, so we could launch surprise attacks and win certain victories." Tra wanted to wear down ARVN by "launching surprise attacks . . . in places very advantageous to us without having to clash with the enemy in places vitally important to them, while at the same time deploying our forces so that we could launch an offensive when necessary." His intent was a vigorous adaptation of a principle the Vietnamese call *tao the* ("creating a position," or what U.S. military strategists call "shaping the battlefield"). These maneuvers would set the stage for even larger attacks. The ultimate result for ARVN, he claimed, "would be chaos and disintegration."[5]

Tra's new attack strategy for the B-2 Front was both bold and arguably as well-crafted as the Highlands campaign, although in many ways it duplicated the 1968 Tet attack missions. After finalizing the design, in late February Tra called together his military commanders to explain the new mission: They would conduct attacks in sectors surrounding Saigon concurrent with the PAVN strike against Ban Me Thuot. The B-2 plan condensed all the 1975 goals for Phases Two and Three together into a new Phase Two. Tra told his commanders that if Communist forces were victorious in the Central Highlands, the situation could change rapidly, and a strategic opportunity might arise. He wanted to be ready if it did.

If the situation developed more slowly, his secondary objectives would be to link the separate "liberated" areas into contiguous zones, destroy a portion of ARVN's military manpower, and prepare secure areas for future assaults. Tra's complex strategy entailed attacks ranging throughout the vast expanse of the B-2 Front, which stretched from the southern rim of the Highlands to the tip of the Delta. The chief blows would be struck by PAVN main-force regulars. In the Communists' Military Region 8 (the northern Delta), the goal was to isolate Saigon from the rice-rich upper Delta by cutting Route 4 and seizing the surrounding countryside. MR-8's newly formed 8th Division and the new 303rd Division would create a contiguous liberated zone from southern Tay Ninh and the Angel's Wing area in Cambodia to the Plain of Reeds in Long An province. Military Region 9 (the southern Delta) would focus on disrupting operations at the large airbase at Can Tho and seizing territory.

Military Region 6, the sparsely populated and long-neglected northern edge of B-2, was also given a significant role in Tra's new plan. The PAVN strategists wanted MR-6 to destroy all ARVN positions from Binh Tuy province on the coast to Lam Dong and Tuyen Duc provinces in the middle of South Vietnam. For the resource-starved MR-6 commanders, clearing such a large area was problematic at best. Still, they dutifully sent their only main-force unit, the 812th Regiment, to carry out its first Phase Two mission: seize the important rice-growing district of Hoai Duc in the remote northeastern part of Binh Tuy province, the area adjacent to the recently captured Tanh Linh district capital.

The heart of the B-2 Front was MR-7, which covered most of III Corps; it would be the scene of the heaviest fighting. The recently formed PAVN 4th Corps would play the key role in this new offensive. Commanded by Major General Hoang Cam, it comprised the 7th and 9th Divisions, along with supporting armor, artillery, sapper, and rear-service units. Tra decided to split the corps in two, sending the two halves to operate in different sectors. The first sector was northwest of Saigon, in Binh Long, Binh Duong, and Tay Ninh provinces. The 9th Division would handle this area, initially attacking the critical Tri Tam district headquarters near Tay Ninh City. The second area was a large zone northeast of Saigon, from Route 20 north through Lam Dong province to Dalat, and from Long Khanh province along Route 1 into Binh Tuy province. The 7th Division, in coordination with the recently activated 6th Division, was assigned responsibility for the northeastern sector. The 7th would seize Lam Dong and Tuyen Duc provinces, while the 6th would strike in Long Khanh and Binh Tuy provinces. Once the 812th Regiment had captured Hoai Duc, it would turn west to assist the 7th Division.

Another important decision was announced at the late February conference: the formation of a second corps in the B-2 Front. The new corps-level unit was made up of the 5th and 303rd Infantry Divisions, plus supporting combat specialty units. Major General Nguyen Minh Chau initially commanded the new corps, called Group 232.[6] His mission was to launch an offensive to the south and west of Saigon. The 8th Division would strike in heavily populated Dinh Tuong province in the Delta. The 303rd would attack from the west and destroy the well-entrenched ARVN territorial forces from the Cambodian border east to the Vam Co Dong River. The 5th Division—minus its 3rd Regiment, which was attached to the 303rd for this campaign—would not participate. The 5th had been devastated by heavy losses in the December 1974 attacks and was busy training over a thousand new replacements.

The South Vietnamese, meanwhile, were making moves to shore up their defenses in the critical region around Saigon. After the loss of Phuoc Long, the III Corps commander, Lieutenant General Du Quoc Dong, resigned. His replacement, named on 4 February 1975, was Lieutenant General Nguyen Van Toan, the Armor School commandant and former II Corps commander. Toan had been fired for corruption in November 1974 and replaced with Major General Phu. It was rumored in Saigon that, in spite of the corruption charges and other gossip that dogged Toan, Ambassador Martin had strongly recommended him to President Thieu. Whether that was true or not, the appointment was logical, since Toan had developed into one of the better ARVN tacticians.

Born on 6 October 1932 in Thua Thien province, Toan went to school in Hue. In 1951 he joined the Army and attended one of the first classes at Dalat, South Vietnam's West Point. After his initial training, he went to armor school in France, and he remained an armor officer his entire career. He served mainly in his native I Corps area, and in 1967 he assumed command of the ARVN 2nd Division. Toan's lifestyle was radically different from the antiseptic revolutionary life led by Tra and his jungle-bound comrades. Toan was a boisterous, heavyset man who enjoyed the perks of high rank. In particular, he had a well-known weakness for wine and women. In early 1972, while still commanding the 2nd Division, he was charged with raping a young girl in the officers' club, but the charges were dismissed.[7] Despite the rape charge and a deserved reputation for corruption, he was appointed to the II Corps command in 1972, mainly because of his ability to work well with the U.S. advisors; his career to that point had been largely undistinguished. Nonetheless, he surprised many observers by his tough and determined campaigning during the Easter Offensive. Regardless of his extracurricular activities, by 1974 he had achieved, in the opinion of Colonel Le Gro, "a deserved reputation as a forceful, if not brilliant field commander . . . [who] employed his forces with considerable skill."[8]

Toan's military style was the polar opposite of Tra's. If Tra's approach in the post-ceasefire period was the crafty maneuver for position, Toan was the poster boy for the American operational method. In II Corps he had constantly moved units to achieve local superiority against PAVN concentrations, and then shifted his units by air to the next hot spot. It was his main tactical principle, one he had honed to great effectiveness in 1973–74, when he rapidly shuttled units about the vast Central Highlands, reacting to one attack after another. Whether he could achieve a similar success in III Corps, given the more powerful PAVN forces and the restrictions on the use of helicopters, was a question no one asked. However, Thieu picked corps commanders on the basis of their loyalty as well as their ability, and there was no questioning Toan's loyalty to Thieu.

Toan, it turned out, had few qualms about his new assignment, or about whether what had worked so successfully in a different environment in II Corps could be effectively transplanted. Toan was the third III Corps commander in six months, and he instantly recognized the seriousness of the situation. With typical gusto, he set about redeploying his regular units from a static defense. Toan wanted to free his divisions from territorial responsibility in order to regain the full mobility he believed so necessary to successfully defend against an enemy able to mass and achieve numerical superiority. While ARVN divisions since 1970 were no longer responsible for protecting a specific area, after the ceasefire they still had the secondary role of supporting RF forces in securing territory. With the departure of American air support and the aid cutbacks, ARVN mobility had sharply decreased in the last two years, and the divisions once again had assumed more of a fixed posture.

With his reduced resources, Toan had to design a more efficient scheme to protect vital points like Tay Ninh, regain territory recently captured by the enemy, and defend Saigon in the event of a major offensive. While Toan's options were limited, he quickly sent out new orders: the 25th Division, formerly responsible for defending Tay Ninh and Hau Nghia provinces, would now focus solely on Tay Ninh. The defense of Hau Nghia province was turned over to the RF/PF. Hau Nghia provincial troops had fought extremely well in 1972, and were considered among the best in South Vietnam. The 5th Division would concentrate on the area north of Saigon, the main avenue of attack during the Tet Offensive in 1968. The 18th would deploy one regiment to Xuan Loc and one regiment to Tanh Linh/Hoai Duc, leaving one regiment free for immediate corps reserve. The 3rd Armored Cavalry Brigade was put on permanent alert as a strike force and general corps reserve, ready to "intervene anywhere."[9]

Toan needed to reconfigure the corps quickly, since U.S. intelligence had picked up ominous indicators of new Communist attacks in March. The Americans' analysis of Tra's plan was nearly perfect. Le Gro wrote: "Main force units are continuing preparations for major attacks, with the principal communist concentrations in Tay Ninh and Long Khanh Provinces. In Tay Ninh, the major goal is reportedly to either overrun or isolate Tay Ninh City. Intermediate objectives may be Tri Tam and outlying GVN positions around the provincial capital. A Communist force structure of 10 to 11 regiments, supported by armor and artillery, could be committed. . . . A Communist attack at Tri Tam could result in its loss."[10]

The accuracy of Le Gro's analysis was even more remarkable given the lengths to which the Communists had gone to hide their plans. At the end of a mid-February COSVN conference, Pham Hung ordered all echelons to carry out this new strategy in the strictest secrecy. Planning was held so tightly that even after attending the conference, the 4th Corps commander was unaware of the full scope of B-2's strategy. Hoang Cam wrote: "We did not know the date and time of the offensive or the specific supporting sectors because during this period the maintenance of secrecy was of paramount importance." All Cam knew was that "the operations of 4th Corps were part of a coordinated plan which also involved [all the other regions of South Vietnam]. We knew these operations were part of the 1975 strategic offensive plan approved by the Politburo, [and] the COSVN Military Headquarters had drafted a detailed plan to carry out its portion of the over-all plan in the B-2 theater of operations."[11] In spite of Hung's admonitions, U.S. intelligence quickly determined most of the likely avenues and locations for attacks.

Using this information, ARVN launched spoiling attacks in each of the divisional sectors in III Corps during the first week of March. Despite these sweep operations, Toan's realignment of forces, and the outstanding U.S. intelligence analysis, the Communists' preparations were mostly unaffected. In the sector northwest of Saigon, Hung and Tra's plans called for twin attacks to cut off and envelop Tay Ninh City. Hoang Cam controlled the northern pincer, while Group 232's commander, Nguyen Minh Chau, directed operations in the area south of Tay Ninh City. Their deputies would direct the other two fronts, Long Khanh and Dinh Tuong.

In the north, the 9th Division, with its 1st, 2nd, and 3rd Regiments, would seize the district capital of Tri Tam, located on Local Route 239 on the edge of the vast Michelin rubber plantation.[12] It would then clear away RF positions east to the Saigon River. COSVN picked Tri Tam rather than An Loc or Chon Thanh because the town was defended by RF troops, while battle-hardened Ranger units defended the other two locations. COSVN also hoped that the capture of Tri Tam would further isolate An Loc and Chon Thanh, and even lead to their abandonment. The southern PAVN pincer, the 303rd Division, would take the district town of Ben Cau and clear away all South Vietnamese regional outposts from the Cambodian border east to the Vam Co Dong River. Three Tay Ninh province local-force battalions would sever Local Route 22 (the road from Route 1 into Tay Ninh City), to prevent ARVN from using the road either for reinforcements or as an escape route. If successful, the pincers would capture two district seats and a large portion of the province. Tay Ninh City, a place of great symbolic importance to the GVN, would be surrounded.

COSVN had distinct reasons for picking these areas. Tri Tam was an important local road junction near Local Route 22. Whoever held it could block movement from Tay Ninh east into Binh Duong province, or south along the river to the Iron Triangle north of Cu Chi. The smaller town of Ben Cau also occupied an important crossroads. Its location along the only passable roads in the local swampy terrain enabled it to dominate the area. ARVN also realized the importance of these district towns. Although only RF battalions and Popular Force platoons defended Tri Tam and Ben Cau, each had solid fortifications with interlocking fields of fire and multiple defensive layers. Because of its location, Tri Tam had the strongest defenses. Three RF battalions and nine PF platoons defended dozens of outposts and blocking positions along the roads and into the countryside. Overall, both were important South Vietnamese resistance points.

Following Tra's plan, a powerful force made up of the 9th Division reinforced by the independent 16th Infantry Regiment, several tank companies, two anti-aircraft battalions, and a dozen artillery pieces, including three of the deadly 130-mm guns, soon began gathering north of Tri Tam. On 10 March (concurrent with the first attack on Ban Me Thuot in II Corps), the three Tay Ninh local-force battalions struck the first blow. They launched ground attacks along the length of Local Route 22 from the junction at Go Dau Ha (where Routes 1 and 22 met south of the provincial capital) almost to Tay Ninh City. While the RF repulsed them in most places, the Communists seized a section of the road near the provincial capital and held it for several days.

With the roadblock in place, the next strike was at Tri Tam. At 5:00 A.M. on 11 March, two 9th Division regiments launched the main assault. Although they penetrated the outer defensive lines, the RF troops put up fierce resistance. Despite three tank-led attacks, the RF troops, backed by heavy artillery fire, held their ground. The RF even resorted to flooding the nearby fields to slow the PAVN tanks.

The stiff RF opposition shocked the 9th Division troops, and the PAVN regulars were forced to pull back. The next morning, however, they launched a stronger wave of attacks. According to the 9th Division's his-

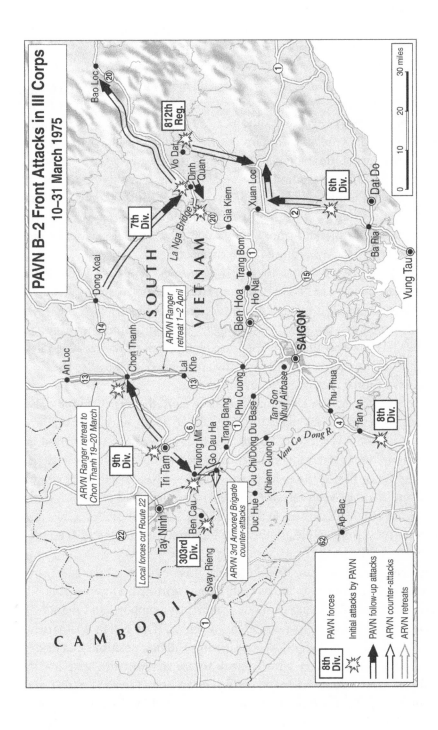

PAVN B-2 Front Attacks in III Corps
10-31 March 1975

tory, "our soldiers fought the enemy for every house and every mound of dirt. The division sent in additional tanks . . . and 85-mm guns forward to provide direct fire support to the infantry. At the same time the division used the attached corps artillery to suppress the fire of the enemy artillery positions. . . . By 9:00 A.M. our troops had captured the communications compound and used explosives to destroy the underground bunker there, the enemy's final defensive position. . . . The soldiers of 2nd Regiment raised [their] flag over the Tri Tam District Military Headquarters at 9:40 A.M. In the area of the triangular fort, enemy troops supported by armored vehicles and artillery continued to resist. On the morning of 13 March, after receiving additional reinforcements . . . 2nd Regiment launched a new attack that overran . . . [the final] concentration of enemy troops. . . . All enemy troops in the area, more than 2,000 men, were destroyed or dispersed on the spot. We captured 929 prisoners."[13]

Despite the PAVN boasts, losses on both sides were heavy. The South Vietnamese claimed ten tanks destroyed and hundreds of North Vietnamese soldiers killed and wounded. However, half of the Tri Tam defenders were either killed, captured, or missing. A thousand others managed to escape. Tri Tam was the fifth district capital to fall in the last five days. Located only twenty-seven miles northwest of Saigon, it was also the closest district capital to Saigon that had been lost.

Shortly after the 9th Division made its assault, the 303rd Division also attacked. The 303rd was made up of the 201st, 205th, and 271st Infantry Regiments, and was reinforced by the 3rd Infantry Regiment, 5th Division, an anti-aircraft battalion, and seven captured armored vehicles. Like Tri Tam, however, Ben Cau was no pushover. ARVN had heavily fortified the area, and the flat, open terrain, cut by many canals and streams, greatly assisted the defenders. The Regional Forces stationed at Ben Cau were six hundred strong, while another five hundred men protected the outer perimeter of the town.

At dawn on 12 March, PAVN artillery fired a concentrated barrage at Ben Cau. Communist infantry then surged forward. However, the RF soldiers fought back using close-air and artillery support, and the PAVN troops were unable to penetrate the defenses. The North Vietnamese pulled back to focus their efforts on clearing outlying positions and bringing their 85-mm artillery guns forward to use as direct-fire weapons. By 2:00 P.M., several South Vietnamese PF platoons were forced to retreat, and the noose tightened around Ben Cau. At 5:00 P.M., PAVN artillery let loose with another heavy volley against the village, and the Communist troops once more charged forward. Again they failed to dislodge the valiant RF. Describing the action, the 303rd's history notes: "The enemy put up an insane resistance. Enemy artillery savagely pounded our troop formations, and infantry launched death-defying counterattacks. When it became completely dark, all elements were forced to temporarily suspend their attacks."[14] The 303rd's assaults on 13 March had been stopped in their tracks by effective fire support and the hard-fighting RF.

Faced with these setbacks, on the night of 13 March, the 303rd commander was forced to rethink his strategy: "In all . . . assigned sectors our units captured a number of outposts and killed or captured enemy troops, but they were not able to overrun the main targets. Faced with the realities of this situation, the division command group met with the regimental commanders . . . and decided that each sector would leave behind enough forces to surround and pressure the enemy while the bulk of the division withdrew to the rear to study its experiences and receive replacements and resupply for the next round of combat."[15]

On the morning of 14 March, the 303rd mounted a fourth wave of attacks against Ben Cau and the outposts on Route 1. Superior numbers and firepower finally wore down the beleaguered defenders, and by late afternoon the 303rd controlled Ben Cau. Fighting throughout the night, North Vietnamese troops cleared the last RF outposts in their areas. After three days of brutal fighting, "The division's mission during the first phase of the campaign was completed. The enemy bases from the western banks of the Vam Co Dong River to the Vietnamese–Cambodian border were crushed. A wide expanse of land from [Tay Ninh] down to the Mekong Delta was liberated."[16]

After analyzing these initial attacks, Lieutenant General Toan concluded that the Communists intended either to take Tay Ninh City or to cut it off by connecting the two pincers at the important road junction of Go Dau Ha and capturing it. Toan was forced to choose one of two options regarding the province: pull the 25th Division, his only regular unit in the immediate area, out of Tay Ninh City in order to launch an attack to recover the lost district positions—thereby leaving the city defenseless and risking its loss—or mass his forces to defend the city.

Toan chose the city. He deployed the 25th's three infantry regiments, the 46th, 49th, and 50th, around the town. He also assigned a company from the 81st Airborne Rangers to protect the city proper. Yet Toan was not totally boxed in. His earlier shuffling of his units had provided him some flexibility. Nor would he sit idly by and watch PAVN troops destroy two key defensive networks. The fire support provided to the besieged RF at Tri Tam and Ben Cau was, according to DAO reports, massive. During the week from 8 to 14 March, ARVN artillery fired almost 26,000 rounds and the VNAF flew 320 attack sorties in III Corps, losing one A-37 to an SA-7 anti-aircraft missile on 12 March. Besides fire support, Toan also committed his corps reserves to meet the threat to Tay Ninh province. On 11 March, Toan directed the 3rd Armored Cavalry Brigade and the 33rd Ranger Group to shift immediately to Go Dau Ha to hold that important road junction. Toan also assigned one battalion from the 7th Regiment, 5th Division, to the 3rd Armored. Brigadier General Tran Quang Khoi's combined force of tanks, Rangers, and infantry would counterattack, with the ultimate objective of retaking Tri Tam. Toan also detached the 48th Infantry Regiment from the 18th Division and lifted it by helicopter to Go Dau Ha. Its mission was to clear Route 1 toward Cambodia.

All these maneuvers were typical Toan: he inserted his corps reserve, stripped less heavily engaged units to deal with a sudden threat, and cross-attached units as necessary. While his moves were a decisive response to a multi-division attack on the western flank, they badly weakened eastern III Corps just as the second, perhaps more important phase of the 4th Corps's attacks was beginning. On the other hand, Toan had few options: the South Vietnamese had virtually no reserves anywhere in the country, and the Tay Ninh area was always viewed as the primary springboard for any major Communist attack on Saigon. Consequently, Toan had decided to use his reserves in the Tay Ninh area and hope for the best in the northeastern sector.

In that sector, Tran Van Tra sought to erode GVN control in Long Khanh province, capture Route 20, and pin down the ARVN 18th Division to prevent its deployment elsewhere in III Corps. His overall goal was to create a "liberated barrier" along the border of II and III Corps. The toughest mission, taking Route 20, fell to the 7th Division. Route 20 ran from Route 1 in Long Khanh province north through Lam Dong province to Dalat. In early February the 7th Division, made up of the 141st, 165th, and 209th Infantry Regiments, was ordered to scout the village of Dinh Quan on Route 20. Dinh Quan was a district capital located fourteen miles northwest of Xuan Loc, and was an important link in the road's defenses. Once it was taken, the 7th would simultaneously attack in opposite directions along Route 20: to the southwest to seize the critical bridge over the nearby La Nga River, and to the northeast to capture Dalat. Capturing the road would sever the Highlands from central III Corps, just as capturing Ban Me Thuot and Quang Duc would isolate the Highlands from western III Corps.

When the 7th Division attacked Route 20, the 6th Division, now in eastern Long Khanh province, would capture Route 2, a road leading south from Xuan Loc to Route 15, the road to Vung Tau. It would then turn north and attack eastward from Xuan Loc along Route 1 into Binh Tuy province. MR-6's 812th Regiment would capture Hoai Duc district and finish clearing northeastern Long Khanh and link up with the 6th Division, thereby isolating the coastal provinces from eastern III Corps. With the western, central, and now eastern sections of the border between II Corps and III Corps captured, South Vietnamese forces in II Corps would be blocked from retreating south. The country would be cut in half.

In late February the 7th Division's unit commanders returned from their reconnaissance of the area. On 5 March Tra's deputy, the newly promoted Lieutenant General Le Duc Anh, ordered the division to move through the jungle from Phuoc Long toward the ARVN outposts along Route 20, with the overrunning of the district capital, Dinh Quan, to be the key opening battle.[17] Despite the Communists' efforts to conceal their movements, U.S. and ARVN intelligence again discovered their plans when captured documents and two soldiers from the 7th who defected to ARVN revealed the presence of the reconnaissance team.

Soon after the Tri Tam/Ben Cau attacks, and after learning of the enemy movement toward Dinh Quan, on 16 March Toan ordered Brigadier General Le Minh Dao of the ARVN 18th Division to send two battalions of the 43rd Regiment to defend the town. The 2nd Battalion, 43rd Regiment, arrived in Dinh Quan that day and was deployed northwest of the town. The 1st Battalion and the regimental headquarters deployed to the La Nga Bridge. Dao left the 3rd Battalion near Hoai Duc to assist the RF in that area against the expected attack by the 812th Regiment. Dao's 52nd Regiment held Xuan Loc and the critical road junction of Routes 1 and 20 northeast of Saigon, called Dau Giay by the Vietnamese. With his 48th Regiment detached to help defend Tay Ninh, Dao was now out of troops, as was the rest of III Corps. The territorial forces stationed on Route 2 south of Xuan Loc and east along Route 1—the targets of the 6th Division and the 812th Regiment—were on their own.

On 6 March the PAVN 7th Division departed Phuoc Long for the long march to Route 20. The Dong Nai River, however, lay between it and the road. With no ford or existing bridge, the division's engineer battalion worked diligently to build a bridge to allow the troops and heavy equipment to cross. It was a tough assignment. "Countless problems and difficulties were encountered moving . . . across the river, but . . . in just three nights the entire division and its attached elements successfully crossed the Dong Nai and in total secrecy."[18]

The delay in crossing the river, however, disrupted Tra's plan to hit Tri Tam and Route 20 at the same time. On 12 March PAVN 4th Corps commander Major General Hoang Cam sent a cable to Bui Cat Vu, his deputy who was leading the Route 20 attack, encouraging him to get moving. Although the element of surprise was now lost, after receiving Cam's message, Bui Cat Vu ordered the 7th Division to attack immediately. Early in the morning of 17 March the 141st Regiment struck Dinh Quan. Savage battles erupted on the ridgeline held by the ARVN 2nd Battalion, 43rd Regiment. After fighting lasting more than twenty-four hours, the PAVN forces finally secured the high ground overlooking the town. The 2nd Battalion retreated south to nearby Tran Mountain and dug in on the high ground near the La Nga River bridge. The 141st Regiment quickly attacked Dinh Quan, and the town fell late on 18 March.

The next target was the La Nga Bridge. The 2nd Battalion was on one side of the river, the 1st Battalion garrisoned the other side. The bridge itself was held by an RF company. But following the original plan, the PAVN forces soon pushed down Route 20. On the morning of 20 March, their commanders threw two fresh battalions from the 209th Regiment against the 2nd Battalion on Tran Mountain. The 141st remained behind at Dinh Quan to recover. The Communist troops charged the 2nd Battalion's positions several times, but were driven off. On the third assault, the 2nd's commander, Major Nguyen Huu Che, ordered two 105-mm howitzers loaded up with anti-personnel rounds and fired straight into the massed Communist attackers. The devastating blasts halted that attack.[19]

Ignoring their losses, in late afternoon the Communists attacked again. To deal with this new threat, Major Che called in air support. Unfortunately, a VNAF F-5E mistakenly hit the battalion's position with its bombs, causing many ARVN casualties. After the errant bombing, Che's hold on the mountain was growing tenuous. In fighting two PAVN regiments for four days, the 2nd Battalion had suffered over eighty casualties. Because of other attacks in Long Khanh province, Brigadier General Dao was unable to reinforce the battalion. With no choice other than to retreat or be overrun, at midnight Dao ordered the battalion to pull back to Xuan Loc. At dawn, the PAVN regiment swept down toward the bridge. Unable to hold off the advancing enemy, the RF commander at the bridge called in an artillery strike directly on his own position next to the bridge abutment. In an effort to prevent PAVN from seizing the bridge, the RF commander had deliberately sacrificed himself. It was in vain. Although the artillery killed a dozen PAVN soldiers, not to mention the valiant RF commander, the bridge still fell to the North Vietnamese. Its flank now unhinged, the 1st Battalion also retreated. The 7th Division had succeeded in its first mission.

Meanwhile, unknown to ARVN, in late February the 341st Division had secretly arrived in the B-2 Front from North Vietnam and was officially assigned to the 4th Corps. On 2 March, after attaching the 273rd Infantry Regiment to the 9th Division, COSVN ordered the 341st Division commander to "Study the Route 20 area from the La Nga Bridge to the Dau Giay intersection and Xuan Loc City. Make all necessary preparations to conduct a large-scale massed battle of annihilation when so ordered."[20] The division commander and his staff officers left to make a personal reconnaissance of this sector. In late March the 4th Corps ordered the 341st Division's two newly arrived regiments, the 266th and 270th, to take over the Dinh Quan area from the 7th Division. The 270th Regiment was to defend the newly captured territory, while the 266th would attack southwest along Route 20 to seize the next district town, Kiem Tan.

Dao was well aware of the need to prevent the Communists from pushing further down Route 20. On 28 March he sent the 2nd Battalion, 52nd Regiment, to recapture the lost territory. As the battalion slowly moved north, it ran straight into the deploying 270th Regiment. This was the regiment's first combat action. The battle raged from early in the morning of 29 March to late the next day, but ended in a stalemate.

On Dao's second front, the PAVN 6th Division timed its road and outpost clearing operation to coincide with the 7th Division's attack. Between 15 and 18 March, the PAVN soldiers swept north along Route 2. The 6th then struck east of Xuan Loc, overrunning Chua Chan Mountain, the important high ground due east of the town. By 28 March, the 6th controlled a thirty-mile section of Route 1 from Chua Chan into Binh Tuy. The last road artery from Saigon to central Vietnam had been cut, preventing ARVN from using Route 1 to assist II Corps.

A few hours before the 7th's attack on Dinh Quan, the 812th Regiment opened fire on Dao's third front, attacking the town of Vo Dac, the Hoai

Duc district headquarters. The stalwart RF troops of Vo Dac, who had survived a thirty-day siege during the Phase One attacks, fought off repeated attacks for three days. Becoming impatient with the failure to seize the district headquarters, Tra demanded on the night of 19 March that the 812th immediately finish off the town. In the early-morning hours of 20 March, after a massive preparatory artillery barrage, the 812th Regiment's assault troops stormed into Vo Dac. After capturing the town, the 812th turned on the last remaining ARVN element in the area, Dao's 3rd Battalion, 43rd Regiment, which was defending some nearby high ground. After two days of fighting, Dao ordered his battalion to retreat back to Xuan Loc. Shortly thereafter, the 812th linked up with a 6th Division reconnaissance element. The 812th had accomplished its mission, and Hoai Duc was added to the liberated area of Tanh Linh. Although badly behind schedule, the 812th now turned to complete the second part of its mission: helping the 7th Division clear Route 20 and capture the provinces of Lam Dong and Tuyen Duc.

A LONELY RETREAT

Back in II Corps, with Major General Phu's attention focused on the column of soldiers and civilians retreating down Route 7B, he had ignored the three surviving provinces in the southern Highlands: Quang Duc, Lam Dong, and Tuyen Duc. Although the South Vietnamese had resettled many civilian refugees from Loc Ninh and An Loc in Lam Dong, the three provinces remained isolated and sparsely populated. Only the city of Dalat in Tuyen Duc province held any true significance for the South Vietnamese. It was the home of their National Military Academy and the old summer residence of the emperor and his family. Many of the country's elite owned vacation residences around the city.

After the PAVN 10th Division's capture of Duc Lap in northern Quang Duc in early March, the three battalions of the 24th Ranger Group pulled back to defend the southern part of the province, including the district seat of Kien Duc and the capital, Gia Nghia. On 20 March COSVN's 271B Regiment surrounded the 82nd Ranger Battalion at Kien Duc, preventing the Rangers from retreating.[21] Shortly thereafter, the 271B left one battalion behind to pin down the Rangers, and then advanced toward Gia Nghia. Two days later the Quang Duc province chief radioed Phu to report that Gia Nghia was under heavy artillery attack, and Communist forces had reached the local airfield. Despite two days of resistance by RF forces, on 24 March the 271B Regiment captured Gia Nghia. The seizure of Quang Duc province secured Dung's southern flank and prevented any counterattack against Ban Me Thuot from that direction.

Although encircled, the 82nd Rangers refused to surrender. On 21 March, in hand-to-hand combat they fought their way through PAVN lines and linked up with the rest of the Ranger group the next day. But with the fall of Gia Nghia, the 24th Ranger Group was stranded far from the coast, without a means of being resupplied with food, water, or ammunition. Since all II Corps helicopters were tied up helping the retreating column on Route 7B, the group commander was ordered to march his unit southeast through the jungle to Lam Dong province to help friendly units defend the city of Bao Loc. It was a long walk to Bao Loc, yet the Rangers set off. Misfortune struck the next day when a Ranger stepped on a mine, killing him and wounding the group commander. The injured colonel was flown out by helicopter, and the 82nd Battalion commander, Major Vuong Mong Long, took over command of the column.

At the same time as the 24th Rangers began their retreat, the PAVN 7th Division turned its attention to taking Lam Dong province and its two major towns, Bao Loc and the provincial capital, Di Linh. The main attack element, supported by tanks and anti-aircraft artillery, drove straight up Route 20 to attack the cities head on. By 4:00 P.M. on 31 March both towns had been captured, the RF survivors were escaping toward Dalat, and Lam Dong province had fallen. Now Tuyen Duc was only the Highland province that remained under South Vietnamese control.

Surrounded by a sea of red, Dalat had been preparing its defenses for an attack. Major General Lam Quang Tho, the commandant of the Dalat Military Academy, had received orders to command Dalat's defense. But with the fall of Di Linh, Tho knew he was surrounded. He had only two options: stay and fight, or retreat. Since the Academy's cadets were desperately needed to recoup the terrible losses the South Vietnamese armed forces had suffered, Tho decided to retreat. After securing Route 11 to the city of Phan Rang, the only road to the coast, the cadets and instructors departed by truck on the night of 31 March. They reached Phan Rang with relative ease on the morning of 1 April and continued on to Binh Tuy province, from which they were airlifted back to Saigon.

However, Tho had left everyone else behind. Shocked by the sudden evacuation of the school, the RF troops crumbled. Monitoring ARVN radio networks, the 812th Regiment learned that Dalat was defenseless, and it moved quickly to occupy the city. It arrived in Dalat on the morning of 3 April and took control of the city. Dalat had fallen without a shot being fired.

The retreating 24th Rangers, however, knew none of this. Cutting through the dense jungle, they stayed alive by ambushing Communist trucks and raiding old guerrilla bases for food and water. The Rangers finally reached the outskirts of Bao Loc on 2 April, but Major Long realized they were too late when he saw "the red flag on the roof of the city hall. We turned north hoping to see a friendly force in Dalat. On 4 April, BBC radio said that Dalat had fallen. . . . On 5 April 1975, I made radio contact with Lieutenant Colonel Loc, who was flying around the Dalat area searching for my force."[22] The 82nd was flown to Phan Thiet and then to Xuan Loc. The other two battalions were picked up over the next couple of days and also taken to Phan Thiet, where they remained to help defend the city. Major Long had led the 24th Ranger Group on a harrowing retreat for almost two weeks, surviving on captured rations and stream water. When he departed Quang Duc, he had 450 men in his 82nd Battalion; only 310 made it to Xuan Loc. But of all the Ranger groups in II Corps, only the 24th survived largely intact.

While Tra's plans were bearing fruit on the western, northern, and eastern side of Saigon, they were not going smoothly to the south, in the Mekong Delta. After receiving the initial COSVN guidance on targets, MR-8 requested permission to instead concentrate its efforts in only three districts west of My Tho, the Delta's second-largest city. These three districts had always been hotly contested, mostly because they were heavily populated, were a rich rice-producing region, and controlled a long section of Route 4. The capture of this territory would enable the Communists to directly threaten My Tho. Tra especially wanted to link his troops in this region with the 303rd Division elements advancing south from Hau Nghia province.

As in III Corps, the South Vietnamese in the Mekong Delta knew the Communist forces were coming and strove to disrupt their plans. In early March ARVN communication intercepts located the PAVN 8th Division headquarters approximately five miles northeast of My Tho. The ARVN 7th Division made several sweeps looking for the division headquarters, and uncovered two large ammunition caches. Between the new intelligence, heavy PAVN casualties earlier in the year, and the ammunition loss,

Le Gro was convinced that any attacks by "PAVN units would be . . . with inexperienced fillers and with inadequate tactical advantage."[23]

He was right again. While several outposts were lost, the ARVN 7th Division kept the critical Route 4 open and repulsed the attacks by the PAVN 8th Division near My Tho. In spite of these successes, however, ARVN prospects in the Delta looked bleak. According to DAO analysts, "The apparent overall objective during the past week has been to expand and consolidate PAVN terrain holdings, while playing upon scare factor to keep ARVN reaction forces locked into potentially critical trouble spots. They have succeeded somewhat on both counts and have forced RVNAF to utilize its entire monthly allotted air support by the 13th of the month. The IV Corps Commander, Major General Nguyen Khoa Nam, recently stated that Communist forces can replace men and equipment with less trouble than RVNAF, and it is just this factor, among others, that the PAVN will try to exploit. Their ability to continue the deterioration process is underscored by the fact that a respectable [series of attacks] was launched following over three weeks of preemptive RVNAF strikes."[24]

While PAVN had made dozens of small but sharp ground attacks all across the Delta, it had not seriously disrupted the ARVN formations or seized any significant territory. It had, however, accomplished the important goal of tying down the three ARVN divisions in the Delta. Any hope of moving units to support III Corps, as had been done with the ARVN 21st Division during the 1972 offensive, was now out of the question, unless the South Vietnamese were willing to cede large tracts of the countryside to the enemy.

KHOI SAVES TAY NINH

While Toan believed the pincers north and south of Tay Ninh City would attempt to link up at Go Dau Ha, the junction of Route 1 and Local Route 22, in fact Tra's plan called for the bulk of the 303rd Division pincer to turn in the opposite direction, into Hau Nghia province. The division left one regiment to take Go Dau Ha while the rest marched away from the town. Unaware of the PAVN strategy, Brigadier General Tran Quang Khoi stopped his efforts to retake Tri Tam and turned his attention to holding Go Dau Ha. Taking advantage of numerous air strikes, Khoi succeeded in holding the town, although enemy elements came within one mile of it. Believing Khoi had stopped the PAVN assault, Toan then ordered him to use his attached 48th Regiment to recapture Route 1 from Go Dau Ha to Cambodia. Using more air strikes and heavy amounts of artillery, the 48th began slowly advancing against stiff resistance. For the North Vietnamese, a successful move by the 48th along Route 1 would dangerously threaten the rear of the 303rd Division as it continued the attack into Hau Nghia. To prevent this potential disaster, the 303rd Division commander pulled back one of the infantry battalions headed to Hau Nghia to reinforce the regiment trying to block the South Vietnamese advance.

Despite the orders to hold Route 1, PAVN gave ground. In one engagement, most of one company was wiped out. Seeing ARVN forces pushing along Route 1, Tra ordered the PAVN 9th Division to attack on Khoi's other flank near Tri Tam to force Toan to pull the 48th back to assist the 3rd Armored against this sudden maneuver. On 23 March one regiment from the 9th drove the newly reconstituted 2nd Battalion, 7th Regiment, 5th Division (the unit that had been decimated at Phuoc Long), from the town of Truong Mit near Local Route 22, shattering the ARVN battalion in the process. Three-quarters of the unit were killed, wounded, or missing.

Khoi immediately reacted to the loss of Truong Mit by sending two of his brigade's combined armor and Ranger task forces to retake the town. The 9th Division was pressing south when it ran into the 3rd Armored. A major battle erupted on 24 March. After fierce fighting, Khoi's tanks and Rangers blasted through the Communist forces and recaptured Truong Mit, killing over one hundred soldiers and capturing many weapons. Still, the 9th Division gambit paid off. Faced with the larger threat at Truong Mit, Khoi pulled the 48th Regiment advancing on Route 1 back to hold Go Dau Ha.

Overall, it was a desperate game Toan and Khoi were playing, with Khoi as fireman, bouncing back and forth between the two flanks within Tay Ninh province, putting out one blaze after another. It was a brilliant orchestration of men and equipment, one that required excellent staff work and logistical planning. But if more units were chewed up as the 2nd Battalion, 7th Regiment, had been, Toan would have even fewer options.

Simply put, Toan needed more reserves. Earlier, at the GVN National Security Council meeting on 13 March, President Thieu had given Toan permission to redeploy his Ranger units. III Corps controlled three Ranger groups: the 31st, 32nd, and 33rd. The 33rd was working with the 3rd Armored. The battle-tested 31st Ranger Group was the former 3rd Ranger Group, which had gallantly withstood the hell of An Loc. It currently defended the town of Chon Thanh on Route 13, but it was surrounded by Communist troops and could only be resupplied by air. The nearest ARVN outpost was ten miles south of Chon Thanh. The 32nd, stationed at An Loc, twelve miles north of Chon Thanh on Route 13, was even more isolated. An Loc was the Binh Long province capital and held the III Corps Ranger Command, but the town's psychological importance was far greater: the heroic defense of An Loc in 1972 had been the most glorious South Vietnamese feat of arms of the war. However, neither An Loc nor Chon Thanh was of any further military value. Each Ranger group had three battalions, and these veteran units were needed to bolster the hard-pressed ARVN defenders closer to Saigon.

Long anticipating another Communist assault on An Loc, the III Corps Ranger commander, Colonel Nguyen Thanh Chuan, had ordered his units to prepare for a long siege. They had stockpiled a ninety-day supply of fuel, food, and ammunition. Colonel Chuan could not imagine abandoning a town that thousands of South Vietnamese soldiers had died to protect. He was stunned, therefore, when the ARVN 5th Division commander, Brigadier General Le Nguyen Vy, arrived by helicopter to deliver the bad news: Lieutenant General Toan had ordered all units to evacuate An Loc. Chuan had five days to prepare to withdraw back to Chon Thanh.

Chuan and many of his Ranger officers were deeply upset at having to abandon An Loc, but they followed orders. Chuan planned a phased evacuation of the city. First, he would lift out his artillery, evacuate the civilians, and burn all supplies and equipment. Once this was accomplished, helicopters would carry out the III Corps Ranger Command, the province headquarters, and one battalion from the 32nd Group. The other two battalions and the regional forces would then march overland and link up with the 31st Ranger Battalion from Chon Thanh, which would be sent to meet them halfway. Secrecy was crucial, for if the enemy got wind of the evacuation and suddenly attacked in the middle of the ARVN withdrawal, it would be disastrous.

Chuan executed the first two parts of his plan without incident. Now his remaining battalions had to walk through a jungle completely controlled by the enemy. The battalions departed at nightfall. In spite of a few small clashes, the Rangers moved swiftly and arrived unscathed in Chon Thanh on 20 March. One reason for their success was that Tra had stripped his regular troops from An Loc to use in Tay Ninh, leaving only local guerrillas to guard Route 13. The successful withdrawal from An Loc caught

PAVN napping, and Tra reacted with fury to this major embarrassment. He ordered the 9th Division to eliminate Chon Thanh immediately.

Anticipating the PAVN attack on Chon Thanh, Chuan quickly developed a new defensive system based on his one RF and six Ranger battalions, plus eleven M-41 tanks and artillery. The Rangers had long ago turned Chon Thanh into a fortress. A ditch surrounded the base, and behind the ditch was a wall of sandbags covered with earth six feet high. Firing ports through which tanks and other heavy weapons could fire had been cut in the wall. With two Ranger groups, Chuan believed he could withstand almost any enemy attack. However, as soon as he had completed his plans, Toan told him to release the 32nd Ranger Group so it could be sent to Tay Ninh. Flabbergasted, Chuan begged Toan to allow him to retain at least one battalion, to which Toan agreed. The 32nd Group was soon lifted out, leaving one battalion behind.

The 9th Division sent most of two regiments, supported by local forces and a battalion of tanks, to attack Chon Thanh. There was no time for reconnaissance or probing attacks. Tra wanted immediate results. The plan was simple: a frontal assault by tanks, followed by waves of infantry. At 9:30 A.M. on 24 March, PAVN launched its first attack. Artillery pounded the Rangers' positions, and then the tanks moved in. The Rangers were waiting for them. Holding their fire until the armor was close, the Rangers cut loose with a ferocious barrage of anti-tank rockets and recoilless-rifle fire. First one, then three, then seven T-54s were burning. As the PAVN infantry tried to move forward, Chuan hammered them with air strikes and artillery. By early afternoon the battle was over. Seven T-54s had been damaged or destroyed, and over a hundred enemy soldiers were dead or wounded. The PAVN 9th Division pulled back to lick its wounds. Many North Vietnamese soldiers had paid for Tra's impatience with their lives.

Realizing the ARVN forces at Chon Thanh would be a tougher foe than the RF troops they had been fighting, the 4th Corps ordered the 273rd Regiment, 341st Division, which had been holding blocking positions on Route 13 south of Chon Thanh, to send two battalions to join the 9th Division in attacking the town. One battalion was left behind to stop any ARVN reinforcements moving up Route 13. Meanwhile, the 9th Division would make another assault on 27 March. Apparently the PAVN commanders had become over-confident, because they did not change tactics. Again they started with a preparatory barrage and then sent in the tanks and infantry. The results this time were even worse. The PAVN columns were smashed before they even got close. After two attacks, ARVN claimed 240 men killed and eleven T-54s destroyed. Colonel Chuan's troops had lost less than fifty dead and wounded.

The 9th Division commander now realized that only a larger force could take the town. He ordered his third regiment to disengage from Tay Ninh and move to Chon Thanh. By 30 March, the 9th Division's three infantry regiments, plus the 273rd Regiment, the remaining tanks, and fifteen heavy artillery pieces, including the three 130-mms, were in position to attack. At dawn on 31 March, the 9th Division commander stood in his command post and gave the order to fire. All hell broke loose as three thousand rounds poured into the Ranger positions. Mortar and artillery shells churned up minefields and smashed bunkers. For over two hours PAVN rained explosives on the surrounded Rangers. Then the attack signal was given. The remaining tanks surged forward, followed by hundreds of North Vietnamese infantrymen attacking from multiple directions. Although heavily outnumbered, the dogged Rangers did not yield. Three times the Communist troops breached the defensive perimeter, but the Rangers, fighting with fierce determination, threw them out. The vastly outnumbered and exhausted Rangers had stopped cold an entire reinforced PAVN division and destroyed even more tanks.

Colonel Chuan's joy, however, was short-lived. One Ranger officer later wrote that while aerial resupply continued, "the amount of supplies we could bring in steadily decreased in the face of the heavy wall of enemy anti-aircraft fire. The enemy anti-aircraft and the artillery attacks raining down on this tiny district capital seemed to be worse than during the battle of An Loc. With the number of defenders we had, the continual attrition, and no reinforcements coming in . . . the pressure was too great. The enemy was determined to take this tiny district capital to open the road for its advance on . . . Saigon. By the ninth day of the siege there were virtually no more medical evacuation or resupply flights. Helicopters were no longer able to land, even if the pilots were skilled."[25] Realizing his predicament, that afternoon, Chuan requested permission to withdraw to Lai Khe. Toan approved the request. Toan believed that the Rangers would soon be overrun anyway, and he desperately needed them for other fronts.

At 10:00 P.M. on 31 March, Colonel Chuan called all the senior Ranger officers together to announce the evacuation. For the Rangers, this second order to retreat was a personal affront to their honor. They had held their ground with enormous courage against a determined foe. To retreat while undefeated was unthinkable. Still, they were soldiers, and soldiers obey orders despite their personal feelings. After quick planning, the exodus took place during the night of 1 April, just as the PAVN forces were massing for another attack the next morning. The VNAF launched a series of heavy bombing raids as a diversion. The Rangers destroyed their remaining tanks and artillery and then infiltrated through the Communist lines. Each of the battalions moved separately, but not without losses. The 52nd Battalion got lost, bumped into an ambush, and took moderate losses. The RF battalion suffered the same fate. Still, while the majority of the 31st Ranger Group retreated in good order and, after refitting, could now be deployed elsewhere, the North Vietnamese had captured all of Binh Long province and had compressed ARVN's defensive line even closer to Saigon.

AN AMBITIOUS GENERAL

Tra's Phase Two attacks were now complete. He had accomplished almost everything he had set out to do. After a month of heavy fighting, the Communists had succeeded in "expanding [our] lines of communications so they could be used to move large numbers of troops and large quantities of supplies and technical equipment to the critical battlefield of [Saigon]."[26] By concentrating his main-force units on RF troops holding district towns, Tra had taken far lighter losses than he would have if he had sent them against regular ARVN units. Still, Tra was not satisfied. He believed his units "were making slow progress and that our armed forces were not strong enough to fully exploit the situation. [Pham Hung] sent several messages requesting the Politburo to urgently send additional forces."[27] Tra hoped the Politburo would follow the strategy discussed during the planning sessions for the offensive—namely, that if the South Vietnamese forces in II Corps collapsed after the fall of Ban Me Thuot, PAVN units in the Highlands would wheel south to attack Saigon.

Writing after the war, Giap is clear that this was also his preferred strategy. However, he was reluctant to overrule Dung, who had given persuasive reasons for wanting to finish the job in II Corps. Dung also resisted an attempt by Tra to tempt him to move his forces toward Saigon. On 22 March, Tra sent a cable to Dung describing the results of the B-2 Front's campaign thus far. As Tra later wrote, while he acknowledged that Dalat was within B-2's area of responsibility, his forces "were small and had to move in close to Saigon and thus could not . . . liberate Tuyen Duc. After the Highlands were liberated our strong forces there could come down to take Dalat, then continue on to [B-2] very conveniently and promptly. Therefore I sent a message to Dung . . . recommending that he send forces down to liberate Dalat because our forces had to advance to Saigon and could not go to Dalat."[28]

Dung did not fall for Tra's trap. On 23 March Tra received a cable from Dung explaining that while Saigon would eventually be attacked, for the moment Dung's forces would continue toward the coast. Dung said he believed PAVN needed to prepare the battlefield first, i.e., clean out the ARVN forces in II Corps to ensure that his rear was secure. While he refrained from saying so, Dung thought that Tra's proposal was premature. While ARVN troops in III and IV Corps had been stunned by the Communist advances, "we had not yet scored any earthshaking victories in [the B-2] area, and so the enemy had not yet fallen apart."[29] Whether Dung was stiff-arming his rival or whether he truly believed that PAVN needed to first secure greater victories remains a matter of conjecture.

Tra, of course, disagreed. He writes that he felt disappointed after reading the message. He believed that if the B-3 forces, especially the 10th Division, had moved into western MR-7, he could have taken Saigon earlier. Oddly, while Tra argued with Dung about the turn toward Saigon, at the same time he was rejecting a similar proposal from one of his own commanders. After reviewing the rapidly changing situation, on 19 March Hoang Cam sent an urgent message to Tra. He recommended that instead of sending the 7th Division north to attack Lam Dong, it continue to advance south on Route 20 to take the Dau Giay intersection and Xuan Loc and destroy the ARVN 18th Division. Cam wrote:

The enemy is now changing his strategic disposition of forces, abandoning a number of locations and pulling back to hold Saigon and the coastal lowlands. In this situation, if we can quickly destroy another element of the 18th Division . . . we will create conditions which will enable us to liberate Xuan Loc. . . . Our first step would be to move 7th Division down to . . . destroy 1st Battalion, 43rd Regimental Task Force. . . . When COSVN's 341st Division arrives, it and 6th Division will liberate [Dau Giay] . . . destroy additional elements of 18th Division, and liberate Xuan Loc. If we delay, the enemy will be able to move elements of his strategic reserves up to reinforce Xuan Loc. In that case we will not only have lost our opportunity, we will also have to leave forces behind to hold [a section of Route 20] and the La Nga Bridge and defend our newly liberated areas. If we expand our attack up to Lam Dong as currently planned, victory will be certain but we will not be able to open fire until 28 March at the earliest. If, on the other hand, we turn around and liberate Route 20 down to Dau Giay the enemy will have no hope of being able to clear the road. In that case Lam Dong will no longer be of any use to them, and they may voluntarily withdraw from Lam Dong as they have from other locations.[30]

It was a bold move that might have produced spectacular results. If the 7th Division had continued south and if the 6th Division had pinned the bulk of the 18th ARVN at Xuan Loc, only one Airborne brigade would have stood between the 7th Division and Saigon. The sudden appearance of an enemy division on Saigon's eastern flank might have sparked panic. Tra, however, denied Cam's request, ordering him to "continue to expand our line of communications to the north in order to create springboard positions for the attack on Saigon in the Route 1 and Route 20 sectors north and east of Saigon."[31]

Then the situation suddenly changed. On the afternoon of 29 March, Danang fell, and Le Duan decided to gamble. Heady with victory, he sent a message to Pham Hung telling him to go for broke with just his existing forces. In the chaotic situation resulting from the collapse of I Corps, one hard push now might topple Thieu. Le Duan's message said: "The revolution in the South has entered a stage of development by leaps and bounds. . . . The enemy has suffered extremely heavy and unexpected setbacks [and] is facing the danger of rapid collapse, militarily and politically. I fully agree with you that at this moment we should act with great timeliness, determination, and boldness. . . . While urgently and promptly carrying out the strategic decision that has been made, I want to stress an urgent requirement: immediately fulfill the mission of carrying out a strategic interdiction and encirclement, and cutting off Saigon. As a matter of fact, we can consider that the campaign for the liberation of Saigon has begun."[32]

Tra was jubilant. "[Le Duan's] message to COSVN affirmed that the situation would develop rapidly, and that it was necessary to step up our attacks and move closer to Saigon. If we won additional victories on the battlefields, Saigon itself might be thrown into chaos."[33] Finally freed from the General Staff's restraints, Tra would not wait for Dung or the arrival of any reinforcements from the North. He would conquer Saigon by himself.

11

"HOW COULD I ABANDON THIS ROCKY SOIL?"

FIGHTING TO SAVE HUE

When the war in I Corps erupted again in 1974, the heavy fighting portended another major attack in the spring of 1975. Given the growing PAVN strength, it was an assault the South Vietnamese were uncertain they could defeat, especially since the terrain heavily favored the attackers. A major ridgeline between Hue and Danang divides the area into two discrete sections. It branches off the Annamite mountain range and ends at the Hai Van Pass on the coast. The pass is the key terrain feature in I Corps. It would take only a few troops to seize and hold it, thereby cutting off South Vietnam's three best divisions. North of the pass are Quang Tri and Thua Thien provinces and the city of Hue, home of the last imperial court. South of the pass is Quang Nam province and Danang, South Vietnam's second-largest city and a strategic seaport. Continuing south are Quang Tin and Quang Ngai provinces. The landscape in I Corps is mostly mountains covered with dense jungle abutting a narrow coastal plain.

As 1975 began, the region's population was slightly over three million, the vast majority of whom were Vietnamese living in the lowlands or the cities. Economically, it was the country's poorest region, yet given the romantic and cultural attachment to Hue, plus Danang's deep-water harbor, it was second in importance only to Saigon. Although President Thieu had considered abandoning the area several times during the past year, he knew it was an impossible task, politically, emotionally, and logistically. Thieu was accordingly forced to invest a significant portion of his military in defending a section of the country that was draining his treasury rather than contributing to it.

Quang Tri and Thua Thien had been the most heavily fought-over ground of the war, largely because of their proximity to North Vietnam. The tiny coastal plain flanked by a long chain of mountains had made it a difficult area for the South Vietnamese to defend. Now it was even tougher. Previously, PAVN offensives had to start from either the Laotian border or across the DMZ. The 1972 offensive had left the Northerners in control of the western mountains from the border to the plains, plus the area from the DMZ south to Quang Tri City. The South Vietnamese held the lowlands along a line from the coast through Quang Tri City along the Thach Han River west to the mountains, and then south to the Hai Van Pass. Since the Paris Accords stipulated a ceasefire in place, the Communists now started with the ball, as so aptly described by Colonel William Le Gro, on ARVN's "30-yard line."

Another factor in previous offensives was that the lack of roads had prevented PAVN forces from building sufficient logistical stockpiles to maintain long offensives, while also providing ARVN units time to detect and react to their movements. Since the areas controlled by the South Vietnamese had better roads and shorter distances, ARVN could shift reinforcements more quickly than the Communists. To mitigate that advantage, after the ceasefire the Communists had invested heavily in building an extensive road network in the area they had captured in 1972. Now PAVN could mass troops and supplies at multiple points in I Corps. Without U.S. air and naval firepower to help stop them, the South Vietnamese were essentially outflanked before a shot was even fired.

Such was the defensive problem for the South Vietnamese in I Corps Forward (Thua Thien and Quang Tri provinces). The Communists could launch a surprise assault from the mountains with overwhelming force against a lightly held position, and then rapidly move a short distance and cut Route 1. Since the coastal plain was only between ten and fifteen miles wide at any point, a successful defense was predicated on three factors: precise intelligence on enemy intentions, adequate troop strength and heavy firepower to blunt the first assault, and reserves to counterattack and seal any penetrations.

However, the commander of I Corps Forward, Lieutenant General Lam Quang Thi, faced constraints in all three areas. Exact intelligence was unobtainable. It was the same problem Truong identified after the Thuong Duc attacks of August 1974. Colonel Nguyen Thanh Tri, the Marine Division's deputy commander, explained that "since we lost access to the intelligence information formerly provided by the Americans, our ability to assess the enemy's situation had become limited. This on many occasions caused us confusion and vagueness in our assessment of the enemy's plans and capabilities."[1] What I Corps intelligence could do, as was true in the other corps, was provide a fairly accurate initial estimate of general enemy intentions. What it could not do was provide clear-cut early warnings on either specific locations or time frames, especially when PAVN commanders suddenly changed their plans, as Giap frequently did.

Moreover, the U.S. aid cuts had severely reduced firepower, and manpower was depleted by the past year's heavy fighting. While the Marines were in good shape, the 1st Division and the Rangers were badly short of men. Mobility, which previously meant movement by helicopter, was now severely crimped because of shortages of fuel and spare parts. That left Route 1 as the main artery for shuttling reinforcements from less-pressured areas. Keeping the road open therefore became crucial, or Truong would face, as Major General Murray had prophesied, "Dunkirk without ships."

The town of Hue in I Corps Forward was the main prize in this hotly disputed land. In 1972 PAVN had attacked into northern Quang Tri from two directions: across the DMZ and from Laos. Its goal, just as in 1968, was to capture the former imperial capital. In 1975, the South Vietnamese still had to defend the same two directions: the current ceasefire boundary and the western mountains. On the Thach Han River, the RVNAF's mission was to guard Quang Tri City and Route 1, which ran straight to Hue. Concurrently, it had to defend a thirty-six-mile left flank, from the Thach Han River south to Hue. Several major rivers flow out of the mountains, each offering access to the lowlands. The Bo River corridor northwest of Hue posed the greatest threat, since it offered the closest, most direct approach to the city.

Now the North Vietnamese had stretched RVNAF defenses further by opening a third front in the crucial hill country south of Hue, an area PAVN had largely ignored during the 1972 offensive. It was ideal country to mount an attack: over forty miles of steep hills and thick forests end where Route 1 meanders through the tight canyons of the Hai Van.

Thi's defensive plan was simple. He did not believe PAVN would cross the Thach Han River, as this would constitute a complete abrogation of the Paris Accords. But if the enemy did attack, and the pressure was too great, he planned to withdraw in phases toward Hue, using the rivers as defensive barriers. From Quang Tri City south to the My Chanh River, approximately halfway to Hue, he had placed two Marine brigades, a Quang Tri–based RF group, and a squadron of the 1st Armor Brigade. From the My Chanh to Hue (the northern half of Thua Thien province), he placed his forces in a defensive arc facing the mountains west of Hue. He deployed a Marine brigade, a 1st Infantry Division regiment, a number of RF battalions, and a second armored squadron.

The remaining three regiments of the 1st Infantry Division defended the hill country from Hue down to the pass. The 1st Division had recently created fortifications on numerous high points to provide mutual fire support. After the heavy battles for Mo Tau and Bong Mountains during 1974, the 1st Division adjusted its tactics from a single defensive line of fortified outposts as far forward as possible, to a defense in depth. This was

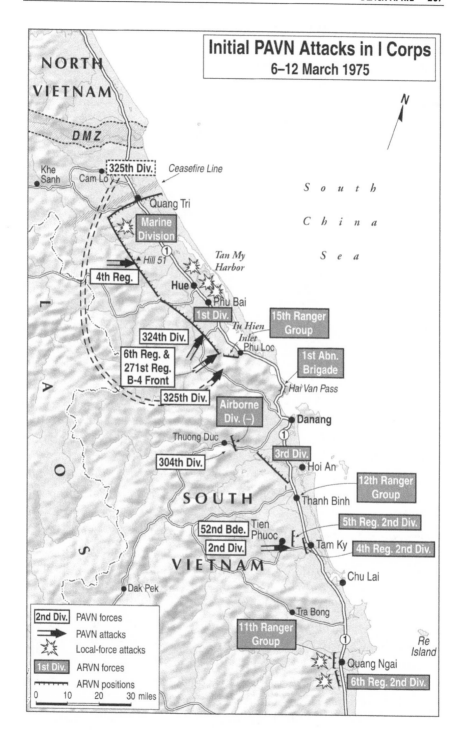

Initial PAVN Attacks in I Corps
6–12 March 1975

NORTH
VIETNAM

DMZ

Khe Sanh
Cam Lo
325th Div.
Ceasefire Line

Quang Tri

Marine Division

Hill 51
4th Reg.

Tan My Harbor

Hue
Phu Bai

1st Div.

Tu Hien Inlet
Phu Loc

324th Div.

6th Reg. & 271st Reg. B-4 Front

325th Div.

Airborne Div. (–)

15th Ranger Group

1st Abn. Brigade

Hai Van Pass

Danang

Thuong Duc

304th Div.

3rd Div.

Hoi An

12th Ranger Group

Thanh Binh

52nd Bde.
Tien Phuoc

2nd Div.

5th Reg. 2nd Div.

Tam Ky

4th Reg. 2nd Div.

Chu Lai

SOUTH

VIETNAM

Dak Pek

Tra Bong

11th Ranger Group

Quang Ngai

Re Island

6th Reg. 2nd Div.

South China Sea

LAOS

N

2nd Div.	PAVN forces
→	PAVN attacks
✴	Local-force attacks
1st Div.	ARVN forces
⊢⊣⊢⊣	ARVN positions

0   10   20   30 miles

designed to defeat PAVN's tactic of penetrating behind the lines to attack unit headquarters.

Previously, Thi also controlled the Airborne Division, but after the battles in late 1974, Lieutenant General Ngo Quang Truong, the I Corps commander, had left two Airborne brigades at Thuong Duc to defend Danang's western flank. This forced Thi to shift a Marine brigade off the ceasefire line to replace the Airborne north of Hue. The third Airborne brigade guarded the Hai Van Pass. Thi held the 15th Ranger Group in reserve.

On Truong's central front, with the Airborne in western Quang Nam, Major General Nguyen Duy Hinh's 3rd Division moved south to protect the rest of the province. Since I Corps intelligence believed that PAVN intended to strike here in the spring of 1975, Truong pulled the 12th Ranger Group from Quang Ngai and positioned it in northern Quang Tin. The 11th Ranger Group and the badly battered 14th Ranger Group would concentrate on expected attacks on Truong's southern front, Quang Ngai province. This left only local RF to defend Tien Phuoc in central Quang Tin, the site of fierce battles in 1974. Since the Quang Tin RF were among the best in I Corps, they rarely received outside help. This was a gap that PAVN would fully exploit.

In addition to his infantry and armor, Truong had the VNAF 1st Air Division, and the Navy's 1st Coastal Zone, which included river craft, short-range patrol vessels, and several deep-water ships. Fully expecting a major spring offensive throughout I Corps, Truong busily prepared for the onslaught by rehabilitating the units that had suffered losses during the tough fighting in 1974. His efforts were paying off, but troop morale remained poor. Low pay prevented the average soldier from adequately feeding his family. Supplies were heavily rationed, medicine and gasoline stocks were depleted, and Truong had expended a considerable portion of his artillery reserve defeating the 1974 attacks. In sum, while Truong controlled the most powerful command within the South Vietnamese military, he had few reserves, his units were under-strength, the terrain placed him at a tremendous disadvantage, and his firepower was drastically reduced.

In comparison, Hanoi had also put its heaviest troop concentration in northern South Vietnam. PAVN had two major commands in the I Corps Forward area: the 2nd Corps and the B-4 Front. The 2nd Corps was made up of the 304th, 324th, and 325th Divisions, an air-defense division, the 203rd Tank Brigade, and artillery, engineer, and signal brigades. The B-4 Front had three independent regiments and eight local-force battalions.

South of the Hai Van Pass, the Communists had major elements of the B-1 Front. These included the 2nd Division in the southern portion of Quang Nam, the 52nd Brigade in Quang Ngai, and almost a dozen independent local-force battalions. In addition, the B-1 Front contained a division equivalent at Thuong Duc, in the form of the two 304th Division regiments and one 324th Division regiment that had taken the town in August 1974.

Strategically, Truong readied for two contingencies. In December 1974, the JGS had predicted that Hanoi's main goals in I Corps for 1975 were to occupy the balance of Quang Tri province and isolate Hue and Danang by cutting Route 1 at the Hai Van Pass. If the Communists attacked with the same forces they had used in 1974, Truong believed he could defeat them.[2] But if the North Vietnamese reinforced the northern front with several strategic-reserve divisions, which it appeared they were doing, then Truong would retreat into a concentrated defense around Hue. If his central and southern fronts also collapsed, he would withdraw into enclaves centered on Danang and the Chu Lai peninsula in southern Quang Tin province. Chu Lai was the site of the ARVN 2nd Division headquarters, and it had a large airfield and nearby port facilities.

Withdrawing into enclaves around the major cities was exactly the plan Hanoi feared. The PAVN planners worried that if ARVN could concentrate its manpower and firepower around strong defensive positions, it would prove costly to break through. On the other hand, what Truong dreaded was Hanoi's dispatching its strategic-reserve divisions to dramatically alter the current balance of power. In November 1974, Truong's suspicions spiked upward when ARVN spies reported that the 308th Division had arrived from North Vietnam. In January, signals intelligence picked up hints that a second strategic-reserve unit, the 341st Division, had moved into Quang Tri province to replace the 325th Division along the ceasefire line.[3] These reports, although unsubstantiated, seemed to confirm the JGS analysis that Quang Tri was Hanoi's primary spring objective.

Overall, Truong's G-2 (intelligence chief) predicted that the enemy would make piecemeal assaults in each province until all PAVN units were engaged. Attacks at first would be strong but brief, building to a crescendo by late April or early May. The G-2's analysis was based upon two main factors. First, PAVN units had also taken heavy casualties during 1974. It would take time to rebuild the units and position new supplies. Second, the weather remained nasty. Normally the rainy season in central Vietnam slackens in January, but this year the rains continued into February. Flooding delayed the start of the offensive, as Communist units engaged in road repair, food production, and training.

PAVN's offensive in I Corps was intended to tie down the two South Vietnamese strategic-reserve divisions, particularly the Airborne, so that Saigon could not shift them to the Central Highlands. However, there were no direct attacks planned against either elite unit, and the various North Vietnamese histories are silent on exactly how PAVN's forces would prevent the Airborne's departure. Perhaps General Giap believed that if his forces threatened a vital target such as Hue, ARVN would be forced to commit the Airborne and the Marines. PAVN would thereby succeed in tying down these units without incurring the risk of directly attacking them. Regardless, it is an interesting exception to Giap's strategy, one that perhaps reveals his true evaluation of his army's strength.

While Giap did not believe his troops could liberate all of Quang Tri and Thua Thien until 1976, he hoped that by aggressively attacking, he might get a lucky break. His goals included destroying a significant portion of ARVN's manpower, capturing part of the lowlands, and gaining control of a large proportion of the rural population. Giap's plan also called for a major attack in Quang Tin. In March 1975 he massed his regulars against the RF, hoping for a quick victory to seize this vital area. The entire PAVN 2nd Division and the 52nd Brigade would shift from their normal operating areas in Quang Nam and Quang Ngai and converge on Tien Phuoc, with the ultimate goal of capturing Tam Ky. Quang Ngai local forces would launch supporting attacks to tie down the ARVN 2nd Division and prevent its reinforcing Quang Tin.

In overall design, it was a repeat of the 1974 plan, only with superior numbers attacking the same positions simultaneously instead of consecutively as they had done the previous year. The General Staff assumed direct control over both the 2nd Corps and the B-4 Front. Giap also assigned a new 2nd Corps commander, Major General Nguyen Huu An, who had just returned from a military school in Russia. He was one of PAVN's best combat leaders, and his promotion would prove instrumental in Hanoi's eventual success. He had risen through the ranks from private to major general, always on the military rather than the political-officer side of the chain of command. He had been a battalion commander in the 1950 Border Campaign, and then a regimental commander at Dien Bien Phu. He later commanded the 325th Division during the unit's infiltration from

North Vietnam in late 1964 and early 1965. He was the field commander during the famous Ia Drang battle at Landing Zones X-Ray and Albany in November 1965, and then commanded the PAVN 1st Division in the Central Highlands. He was then sent to Laos in 1968 to become the commander of the 308th Division. He fought in Laos during Lam Son 719, and was then detached to command the PAVN offensive in the Plain of Jars. When the Easter Offensive bogged down, An was brought back to take over the 308th Division, leading it against the South Vietnamese counteroffensive until the Paris Peace Agreement was signed.

After receiving Giap's strategic guidance, the 2nd Corps and B-4 Front drew up a plan to combine forces and attack northern Thua Thien. Their goal was to penetrate and then hold part of the lowlands. Logistics teams began stockpiling supplies for an attack, and reconnaissance troops were dispatched to scout ARVN positions. In early February a group of senior officers traveled to Hanoi to gain Giap's approval for their plan.

However, after several days of discussions, the plan was rejected. The rationale was straightforward: the Marine defenses in northern Thua Thien were simply too stout. A new plan called for the 2nd Corps to instead shift south and attack the hill country below Hue. The 324th Division would attack the same positions it had attacked the previous year, the Bong Mountain/Mo Tau area. From the hilltops in both areas, PAVN could bring artillery to bear on Route 1 and Hue's main airport, Phu Bai, effectively shutting them down and isolating I Corps Forward except by sea. The 325th Division would secretly depart the ceasefire line in Quang Tri and occupy the right flank of the 324th Division. It would assault the hills near the Truoi River, closer to the Hai Van Pass. This multi-division thrust would be the primary sector for the entire Quang Tri/Thua Thien battlefield. Although both divisions sought to destroy ARVN units, the 325th's main mission was to cut Route 1. At the same time, the B-4 Front would draw Truong's attention to northern Quang Tri by means of a feint. Afterwards, it would attack northern Thua Thien to prevent ARVN from reinforcing the defenders south of Hue.

Giap's forces in I Corps would attack in two phases. Phase One would occur from March to early May. It was timed to coincide with the attacks in II Corps, and so the opening date was critical: no later than 5 March. Phase Two would last from July to August. Each phase required two plans: a Basic Plan and an Opportunity Plan. The Basic Plan was the main concept, while the Opportunity Plan was in case of a sudden breakthrough. The opening blows would be sapper attacks against supply facilities and bridges. Giap also ordered that no tanks or heavy artillery, the deadly 122-mm and 130-mm cannons, could participate in the first phase. Giap needed to husband his remaining heavy weapons for the final attacks.

Using the same strategy as in the Central Highlands, Giap decided to secretly reposition a combat unit from the northern portion of the theater—in this case, Quang Tri province—south to what he viewed as a more weakly defended area. Just as surreptitiously infiltrating the 316th and 341st Divisions from the strategic reserve into South Vietnam was a major factor in Hanoi's successful spring offensive, shifting the 325th Division south within I Corps was another. ARVN had barely contained an attack by the 324th Division in the hill country in the summer of 1974. If a second division was added, the two would almost certainly prove unstoppable. Giap's movement of the 325th Division from northern Quang Tri to south of Hue had a tremendous impact on the tactical situation in I Corps Forward. He achieved this advantage not by reinforcement from the strategic reserve, as Truong feared, but by maneuver. Giap's stratagem enabled him to use his reserve divisions on other battlefields, thus affecting theaters across the country.

Giap's instructions regarding the change, however, were not transmitted until early February, and since the attack date was 5 March, the short time frame created major difficulties for his frontline units. According to Major General Nguyen Huu An, "The problem we faced was that . . . we had only thirty days from the time we received our orders until the time we were to open fire, and in that period we had to virtually begin our campaign preparations from scratch. All our previous logistics preparations had been focused on [northern Thua Thien]. Now all these supplies had to be loaded onto the shoulders of our transportation troops and carried up and down scores of steep, muddy mountain slopes."[4]

As the PAVN 2nd Corps engineers began to carve rough roads out of the rocky terrain to move vehicles, heavy weapons, and supplies to the new front, Major General An decided it would be impossible to meet the attack deadline. The 325th Division needed time to reposition, and the corps did not have enough supplies stored in the area south of Hue to support two divisions. Despite Giap's orders to open fire on 5 March, Nguyen Huu An decided to have the 324th open fire on 10 March, followed three weeks later by the 325th.

On 26 February An's deputy, Major General Hoang Dan, arrived in Hanoi to brief Giap and Deputy Chief of Staff Le Trong Tan on the changes. Although the basic design was quickly approved, when Tan heard about the proposed delay, he exploded in anger: "With a major campaign of strategic significance that is being coordinated with many other battle-fields, do you think that you can start your attacks any time you want? If you delay the start of your attacks the enemy may send the airborne divi-sion to the southern Central Highlands, which will shatter our campaign in the primary theater of operations! Then what will happen to our Gen-eral Offensive? After all the times we have brought you up here to attend the meetings, all the representatives we have sent down to disseminate our plans to you, and all the reminder cables we have sent, is it possible that you still do not understand this?"[5]

Despite Tan's outburst and the compelling strategic needs, the logistics were immutable. Dan tried to explain that the 2nd Corps had to provide food and ammunition for four infantry regiments plus support troops while moving supplies and artillery in difficult terrain in the midst of ter-rible weather. A compromise was reached: The B-4 Front would open fire by itself on 5 March in Quang Tri to draw ARVN's attention. On D-Day + 3, one 324th Division regiment and two B-4 Front regiments would assault Mo Tau and other nearby hills. On D-Day + 21, one regiment of the 325th Division would commence an assault on the 324th's right flank.

As Dan prepared to leave, Giap called him back to forcefully reiterate the time schedule. He told Dan, "Remember that this campaign is not like previous campaigns. You people down there may be able to use new ideas to fight really well and over-fulfill the goals set by the plan. How-ever, you must also remember that there is absolutely no flexibility on those elements that the General Staff has laid down in our instructions, and you must follow them to the letter."[6] Dan got the point: Open fire on schedule.

By early March the 2nd Corps had completed a road that vehicles could traverse, and built more than fifty miles of side roads to a number of hills along both sides of the Truoi River. It was an impressive engineering feat under tough conditions. As Major General An later wrote, "Do you think that, with a brand-new dirt road and the constant late-season rains, with people and vehicles constantly moving up and down these roads, that there would be problems? You are right! There was mud, mud, and more mud. People were always ankle-deep in mud, and vehicles moved as slow as tor-toises, often spinning their wheels and forcing the troops to get out and push. 105-mm howitzers . . . had to traverse grades of between 20 and 40 degrees in a driving rain. Only with the help of infantry troops was the artillery finally able to move its guns into position. The problems we had moving the guns into place were just as bad as anything we faced at Dien Bien Phu."[7]

To implement Giap's plan to draw ARVN's attention northward, on 5 March PAVN held a large-scale field exercise near Cua Viet to give the impression of an impending offensive. The B-4 Front shifted troops around, and it sent out tracked vehicles to drive through a number of areas. To deceive allied signals intelligence, the B-4 Front commander ordered the 46th Regiment (an independent unit in North Vietnam) to use "the unit code designation of the 308th Division in its communications. Regimental cadres sent out to reconnoiter the terrain all used the radio unit code designations of the different regiments of the 308th Division. At the command level, the Military Region Headquarters sent messages over its communications channel as if it was commanding an important sector in a real offensive campaign."[8]

Various Communist histories claim that the field-exercise feint achieved its purpose, since RVNAF forces were not shifted south to bolster the hill country. Yet no South Vietnamese account even mentions it, and U.S. records barely discuss any activity in this area. It may have been ignored or may have simply gone unnoticed. More effective was the 46th Regiment's fake radio messages, as the possible presence of the 308th Division deeply concerned the ARVN commanders. Both I Corps deputy commanders wrote in their memoirs that when PAVN forces attacked across the Thach Han River on 19 March, they were led by the 308th. Others, including Generals Cao Van Vien and Ngo Quang Truong, believed it was the 341st Division. It was neither. The 308th remained in the Hanoi area, and the 341st was in III Corps. In fact, the PAVN units that came across the Thach Han River were Quang Tri provincial forces, supported by armor. But even the radio fakery was not particularly effective. Just as he had done in late 1974, Lieutenant General Thi eventually stripped the Thach Han River line of all but Regional Forces and Rangers, daring Hanoi to breach the ceasefire line.

In early March, when sappers destroyed an ARVN 3rd Division ammunition dump and damaged the critical An Lo Bridge over the Bo River north of Hue, Truong was convinced that PAVN's spring offensive was imminent. But the South Vietnamese, tied down defending large tracts of land, could only sit in their bunkers and wait for the coming PAVN onslaught.

THE ATTACKS BEGIN

In accordance with Giap's orders, the B-4 Front infiltrated sappers, political cadres, and five infantry battalions into the lowlands. After conducting the fake field exercise near Cua Viet, the 9th Regiment, 304th Division, departed for Thuong Duc on 6 March. It would replace the 324th Division regiment at Thuong Duc, and that regiment would shift north to take part in the attacks in the hill country. Major General An wanted the 324th at full strength, hoping he could chew up the ARVN 1st Division and make it easier for the 325th Division to break through to Route 1.

On 8 March Communist local forces made a series of attacks across Quang Tri and Thua Thien. In northern Quang Tri, most RF positions held, but one outpost was destroyed, allowing Communist forces to penetrate into the area east of Route 1. Fifteen hamlets were seized, but hard-fighting Quang Tri Regional Forces drove the Communist troops out in two days. In northern Thua Thien, North Vietnamese gains were slight, except for one major target, Hill 51, which was overrun after a stiff fight. Defended by a lone Marine platoon, it was attacked by the B-4 Front's 4th Regiment. Although the Marines repulsed several assaults, by late afternoon the North Vietnamese troops had penetrated their bunkers. About to be overrun, the Marine lieutenant in charge called for an artillery strike directly on his own position. He was killed, but his unit's stalwart defense delayed the PAVN advance, and enabled the 4th Marine Battalion to counterattack the next day. Using pinpoint air strikes, the Marines crushed the Communists, killing over one hundred and capturing numerous weapons.

Southeast of Hue, two Communist local-force battalions penetrated behind ARVN lines and moved to the coast. Their mission was to annihilate the governmental structure in the area. The North Vietnamese marched into several villages and called on the people to rise up against their "oppressors." The population immediately rejected the Communists' appeals. Lieutenant General Thi organized a task force to regain the lost territory, and the ARVN counterattack destroyed one battalion and mauled the other.

Overall, the initial Communist efforts in Quang Tri ended in dismal failure. By 12 March, the survivors had withdrawn back into the mountains. The Communist forces' only meaningful accomplishment was that the fighting in northern Quang Tri caused a hundred thousand civilians—

approximately half the population—to flee to Hue. Entire villages fled. Fifty thousand people had arrived in Hue by 10 March, and another fifty thousand arrived the next day. About twenty thousand people from Thua Thien ran to Danang. Both city governments moved quickly to assist this massive influx of people. The Vietnamese Red Cross began distributing food, while other volunteer and government agencies worked to provide shelter and medical care. These various agencies efficiently assisted the refugees, but despite the authorities' urgings, most people refused to return to their homes. While they were reassured by the effective military response to the attacks, they remained terrified of the Communists. The North Vietnamese 1972 shelling of retreating civilians on Route 1 heading south from Quang Tri City, nicknamed "The Highway of Death," and the 1968 massacre in Hue remained fresh in their minds.

South of Hue, the time for the 2nd Corps to open fire had arrived. Despite tremendous efforts by Nguyen Huu An's logistics teams, the corps could provide only about 50 percent of the necessary campaign supplies. Regardless, An ordered the 324th Division to attack. On 8 March, two regiments from the division struck ARVN positions on Mo Tau, while two B-4 Front regiments attacked several other important hills. The fighting was ferocious. Time and again PAVN troops charged ARVN defenses. Mo Tau was overrun, but numerous air strikes, some coordinated personally by Lieutenant General Thi, enabled a counterattack to regain the hill.

After two days of fighting, the PAVN forces' casualties were high, and their success was minimal. Several small hills were captured, along with one major one, Hill 224, the gateway to Bong Mountain. Hill 224 dominates the north side of the Truoi River, and stands between Mo Tau and the Mom Kum Sac hills, which command the river's south side. When a battalion of the 1st Division was overrun on Hill 224 in heavy fighting, Thi ordered a counterattack. The 1st Division soon recaptured half of Hill 224, while Mo Tau and the majority of hills remained firmly in South Vietnamese hands. In general, the 1st Division's new defensive strategy worked perfectly, and the 324th was driven back with heavy losses.

On Truong's other fronts, North Vietnamese forces were quiet in the central sector, but attacks were successful at ARVN's weakest point, the RF defending the district town of Tien Phuoc. After secretly massing the entire PAVN 2nd Division plus major elements of the 52nd Brigade from Quang Ngai, they attacked at 12:30 A.M. on 10 March. By 4:00 P.M., they had shattered the RF defenses and captured the town. The survivors pulled back to regroup on the main road heading to Tam Ky.

On 11 March Brigadier General Tran Van Nhut, the ARVN 2nd Division commander, hurried to Tam Ky from Quang Ngai to make preparations for a relief operation to recapture Tien Phuoc. Truong also dispatched his reserve, the 12th Ranger Group, to reinforce Tam Ky. The next day, the 5th Regiment, 2nd Division, arrived from Quang Ngai to conduct the attack. Radio intercepts and prisoners quickly revealed the size of the North Vietnamese forces in the area, and the 5th Regiment prudently halted its attack well short of the town.

Losing Tien Phuoc was a blow, but Truong's main concern was the hill country. Several captured B-4 Front soldiers informed their ARVN interrogators that Quang Tri local forces had replaced the 325th Division along the ceasefire line. When prisoners from the 324th Division confirmed the arrival of the 325th in the hill country south of Hue, Truong immediately took action. He realized that the 325th's presence enabled PAVN to strike in multiple directions, either to put additional pressure on his 1st Division, to seize the Hai Van Pass, or to attack Danang from the north. On 10 March, while the PAVN 304th Division at Thuong Duc remained in its bunkers, he shifted one Airborne brigade to cover Danang's northern approaches. He also ordered the 14th Ranger Group to depart Quang Ngai and fly to Danang to reconstitute his reserve, and moved a 3rd Division regiment to cover northern Quang Tin after the departure of the 12th Rangers.

Little did Truong know that the 304th was so badly battered from the previous year's battle at Thuong Duc that it was incapable of operations. Only the division's 9th Regiment, on its way from Quang Tri, was combat-ready. This was ARVN's third intelligence breakdown in this campaign. First was the false intelligence that the 308th and/or 341st Divisions were on the ceasefire line, which caused the South Vietnamese to keep larger forces in northern Quang Tri than necessary. Next was missing the 325th Division's southern shift. Third, the failure to accurately gauge the 304th's status led Truong to tie down his best troops and, more importantly, affected his military decision-making. With the 304th encamped west of Danang, he believed he had to concentrate a sizable blocking force to defend his capital, and this worked to the detriment of his other fronts. While intelligence is never perfect, when combined with Thieu's subsequent decisions and the collapse of morale, these failures led directly to the fall of I Corps.

Despite the loss of Tien Phuoc and a few positions south of Hue, after the first week of action Truong was confident that he had halted the North Vietnamese offensive. Only the looming presence of the 325th Division gave him any pause, but with his shift of the Airborne and the 14th Rangers, the situation seemed fairly secure. In the midst of this confidence, on 12 March, the JGS cabled Truong ordering him to release the Airborne Division for an immediate return to Saigon. With ARVN's strategic reserves tied down in I Corps, the JGS needed the division to help retake Ban Me Thuot and defend Saigon. In fact, there was almost no second line of resistance around the capital.

To Truong and his commanders and staff, this order was insane. With the 325th Division poised in the hills, and the 304th Division entrenched west of Danang, removing the Airborne would strip Truong's defenses around South Vietnam's second-largest city. He immediately requested and was granted an audience with the president.

Arriving in Saigon on 13 March, Truong passionately tried to dissuade Thieu. Taking his best unit in the midst of an enemy offensive was folly, Truong exclaimed. Without the Airborne, he would need to shift the Marines from Quang Tri to cover his lines west of Danang. The resultant transfer of forces to protect the city meant in essence abandoning Quang Tri. Defending Hue would also prove problematic. Further, the loss of the Airborne would adversely affect military and civilian morale. The civilians were well aware that the Red Berets were essential to the region's defense, and they would interpret the Airborne's removal as the government giving up I Corps. The population would subsequently flee, compounding Truong's already massive refugee problem. If Thieu's order stood, the sweeping changes it would entail threatened to destroy I Corps.

The president, however, was adamant. Thieu explained to Truong his new strategic concept. With the severe aid cuts, and no hope of U.S. airpower to help stem the North Vietnamese attacks, his best option was to consolidate his forces, conserve his logistics, and try to survive the dry-season offensive. Afterwards, the military would prepare for what he was sure would be a major North Vietnamese offensive in 1976. Thus, he had made the decision to defend only those areas critical to the survival of South Vietnam. It was better, Thieu stated, to lose part of the country than to enter into a coalition with the Communists. Turning to a map, he outlined for Truong his vision of the future of South Vietnam. In I Corps, only Danang and the surrounding areas were to be held at all costs. All other areas, including Hue, could be abandoned to permit Truong to preserve his combat strength for Danang's defense. Truong was ordered to develop a plan for the necessary redeployments. He would receive the newly formed 468th Marine Brigade as a replacement for the Airborne, who would start moving by 17 March.

Faced with Thieu's refusal, Truong begged to phase the withdrawal. Once the situation was stable, he could shift forces, but rapid changes would invite panic. Thieu instead offered a compromise. Truong could stagger the movement one Airborne brigade at a time, but the entire withdrawal was to be completed by the end of March.

A devastated Truong later described Thieu's decision to colleagues as "irrational," and he contemplated resigning. He later wrote: "I was bitter and angry because the order was so sudden, beyond anything I ever anticipated or desired . . . although the situation in Hue, Quang Ngai, and Danang was rather serious because of the enemy's continuous attacks, I had sufficient strength to resist and planned to send the Airborne and Marine Divisions to those areas to regain a position of superiority. I meticulously explained my ideas and my plans to the President and the Prime Minister but these ideas and plans were rejected."[9]

Why Truong was so surprised about the Airborne's withdrawal is a mystery. Removing Airborne units to meet a major threat to Saigon had first occurred in June 1974, when a brigade was rotated back during the Iron Triangle battle. Further planning occurred, according to General Vien, at the December 1974 National Security Council meeting, which outlined the JGS's plans for 1975: "The I Corps was told to rearrange its forces so that the Airborne Division could be redeployed to Saigon or elsewhere within seventy-two hours."[10] That short time frame precisely fits Thieu's subsequent order. Frank Snepp, the CIA's main analyst in Vietnam, recounts that in February 1975, Thieu had again informed Truong to "hold [the Airborne] in reserve for a possible transfer to Saigon."[11]

But even though Truong knew in principle that this was a possibility, to have the withdrawal called for so hurriedly and in the midst of an enemy offensive was a severe blow. Additionally, Thieu was now changing to a Danang-only enclave from the previously-agreed-upon three-enclave plan (Hue, Danang, and Chu Lai). While Truong understood the requirement for a strategic reserve, he felt that Thieu vastly underestimated the psychological impact of rapid troop redeployments on a population that feared the Communists after years of depredations.

One other factor deeply concerned Truong. He suspected that the real reason Thieu wanted to pull the Red Berets south was to prevent a coup. With Thieu, it is often difficult to separate policy from personal motivation, since he rarely revealed his inner thoughts. But by 1975, the military had been mostly weaned from its previous coup mentality. Still, Thieu's suspicious nature constantly was on the lookout for challengers, and the one general officer who had the national reputation to threaten the president was Truong.[12] The president's political wariness of Truong probably affected how clearly he explained this and subsequent decisions to his general. For example, there is some confusion as to whether Thieu informed Truong that his idea was to seek a "last enclave, a beachhead along the coast that would serve as a landing area if the Americans decided to return."[13] He wanted to maintain this enclave so that the Americans could not say there was nowhere to land. Moreover, by concentrating three divisions and four ranger groups around Danang, Thieu hoped to lure PAVN into a set-piece battle, where ARVN's superior firepower could inflict severe casualties on the North Vietnamese. Whether Giap would have taken the bait and mounted repeated charges against Danang is debatable. Regardless, the hasty withdrawal of the Airborne helped trigger the downfall of I Corps.

When Truong returned to his headquarters, he did not inform his subordinates of everything Thieu had told him. According to Truong's Navy commander, Commodore Ho Van Ky Thoai, Truong was following orders. Truong told him after the war that Thieu had instructed him "to keep this information absolutely secret and not to disclose to his division commanders, province chiefs, or his Navy and Air Force commanders that we were going to abandon Central Vietnam."[14]

On 14 March Truong convened a meeting with his senior officers, but, per his orders, he discussed only the withdrawal of the Airborne Division and not the enclave plan. Thieu, fearful of Communist spies, had hamstrung Truong's ability to inform his commanders, which prevented them from making sufficient preparations for a full-scale retreat. While Truong told them to make "contingency plans" for a withdrawal to Danang, his primary directive was for them to hold their ground. He did share the full news with his chief of staff, ordering him to commence planning for a retreat into multiple enclaves, but he was unable to do much on his own. Thus, when the decision came to pull back to Danang, the ARVN retreat was a haphazard affair that immediately broke down because of thousands of panicky civilians on the road and PAVN forces pressing hard on their heels.

Despite Truong's bitterness, he ordered the 369th Marine Brigade to depart Quang Tri and replace one of the Airborne brigades at Thuong Duc. The 258th Marine Brigade and the Marine Division headquarters would shortly follow and replace the other Airborne unit. Truong also ordered Lieutenant General Thi to ship his 175-mm artillery battalion and an M-48 tank company to Danang, along with engineering equipment and ammunition stocks.

Thi was extremely upset about the loss of the two elite brigades. He did not believe he could hold Hue against a determined enemy thrust without them, and asked that Truong do the utmost to secure Route 1. Otherwise, he would be cut off. In response, Truong altered the Marine redeployment and shifted forces to help Thi. In return for the 369th Marine Brigade, Truong gave Thi the 14th Ranger Group. He left the 147th Marine Brigade and Marine deputy division commander, Colonel Nguyen Thanh Tri, north of Hue. Truong also put the 258th Marine Brigade headquarters and one battalion on the Hue side of the Hai Van Pass, while another battalion remained near Hue. The third battalion went with the 369th Marine Brigade to Thuong Duc. Not until the 468th Marine Brigade arrived from Saigon on 21 March did he shift the 258th Marine Brigade headquarters into Quang Nam province.

While Truong was still digesting Thieu's order, the PAVN 324th Division resumed the assault. The fighting was especially ferocious at Hill 224. Over several days, control shifted back and forth. ARVN artillery and air strikes pummeled the PAVN troop concentrations, and by 16 March ARVN counterattacks had recaptured the entire peak. While the surrounding hills remained in enemy hands, supply problems prevented the 324th from launching further attacks.

Meanwhile, in Quang Ngai province, low-level fighting continued, but neither side could make any headway. On 13 March, noticing the pullout of the 14th Rangers and the 5th Regiment, local Communist forces pushed forward. By 16 March they were pressing toward Quang Ngai City, forcing back a regiment of the 2nd Division. To shorten his lines, Truong ordered the abandonment of two western districts in Quang Ngai, hoping that he could use the troops to strengthen his defenses along Route 1. Truong supervised the air evacuation of one ranger battalion and numerous civilians from one of those districts. Over two days, some 2,500 GVN civil servants and their families were rescued.

Late on 16 March, the 14th Rangers arrived in Quang Tri and replaced the 369th Marine Brigade along the Thach Han River on the western side of Route 1. The 14th Rangers were badly under-strength; they had roughly 1,400 soldiers present for duty (out of a full complement of 2,324), with an average strength of less than 300 men per battalion (out of 683). They were replacing a full-strength, 3,500-man Marine brigade. The Rangers put one battalion on the river and another facing the mountains, and held one in reserve. The next day, the 258th Marine Brigade departed from the eastern side of Route 1, leaving only the Quang Tri RF group to continue defending the area. The last Marine brigade, the 147th, remained dug in northwest of Hue. Once again Thi had deliberately placed his weakest units on the ceasefire line, gambling that the North Vietnamese would not cross it.

On 15 March Nguyen Huu An held a staff meeting to evaluate the campaign. While An was pleased that his units had overrun an ARVN infantry battalion on Hill 224 and captured a few other hills, he was jubilant that his units had opened fire exactly on schedule. Yet despite the importance he placed on accomplishing Giap's prime directive, An was no political hack. He admitted that "our concrete achievements were not impressive" and that, because of a host of problems, "the corps's combat efficiency during this phase of the operation was low."[15] Many on his staff recommended that he employ the 325th Division to assist the 324th in its attacks, but he decided against that move. Instead, he directed the 325th to stick to the original plan and open fire on 21 March against ARVN units in the Mom Kum Sac hills south of the Truoi River. He informed Giap of his decisions, and then went to the 325th's headquarters to inspect its combat preparations. His refusal to adjust his plans, despite the real difficulties the 324th had encountered in penetrating ARVN defenses, would prove critical.

On the night of 15 March, PAVN strategic intelligence reported to Giap that the 14th Rangers had shifted to Danang. Although Giap was focused on the Central Highlands, upon studying the Rangers' movement, combined with the pullout from Pleiku, he now discerned a pattern. He suspected ARVN was retreating into the long-feared enclaves. He immediately ordered new attacks in I Corps to prevent an enclave from forming at Danang. On 17 March he cabled Nguyen Huu An to shift to the Opportunity Plan: liberate Hue, the rest of Thua Thien, and Quang Tri now. Giap wrote: "The situation is developing quickly and the big opportunity is arriving sooner than we had anticipated. The enemy is now being forced to deal with our attacks . . . and he has begun to carry out strategic withdrawals and regrouping. Tri-Thien must intensify its operations on all fronts. Specifically, step up your attacks from the west against the enemy's regular army units, cut off and strategically divide Hue from Danang, [and] boldly send forces down into the lowlands to . . . push in the enemy's defensive blocking lines."[16]

On 18 March, Giap received more vital intelligence. North Vietnamese spies reported that the Airborne was withdrawing to Saigon. Giap's attention was now riveted on I Corps. Noticing the very thin ARVN defenses along the Thach Han, Giap's staff concluded that the South Vietnamese were abandoning Quang Tri province. As soon as the morning staff meeting was over, Giap sent a cable to the two PAVN commands. They were instructed "to take immediate and daring action. [B-4] must immediately send forces down into the lowlands and intensify operations deep within the lowland area. You are to send not just battalions, but . . . entire regiments to . . . attack."[17] In ordering the B-4 Front to attack across the cease-fire line, Giap had just called Lieutenant General Thi's bluff.

Later that day, the PAVN commanders received a second important message. It provided the intelligence on current South Vietnamese plans, and outlined Giap's main strategy: "In Danang the Airborne Division is being withdrawn to Saigon. The Airborne will be replaced by the Marine Division. It is possible that the enemy will abandon the area from north of Hue to the Thach Han River. These redeployments are part of a major retrenchment and strategic withdrawal plan for all South Vietnam. Because the situation is currently so advantageous for us, you all must direct the units under your command boldly and urgently. You must not allow the enemy to abandon the area north of Hue, withdraw his forces safely, and bring all their people, including civilian reactionaries, back to make their stand in Danang, because if they are able to do that we will run into problems. You must quickly attack down to Route 1, cut the road and attack the airfield and supply warehouses and facilities at Phu Bai."[18]

In less than a week, Giap had become privy to the single most important piece of the South Vietnamese government's strategy. This critical information gave him a rare opportunity to adapt his tactics, and he took full advantage. On 18 March the Politburo met to assess the situation. Giap's speech outlined his belief that ARVN was pulling back into enclaves and that it was crucial to push hard now in order to prevent this.

Strongly supported by Le Duan, he recommended that his armies attempt to conquer the South in 1975, and that Saigon be made the primary direction of attack. However, while Saigon remained the ultimate prize, the first goal would be to destroy the RVNAF forces in I Corps and liberate Hue and Danang.

While the Politburo was making these far-reaching decisions, the sudden and unexplained shift of the Marines from Quang Tri had brought about precisely what Truong had dreaded: the remaining civilians became demoralized and immediately left their hamlets and villages. On the morning of 17 March, a new wave of refugees reached Hue bearing news of the Marines' abrupt departure. And it was not only the civilians who were affected. Lieutenant General Thi noted that "The Marines' departure had a devastating effect on the courage and morale of the RF units."[19] The Quang Tri RF troops, who had fought superbly two weeks earlier against the first enemy incursions, now felt abandoned. Moreover, rumors that the GVN was preparing to cede much of I Corps to the Communists began to spread. The outlines of Thieu's truncation plan had leaked out, and had morphed into a nefarious "secret deal" to discard part of the country. Many South Vietnamese were convinced this had been arranged by the superpowers. When people learned of the withdrawals from Kontum and Pleiku beginning on 15 March, the rumors were only reinforced. That night and into the next morning, a flood of people headed for Danang. Massive numbers of civilian vehicles flowed south on Route 1, and the civil governments in Quang Tri and Hue crumbled as many officials evacuated.

Truong called Prime Minister Khiem every day to plead for help in coping with the refugee problem. With the roads jammed with civilians, Truong was losing the ability to maneuver his forces. He told Khiem it was already almost impossible to execute Thieu's order to withdraw via Route 1 into an enclave around Danang. On 17 March Truong tried to set up checkpoints at the Hai Van Pass to control the flow of refugees into Danang, but traffic immediately backed up. Truong feared the Communists would shell the road as they did in 1972, so for humanitarian reasons he opened the checkpoints. Consequently, Danang became terribly overcrowded. People slept on the sidewalks, and food and sanitation were becoming serious issues.

Given this news, Thieu ordered Khiem and the entire Cabinet to make an inspection tour of I and II Corps. They arrived at Danang the morning of 18 March. Truong assembled his staff, the province chiefs, and senior military officers to brief Khiem. Before the main meeting, Truong gave the prime minister an update on the military situation. He warned him that North Vietnamese attacks against Hue and Danang were imminent, while upwards of a half-million refugees were heading toward Danang. Shocked, Khiem ordered Truong to report directly to Thieu the next day.

Beginning the meeting, the province chiefs took turns describing the difficult refugee situation. Several recommended that Thieu issue a statement denying the rumors of a secret deal, and that military dependents be evacuated so that the soldiers could fight without worrying about their families. The province chiefs also informed the prime minister that upwards of 350,000 people wanted to leave I Corps. Khiem promised he would arrange for sea transportation, but he claimed he needed four days to arrange for the ships. He promised to appoint a special group of Cabinet ministers, headed by Deputy Prime Minister Phan Quang Dan, to deal with the refugees and plan for their movement south.

Despite Khiem's promises, little was subsequently accomplished. Instead of remaining in Danang and assisting, he and the Cabinet immediately departed, although Khiem stopped off at Nha Trang to meet with Major General Phu and assess the situation in II Corps. Afterwards, Khiem returned to Saigon. While he has rightly received much criticism for the government's lackadaisical response, Khiem did keep one promise. Within a day, Deputy Prime Minister Dan, whose work in resettling the refugees from the 1972 offensive is a significant but overlooked accomplishment of Thieu's government, was appointed to solve this new refugee problem. Dan immediately began working to move people out of Danang.

After meeting with Khiem, Truong flew to Hue. Gathering various religious, political, and civic leaders together, he outlined the critical military situation and asked for their help in defending the city and coping with the refugees. They wholeheartedly agreed, but stated that the refugee situation was growing worse by the hour. They urged that something be done to give the people some hope. The eager response from the Hue civilian leaders convinced Truong that the city could be defended. It was the best way to stem the refugee problem. If the people saw that the military intended to fight, they would be less likely to flee. Truong decided to "do everything in my power to hold Hue and I Corps. . . . How could I abandon this rocky soil that so many of my comrades-in-arms had shed their blood to defend, especially during the 1968 Tet Offensive?"[20] Truong had commanded the 1st Division during the Tet Offensive, and his stalwart fight for the city had earned him the admiration of the citizens of Hue and Thua Thien province. Still, a cautious Truong called Khiem that night to inform him that the earlier estimate of 350,000 people who wished to leave I Corps was too low.

Following Khiem's order to report directly to Thieu, Truong flew to Saigon again on 19 March to brief the president on the withdrawal plans he had developed. Truong offered two options: either a retreat north and south along Route 1 to Danang, or a pullback into enclaves centered on Hue, Chu Lai, and Quang Ngai City, and then a withdrawal by sea. Since refugees already jammed Route 1, the enclave/sea withdrawal was the better option. In particular, it was Truong's judgment that a withdrawal from Hue by road was already impossible. Truong recommended defending the enclaves as long as possible, and then withdrawing to Danang if the pressure became too great. He would give up Chu Lai and Quang Ngai first, and only then Hue. Truong especially wanted to fight for Hue, as he had good defenses around the city. One also suspects the city held great significance for him after the fierce battles in February 1968 to retake it from the Communist forces.

Both General Vien and President Thieu recommended a different plan. They wanted Truong to withdraw in successive phases toward Danang, as Thieu believed that PAVN would make a strong effort to cut Route 1 at the Hai Van Pass. Vien did not believe that the Navy had enough ships to supply three enclaves simultaneously. It was his way of saying he did not believe Truong could hold both Hue and Danang. Prime Minister Khiem and Vice President Huong were more forthright. They recommended abandoning Hue. But despite their opposition to Truong's plan, Thieu agreed to let him defend Hue. In supporting his commander, Thieu went against his own instincts and the counsel of his senior advisors. However, he warned Truong that if he could not hold Hue, Route 1 and the Hai Van Pass must remain open so that the 1st Division could safely withdraw to Danang. Thieu also promised to make a TV and radio broadcast that night to reassure his people.

Before leaving, Truong asked Thieu about the government's plans for the Marine Division. A Marine withdrawal would drastically influence his own plans, and he needed to know. Thieu now faced a remarkable moment of his presidency. Would he inform Truong that he intended to strip him of his best remaining troops at the exact moment the enemy was about to strike? According to General Vien, Thieu flinched from this difficult decision. Although Vien acknowledges that Thieu was in an "excruciating position," he states that Thieu denied that there were plans being drafted to recall the Marines. Thieu simply told Truong to "hold onto whatever territory he could with whatever forces he had now."[21]

Truong, however, was well aware of Thieu's propensity for giving generalized instructions and expecting his subordinates to work out the details. Truong wanted clear-cut instructions that he could implement, while Thieu wanted to give strategic direction and then let his general determine how to implement his decisions. The circumstances were eerily similar to the meeting with Pham Van Phu at Cam Ranh Bay. Although Phu claimed he was instructed to withdraw from Kontum/Pleiku within three days, Thieu (and Vien) later claimed the timing and planning were left to Phu's discretion. Regardless, it was another miscommunication that contributed to the destruction of the Republic of Vietnam.

Returning to Danang that evening, Truong received an urgent phone call from Lieutenant General Thi. He reported that at 3:00 A.M. PAVN forces had attacked across the Thach Han River in Quang Tri. Although Thi and others believed the attackers were the 308th Division, in reality only one local sapper battalion had crossed the river, while three Quang Tri local-force battalions attacked from the mountains. In any case, the two defending Ranger battalions were quickly engulfed in heavy fighting. At daybreak, another local PAVN unit and four T-54 tanks of the 203rd Armor Brigade pushed southward along the coast undetected and reached a point six miles behind ARVN lines. An RF unit finally spotted and reported the vehicles, and then fled. So did many of the remaining Quang Tri regional troops. With their families and the Marines gone, and nothing but deserted villages all around them, they had little to fight for. Facing no opposition, the PAVN column turned inland and slowly headed for the district town of Hai Lang, which sits on Route 1 south of Quang Tri City. The 14th Ranger headquarters was positioned in Hai Lang, and if the armor reached it, the Rangers would be overrun.

Colonel Nguyen Thanh Tri, the Marine deputy commander and the commander of Lieutenant General Thi's northern front, requested air strikes to destroy the armor, but none were available. At 4:00 P.M. the PAVN column seized the former headquarters of the 258th Marine Brigade, less than two miles from Hai Lang. Meanwhile, the 14th Ranger commander reported that he had lost contact with his units along the Thach Han, and that Communist troops had captured Quang Tri City. With his flanks crumbling, Tri ordered the Rangers and the Quang Tri RF to retreat and take up defensive positions along the My Chanh River. He also ordered the 7th Marine Battalion, 258th Brigade—currently sitting at the Thuan An port outside of Hue awaiting ships to withdraw to Danang—to halt its redeployment. The Marine battalion would bolster the RF defenses along the My Chanh on the eastern side of Route 1.

During the 1972 offensive, the North Vietnamese lost the cream of their army trying to conquer Quang Tri province. After three months of terrible fighting in 1972, ARVN finally halted the PAVN advance at the My Chanh River. ARVN then spent another three months and thousands of casualties recapturing half of the province and Quang Tri City. This was the most blood-drenched, bomb-wracked, fiercely contested land in all of Vietnam. Now the Communists had retaken it in just one day. When combined with news reports about the horrific retreat from the Central Highlands, the loss of Quang Tri crushed South Vietnamese morale.

After receiving a report on the disastrous developments from Lieutenant General Thi, Truong called the president. He recommended that Thieu hold off on his speech about defending Hue until Truong could better understand the situation. Truong further asked to retain the last Airborne brigade until 31 March. This would give the population some confidence that the government intended to defend the land. Thieu agreed, but on the condition that the Airborne not be used in combat.

At dawn the next morning, Truong flew to see Thi and his subordinate commanders. Truong informed them that Hue would be defended at all costs. His officers responded that they could hold. Despite the setback in Quang Tri and sporadic artillery fire hitting Hue, their positive attitude buoyed Truong. Still, he ordered Thi to prepare contingency plans for a retreat to Danang by the Marines and the 1st Division if the situation became too difficult.

Despite Truong's caution, Thieu went ahead with his speech on 20 March. Speaking on the radio, the president was short on specifics. Mentioning that ARVN had faced "four to one odds" at Ban Me Thuot, he did not reveal that he personally had ordered the retreat from the Central Highlands. He simply said that "to preserve their strength and create conditions for more effective combat in the present stage . . . our armed forces did not defend Kontum and Pleiku cities."[22] Yet even with the situation at Hue still unclear, he stated, "We are determined to defend our territory until the end. Reports about the abandonment of Thua Thien, Dalat, and other localities are nothing but completely false, groundless rumors aimed at sowing confusion among the people." Concluding with a plea for the people to rally, he unfortunately offered no solutions other than that he had instructed the "government to take emergency measures to meet the requirements of the situation." Unfortunately, Thieu's speech had little effect on troop morale or the refugees. Whatever his intent, he had not delivered the forceful denunciation of a secret deal to partition the land that civilians and the military alike needed to raise their morale. Thieu had missed an opportunity to give his countrymen some hope.

Feeling that the situation was difficult but still tenable, Truong returned to Danang that night. Upon arriving at his headquarters, he found a cable from the JGS awaiting him. The message, flown to Danang by special courier, was a bombshell. It stated: "Limited air and naval resources available are only sufficient to support one enclave. You are therefore to conduct a delaying action by withdrawing to the Hai Van Pass if the situation permits."[23] Despite the earlier agreement with Thieu to fight for Hue, a stunned Truong interpreted the cable to mean that he was to abandon the city and retreat to Danang. Shortly thereafter, a second cable arrived from JGS countermanding Thieu's permission to retain the Airborne brigade. Enormously upset, Truong penned a quick reply to General Vien: "I feel weak and confused. I am afraid I am not capable of carrying out my duties. I request that you accept my resignation, and 'That is all.'"[24]

After receiving Truong's resignation cable, Thieu immediately clarified his message. His intent had been to provide Truong the flexibility to deal with the situation, not to give the impression that he had abruptly changed his mind about Hue. Thieu had the JGS send a clarification to the original message: "To put it more accurately, when the situation so demands and conditions allow this to be carried out in a timely manner."[25]

While temporarily mollified, Truong knew he still faced major difficulties. The worst problem was the 300,000 refugees who had already poured into Danang, with another 500,000 on the way. His troops had also suffered; in the two weeks from 5 to 19 March, I Corps had lost 334 dead, 1,427 wounded, and 236 missing in action. The Air Force had flown over five hundred sorties and lost two airplanes to ground fire. Over 200,000 artillery shells had been fired, the highest amount since March 1973.[26] At that rate, serious shortages would soon appear. By comparison with the 200,000 artillery rounds ARVN had fired, the North Vietnamese claim that "thanks to economy measures and scraping together our reserve stocks for two years, we had about 40,000 rounds. During Phase One of the campaign we had used only 85-mm, 100-mm, and 122-mm guns. The number of 122-mm and 130-mm shells used during Phase One was insignificant, and these rounds were being saved for use when a major opportunity developed."[27] Despite the huge disadvantage in the number of shells, ARVN reports repeatedly mention the improved accuracy over 1972 of the PAVN gunners. Part of the reason is that the Communist gunners were no longer under repeated air attack and counter-battery fire.

Overall, Truong found himself roughly in the same situation now as at the start of the attacks: waiting for the next blows to land, and hoping he could, by some miracle, fend them off once again.

"MAINTAIN A FIRM GRIP ON ROUTE 1, NO MATTER WHAT THE COST"

In Saigon, Wolfgang Lehmann watched Danang's growing refugee problem with concern. On 18 March he cabled Washington and recommended that "it would not be too early to think in terms of a possible sea lift to move large numbers of people" out of I Corps. If PAVN attacked Hue, hordes of people would flee to Danang, greatly aggravating that situation. Lehmann wrote: "In such a contingency I should think that a sea lift of refugees . . . using suitable U.S. Navy assets, and perhaps augmented by ships from other countries . . . would be the right thing to do on plain humanitarian grounds alone."[28] At the same time, Lehmann ordered the evacuation of all non-essential U.S. personnel from I Corps. Embassy officers in those provinces would man their offices during the day, and then leave at dusk by helicopter for Danang.

As recounted in chapter 9, Lehmann met with Thieu on 20 March at the insistence of the State Department to obtain from the president his precise military intentions. In a wide-ranging discussion about the country, Thieu stated in regard to I Corps that he would not abandon Thua Thien. Aware that removing the Airborne had made the situation worse, Thieu said he had instructed Truong to do "his best with the forces he has at hand. Hue would not be abandoned."[29] He did not, however, think Truong could hold Hue, and he believed that forming an enclave at Danang was the best option. "It would have to be decided later whether to try to hold that enclave. If it were to be useful as a beachhead for the future recapture of other territory that was one thing, but if it were to be held simply as a suicide mission that would be another." It was Thieu's way of gauging U.S.

intentions, and slyly offering an opening for an American return. No U.S. official grasped the president's subtle message.

While Lehmann was attempting to divine Thieu's intentions, on 17 March ARVN received a piece of excellent intelligence. A defector from the 325th Division told his interrogators that the division intended to launch a two-regiment assault toward the district town of Phu Loc on Route 1 near the northern entrance to the Hai Van Pass. Truong immediately moved the 8th Marine Battalion, 258th Brigade, to the town. He also began air strikes and long-range 175-mm artillery fire onto the suspected location of the 325th Division in hopes of delaying its movement. It was the best he could do. The presence of the 304th Division in Thuong Duc continued to force Truong to maintain a Marine brigade in western Quang Nam to guard against a thrust by that unit. Truong simply had no troops left.

The defector's intelligence was accurate: renewed assaults in Thua Thien province were imminent. PAVN's plan called for the B-4 Front to attack the Marines defending the Bo River northwest of Hue while concurrently sending forces across the My Chanh River. South of Hue, the 324th Division would again strike Bong and Mo Tau Mountains and Hill 224. Simultaneously, the 325th would cut Route 1 to prevent ARVN troops from retreating to Danang. Nguyen Huu An had just received a directive from Hanoi that he must cut Route 1 between Hue and Danang on 21 March, no matter what the cost. He immediately diverted his campaign's primary focus away from the 324th Division to the strike by the 325th. That division would now have priority for fire support and logistics. After inspecting the 325th's preparations, he ordered it to attack on 21 March.

The key to the 325th's assault was that it had spent almost a month secretly positioning artillery on the high ground near the Mom Kum Sac hills. The plan was to mass cannon fire directly on the Ranger defenses to soften them up before the main assault. Press-ganging its infantry as porters, the 325th hauled twenty-four artillery pieces and almost three thousand rounds of ammunition up brush-covered slopes into eight separate firing positions. After three weeks of intense labor, its guns now had Route 1 and other vital targets within range. Once the opening barrage was complete, infantry would assault the 60th and 61st Battalions, 15th Rangers, which were holding these hills. Once the hills were overrun, Route 1 was only a mile away. Hue would be cut off, and thousands of South Vietnamese soldiers, Marines, and civilians would be trapped.

The two main Ranger positions in the Mom Kum Sac range were on Hill 560 and Hill 312. Two battalions from the 18th Regiment, 325th Division, would make the primary assault on Hill 560. The 18th Regiment's mission was to overrun the 61st Rangers and then cut Route 1. Another two battalions from the 101st Regiment, 325th Division, would strike the 60th Rangers on Hill 312. The mission of this regiment was to destroy the Rangers, then penetrate into the lowlands and attack the 15th Ranger Group headquarters on Route 1 at the village of Luong Dien. This was the last ARVN blocking position before the bridge over the Truoi River. There were no ARVN defenses between the bridge and the southern entrance to Hue.

Giap had placed his troops in the perfect position. The 325th Division was at full strength—the People's Army had spent considerable effort rebuilding it after it had been virtually destroyed in 1972. The division had been re-equipped and extensively trained. Facing the 325th were only two badly under-strength Ranger battalions. While the Rangers' fortifications and fire support were excellent, the large amount of ground they held stretched the too few defenders beyond their limit.

Commanded by Major Do Duc Chien, the 60th Rangers were typical of Ranger units in 1975. The Rangers were originally designed as elite light infantry, conducting reconnaissance and long-range patrols. Now they were corps-level reserves guarding static positions against main-force PAVN infantry. It was a tough assignment, especially since they were at the bottom of the ARVN logistics system for troop and weapon replacements. For example, Chien's unit had only two hundred men, and most of his officers had been killed or wounded in the savage fighting for Mo Tau the previous year. He had received new officers to serve as company commanders, but sergeants commanded his platoons in place of lieutenants. His weapons situation was even worse. Only 30 percent of his grenade launchers worked, and soldiers were being killed by exploding gun barrels because he had no substitutes. Radio batteries were in short supply, which severely hampered communications.[30] His unit was being asked to defend against an enemy force five times its size supported by artillery.

After a ten-minute delay due to fog, at 5:50 A.M. on 21 March, the PAVN Phase Two attacks in the hill country opened with a roar. Volleys of murderous fire exploded on the Ranger bunkers and trenches. After an hour, the shelling shifted to pound ARVN artillery bases and targets ranging from Phu Loc to ships in nearby waters. When the artillery fire lifted, the PAVN infantry charged forward against elements of the 61st Rangers. Within an

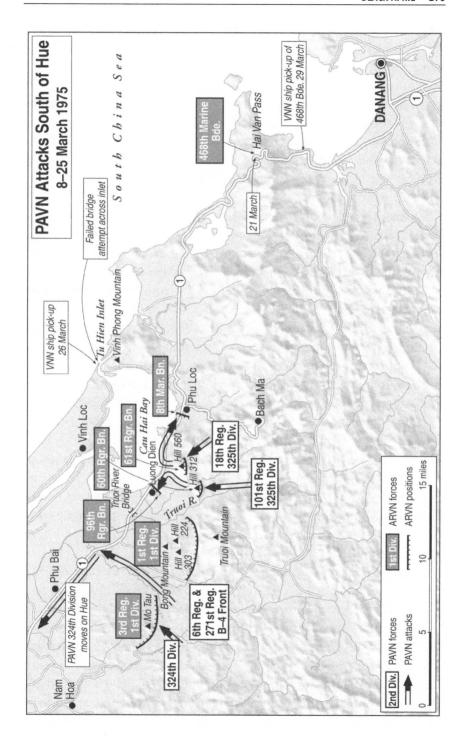

PAVN Attacks South of Hue
8–25 March 1975

South China Sea

VNN ship pick-up 26 March

VNN ship pick-up of 468th Bde. 29 March

DANANG

Failed bridge attempt across inlet

468th Marine Bde.

Hai Van Pass

21 March

Tu Hien Inlet

▲Vinh Phong Mountain

8th Mar. Bn.

● Vinh Loc

60th Rgr. Bn.

61st Rgr. Bn.

Cau Hai Bay

Truoi River Bridge

Luong Dien

Hill 560

● Phu Loc

● Bach Ma

96th Rgr. Bn.

1st Reg. 1st Div.

Hill 312

18th Reg. 325th Div.

101st Reg. 325th Div.

Truoi R.

Hill 303 ▲

Hill 224 ▲

Bong Mountain ▲

Truoi Mountain ▲

● Phu Bai

PAVN 324th Division moves on Hue

3rd Reg. 1st Div.

Mo Tau ▲

6th Reg. & 271st Reg. B-4 Front

324th Div.

● Nam Hoa

Legend

PAVN forces

PAVN attacks

2nd Div. — PAVN forces

ARVN forces

1st Div. — ARVN positions

ARVN positions

0   5   10   15 miles

hour, the Communist troops had captured several strong-points near Hill 560, but the hill remained in ARVN hands. In the face of heavy fire, the Rangers held their ground and rained mortar rounds and machine-gun fire onto the attackers. ARVN batteries along Route 1 returned the artillery fire and pummeled the enemy formations. Yet despite the casualties, the attackers pressed forward to take Hill 560. Cutting through the perimeter obstacles, they reached the Ranger bunkers. Hand-to-hand fighting broke out, but despite being outnumbered, the Rangers threw out the attackers. With his main assault force stymied, the PAVN commander pulled back to re-evaluate the situation.

Looking for a new breach point, the commander noticed a gap in the Ranger defenses. The eastern side of the hill was very steep, and the Rangers had positioned their troops elsewhere and used a minefield to protect that section. The North Vietnamese commander made a bold decision: using the thick jungle as cover, his men secretly removed the mines so they could make an assault straight up the nearly vertical slope.

By 2:00 P.M., they were ready. Climbing the slope, PAVN infantry surprised the Rangers from behind. They overran the 61st Rangers' command post and captured their commander. The battle was over in an hour. The Rangers had been routed from the hill, but not without cost. The North Vietnamese had lost forty dead and one hundred wounded capturing Hill 560.

At the same time, elements of the 101st Regiment, 325th Division, attacked the 60th Rangers on Hill 312, but Chien's Rangers drove them off with a barrage of mortar rounds. Several more times the enemy troops assaulted his positions, but his men stopped them cold. Then the group commander radioed Chien that the 61st Rangers had been overrun, and he ordered Chien to retreat back to the group command post at Luong Dien. Of the five hundred Rangers who had marched up into the Mom Kum Sac hills, only about three hundred escaped.

In the 1st Division's sector, the 324th Division struck Hills 224 and 303, and Bong and Mo Tau Mountains. Within a short time, Hill 224 was captured, but the PAVN advance was halted at Hill 303 by tough resistance. On Bong Mountain, a battalion from the ARVN 1st Regiment, 1st Division, was pushed off with heavy casualties, but a counterattack by a sister battalion reclaimed the high ground. Savage fighting continued to roil across Bong Mountain, which changed hands multiple times. Finally, on the morning of 22 March, the 1st Regiment regained control of the mountain. On Mo Tau, elements of the ARVN 54th Regiment, 1st Division, repulsed several assaults. A prisoner reported that PAVN casualties were extremely heavy, and that one battalion was almost wiped out. The 1st Division had held once more, but the 324th's assault prevented the 1st Division from assisting the 15th Rangers on its flank.

Later that afternoon, the 2nd Corps and B-4 Front received a message from Giap. His cable outlined the goals agreed upon at the 18 March Politburo meeting. Announcing that the enemy had begun to withdraw in Thua Thien/Hue, Giap wrote: "The mission of 2nd Corps and B-4 Front is to take quick and bold action to block the enemy withdrawal . . . destroy the entire 1st Division and other forces in the area . . . completely liberate Tri-Thien and Hue, and occupy the entire Hai Van Pass. Our forces must completely cut off all traffic on Route 1 from Hue to Danang by the end of the day on 21 March 1975. B-4 forces must not stop at My Chanh. Instead they must quickly develop the attack in the direction of the Thuan An harbor entrance . . . 2nd Corps and B-4 are authorized to use any of their forces to destroy the enemy, including artillery and tanks. . . . Because of the enemy evacuation artillery positions must be moved so that they can reach and control the Thuan An harbor entrance."[31]

Nguyen Huu An immediately ordered the artillery supporting the 325th Division to begin firing on Route 1 to block any vehicular movement. Within minutes, artillery rounds began to hit the highly congested road. Vehicles exploded, and many civilians died from the shelling. While a few braved the fire, most panicked and drove back to Hue. While it was not the bloody carnage that was Route 1 in 1972, the civilian fears of indiscriminate PAVN fire once again proved true. GVN authorities began shuttling civilians toward the Thuan An port to be evacuated by ship. Within hours, the first manifestations of the "family syndrome" in I Corps began to be seen, as some 1st Division soldiers deserted to find their families. RF/PF and rear-service units also began to melt away. It started slowly, but within days the phenomenon enveloped almost every unit save the Marines.

Nguyen Huu An then ordered the 325th Division to move from the hills and cut Route 1. The 325th sent three battalions on an all-night march through driving rain and heavy brush to block the road. The PAVN troops reached the lowlands at dawn on 22 March. RF troops in nearby positions spotted them and opened fire, but the North Vietnamese soldiers soon cleared the RF bunkers and occupied a two-mile stretch of road.

Learning of the loss of Hill 560, Lieutenant General Thi immediately called Truong and requested permission to use the 8th Marine Battalion in

Phu Loc to recapture the hill. He also called Brigadier General Nguyen Van Diem, the ARVN 1st Division commander, who was in command of Thi's southern front, and ordered him to make a diversionary assault to assist the Marines. He also sent in his last reserve, the 94th Ranger Battalion, 15th Group. But instead of attacking to recapture the Mom Kum Sac hills, the Marines and Rangers now had to deal with the sudden appearance of PAVN forces on Route 1. Heavy combat raged all day as the Rangers and Marines assaulted both sides of the roadblock. Despite multiple assaults and heavy air support, the counterattack failed. Exhausted, both sides dug in as night fell.

The 2nd Corps history rightly calls cutting Route 1 "the most effective blow of the entire offensive."[32] Although the 325th Division troops had now been awake for forty-eight hours, Giap offered them no respite. In a message on the afternoon of 22 March, he commended the 325th's cutting of Route 1 as "a tremendous achievement." However, "no achievement would be sufficient to balance the criminal mistake the division would make if it allowed the enemy to re-open the road. The division had to maintain a firm grip on the newly captured section of Route 1, no matter what the cost."[33] During the night, the 325th Division commander brought most of his two regiments to Route 1, leaving only a battalion behind to garrison the Mom Kum Sac hills.

Given Giap's new orders, and with the 324th's inability to capture the hill positions, at noon on 22 March, An decided to shift strategy. He ordered the 324th Division to bypass the 1st Division and penetrate directly into the lowlands. Concurrently, the 325th would resume the attack and send one regiment north on Route 1 toward the 15th Rangers' headquarters at Luong Dien. Once Luong Dien was captured, the regiment would attack Phu Bai airport in coordination with the 324th. The 325th's other regiment would strike toward Phu Loc. On the night of 22 March, the 324th left one regiment behind to pin down the 1st Division, and sent its other two regiments to attack Hue from the south.

Making a rapid attack against the ARVN defenses south of Hue presented Nguyen Huu An with two major problems. First, his troops were burning through supplies. Some units reported they were dangerously low on ammunition and food. The continuing rains turned the makeshift roads into impassable rivers of mud, and few supplies were coming forward. He faced a difficult choice: Halt his advance and give his logistic teams time to resupply his troops, or go for broke. While he was considering his options, his supply troops found the solution. They used captured ARVN weapons, and they stole food from local villagers to resupply the soldiers.

An's second issue was firepower. Per Giap's original order not to use the corps's armor and heavy artillery, An had left them deep in his rear. Now Giap had suddenly approved the use of armor, but An had only one tank company close enough to get into battle. Having just returned from a Soviet school, he was disappointed by Giap's earlier caution. Contemplating the tactical situation on 22 March, An later wrote: "If only the General Staff had approved the recommendation made by 2nd Corps Headquarters at the start of the campaign, to allow us to position one tank battalion and one battalion of long-range artillery right behind the corps's attack formation, this force would have been a priceless asset to us now. Later, when I thought about this issue, I decided that during this period the General Staff should have given us broad authority to use all forces subordinate to the corps, so that when an opportunity arose it would have been easier for us to react. If that had been done, I am certain that the pace of our attack would have been more rapid."[34] Whether he is correct is open to debate. An armor thrust would have exposed his tanks to air attack, and he would have faced the same clogged Route 1 that ARVN confronted.

Lieutenant General Thi, meanwhile, was well aware he needed to stop a PAVN thrust into the undefended land south of Hue. Consequently, on the night of 22 March he pulled in his defenses. He ordered the 15th Rangers to withdraw across the Truoi River, while the 1st and 54th Regiments were told to withdraw from their hilltops and move closer to Hue's southwestern flank. Together they would to form a new defensive line to protect Hue's soft underbelly. The division's other two regiments would remain in their positions west of the city.

That afternoon, Truong received another distressing message from the JGS. Thieu had changed his mind. Vien repeated his earlier warning that Saigon was capable of supporting only one enclave. "For this reason, by every means possible, quickly, and as the situation permits, form an enclave at Danang. During the initial phase, 1st Infantry Division, 3rd Infantry Division, and the Marine Division will move into the Danang enclave. In Phase Two, 2nd Infantry Division will move into the enclave as well. When the entire 2nd Infantry Division has arrived, you will immediately return the Marine Division to the National Level Command Authority."[35]

This was the final blow for I Corps. Whatever Thieu's intent, upon receipt of these orders, Truong ordered the 8th Marine Battalion to cease its efforts to reopen Route 1, and to establish positions closer to the Hai Van Pass. Despite Thieu's earlier orders to ensure the road stayed open so that the 1st Division could use it to withdraw, his new orders ensured that Truong could not comply. Truong is reported to have said that with no way out of Hue, he hoped the troops would stop deserting, as "they would have no alternative except to fight."[36] Truong was wrong. Instead of settling down along a defensible perimeter, his troops felt abandoned. Desertions increased, and commanders soon began losing control over their soldiers.

This could not have come at a worse time, as Giap was determined to take advantage of South Vietnamese turmoil. After disseminating the various orders to the 2nd Corps, Giap sent a cable on 22 March to Van Tien Dung in II Corps summarizing the Politburo's decisions. "The tremendous, strategically significant victory we have just won signals a new step in the collapse of the Americans and their puppets and marks a turning point in the military and political character of the war in South Vietnam. The enemy has displayed his intention of conducting a large-scale strategic withdrawal throughout the entire South Vietnamese battlefield aimed at pulling his forces back and concentrating them to defend primarily just Saigon and the Mekong Delta. After his retreat from the Central Highlands, he is now in the process of withdrawing from Hue and we cannot exclude the possibility that he may also withdraw from Danang. In view of this situation, the Politburo's resolve, as has already been transmitted to you, is to move as fast as possible, acting with daring and surprise . . . in order to defeat the enemy's plan and quickly achieve our strategic resolve in the key, focal-point sector."[37]

The key sector was Saigon, the heart of South Vietnam. But first, Senior General Vo Nguyen Giap intended to destroy I Corps, once and forever.

12.

"THE HOURS OF HELL"

THE COLLAPSE OF I CORPS

After retreating from Quang Tri, on 20 March Marine Colonel Nguyen Thanh Tri redeployed his forces along the My Chanh River line. He assigned the 14th Ranger Group and the remnants of the Quang Tri RF, along with the still full-strength 7th Marine Battalion, to guard the area from the bridge on Route 1 over the My Chanh River east to the sea. An eleven-mile front was being covered by fewer than two thousand men. Elements of the 1st Armor Brigade protected Route 1 from a PAVN armor thrust. The 147th Marine Brigade was arrayed along the western side of the bridge along the My Chanh River to the mountains, and then south to Hue. The 1st Division was deployed from west of Hue south along the mountains down to the Truoi River, where the 15th Rangers took over from the river to Phu Loc. The 8th Marine Battalion held Phu Loc, and a Thua Thien RF Group guarded the Hai Van area. This left Lieutenant General Thi with no reserves to call upon if his lines were penetrated. Only the VNAF and, occasionally, ships offshore provided any additional fire support.

RVNAF forces in Thua Thien would get no respite, as that same day, Deputy Chief of Staff Le Trong Tan cabled the B-4 Front, telling them that while "the capture of the entire province of Quang Tri is very commendable, the troops must not stop at My Chanh but must instead continue to attack."[1] Tan wanted the B-4 Front to attack simultaneously with the 2nd Corps assault on 21 March, destroy all RVNAF forces north of Hue, and capture the city.

The B-4 Front planned its main assault against the RF positions near the coast. Opposite the ARVN troops, the B-4 Front had three Quang Tri local-force battalions positioned on the eastern side of Route 1, and the reinforced 4th Regiment on the western side. It would send two Quang Tri battalions, supported by seven tanks, to puncture the RF lines and capture the district capital of Huong Dien. It would then continue south along the coastline and strike the Thuan An/Tan My ports, the only remaining escape route for the RVNAF units trapped in the Hue pocket. The Thuan An/Tan My harbor area and warehouse facilities are located next to the coast on the Perfume River about five miles east of Hue. Only small ships could sail into Hue. Although Tan My had several LST ramps, silting prevented the LSTs from entering the harbor, which is why Major General Murray had wanted to dredge it. The Tan My port is connected to the Thuan An port by a floating bridge across the Tam Giang Lagoon.

The third Quang Tri battalion would attack near the bridge on Route 1, while the 4th Regiment would assault the 147th Marines. The two other

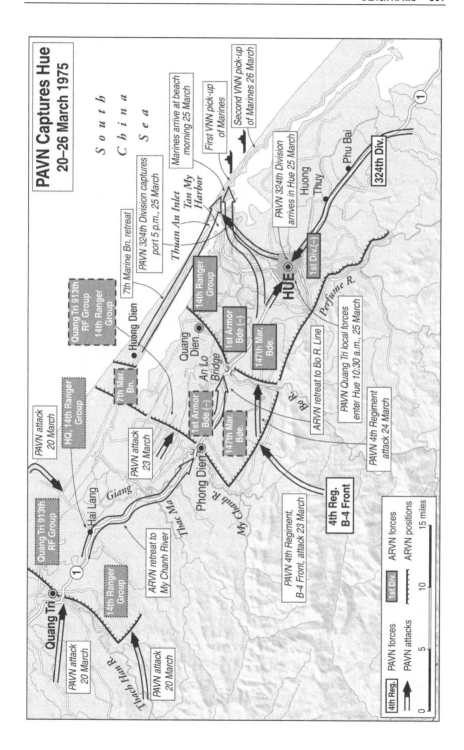

PAVN Captures Hue
20–26 March 1975

B-4 Front regiments, although badly battered from the earlier fighting, were southwest of Hue and prepared to strike from that direction. The independent 46th Regiment, recently arrived from North Vietnam, was in reserve.

Concurrently with these attacks, the B-4 Front ordered two Thua Thien local-force battalions "to cut off and control the Tu Hien Inlet, no matter what the cost. Local forces will carry out all other missions. This order supersedes all previous orders."[2] On the night of 22 March, the two battalions slipped by ARVN outposts and marched to a position on the coast just south of the inlet. The next night, they crossed the Cau Hai Bay and began firing at the naval base located at the Tu Hien Inlet. It would prove to be a key maneuver in the final battle for Hue.

As Colonel Tri surveyed his defenses on 20 March, he was deeply concerned about the Quang Tri RF. He knew they were not cowards, but he also knew their morale had been shattered. As Tri wrote after the war, "the RF soldiers saw in front of them lines of people abandoning their villages and homes, carrying their worldly possessions on poles and with their children in their arms. Included among these fleeing crowds of people were their own wives, children, and other relatives. Faced with such a situation, how could the morale of the RF soldiers fail to be affected?"[3]

Preparing his defenses, on 21 March Colonel Tri ordered the engineers to blow up the bridge on Route 1 over the My Chanh River to prevent enemy armor from crossing. At the same time, a few artillery rounds struck Hue. It was enough to set the remaining population fleeing toward Tan My, further unnerving the already distraught RF troops. The same day, the 468th Marine Brigade arrived from Saigon. Its two battalions (its third battalion was still forming in Danang) replaced the 1st Airborne Brigade at the Hai Van Pass. The 258th Marine Brigade headquarters soon departed the pass, but left the 8th Marine Battalion behind. Why Truong did not order the 468th Brigade to assist the 8th Marine Battalion in opening Route 1 remains a mystery. He did not receive the message to return the Marine Division to Saigon until late on 22 March, and clearing Route 1 was critical if Lieutenant General Thi's forces were to have any chance of escaping. Perhaps he was not confident the newly formed unit was combat ready. Still, leaving the 468th Marines sitting in their foxholes instead of attacking the roadblock was a crucial mistake by Truong.

Because of poor coordination, the B-4 Front was unable to launch its main attack north of Hue until the morning of 23 March. When it finally did attack, the RF initially held, but by noon they began to give way. Given the recent shelling of Hue and the blocking of Route 1, many troops had deserted to find their families, and the remaining few were in little mood to fight. Although Colonel Tri attempted to send a Marine company and tanks to support the RF, the North Vietnamese began shelling the 147th Brigade positions, halting that plan. In mid-afternoon, the RF collapsed and began streaming back to the final defensive line north of Hue behind the An Lo Bridge on the Bo River, only twelve miles from the city.

As the Communist troops slowly pursued the fleeing RF, at 3:00 P.M. the 4th Regiment launched its attack and caught a Marine battalion off guard. The Communist troops cut off two platoons and pushed back the Marine defenses. With his right flank unhinged by the collapsing RF, and no reserves to seal the breaches, Colonel Tri ordered a retreat back to the final Hue defensive line along the Bo River. That night the cut-off platoons escaped and linked up with their parent unit. Tri deployed the 14th Rangers from the An Lo Bridge to the Thuan An Lagoon, while pulling the 7th Marines back to defend Huong Dien. The 147th Brigade retreated behind the Bo River. The Quang Tri RF had virtually disintegrated as a fighting force. Most of their men fled into Hue despite the efforts of Marine officers and province officials to stop them.

On the morning of 23 March, PAVN also resumed the attack south of Hue. After reviewing the situation, Major General Nguyen Huu An ordered the 325th Division to send its two regiments to attack in opposite directions along Route 1. The previous day, one battalion from the 325th Division's 101st Regiment was mauled taking a hill from the Rangers, but still managed to capture it. This placed the 101st in position to assault the Ranger base at Luong Dien. Taking Luong Dien would outflank ARVN forces defending Hill 303 and Mo Tau. On the morning of 23 March, the 101st Regiment assaulted Luong Dien. After a day-long battle, the Rangers retreated over the Truoi River and blew up the bridge behind them. By nightfall, they had withdrawn to Phu Bai. On the other flank, the 325th Division's 18th Regiment overran Phu Loc after the 8th Marines pulled out.

To pin down the ARVN 1st Division, the remaining 324th Division regiment simultaneously attacked Hill 303 and Bong Mountain. The ARVN positions held out until a tank attack in the afternoon finally captured the two positions. With his defenses south of Hue being compressed, Brigadier General Diem ordered his two regiments defending the Mo Tau/Bong Mountain/Hill 303 complex to retreat to Phu Bai. They would block the enemy advance on Route 1 and backstop the Rangers. If Phu Bai fell, it was only ten miles to Hue. Diem also pulled the other two regiments west of Hue closer to the city.

While Truong's northern front was embroiled in heavy fighting, his southern front was relatively quiet. That was about to change. ARVN Brigadier General Tran Van Nhut had pulled his units back to screen the populated lowlands and major cities. In a line running south from northern Quang Tin to the Binh Dinh province border, a distance of ninety miles, Nhut had the 5th Regiment and the 12th Ranger Group defending Tam Ky, the 4th Regiment at Chu Lai, and the 6th Regiment and the 11th Ranger Group in Quang Ngai City.

At the start of the campaign, the B-1 Front's goals were to capture Tien Phuoc and eliminate several ARVN battalions. Now the B-1 commanders sensed an opportunity to destroy Nhut's entire 2nd Division and capture all of Quang Ngai province. On 16 March they changed plans. The new design called for a major attack against Tam Ky that would draw in 2nd Division forces to defend the city, whereupon they would be surrounded and cut off. The 52nd Brigade would then liberate Quang Ngai. On 21 March PAVN artillery began blasting away at RF defenses near Tam Ky. Company-sized infantry probes whittled away at RF positions. Nhut reacted to the attacks precisely as the B-1 Front hoped: he moved the 4th Regiment from Chu Lai to reinforce Tam Ky, and he pulled a battalion from the 6th Regiment to protect Chu Lai.

Nhut, however, had another, growing problem. Troop morale was rapidly sinking as the men learned of the bloody retreat from the Highlands and, closer to home, the desperate situation in Hue and the growing refugee problem in Danang. Many of his soldiers were from Hue or Danang, and they were very worried about their families. Thus, when the main assault against Tam Ky began in the early morning of 24 March with concentrated artillery barrages followed by tank-supported infantry attacks, Nhut's defenses collapsed. Two North Vietnamese infantry battalions soon penetrated the defenses south of the city, while another infantry battalion assaulted the city directly from the west.[4] Nhut's 4th Regiment retreated and was picked up by helicopters on a nearby beach; meanwhile, PAVN forces north of the city were slow to close Route 1, allowing the rest of the ARVN soldiers to escape. The 5th Regiment and most of the RF fled south to Chu Lai, while the 12th Rangers and thousands of civilians retreated north toward the Quang Nam border.

It was no different in Quang Ngai City. Learning of the Tam Ky disaster, Quang Ngai Regional Forces, the 11th Rangers, and elements of the 6th Regiment pulled back to the city's western defensive line. At 1:00 P.M. on 24 March, the PAVN forces attacked. Tanks rumbled forward, artillery shells crashed down, and the 52nd Brigade and several local-force battalions charged the city's outskirts. With his defenses crumbling, the Quang Ngai province chief radioed Nhut and requested that his forces be permitted to withdraw to Chu Lai. Truong approved the request. The ARVN units in Quang Ngai City formed a convoy and departed that night for Chu Lai. Tipped off to the evacuation by a radio intercept, PAVN forces repeatedly ambushed the convoy, causing 50 percent casualties. At midnight, Quang Ngai City fell to the North Vietnamese. Truong's southern front had collapsed, more from poor morale and panic than from enemy pressure. Worse, thousands of new refugees were now streaming to Danang.

Besides his collapsing fronts, Truong faced another serious predicament. After receiving the 22 March JGS message to send the Marine Division back to Saigon, Truong ordered Lieutenant General Lam Quang Thi to meet him in Danang the next morning. When Thi arrived, Truong ordered him to continue defending Hue, but also to draft contingency plans to withdraw his forces to Danang. In discussing this possibility, Thi laid out his design. He wanted the Navy to sink ships across the eighty-yard-wide Tu Hien Inlet, and the Marines to secure Vinh Phong Mountain, which dominated the southern side of the inlet. Then the 1st Division, Thua Thien RF, and 15th Rangers would march across the ships and link up with the Marines, thereby bypassing the roadblock at Phu Loc. The forces north of Hue would retreat to the Tan My port and be picked up by Navy ships. When Truong and his staff agreed to these plans, Thi returned to Hue.

Thi spent 23 March preparing for the move. He began by shifting his headquarters out of Hue to the Thuan An naval base. On 24 March he called a meeting with Colonel Tri, Brigadier General Diem, and several other officers to discuss the situation. Gathering at the naval base, the officers described the grim situation. Hue was abandoned, thousands of civilians and vehicles were clogging the road to Tan My, the 1st Division was under heavy pressure, and radio intercepts revealed that enemy forces were preparing to launch more attacks. Given wavering troop morale and no reserves, they concluded that defending Hue was hopeless. Worse, Diem stated that if they did not move immediately, PAVN would soon punch through his lines and attack Tan My. At best they had a day before his lines collapsed.

The decision was made to have the Marines retreat to Tan My, cross the inlet, and then move along the beach away from the civilians to a pick-up point about three miles south. The 14th Rangers and 1st Armor Brigade would fight a rear-guard action and then join the Marines. The 1st Division would move to the Tu Hien Inlet, with the 15th Rangers and Thua Thien RF screening the beachhead. All supplies and heavy equipment, including artillery and tanks, would be destroyed. Diem told Thi that only two of his four regiments would be able to escape.

Thi ordered Diem and his chief of staff to fly to Danang and present the withdrawal plan to Truong. Meeting with Truong, Diem categorically stated the defense of Hue was impossible, so at 6:00 P.M. on 24 March, Truong ordered the evacuation. Concurrently, he told Nhut to withdraw all of his forces in Quang Tin and Quang Ngai provinces and prepare for the final defense of Chu Lai. Truong then called Thieu, who agreed that Hue was rapidly becoming untenable. Thieu approved the withdrawal plan, and Diem and his chief of staff flew back to deliver the news to Thi.

The final battle for I Corps was about to commence.

RESCUING THE PEOPLE

Back in December 1973, Major General John Murray had made two predictions about I Corps Forward. First, unless the Tan My port area was dredged to allow larger ships to dock, Truong's forces could not effectively use the port to escape if Route 1 was blocked. Second, given the denial of the request for six additional LSTs by the DOD and State Department lawyers, the South Vietnamese would not have enough shipping to rescue the people and equipment trapped north of the Hai Van Pass.[5] Now Murray's prophecies were coming true with a vengeance. At the port, GVN authorities were desperately loading refugees onto various small ships, but there were too many people. The JGS, acting without authorization, managed to requisition one commercial South Vietnamese ship, which arrived at Tan My port on 23 March. Five thousand family members from the 1st Division were loaded onto the ship, and then it sailed for Danang. But approximately fifty thousand more remained trapped in a rapidly shrinking pocket, defended by troops whose morale was failing.

If Hue's situation was dire, Danang was a looming calamity. On 22 March, Deputy Prime Minister for Social Welfare Dr. Phan Quang Dan arrived in Danang. He had been attending a conference in the Philippines when he received instructions from Prime Minister Khiem to hurry home and direct the government's emergency refugee relief. Upon arrival in the beleaguered city, Dan announced the establishment of a local committee to coordinate refugee care. The committee, which included the mayor and several other prominent citizens, had actually been formed two days before. Oddly, however, despite thousands of people sleeping on the sidewalks and defecating in the streets, the mayor had waited until Dan's arrival before taking any action.

Aware of Thieu's design to truncate the nation, Dan planned to move the refugees south, but given the massive numbers, it was an impossible task for South Vietnam alone. Dan needed foreign assistance to help his countrymen.

In response to Lehmann's 18 March recommendation that the U.S. begin planning for the sealift of vast numbers of civilians, on 20 March the State Department called a meeting of the Washington Special Actions Group (WSAG). The purpose of the meeting was to draft plans to support South Vietnam's refugees, but only one idea was endorsed. Since U.S. government lawyers had banned the use of U.S. military ships in any sealift, the WSAG suggested that the GVN request the loan of six LSTs from Indonesia, South Korea, and Taiwan.

The GVN immediately agreed. Dan returned to Saigon on 23 March and began coordinating humanitarian aid. His first meeting was with the Philippine and Japanese ambassadors. Manila offered one LST; Tokyo replied that it could not provide shipping but would furnish nine billion yen to buy food and supplies. Dan then held a conference with General Vien, who recommended that he requisition all South Vietnamese civilian ships to assist with the refugee movement. Dan agreed and drafted the decree, but in another display of bureaucratic bungling, the minister of public works declined to sign the order. It sat on Dan's desk for a week before he could return to Saigon and sign it himself.[6] The delay botched any internal shipping support except for the one civilian vessel that had been requisitioned earlier.

Later that day, Dan met with Lehmann and the South Korean and Taiwanese ambassadors to discuss relief efforts. Dan said that there were currently six hundred thousand refugees in Danang, with many more on the way, along with the city's population of four hundred thousand. The GVN could not care for that many people in one place, and it had only enough shipping to move sixty thousand refugees per month. Dan asked the South Korean and Taiwanese governments for ships to move people, and he solicited $4 million in humanitarian aid from Korea. Both ambassadors said they would pass the requests along to their governments. Lehmann then told Dan that he was arranging for civilian aircraft to ferry people from Danang. Dan suggested moving everyone first to Cam Ranh Bay, but said he would need several days to prepare for an influx of refugees.

The State Department also ordered the U.S. Embassies in Indonesia, South Korea, and Taiwan to query their host governments about using LSTs to help South Vietnam. The initial responses were lukewarm. The Indonesians declined, given their participation in the International Commission of Control and Supervision, the body set up to monitor compliance with the Paris Accords. The Koreans also proved reluctant to loan any ships. Nor were they overly thrilled about the $4 million request. Only the government of Taiwan was willing to consider the idea, but it wanted U.S. assurances that its ships would be returned in good shape and that the U.S. would pay all costs.

En route from the Middle East to Washington, Kissinger directed the American ambassadors in Taiwan and South Korea to implore their hosts to reconsider. Because Kissinger had no funding authority, nor could he guarantee that the ships would be returned undamaged, his only option was to plead. He directed the ambassadors to deliver a simple message: Since the Philippines had agreed to help despite the risk and without seeking reimbursement, and given the dire situation, could the governments assist solely out of humanitarian concern? Between Dan's direct supplications to the ambassadors in Saigon and the U.S. entreaties in Taipei and Seoul, the pleas worked. Korea and Taiwan agreed to send two LSTs each, and aircraft if needed. Taiwan also quietly dropped its earlier condition that the U.S. pay for the trip and guarantee the ships' safe return.

But there was one further snag. The LSTs in question had been manufactured in the U.S. and sold to South Korea and Taiwan. By law DOD was required to notify Congress fifteen days in advance that U.S.-originated material was being transferred. The GVN also had to commit in writing that it would not turn over the ships to a third country. With time absolutely critical, President Ford decided to let the ships sail and inform Congress afterwards.

The LST loan, however, was only a minor irritant to Congress. The aid debate had recently been roiled by a novel proposal from Senator Sam Nunn (D., Ga.), who had traveled to South Vietnam in January 1975. His trip report recommended that the U.S. match its aid to South Vietnam to that given North Vietnam by the Russians and Chinese. Nunn requested that the administration prepare a detailed analysis comparing aid to the two countries, although he acknowledged in his trip report that "the intelligence community is not able to put a dollar value on Soviet and Chinese aid to North Vietnam," which seemed to undercut the idea.[7]

The CIA knew Nunn's request was a ridiculous task. It was impossible to gauge how much it cost the Russians and Chinese to manufacture and ship equipment to the DRV. The CIA could not even accurately measure the amount of aid the North Vietnamese had received. Almost all intelligence on aid was derived from photo reconnaissance over North Vietnam, which had been halted in 1973. The CIA produced an initial report in January 1975 based mainly upon guesswork; it declared that the GVN had received significantly more aid than the DRV. When NSC staffers complained, the CIA tried a second time. An updated report on 5 March was filled with so many caveats as to be virtually useless, but the final tally was roughly the same.[8] Since it appeared that Hanoi was doing more with less assistance, this only strengthened the impression of a weak South Vietnamese military.

Upon the return of the congressional delegation from Vietnam in early March, another round of hearings was held before the appropriate subcommittees to discuss the supplemental request. Despite battlefield events, the House Democratic Caucus remained deeply hostile to sending additional money, and on 12 March it voted overwhelmingly against further military aid to either South Vietnam or Cambodia. The Senate subcommittee, however, had voted a few days earlier to provide military aid to Cambodia. Shortly after the caucus vote, the House subcommittee met and forged a compromise. It would also vote for new aid for Cambodia, but with a major stipulation: a cut-off date of 30 June for military aid, although economic aid would continue. When the administration signaled that it would not accept this condition, the compromise was defeated, and no aid was voted on.

Senate aid opponents then pounced upon the House's idea. On 17 March, the Senate Foreign Relations Committee accepted its subcommittee's recommendation and voted to provide military aid to Cambodia, but several senators added a terminal date of 30 June to the bill. Two other senators subsequently introduced an amendment to the FY76 Defense Appropriations Bill to cease all military aid to South Vietnam after 30 June. On 18 March, Republican leaders met with President Ford to discuss the compromise: continued aid, but with a cutoff date. Ford again rejected the offer, saying it would interfere with his conduct of foreign policy. With Ford's rebuff, congressional leaders decided to postpone action on the supplemental until after Congress returned from its normal two-week Easter recess. On 25 March Congress passed the overall foreign-aid bill for 1975. It was for $3.6 billion, which was $2.27 billion short of what Ford had requested. This was the biggest cut ever by Congress, and even that barely passed, as many legislators argued that the money could be better spent at home during a recession.

Whether the Democratic leadership realized how precarious South Vietnam's situation was, or even cared, this action essentially killed the president's 28 January supplemental request for $522 million for South Vietnam and Cambodia. The gap between the administration's and Congress's views on Indochina appeared unbridgeable. Ford and Kissinger believed that aid would allow South Vietnam and Cambodia to defend their countries, forcing North Vietnam to conclude that a military victory was impossible. Weakening Saigon would not compel Hanoi to negotiate a settlement; it would only invite the Politburo to launch a full-scale offensive. Moreover, the U.S. had a moral obligation to assist these countries, not only to honor the 58,000 Americans who had lost their lives defending South Vietnam, but also for the people whom we had encouraged to reject Communism. To betray them would be a national disgrace. Lastly, American credibility was at stake, for if we abandoned Indochina, our enemies around the world would be encouraged and our allies disheartened. In particular, the Chinese had reversed years of deep hostility and staked their policy on our image as a reliable partner against the Soviets. If we quit Indochina, it would have a dramatic impact on U.S. foreign policy around the globe, especially in Europe and the Middle East.

The congressional desire to terminate aid was based upon beliefs that were polar opposites to Ford's and Kissinger's. Many felt the war was lost and more aid was useless. If South Vietnam could hang on, reducing aid to Saigon would force Thieu out of power and hence allow a political solution that would include the Communists in the government. One freshman member of the House, Representative Henry Waxman (D., Calif.), expressed that view clearly: "We cannot promote the peace by providing the means of war. . . . Providing more military aid to Saigon only increases resistance to substantive negotiations."[9] Many legislators did not believe that South Vietnam was in great peril, or that cutting money would decide South Vietnam's fate. More supplies would simply prolong a war many were convinced Thieu was guilty of re-starting. Regardless of the facts on the ground, one analyst of congressional intent later wrote: "it is clear that many critics believed that to approve Ford's request would mean surrendering to a policy that had gone on for decades and would go on into the indefinite future. There was no light at the end of the tunnel."[10]

But with South Vietnam's desperate situation, the Ford administration could not wait for congressional action. Returning from the Middle East, Kissinger immediately began to coordinate the administration's response to the growing crisis. Because of the lock Kissinger held on American foreign-policy-making, plus the lack of information on Thieu's plans, little other than the LST idea had been broached until he arrived home. On 24 March he chaired a State Department meeting to talk over possible initiatives. After a lengthy discussion, Kissinger confirmed that the administration not only would continue with the supplemental request, but would ask for even larger sums. Despite the remote chance of success, he stated: "We will go up there and ask for what is right and not worry if we get creamed."[11]

Kissinger's staff concluded that reopening direct negotiations with Le Duc Tho would accomplish little. They felt Tho would simply stall until all of Hanoi's military objectives were met. The best diplomatic effort the attendees could think of was to send letters to the Soviets and the Chinese asking them to rein in their ally. Kissinger realized the futility of diplomatic initiatives to halt Hanoi's offensive without the threat of force, proclaiming that "I am convinced that North Vietnam will do absolutely nothing except under military pressure." But the attendees knew that any military warnings were simply posturing as long as the legislation banning U.S. military action remained in effect. Ford would not risk a constitutional crisis by ordering air strikes. Even if he were willing to gamble on a showdown with Congress, Kissinger believed it would be a "disaster and mistake. We could not get any money at all if we did that."

Other measures included a decision to draft a presidential statement asking for refugee assistance and condemning the North Vietnamese invasion. Ambassador Graham Martin, who was attending the meeting after being told to cut short his recuperation from dental surgery, was directed to write another letter from Ford to Thieu. It was one more in a long line of letters offering little more than moral support and promises. In essence, the administration was reduced to begging Congress for more aid while trying to find some feasible diplomatic steps to halt North Vietnam's offensive, as if words were effective anti-tank weapons.

On 25 March, Ford dispatched General Frederick C. Weyand—who had been the last commander of U.S. military operations in Vietnam—on a fact-finding trip to South Vietnam. Martin would accompany Weyand and deliver the presidential letter to Thieu. That morning, Ford gathered in the Oval Office with Weyand, Kissinger, and Martin. Weyand's mission was to assess the situation and write a report that could be used to persuade Congress to appropriate whatever aid the GVN needed. Ford told Weyand that "this is one of the most significant missions you have ever had. You are not going over to lose, but to be tough and see what we can do. . . . We want your recommendations for the things which can be tough and shocking to the North."[12] Ford, however, remained loath to press Congress to re-intervene with airpower. "I regret," he said, "I do not have the authority to do some of the things President Nixon could do." If Weyand ever needed confirmation that the B-52s would not return, this was it.

While Weyand assessed Saigon's military needs, Martin was to provide the political support, such as it was. The letter Martin had drafted for Ford's signature was designed to be supportive but not precise as to actions. The letter began by lamenting that "events over the last twelve months . . . resulted in a diminution of the American material support which your government had fully expected to receive."[13] After expressing an understanding of Thieu's decision to retrench, Martin wrote: "you may rest assured that we will make every effort to secure from Congress adequate amounts of aid for South Vietnam. We fully realize this must be done promptly." To ensure that "our military aid requests are specifically designed to meet your actual current needs," Ford had dispatched General Weyand to assess the situation. Ending the letter, Martin wrote: "You and your people may be assured . . . of my resolve to do everything I can to help the Republic of Vietnam." Everything except B-52s, something the South Vietnamese needed at the moment even more than aid.

Faced with heavy opposition from the Democratic-controlled Congress, Kissinger and Ford decided to resurrect the early-March proposal to Senators Pearson and Church for a three-year aid option. Ford was desperate to get something enacted, since on 21 March the White House Congressional Liaison Office had warned the president about the Senate bill to terminate all military aid to South Vietnam on 30 June. Given this new stipulation, the liaison office believed that Church and Pearson's compromise offer was dead.

At a news conference on 26 March, Kissinger explained that because of congressional resistance, the administration was willing to consider a compromise as an alternative to losing the supplemental vote. Moreover, Kissinger appealed to America's moral commitment to Indochina, stating that cutting off aid would "deliberately destroy an ally in its moment of extremity."[14] His plea was in vain. As the White House liaison office predicted, after the news conference, Senator Pearson declared that the vast gulf between the two sides' aid amounts plus the 30 June cut-off amendment had killed the deal. President Ford's last chance to gain aid for South Vietnam was gone.

BLOOD IN THE WATER

On the afternoon of 24 March, the Politburo hurriedly met in response to the swiftly changing battlefield. It had planned to gather on 25 March, but the collapsing Hue pocket and the capture of Tam Ky caused it to reconvene sooner. After Lieutenant General Le Trong Tan summarized the military situation, Le Duan took the floor. Clearly, he claimed, the South Vietnamese were reeling. With Danang teetering on collapse and ARVN retreating to Saigon, the People's Army needed to step up its attacks. The Politburo decided to rapidly assault Danang while preparing to conquer Saigon, the ultimate prize. At this point, the old quandary surfaced: Should North Vietnam wait until the divisions from the B-3 Front could join Tra's units before attacking Saigon, or should it attack with just Tra's forces?

Although the Politburo agreed that PAVN needed to mass its forces, Le Duan wanted to take a stab at Saigon now. Laying out his reasoning, he stated: "We must mass sufficient main force strength on Saigon's outer perimeter to destroy three divisions. . . . [But] If we are able to advance quickly, then we must advance, without worrying about whether we have time to consolidate and regroup. . . . The best leap forward that the revolution can make is to launch attacks and uprisings. Just go ahead and make military attack, because when we do uprisings will break out immediately."[15] Le Duan, despite hordes of civilians fleeing his advancing troops, still fervently believed that the South Vietnamese people were waiting to be liberated, and would storm the proverbial castle gates at the first chance.

On 25 March the regular Politburo meeting was held. The members concluded that the long-heralded "strategic opportunity" had finally arrived. Besides affirming their previous judgment that the People's Army should quickly defeat I Corps while concurrently moving more troops to Saigon, they made several other major decisions. First, Lieutenant General Tan was assigned as the overall commander of Communist forces in the campaign to conquer Danang. Second, the 3rd Corps was formed from the separate units in the B-3 Front. Third, Le Duc Tho would go south and meet with Van Tien Dung to explain the Politburo's reasoning, and would then proceed to COSVN to oversee the assault on Saigon. Most important, the Politburo once again advanced its timetable for liberating South Vietnam. The original plan had called for 1976. Then, after the liberation of Ban Me Thuot, the target date was changed to late 1975. Now, with the imminent destruction of I and II Corps, the Politburo decided to conquer Saigon in May, before the onset of the rainy season.

After the Politburo meeting, the General Staff worked throughout the night preparing plans to assault Danang. On 26 March, Tan met with Giap to present his strategy. Giap began the meeting by offering his opinion that ARVN would either rapidly withdraw from Danang, or defend it to the death. Given these two possibilities, Giap asked Tan, "How do you propose we fight?"[16] Tan told Giap that he expected the South Vietnamese to defend Danang, and that it would take him five days to coordinate the assault. Giap then turned to the deputy head of Military Intelligence and asked: If the ARVN troops withdraw from Danang, how long will it take? "Three days" was the reply. Giap suggested that Tan draft plans to attack in three days. A stunned Tan exclaimed: "It is impossible to prepare to fight like that!" Giap recounts that for the first time, he showed "discontent" with Tan. Admonishing him that the ARVN forces might escape if he dithered, Giap followed Le Duan's dictum and ordered Tan to toss caution aside and advance without regard to careful planning. Tan agreed, and he departed for Danang.

THE FALL OF HUE

After the meetings in Danang with his commanders from I Corps Forward, Lieutenant General Truong ordered the Navy to prepare for the evacuation of Hue. Truong's naval commander, Commodore Ho Van Ky Thoai, formed a task force to rescue the South Vietnamese heading to the embarkation points. The Navy headquarters in Saigon also "committed every asset available, including LST *Danang* (HQ-501), which departed Saigon with one engine inoperative and with shipyard personnel embarked."[17] The warships of the Fleet Command created a screen stretching for ten miles around the Thuan An Inlet to guard against North Vietnamese patrol boats that might attempt to disrupt the evacuation, or to lay mines near the narrow entrance. Twenty-two landing craft—small World War II boats—from the Army's Military Transportation Command were placed under the Navy's control and ordered to ferry people out to the larger ships.

On 24 March the naval base at Tu Hien was charged with lashing several craft together so the 1st Division could cross, but the effort failed because the current was too swift. Sinking a ship was also determined to be unfeasible, so the Navy decided to tow a floating bridge from Danang. When the floating bridge finally arrived, enemy shelling from Vinh Phong Mountain by local forces that had infiltrated the night before prevented the Navy from accomplishing its mission. For some unknown reason, the Marines had failed to secure the high ground despite Lieutenant General Thi's repeated requests.[18]

North of Hue on the morning of 24 March, the 4th Regiment crossed the Bo River in two places and assaulted the Marines. Heavy fighting raged, but the Marines held their ground. To support the Marine defenders, the 14th Rangers backed by armor counterattacked several times into the PAVN flank, but they did not succeed in destroying the two bridgeheads. However, after the decision in the late afternoon of 24 March to withdraw from Hue, Colonel Nguyen Thanh Tri ordered the Marines to retreat. The 1st Armor Brigade and the 14th Rangers acted as rear guard. After the Marines left, the Rangers retreated and blew up the An Lo Bridge behind them.

Marching almost twenty miles that night, by the morning of 25 March the exhausted Marines had gathered on the beach several miles south of the Thuan An port. After the Marines formed a defensive perimeter, Colonel Tri and his headquarters boarded a small transport ship and moved offshore. The 1st Armor Brigade was forced to abandon much of its equipment several miles from Tan My. Thousands of other troops, including logistics, engineers, and RF/PF, jammed the port, while abandoned vehicles and equipment littered the road. Numerous buildings burned from enemy artillery shells, and people lay dead in the fields, killed by shrapnel or marauding soldiers. The 14th Ranger Group held the rear, and its reconnaissance company was the last ARVN unit to withdraw from Hue. Fortunately for the South Vietnamese, the B-4 Front forces did not pursue with zeal. Not until late that night did the B-4 Front order its reserve, the 8th Quang Tri Battalion, to seize Hue.

After receiving sporadic artillery fire at the Thuan An naval base, around 6:30 P.M. on 24 March, Lieutenant General Thi and his staff boarded a Navy ship. At this point, Thi lost control of his units. Worse, upon returning from his meeting with Truong, Brigadier General Diem gathered his staff for a final conference. While there remains confusion as to his exact orders, instead of leading his division in its most critical hours, Diem disbanded his unit and told his senior officers to make their own way to the pick-up point at Tu Hien. While the division had fought valiantly to this point, by midnight of 24 March, it had collapsed. Diem's dissolution of the division doomed the Hue pocket. The end of resistance south of Hue opened an easy path for the PAVN regiments to reach the Marine laager point, not to mention the Tan My/Thuan An ports. Why Diem, a native of Hue who had served for years in the 1st Division, disbanded his unit is unknown: he died several days later in a helicopter crash and left no explanation.

Despite the mobs at the ports, the landing craft continued to shuttle people from Tan My out to the LST *Can Tho* (HQ-801). They rescued about six thousand civilians on 24 March. While the evacuation continued that night, rough seas and enemy shelling were making it increasingly hazardous. By midnight, over half of the landing craft had abandoned the rescue and fled to Danang.

For the Marines on the beach, dawn on 25 March revealed heavy waves and strong currents. The Navy shifted from the ports to the beach in order to rescue the Marines, but the poor conditions prevented the small landing boats from coming ashore. At 1:30 P.M., the order was given for the *Can Tho* to beach. The LST could only get within ninety yards of the shore, where it halted and dropped rope ladders over its sides. While the Marines had maintained unit discipline, ARVN troops had not. Several thousand civilians and leaderless soldiers had followed the Marines. The 5th Marine Battalion commander described the horror as people frenetically surged toward the ship. "Those who did not know how to swim desperately clung to anyone who did, struggling against the angel of death there in the ocean waves. A few M-113s swam out, driving right over them. Screams filled the air. One wave would pick them up and the next would drive them underwater. Heads bobbed up and down, and many bodies sank under the waves and disappeared as the ship sat there with its engines running, waiting."[19] With the current growing stronger, after less than an hour, the *Can Tho* reversed engines and pulled back to avoid becoming grounded. Only one hundred people had made it onboard.

The Marines decided to shift further south along the beach to avoid the mobs of soldiers and civilians. After marching south a mile, the Marines spread out and dug foxholes in the sand. While many civilians and soldiers followed them, the Marines expelled them from their perimeter, and they shot several people they considered Communist infiltrators. It was the first crack in the vaunted Marine discipline. The VNN ships, however, had no better luck finding a suitable landing area in the new position.

After the Marines retreated, the People's Army north of Hue slowly moved forward. Local-force units pushed toward Thuan An, while the 4th Regiment moved west of Hue along the edge of the mountains. The 8th Quang Tri Battalion crossed the Bo River on Route 1 and by 9:00 A.M. 25 March had captured a district town only three miles outside of Hue. It then sent a reconnaissance element to seize another bridge on the city's edge. While the reconnaissance troops were at the second bridge, two underground agents rode up on a motorcycle and announced that ARVN had abandoned the city. Commandeering a Marine jeep, three men from the 8th Battalion and the two underground agents entered the city. At 10:30 A.M. they raised their flag over the Hue Citadel, on the same flagpole many ARVN 1st Division soldiers had died retaking in 1968. At noon, advance elements of the 3rd Regiment, 324th Division, riding on captured tanks, entered Hue from the south. Continuing their advance toward the ocean, B-4 Front units and the 2nd Regiment, 324th Division, which was moving toward Tan My, linked up around 5:00 P.M. Both ports had now been captured.

Lieutenant General Thi, learning that Tu Hien was under enemy fire and that the Navy had not erected the bridge across the inlet mouth, ordered the ships to proceed south to pick up the troops stranded there. The vast majority of VNN ships departed at 4:45 P.M. One 1st Division regiment had arrived at the Tu Hien Inlet, but the naval officer commanding the coastal squadron moved his ships out to sea after an Army officer pulled out his pistol and threatened to kill him if he did not transport his troops to the other side. Now stranded, some soldiers stole local fishing boats while others attempted to swim across the inlet. Many drowned in the swift currents. With the arrival of the Navy ships at Tu Hien around midnight 25 March, the small landing craft began shuttling troops. By dawn, they had managed to rescue about 1,100 soldiers.

With the bulk of the Navy at Tu Hien, Colonel Tri arranged for three other landing craft to beach at dawn, 26 March, to rescue his four thousand stranded Marines. Tri ordered that the wounded and dead be loaded first, then the brigade headquarters, and then the rest of the Marines. The 7th Battalion would hold the line and board last. When the first landing craft hit the beach that morning, the Marines loaded in an orderly fashion, but after an hour, the enemy arrived. As the ship sat exposed, a PAVN unit fired an AT-3 Sagger anti-tank missile. The missile hit the ship, wounding the 147th Brigade commander. Fearful of more missiles, the ship quickly backed away. Only eight hundred Marines had made it onboard. To avoid the encroaching enemy, the Marines again moved south on the beach.

Around noon, another landing craft beached. This time, Marine discipline gave way. Hundreds of men swarmed the ship, and it became overloaded and stuck in the sand. Many of the trailing civilians and soldiers also tried to rush onboard. Since the Marines had been told this ship was reserved for them, they began shooting people to rid themselves of the weight. This total collapse of Marine discipline would manifest itself again in Danang and in further evacuations. As the ship lay immobilized, the PAVN gunners suddenly found the range. Several rounds hit the ship, wounding and killing dozens. Realizing they were sitting ducks, a Marine battalion commander ordered everyone off. As the bow door opened, Communist machine-gun fire cut down dozens more. The remaining Marines desperately dug defensive positions and tried to fight back, but they were almost out of ammunition.

As night fell on 26 March, firefights with PAVN troops continued. The Marines had nowhere to hide, and the senior commanders decided they had no choice but to try and fight their way to the Tu Hien crossing. Forming a column, the remaining troops moved south along the beach. Very few Marines made it to Tu Hien, and most were captured the next day. Many committed suicide with grenades rather than surrender. The 147th Marine Brigade died on the beach; only about one in four Marines were rescued. PAVN figures for South Vietnamese losses in the Hue pocket are staggering: they claim they captured thirty thousand soldiers, including RF/PF. In addition to the Marine brigade, the 1st Division, 14th and 15th Ranger Groups, 1st Armor Brigade, several artillery battalions, and fifteen RF battalions were destroyed. Equipment losses were enormous; the Communists captured one hundred forty tanks and personnel carriers, eight hundred trucks, and ten thousand tons of ammunition.[20]

The situation was also desperate on Truong's southern front. Brigadier General Tran Van Nhut spent the night of 24 March in his helicopter overseeing the retreating convoy from Quang Ngai. The column arrived at Chu Lai on the morning of 25 March. According to Nhut, when he arrived the "base was flooded with RF and PF units, police, government officials, and civilians from the provinces of Quang Tin and Quang Ngai. The dock area swarmed with people who could see an LST troop transport anchored in the Chu Lai harbor. Twice I personally had to use a bullhorn to warn the troops to return to their units and take up defensive positions against a possible enemy attack, but it seemed as if no one was listening. The soldiers were afraid of being abandoned in Chu Lai, as had happened to other troops during the evacuation of II Corps."[21]

With the base jammed, Nhut called Truong and asked permission to withdraw to Re Island, twenty miles offshore. Despite JGS orders to bring the 2nd Division to Danang to replace the Marine Division, with Danang overflowing with refugees, Truong agreed.[22] Nhut flew out to see the captain of the ship, the LST *Nha Trang* (HQ-505). While Chu Lai had a large pier that could accommodate the ship, the dock was packed with an unruly mob of approximately ten thousand people. Nhut decided to avoid the civilians and have the LST land that night on a nearby beach to pick up his troops. He quickly gathered his staff and commanders to plan the evacuation. According to Colonel Le Thuong, the division artillery commander, "A detailed time schedule was established and issued verbally in a general meeting attended by the entire division headquarters staff and the commanders of all units of the division. The evacuation order laid out a plan to destroy all artillery pieces, armored vehicles, and heavy equipment which could not be evacuated; to destroy all ammunition dumps and fuel storage tanks; and to burn down the barracks and headquarters buildings."[23] To assist with the evacuation, the Navy ordered the LST *Vinh Long* (HQ-802) and the smaller Landing Ship Medium (LSM) *Huong Giang* (HQ-404), plus six small landing craft from Qui Nhon, to divert to Chu Lai.

At 9:00 P.M. on 25 March, the LST *Nha Trang* moved to the beach, where about five thousand soldiers and several M-113 personnel carriers had gathered. Once again the water was too shallow, and the ship went aground one hundred yards offshore. This caused a repeat of the horrific scenes on the beach near Tu Hien. As Colonel Thuong recalls: "Fear grew quickly in the darkness as ear-shattering explosions from the exploding ammunition dumps split the night, and flames from burning fuel tanks lit a whole section of the sky. Inside the base, all the buildings began to burn, filling the air with smoke and causing men to lose their grip and their very ability to reason. The situation became irreversible and there was no solution, no one was issuing orders, and military discipline collapsed. Everyone tried only to save his own skin—some swimming out to the ship, others climbing aboard M-113s which drove recklessly into the surf, ramming into each other in the struggle to reach the ship. Untold numbers of men died in the confusion."[24] After panicky soldiers tossed hand grenades and killed several people on the ship, the *Nha Trang* backed away from the beach. Nhut ordered the ship to dock at the pier.

To prevent the mob from storming the ship, the *Nha Trang* halted ten yards from the dock and erected a makeshift gangplank between the pier and the ship. This forced the people to load single file, which greatly reduced the hysteria. At around 1:00 A.M. on 26 March, the other ships arrived at Chu Lai harbor. With the tide running out, only the *Huong Giang* could enter. It tied up behind the *Nha Trang* and also took on people. By noon, the majority of the people were loaded and the ships left the harbor. They attempted to return later that night to pick up the 6th Regiment, which was serving as rear guard, but they were unable to enter the harbor because of enemy fire from the banks.

While the withdrawal was chaotic, and all the heavy equipment and many small arms were lost, the Navy had managed to evacuate 10,500 troops and civilians. According to Navy Captain Pham Manh Khue, "4,000 of them were 2nd Division personnel, 4,000 from RF units of Quang Tin and Quang Ngai, and the rest were policemen, dependents, and civilians. On 27 March 6,000 servicemen and their dependents disembarked at Re Island, and the rest were shipped to Danang."[25]

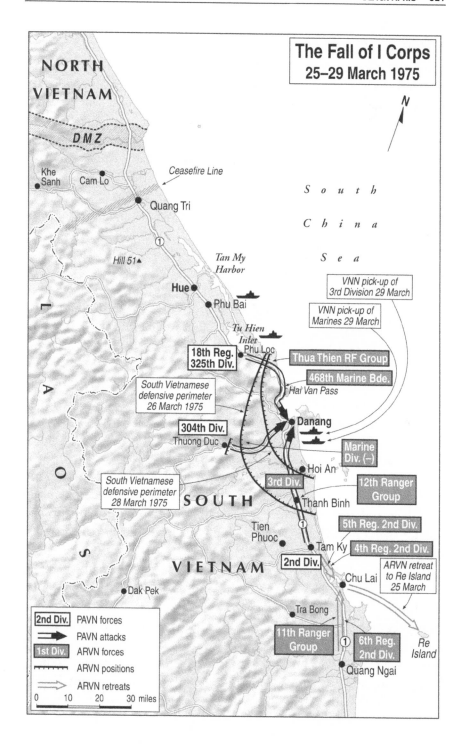

The Fall of I Corps
25–29 March 1975

NORTH VIETNAM

DMZ

Khe Sanh
Cam Lo

Ceasefire Line

Quang Tri

South China Sea

Hill 51▲

Tan My Harbor

Hue
Phu Bai

VNN pick-up of 3rd Division 29 March

VNN pick-up of Marines 29 March

Tu Hien Inlet
Phu Loc

18th Reg. 325th Div.

Thua Thien RF Group

468th Marine Bde.

Hai Van Pass

South Vietnamese defensive perimeter 26 March 1975

304th Div.
Thuong Duc

Danang

Marine Div. (--)

South Vietnamese defensive perimeter 28 March 1975

Hoi An

SOUTH

3rd Div.

12th Ranger Group

Thanh Binh

Tien Phuoc

5th Reg. 2nd Div.

Tam Ky

4th Reg. 2nd Div.

2nd Div.

VIETNAM

Chu Lai

ARVN retreat to Re Island 25 March

Dak Pek

Tra Bong

11th Ranger Group

6th Reg. 2nd Div.

Re Island

Quang Ngai

L A O S

2nd Div. PAVN forces
➡ PAVN attacks
1st Div. ARVN forces
⊤⊤⊤ ARVN positions
⇨ ARVN retreats

0   10   20   30 miles

THE FINAL COLLAPSE

While events in I Corps were spiraling out of control, discontent was growing among Thieu's senior officers, who openly questioned his conduct of the war. Aware of the disgruntlement, on 24 March Thieu sent an "eyes-only" message, part exhortation and part explanation, to his military commanders and province chiefs. "Our nation is currently undergoing a period of very grave challenges," he wrote. "The current situation can easily cause fear and confusion among the army and the civilian population. . . . Today I feel I must call your attention to the following points. . . . The recent actions taken by the government and the army were courageous decisions that were implemented by the National Security Council after very careful consideration, and were done to preserve our forces in order to firmly protect the most heavily populated and richest parts of our nation. In my speech on 20 March 1975 I emphasized that all the remaining portions of the country that we still hold will be defended to the last. All rumors and irresponsible speculation contrary to the above-mentioned facts is part of a Communist plot aimed at using psychological warfare to sabotage the fighting spirit of our soldiers."[26]

To reinforce his guidelines, the next day Thieu fired off another message. This communication, sent only to his four corps commanders, was unambiguous: "All provinces and territory that we still possess as of today, 25 March 1975, must be defended to the death. At every location we must make efforts to inflict the maximum destruction on the enemy, slow the enemy's rate of advance, strengthen and consolidate our defenses, and use every idea and resource to launch counter-attacks. Corps . . . commanders bear the responsibility for directing, guiding, and monitoring all unit and territorial commanders under your command to ensure absolute compliance with these orders."[27]

The messages demonstrated that Thieu would not alter his habit of bypassing the JGS, thereby preventing centralized military planning. By dividing authority, Thieu's system had effectively prevented any general from accumulating sufficient power to overthrow him. However, during a national crisis when strategic decisions were required, the system broke down. With no national planning process, the individual corps had been left alone to handle a major Communist offensive. More important, Thieu's "defend to the death" order–especially in I Corps, where two enclaves were evacuating–indicated a growing disconnect between the Palace and reality on the ground.

That was partly due to poor information flowing from regional headquarters back to Saigon, but the bigger reason was that Thieu was consumed with political maneuvering. The same day as his "defend to the death" message, the government announced that Thieu had directed Prime Minister Khiem "to reshuffle the government structure" in order to improve the situation. At the same time, he invited "anti-communist nationalists, who are qualified and willing to dedicate themselves to the national cause, to participate in the cabinet."[28] For the first time, Thieu was bowing to the wishes of the opposition and opening his government. The key phrase, however, was "willing to dedicate themselves to the national cause." It was Thieu's way of saying: No political machinations to oust him.

On 26 March Thieu made his second national radio broadcast. Reading an "Order of the Day" to the nation, he told the people that faced with the Communists' "obvious superiority in numbers and firepower, we have to reduce the scope of our defense in order to ensure that it is consistent with the facilities and capabilities at our disposal in these two Military Regions."[29] Rationalizing the retreats as due to a lack of "facilities and firepower" (meaning U.S. aid and airpower), Thieu never mentioned the capture of Hue, and he downplayed the heavy ARVN losses. Attempting to bolster morale, he reminded his countrymen that they had stopped countrywide Communist attacks during the 1968 and 1972 offensives.

To re-emphasize his points, he spoke on TV later that day. He admitted that provinces in I Corps had fallen, but he did not mention that Hue had been lost. Because of the imbalance of forces, Thieu said, Lieutenant General Truong had been forced "to withdraw to ensure the life or death defense of Danang and Quang Nam."[30] Stating that he had ordered the military to "defend to the death," he sought to inspire the "anti-communist, nationalist spirit of all the compatriots." He had directed Prime Minister Khiem to create a "fighting government" that will not "solicit surrender to the communists, recognize the existence of a second nation in the south, or accept a solution calling for a coalition with the communists that will allow them to easily take over our south." Moreover, he and the National Assembly had taken "the necessary moves vis-à-vis the U.S. government and Congress, so the latter will take strong, immediate action to rapidly provide a sufficient volume of necessary facilities to our armed forces so they can fight.

I eagerly await the results of these moves." He closed by appealing to the people to support the government, and to assist the refugees.

Despite his brave words, the two speeches failed to squelch the persistent rumors that the withdrawal orders were part of a secret and nefarious deal to cede control of the northern half of South Vietnam to the PRG. After the war, Thieu came under much criticism from South Vietnamese for not addressing this rumor, which as we have seen had a terrible impact on troop morale. He was also criticized for not speaking to the people more often to explain the situation. The criticisms are valid, as Thieu waited until 20 March to make his first broadcast, and it was not until 26 March that he explained his strategy. Although the South Vietnamese population had responded to Thieu's previous appeals, this time his efforts, while a remarkably transparent outline of his policies for a man accused of being a dictator, were too little and too late. The South Vietnam of March 1975 was a different country from the South Vietnam of 1972: isolated, lacking American airpower, near bankruptcy, and with a war-weary population that blamed Thieu for its economic and military predicament.

At the same time Thieu was trying to rally the country, Lehmann kept his promise and arranged for flights to Danang to begin on 26 March. He contracted with World Airways out of Oakland, California, for twenty flights to remove refugees. World Airways, which was then airlifting rice and ammunition to the beleaguered Cambodian army, had a long history of chartered contracts to fly U.S. troops and supplies around South Vietnam. The company immediately dispatched one Boeing 727 to Saigon. On 26 March, the first World Airways flights were made to Danang, taking out over two thousand people. At the same time, Major General Homer Smith shifted six tugs and five barges that had been engaged in the Mekong River convoys hauling supplies to Cambodia to assist in the evacuation. On 25 March the Military Sealift Command (MSC) alerted ten ships to steam toward Danang to pick up equipment and supplies. The first ship, the *Pioneer Contender*, pulled into Danang on 27 March. During the next several days four of the tugs Smith dispatched, and three other MSC ships, the *Sgt. Andrew Miller*, *Pioneer Commander*, and *American Challenger*, also arrived.

On 24 March the GVN made a worldwide plea for assistance with the massive influx of refugees in Danang. Kissinger used this appeal to get the U.S. bureaucracy moving. On 27 March, Kissinger and Secretary of Defense Schlesinger made the decision to mount a massive sea- and airlift to move the refugees south using U.S. Navy LSTs based in the Philippines, which could arrive more quickly than the Korean and Taiwanese ships. Given the War Powers Resolution, plus the debacle at Chu Lai, Schlesinger ordered that no American combat ships enter South Vietnamese ports. The ships would anchor offshore and the people would be lightered out.

The next day, a message was sent to the U.S. Embassy asking if Truong could provide adequate security for a substantial American rescue effort. Ambassador Martin, who had just arrived in Saigon with General Weyand, quickly replied: "Danang is swollen with what is certainly around a million refugees, and the actual number may be 1.5 million, plus the normal population of 500,000. This sheer mass, even if orderly and calm, would strain civilian government to the breaking point. The populace of Danang is neither orderly nor calm. The airport is being mobbed as are virtually all conceivable ship and port embarkation points. . . . Further compounding the problem is a large number of armed ARVN stragglers who have no cohesion or discipline. You have, in short, a city under siege and perhaps on the verge of being attacked with over two million people milling around, many out of control, and effective law and order breaking down."[31] Martin requested that U.S. combat units be utilized, along with the fleet currently standing by to evacuate the U.S. Embassy in Cambodia.

Kissinger turned him down on both counts, and Martin reacted with indignation. "It seems that the extreme emergency nature of the situation and the very real potential for a massive tragedy is still not understood. The fact of the matter is that the situation is so extremely serious that nothing but an all-out effort with every available resource will be minimally adequate."[32] Martin stoked the fire by stating, "we believe that failure on our part to move massively and without restrictions in this human emergency will not be understood." This was the first clash between him and Kissinger, a rift that would only grow wider as Martin tried to bully Kissinger into actions that congressional restrictions would not let him take.

Separately, Kissinger had concluded that South Vietnam would not survive. While he remained convinced that Thieu's decision to withdraw was based upon congressional aid cuts, he told President Ford on 28 March that "the force ratios are so bad I don't think Vietnam can make it. Cambodia certainly could have lasted had we not deserted them. It is a moral collapse of the United States."[33] The next day at a staff meeting, he lamented that if Thieu had stood and fought, making PAVN "suffer at each point in Vietnam over the past few weeks, things might have been different. But the disgrace is ours." When a staffer remarked that the Soviets should be held accountable for equipping the North Vietnamese, Kissinger brushed aside that point, stating, "we can't ask the Soviets in the spirit of détente to save us from ourselves."[34]

In Danang, the situation was growing worse by the hour. Despite the visit by Deputy Prime Minister Dan and the creation of the refugee committee, the sheer number of people overwhelmed GVN efforts. With over one million people crowding Danang's streets, on 26 March Truong ordered his deputy, Major General Hoang Van Lac, to fly to Saigon and plead for transportation. Lac's message was simple: Moving the refugees would give Truong a chance to restore order and stiffen the defenses. Otherwise, all was lost.

Despite Lac's efforts, until the ships arrived, airplanes were the only means to move people out. While the initial World Airways flights went smoothly, on the early afternoon of 27 March the growing legion of people at the airport suddenly became disorderly and rushed a plane, and the field was shut down. The city's streets were no better. With increasing chaos caused by armed stragglers fighting with civilians over food, the police began to melt away. Control broke down, leading to riots and other serious crimes. After the first ships arrived, people rushed to the docks, creating more madness.

To make matters worse, the JGS warned Truong that signal intercepts indicated the enemy intended to shell Danang at 7:00 P.M. on 28 March. With morale shaky, Truong ordered the Marines and Major General Hinh's 3rd Division to pull their troops back to a final defensive line around Danang. This meant Hinh's regiments south of Danang were now just ten miles away, placing South Vietnam's second-largest city well within enemy artillery range. The 468th Marine Brigade continued to defend the Hai Van Pass, while the 369th Marine Brigade held the center of the perimeter. Hinh, however, had a growing desertion problem. On 27 March he noted: "Almost all personnel assigned to 3rd Division rear base support units and to the division headquarters have deserted to go take care of their families. My [main] base at Hoa Khanh is gradually emptying out."[35]

Sensing that ARVN's final collapse was at hand, on 26 March Giap's staff issued orders for PAVN units to rapidly advance on Danang. The plan called for the 2nd Division to attack from the south on Route 1, while the 304th Division at Thuong Duc would move forward from the west. The 2nd Corps would capture the Hai Van Pass and assault Danang from the north. Nguyen Huu An was told to "send additional artillery pieces [to the

Hai Van] . . . so that, when the order is given, this position can immediately begin shelling the Danang airfield. You must do whatever is necessary to overcome all terrain obstacles in order to move your artillery forward far enough to reach the Danang harbor and port area."[36]

To accomplish this task, An had to overcome some major problems. Only the 18th Regiment, 325th Division, was close to the Hai Van Pass. His other units were all in Hue, the bridge on Route 1 over the Truoi River had been destroyed, and his logistics were scattered across two provinces. He immediately tasked his deputy, Major General Hoang Dan, with directing the assault against the Hai Van Pass. To bring his combat power to bear, he told his engineers to rebuild the Truoi River bridge so that he could truck his soldiers to the Hai Van. He also sent two tank companies and two batteries of 130-mm guns to reinforce the 18th Regiment. An would join the 304th Division west of Danang, bringing with him a battalion of tanks. He ordered his corps rear services to unsnarl any logistics jams and to use ARVN equipment to replace or augment their own. Each sector would employ the Soviet tactic of "attack from the march," meaning that if the troops encountered any resistance, they would immediately attack instead of stopping to prepare.

Responding rapidly to An's orders, on the morning of 28 March, Hoang Dan pushed forward. Throughout the day, the soldiers of the 18th Regiment engaged RF troops holding positions near the pass. Dan's troops finally pushed through, but then faced another problem: a bridge on Route 1 that had been blown up by PAVN sappers a week earlier. The engineers were unable to repair it in time, so Dan left his heavy armor and artillery behind and moved forward with seven amphibious PT-76 tanks. At 5:30 A.M. on 29 March, a battalion from the 18th Regiment, followed by the PT-76s, assaulted the Hai Van Pass.

An's artillery, meanwhile, had moved into position, and just as JGS intelligence had predicted, they began firing at 7:00 P.M. on 28 March. Three hundred rounds hit the airfield and logistics centers around Danang. They struck Truong's headquarters, forcing him to move to the Danang naval base. Communications with Saigon were cut, but not before the JGS warned Truong that signals intelligence had now gleaned that PAVN intended to launch a full-scale assault at 5:00 the next morning. On the basis of that information, Truong made the decision to abandon the city. That night, he called a meeting with his commanders and told them to move their troops to the beaches. Hinh protested, saying that he could not plan a move with so little time. When Truong said nothing, Hinh realized he had no choice.

The Navy immediately moved to pick up units from the beach. The 468th Marine Brigade was successfully evacuated by the LSM *Lam Giang* (HQ-402) at the foot of the Hai Van Pass at 6:00 A.M. on 29 March. The 369th Marines retreated to a beach south of Danang, with the 304th Division in hot pursuit. The brigade began to board the LSM *Huong Giang* (HQ-404), the same ship that had helped rescue the 2nd Division at Chu Lai. The water was not deep, but the sea conditions were rough, with high waves. Colonel Nguyen Thanh Tri helped Lieutenant General Truong wade out to the ship. As the Marines loaded, PAVN gunners began to shell the beach. The *Huong Giang* was forced to back away after picking up about five hundred Marines. When PAVN forces arrived, the Marines resisted for several hours, but eventually three thousand surrendered. The 369th Brigade commander was probably killed by enemy fire on the beach. In the 3rd Division, only one of Hinh's regiments made it to the landing zone, where the HQ-402 picked them up. Only about a thousand of his men out of approximately twelve thousand made it onto the ship; the rest were stranded.

South of Danang, the PAVN 2nd Division moved north on Route 1. Despite orders not to tangle with South Vietnamese defenses, the lead regiment kept stopping to engage RF troops. After the third incident, the 2nd Division commander sacked the regimental commander for not bypassing the defenders. All PAVN columns reached Danang by mid-morning 29 March. They entered the city, and by 3:00 P.M. Communist flags flew over Danang. I Corps had disintegrated in one of the most remarkable defeats in modern military history. The losses were enormous, akin to battles on the Eastern Front in the opening days of Germany's attack on Russia in World War II. According to North Vietnamese figures for the entire campaign from 5 to 29 March, PAVN forces "eliminated almost 120,000 enemy personnel from the field of battle (only 6,000 enemy troops managed to escape). Of this total, 55,000 were captured on the battlefield, while the rest deserted their units and turned themselves in."[37] They captured "129 aircraft, 179 tanks and APCs, 327 artillery pieces, 47 ships and boats, 1,084 military vehicles, and large quantities of ammunition and fuel."

So much has been written about the chaos at Danang's ports, there is little reason to repeat it here. For the South Vietnamese who escaped, the city's fall would forever be known as "the hours of hell" (*Gio Dia Nguc*).

Danang's panicky and very public collapse only confirmed long-held impressions in the West that ARVN was a house of cards waiting for the first strong gust to blow it over. While the panic displayed at the evacuation points was a disgrace, however, for the most part South Vietnamese forces had fought well. It was not until late in the campaign that numerous factors caused a sudden and irreversible breakdown of morale. While many have cited the withdrawal of the Airborne Division as the primary cause, the cutting of Route 1 south of Hue was just as important. Also critical was the U.S. Congress's denying aid in the middle of the offensive. After the fall, a senior CIA officer with close ARVN ties reported that "the general consensus among the officers and men was that they could have held out for some time longer, but it seemed useless in view of probably total discontinuance of U.S. military aid."[38] The news of the disastrous retreat from the Highlands plus the rumors of partition also played a large role.

More important still was the mass of refugees. Truong later wrote: "The most significant problem facing me were the hundreds of thousands of refugees who moved in an uncontrollable mass to Danang. This force represented a greater danger and contributed more to the defeat of the ARVN than did the enemy. Combat units attempting to deploy ... were swallowed up in the mass of humanity which choked Route 1 and intermediate land routes. Confusion, frustration, and ultimately panic began to grip some combat units."[39]

Most important of all was the family syndrome. While not excusing the ARVN collapse, the family syndrome is the key to understanding the events of late March 1975. As the I Corps Navy commander remarked after the war about the impact of housing relatives near the units, "Do you think that you would have the courage to abandon [your wife and children] there and go to the bunker to fight back? Let them just take care of themselves?"[40] Thoai's analysis rings true for any army, not just the South Vietnamese.

13

"THE SEA IS OUR ONLY HOPE"

THE BATTLE FOR THE COASTAL CITIES

When Major General Pham Van Phu received President Thieu's 25 March cable ordering all corps commanders to defend the areas that remained under their control, no matter what the cost, his course of action was now clear. He had to protect a semi-contiguous line comprising three fronts along a narrow coastal strip from Binh Dinh province through Tuy Hoa down to Nha Trang. However, given the destruction of the Ranger groups on Route 7B, he no longer had the men or equipment to accomplish this task. Still, from 25 to 29 March, Phu attempted to reorganize the shattered Rangers and the 23rd Division, and to rebuild badly shaken morale, which was just as crucial as material to restoring the military balance. The Communists, however, moved swiftly to deny him the breathing room he needed to consolidate his defenses.

On 25 March Phu issued a draconian order: His troops would shoot any deserter who was caught committing a crime. He further ordered that all stragglers be rounded up and used to reconstitute two Ranger groups. Further, after learning of the chaos swamping Danang, on the afternoon of 29 March Phu held a staff conference at his headquarters in Nha Trang. He ordered the imposition of strict disciplinary measures throughout II Corps. All soldiers were restricted to base, and military courts would conduct immediate trials—and executions if necessary—of any soldiers who violated military disciplinary regulations. Phu was determined "not to allow a second Danang to happen here."[1] Moreover, to answer the growing chorus calling for his dismissal, Phu informed the Vietnamese press that he had "declared martial law in II Corps. Looters will be executed on the spot ... Phu has personally directed the ... Military Court to utilize emergency procedures to try any person who claims to represent the military to extort money from or to harass the civilian population."[2]

The Communists were equally determined not to let Phu rally his troops. At its 25 March meeting, the Politburo's overarching decision was to liberate South Vietnam before the rainy season began, but the meeting also addressed a number of specific issues. These mainly concerned the rapidly accelerating events in I Corps, but the Politburo also commenced planning to complete the conquest of South Vietnam. First, it decided to send Le Duc Tho south to join Pham Hung and Van Tien Dung in directing the forthcoming attack on Saigon. Dung was ordered to rendezvous with Tho at Ban Me Thuot so that he could learn the Politburo's latest decisions. Pham Hung and Tran Van Tra from the B-2 Front, and Vo Chi Cong and Chu Huy Man from B-1, were also instructed to attend the meeting at Ban Me Thuot.

Further, for the third time that month, Giap sent a cable to Dung ordering him to cease his attack to the coast, and instead turn toward Saigon. Giap wrote: "Concentrate three main-force divisions . . . in the Ban Me Thuot area for rapid reorganization, ready to move out and prepare to attack . . . Saigon. . . . In the Route 7 sector, use only local forces to expand the attack down to Tuy Hoa. In the Route 21 sector, expand your offensive to the east and, depending on your capabilities and if the situation is favorable, move down to take Nha Trang and Cam Ranh."[3]

Immediately afterwards, Le Duc Tho sent a follow-up message to Dung. In preparation for his trip to meet Dung, "the other day I sent you a cable discussing the decision by the Politburo and the Central Military Party Committee on implementing Plan One [the attack on Saigon] in the immediate future, and I am sure you understood. Now the extent of the development of your attack has reached the proper level and you should not advance further. Instead, you need to quickly regroup and consolidate your forces and establish solid defenses for the newly captured areas."[4] Tho stated that Danang would fall quickly, enabling PAVN forces to sweep down from the north and finish conquering II Corps. "For that reason, you need to immediately realign your forces so that when I arrive the lead element will be able to move out immediately so that we can implement Plan One as quickly as possible. . . . Currently the situation is developing very favorably for us, it is advancing by leaps and bounds, so at this time when the enemy is frightened, confused, and suffering large-scale disintegration, we must seize the moment and act even more quickly."

Dung again rejected this plan. While he did not want to be viewed, as Tran Van Tra was, as someone who argued with his superiors, Dung's instincts told him to finish off the retreating ARVN forces before turning south to attack Saigon. For Dung, the question was: "Should the 320th and 10th Divisions stop chasing down the enemy and shift immediately. . . . Or should we let them continue on into the lowlands, liberating Phu Yen and Khanh Hoa provinces, go on to Nha Trang and Cam Ranh, and then [turn south]?"[5] Dung believed that his troops could capture the coastal provinces and still meet the Politburo's timetable for the attack on Saigon. He replied to Giap asking that his "units be allowed to fight on down toward the plains for a few more days . . . we could liberate a number of areas that were crucial . . . [Yet] we could still guarantee that we would meet the Political Bureau's schedule." To pacify the Politburo, Dung agreed to send the 316th Division, currently garrisoning Ban Me Thuot, to Tay Ninh province.

The next day the Politburo reluctantly agreed once more. Dung was told to destroy the remaining II Corps forces, but afterwards his forces must be "concentrated and strengthened quickly to move into [III Corps] to strike the enemy's nerve centers in accordance with the new strategic decisions."[6] On 27 March an elated Dung held a conference with his senior officers and announced that he was authorized to continue the attack to the coast, and that the three B-3 Front divisions would be combined to form a new strategic Army corps: the 3rd Corps. The corps commander would be Vu Lang, and Dang Vu Hiep would be the corps political commissar.

Mission orders soon went out to the three divisions. The 316th would move southwest to Tay Ninh province; the 10th would destroy the 3rd Airborne Brigade near the M'Drak Pass and then press forward to the coast; while the 320th would capture Tuy Hoa.

The 320th Division had the most difficult mission. It was given one week to capture a large area along the coast. It would then return to Ban Me Thuot, and then move south to accomplish its mission. This meant that it needed, as the division history noted, to "clear [Route 7B] to move our tanks, heavy artillery, technical equipment, and supplies down to the jumping-off point for the attack. Route 7[B] from Cung Son to Tuy Hoa had been heavily mined, both by our own local forces as well as by the enemy. If we wished to use this road, it would have to be swept and cleared very carefully. This heavy responsibility was entrusted to the division's engineer battalion. For several days and nights the engineers worked around the clock . . . to clear the road to enable the division to march into battle. Not a night went by without a mine exploding or without men being killed. The division command group closely monitored the progress of this difficult mission. One night the division commander himself rode in an armored personnel carrier down to the road, driving right behind the engineers' mine-clearing vehicles to bolster the morale of the troops and to inspect and direct the work of the engineers."[7]

As Dung's troops pressed forward, now for a fourth time, the Politburo again changed its mind. Despite the earlier authorization to destroy II Corps, immediately after the fall of Danang the Politburo reversed itself: "The Central Military Party Committee, with the unanimous agreement of the Politburo, decided to mass all of our units in the southern Central Highlands and rapidly send this force straight down to eastern Cochin China."[8]

Accordingly, Dung was supposed to immediately shift the 3rd Corps toward Saigon, while the B-1 Front would attack the ARVN 22nd Division and capture Binh Dinh, using the 3rd and 968th Divisions and Binh Dinh local forces. These would then wheel south on Route 1 and link up with local forces to finish seizing the coast. The Politburo also decided to move the 10th Division south via Route 20. However, the change in plans did not occur until the late afternoon of 29 March, long after the 10th had initiated its campaign to destroy the 3rd Airborne along Route 21 and then advance to the coast.

Once again, Dung quickly cabled Giap, saying that his forces could "annihilate the remaining airborne troops and other enemy troops on Route 21, rapidly advance southward to take Nha Trang and Cam Ranh, and then advance southward along the coast."[9]

For the fourth time, Dung's pleas worked. Giap replied to Dung: "We have discussed this subject with [Le Duan] and have agreed that we must maintain a very flexible policy in order to be able to exploit this opportunity. This means you may mass the 10th Division to quickly destroy the airborne unit and enemy remnants, rapidly capture Nha Trang and Cam Ranh, and then south." The Politburo's final decision regarding the 10th Division sealed the fate of ARVN units along the coast. Thrilled at the turn of events, Dung sent Giap a note thanking him.

The 10th Division had its three organic infantry regiments, the 24th, 28th, and 66th, along with tank, anti-aircraft, and artillery units, plus the 25th Regiment, which was newly attached to it. But seizing the M'Drak Pass would not be easy. The pass runs through an arm of the Annamite Mountain chain that separates the Khanh Duong district capital from Ninh Hoa on the coast. The terrain is very rugged, and the road twists and turns through mountain canyons and over numerous bridges and culverts. To delay the PAVN advance, the commander of the 3rd Airborne Brigade, Lieutenant Colonel Le Van Phat, instructed his men to destroy the bridges on Route 21 west of the pass after the last escaping ARVN troops had passed through. However, Phat's belief that destroying the bridges would impede the PAVN advance did not account for the superbly efficient PAVN engineers. As the 10th Division history later recounted, the "engineers and reconnaissance troops quickly completed a road west of the pass . . . and simultaneously widened a footpath from western Khanh Duong . . . to enable trucks to use it. The 24th Regiment, the blocking force that was being sent to take up a position east of the pass, [used] the road completed by the engineers."[10]

Given the rugged terrain, an assault straight down the road would be difficult, so the 10th planned to outflank the Airborne defenders. It would send the 24th Regiment looping to block the eastern side of the pass. A second regiment would attack the western entrance. The third regiment would move north and then turn and attack into the middle section of the pass.

Although the Airborne troops were dug in and waiting, Phat soon learned from his reconnaissance teams that he faced superior PAVN forces that were trying to outflank him from two directions. There was little he could do about it. His three battalions simply could not cover the nine-mile pass, plus stop the flanking movements. When a resupply convoy was ambushed on 28 March on the eastern side of the pass, Phat knew that a full-scale attack was imminent. Realizing he could not allow the Communists to cut off his only avenue of retreat, he sent his 2nd Battalion to the eastern end to clear Route 21 back to the Ranger Training Center at Duc My.[11] His 5th Battalion continued to guard the pass's western entrance, while the 6th Battalion held the middle.

Phat's intuition was correct. At 3:00 A.M. on 29 March, the 10th Division launched a massive artillery assault. For almost six hours the Airborne batteries exchanged fire with the Communist artillery, which mainly consisted of former ARVN howitzers captured at Ban Me Thuot, along with truckloads of ammunition shipped from the Mai Hac De supply depot there.

At 9:30 A.M. on 30 March, PAVN simultaneously struck each Airborne battalion with a regiment. Fighting raged all day, but the 5th and 6th Battalions, backed by numerous air strikes, held their ground. At the eastern end of the pass, however, the 2nd Battalion suffered heavy losses. A large unit attacked the battalion's command post, defended by only thirty support personnel. With such a tiny force, the 2nd Battalion commander, Major Tran Cong Hanh, had little hope of holding out. While he managed to beat back the initial assault, he soon heard bullhorns demanding his surrender. He refused, and despite being saddled with non-infantry headquarters personnel, he made a mad dash through enemy lines. For five miles the PAVN forces chased Hanh and his men. Finally, he made radio contact with the brigade deputy commander, Lieutenant Colonel Tran Dang Khoi, who swooped in with helicopters and rescued Hanh and the survivors.[12] Hanh's infantry companies, perched on isolated hilltops in the surrounding hills, were attacked separately by enemy battalions and suffered heavy casualties.

While the Airborne had stopped the initial attack, the 2nd Battalion on the eastern end was surrounded. Notwithstanding the plentiful air support, Phat knew he could not hold without reinforcements. Learning from three prisoners that the 10th Division would commit every soldier it had, together with tanks, to capture the pass, Phat radioed II Corps on the night of 30 March and asked permission to retreat. Phu refused, but told Phat that he was urgently seeking reinforcements for him.

The 10th Division's signal-intercept unit picked up Phat's transmission, and, believing he intended to withdraw, the division immediately attacked. Early in the morning of 31 March, one regiment with tanks assaulted the 5th Battalion at the western end. A second regiment attacked the 6th Battalion from the north, while the 24th Regiment moved down from the hills and seized Route 21, cutting off Phat's brigade. The 72nd Ranger Battalion, 21st Group, re-forming at the Duc My training camp after its retreat from Ban Me Thuot, tried to break through and assist the Airborne. The 21st Ranger Group commander, Lieutenant Colonel Le Qui Dau, confirmed that "I was given orders to place my 72nd Battalion under the operational control of 3rd Airborne Brigade, but it was too late to save the situation, even though we tried very hard. Most of the airborne forces in forward positions were cut off and isolated. During this operation 72nd Battalion suffered significant losses because it had no support other than its own individual heavy weapons, while the enemy's attack spirit was high and they had ample fire support."[13]

The 10th Division history confirms Dau's description of intense fighting: "At dawn the enemy concentrated their artillery . . to shell the 24th Regiment's blocking positions. The shelling was coordinated with savage air strikes on these positions. . . . Flight after flight of A-37s took turns dropping bombs and napalm on the regiment's positions. Enemy infantry made death-defying charges in an effort to push the regiment out of its blocking positions and clear the road."[14] The 10th Division shifted the regiment attacking the 6th Battalion plus four tanks to reinforce the 24th Regiment. Air strikes knocked out the four tanks, and PAVN sent in four armored personnel carriers. The additional troops helped PAVN hold the eastern end of the pass. The 3rd Airborne was cut off and in danger of being overrun.

Phat radioed II Corps all day asking for reinforcements, and Phu was desperately trying to find some. Early in the morning of 30 March, Brigadier General Tran Dinh Tho, the chief of the J-3 (operations) staff of the JGS, called Phu and promised him that "the Marine Division would arrive at Cam Ranh Bay on LSTs that afternoon. The Marines would stay on the Cam Ranh peninsula. One brigade of Marines would be immediately reorganized and re-equipped and sent to reinforce the Khanh Duong front. General Phu greeted this news with great jubilation."[15] Phu's newfound optimism was short-lived, however, when Brigadier General Phan Dinh Niem, the commander of the 22nd Division, flew in at noon to tell him that the situation in Binh Dinh was critical. Niem's three regiments were still holding the Communists at bay, but enemy local forces had made a sudden attack into his rear near Qui Nhon and scattered many of the province's RF troops. Phu told Niem to guard the Qui Nhon waterfront and protect the city.

Later that afternoon, Phu flew to Cam Ranh to meet Lieutenant General Ngo Quang Truong, who had just arrived in the port. Truong had been Phu's boss in 1972 when Phu commanded the 1st Division. Phu wanted Truong to release the Marines, but Truong refused to speak to him. It was Truong's strangest action of the war, for without the Marines, Phu had no chance. The main reason was Truong's anger at Phu for the disastrous retreat from the Central Highlands, which had helped destroy I Corps.

Truong, however, was also depressed and in poor physical condition. According to a CIA report, he required "intravenous injections [and] was suffering from a severe stomach ailment; he also appeared dejected and in poor morale due to the loss of MR-1."[16] When the JGS ordered the Marines to disembark at Cam Ranh and told Truong to return to Saigon alone, he refused. He told the ship's captain "to call the General Staff to ask that the Marines be allowed to return to Saigon along with me for a rest. If this request was refused, I would remain in Cam Ranh with the Marines and would fight at their side."[17] Truong probably feared that if he returned alone, Thieu would arrest him for the loss of I Corps. He wanted to stay with the Marines because they provided him protection. Truong was no coward, but he was not a fool either. The JGS quickly rescinded the order, and told the Marines to get back on the ships and return to Saigon. The next day the Marines sailed away, and Phu's last hope for reinforcements from outside II Corps vanished with them.

Phu's desperate search for reinforcements grew even more frantic. He again issued orders to gather every available soldier in the Nha Trang area and form units to help hold the remaining section of the coast. Locally, Phu had only the 40th Regiment, 22nd Division, but it was needed to hold the western outskirts of Nha Trang. Even if the Airborne successfully defended the pass, the 10th Division could bypass it via old logging roads that led directly to the city.

Phu sent Brigadier General Tran Van Cam to Tuy Hoa to organize the defense of that city. Cam was to secure Route 1 from Tuy Hoa to the critical Ca Pass, located eighteen miles south of the town. The Ca Pass is seven miles long, with sheer rock cliffs on one side and the sea on the other. A determined defender backed by air strikes and naval gunfire could easily hold it even against major enemy forces. If Cam held Tuy Hoa and the Ca Pass, Communist units from the north would be unable to advance south. On 30 March, Phu told a visiting Vietnam Press correspondent that Ranger units had turned the Ca Pass into "a strong line of defense."[18]

It was a fantasy. Only the battered 34th Ranger Battalion was holding the pass. Despite Phu's orders, the Rangers who had survived the ordeal on Route 7B had not been reorganized. Many had been sent to the Duc My training center, but the commander of the training center insisted on re-forming the original units instead of creating ad-hoc elements to defend the region.

The reorganization of the 23rd Division remnants that made it to Nha Trang after the disastrous attempt to retake Ban Me Thuot was also moving too slowly. They were being grouped at an old Special Forces camp on Route 1 near Cam Ranh. Despite efforts by Colonel Le Huu Duc to turn what was left of the 23rd into a coherent military formation, the battered soldiers were still just a disorganized rabble. In addition, most of Khanh Hoa province's resources were going into the effort to care for 13,000 civilian refugees being housed at a camp about three miles north of Nha Trang. But whatever the reason for ARVN's failure to regroup the soldiers who had survived the retreats on Routes 7B and 21—shattered morale, lack of time and resources, or both—that failure would cost the South Vietnamese.

Phu's efforts to hold the coast began to disintegrate on the morning of 31 March when rockets hit the Duc My training center, setting some of the student barracks on fire. Sensing the Airborne's imminent defeat, and hoping to save the trainees, the commander of the training center decided to flee. Packing food into several trucks, hundreds of Ranger cadres and students departed that night and began walking toward Nha Trang, which they reached on the morning of 1 April.[19] There they were greeted by a rapidly disintegrating city. Late the previous afternoon, rioting had broken out as soldiers flowing in from the ships that had arrived from I Corps began looting and robbing civilians. Seeing the column of retreating Rangers, the thousands of refugees in the temporary holding camps also began pouring into the city. Efforts were made to stop the disorder and to execute undisciplined troops on the spot, but the police were able to stabilize only part of Nha Trang. Any chance of preventing "a second Danang" was slipping away.

A RETREAT TO THE SEA

With no other options, Phu went to Commodore Hoang Co Minh at the 2nd Coastal Zone headquarters in Cam Ranh to discuss plans to retrieve the 22nd Division from Qui Nhon and bring it to Nha Trang. The 22nd was the only viable unit left in II Corps. According to Phu's biographer, Pham Huan, Phu ordered "the 22nd Division to fall back to Qui Nhon to hold and defend the city, and particularly the military port area, in order to have a route of withdrawal so the division could board Navy ships to be transported down to Khanh Duong, Nha Trang, and Phu Yen."[20] Minh immediately informed Naval Operations in Saigon, which agreed to the plan and sent him the destroyer *Tran Nhat Duat* (HQ-03) to help ferry the men back from Qui Nhon.

Although Minh had contacted Saigon, however, he was reluctant to go himself. He believed that "if I leave Cam Ranh it would be very dangerous because my presence as the commander was very important." Minh's prediction was proven true: "The problem was not fighting; the problem was morale. My staff at Cam Ranh said they needed me very much."[21] This was the predicament many South Vietnamese commanders found themselves in. Their presence reassured their staff, which in turn kept the military operations semi-functional. Yet given the torrid pace of combat operations countrywide, commanders frequently had to leave their base to take direct command of far-flung battles. Since many South Vietnamese believed that a secret deal had been struck with the Communists to partition the country, when the commander left, the staff promptly fled, disrupting communications and leading to more confusion among the combat units. Despite his misgivings, however, Minh gathered all available vessels in the 2nd Coastal Zone and departed that evening.

In Binh Dinh, meanwhile, on 27 March Brigadier General Phan Dinh Niem ordered the 41st and 42nd Regiments to continue defending Route 19. Niem also ordered Colonel Le Cau to withdraw his 47th Regiment from the northern part of the province and establish defenses on Route 1 closer to Qui Nhon. Without any transportation, Cau's soldiers had to walk the twenty-eight miles to their new position. As his units started withdrawing, the local civilians joined them. Soon his battalion commanders began reporting that it was increasingly difficult to control their troops, as the soldiers were becoming intermingled with the civilians. Cau told his men to move off the road, leaving the hardtop to the civilians.

On 24 March the B-3 Front began shifting units to occupy the coast. Its first move was to order the 968th Division to shift east from Pleiku on Route 19 and, in conjunction with the 3rd Division, to trap and destroy the ARVN 22nd Division.

On 26 March new orders also arrived for the PAVN 3rd Division. The B-1 Front's instructions to the 3rd Division read as follows: "[The] Party Committee has decided to annihilate or disperse the entire remaining [ARVN forces] in the region and liberate [Binh Dinh] as quickly as possible. This is now a practical fact, not just a possibility. During the course of twenty days and nights of continuous combat the Yellow Star Division has properly accomplished its mission . . . but its percentage of casualties is still too high. The division's immediate mission is to surround and destroy the 22nd Division, prevent it from escaping, and, fighting alongside local armed forces, stand ready to liberate Qui Nhon."[22]

To accomplish this mission, the 3rd Division attempted to cut off the 41st and 42nd Regiments on Route 19 by circling a battalion to their rear and seizing a bridge just behind them. The 3rd also focused on building roads to bring its artillery close to the battlefield to support its attacks against the two ARVN regiments. The efforts to bring artillery forward failed, however, and when the battalion attacked, the 42nd Regiment drove it off, causing heavy casualties. For several days the North Vietnamese continued to attack, but with little success. The failure caused the Yellow Star commander to fly into a rage. Blaming the failed attacks on poor fire support, he relieved the artillery regiment's commander. He also sacked the transportation battalion commander for not shipping enough ammunition to the front lines.

At the same time, following orders to smash the South Vietnamese defensive line north of Qui Nhon, on 30 March three newly formed local-force regiments attacked RF/PF positions. Most of the RF/PF troops fled or were overwhelmed by the assaults, allowing the Communists to cut Route 1 and block Colonel Cau's retreat. With the 22nd Division's rear now in chaos, the PAVN trap was closing. The 968th Division reached an assembly area near Binh Khe on 27 March, and the 3rd Division reinforced the battalion fighting behind the 42nd Regiment.

As the situation in Binh Dinh worsened, at 8:00 P.M. on 30 March Brigadier General Niem called Phu again. Niem reported that almost all the RF units had deserted, PAVN sappers had entered Qui Nhon, and the city was in danger of falling. Phu promptly called the JGS and briefed several senior officers on the rapidly deteriorating situation, but they could offer little help. Phu was faced with a momentous decision. Without outside reinforcements for the Airborne, he believed he had no choice but to retrieve the 22nd, his last organized unit, to reinforce Tuy Hoa and the Airborne on Route 21. That night, according to Pham Huan, while "Phu initially intended to issue orders to 22nd Division to pull back to Qui Nhon ... to defend the military port and wait for Navy ships to pick the division up and bring it back to help defend the Khanh Duong and Phu Yen fronts, General Tat protested, saying that if we evacuated Qui Nhon, Nha Trang would fall just that much faster. For that reason General Phu hesitated and remained undecided about the decision to evacuate Qui Nhon and bring 22nd Division back on the night of 30 March 1975."[23]

The delay was costly, as it allowed the PAVN 3rd Division to close in behind the ARVN regiments on Route 19. Further attacks in Binh Dinh later that night convinced Phu he had to act. At 11:00 A.M. on 31 March, Phu ordered Niem to retreat to Qui Nhon and defend the city. Niem quickly ordered his two regiments on Route 19 to withdraw, but the trap was sprung. PAVN now had a regiment of the 3rd Division behind both the 41st and 42nd Regiments, while the 968th Division was pressing against them from the west. The 41st Regiment commander, Colonel Nguyen Thieu, described what happened to his unit during its retreat eastward to try to link up with the 42nd Regiment:

I assigned 2nd and 3rd Battalions to make a two-pronged attack to clear the road while 1st Battalion served as our rear guard. When the 41st Regiment reached the town of Phu An on Route 19 it clashed with enemy forces. The battalions made a concerted attack, and after half an hour of fighting shattered and dispersed the enemy force at Phu An. At about 5 that afternoon, however, just as it reached [the 42nd Regiment], units of the 3rd Division blocked its way. While 3rd Battalion, 41st Regiment, formed a spearhead that tried unsuccessfully to punch a hole through, 1st Battalion, 41st Regiment, in our rear began to be attacked by the lead units of the enemy's 968th Division, and enemy artillery began to adjust fire into the area where the troops of 41st Regiment had halted. . . . Because we could not allow our units to suffer continued losses from enemy artillery, 41st Regiment decided to use the firepower of our accompanying platoon of M-113 armored personnel carriers to clear the road while infantry stuck close behind them, expanded outward to cover both sides of the road, and provided security along the route of march. In spite of these efforts, enemy forces pressing in on both our flanks inflicted significant losses on the 41st Regiment. When night fell and it grew completely dark, and when the sound of gunfire faded to a few scattered shots, the units of 41st Regiment resumed their movement eastward to where the 42nd Regiment was located.[24]

While the 41st Regiment fought its way east along Route 19, the situation in Qui Nhon was deteriorating further. On the morning of 30 March, the commander of the Phu Cat airbase reported that all the RF defenders assigned to the airbase had deserted. Spotting the abandonment, at midafternoon on 30 March, Communist local forces attacked the airbase. The base's Air Force security forces held them off, but with the discovery of more Communist local forces racing to join the fight, the airbase commander phoned Colonel Le Van Thao, commander of the VNAF 92nd Air Wing at Phan Rang, and begged him for help. The enemy would attack that night, and Phu Cat had few defenses.

Thao immediately gathered every available A-37, some forty aircraft, and took off. His mission was tricky at best. He would arrive at night, and the A-37 was not equipped for night missions. Thao, however, had extensively trained his unit to fight at night; it was perhaps the only such unit in the Vietnamese Air Force. He had succeeded in developing an all-weather bombing capacity by creating a method using the plane's instruments, timing, and a beacon-based navigation system. He would now test that training under the most demanding circumstances, a close air strike at night. His only hope of smashing the attack was to simultaneously unload the bombs of all forty planes directly on the suspected location of the enemy's assembly area. And the location was right next to the base. If Thao's timing was off by even a few seconds, his planes would bomb his own people. Even if he did hit the enemy, his forty aircraft carried only two bombs apiece. Each bomb weighed 250 pounds. Taken together, his eighty bombs roughly equaled the destructive punch of one B-52.

As Thao's formation neared the base, he radioed the tower and confirmed the location to hit. Gripping the stick tightly, as he flew over the spot, he hit the button releasing his bombs and informed his other pilots to drop theirs. He immediately switched to the tower radio frequency and called the tower as he saw the bombs explode. Within seconds the base commander was on the air confirming that he was okay and that Thao's daring night raid had hit the exact spot. Thao's men had accomplished one of the most astounding air strikes in the war, a massed formation of forty A-37s concurrently releasing their payload at night without guides on a location that was dangerously close to the pilots' fellow VNAF personnel.

At dawn the 2nd Air Division hastily abandoned Phu Cat. Only thirty-two aircraft managed to get out, leaving more than fifty others to fall into enemy hands. PAVN forces moved in and captured the airbase by late afternoon on 31 March.

Meanwhile, Le Cau's 47th Regiment, moving south along Route 1, broke through the local-force blockade and headed toward Qui Nhon. As Cau struggled to control his troops amidst the many civilians retreating with them, his men were attacked a second time. Between the two battles, about half of his regiment was killed or captured. The rest broke into small teams and continued moving south through the countryside toward Qui Nhon, but the 47th Regiment was no longer combat-effective.

On the afternoon of 31 March, Phu briefed President Thieu on the deteriorating Binh Dinh front. Thieu ordered Phu to defend Qui Nhon and prevent any chaos. Meanwhile, to support Commodore Minh's efforts to retrieve the 22nd Division, earlier that day the new Navy commander, Admiral Chung Tan Cang, assigned Commodore Ho Van Ky Thoai, the I Corps Navy commander, to take command of all naval forces supporting the Qui Nhon battlefield. To reinforce Minh's flotilla, at noon Cang ordered all VNN ships still picking up refugees off the coast of Danang to sail to Qui Nhon immediately. Despite Thieu's orders, Phu was under no illusion that the retreating 22nd Division units could prepare an adequate defense of the city against the onrushing PAVN.

In fact, Communist local forces were already closing in on Qui Nhon. The Binh Dinh province history states: "At 10:00 A.M. on 31 March the forward headquarters ordered all district forces to quickly attack and capture their district capitals. Enemy forces . . . hurriedly retreated, and a number of officers and governmental officials fled from Qui Nhon back to Nha Trang. In the face of this favorable opportunity . . . the headquarters of the province military unit issued orders to all forces to besiege and destroy enemy forces and liberate Qui Nhon."[25]

At noon on 31 March a Communist local-force regiment poured into the city from the north, brushing aside RF troops holding the outskirts. By 6:30 P.M. it had captured the province headquarters and the city center. A short time later, Niem reported to Phu that enemy troops had taken the city. After receiving the earlier orders to hold the port, Niem had been flying back and forth in his helicopter trying to help his troops, but the situation seemed hopeless. His 47th Regiment was decimated, and with his two other regiments plus his divisional armor still on Route 19, caught between the local forces holding Qui Nhon and the main-force PAVN units pressing from behind, he was faced with the destruction of his beloved 22nd Division. It was too much for Niem. With the city's fall, and fearing his units would be destroyed, early in the evening a mentally and physically exhausted Niem flew out to a VNN ship and collapsed.

Hope appeared at 9:00 P.M. with the arrival of Minh's flotilla to rescue what remained of the 22nd Division. Upon being briefed on the current situation, Minh radioed Phu and told him about Niem's collapse. Listening to the radio at VNN headquarters in Saigon, Navy Captain Do Kiem, the head of operations for the Navy, quickly informed Admiral Cang of the impending disaster. Thinking quickly, Kiem proposed to Cang that with the firepower from the combined naval groups and their better communications, Minh could establish a defensive perimeter and perhaps even retake some of the outlying areas. Cang agreed, and he and Kiem hurried to see Lieutenant General Dong Van Khuyen, chief of staff of the JGS, who accepted the plan. Khuyen promptly visited President Thieu, who signed a decree appointing Minh commander of the Binh Dinh Front. Kiem radioed Minh at 2:00 A.M. on 1 April, telling him that his mission was to hold the city and withdraw the 22nd Division.[26]

But given the chaos in Qui Nhon and Niem's collapse, Minh was having difficulty contacting any 22nd command elements. Finally, he reached a logistics officer near the beach who was monitoring the division's command frequency. As this officer later wrote, Minh "read [a] message informing us that . . . the Joint General Staff had appointed Commodore Hoang Co Minh as acting commander of the 22nd Infantry Division, replacing Brigadier General Phan Dinh Niem, who was being removed for reasons of health. He then told me to immediately report to the Deputy Division Commander that at exactly 12:30 P.M. [Minh] would send in five LCM landing craft. Each LCM was capable of carrying 500 men. Each landing craft would make a number of round trips to take the soldiers out to our warships off the coast. Before boarding the LCMs all soldiers were to throw their weapons and military equipment into the sea."[27] Since the Qui Nhon pier was not strong enough to hold many troops, and since ships had beached many times before on the city's coastline, the decision was made to load the soldiers from the shore.

More good news came with the arrival in Qui Nhon of the 41st and 42nd Regiments. After continuing along Route 19 all night, early in the morning of 1 April the two regiments and the division's armored squadron successfully reached the junction of Route 1 and the local road into Qui Nhon. At 11:00 A.M. they were told to move toward the shore and board Navy ships to evacuate. The decision was made to have the 42nd Regiment and the armor lead the way, followed by the artillery, with the 41st Regiment acting as rear guard.

As the first 22nd Division elements reached the outskirts of the city, Communist local forces firing from buildings blocked their path. Colonel Thieu brought up a 105-mm howitzer and began blasting at the enemy positions. Resistance soon crumbled, and the 22nd forces punched through.

Pushing toward the sea, the 41st and 42nd Regiments destroyed two more enemy positions before reaching the beach, where they set up a defense to secure the landing points. The units soon began embarking, but by 7:00 P.M. they had to halt because of heavy enemy fire. At 9:00 P.M., the LSM *Ninh Giang* (HQ-403) tried to reach the beach, but it was hit by B-40 rockets and was forced to retreat. When Minh directed another ship to beach nearby, it was also hit. Since Minh could not risk the loss of his larger transport ships, he ordered the smaller coastal gunboats to pick up the men. At dawn on 2 April, with PAVN firing at any approaching ship, the word was passed to the remaining ARVN elements to swim out to the ships. The operation lasted until 11:00 A.M. When it was completed, only about half of the two regiments had made it to the ships. Figures on the total number of men picked up vary widely, from a few thousand to a high of seven thousand. And meanwhile, another major city had fallen.

While the ARVN 18th Division would later become renowned for its stalwart defense of Xuan Loc, near Saigon, the 22nd Division, far out of sight of Western reporters, had also accomplished an amazing feat of arms during the 1975 offensive. It maintained unit integrity through twenty-five days of major combat and inflicted heavy casualties on the North Vietnamese. During its retreat, not only did it smash through three Communist roadblocks to reach the sea, its men did not panic or desert. As Major General Homer Smith wrote, "the 22nd Division defended strongly with great perseverance against determined and heavy PAVN attacks. Outflanked, outgunned, and eventually cut off, the 22nd fought its way back to the beaches and was eventually evacuated."[28] The 42nd Regiment's commander, Colonel Nguyen Huu Thong, after his last man was picked up, waved goodbye, went to a nearby house, and committed suicide. The 47th's commander, Colonel Le Cau, was moving with his reconnaissance company when he stepped on a land mine. He told his men to leave him, but they refused. They tried carrying him, but were soon surrounded and forced to surrender. Only the 41st Regiment's commander, Colonel Nguyen Thieu, was rescued with his troops. When the division landed at the port of Vung Tau near Saigon, he helped form the remaining men into two regiments.

As for the PAVN 3rd Division, despite its heavy casualties, its history brags about its victory: "Enemy bodies, vehicles, and artillery lay scattered . . . all the way down to the Qui Nhon docks. . . . The 22nd Division, the long-time combat opponent of the Yellow Star Division through nine long years of ferocious battles, had been destroyed. Binh Dinh Province, the birthplace of the division, had been liberated."[29]

THE FALL OF TUY HOA

As Qui Nhon was falling and the regiments of the 22nd were fighting their way to the shore, the PAVN 320th Division—the unit that had chewed up the troops and civilians retreating from Cheo Reo—was finalizing preparations to take Tuy Hoa, 110 miles south of Qui Nhon. The city, built alongside Route 1 near the sea, had a population of roughly 300,000 people, mostly Vietnamese. A large river ran south of the town, and the area surrounding it was mainly rice paddy cut by irrigation canals. Two hills to the north dominate the terrain.

The 320th Division—with three infantry regiments, one tank battalion, and several battalions of anti-aircraft guns, artillery, and engineers—along with the Phu Yen local forces, decided to assault the city in three prongs. The primary assault sector would be from the west into Tuy Hoa itself. The main assault would use two infantry regiments plus field artillery, anti-aircraft battalions, and the tank battalion. Roadblocks would be established north and south of the city along Route 1. An infantry battalion would swing south to block any ARVN reinforcements coming from the Ca Pass area. Local forces would cut Route 1 north of the town and support the two main attack sectors.

Defending the city and lengthy portions of the coast against this onslaught were multiple battalions of Phu Yen Regional Forces and the remnants of the 96th Ranger Battalion, 21st Group. Several RF battalions ringed the city to protect it from attack from either north or south along Route 1. On the western approaches, the RF had built a series of interlocking defensive positions. For fire support, they had a battery of 105-mm guns and some M-113s. Brigadier General Cam had been ordered by Phu to defend the city and prevent PAVN from moving south along Route 1. However, Cam was outmanned and essentially blind, without any intelligence to indicate when and where the Communists would attack.

The 320th's plan called for its forces to maneuver close to Tuy Hoa by 31 March. On 2 April they would "open fire, attack and liberate the city during daylight hours, then expand the attack to seize the . . . Ca Pass. . . . After capturing the city, all units would be re-supplied with fuel and food rations to be ready to advance as soon as orders were received."[30]

The last part of that plan could not be carried out. By the night of 29 March, the PAVN engineers still had not completed rebuilding the bridge across the Ba River. Many of the Communist forces' supplies were still en route to Tuy Hoa, and some 320th Division units had not yet arrived. Despite this, when a signal intercept indicated that ARVN was preparing to withdraw—which was incorrect—Division Commander Kim Tuan ordered the attack moved up one day. Several elements immediately shifted forward and overran two outlying RF positions. At 5:30 A.M. on 1 April, PAVN artillery began pounding Tuy Hoa. An hour later, the artillery fire lifted, and the tanks and infantry rolled forward. The RF troops offered little resistance against the North Vietnamese regulars. Cam radioed Phu that he was under massive attack. By 7:30 A.M., the North Vietnamese armor was inside the city, poised to attack the sector headquarters. The few Rangers holding the city center fought back, but the headquarters was captured in thirty minutes. By noon, the Communist soldiers had captured Brigadier General Tran Van Cam. He was the first South Vietnamese general officer captured in the 1975 offensive. Turning its forces north and south, the 320th Division was in full control of Tuy Hoa and its outlying districts by 3:00 P.M. on 1 April.

Not stopping there, a battalion of the 320th advanced south. Supported by Phu Yen local forces, it seized control of the Ca Pass. Despite the excellent defensive terrain, the 34th Rangers held out for only a short time. South Vietnamese patrol boats sailing south of Qui Nhon reported to Captain Kiem at the Navy Operations Center in Saigon that convoys of PAVN tanks and trucks were seen driving down Route 1, but that the boats' short-range guns could not reach these targets. The Navy tried but failed to obtain air support to destroy the bridges and stop the advance. Admiral Chung Tan Cang ordered his larger warships with longer-range guns to bombard and destroy the bridges from Qui Nhon to the Ca Pass, but they were ineffective. Consequently, not only had Route 1 been cleared of ARVN forces all the way to the Phu Yen/Khanh Hoa province border, but more important, several of the natural barriers to invasion from the north—the critical passes on Route 1—were captured. PAVN now had an easy motorway leading direct to Saigon.

THE FALL OF THE COAST

For South Vietnam, 1 April was a decisive day. At dawn, the North Vietnamese 24th and 28th Regiments, 10th Division, supported by tanks and large concentrations of artillery, launched a full-scale assault against the 3rd Airborne Brigade. Within half an hour, the last defensive lines of the Airborne in the M'Drak Pass were crushed. Lieutenant Colonel Le Van Phat ordered his troops to retreat to high ground and wait for helicopter evacuation. The 10th Division took full advantage of the breach in the ARVN lines. As the division history recounts, "3rd Airborne Brigade was destroyed, Ninh Hoa's western defenses were shattered, and the road to the lowlands was clear. Without a moment's rest . . . 3rd Battalion, 28th Regiment, reinforced by tanks, anti-aircraft guns, and field artillery, quickly surged forward and launched a coordinated attack with 6th Battalion, 24th Regiment, capturing the Duc My base."[31] The 10th Division spent that night at the Duc My training center.

At II Corps headquarters near the Nha Trang airfield, the South Vietnamese military command was stunned at the rapid disintegration of the ARVN defenses at Tuy Hoa and the M'Drak Pass. At 10:30 A.M., after returning from overflying Tuy Hoa, Phu held a staff meeting with Lieutenant General Pham Quoc Thuan, the commander of the Dong De NCO Academy, and Brigadier General Pham Duy Tat. Pham Huan claims that "Phu requested the generals . . . [to] each handle their own defensive arrangements for their own units. He said all II Corps's resources would be devoted to the Khanh Duong front. . . . With regard to providing regular units to defend Nha Trang, Phu said that would have to await the arrival of troops from the 22nd Division."[32] Phu sent Tat in a helicopter to the Ca Pass to make contact with the 34th Rangers, but Tat was too late. The Ca Pass, heralded by Phu as a primary defensive position along the coast, had already fallen.

As the meeting was breaking for lunch, an operations officer ran in and reported that reconnaissance aircraft had spotted PAVN tanks at Duc My and Ninh Hoa. In fact, although PAVN tanks had reached Duc My, they were not yet at Ninh Hoa, but it did not matter. The news of the tanks and the destruction of the Airborne defensive line was the final straw at II Corps headquarters. Panic set in, and officers and guards began running for the door.

Unable to halt the fleeing soldiers, Phu stood motionless for a few minutes, trying to think what to do. Like Commodore Hoang Co Minh two days before, Phu was caught in a terrible dilemma. Should he stay at his headquarters and try to establish radio contact with the field units, or should he leave and try to contact them from his helicopter? Phu chose to leave for the front. He jumped into his jeep and drove over to the Nha Trang airfield, where he ordered the base closed to anyone trying to enter. Lieutenant General Thuan soon joined Phu, and they took off in a helicopter to try to contact any units still manning their positions in the Nha Trang area.

With Phu's departure, the remaining staff officers fled, causing a chain reaction in the combat units. Unable to contact II Corps headquarters for instructions, and with no contingency plans, Colonel Duc decided to withdraw the 23rd Division and the two battalions of the 40th Regiment, 22nd Division. The Regional Forces did the same.

Seeing the collapse of II Corps headquarters, the American consulate also decided to evacuate. It was not pretty. The journalist Arnold Isaacs wrote, "The U.S. consul-general for II Corps, Moncrieff Spear, and his staff also hurriedly left Nha Trang on the afternoon of April 1. As they prepared to go, hundreds of Vietnamese tried to climb over the whitewashed walls . . . the evacuation was so chaotic that more than one hundred Vietnamese consular employees, who had been promised flights to Saigon, were left behind, some of them ordered away from planeside by U.S. officials who trained rifles on them."[33]

Despite Phu's best intentions, the bedlam that had swept Danang was repeating itself in Nha Trang. The city was coming apart at the seams. At mid-morning almost 1,100 soldiers held in the local prison for a variety of crimes overwhelmed their guards and swarmed into the city. They ransacked houses and the market along Nha Trang's main road. Soon fires were burning in the market. Looters stole cars and bicycles, and many robbed any civilians they could find. The population fled Nha Trang to escape the rampaging criminals. As one ARVN officer leaving with his family later wrote, "The chaotic scene seemed to unfold endlessly as . . . thousands of people poured onto Route 1. . . . Traffic jams blocked movement almost every ten yards. Nha Trang city, once . . . fresh in appearance like a young girl at sweet 16, was already bearing a dismal look. Most of the shops . . . were ruined. Some were still burning; walls of others had collapsed, and their entrance doors were shattered or broken by gunfire . . . the roads and streets were covered with trash and the trunks of fallen trees."[34]

Many fled to the city dock, called the Stone Pier, to reach Vietnamese Navy ships. Years later, a woman named Tran Thi Minh Canh, who had lived in Nha Trang, wrote about those days. She related how fear of the Communists drove them to escape: "Tonight we are running in agonizing terror that supersedes all other needs, all other considerations. Others run alongside us but we hardly notice them in our feverish race to the sea. Friends become foes; neighbors become enemies as we rush to reach our salvation. The sea is our only hope. . . . We left with nothing except a few satchels of clothing and as many pieces of jewelry as we could hide on our bodies to trade for food or shelter, or our lives."[35]

For the escaping civilians, the nightmare of Hue, Danang, and Chu Lai was being reborn in Nha Trang. The LSM *Han Giang* (HQ-401), which was docked at the pier, was quickly swamped by hundreds of civilians as they jammed their way on board. As Canh writes, "From somewhere within the deep recesses of memory, inhuman instinct subjugated human conscience, and the law of survival propelled the masses. The weaker fell and were kicked aside by the stronger; the slower became prey to the swift. The screaming and shouting and crying blended together in a single guttural refrain of human desperation . . . [At the ship], the terrified crowd moved as one huge mass, pressing to the loading point with crushing force. Luggage and packages were tossed aside in the frantic rush to safety. . . . Those who did not assert themselves were felled and . . . were trampled to death by the stampede. People clambered aboard as ants over candy. Children were separated from their parents, and then crushed or propelled into the water to be forever lost from this life. On board, the dangers were no less terrifying. We were at the mercy of the masses surging onto the deck. Bodies were kicked about like discarded rag dolls after having been trampled. There was no mercy; no one else mattered to anyone."[36]

The ship filled so rapidly that it began to list, forcing the captain to back away from the pier. Seeing the masses of clamoring civilians, and mindful of the terrible tragedy at Danang, the local Navy commander refused to allow any more of his ships to dock at Nha Trang. Soon they weighed anchor and sailed to Cam Ranh.

Although Phu reached the Khanh Duong front, he was unable to contact either the Airborne or any other units defending Nha Trang. Running low on fuel, he headed for Phan Rang, where he then switched to his C-47. Before leaving, however, Phu spoke to Lieutenant General Khuyen at the JGS over the telephone. A screaming match ensued when Khuyen demanded to know why Phu was madly rushing around in the air instead of seeing to the defense of Nha Trang. Slamming the phone down on Khuyen, Phu again flew over the M'Drak Pass, where he managed to briefly contact the 3rd Airborne headquarters. He was informed that the Airborne's defensive lines had been shattered and it was retreating. The ground station then shut off. Phu's airplane flew aimlessly overhead for a few minutes and then returned to Phan Rang, where Phu boarded his helicopter and returned to the Nha Trang airbase.

Late in the day, an exhausted Phu entered Brigadier General Nguyen Van Luong's office at the Nha Trang airbase. Shortly thereafter, Luong and the Nha Trang base commander, Air Force Brigadier General Nguyen Van Oanh, went to Luong's office looking for Phu. They informed him that Lieutenant General Khuyen had placed them in charge of defending Nha Trang. Phu immediately called Khuyen, who once more chastised him for the rapidly collapsing situation. After a short shouting match, Phu again hung up on Khuyen. He walked out the door, telling "Oanh that he had full authority to take any necessary action in his capacity as battlefield commander."[37] Phu got into his helicopter and flew off to Phan Rang. It was his last act as II Corps commander.

Phu spent the night of 1 April "lying on an army cot without a mattress or a blanket, at the headquarters of a Ninh Thuan province RF battalion assigned to guard the Phan Rang Air Force base. The night was one of rioting, disorder, and looting in the cities of Phan Rang, Cam Ranh, and Nha Trang."[38]

Early in the morning of 2 April, Phu left for Phan Thiet to meet with the III Corps deputy commander, Major General Nguyen Van Hieu. Phu, mentally and physically exhausted, stood waiting for Hieu on a hilltop near the city. All that was left from his staff was Pham Huan, two aides, and Colonel Duc, the 23rd Division commander. When Hieu landed, he informed Phu that II Corps was dissolved, and that General Cao Van Vien had ordered Ninh Thuan and Binh Thuan provinces incorporated into III Corps. In addition, President Thieu had ordered that ARVN hold Phan Rang, the capital of Ninh Thuan. Phu was to depart at once for Saigon and report to General Vien.

For Major General Pham Van Phu, the calamitous events of March were over, and so was his command. In great despair, he flicked his cigarette to the ground and drew his pistol from its holster. Before Phu could commit suicide, Colonel Duc knocked the revolver from his hand. His aides then escorted him to his helicopter, and they flew to Saigon.[39] Most histories state that Phu panicked on 1 April and deserted his post, flying to Saigon to escape the Communist advance. He did not. In reality, Phu had tried desperately to organize a defense of the remaining coastal provinces, but failed because of the relentless PAVN attacks, the broken morale of the ARVN forces, and the inability to simultaneously command three fronts stretching for almost 180 miles.

General Van Tien Dung had made the correct analysis, and his final push had cleared the coast for other PAVN forces to easily advance on Saigon. If Dung had turned his forces around as the Politburo wished, he would have given Phu the breathing room to steady his troops and erect much tougher defenses. The PAVN columns would then have had to fight their way through, delaying the final assault on Saigon. Dung's choice to first clear away II Corps and then move toward Saigon was one of the most critical, though little-known, strategic decisions of the final offensive.

With the collapse of ARVN defenses, the coast stood wide open. The PAVN command learned from radio intercepts that ARVN forces were withdrawing from Cam Ranh and that on 1 April the II Corps headquarters had fled toward Phan Rang. Further, the "General Staff reported the enemy's situation to the [10th] Division and urged it to . . . develop its attack as rapidly as possible in the direction of Nha Trang and Cam Ranh. The message stated that if necessary it should send a small unit in advance to prevent the enemy from destroying technical bases and loading people abroad ships."[40] Spurred on by news of the retreating ARVN, on the morning of 2 April the 10th Division tanks surged down Route 21. Shrugging off air strikes, at noon the 10th Division marched into Ninh Hoa. Finding the city already in the hands of an alert Communist local-force unit, the 10th quickly pushed south on Route 1 to seize Nha Trang and Cam Ranh. Although the 10th had to fight its way through some rear-guard Ranger elements on Route 1, by 5:00 P.M. the division was advancing into Nha Trang. Another coastal city had fallen.

At Cam Ranh Bay on 1 April, the *Pioneer Commander* arrived from Danang. Cam Ranh was supposed to be the safe haven for the South Vietnamese troops and civilians being transported from I Corps by the American Military Sealift Command (MSC). Although the captain repeatedly radioed MSC headquarters about a band of thugs who were terrorizing the people on the ship, no one in Saigon alerted the South Vietnamese military at Cam Ranh. When the ship docked, the thugs disembarked and went on a rampage. They easily overwhelmed the guard force at the ARVN 5th Logistics Center, commandeered a number of vehicles, and shot and seriously wounded the Logistics Center commander, who tried to stop them from stealing his vehicles. The looters formed a column and headed south toward Phan Rang.

Only a few Americans still worked at the once-bustling port of Cam Ranh. They were ordered by the MSC to assist with the refugee evacuation. Given the thugs terrorizing the ships, the *Pioneer Commander* and the *Pioneer Contender* were told to drop off their loads of refugees from Danang and continue south. Another MSC ship, the *Sgt. Andrew Miller*, would pick up the refugees. The *Sgt. Andrew Miller* arrived the morning of 2 April and began loading from the dock. No panic was displayed, and the worn refugees glumly boarded. Late in the afternoon, the vessel backed away from the pier and moved out to sea. The lines of waiting evacuees, however, continued to lengthen.

Soon another MSC ship, the *Greenville Victory*, entered the harbor, but it did not pull up to the pier. It anchored in mid-harbor, under orders from

MSC headquarters to use a barge fastened to the tugboat *Chitose Maru* to ferry the refugees to it. However, the pier was ten feet higher than the barge, and when the brightly lit *Greenville Victory* did not tie up to the dock, the civilians began to panic. As the barge neared the pier, jostling refugees knocked the first row of people into the water, where the barge crushed them. As the barge made contact with the pier, rows of people—the old, the young, women and children—were jostled from the pier, smashing onto the deck of the barge. Screams from the injured and frightened drowned out the voices of the tugboat's crew as it tried to maintain order.

What had happened in Nha Trang was now repeated in Cam Ranh. Hundreds of people leapt onto the barge. Many were crushed under the weight of so many bodies. When the barge was full, the tugboat pulled away from the dock and headed to the *Greenville Victory*. There it confronted a new danger. Small vessels trying to reach the MSC ship cut in front of the tug. As the tug turned to place the barge against the ship, its powerful wake swamped some of the smaller boats. Cutting his engine, the captain of the *Chitose Maru* slowly pulled up to the much larger ship. Using cargo nets draped over the side of the *Greenville Victory*, people from the barge began climbing up the ropes. People from the sampans and other small vessels also tried climbing aboard. Many lost their grip and fell into the sea. Children and infants were thrown from the cargo nets up to the larger ship, but if no one on deck was able to catch them, they fell into the water. Many children and adults were smashed between the two hulls.

The scene was repeated all night. As one American present later wrote: "When the last refugee had left the barge [on the first trip], only the debris-littered deck remained as evidence of the human tragedy the evacuation had become. We agonized over the injury and loss of so many people, and we struggled with the fact that we had no control over the terrible fear that drove the refugees. . . . Returning to the pier, we could only watch again as waves of panic-driven Vietnamese [were] falling, scrambling, shoving, and fighting their way onto the barge. The terrible cacophony of the tug's engine and horn blaring, people's screams and cries . . . filled my ears until they hurt. The appalling scenes were nightmarish and our only relief came when the barge was full again."[41] By mid-evening, the *Greenville Victory* was filled with nine thousand people, and it sailed off. A new ship moved in, the S.S. *American Challenger*. It continued loading until dawn, when it was replaced by another vessel.

On the morning of 3 April, a 10th Division assault force advanced south on Route 1 to capture Cam Ranh. Despite the VNN's withdrawal, the South Vietnamese still fought back. As the 10th Division history put it, "Enemy aircraft savagely bombed and strafed our forces in an effort to stop our advance. Pockets of resistance along the sides of the road continuously opened fire on our advancing forces."[42] It was for naught. At 2:00 P.M. on 3 April the huge military port at Cam Ranh was captured. Nothing but a mob of retreating soldiers stood between the 10th Division and the next major town heading south, the port city of Phan Rang. But instead of sending the 10th south on Route 1 to assault the city, Giap ordered it to halt and prepare to move toward Saigon. It would prove a costly mistake.

14

"LIGHTNING SPEED, DARING, SURPRISE, CERTAIN VICTORY"

PAVN SURROUNDS SAIGON

A s PAVN forces stood poised to sweep into Qui Nhon, Tuy Hoa, and Nha Trang, the Politburo assembled for a fateful meeting. For the hardened revolutionaries who made up the North Vietnamese political and military leadership, the battlefield reports pouring in over the past two weeks were stunning; their forces were seizing territory and population at a dizzying pace. After decades of "struggle," a term embodying Ho Chi Minh's vision of an unrelenting effort to unify the country under the Communist banner, they now stood on the brink of victory. The "struggle" philosophy had been cobbled together from militant Marxist/Leninist ideology and fervent Vietnamese nationalism. It had provided the theoretical framework that enabled the Communists to persevere through the long, difficult war years. Now, as events in South Vietnam unfolded with a rapidity that made previous timetables and plans irrelevant, the Politburo gathered to discuss the next moves toward achieving their long-sought dream.

The Politburo meeting of 31 March was to discuss the third strategic blow in the campaign, the final attack on Saigon. As the men took their seats, Le Duan opened the meeting. After laying out the basic issues, he asked Giap to report on the battlefield situation. Giap's views were clear. In a fiery call to arms, he urged his Politburo colleagues to strike now: "Our army is in a position to launch an all-out attack to exploit our victory. We are fully capable of massing the maximum number of forces from throughout our nation to confront the enemy with overwhelming force on the primary battlefield, Saigon. *We now have a great opportunity.* It is certain that we can achieve complete victory in this final, decisive strategic battle. I recommend that we quickly develop a battle plan, strategically surround Saigon/Gia Dinh from the east and the west, and use a powerful mainforce 'fist' to make a surprise deep strike aimed at destroying the enemy. One attack will bring us victory. The formula for this strategy is *'lightning speed, daring, surprise, certain victory.'*"[1] (Emphasis in the original.)

After Giap finished, other Politburo members, including the old ideologue Truong Chinh, also spoke in favor of throwing the full weight of the People's Army against the remaining ARVN forces. Chinh's speech swept aside any remaining doubts. If the former guerrilla-warfare advocate was suddenly a main-force supporter, surely a large-scale conventional attack was the proper course. In this heady atmosphere, a vote was taken. The decision was unanimous: South Vietnam was collapsing, and it was time for decisive action.

In perhaps the most momentous message sent during that fateful year of 1975, on 1 April, Le Duan sent new instructions to Pham Hung, Le Duc Tho, and Van Tien Dung, instructions that sealed the fate of the Republic of Vietnam. Summarizing Giap's briefing, he told them: "We have wiped out and disbanded 35% of the enemy effectives, killed or put out of action two enemy army corps . . . and destroyed more than 40% of their material and logistical bases, liberated 12 provinces and increased the population of the liberated zones to nearly 8 million." Furthermore, "our armed forces have matured immeasurably, there have been few military casualties . . . [and] there has been inconsiderable loss of weapons and ammunition on our part. . . . In this context, the Politburo has arrived at this conclusion: strategically, militarily and politically we have an overwhelmingly superior force, the enemy is facing the danger of collapse. . . . The Americans have proved completely powerless, and no reinforcements from the U.S. can salvage the situation. . . . From this moment the last strategic decisive battle of our army and people has started. . . . Therefore the Politburo has decided [to] successfully end the war of liberation in the shortest time. The best way is to start and end it in April of this year, without any delay." To his southern commanders, he then outlined what the next steps would be: "Immediately—at a higher speed than planned—we have to send more reinforcements to the west of Saigon as a matter of great urgency . . . In order to carry out [this] strategic orientation . . . the Central Military [Affairs] Committee has decided to swiftly move 3rd Corps . . . [to Saigon] . . . and has decided to bring in the Army reserve corps."[2]

This historic Politburo meeting approved three significant items: send the 1st and 3rd Corps to help conquer the South Vietnamese capital; use the B-2 Front forces to attack ARVN units in III Corps to see if they would immediately collapse; conquer Saigon by the end of April. In his memoirs, Giap sketched the basic North Vietnamese battle plan: "With regards to our strategic disposition of forces, the Politburo decided to quickly strengthen our forces on the western approaches to Saigon, strategically encircle and isolate the city from the southwest, and completely cut Route 4 to isolate Saigon from the Mekong Delta. Our forces east of Saigon would attack and capture important targets and encircle and isolate Saigon from Ba Ria and Vung Tau. Our main-force punch would be truly powerful, including the use of [tanks, artillery, and anti-aircraft], and would be prepared to strike directly into the most critical enemy targets in the center of Saigon when the opportunity presented itself."[3]

After the 31 March meeting, Giap's staff now focused on three mission-critical tasks: First, monitor the battlefield situation. Second, supervise the deployment of forces to the Saigon battlefield. Third, study and recommend strategic and campaign fighting methods for the coming attack on the capital. That night, the General Staff shifted half of the 1st Corps—the last remaining strategic-reserve unit, which until now had been held in North Vietnam—toward the DMZ. The 1st Corps history states that a "corps advance element . . . moved to the assembly position. Eight military trains . . . transported corps forces southward. . . . More than 1,000 vehicles left the assembly position and, throwing up an enormous cloud of dust, began rolling south down Route 1. At Vinh City [north of the DMZ] the corps advance element divided into two sections. The 66th Mechanized Infantry Battalion and 2nd Artillery Battalion moved down to Vinh harbor and were transported by sea on Navy ships down to Quang Tri. The rest of the advance element, consisting primarily of 320B Division and 367th Air Defense Division . . . continued a motorized movement down the highway."[4]

The next day Giap visited the 1st Corps headquarters to personally issue the order for the corps to move into South Vietnam. Only the 308th Infantry Division, long considered PAVN's most elite division, would remain behind to defend the North. The 1st Corps's ultimate destination was an assembly area at Dong Xoai in Phuoc Long province, fifty-six miles northeast of Saigon. It was to arrive by 15 April. With no time for elaborate preparations, Giap made it clear that the men of the 1st Corps would have to follow the time-honored PAVN slogan of self-reliance (*tu tuc*) and overcome most obstacles on their own—finding fuel and food, making repairs, fixing roads and bridges. For Giap, in another oft-repeated slogan, "Time is now strength," and with ARVN seemingly on the verge of collapse, he had no time to waste.

Implementing the Politburo's ambitious war plans, however, would not be easy. Shifting an entire corps 1,050 miles over dirt roads and high mountain passes, across numerous streams and deep valleys, was an enormous logistics challenge. The Rear Services Department and unit staffs had to quickly determine how to ship south all these troops and supplies. Next, they needed to develop a workable road-march timetable that would not generate huge traffic snarls or make tempting targets for South Vietnamese or American bombers. The staffs would then need to organize, move, feed, and support a massive number of troops from the 1st and 3rd Corps—and soon the 2nd Corps—in an incredibly short time. Yet they were totally inexperienced in an effort of this scale. Moreover, the roads in the western part of South Vietnam were rough and choked with dust—it was the end of the dry season—and the Communists' trucks and armor were generally worn older models. Although the Rear Services Department sent a large number of mechanics south to help with repairs, it was unclear how much of the 1st Corps's aged Soviet Bloc gear would survive such a long and fast-paced journey. While the North Vietnamese had captured and pressed into service enormous quantities of ARVN war booty, the leadership was taking a huge gamble that the entire road and logistics system could handle such a substantial influx of men and equipment without completely breaking down.

Fortunately for the North Vietnamese, PAVN had been preparing for this since before the signing of the Paris Accords. In October 1972 the Rear Services Department had begun replenishing PAVN's stockpiles of food and ammunition in the South. Once the process of rebuilding the supplies in the South was nearly complete, PAVN instituted a wide array of logistics programs. As the *History of the People's Army* notes, "during the two years 1973–74 all units throughout the armed forces carried out a general inventory of their property and finances and organized the retrieval, collection, and repair of their equipment, thereby resolving at least a portion of our difficulties in providing supply and technical support. Units operating on the battlefields were ordered to economize on their usage of ammunition, and especially of large-caliber ammunition. Units were also ordered to improve and repair weapons and equipment captured from the enemy so that we could . . . use these weapons and equipment to fight."[5]

The various military branches also worked diligently to repair their own vehicles and equipment: "The Artillery Branch established a number of collection teams to retrieve damaged artillery pieces located on the various battlefields and bring them back to North Vietnam for repair. . . . The Armored Branch . . . [raised] the Branch's combat availability from 60% in 1973 to 98% at the end of 1974. The Signal Branch put into service more than 1,000 radios captured from the enemy and repaired 2,300 inoperable radios, 3,000 telephones, and 1,000 generators. The 2nd Corps alone repaired more than 1,000 vehicles and almost 10,000 weapons and other pieces of equipment. . . . The number of technical personnel and mechanics sent to the battlefields during the two years 1973–74 reached 15,000 men."[6]

The PAVN history goes on to state that the most important aspect of this considerable logistics effort was the expansion of the fuel network to support the tremendous increase in the number of vehicles: "Paralleling the strategic transportation and troop movement corridor was a petroleum pipeline network 1,050 miles long with 101 pumping stations, of which 814 miles was newly constructed during the two years 1973–74. Overcoming many technical, terrain, and weather difficulties, our POL [petroleum, oil, lubricants] troops brought the gasoline pipeline over mountain peaks [more than] 1,000 meters high and across rugged terrain, building flat places for the placement of pumps along steep mountain slopes, etc. On 15 January 1975, for the first time the flow of gasoline through the pipeline reached [Quang Duc]."[7]

New buildings were constructed to store the vast amounts of material shipped south: "The various warehouse units along Group 559's [the element commanding the Ho Chi Minh Trail] strategic corridor reorganized their forces and . . . a large number of warehouses with storage capacity in excess of 10,000 tons were built. . . . This network of warehouses [was] directly linked with the great rear area in North Vietnam and with the rear-services bases and networks of the battlefields . . . via the strategic and campaign road networks including both land routes and sea routes through the ports of Cua Viet and Dong Ha. This created a continuous, solid rear-services network with a large supply storage capacity, a relatively complete force of support personnel, and a powerful motorized transport force."[8]

On the basis of these improvements, the Rear Services Department rightfully boasts that "The success of the army's rear services task during the . . . [1975] offensive was the result of preparations made during the previous years, especially 1973 and 1974. . . . By the time of the general offensive we had a whole integrated road network extending from the rear area south to the most distant battlefields. . . . In addition to the road network there was a whole network of POL pipelines. . . . [This enabled] the extensive use of mechanized transportation forces, especially trucks, to transport troops and equipment to the front. This truly became the principal formula for success. [During the offensive] nearly all transportation of material and equipment to the fronts . . . was done by means of mechanized equipment."[9]

In order to build this massive road complex, the PAVN Engineer Branch greatly expanded the size and upgraded the equipment of the engineer forces assigned to Group 559 and to the various military commands.[10] In 1973, the "engineers of the military regions were reorganized into regiments, were reinforced with mechanized river-crossing components, [and were given] the mission of making strategic preparations and of preparing a network of campaign roads . . . The military engineers of . . . such combat arms as armor, artillery, missiles—forces which accompanied the units— were strengthened with regard to organization and equipment in order to increase their capability to meet their own mobile requirements."[11]

This strengthening of engineer forces would eventually pay another huge dividend for the North Vietnamese. As the PAVN tanks and trucks advanced forward, the South Vietnamese continually tried to slow them down by destroying bridges and culverts. Yet the engineers, well practiced in the art of hasty repairs, rapidly fixed the damage. This enabled PAVN to hotly pursue the retreating South Vietnamese, denying them the time to regroup their forces. Besides the other logistics factors, this expanded engineer force is another critical element in the military success of the 1975 offensive.

While the peasant soldiers of North Vietnam no longer had to walk down the Ho Chi Minh Trail, their commanders now faced a new problem: efficiently commanding the larger combat units they had formed. Recognizing this predicament, the Signal Branch expended tremendous energy improving PAVN's radio, telephone, and military postal networks. Multiple communications networks were installed to assist the command echelons. Of special importance was the completion of a system of telephone cables, called "Unification," which ran from Hanoi all the way down to the B-2 Front. The senior PAVN signal officer describes the result: "The armed forces concentrated . . . on installing cables along with multi-circuited high-frequency telephone equipment . . . to link it with [the various fronts] and to combine them with the radio relay axis going parallel with them so as to support one another. This was a very great effort on the part of our signal troops, who overcame . . . complicated terrain, high mountains, deep streams and inclement weather in order to install hundreds of miles of cables and tens of switchboard stations . . . the units also installed tens of radio relay stations at altitudes ranging from 1,500 to 2,000 meters. . . . At the same time, we also designed and steadily developed the short-wave radio network and installed receiving and transmitting stations . . . of great power. As a result, the [signal forces] were able to maintain uninterrupted communications . . . [for] the leadership and command of various strategic and combat echelons during the general offensive. . . . After our victory in Ban Me Thuot . . . the short-wave radio network was extended to the units taking part in the campaign . . . to reach division and provincial military commands."[12]

Moving virtually the entire North Vietnamese army south to attack Saigon required senior leadership able to act on Politburo decisions. While the Politburo was meeting, Van Tien Dung was waiting for other high-ranking leaders in the South to join him for the scheduled meeting with Le Duc Tho at Dung's headquarters on Route 14 near Ban Me Thuot. But after the Politburo had made the decision to mass the People's Army to attack Saigon, Le Duan sent a flash telegram canceling the meeting. He had decided instead to send both Dung and Tho to the B-2 Front to form a new campaign headquarters for the coming battle. As long as the Americans had been involved in the war, sending senior officials like Dung and Tho that far south was fraught with danger. Since that menace no longer existed, the Politburo had decided to provide direct high-level supervision to ensure victory.

On 2 April, Dung and his forward command, code-named Group A-75, left for COSVN headquarters in Cambodia, just across the border from Tay Ninh. They arrived on the night of 3 April. Tho would meet Dung at COSVN. As the North Vietnamese struggled to synchronize their different battlefields, the greatly improved command-and-control structure was another critical factor in their success.

While half of the 1st Corps—the 320B Infantry and 367th Air Defense Divisions, plus artillery, tank, and engineer brigades—was moving toward Quang Tri, the other half—the 312th Division, 202nd Armor Brigade, and assorted rear-service units—was preparing to deploy. But despite Hanoi's constant urging of speed, PAVN had only enough trucks to move one division at a time. Consequently, it had to implement truck shuttles, with the 320B Division moving first. For instance, when the 320B reached Dong Ha (a small river port inland from the coast just north of Quang Tri City) on 2 April, it switched to trucks belonging to Group 559, while the trucks it had been riding in returned north.

On 5 April, as the 320B Division sped through southern Laos, behind it the 312th Division reached Dong Ha after a long trip on the same trucks that had ferried the 320B to the town. The corps headquarters then contacted Group 559 to switch vehicles again, and the trucks that had brought the 312th south returned to North Vietnam to pick up more troops. The 312th Division would continue south along the same route and on the same trucks used by the 320B. Despite the stretches of bad road and heavy traffic, by ferrying in this manner, the 1st Corps elements were able to move south fairly rapidly.

March orders from the 1st Corps to its units were straightforward. The convoys would travel between eighteen and twenty hours per day. Each vehicle would have two drivers. Troops would sleep in the vehicles. Drivers would be given priority for rations and sleep. The average speed would be nineteen miles per hour, but trucks that could move faster were allowed to pass those that could not. If a truck broke down, the men riding in it were responsible for fixing it.

While the infantry, air-defense, and engineer troops of the 1st Corps were rolling forward in rickety trucks through a huge cloud of dust, the General Staff was paying particularly close attention to one unit, the 202nd Armor Brigade, which was the most powerful 1st Corps combat element. PAVN had invested an enormous amount of effort in creating the 202nd. It was formed in North Vietnam during late 1973 by combining a mechanized infantry regiment with tanks from another armored battalion and the tanks assigned to the Armor School. The brigade comprised the 3rd and 198th Tank Battalions, the 66th and 244th Mechanized Infantry Battalions, one engineer battalion, six support companies, and the brigade headquarters. On 27 December 1973, the brigade's organization was completed, and it was assigned to the 1st Corps.

Given the difficulties in moving tracked vehicles these great distances, the General Staff copied the American method: It moved the vehicles and their personnel by ship. The Navy had also spent the last two years preparing for this day. The Navy's history notes: "we built the [Cua Viet] base and the Dong Ha Harbor into an important maritime communications and supply line linking into our supply artery leading from our great rear area in North Vietnam into South Vietnam."[13]

The 66th Mechanized Infantry Battalion, 202nd Armor Brigade, was the first corps element sent south. After the battalion had moved by train to the Vinh City rail station, "Navy vessels then transported the battalion, together with elements of corps artillery, to the Cua Viet harbor."[14] For the first time in the war, North Vietnamese Navy ships carried a complete armored unit to the South. The Navy would eventually transport "17,343 cadres and enlisted men, 40 tanks, and 7,786 tons of weapons and fuel forward to fight in the Spring 1975 Campaign to liberate South Vietnam."[15]

Aircraft also carried men and equipment south. According to the Air Force history, "On 5 April 1975 the first transport aircraft flight landed at the Phu Bai airfield [outside Hue]. Two days later the first transport flight landed at Danang. During succeeding days we began sending flights from Danang to the newly liberated airfields in the Central Highlands. . . . By the end of April, our aircraft had conducted a total 163 flights south, transporting 4,250 officers and enlisted men and 120.7 tons of weapons and technical equipment, including 48 tons of main gun ammunition for tanks, Saigon city maps, and large quantities of flags and leaflets to meet the urgent requirements of the campaign."[16]

On 26 March the 202nd Armor Brigade received orders to send its remaining units forward to the front. On 4 April the 66th Battalion was ordered to take Route 14 straight down to Dong Xoai in Phuoc Long province. Despite the importance of the tanks to the coming attack, like all other units, "the battalion had to send reconnaissance teams to check on and repair the road even while it moved forward, repairing its own vehicles and weapons when they broke down, locating sources of fuel on its own, and finding its own fords and river crossing points. The battalion crossed six rivers and drove over hundreds of steep passes to reach its designated assembly point. On 9 April the [202nd] brigade headquarters, 244th Battalion, and 10th [Reconnaissance] Company set out, continuing its journey along Routes 9, 22, and 14 through the Central Highlands and then down [to the B-2 Front area]. Long columns of dusty tanks and armored vehicles drove day and night through newly liberated areas."[17]

Traveling in shifts, the advance corps elements, mainly from the 320B Division, arrived in Dong Xoai on 11 April. By 14 April, all remaining corps units except the 202nd Brigade had also arrived, one day earlier than the General Staff's plan. Although other units continued to straggle in, the 1st Corps had accomplished an amazing feat, rapidly traveling over a thousand miles while not leaving a trail of broken-down vehicles along the road. In two short weeks, the most powerful combat unit the North Vietnamese had ever assembled had driven unopposed from North Vietnam down the long Ho Chi Minh Trail and through South Vietnam itself to the very gates of Saigon.

While the 1st Corps was rolling south, on 1 April Giap recalled Deputy Chief of Staff Le Trong Tan from Danang back to Hanoi to receive a new assignment. Simultaneously, the General Staff ordered the 2nd Corps to detach the 325th Division, the 203rd Tank Brigade, and one anti-aircraft regiment to reinforce the 1st Corps, now arriving at Dong Ha. Major General Nguyen Huu An and the other senior 2nd Corps officers were deeply upset by this order, and they went to see Tan before he left for Hanoi, to try to get him to reverse this decision.

For An, the movement south and the attack on Saigon were precisely what the Soviets had trained him for, and he was determined not to miss this opportunity. Trapped by PAVN's tradition of obedience to General Staff mandates, he could not directly protest the orders. Nonetheless, he had vast experience in PAVN command circles as well as in battle, and he knew how to manipulate the system while still appearing obedient. He cleverly side-stepped military etiquette by telling General Tan that he and his fellow officers were "concerned about the order for 2nd Corps to send 325th Division, 203rd Tank Brigade, and an anti-aircraft regiment to reinforce 1st Corps. However, if we suggest an alternative plan I am afraid it might upset the plans of our superiors."[18] He then requested permission to present another option. Tan agreed. Seizing his chance, An asked that the entire 2nd Corps remain together and be sent south, emphasizing "the mobile capabilities of the corps, the fact that we have trucks, vehicles, ships, and good roads, and that we are capable of fighting during the advance and attacking from the march." Convinced by An's passion, Tan promised to present his proposition to Giap.

As Le Trong Tan flew back to Hanoi, another Politburo member also had strong feelings about the proper disposition of the North Vietnamese forces. Right after Giap and Le Duan accepted Van Tien Dung's argument regarding the use of the 10th Division, Giap sent a conciliatory message to Le Duc Tho advising him that "according to Dung, it will require no more time than turning around and taking the old route. We feel that it is advantageous and [Le Duan] agrees."[19] While Le Duc Tho had supported Tra's request to send additional divisions to the B-2 Front, when he learned that Le Duan had approved Dung's recommendation concerning the 10th, he dropped his objections. But then he recommended a new course of action.

On 3 April, he sent a message back to Hanoi, outlining another strategy. "If the 10th Division has advanced that far south, we should consider having it and another division from [B-1 Front] liberate Phan Rang and Phan Thiet and advance south to liberate [Vung Tau]. . . . That would be very unexpected, and we could quickly approach Saigon from the east. Although the supply line might be stretched out, we can take advantage of Route 1 . . . to move cargo more rapidly and conveniently than advancing from [the west]."[20]

The General Staff now faced a dilemma. Should it reinforce the 10th Division with the 3rd Division, send them to attack the coastal cities of Phan Rang, Phan Thiet, and Ham Tan, and then use this force, along with the B-2 Front's 4th Corps, to attack Saigon from the east? Or should it send the 10th back to the west to link up with the rest of the 3rd Corps? Moreover, what was the best way to use the 2nd Corps? Should part of it strengthen the 1st Corps, or should the General Staff keep it intact and send it to help complete the conquest of the coast—which would mean a long drive down Route 1—and join the attack against Saigon from the east?

These questions and more faced the senior leadership at the General Staff meeting on 4 April. As the options were discussed, Tan kept his promise to Nguyen Huu An. According to Giap, Tan "suggested that we should form a coastal column made up of the forces that had just liberated Danang to quickly move down the coast, attacking the enemy from the march, to destroy enemy forces and gain control of the strategic positions from Nha Trang south in order to prevent enemy forces from pulling back and regrouping to defend Saigon."[21] The General Staff pondered both Le Duc Tho's and Tan's recommendations, but they soon realized that even with the addition of the 3rd and 10th Divisions to the 4th Corps on the eastern approach, that side would be much weaker than the columns from the north and west of Saigon. In addition, the eastern force would have to deal with ARVN forces on two flanks: in the Bien Hoa/Long Thanh areas, and in its rear at Vung Tau. After considering all the options, and after a flurry of messages between Hanoi, the various southern commands, and Le Duc Tho, both Giap and Le Duan approved Tan's suggestion. In one of the key strategic decisions of the "Great Spring Offensive," they formed a "Coastal Column" comprising the 2nd Corps, several units from North Vietnam, and the 3rd Division. Le Duan quickly issued orders naming Le Trong Tan as commander of the newly organized Coastal Column and Major General Le Quang Hoa as political commissar. Both were told to report immediately back to Danang.

It was a logical decision for a number of reasons. Given the crush of trucks and PAVN elements moving down Route 14 toward the western side of Saigon, trying to push parts of the 2nd Corps down that same road would have resulted in a major traffic jam. It would also have resulted in an imbalance of forces between the western and eastern approaches to Saigon. Moving the units down Route 1, while a longer journey and subject to air strikes, naval gunfire, and blown-up bridges, provided them an excellent road unrestricted by the movement of other units. It also put another full corps on the eastern side of Saigon, thus balancing PAVN forces for the assault.

These new decisions necessitated other changes as well. When the 320th and 10th Divisions departed for assembly areas north of Saigon, a vacuum would be created along the coast. The PAVN commanders could not leave the independent 25th Regiment and local forces all alone to garrison that area, while simultaneously manning the front line at Phan Rang. Realizing their vulnerability, on 2 April the General Staff ordered the 968th Division, then still in Binh Dinh, to immediately move south to take over the coastal defense. The division reached Nha Trang on 6 April and replaced the 10th Division. The 968th would remain in this area until the end of the war. In addition, the General Staff ordered Ninh Thuan province local forces to clear away remaining South Vietnamese positions near Phan Rang and along Route 11, the road from Phan Rang to Dalat. At the same time, the 812th Regiment received orders to advance on Phan Thiet and pin down ARVN in that city.

On 5 April, Le Trong Tan returned to Danang, where he held a meeting with Nguyen Huu An in the former headquarters of the ARVN 3rd Division. Earlier, Tan had sent Major General An a cable telling him the Central Military Affairs Committee had agreed with his recommendation. At the meeting, the decision was made to leave behind the 324th Division to guard the Danang area and the 2nd Division to guard the Quang Nam/Quang Tin area, while the 3rd Division and the 5th Armored Battalion would join the 2nd Corps. The 46th Infantry Regiment was attached to the 325th Division to replace its 95B Regiment, which was still in the Central Highlands. Tan informed the 2nd Corps staff that the lead element must depart by 7 April and be in an assembly area northwest of Xuan Loc by 25 April. To prepare for this long journey, Giap "decided to reinforce the Corps with additional transportation resources. The 571st Truck Division [from Group 559] and the 83rd River Crossing Engineer Regiment were attached to the Corps . . . and Navy transport vessels were provided to transport 9th Regiment, 304th Division, from Danang to Qui Nhon."[22]

Giap immediately pressed the commander of Group 559 to help the 2nd Corps. In a cable he outlined his orders: "The requirements of the front are extremely urgent, and must be figured in days and hours. At this moment, *Time is force; time is power.* You must use every possible means to ensure that the units marching to the front move extremely quickly, that supplies move with great urgency, and that you properly complete this urgent supply campaign."[23] In response, Group 559 established a headquarters in Qui Nhon. Giap also sent Hoang Minh Thao from the Central Highlands campaign to establish a headquarters in Nha Trang to organize and direct the movement of units down Route 1.

But it was not enough. Group 559 was running out of trucks. The Rear Services troops were still also transporting the 1st and 3rd Corps, and ensuring that all necessary supplies and transportation would be available for them. Now they had to help Tan's forces cover more than four hundred miles along Route 1 to reach Phan Rang, and they needed to do it quickly, before ARVN could recover and prepare defenses to block their advance. As one senior officer recalls, "The 571st Division was given the continuing responsibility for helping to transport 2nd Corps forward. At this time, while the main portion of 571st Division was helping to move 1st Corps and 3rd Corps south, the rest of the division's trucks were working to transport rice and ammunition from Dong Ha to Danang to support 2nd Corps."[24] Under Giap's prodding, the 571st Truck Division headquarters radioed all units to concentrate everything they had to carry out this new mission. They managed to round up almost seven hundred trucks from Danang to assist the 2nd Corps's rapid advance.

After his meeting with Tan, a jubilant 2nd Corps commander now discovered that his earlier analysis of his corps's mobility had been overly optimistic. Danang is four hundred miles from Cam Ranh. Writing in his memoirs, Nguyen Huu An admitted that "Although we understood that we would run into many problems when conducting such a long march, we had not fully anticipated how great these problems would be. When we officially began our preparations for the journey, almost half of the vehicles and weapons of our 673rd Air Defense Division and of the . . . 203rd Tank Brigade were still stuck [in the hills]. . . . When we assembled all our transportation resources, including a number of trucks from the 571st Division that had just arrived to reinforce us, we had only enough to transport a bit over two-thirds of our forces. Along the road our corps would have to cross 569 bridges, of which 14 spanned large rivers. We had just learned that the enemy had destroyed [numerous bridges], but the corps river-crossing engineer element was tiny and only able to assembly four fifty-ton ferries."[25]

While the 2nd Corps was trying to figure out how to haul itself south, the 3rd Corps units were also receiving movement instructions. The 320th Division would depart from Tuy Hoa, the 10th from Cam Ranh, and the 316th from Ban Me Thuot. The 316th was told to move first and arrive in Tay Ninh province on 3 April. Soon afterward, the 320th was ordered to depart from Tuy Hoa on 10 April. Following Route 7B to Route 14, the 320th ran into its "twin," the 1st Corps's 320B Division, which had been cloned from the original 320th back in 1965. Together, the lead elements of the division arrived in Tay Ninh on 15 April.

The 10th Division, meanwhile, had a much tougher time than the other units. Its history notes: "The greatest problem confronting the division at this time was transportation. Even though 3rd Corps Headquarters gave the division top priority for the use of trucks, the division was still sixty trucks short of its transportation requirements. To resolve this problem the division headquarters sent . . . the Division Chief of Political Affairs back to personally work with the Nha Trang and Cam Ranh Military Management Committees to persuade the local citizens to provide vehicles to help our troops. At the same time the maximum use was made of captured enemy vehicles for transporting our forces into battle."[26]

When the 10th Division finally departed on 9 April, the North Vietnamese forces' road march turned deadly for the first time. The 10th's delay had allowed the South Vietnamese the breathing room they needed. The division's route was uncomfortably close to ARVN positions; at one point it was only twelve miles from the South Vietnamese Air Force base at Phan Rang. When spotter aircraft detected the division's movement, Colonel Le Van Thao's A-37s pummeled the moving convoy. The 10th Division history details the deadly effects. "After 72 hours of preparations at Cam Ranh, the entire division moved out down Route 450 [a small road leading from Cam Ranh across the mountains to Route 11] . . . the division advanced through a ferocious storm of enemy bombs and shells. On 10 April the 7th Engineer Regiment's river-crossing battalion lost six vehicles transporting vehicle ferries. On 11 April the enemy destroyed five of 28th Regiment's trucks. On 12 April the division headquarters and 4th Regiment lost seven trucks. On 13 April the 24th Regiment had nine trucks destroyed. Route 450 turned into a flaming hell. However, the entire convoy, numbering hundreds of vehicles filled with troops, guns, ammunition, and food, kept moving forward. . . . On the afternoon of 13 April [most of the division], having survived the enemy bombing attacks, reached . . . Dalat."[27]

The 3rd Corps urged the division to hurry, but it faced logistical conditions every bit as difficult as the other PAVN elements had faced. The division history states: "our vehicles drove constantly, night and day. The soldiers were allowed only short stops to cook rice and boil drinking water before continuing . . . Riding on uncovered vehicles, the sun and the dust blackened the faces of our troops."[28] Despite these hardships, the division arrived at the campaign assembly area in a rubber plantation in Tay Ninh on the night of 22–23 April. The 3rd Corps, the fourth main-force "fist" of Dung's powerful army, had gathered outside of Saigon.

Meanwhile, the 2nd Corps, after a rapid inspection of captured equipment, determined that it could use a significant number of American weapons and vehicles to alleviate shortages. As Nguyen Huu An noted: "In the space of only a few days the 203rd Tank Brigade confiscated and incorporated into its ranks dozens of enemy M-113s and M-48 tanks. Our artillery took large numbers of enemy trucks, artillery pieces, and ammunition to replace their old equipment. More than one-third of the guns in our artillery units were now captured weapons. . . . The units also put into use the communications equipment mounted on the enemy vehicles, high-powered radios that were excellent for command and control. Infantry units also switched to the use of many types of enemy weapons and technical devices. Almost every company and battalion was now equipped with U.S.-made PRC-25 radios."[29]

Given Tan's order to depart on 7 April, the 2nd Corps headquarters convened a meeting of all subordinate elements to issue mission orders and march plans. The reconfigured 2nd Corps now comprised the 3rd, 304th, and 325th Infantry Divisions, plus the 673rd Anti-Aircraft Division. Separate artillery, engineer, and signal brigades augmented the infantry, along with the powerful 203rd Tank Brigade.

The corps organized itself into five separate march elements. In the First Element was a regiment from the 325th Division, an armored battalion from the 203rd Tank Brigade, an anti-aircraft regiment, and two engineer battalions. Follow-on elements would be equally balanced, meaning that the entire corps was organized into five separate combined-arms attack formations. Each element had a combat organization powerful enough to protect itself from small-scale attacks during the advance, yet it also had the capability, through the engineer brigades, to resolve any problems along the road.

As the 2nd Corps prepared to depart on the morning of 7 April, Giap sent a handwritten cable to the front, exhorting his forces racing toward Saigon to move as fast as possible: "Speed, ever greater speed. Daring, ever greater daring. Exploit every hour, every minute. Rush to the battlefield to liberate the South. Resolve to fight to secure total victory. Immediately disseminate this message to every cadre and every soldier."[30] Unit political officers immediately turned this cable into a psychological weapon. They ordered the soldiers to inscribe the slogan "Speed" onto rifle butts, tank barrels, and truck bumpers. It was an effective motto; it provided a clear-cut sense of mission to the young troops by emphasizing that the final battle to end this long and costly war was about to commence.

Despite the tremendous organizational improvisation, the shortage of trucks continued to plague the 2nd Corps. The First Element was split into two groups and shuttled south in a manner similar to the 1st Corps. Notwithstanding the scarcity of trucks, the Coastal Column was the largest North Vietnamese force ever massed during the war. It consisted of a total of "2,276 vehicles to transport supplies and personnel . . . 223 towed artillery pieces . . . 89 armored vehicles, of which 54 were tanks. A total of 32,418 personnel took part in this road march."[31] The Column was a steamroller headed straight for Phan Rang.

The first section of the First Element, consisting of the 325th Division's headquarters, its 101st Regiment, artillery and anti-aircraft elements, and the advance guard, set forth at 9:00 A.M. on 7 April. Barreling down the road, its men quickly repaired eight major bridges and dozens of smaller ones destroyed by ARVN units, and built detours around several more they could not fix. Their reward for rapidly reaching Khanh Hoa province was air strikes from Colonel Thao's A-37 wing. The blown-up bridges and the air strikes, however, did not appreciably slow the 2nd Corps's movement. At one point, one section traveled an incredible 115 miles in one day.

In Binh Dinh, the 3rd Division was also preparing to move. While the troops rested and conducted training for urban combat, the division's Rear Services personnel scrounged every available vehicle that could carry men and supplies. Over one thousand new replacement soldiers from North Vietnam arrived to make up the division's heavy losses. After securing a total of 924 vehicles ranging from civilian buses and cars to captured ARVN trucks driven by press-ganged South Vietnamese soldiers, on 8 April the division began its road march south.

The timing of the various movements was near perfect. As the 968th Division arrived to assume the defense of Cam Ranh Bay, the 10th Division moved out. On 10 April, just after the 10th's units departed, the lead section of First Element and some 3rd Division support units flowed down the road and bivouacked near Cam Ranh. Integrating itself into the second section of First Element as it passed through Binh Dinh, the 3rd Division arrived at the assembly area twenty-five miles northeast of Phan Rang on 11 April. The Coastal Column's movement of more than 2,200 vehicles and thousands of soldiers over four hundred miles, repairing blown-up bridges and fighting off air strikes and naval gunfire along the way, was a magnificent achievement, accomplished through the combined effort of soldiers and officers alike.

The Communists' success in moving three entire corps that far and that fast was for them a logistics feat unparalleled in the war, surpassed only by the building of the Ho Chi Minh Trail. It was a wildly improvised orchestration of men and machines down hundreds of miles of dusty, rutted, sometimes mud-clogged roads, and over dozens of bombed-out bridges and steep mountains. Surely it is one of the most unheralded military movements in history. That the PAVN technical staff somehow managed to hold all of those old trucks, T-54s, and Chinese APCs together on that long journey south is by itself a remarkable triumph.

If improved armor tactics, skillful engineering, and increased command and control were now decisive on the battlefield, this success was made possible only by the earlier efforts of the PAVN Rear Services troops. In the two years since the Paris Accords, they had labored long and hard—and in gross violation of the peace agreement—to develop this critical logistics network. Most important of all was the fuel line running all the way to Loc Ninh, for without gas and oil, the trucks and tanks would have been useless.

No doubt the huge quantities of captured equipment also contributed mightily to the PAVN exploits. Also deserving of emphasis is the sense of urgency instilled in each soldier and cadre. The notion that final victory lay within their grasp—an idea repeatedly impressed upon them by their officers and reinforced by the relentless exhortations of their political officers—also undeniably played a major role in the successful movement of over a hundred thousand men and tons of equipment to a distant battle-field. Victory does wonders for morale.

PAVN, however, was not immune to weaknesses similar to the ones that so afflicted ARVN during the final offensive. Notably, PAVN had its own version of the family syndrome. As one senior Group 559 officer drove down the Ho Chi Minh Trail, his car ran into a traffic jam at a control station. The officer got out of his vehicle and walked to the station to find out the reason for the delay. The local commander told him that after word spread in North Vietnam that the Central Highlands had fallen, a large number of drivers coming from the North allowed family members and friends to hitch a ride aboard their trucks to "visit relatives" in the South. In fact, these people were trying to stake a claim to land and property in the vast and rich newly liberated areas. Since none of the civilians had valid travel documents, the control station had ordered them off the trucks. This left a tremendous crowd milling around and provoked a dangerous confrontation between the angry drivers and civilians and the tiny traffic-control team. Rapidly assessing the situation, the quick-thinking officer came up with a Solomonic solution. Any civilians who were immediate relatives of the drivers, including in-laws, would be allowed to accompany the trucks southward. Those civilians who were not immediate relatives would be loaded aboard the next truck convoy headed back north. All civilians, both those continuing south and those returning, would be required to arrange for their own food and housing. Soon the detained vehicles were released, and traffic was again flowing smoothly.[32]

THIEU'S GRIP ON POWER BEGINS TO LOOSEN

As the military situation worsened, President Thieu came under intense pressure to broaden his government in order to rally the nation. This was not the first time Thieu's political opposition had exploited military reversals in an attempt to gain power. During the 1972 offensive, some of the same issues that bedeviled Thieu now had also arisen. Opposition parties had called for a broader government to rally the people after the fall of Quang Tri City in April 1972. Elements in the JGS had grumbled then about Thieu's military moves, as rumors began circulating of super-power connivance to end the war at South Vietnam's expense. However, after ARVN, with the help of U.S. airpower, had stabilized the situation in July 1972, much of the discontent had receded. Now once again faced with military reversals, a number of South Vietnamese began searching for an accommodation with the Communists that would offer a chance at nominal independence, not to mention personal survival. The quick answer was to remove Thieu. This is why Hanoi dangled the possibility of a coalition government. By exploiting Thieu's image as an uncompromising hawk while playing on South Vietnamese fears of U.S. abandonment, the Politburo hoped to unravel Saigon's command structure in order to ease its military conquest.

The opposition ranged from moderates who could work with Thieu but wanted to add to his government people whose talent extended beyond simple loyalty, to hard-core militants who demanded the president's overthrow. The 15 March visit to Thieu by Bui Diem, Tran Van Do, and Tran Quoc Buu was the initial effort by the moderates. It was soon followed by a 21 March statement by the opposition bloc in the Lower House criticizing the retreats. Thieu quickly announced on 25 March that Prime Minister Khiem would form a new, broad-based government, but he failed to inform Tran Van Do beforehand. Do viewed this as a tactic by Thieu to fend off his demand to completely overhaul the government, including replacing Khiem. Hence the opposition immediately mobilized to draft a response to Thieu's announcement.

One new participant in the opposition was Nguyen Cao Ky. Thieu's former running-mate had been living on a farm in Darlac province since pulling out of the 1971 presidential election. Given the enmity between the Ky and Thieu, Ky's presence in the opposition clearly had the potential to create political mayhem. Yet both Do and Dang Van Sung, publisher of *Chinh Luan* (the paper that had printed both Nguyen Tu's articles on the retreat from the Highlands and the 21 March opposition statement), wanted to bring Ky into the fold. Father Tran Huu Thanh, founder of the People's Anti-Corruption Movement, which had conducted anti-corruption and anti-Thieu demonstrations in September 1974, also sought out Ky. After hearing their supplications, the former Air Force commander offered the Tan Son Nhut VNAF Officers' Club as a meeting venue. Gathering on the afternoon of 26 March, the group consisted of about thirty opposition members, including Father Thanh, Tran Van Do, and Dang Van Sung. Notably absent were representatives from the An Quang Buddhist sect and the left-wing Catholics, since they considered themselves part of the Third Force and not of the anti-Communist nationalists whom Thieu had requested to join his government.

Most of the participants wanted Thieu's resignation, but Tran Van Do convinced them to call instead for a change in the government and for the formation of an "Action Committee to Save the Nation." The price Thieu would have had to pay for Do's co-operation, however, was steep. While the resolution did not directly call for Khiem's resignation, Do wanted Khiem gone and the new Cabinet to have greater autonomy from Thieu, particularly regarding personnel changes and anti-corruption measures.

At first, Ky's sponsorship of the meeting did not produce any fireworks. Ky claimed that he did not want to participate in politics, and stated that he would immediately ask anyone who even mentioned a coup to leave. To maintain his neutrality, Ky refused to sign the proclamation.

Thieu's desire to broaden his government was cast in doubt, however, when he ordered the arrest that night of ten people on charges of "plotting" to overthrow the government. Since those arrested included two individuals who had attended the meeting, plus several journalists who worked for Sung and people who were known to be associates of Ky, it was generally assumed that the arrests were a response to the meeting.[33] Ky reacted with fury, believing that Thieu was threatening him. Police Chief Nguyen Khac Binh denied that the arrests were an attempt to pressure Ky, but the damage was done.

The arrests spurred the Action Committee to meet again the next day. With Ky attending, the participants elected Father Thanh as their chairman. After the meeting, Thanh and Ky held a news conference. Going far beyond the previous day's innocuous statement, Thanh demanded that Thieu turn over all power to a new government. Although Thieu could remain as president, he would become a figurehead. Ky once again declared that he had no intention of staging a coup, and he was not seeking political power. Instead, he wanted to lead the military to a victory to lift morale. Displaying a dissociation from reality, he publicly offered to "take eighty tanks and two regiments of infantry and go reoccupy Ban Me Thuot in three days, with me in the lead tank."[34] Earlier he had broached this concept to General Cao Van Vien, who had politely declined. Ky did depict himself, however, as a binding force for the various opposition groups, which seemed to puncture his earlier denials that he was seeking political power.

Thieu's arrest of the ten men had destroyed the fragile effort at reconciliation between the opposition and himself. It had also forced Ky to attend the next meeting and back Thanh. Since within the nationalist opposition Thanh was the most involved in personal attacks against the president, supporting Thanh guaranteed the reconciliation effort's demise. In some ways, though, Thieu did not care. He did not believe that Hanoi would negotiate with a government headed by Ky (or anyone else, for that matter), especially given that the North Vietnamese now had the upper hand on the battlefield.

Apart from the arrests, however, Thieu generally ignored the growing opposition requests for consultations and change in government. Why? Because Thieu, besides fighting the war and trying to find new sources of aid, was secretly attempting to organize a new Cabinet on his own. Shortly after the 21 March opposition statement, he ordered Prime Minister Khiem to ask various opposition figures to join his government. When they all declined, on 28 March Thieu asked Senate Chairman and former Foreign Minister Tran Van Lam and House Speaker Nguyen Ba Can to meet with him. Thieu wanted them to help Khiem form a new government. Lam, however, was under pressure from his Senate colleagues to take a different course. On 20 March the Senate had voted to request that Prime Minister Khiem appear before the assembly to discuss the military situation. When Khiem declined, various senators, both from the opposition and from Thieu's Democracy Party, jointly asked Lam to convene an emergency session. The intent was to request Thieu's resignation. Lam had scheduled the session for 2 April.

The collapse of Danang and its attendant horrors destroyed Thieu's final hope of forming a new government on his terms, as the last remaining pro-Thieu civilians also began demanding his resignation. On 1 April Thich Tam Chau, the head of the Buddhist pro-government Quoc Tu faction, sent a letter to Thieu denouncing the president's military blunders and asking him to resign. The next day, the Senate followed suit and issued a public appeal for a new government and a "change in leadership," a subtle way of calling for Thieu's resignation without saying so directly. On 3 April the head of the Catholic Church in South Vietnam, Archbishop Nguyen Van Binh, published a letter supporting the Senate's appeal. Binh deliberately couched his letter in the same terms as the Senate's appeal so that other Vietnamese bishops would then be free to publicly agree or disagree with him.

After the Senate's demand for Thieu's resignation, Tran Van Lam called on the president. Lam wanted Thieu and Vice President Tran Van Huong to resign and turn over their powers to him. Lam's intent was to form a national-unity government, with Ky as the head of a council that could negotiate an accommodation with Hanoi or a coalition with the Provisional Revolutionary Government. Lam, however, had badly misjudged Thieu. According to Lam, "Thieu reacted . . . abusively, [and accused] his former supporters of having deserted him. He refused to consider either resigning or handing over real power to a new government."[35]

Although most civilian leaders were calling for his head, and there was much badmouthing in the military, Thieu retained the loyalty of the senior military officers. As long as they supported him, the president could fend off the political calls for his resignation. General Cao Van Vien, the chief of the General Staff; Lieutenant General Nguyen Van Toan, the commander of III Corps; and even the Air Force commander, Lieutenant General Tran Van Minh, continued to back Thieu.

Yet Thieu needed a scapegoat, and he found one in Prime Minister Khiem. Khiem's inability to form a new government, the military reversals, and the opposition's calls for a new government provided Thieu the excuse he needed. On 4 April Thieu asked Khiem to resign, along with the entire Cabinet. Concurrently, Thieu announced that the Speaker of the House, Nguyen Ba Can, had accepted the position of prime minister. Can's marching orders were to form a broad government, what Thieu termed a "fighting Cabinet."

The same day, Thieu made a lengthy TV speech to the nation. He admitted that he had ordered the withdrawal from the Central Highlands, but stated that it was with the intention of regrouping to retake Ban Me Thuot. He espoused the view that the fall of Danang was due to the Communists' overwhelming strength. Finally, Thieu denied that a deal had been made to divide the country, and asserted that he was determined to defend all remaining territory. He also stated that he was prepared to return to the negotiating table if the North Vietnamese ceased their attacks. Lastly, he proclaimed that the Communists were attempting to destroy the South Vietnamese government by urging a coalition government. Thieu insisted that the constitution must be preserved in order to support any negotiations. The next day, according to Van Tien Dung's account, Thieu sent out an order mandating the "urgent strengthening of the Phan Rang defense line, and reprimanded those of his generals who favored an early regroupment around Saigon/Gia Dinh for being defeatist."[36]

As he had done so often in the past, Thieu had outmaneuvered his domestic opponents. Still, his hold on power depended entirely upon continued American support and, just as important, upon reversing the military tide.

INFORMING WASHINGTON

As the PAVN juggernaut closed in on the South Vietnamese capitol, both the CIA and the DAO told Washington that South Vietnam was doomed. On 29 March the CIA's Saigon station chief, Tom Polgar, stated: "Unless the U.S. takes prompt action to halt the North Vietnamese aggression—not necessarily through military means—the situation . . . is likely to unravel quickly over the next few months, resulting in the actual or effective military defeat of the GVN in a very short time."[37] Polgar's views hit home. An interagency report, coordinated by the CIA, DIA, and State Department, and published on 4 April, was unequivocal: "The only question over the defeat of the Republic of Vietnam is timing—whether it will collapse or be militarily overwhelmed in a period of weeks or months. The North Vietnamese have recognized South Vietnam's vulnerability and appear determined to take rapid advantage of it."[38]

American intelligence soon confirmed the Politburo's intention to go for the kill. According to Frank Snepp, on 8 April "the Station's best agent supplied us with a crucial update of the intelligence already in hand. The Communists had just issued a new 'resolution' calling for . . . a move against the capital at an as yet unspecified date, with no allowance whatsoever for a negotiated settlement. All the 'talk' of negotiations and a possible coalition government, he emphasized, was merely a ruse to confuse the South Vietnamese and to sow suspicion between them and the Americans."[39]

This was a great intelligence coup, for the CIA's best source was reporting a brand-new COSVN resolution. Known as COSVN Resolution 15, it called for the seizure of South Vietnam by the end of 1975. Although Resolution 15 merely reflected the Politburo's 18 March decision and not the latest decision to end the war by the end of April, this critical intelligence should have left no doubt about North Vietnamese intentions.

On 10 April, Colonel William Le Gro disseminated similar intelligence in what would prove to be the last Monthly Intelligence Survey and Threat Analysis (MISTA) produced by the DAO. Ambassador Graham Martin, however, disagreed with both the DAO's and the CIA's analysis of the new intelligence. While Martin accepted the estimate of PAVN's military capabilities versus ARVN's, he appended a dissent to Le Gro's report. He laid out his belief that "the enemy's capabilities will not be exercised to their fullest because factors exterior to the local tactical situation will operate to deter the DRV. Most significant in the exterior factors considered will be international diplomatic pressures. The prompt and adequate provision of US military assistance, not repeat not including the employment of US airpower in SVN, will in the Ambassador's view give the defending forces . . . material and psychological strength to prevent the necessity of capitulation while the international pressures work to provide the basis for a new political settlement."[40]

For Martin, it was a desperate wish born of a desire to see South Vietnam survive with some semblance of independence, and to see America extract itself from the Vietnam quagmire with a modicum of dignity. For his numerous critics, the ambassador's assertion that a political solution could be found in time to stave off a PAVN march into Saigon was the culmination of what they saw as his "head-in-the-sand" approach. Instead, it was a man grasping at proverbial straws. No alternative existed except an abrupt and humiliating run for the exits by U.S. officials. Leaving as enemy tanks enter a doomed city is one thing, but cutting and running while life still breathes in your ally is quite another, and Martin would have none of that.

Regardless, there was little the CIA or the DAO could do about the torrent of North Vietnamese forces rushing toward them but report it and hope for a miracle. Writing to General Weyand at the end of March, Colonel Le Gro noted that "the 320B Division is currently enroute to III Corps and that two other divisions currently deployed in the south or from the . . . reserve will also move to III Corps in the next one to three months."[41] What Le Gro did not realize is that at that moment the Communists were in the process of sending *eight* more divisions to Saigon, and that they would arrive in two weeks, not in one to three months.

Now the destiny of a country so many Americans had fought and died for hung on the outcome of the race between the South's efforts to reorganize its shattered units from the northern military regions, and the Communists' ability to deploy forces into III Corps. For the moment, however, as PAVN prepared for the battle for Saigon, the South Vietnamese were tired of badly botched withdrawals. If Giap wanted Phan Rang, the peasant soldiers of the People's Army would have to fight for it.

"HOLD FAST THE REMAINING LAND"

THE SOUTH VIETNAMESE FIGHT BACK

With the hectic events of 1 April—the shattering of the 3rd Airborne Brigade's defensive line at the M'Drak Pass, the appearance of North Vietnamese tanks at the town of Ninh Hoa, and the news that Phu's headquarters had fled Nha Trang—South Vietnamese control along the central coast disintegrated. Chaos, spreading like a plague borne by thousands of fleeing civilians and retreating ARVN troops, quickly reached south to Cam Ranh Bay and nearby villages and towns. By late afternoon on that day, only the sleepy town of Phan Rang, the next major city south on Route 1, remained largely free of panic. Phan Rang was the capital of Ninh Thuan province, and is located fifty miles southwest of Nha Trang,

That would not remain true for long, however. After returning from Pham Van Phu's mid-morning meeting in Nha Trang—his last meeting as commander of II Corps—Air Force Brigadier General Pham Ngoc Sang, commander of the 6th Air Division, faced a rapidly deteriorating situation at his headquarters at Thanh Son airbase outside Phan Rang.[1] Crowds of civilians and soldiers had forced their way onto the airfield, looking for a plane ride to Saigon. To add to the confusion, following orders from VNAF headquarters in Saigon, the Air Force units at Nha Trang had hastily abandoned the city that afternoon and withdrawn to Thanh Son. Instead of conducting an organized departure, the VNAF crews had grabbed their families and ferried them to Thanh Son, stranding everyone else. Sang now had most of two air divisions—the 2nd and the 6th—crowded onto the airbase.

As night fell on 1 April, the situation confronting Sang was grim. He later wrote: "the base was very empty because a large number of the RF soldiers guarding the perimeter of the airbase had deserted. On the base itself a number of young soldiers were firing their guns wildly out of ignorance and fear. In the city . . . the population was in a state of shock and confusion. Convoys of military and civilian vehicles crammed with people jammed Routes 1 and 11 as they drove south, fleeing the enemy."[2] The men of his 6th Air Division were frightened and worried. To prevent further disruption, Sang ordered the gates closed and the base sealed to entry. There were simply too few men to guard the massive airbase—built for American jet aircraft, Thanh Son airfield formed a square, roughly three miles in each dimension. However, like a gift from the heavens, late that night Lieutenant Colonel Le Van Phat, together with his 3rd Airborne Brigade headquarters and a portion of one battalion, arrived at the base entrance on trucks and requested permission to enter. Sang checked with VNAF headquarters in

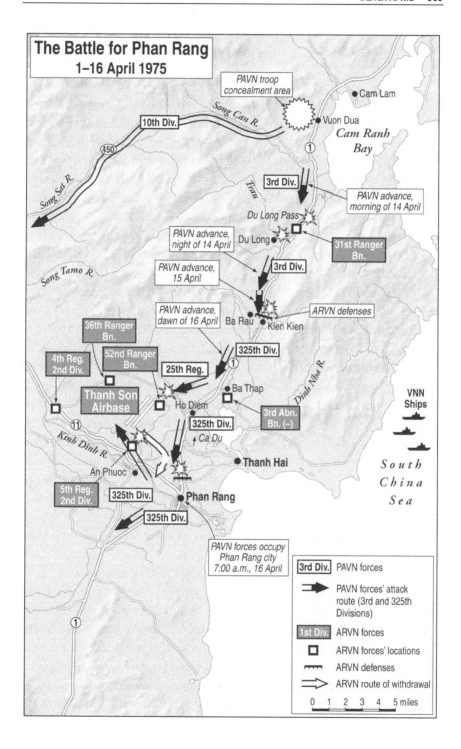

The Battle for Phan Rang
1–16 April 1975

PAVN troop concealment area

Cam Lam

Song Can R.

10th Div.

Vuon Dua

Cam Ranh Bay

450

Song Sat R.

3rd Div.

PAVN advance, morning of 14 April

Trau

Du Long Pass

Song Tamo R.

PAVN advance, night of 14 April

Du Long

31st Ranger Bn.

PAVN advance, 15 April

3rd Div.

PAVN advance, dawn of 16 April

Ba Rau

ARVN defenses

Kien Kien

36th Ranger Bn.

325th Div.

4th Reg. 2nd Div.

52nd Ranger Bn.

25th Reg.

Ba Thap

Dinh Nha R.

VNN Ships

Thanh Son Airbase

Ho Diem

3rd Abn. Bn. (–)

325th Div.

Ca Du

An Phuoc

Kinh Dinh R.

Thanh Hai

South China Sea

5th Reg. 2nd Div.

325th Div.

Phan Rang

325th Div.

PAVN forces occupy Phan Rang city 7:00 a.m., 16 April

3rd Div.	PAVN forces
⟹	PAVN forces' attack route (3rd and 325th Divisions)
1st Div.	ARVN forces
☐	ARVN forces' locations
⊓⊓⊓	ARVN defenses
⟹	ARVN route of withdrawal

0   1   2   3   4   5 miles

Saigon, which swiftly granted authorization. Sang asked Phat to have his troops assist in base security and clear away some local guerrillas who had crept close to the airfield.

Phat's arrival, while solving the security problem at Thanh Son, did nothing to stem the bedlam. Early in the morning of 2 April, Air Force Brigadier General Nguyen Van Luong, commander of the 2nd Air Division, departed the Phan Rang airbase in his C-47 for the Tan Son Nhut airbase in Saigon. As soon as Luong left, the helicopters and airplanes from his 2nd Air Division that had fled Nha Trang to Thanh Son quickly followed, setting off a frenzied exodus. One of Sang's senior officers remembered it later: "The sight of aircraft flooding out onto the runway and competing with one another in a race to take off turned Thanh Son Air Base, which had been peaceful, into a place of total chaos. Thousands of soldiers and their families, who were waiting for evacuation at the control tower, suddenly panicked, and all semblance of order collapsed. Every time an aircraft arrived, everyone surged toward it, fighting to get on board. The MPs and the control-tower personnel were helpless, especially since the crowds of soldiers included men with weapons that began firing indiscriminately."[3]

In the midst of this bedlam, fortune again smiled on Brigadier General Sang. The Australian government had responded to South Vietnam's pleas for humanitarian assistance with its massive refugee problem by sending several C-130 military transport planes to assist in the evacuation. The first one arrived at Tan Son Nhut on the morning of 31 March, with its initial mission to help move civilians out of Thanh Son. The Australian C-130 flew to the airfield on 1 April, but because of the chaotic conditions resulting from the arrival of the airplanes and helicopters from Nha Trang, it was unable to land. It returned to Tan Son Nhut. A second C-130 arrived in Saigon later that same day, and another attempt was made with both planes on 2 April.

At first the flights went smoothly, but turmoil soon broke out again. According to an Australian historian, "In the course of making five or six flights that day, the two aircraft became caught up in the pandemonium associated with the evacuation of the city in the face of the expected enemy onslaught. At one stage a C-130 was mobbed by refugees and ARVN personnel who panicked when four rockets landed about 400 [yards] away, prompting a soldier to fire warning shots into the air. Unfortunately this man was standing under the aircraft's elevator at the time, and several rounds holed the aircraft's tail. . . . Later . . . on the last flight of the day, [the plane was] blocked by two fuel tankers while the control tower sought some assurances that [the planes] would be returning. Although he knew this would not be the case, only after [the pilot] said they would be back were the tankers driven aside to let him take off. In the course of this day's operations some 1,500–1,800 refugees were taken out to Can Tho."[4] Given the chaos, the Australians decided to halt the emergency flights.

Meanwhile, in addition to the hundreds of civilians mobbing the airbase, thousands of other people escaping south on Route 1 were now engulfing Phan Rang. Worse, the ARVN deserters from I Corps who had arrived on the ships docking at Cam Ranh Bay, plus the remnants of some II Corps units, had formed a convoy and were streaming down Route 1, looting as they went. Unable to cope with the armed rioters, and fearing the imminent arrival of PAVN tanks, the Ninh Thuan province chief fled Phan Rang on 2 April, along with most of the local police, provincial administrators, and RF troops. Only a Catholic priest in the small village of Ho Diem on Route 1 east of Phan Rang, who also commanded the local Self-Defense Force, held his position and prevented local guerrillas from entering Phan Rang. After the province chief deserted, communication with Saigon was lost. The communication breakdown and the hurried departure of the 2nd Air Division from Nha Trang led to speculation in U.S. intelligence circles that the VNAF had abandoned the Thanh Son airbase, and that Phan Rang had fallen to the Communist advance.

In reality, Sang's airmen and Phat's troopers were still holding fast. On 3 April, communications between Saigon and Phan Rang were re-established. Phat was ordered by the Airborne Division headquarters in Saigon to remain and defend the airbase. That morning he sent his brigade reconnaissance company out to recapture the nearby high ground from local guerrillas. Although his men accomplished this mission, Phat soon realized that his battered unit would be unable to completely control the large base and secure the perimeter. Phat recommended to Sang that he ask for another Airborne unit as reinforcements. He did, and the JGS quickly granted the request. Later that afternoon, fresh troops from the 3rd Battalion, 2nd Airborne Brigade, were flown in. Phat immediately positioned them in the hills surrounding the base. The Airborne reinforcements steadied the morale of the civilians and Air Force personnel. By late afternoon, with most of the refugees cleared from Thanh Son, and the Airborne in complete control of the airfield, base functions returned to normal.

As calm slowly returned to Thanh Son, more help came, this time from the sea. On 3 April, four U.S. Navy ships arrived off the coast of Vietnam. As they held position in the waters off Phan Rang, the cargo ship U.S.S. *Durham* was sent in to investigate. Dozens of small boats loaded with refugees quickly surrounded the American vessel. Over the next two days, the *Durham* picked up almost 3,500 Vietnamese refugees. Alerted to the Americans' presence, Sang dispatched the commander of his helicopter wing, Lieutenant Colonel Le Van But, out to talk with them. Lieutenant Colonel But relayed two questions from Sang: Would the Americans provide naval gunfire support to the South Vietnamese defenders, and would they help with the evacuation? After a half-hour meeting, Lieutenant Colonel But left the ship, deeply discouraged by the American response. While the U.S. ships would assist any refugees, there would be no military assistance from South Vietnam's former ally.

That same afternoon, Sang flew to Phan Thiet to meet with III Corps Commander Lieutenant General Nguyen Van Toan. Toan was carrying orders from General Vien. Effective 4 April, the two remaining II Corps provinces under South Vietnamese control, Ninh Thuan and Binh Thuan, would be incorporated into III Corps. Vien was sending reconnaissance teams from the Strategic Technical Directorate to the northeast and northwest of Phan Rang to determine the current location of the Communist forces. Following Thieu's orders for no further retreats, Phan Rang would be held.[5] Sang was designated the officer responsible for the defense of the city. He and his Air Force technicians and pilots had suddenly become South Vietnam's front line.

CLOSING THE CIRCLE

As the 10th Division swept unopposed into Cam Ranh, COSVN ordered MR-6 to destroy any remaining South Vietnamese RF outposts along Route 11 on the western flanks of Phan Rang, and to move swiftly to occupy all land right up to the very gates of the provincial capital. It was a tough task; the only Communist forces in the area were small bands of local guerrillas. Still, between 1 and 5 April almost all of the hamlets along Route 11 were captured. Further, the critical district town of Du Long, located near the important Du Long Pass on Route 1 between Cam Ranh and Phan Rang, was abandoned by South Vietnamese Regional Forces. Guerrillas moved in quickly and took over the district capitol.

Ninh Thuan was a small province (it was dissolved after the war), 220 miles northeast of Saigon, with a population of more than 300,000. About 17,000 of those were ethnic Chams, an ancient people who had once ruled all of central Vietnam. The rest were Vietnamese and a mix of other ethnic groups. The terrain is mostly mountainous. Phan Rang is located in the southern portion of a narrow valley bordered by mountain ranges on the west, the north, and the northeast. The valley begins at the Du Long Pass, nine miles east of Phan Rang; Route 1 runs through the Du Long Pass to Phan Rang. The Thanh Son airbase is three miles north of Phan Rang along Route 11. The villages of Ba Rau and Ba Thap are located on Route 1 midway between Phan Rang and Du Long. Phan Rang has two ports: Tan Thanh and Ninh Chu.

While Communist local forces were seizing villages around Phan Rang, MR-6 was preparing a second and even more ambitious plan. After capturing Dalat, the 812th Regiment sent two infantry companies to Phan Rang to support the local forces there, but the rest of the regiment moved toward Binh Thuan province to attack Phan Thiet, the next provincial capital south of Phan Rang on Route 1. Sending the 812th toward Phan Thiet instead of Phan Rang was a cunning move. If the 812th succeeded in capturing Phan Thiet, it would cut off any ARVN forces retreating from Phan Rang, forming a pocket from which the only escape would be by sea or by air. If this strike was coordinated with an all-out push from the 10th Division, Phan Rang and Phan Thiet would fall easily to the Communist troops.

However, while this was a good plan on paper, the 812th Regiment was too far away and too immobile to strike Phan Thiet in a reasonable amount of time. Further, the 10th Division was exhausted after nearly a month of heavy fighting. Elements of the division were strung out along Route 1 from Ninh Hoa to Cam Ranh. They had fought two ARVN infantry regiments, the 21st Ranger Group, the 3rd Airborne Brigade, seven RF battalions, and two armored troops. They had captured Duc Lap, Phuoc An, Khanh Duong, Ninh Hoa, Nha Trang, and the critical military port of Cam Ranh Bay. During March, few Communist units fought as long or as effectively as the 10th Division. Recognizing its achievements, Van Tien Dung sent a telegram to the 10th praising its efforts. He wrote: "The . . . 10th Division made a significant contribution to the victory of the Central Highlands Campaign and helped to change the very character of the war in a short period of time."[6] However, the 10th needed time to assert control over the newly liberated territory. Given the situation, on 4 April the division was ordered to halt and secure Cam Ranh.

Although the local guerrillas had captured numerous villages and had walked into the critical Du Long district capital without opposition during the first week in April, the 10th Division's halt gave ARVN some badly needed breathing room. Brigadier General Sang's stand, the arrival of the Airborne, and the enemy's delay—all provided a little time for the South Vietnamese to recover.

On 4 April—the day Ninh Thuan and Binh Thuan provinces were incorporated into III Corps—Lieutenant General Nguyen Vinh Nghi, the former IV Corps commander, arrived to take over the Phan Rang front from Brigadier General Sang. Most accounts indicate that Nghi volunteered for this assignment. Why he wanted this almost impossible job is open to speculation, but he was probably attempting to redeem his reputation, having been sacked for corruption on 30 October 1974. Nghi supposedly brought with him Thieu's personal promise that two divisions would be assigned to defend Phan Rang. Thieu hoped that the troops recovered from I Corps could be formed into cohesive units and sent to stabilize the front.

That a senior officer like Nghi believed this pipe-dream is indeed strange. In any case, the only troops Nghi brought with him were a few staff officers to form a III Corps Forward Headquarters. He set up his command post at Thanh Son airbase, and his staff quickly established communications with the III Corps Headquarters in Bien Hoa. After Sang briefed him on the situation, Nghi outlined his operational plan. Once the promised reinforcements arrived, Nghi would retake Du Long and anchor his main defensive line on the Du Long Pass. Here Route 1 runs between narrow mountain cliffs, and as such the pass offered the primary defensive position between Cam Ranh and Phan Rang. Nghi would create a secondary blocking position on Route 1 at the villages of Ba Rau and Ba Thap. Nghi also wanted to re-establish the defenses along Route 11 in order to halt Communist incursions and protect the western and southern approaches to the airbase. Unfortunately, Nghi would need a sizable number of troops to accomplish this, and all he had was the remnants of Lieutenant Colonel Phat's brigade and the newly arrived 3rd Airborne Battalion. Despite Thieu's promise, what Nghi would eventually obtain was far less than two divisions.

One potential source of manpower was the Airborne units that had retreated into the hills around the M'Drak Pass. On 2 April, shortly after helping to stabilize the airbase, Phat appealed to Sang for assistance in rescuing his stranded men. Sang agreed, and he sent Lieutenant Colonel Le Van But and Phat's deputy, Lieutenant Colonel Tran Dang Khoi, to fly out and examine the situation. Cut off and without resupply, the 5th Battalion, plus portions of the 2nd and 6th Battalions, had followed Phat's orders and assembled on the hilltops near the pass. Some troops had been captured on 1 April, including the 6th Battalion commander, but almost six hundred soldiers had escaped. Now the tough Airborne troops were patiently awaiting rescue. On the eastern end of the pass, while a few 2nd Battalion soldiers had escaped to Phan Rang, another two hundred hardy survivors remained trapped. Luckily, the Communists had ignored them.

Circling over the pass, Khoi made radio contact with the units. The 2nd Battalion commander, Major Tran Cong Hanh, had taken a separate helicopter to search for his missing troops. After examining the situation, Lieutenant Colonel But quickly realized that his two squadrons of Huey transport helicopters were not enough. Plus, an operation of this size would require meticulous planning to prevent a disaster in case of panic or an enemy attack. Ticking off the mission requirements in his mind, But realized he would have to secure a landing zone to defend against a possible attack, load the troops as quickly as possible, and then return to Thanh Son without running out of fuel. It would be a very close call, since the trip was at the ragged edge of the range of his helicopters. Both But and Khoi returned to Thanh Son to plan the operation with Sang.

After a short briefing, Sang made another urgent call to Saigon for assistance. Within hours, six giant Chinook helicopters, each capable of carrying five or six times as many men as a Huey, were sent from Bien Hoa airbase, twenty miles northeast of Saigon. Sang also had extra fuel flown up in C-130s, since the airbase's regular source of fuel had been lost with the capture of Cam Ranh. Working fast to come up with a plan before the Communists could react, Sang decided to launch every helicopter he could muster—more than forty Huey transports, twelve helicopter gunships, the six Chinooks, and But's own command-and-control helicopter—in a daring operation to rescue the Airborne. Two flights of A-37 bombers would provide air cover.

The helicopter armada took off at first light on 3 April and flew straight toward the main body of trapped soldiers. As the helicopters approached the target area, a group of Hueys split off to pick up the scattered 2nd Airborne troops on the eastern end of the pass. Upon reaching the main landing zone, But sent the gunships to search the nearby hills carefully for signs of an enemy ambush. Finding none, he gave the all-clear signal. The six giant Chinooks moved in first. Landing one at a time, they swooped in and dropped their ramps. The Airborne, maintaining the strict discipline for which they were renowned, swiftly loaded. As soon as the Chinooks left, the Hueys began landing. As each helicopter finished loading, it took off and headed straight back to Thanh Son, while the A-37 escorts continued to circle overhead. Within an hour, six hundred men had been evacuated from the main landing zone, while another two hundred were rescued from the 2nd Battalion positions. When the last helicopter had finished loading, Lieutenant Colonel Le Van But pulled pitch and headed back to the airbase. By the time he landed, his fuel warning light was on. Sang's airmen had completed a daring rescue of eight hundred desperately needed elite ARVN troops without a single enemy shot being fired.[7]

The Airborne were not the only ARVN troops being rescued at that time. Late in the afternoon of 1 April, the LST *Danang* (HQ-501), carrying what remained of the ARVN 2nd Division, arrived at the port city of Ham Tan in Binh Tuy province, south of Phan Thiet. After being evacuated from Chu Lai to Re Island as I Corps disintegrated, the remnants of the 2nd Division had lost contact with I Corps Headquarters and had been stranded on the island. Fortunately for the troops, one of the *Danang*'s engines broke down as it was sailing south from I Corps. An alert soldier spotted the ship when it hove to off the island to make repairs. Brigadier General Tran Van Nhut personally flew the last operational 2nd Division helicopter out to the HQ-501. After a short discussion, the LST captain agreed to transport Nhut's troops to Cam Ranh Bay. En route, Nhut received orders to divert to Ham Tan instead.

Several days after the 2nd Division disembarked, the ragtag convoy of ARVN deserters that had bedeviled Phan Rang on 2 April and Phan Thiet on 3 April arrived at Ham Tan. When the caravan reached the small port city, both Nhut and the province chief went out to meet it. A deal was quickly struck. Nhut told the men that since Route 1 was cut near Xuan Loc, they would be unable to reach Saigon by road. In return for their disarming and handing over all weapons and vehicles, Nhut and the province chief would arrange for sea transportation to Vung Tau, where the men could take a bus to Saigon. Nhut also threatened to shoot any soldiers caught raping or looting.

For Nhut, who had been ordered by the JGS to re-organize his division within one week and prepare for combat, the weapons and vehicles from the convoy were an unexpected windfall. He picked up some APCs, plus several artillery pieces and a large quantity of individual weapons. While the 2nd Division was the only I Corps unit (other than the Marines) that had succeeded in evacuating a portion of its manpower, the division's infantry regiments were badly under-strength. Lieutenant General Toan transferred two RF battalions from III Corps to replace some of the division's losses. Toan also sent a few 105-mm howitzers recently arrived from the U.S., but the guns lacked sights and spare parts.

It was all Toan could do. The 2nd Division was in the best shape of the three regular ARVN divisions from I Corps, but that was not saying much. Even with the RF fillers, and scraping together other troops who had made it south, Nhut could field only two battalions per regiment. The troops' morale had plummeted after the horrors of Chu Lai and having to leave their families behind. With little time to train and rebuild unit cohesion, Nhut knew that the 2nd was an empty shell. He recommended that the division stay in Ham Tan to defend the port, but mainly to recover and regain some semblance of fighting strength. Toan rejected his request. The 2nd was among the few pawns Toan had left, and on 7 April he ordered Nhut to prepare his troops to move north to help defend Phan Rang and Phan Thiet.

TRYING TO STEM THE TIDE

The South Vietnamese had been slow to re-organize their forces that had escaped from I and II Corps, but under the DAO's prodding they soon began reconstituting units. Other efforts to bolster troop strength were also undertaken. RF soldiers were used to fill out ARVN regiments. Although desertions were heavy, many of the deserters were rounded up, and the net inflow of men was greater than the losses. The process of merging under-strength RF units in IV Corps to form complete units was also quickened. General Vien and other senior officers made pleas to the troops to maintain their fighting spirit. In the command arena, on 3 April Lieutenant General Nguyen Van Minh, former commander of III Corps and now ARVN inspector general, was placed in command of the Capital Military District, replacing Admiral Chung Tan Cang. Cang was put back in charge of the Navy, replacing acting chief Admiral Lam Nguon Tanh.

President Thieu's decision to reinstall Cang, a staunch supporter, was not made to improve naval efficiency. It was to prevent Nguyen Cao Ky from using the Navy to support a coup. Cang's first action as Navy commander was to create a new Riverine Task Force, TF 99. Captain Le Huu Dong, who had served previously with Cang on the Delta's muddy rivers, took command of TF 99. Dong reported directly to Cang, and the TF was deliberately based at Nha Be, close to Saigon. The LST *My Tho* (HQ-800) was anchored nearby to provide a headquarters for the new task force. Cang formed TF 99 from parts of two existing task forces in the Delta, TF 212 and TF 214.[8] This decision also had political motivations. Commodores Nghiem Van Phu and Dang Cao Thang commanded TF 212 and 214 respectively, and they were part of the group that in 1963 had kicked Cang out of the Navy. Later, they had supported Ky against Thieu. In order to reduce the forces of his old rivals, Cang took their best units and merged them into the new TF 99. Ostensibly, Cang created TF 99 to protect the Saigon and upper Mekong Rivers from increased sapper interdiction. In reality, the formation of this new unit was to provide a loyal military force on the waterways close to Saigon, and to deny any pretext for TF 212 and 214 to be near the capital. Ironically, this move would pay huge dividends in the fight for the Delta.

On the military front, as the situation stabilized around Phan Rang, Lieutenant General Nghi and Brigadier General Sang went back on the offensive. Although Sang strongly disagreed with the decision that his air division should remain so close to the front lines and subject to Communist shelling, Colonel Le Van Thao's A-37 wing soon resumed bombing operations. Striking targets in the Cam Ranh Bay area, it flew round-the-clock missions against the advancing PAVN troops. Despite several successes, however, notably against the 10th Division moving on Local Route 450, Thao's operations were hampered by the lack of ground controllers and by the desire to avoid civilian casualties. His losses were also mounting. One A-37 was shot down when the pilot came in low to bomb a bridge and at the last second noticed that the Communists had tied civilians to it. Pulling up, he swung around to look for another target when an SA-7 team, lying in ambush, hit him with a missile.

Moreover, the aircrews at Phan Rang were attempting to load bombs and refuel the aircraft under difficult conditions. Constant rocket attacks forced technicians to wear flak jackets while struggling to load 250-pound bombs in the tropical heat. Worse was the lack of food and other supplies. With Route 1 cut east of Xuan Loc, supplies were arriving only by air. Often Thao's pilots, who were flying four sorties per day, would get only one meal. Many were not sleeping because of the constant need for air support, or the simple fear of being left behind if an evacuation suddenly was ordered. The dread of abandonment was so great that some helicopter pilots took to sleeping on cots next to their parked aircraft. Thao's solution was to rotate half his wing to Saigon each day, both to re-arm and re-fuel, and to catch some sleep and get a meal. In the morning they would fly back to Phan Rang, where Thao would direct them on armed reconnaissance missions along Route 1. However, while his attacks stung the PAVN forces, one A-37 wing alone could not halt the PAVN advance.[9]

On 7 April, Nghi's promised reinforcements began arriving. The 2nd Airborne Brigade, commanded by Colonel Nguyen Thu Luong, flew into Thanh Son. Luong's unit was to replace the 3rd Airborne Brigade so it could return to Saigon to regroup.[10] The 2nd Brigade had departed I Corps and arrived at its rear base at Bien Hoa on the afternoon of 21 March and had been placed on full alert. The men were not even allowed to visit their families. This was particularly onerous. As Luong later wrote, "We spent three years straight, from 1972 until 1975, conducting continuous operations in I Corps. Even when the cease-fire agreement was signed in 1973 we still did not get to return to our rear base to rest, regroup, re-equip, and conduct training. Instead we were sent out to the farthest front-line positions and assigned to defend hill positions along the Annamite Mountain Chain. . . . The days when the weather was sunny and dry were not so bad, but the days when . . . [there was] a cold drizzle falling through a north wind were particularly miserable. Stationed atop high hills and mountains, living in tents made from our own ponchos . . . cold and wet, we had difficulty cooking anything, and always we were face to face with the enemy. . . . One thoughtless moment could cost a man his life [from] enemy mines, booby-traps, and mortar shells, because the enemy never respected the cease-fire agreement."[11]

Colonel Luong arrived at Thanh Son on the first plane. The rest of the 2nd Airborne Brigade, including the 7th and 11th Battalions, an artillery battalion, and support and logistics units, were transported from Bien Hoa to Thanh Son by C-130. The airlift was completed at 2:00 A.M. on 8 April. Luong immediately went to see Lieutenant General Nghi, who provided him his new missions: conduct operations to recapture lost territory, and defend Phan Rang and Thanh Son. Luong would be allowed to retain the 5th Battalion, 3rd Brigade, for five more days. While the situation had stabilized, the outlook was still critical. Guerrillas were holding the Du Long

Pass and the important villages of Ba Thap and Ba Rau on Route 1. They had also crept back close to the airbase perimeter.

Colonel Luong immediately formulated an operation to accomplish the missions Nghi had given him. While the 5th Airborne Battalion would continue to guard the base and assist in clearing Route 11, the 3rd Battalion would clear Route 1 and recapture Ba Rau and Ba Thap. Once that was accomplished, Luong would leapfrog his 11th Battalion over the 3rd Battalion in a helicopter assault to attack Du Long town, and then recapture Du Long Pass.

Wasting no time, early in the morning of 8 April, Colonel Luong executed his plan with precision. Communist local forces were pushed back on all fronts. After the 3rd Battalion recaptured Ba Rau, Luong then air-assaulted the 11th Battalion into Du Long and the high ground. His troops quickly recaptured the town. Much to their surprise, they snared a small PAVN truck convoy. The drivers told the Airborne that their commanders had informed them that Phan Rang was already captured. The Red Berets had just proven them wrong.

"THE DECISIVE BATTLE HAS NOW BEGUN"

While the Airborne troops were busy recapturing territory near Phan Rang, PAVN's attention was focused elsewhere. The General Staff had no intention of allowing ARVN any breathing room, but, as we have seen, there had been a major difference of opinion over how to proceed next. Many of Hanoi's military and political leaders (Tra, Le Duc Tho, Le Duan, and Giap) wanted to strike Saigon quickly, while Dung wanted to secure I and II Corps, mass the PAVN forces, and then attack the capital in one overwhelming strike. Despite Dung's disagreement, the sudden victories over I and II Corps persuaded his Politburo colleagues to move against Saigon immediately instead of waiting to mass their forces. The hope that a strong push from Tra's B-2 Front might topple Thieu proved irresistible.

But how best to accomplish that mission? Giap recognized that ARVN "still worked stubbornly to establish a defense line from Phan Rang south to keep our armed forces at arm's length. [ARVN] hoped to block and push back our attacks in order to hang on until the rainy season."[12] Giap feared that if the South Vietnamese could hold on, the Americans might increase aid, or any number of other scenarios might occur to deny a complete victory. That is why at the 31 March Politburo meeting, Giap recommended immediately sending the entire People's Army south. He also suggested that Tra launch attacks against Saigon from multiple directions. When ARVN panicked, Giap said, sapper and commando forces already infiltrated into Saigon would launch a "mass uprising" in coordination with the PAVN assault. If the Communists' plan succeeded, Saigon would be overwhelmed by a combination of external main-force blows and internal uprisings long before the other three North Vietnamese corps arrived. It was a risky move. Attacking Saigon when the ARVN forces were reeling might be a killer blow, but if they stood their ground, Giap risked a major defeat. Moreover, that might provide the South Vietnamese a badly needed morale boost, or convince the U.S. that South Vietnam was still salvageable.

Tra also advocated a sudden push. Regardless of the facts on the ground, he had been wedded to this strategy for too long to turn back now. Immediately after receiving Le Duan's 29 March message, and without waiting for specific attack guidance, Tra traveled in a jeep from COSVN to meet 4th Corps Commander Hoang Cam at a secret location near the Dong Nai River. He arrived late at night on 31 March. By mid-afternoon on 1 April, Cam, his deputy, Bui Cat Vu, and the 341st Division commander, Tran Van Tran, had also arrived. The next day, Tra began the meeting by explaining to the others the overall situation in South Vietnam. He then got to the heart of the matter: he had received authorization from the Politburo to take the initiative and not wait for reinforcements.[13]

Tra then outlined the new attack plan. His main attack on Saigon would be from the east and the south. Hoang Cam was given the mission of destroying the ARVN 18th Division at Xuan Loc and taking the town, and then capturing the Bien Hoa airbase on the outskirts of Saigon.[14] The 6th Division would be attached to the 4th Corps, giving Cam three divisions— the 6th, the 7th, and the 341st. Cam asked Tra to delay the assault until 9 April to give him time to plan and adjust his forces. Tra agreed.

South of Saigon, Tra's initial plan called for units of the 303rd and 5th Divisions to capture Moc Hoa, the capital of Kien Tuong province in the Plain of Reeds, and destroy the ARVN 9th Division. This was a continuation of the earlier border-clearing mission conducted by the 303rd Division, and was designed to turn the Plain of Reeds into an operational base for Group 232. Once this base area was established, the 5th Division could use the local roads to move heavy equipment from its Cambodian border bases to cut Route 4 and destroy the ARVN 7th Division. To reinforce the attack from the south, Tra recalled the 271B Regiment from Quang Duc and began trucking it toward the Delta. Tra hoped that if his forces were able to destroy these three ARVN divisions, "the puppet army and regime would vacillate and become chaotic and not be able to defend Saigon effectively, or else there would be an important political upheaval within the ranks of the puppets [a coup], or between the puppets and the Americans, in which case we would immediately . . . attack . . . in order to liberate all of the B-2 theater."[15]

Tra departed on the afternoon of 3 April and returned to COSVN headquarters in the early hours of 4 April to meet Dung, who had arrived the day before. One can only speculate as to what Tra must have felt seeing Dung, although he claims that when they met, they "happily embraced."

Regardless of the appearance of his rival, Tra's earlier reading of the Politburo tea leaves was correct. When he returned to his headquarters, Le Duan's 31 March message ordering him to create a new action plan in B-2 awaited him. As usual, Giap had also sent a follow-up message on 1 April, outlining his concept for the attack on Saigon:

Just as the Politburo says, our revolutionary war in South Vietnam is now entering a period of growth by leaps and bounds. At present we already have sufficient forces and capabilities to achieve complete victory in a much shorter time than we had initially projected. The decisive issue is that we must seize our opportunity in a timely fashion. . . . we must try to begin a massive assault on Saigon by mid-April. If we can meet that time schedule it will be to our maximum advantage and will ensure our most resounding victory. We can no longer surprise the enemy with regards to the direction of our main attack. The enemy knows that we must attack Saigon, but he believes it will take us one or two months to prepare such an attack. For this reason, at present the achievement of surprise is now a question of timing. On the one hand we must move forces rapidly, speedily, while on the other we must immediately use the forces we have on hand to take timely action, without waiting to concentrate all of our forces. . . . That is the meaning of the Politburo's declaration that the decisive battle of Saigon has now begun. . . . With regards to the two basic formulas for action: the first being a long-term siege to create the conditions for us to finally attack and overrun the target; and the second being a daring, immediate attack . . . we should now select the second formula. This means we should act in a truly rapid and daring manner, while at the same time making preparations so that, under certain conditions, we can switch to Formula One and still achieve final victory within a short period of time. . . . Using the forces you currently possess, you need to take quick action to exploit every opportunity the enemy's terror and confusion may present to you. . . . We now must count time in days.[16]

Giap's message laid out in unequivocal terms his desire to strike at Saigon now. He and Le Duan anticipated that, as in Danang, South Vietnamese forces near Saigon would collapse and PAVN troops would easily enter the city. Only Van Tien Dung remained cautious, believing that the conditions were not yet right for such a risky venture.

After reviewing Tra's plan, Giap accepted most of it, but he canceled the 5th Division's attack at Moc Hoa. Instead he ordered Tra to use the 5th Division to cut Route 4 south of Saigon and seize the towns of Tan An, the capital of Long An province, and Thu Thua, a village north of Tan An. The 303rd would launch secondary attacks near Moc Hoa to assist the 5th Division. Because of the failure to take Route 4 in March, this time Giap choose the attack location, a point where he thought the ARVN defenses were weakest. He selected a section of Route 4 in Long An that was defended solely by Regional Forces. The South Vietnamese had only three RF battalions shielding the road and the various canals. The closest South Vietnamese regulars were the 12th Regiment, 7th Division, miles away in Dinh Tuong province. However, the RF did have some help. Five ARVN artillery bases offered fire support, river patrol boats supplied security along the waterways, and VNAF aircraft from Can Tho, south of the Mekong River, provided air cover for the Route 4 corridor.

For Giap, the decision to bypass Moc Hoa and attack Route 4 directly was another gamble. The 5th Division had only just finished rebuilding after its losses in December 1974, and MR-8 forces had attacked a stretch of Route 4 south of Long An in March without success, mainly because of the excellent performance of the ARVN 7th Division. Still, both Tra and Giap desperately wanted to seize the Route 4 corridor in Long An for a variety of reasons. Doing so would disrupt food supplies to Saigon, and would block ARVN from falling back into a Delta enclave. Most important, it would create another "liberated zone" for staging troops and equipment to provide a second attack prong from the south.

After Tra's earlier exultation over Hanoi's newfound acceptance of his strategy, he claims that, when he received the changed orders, he spent a "sleepless night" worrying how his forces could move their heavy equipment through the marshy Delta.[17] Without capturing Moc Hoa and the nearby roads, his new corps, Group 232, would have to launch its assault against Saigon from the southwest across the marshy Vam Co Dong River, a very difficult mission. The river was two to three hundred yards wide, and both banks were mostly swamp covered with thick vegetation. Group 232's heavy equipment would be forced onto tiny Route 10, which would also mean rebuilding a destroyed bridge and traversing another swamp, this one two miles wide. If the VNAF caught the Communist troops on the road, they would be slaughtered.

Tra was particularly worried that airpower could turn the tide against him if the South Vietnamese chose to stand and fight. Therefore, his plan had another key element: interdict the South Vietnamese airfields, especially the major airbases at Bien Hoa and Can Tho. Tra sent one 130-mm battery to reinforce the efforts of the sappers who were responsible for shelling Bien Hoa. However, captured documents alerted the South Vietnamese to this strategy, and ARVN sweep operations prevented the sappers from achieving their goals.[18]

Although Giap had approved Tra's plan, with the modifications noted above, when Dung arrived at COSVN headquarters, he immediately began analyzing it. While Dung realized he knew little about the B-2 area, he had no enthusiasm for Tra's strategy, but realized there was little he could do to change it now. Dung was lower in the Politburo than Pham Hung, who had worked with Tra in formulating the strategy. With Giap and Le Duan backing Hung's and Tra's plan to use the B-2 forces to launch an early attack, Dung was boxed in. However, after "three days of quite detailed reports by the regional staff on all aspects of the situation in Saigon," Dung now had "a firmer basis for discussing plans for the general offensive."[19]

The arrival of Le Duc Tho at COSVN changed everything for Dung, because Tho was carrying instructions that provided Dung the clout he needed. On 7 April Tho held a conference and announced the formation of a new campaign headquarters to oversee the attack on Saigon. Dung was given overall command of the final offensive, a decision, according to Tra, that "everyone supported."[20] Tra and Le Duc Anh would command the forces on the western approaches, while Le Trong Tan would command the two corps on the eastern approaches. Pham Hung would act as political commissar.

According to Giap, at the conference Le Ngoc Hien, the General Staff's chief of operations, presented the General Staff's campaign battle plan.

Hien had based the plan on Giap's guidance in his 1 April cable. The plan was divided into two phases. The first phase, which would begin on 8 April, involved attacks "to strategically cut off . . . and surround the enemy . . . and attack [Saigon's] outskirts and eight separate targets within the city in preparation for the general offensive. If the situation was favorable and the enemy began to disintegrate, a deep penetration strike would be launched immediately, in coordination with mass uprisings designed to capture the city."[21] Phase Two, which was projected to begin between 15 and 20 April, would involve an assault on Saigon from five separate directions. "If the [ARVN] 18th Division could be destroyed and if we were able to cut off and isolate Saigon, we would shake the very foundations of enemy power and new opportunities would then present themselves. If the enemy pulled back and tightened his defenses, we would prepare additional forces to reinforce our attack [switch to Formula One], but we still would have to complete the capture of the city during the month of April."

Although the COSVN conference unanimously approved the plan, Dung remained convinced that B-2 was not strong enough to succeed in its new mission, and that the North Vietnamese needed to wait until all their forces were together to make one massive assault. He was worried that the ARVN troops would fall back into Saigon, where costly, destructive, and protracted house-to-house fighting would be required to defeat them. Since the first attack was scheduled for the next day, Dung was forced to accept Tra's approach. However, he made sure the Politburo was aware of his views. He sent a cable to Hanoi recommending that the Politburo and the Central Military Affairs Committee rapidly move reinforcements to the B-2 Front.

After studying Dung's cable, the Politburo seemed to back away from its exhortations of 29 March. No doubt the euphoria stemming from the resounding victories in I Corps had slowly been replaced by the realization that it would take time for the forces already speeding south to assemble within striking distance of Saigon. On 9 April Le Duan sent a cable to Pham Hung and Le Duc Tho: "I just received [Dung's] cable . . . this morning. After discussions with [Giap] and the comrades at the General Staff, I believe that you all need to wait to prepare for a few more days and for the bulk of 3rd and 1st Corps (including both infantry and heavy weapons and technical equipment) to arrive before beginning the [main] assault. From now until the big attack begins, the western and southwestern wings . . . should step up [their] operations to cut Route 4 to force the enemy to disperse his forces to deal with our attacks in order to cause additional disruption and fear within the enemy's ranks and make it difficult for him to guess our campaign plans. At the same time, you should also order the urban commando teams to infiltrate into the city. The other sectors should also take appropriate actions to support the big attack. You need to ensure that once the attack is launched, you attack hard, continuously, and repeatedly until complete victory is achieved. . . . That is the basic plan and the plan most certain of victory. . . . I also agree with your projection that we need to make preparations to deal with the possibility that the fighting may become long and protracted, for a certain period of time at least."[22]

Le Duan was too late. Tra's troops had already opened fire.

STANDING FIRM IN THE DELTA

Shortly after Tra received the new orders from Giap, he sent the 5th Division toward Long An province. After three days of tramping across canals and dusty paddy, the regiment reached an assembly area near Tan An, the provincial capital. A second regiment was sent to attack Thu Thua, north of Tan An. A third was held in reserve near Tan An. This section of Route 4 was squeezed between the Vam Co Dong (Eastern Vam Co) and Vam Co Tay (Western Vam Co) Rivers. A network of lateral canals cut across the land. If PAVN forces succeeded in capturing Tan An plus the bridges on Route 4 over the two Vam Co Rivers, they would sever Saigon from the Delta and prove difficult to dislodge.

To support the main attacks at Xuan Loc and along Route 4, at dawn on 7 April, the 303rd Division launched a series of diversionary raids near Moc Hoa, but it had minimal impact. In III Corps, sappers shelled Bien Hoa airbase with 122-mm rockets on 8 April, again doing little damage. In Tay Ninh, PAVN forces attacked Brigadier General Tran Quang Khoi's 3rd Armored Cavalry Brigade, but to no avail. Despite Tra's convictions that any attack would cause a South Vietnamese collapse, ARVN easily repulsed these surprisingly weak attacks.

After finally reaching their positions, early on 9 April the two 5th Division regiments attacked the Long An RF forces guarding Thu Thua and Tan An. Another PAVN element set up a roadblock on Route 4 near the Long An/Dinh Tuong provincial border to block ARVN 7th Division reinforcements coming from the south. The first objective at Tan An was to secure the airfield and then sweep into the city. As dawn broke, a long line of Communist infantry surged forward and captured a small section of the airbase, but stiff resistance from the local RF prevented further losses. Caught out in the flat Delta terrain and unable to advance, the exposed troops were soon forced by artillery fire to retreat. The RF counterattacked, and by mid-afternoon the Communists had been badly beaten, leaving one hundred dead on the battlefield.

The ARVN 7th Division quickly responded to the attack. Reinforced by the division's M-113 squadron and reconnaissance company, the 12th Regiment, commanded by Colonel Dang Phuong Thanh, immediately moved from its position further south in Dinh Tuong province to support Tan An. Crossing a corps boundary was a rare occurrence, but according to the 7th Division's chief of staff, "Since Long An was closer to the 7th Division . . . than to [Long An's] parent III Corps headquarters, we had prior permission to coordinate and provide necessary support to that province."[23]

After clearing out the roadblock on Route 4, the 12th Regiment continued moving north and caught the PAVN 5th Division from behind. Over the course of the next four days, ARVN fought a series of battles with two regiments of the 5th, completely shattering one of them. Communist losses were high: four to five hundred killed, along with thirty men and numerous weapons captured. The PAVN soldiers were mainly teenagers recently infiltrated into South Vietnam. Scared, unfamiliar with the terrain, and poorly trained, they took a beating at the hands of the Long An RF and regular ARVN forces. But the victory was not without cost. The 12th lost thirty-seven killed and ninety wounded.[24]

The results were the same in Thu Thua. Only local Popular Forces guarded this important town. Thinking it would be an easy target, the Communists had sent only a small sapper unit for the initial attack. The sappers moved in before dawn, infiltrating through the local market and trying to overrun the district headquarters with a quick raid. They timed their attack to avoid the Long An province riverboat company, which normally did not return from night patrol until after sunrise. Unfortunately for them, this morning the boats had returned early. Catching the sappers out in the open, the heavy fire from the ships decimated them. A few managed to penetrate into the town, but they were driven out by local police. After the battle, the Long An province chief reinforced Thu Thua with two RF battalions.

The next day, the district chief ordered the boats to hide in a nearby small canal, while he used the RF to search for the Communist troops. As the RF swept across the dry fields, suddenly they came under intense fire from a large number of Communist forces. The 5th Division's reserve regiment had been committed. The RF retreated to a canal bank, but they were pinned down and faced destruction. The district chief quickly counterpunched with the hidden boats:

> After powerful barrages of heavy weapons, Communist forces began their assault. The [North Vietnamese] swarmed out in a black cloud all across the entire field in front of me [in] a human-wave attack. . . . When I gave the order, our navy boats . . . surged forward to enter the fray. My orders were very clear: "Move up and down the river, firing all the time." Six river patrol boats gave us eighteen heavy machine guns, each of which could fire 350 rounds per minute. The boats had plenty of ammunition. Six landing craft with eighteen machine guns and firing almost 6,000 rounds every minute sailed in a column up the river firing their weapons. The river assault company commander received clear orders that if any boat was sunk by an enemy B-40 rocket it was to be abandoned. No boat was to stop to try to save it. Every boat was to continue firing until the enemy assault was repelled. The enemy troops charged excitedly forward to what they thought was victory, when suddenly they came under heavy fire from the river patrol squadron, cutting them down in droves. The Communists reacted quickly, firing B-40 and B-41 rockets and all types of mortars that exploded in the river, sending columns of water into the air which then fell back down like rain. Luckily the riverboats were moving, so not one vessel was hit and the boats were able to stop this massive assault. The boats created a curtain of fire. . . . The enemy survivors, and there were not many, pulled back a long distance. They were unable to recover the bodies of their comrades, who lay covering an entire large, open field.[25]

The attack cost PAVN dearly. The DAO reported that 122 North Vietnamese were killed. But the Communists did not retreat. They began attacking the small PF outposts surrounding the district seat, while using artillery to soften up the town's defenses. Despite the determined stand by the Long An RF/PF, the PAVN ring slowly tightened around Thu Thua.

PAVN also planned major attacks to seize Can Tho, the capital of the lower Delta and the IV Corps Headquarters, but ARVN intelligence discovered these plans. On 1 April, IV Corps intelligence intercepted a radio message that the Communists intended to launch an offensive that month. The next day, ARVN further learned that a local-force regiment had been assigned to operate with the three regiments of the PAVN 4th Division to attack Can Tho and capture the city. Soon thereafter, ARVN detected the division moving from the U Minh Forest. Another COSVN message was intercepted ordering MR-9 to launch the attack no later than 8 April.

On the basis of this information, ARVN IV Corps Commander Major General Nguyen Khoa Nam ordered the 21st Infantry Division, then conducting an operation along the edge of the U Minh Forest, to immediately pull back and defend the city. The 21st had three infantry regiments; the 31st, 32nd, and 33rd. It also had the 9th Armored Squadron, made up entirely of M-113 APCs. Nam reinforced the division with the 11th Regiment, 7th Infantry Division, and the newly formed 63rd Infantry Regiment, a unit that had been created out of an An Giang province RF group. All nearby corps and territorial artillery was organized into a fire-support network to directly assist the 21st.

Colonel Mach Van Truong commanded the 21st. One of the original cadres who formed the unit in 1959, Truong had commanded a regiment of the ARVN 5th Division at An Loc in 1972, and most recently had been Long Khanh province chief. He was close to Major General Le Van Hung, who had been the 5th Division commander at An Loc. Truong assumed command of the 21st in October 1974 when Hung became the deputy corps commander.

To block the enemy attack, Truong positioned his 32nd Infantry Regiment and the attached 63rd and 11th Infantry Regiments, together with RF territorial forces, in defensive fortifications along the highway into Can Tho, which the Communists called the Arc Road. He kept a second regiment in reserve, and combined his 9th Armored Cavalry Squadron and the 33rd Infantry Regiment into a new Task Force 933. He stationed TF 933 outside his defensive positions as a mobile force that could attack the enemy's rear and block reinforcements from entering the area from the outside. According to Truong, "On the night of 8 April, the [PAVN] 4th Division reached the Arc Road and secretly crossed the river (they had to swim across the river individually, so they were only able to bring light equipment with them). They attacked just before dawn. Our units fought back ferociously from our heavily fortified positions, and pre-arranged artillery barrages blocked [the PAVN] attacks. Then helicopter gunships and Air Force fighters from the Tra Noc and Binh Thuy Airfields flew in to bomb and strafe the area. On the outer perimeter, to the enemy's rear, TF 933 sealed off the rear to block any reinforcements. The enemy dug in and fought for the entire day under continuous fire from our aircraft and artillery.... They suffered very heavy losses. On 10 April, the 4th Corps G-2 [intelligence] Office intercepted secret messages from COSVN Headquarters and MR-9 ordering the 4th Division to pull back."[26]

The stiff ARVN defense cost the Communists over four hundred men killed and wounded. From their perspective, "the act of sending a large force of troops through the Arc Road line and then withdrawing them back again had an effect on the fighting strength of the troops ... enemy artillery positions shelled 4th Division's regiments continuously. Our ammunition stocks were low and we were unable to suppress the enemy artillery fire (at this point the Region's ammunition stockpile totaled only ten tons of ammunition of all types). On 15 April, the ... Military Region Party Committee met to assess the situation. They concluded ... that the enemy was determined to hold Can Tho [and] it was not yet possible to coordinate the attack ... with the attack to capture Saigon ... on 18 April, [MR-9] received an order from COSVN [to stop attacking until 26 April]."[27]

In response to the 4th and 5th Divisions' setbacks, MR-8 forces launched attacks to draw ARVN units away from Route 4. On 13 April two PAVN 8th Division regiments and two Long An local-force battalions attacked Tan Tru, an important district town east of Tan An where the Vam Co Tay and Vam Co Dong Rivers converge. For four days the valiant PF, backed by numerous VNAF strikes and reinforcements from one Long An RF battalion, fought off the Communists. To assist the PF, Lieutenant General Toan ordered recently arrived elements of the ARVN 22nd Division to help defend Tan Tru. Although the 22nd was a shadow of its former self, one of its newly reconstituted regiments quickly pushed the PAVN forces back. After failing to seize any territory in Long An, the 8th Division abandoned its efforts and turned north, reaching an assembly area near Saigon on 25 April.

Despite the serious defeats suffered by PAVN, the fighting for Route 4 was not over. To help ARVN forces in the Delta, Admiral Cang ordered TF 99 to sail south and maintain control of the upper Delta's waterways. On 16 April Captain Dong led his assembled task force toward Long An province. His vessels helped turn back the Communists at Tan Tru, but their greatest victory came the next day. Sailing up the Vam Co Tay River toward the Thu Thua canal, TF 99 stumbled onto a large Communist unit bathing in the river. Dong's ships immediately attacked. Machine-gun fire spurted from the decks, sweeping the river, but the Communist troops on the banks quickly returned fire. Rocket-propelled grenades and mortar rounds began hitting the water. Then Dong unleashed two flame-thrower boats, called Zippos. Spewing fire, the two boats incinerated dozens of North Vietnamese troops. The surviving enemy soldiers fled in panic, leaving dozens of burned and blackened bodies floating in the water. For the next week, Dong's forces fought every day, severely restricting the Communists' supply efforts, and preventing them from easily moving troops along the numerous waterways. After the repeated beatings, PAVN decided to halt operations in IV Corps until the main Saigon offensive. Tra's design for cutting off Saigon from the south had failed miserably. ARVN had held the Mekong Delta.

After the disastrous losses for the South Vietnamese in I and II Corps, which had lowered morale throughout the country, ARVN commanders in the Delta had spent time calming the fears of their troops. Consequently, the South Vietnamese at all levels put up tough resistance. The relative weakness of the Communist units in the region also contributed to the results. But more important was a serious mistake on Tra's part. Recognizing the importance of the Route 4 corridor through Dinh Tuong and Long An provinces, he had used the 8th Division to make attacks in March, and then the 5th Division to make similar attacks in April. If he had launched a simultaneous attack with both divisions in the two provinces, and had concurrently swung the 4th Division into action near Can Tho, ARVN would have been hard pressed. Tra's piecemeal attacks gave ARVN time to recover, steady its nerves, and shift forces to defeat the attacks.

Although ARVN had again performed well in the Delta, the overall situation remained bleak. The DAO stated: "In sum, RVNAF has weathered week without conceding major territorial losses or sustaining critical defeats. . . . [However], it may well be confronted with even more critical battles to preserve security along Route 4, hold . . . Can Tho and cripple [PAVN main-force] units. RVNAF must accomplish this without taking high casualties. In its current state of overextension, decisive defeat of even one ARVN regiment would . . . have dangerous ramifications."[28] Despite Tra's tactical error, his attacks continued to accomplish one feat: hopes that the South Vietnamese could either retreat into a Delta redoubt or send a division north to help III Corps were fast fading.

GETTING READY TO ATTACK

In Phan Rang, with the completion of the successful Airborne attacks, the situation was now completely stabilized. The ARVN Central Logistics Command established an ammunition and fuel-supply point at Phan Thiet. The Ninh Thuan province chief, who had fled to Phan Thiet on 2 April with the flood of civilians pouring down Route 1, returned to the province on 7 April with a number of his administrators. His return was not voluntary: Lieutenant General Nghi had sent a cable to the Binh Thuan province chief, ordering him to find his wayward counterpart and send him back immediately. With no enemy pressure, the reassuring presence of the elite Airborne, and Thieu's promise of fresh troops still dancing in his head, Nghi began to seriously consider the possibility of retaking Cam Ranh and perhaps Nha Trang. However, ARVN radio-intercept operators, including ones on an EC-47 aircraft, had begun picking up a large volume of Communist chatter. Although this signaled a potential massing of PAVN forces, Nghi still believed that he could recapture the two cities. He became even more excited when he learned that the PAVN 10th Division had left Cam Ranh. Retreating ARVN soldiers who managed to slip through the lines also provided intelligence on enemy dispositions at Cam Ranh, leading Nghi to believe that the area was lightly held, which it currently was.

Unfortunately for Nghi, he had no inkling that the massive Coastal Column was pouring down Route 1 toward his forces. To make matters worse, on 9 April, after two days of heavy fighting, the PAVN 812th Regiment and a local-force sapper battalion seized Thien Giao, a district town only ten miles from Phan Thiet. MR-6's plan was slowly coming to fruition, and Phan Rang was becoming an isolated outpost.

While PAVN's battlefield momentum had slowed, the 968th Division reached Ninh Hoa on 6 April and moved in to secure Cam Ranh and Nha Trang after the 10th Division's departure. Units of the 3rd (*Sao Vang*) Division followed hot on the heels of the 968th. After sending an advance party ahead to coordinate the road movement and arrange for fuel and food, the 3rd departed Binh Dinh on 8 April and arrived north of Phan Rang on 11 April.

On 12 April Le Trong Tan and the Coastal Column headquarters reached the assembly area, a small village near Cam Ranh Bay. The day before, the General Staff had sent Tan a cable informing him that ARVN was strengthening Phan Rang's defenses. North Vietnamese spies were continuing to supply timely intelligence on ARVN plans. Tan was given the option of bypassing Phan Rang if he felt it would be too difficult to conquer. Shortly after Tan arrived at the assembly area, he held a meeting with the various commanders. Local forces would play a crucial role as guides if Tan decided to attack, since none of the Coastal Column forces had any knowledge of the terrain. Initially, there was some discussion as to whether it would be quicker to bypass Phan Rang. In the light of the pummeling the 10th Division had taken from the VNAF, however, Tan decided it was important to move against Thanh Son airbase. Moreover, Tan's supply situation was excellent. His troops had captured two thousand tons of rice and over four thousand tons of gasoline and oil at Nha Trang. The movement south had been relatively easy. With no logistical limitations, and his units advancing steadily, Tan felt no need to bypass the pesky ARVN at Phan Rang. He ordered the 3rd Division to attack along Route 1 and capture the Du Long Pass and Phan Rang. A secondary but still important attack would be made by the B-3 Front's 25th Regiment, now under the operational control of the 3rd Division, to capture Thanh Son. Tan gave the 3rd Division one day to prepare. Given the division's lack of familiarity with the terrain (when it departed Binh Dinh, it did not have a single map of the Phan Rang area, and it was issued only one small general map when it arrived at the assembly area), and since it had just finished a long road march, the division commander requested and was granted a one-day extension.

Following Tan's orders, the 3rd decided to send two spearheads along Route 1. One battalion would strike Du Long, while another would swing behind the pass and attack Ba Rau, the village halfway between Du Long and Phan Rang. The division staff knew this second approach would be difficult, but they believed that if they could take Ba Rau, Du Long's defenses would crumble. Another regiment would punch toward the sea and follow the coast to cut off escape in that direction. The 25th Regiment, reinforced with light artillery and a battery of anti-aircraft guns, would attack the airbase. Another regiment would be held in reserve. The attack would begin at dawn on 14 April. The 3rd Division's mission was clear: "Destroy all enemy forces in Phan Rang, liberate all of Ninh Thuan province, confiscate all technical support facilities, especially air force equipment, and be prepared to continue to advance to the south."[29]

Unaware of the gathering enemy, on 12 April Lieutenant General Nguyen Van Toan informed Nghi that the 2nd Airborne Brigade would be withdrawn back to Saigon the next day. The 5th Airborne Battalion, 3rd

Brigade, had already left Phan Rang the day before. The 31st Ranger Group, which had recently fought at Chon Thanh and was now recuperating at the major ARVN supply depot at Long Binh near Saigon, and the 2nd Infantry Division, with two reconstituted regiments, a few APCs, and an artillery battery, would replace the Airborne troops. Although Nghi protested, the III Corps commander was adamant. After sending the 1st Airborne Brigade to Xuan Loc, Toan needed to restore his reserves around Saigon. As Toan later told the author, "Saigon was more important than Phan Rang."

At 6:00 A.M. on 13 April, the 31st Ranger Group, with its three battalions and assorted support units, assembled at Bien Hoa airbase for transportation to Phan Rang. By 4:00 P.M., the group's transfer was complete. The 2nd Division, consisting of the 4th and 5th Regiments (the 6th Regiment and one artillery battery had moved to Phan Thiet on 12 April to assist in the defense of that city), also began moving to Phan Rang. On 13 April the 4th Regiment arrived by truck, with the 5th Regiment arriving the next day. The 5th was Nhut's weakest unit: it consisted of a Long An RF battalion and a second battalion of men scraped together from various 2nd Division and other units. The division headquarters arrived on the morning of 15 April.

Toan's moves could not have come at a worse time. Switching units on the front lines is tricky, especially under pressure. The replacements need a period of time to acquaint themselves with the terrain and the enemy situation. Support units like artillery and logistics also require time to organize. While airpower was plentiful, if PAVN began shelling the airbase, that support would quickly disappear. Artillery was in short supply, as were sighting mechanisms, ammunition, and spare parts. Radios were few, and most other stocks were low as well.

After meeting with Nghi and Sang, the Ranger Group commander, Colonel Nguyen Van Biet, sent the 31st Ranger Battalion to replace the 11th Airborne Battalion at the Du Long Pass. The 11th Battalion commander and one infantry company withdrew to Thanh Son, while the other three companies took up defensive positions on hilltops along Route 1 just north of Phan Rang. They would move to Thanh Son the next morning and then fly back to Bien Hoa. Another Ranger battalion would be sent to replace the 3rd Airborne Battalion at Ba Rau. Colonel Biet held his last battalion at the airport in reserve. The 4th Regiment, 2nd Division, would guard Route 11. When the 5th Regiment arrived, it would also remain near the airbase.

Coordinating his departure with the arrival of the Ranger elements, Colonel Luong moved the 7th Battalion and most of his headquarters out on the same planes that flew in the Rangers. The 3rd and 11th Battalions would depart on 14 April, completing the withdrawal of the Airborne except for the artillery, which would stay an extra day.

Major Nguyen Van Tu's 31st Ranger Battalion arrived at the Du Long Pass around 6:00 P.M. on 13 April. After an orientation and examination of the Airborne defensive works, Tu completed the replacement around 10:00 P.M. While it was relatively quiet on South Vietnam's front line, Tu was deeply worried. The only troops close by were some RF in Du Long town who had just returned after earlier fleeing in panic. When Tu asked Colonel Biet about fire support, Biet reassured him that even though artillery was not available, there was abundant airpower. However, lack of artillery and reinforcements was not Tu's only worry. His unit was badly understrength. Around two hundred men, less than half the unit's authorized strength, had made muster at Bien Hoa that morning. While absent ARVN soldiers typically filtered in several days after the start of an operation, Tu had no idea how they would reach distant Phan Rang.

As Tu surveyed the hills, he pondered his two-fold mission: to hold the line at the Du Long Pass, and to act as a traffic checkpoint on Route 1. He was to monitor civilians traveling south, as enemy commandos often disguised themselves as local peasants. Any soldiers were to be grabbed and sent to the rear for use in forming new units. As Nguyen Van Tu, a soldier since 1963, went to sleep under Vietnam's stars, it would be one of the last peaceful nights he would know for many years.

THE BEGINNING OF THE END FOR PHAN RANG

At 5:30 A.M. on 14 April, Communist artillery shells began exploding on various positions near Du Long, Ba Rau, and smaller villages along Route 1. For an hour PAVN rained hot steel on the Rangers' bunkers at Du Long Pass and the Airborne's at Ba Rau. At 6:30 A.M. several tanks and waves of infantry tried to punch through Major Tu's lines, but the Rangers held them off. Two A-37s appeared overhead thirty minutes later. As the jets dove in to strike the attackers, their bombs fell short and hit a Ranger position, wounding a dozen of Tu's men. Despite the friendly fire and the heavy attacks, the Rangers held.

Unable to break through on Route 1, the North Vietnamese cut through the hills, bypassing the Ranger positions, and attacked Du Long town. After a short fight, the RF forces crumbled and the town was captured. Although Tu was still holding, he was now outflanked. He called Colonel Biet for orders and was told to maintain his position, as reinforcements from the 52nd Ranger Battalion were on the way. Although the troops of the 52nd rushed forward, they were pinned down by the second 3rd Division column and were unable to advance any further. At 4:00 P.M., Colonel Biet ordered Tu to retreat, telling him to get his men back to the airport.

Tu decided to infiltrate his men in small groups through the Communist lines. After issuing orders and directions to his remaining men, Tu began moving with his headquarters staff. As he scrambled down a hill, he suddenly saw a T-54 swing its turret around and point the long barrel of the main gun at his group. Shouting for the others to run, Tu dashed down the hill, trying to draw the tank's attention away from his men. It worked. The T-54 fired a round at him, which exploded nearby. He fell to the ground, dazed. Noticing wetness running down his backside and right leg, Tu suddenly felt fear, wondering how badly he had been wounded. Reaching carefully around behind him, he put his hand on his wet fatigue pants. Much to his relief, he discovered that a shell fragment had hit and broken his canteen, splashing water on his legs. Getting up, Tu continued moving, and by the next morning, he and most of his battalion staff had made it to the airbase. However, only eighty of his soldiers escaped. The Du Long Pass, regarded as the key to ARVN's ability to defend Phan Rang, had fallen.

While artillery bombarded the 31st Rangers' positions, elements of the PAVN 25th Regiment began moving toward Thanh Son. Helicopter patrols soon spotted a large number of men camouflaged with leaves and branches heading toward the airbase. Lieutenant Colonel But's gunships tried to hold them off, but they penetrated the airbase and rushed toward the hangar area. Lieutenant General Nghi immediately ordered Colonel Luong to lead the portion of the 11th Airborne currently waiting near the runway for their ride back to Saigon to stop the attackers. Luong protested, telling Nghi that responsibility for the defense of Thanh Son had been turned over to the 2nd Division. Nghi insisted, and Luong reluctantly obeyed.

Luong requested that four armored personnel carriers that were parked on the airfield be placed under his command to support the attack. Nghi granted this request. Fortunately, the combined fire support provided by the APCs and armed helicopters was extremely effective in stopping the advancing PAVN troops. As the Airborne pushed outside the airbase, the fighting became fierce. The 11th Battalion commander noted: "Just after the troops moved beyond the perimeter fence enemy forces began firing heavily. One M-113 was hit by a B-40 rocket and burst into flames. The two airborne companies launched an all-out assault, while armed helicopters . . . from the airfield strafed the enemy force that was trying to surround the two airborne companies. Flights of A-37s bombed enemy mortar positions in the foothills next to the airfield. Communist forces popped all different colors of smoke to try to trick and confuse the bombers. The airborne troopers fought a close-quarters battle using grenades and bayonets. The heroic assault by 11th Airborne Battalion inflicted heavy losses on the enemy force . . . leaving behind more than one hundred bodies. . . . Our side suffered six soldiers killed or wounded and one M-113 destroyed."[30]

After defeating the attack by the 25th Regiment, Luong attempted to convince Nghi that the situation was calm. He took Nghi and Sang on a jeep ride to visit Ba Rau. When they returned, a cable was waiting informing Nghi that the newly appointed Defense Minister, Tran Van Don, accompanied by Lieutenant General Toan, would arrive on 15 April for a visit. Nghi requested that Luong stay another night so that Luong could personally take Don and Toan on a tour of the area. Grumbling, Luong agreed. The day before, Don had issued an appeal to "see to it that every inch of land is safeguarded, as we are determined to hold fast the remaining land."[31]

As night fell on 14 April, the ARVN forces had managed to hold off the 3rd Division's attacks. The North Vietnamese had grabbed Du Long town and the pass, and the high ground near Ba Rau, but they had failed to penetrate much further down Route 1. The Communist commanders decided to send an additional battalion to reinforce the 25th Regiment, move their artillery closer to the front lines, and resume their attacks and seize Ba Rau the next day.

At dawn on 15 April, PAVN artillery resumed its heavy shelling, this time concentrating its fire on Ba Rau and the nearby smaller hamlet of Kien Kien, held by the 3rd Airborne Battalion. The 3rd Battalion's commander, Major La Qui Trang, had three companies positioned on the high ground west of Route 1, and his headquarters and another company east of the road at Kien Kien. Two companies from the 11th Battalion supported him, plus elements of the 52nd Rangers. After another massive artillery barrage lasting an hour, PAVN attacked. Trang's companies on the west side of the road soon found themselves in dire straits. They held out for several hours against the numerically superior PAVN troops, but the artillery and the constant attacks wore them down. At noon, Trang radioed Luong, asking to retreat. Luong granted permission, and Trang ordered his men on the west to disperse and infiltrate back to Thanh Son. He pulled his remaining troops onto high ground east of Route 1, and called in air strikes that destroyed the bridge on Route 1 at Kien Kien. The PAVN troops were forced to halt their advance while their engineers built a bypass. Another day had passed. Although the North Vietnamese were slowly gaining territory, at this rate it would take them a week to reach the provincial capital. Such a delay threatened the Coastal Column's ability to reach Saigon in time to participate in the attack. New measures were called for, and Nguyen Huu An's recent Soviet training would now pay huge dividends.

16

"NO MATTER WHAT HAPPENS, DO NOT STOP YOUR ATTACK"

CAPTURING PHAN RANG

On 13 April, the lead sections of the Coastal Column's First Element, which had departed Danang on 7 April—a battalion of the 203rd Tank Brigade and the 101st Regiment, 325th Division—arrived at Cam Ranh Bay. Traveling right behind them was Major General Nguyen Huu An. Given the Coastal Column's tight timetable and the fighting the last two days against the ARVN blocking positions on Route 1, Lieutenant General Le Trong Tan told An to commit the newly arrived armor and infantry to a deep-penetration strike to capture Phan Rang. An promptly drafted a daring strike straight down Route 1 to capture the besieged city.

An's attack plan consisted of an armor spearhead of twenty tanks and armored personnel carriers from the 4th Tank Battalion, 203rd Tank Brigade, reinforced by an infantry battalion from the 101st Regiment. Some infantry would ride on the armor while the rest would travel in trucks interspersed among the tracked vehicles. A small tactical headquarters from the 101st Regiment, defended by several 37-mm anti-aircraft guns, would follow closely behind the lead element. Next would be a truck convoy carrying the remaining two 101st Regiment infantry battalions, along with long-barreled 85-mm artillery pieces to provide direct fire support. An air-defense battalion at the column's rear would protect against the A-37s. The column would use the speed and firepower of the massed armor, infantry, and anti-aircraft artillery, called an "attack from the march," to overwhelm the defenders. This type of fast-moving assault was a Soviet armor tactic designed to penetrate an enemy defensive position and rapidly reach the enemy's rear, thereby creating havoc. If the first spearhead failed, An would commit a second column comprising the 18th Regiment, 325th Division, and the 5th Armored Battalion. To concentrate artillery for the attack, the 325th Division would deploy its artillery next to the 3rd Division's artillery so that they could coordinate their fire. Since the 325th Division attackers were not familiar with the area, the deputy commander of MR-6 would ride on one of the first tanks.

An gave missions to the other PAVN elements as well. Since successful air strikes would slaughter the infantry riding in the trucks, the corps staff assigned two air-defense regiments to cover the two columns, and it gave the 673rd Air Defense Division overall air-defense responsibility for the attack. The 3rd Division would hold its positions and let the deep-penetration column pass through. Then the division would launch a secondary attack with two organic regiments and the independent 25th Regiment. One regiment would advance down the western side of Route 1 and seize villages and key terrain right up to the airbase perimeter. Another regiment would attack on the eastern side of Route 1 and capture the small port of Ninh Chu, located a mile north of Phan Rang. The third regiment would remain in reserve. The reinforced 25th Regiment would launch another assault against the Thanh Son airbase. A recently formed local-force battalion would attempt to cut Route 11 between Thanh Son and Phan Rang, while guerrillas would harass the Airborne and Ranger positions throughout the night before the main assault. The main elements would depart from an assembly area near Cam Ranh at 10:00 P.M. on 15 April. The attack would begin at 5:00 the next morning, and the 325th Division was ordered to capture all targets by the end of the day.

This strike was, to this point in the war, the largest PAVN combined-arms operation ever conducted. It showed just how far the North Vietnamese had come since the Easter Offensive. There would be no repeat of An Loc in 1972, when armor attacked without adequate infantry and anti-aircraft support. No American unit in Vietnam ever faced anything remotely as powerful as this assault. In essence, PAVN had massed forty armored vehicles and two infantry regiments, supported by an air-defense division and two artillery regiments, into an enormous one-two punch that would barrel straight down South Vietnam's best highway to capture a target ten miles from its starting point. Once the column punctured the ARVN lines and entered Phan Rang, units in the lead element would fan out in several directions to secure the city. They would then assist the assault on the air-base, and set up a blocking position on Route 1 south of Phan Rang to seal off ARVN's overland escape route.

Nguyen Huu An was worried about the South Vietnamese bombers, but he felt confident that his artillery barrages against Thanh Son would restrict Air Force operations enough to enable his assault column to enter Phan Rang before the planes could react. Absolute secrecy was to be maintained to ensure the element of surprise. To emphasize the corps commander's intent, the chief of the Armor Branch personally issued instructions to the 4th Tank Battalion's commander: "You must attack at high speed, use heavy firepower to break through the enemy's outer defense lines, and rapidly penetrate all the way into Phan Rang. No matter what happens, do not stop your attack."[1]

The South Vietnamese (and the Americans) were completely unaware of the PAVN plan. It was on 14 April that Lieutenant General Nghi received the top-secret cable informing him that Tran Van Don, the former general and recently appointed minister of defense in the new Nguyen Ba Can government, would arrive at Thanh Son. Don was coming for an inspection, and he arrived at noon on 15 April. Don was not the only visitor. On 13 April, James Lewis, a former Special Forces officer now secretly assigned to the CIA, arrived at Thanh Son. Lewis spoke fluent Vietnamese and knew the area well. He had been stationed at the Nha Trang consulate until the evacuation. Lewis's job at this point was to provide the CIA with information on the situation at Phan Rang.

On the morning of 15 April, after the first Cabinet meeting of Can's government, Defense Minister Don called together ARVN's senior leadership, including Cao Van Vien and Nguyen Van Toan, to formulate a strategy to defend the country. After the meeting, Don and Toan flew to Thanh Son. As Nghi had requested, Colonel Luong took Don and Toan on an inspection tour. The group then returned to the airbase for a more formal briefing by Nghi and his staff.

After Nghi outlined the situation, he requested the return of the 2nd Airborne Brigade, and specifically asked to retain one of the Airborne battalions still present at Phan Rang. Colonel Biet from the Rangers and Brigadier General Nhut, commander of the 2nd Division, then outlined the problems their units faced: lack of supplies, fuel, and equipment, and low morale. Don empathized with his former colleagues, and promised that when he returned to Saigon, he would order the JGS to send Luong's 2nd Brigade back to Phan Rang. He would also try hard to find the equipment the units defending Phan Rang lacked, such as radios, sighting devices and ammunition for the artillery, and fuel for the airplanes and M-113s. Regarding the political rumors, Don told them a partition line would be created to form a new Republic of Vietnam, with Nha Trang as the end point of a line running from Tay Ninh to the coast. To solidify RVN claims to this territory, Don ordered Colonel Luong to retake Nha Trang. A flabbergasted Luong informed Don that it would require the entire Airborne Division to recapture Nha Trang, hardly a feat his two remaining battalions could accomplish. Don and his party, disheartened by the state of affairs at Phan Rang, departed in mid-afternoon.

As night fell on 15 April, and as Nguyen Huu An was preparing to drive a dagger into the heart of Phan Rang's defenses, the South Vietnamese forces in Ninh Thuan province were arrayed in the following manner: The Air Force would provide air support from Thanh Son airbase, while the Navy cutters *Tran Nhat Duat* (HQ-03) and *Tran Binh Trong* (HQ-05) and several other ships sailed along the coast supplying naval gunfire support. Commodore Hoang Co Minh commanded this ad-hoc naval task force.

On the ground, ARVN units were concentrated around Thanh Son airbase. Nhut had his 4th Regiment defending the western side along Route 11, while the 5th Regiment held the area south of the airbase. Since Colonel Luong was in the process of withdrawing, he had placed most of his brigade in close proximity to Thanh Son. He had only three companies from the two remaining Airborne battalions still protecting the Route 1 avenue of approach: one company from the 3rd Battalion was still at Kien Kien, while the two companies from the 11th Battalion had withdrawn south to Ca Du Mountain, the high ground that controlled the western approach to Phan Rang on Route 1. The 31st Ranger Group had one battalion north of the airbase, while the elements of the 52nd Ranger Battalion at Ba Rau also had pulled back to guard the airbase perimeter. (Nguyen Van Tu's 31st Ranger Battalion had been destroyed at the Du Long Pass.) Artillery was limited to a few guns. One battalion of RF troops defended Phan Rang, while another helped secure the airbase.

Only a few ARVN troops stood on Route 1 between the PAVN forces and the city. It is not clear why Nghi left the highway so lightly defended. Perhaps he thought PAVN would be unable to make any direct attack on Phan Rang for another week, since Colonel Le Van Thao's pilots had reported that the bridges on Route 1 from Cam Ranh to the Du Long Pass had been destroyed. Therefore, on the crucial morning of 16 April, at the place at which the South Vietnamese had their last realistic hope of preventing the massive Coastal Column from advancing and participating in the attack against Saigon, the entire ARVN force physically present on Route 1 consisted of one platoon of paratroopers. The remaining Airborne soldiers along Route 1 were dug in on the hills overlooking the highway. After having been conditioned for years in infantry tactics, which in this case meant holding the high ground and covering the road with artillery and airpower, the South Vietnamese were completely unprepared for a high-speed armor attack.

A LIGHTNING STRIKE

Despite An's orders that "absolute secrecy" be maintained, at 2:00 A.M. on 16 April, the orbiting EC-47 radio-intercept plane began picking up clear-text messages being transmitted from a PAVN headquarters element (probably the forward headquarters of the 325th Division) code-named "Red River." The headquarters was trying to coordinate the movement of the various mechanized and infantry units for the attack. The EC-47 landed at Thanh Son and immediately informed Colonel Thao that the Communists planned to launch a large armor assault at 5:00 A.M. Thao quickly informed Sang and Nghi of this new intelligence, and requested permission to bomb the PAVN forces. Sang agreed, and Thao's pilots spent the night flying missions into the Du Long Pass area, attacking enemy convoys on Route 1.

Based on reports from the returning pilots, at 3:00 A.M. on 16 April, Thao informed Nghi that a large number of enemy vehicles were moving through the Du Long Pass. Nghi was stunned. He demanded to know how PAVN had moved so close if the bridges had been knocked out. Sang and Thao were perplexed, and started quizzing some of the pilots. They soon discovered the answer: the over-stressed pilots, afraid of the growing SA-7 threat, had dropped their bombs as close to the bridges as they could and then reported them destroyed. The Army had not destroyed the bridges during the initial retreat, in order to enable the civilian population to escape. Only a few bridges near Kien Kien had been knocked out, leaving many others closer to Phan Rang untouched. Worse, in the absence of instructions, ARVN had failed to wire the bridges with explosive charges so that in an emergency they could be quickly destroyed. It was another major mistake.

While Nghi, Sang, and Thao were absorbing this information, local Communist guerrillas, per Major General An's plan, launched the first attacks. Colonel Luong's troops on the airbase perimeter and on Ca Du Mountain were hit with shelling and infantry probes, as were the Rangers north of the base. Nghi's headquarters had spent the night trying to raise the JGS in Saigon to warn it of the impending attack and to ask for immediate resupply, but his communications team was unable to contact Saigon.

At precisely 5:00 A.M., the Communist artillery batteries opened fire. Explosions shook the foxholes of the Airborne platoon along the shoulders of Route 1 near Kien Kien. Soon the deep-penetration column of tanks, armored personnel carriers, and trucks loaded with infantry rumbled forward and passed through the positions held by the 3rd Division. When the lead tank appeared in front of the ARVN lines, an anti-tank rocket knocked it out, but other tanks quickly returned fire. The PAVN infantry jumped off their vehicles and dispersed the paratroopers, and the column soon resumed its advance down Route 1.

Despite the heavy shelling and the fact that they were exhausted from the previous night's missions, Thao's A-37 pilots took off again. The distance between Thanh Son and the enemy tanks on Route 1 was so short that the pilots barely had time to retract their landing gears before they were dropping bombs. Despite the early-morning fog, the smoke from the artillery rounds, and the heavy barrage of anti-aircraft fire, the pilots pressed in. First one, then another tank was hit. Still the armor kept coming. Repeatedly the A-37s dove in, their bombs setting trucks and tanks on fire. Armed gunships from Le Van But's squadron soon joined the fray. The deep-penetration column, however, fought back hard, blazing away at the A-37s with numerous anti-aircraft weapons. Several planes sustained heavy damage and limped back to base. Despite the air assault, the PAVN tanks grimly pressed on. Bypassing the blown-up bridges near Kien Kien, within an hour, the lead tanks had reached the outskirts of Phan Rang.

The rapid reaction of Thao's airplanes and But's helicopters, however, had dramatically slowed the second part of the lead column, the trucks carrying the rest of the 101st Regiment's infantry. While the armor pushed ahead, the trucks had to stop and take cover from the constant air bombardment. Worse for the North Vietnamese, the anti-aircraft units that were supposed to support them had not kept pace. Consequently, the truck column had outrun its anti-aircraft umbrella but fallen behind the lead armor. Spotting this development, the Air Force bored in, and the North Vietnamese once again felt the sting of Thao's A-37s. According to the 2nd Corps history: "Between 6:00 A.M. and 9:00 A.M. enemy aircraft made thirty-seven bombing sorties attacking the [second] assault formations of 101st Regiment. These attacks destroyed six vehicles, damaged ten other vehicles (including one tank), and killed or wounded a number of cadre and enlisted men. The cadre and soldiers . . . resolutely continued their advance, but the savage air and artillery attacks on the column greatly slowed their progress. . . . The 120th Anti-Aircraft Battalion, however, was still in the Du Long area and its guns did not have sufficient range to cover the skies south of [Ho Diem]. The howitzer positions of 3rd Division and of the [325th's] Artillery Regiment were too far back to reach and paralyze Thanh Son Airbase and had not yet been able to suppress the enemy artillery positions firing from inside the airbase and from the area of Ca Du Mountain."[2]

With his forces caught out in the open, the 325th Division commander personally took control of the two battalions of the 101st Regiment. The 2nd Corps headquarters ordered the air-defense commander to push his units forward to provide cover for the beleaguered infantry, but his units remained too far back to protect the trapped truck column. The advancing armor was slowly being stripped of its badly needed infantry support.

At this moment, the 3rd Division came to the rescue. Following the original plan, after the lead tank element had passed its positions, the troops of the 3rd started attacking. However, after one battalion had captured several villages west of Route 1, moved up close to Thanh Son airbase, and pinned down the Rangers, the regiment deviated from the original plan. It sent another of its battalions to capture Ca Du Mountain and block the Airborne troops from moving down to the road and attacking the advancing armor with anti-tank weapons. The 3rd Division infantrymen then joined the lead element while the 3rd's other regiment advanced on the eastern side of Route 1. With the new infantry reinforcements, the composite force on Route 1 quickly resumed its advance. The attackers soon ran into the last South Vietnamese defenders outside the city, an RF unit dug in outside Phan Rang. After forty-five minutes, they routed the RF, but only after losing two more tanks and dozens of men. Having destroyed the final barrier, the armored column roared into the city and quickly captured the province chief's headquarters. Although the lead element had lost a quarter of its tanks and much of its accompanying infantry, by 7:00 A.M. PAVN controlled the city. Phan Rang had fallen.

Following their battle plan, several tanks and trucks quickly split off from the main column. One group headed for the main port and another to an important bridge on Route 1 just south of the city. Grabbing the bridge in a quick firefight, the Communists continued south and captured a nearby district capital, effectively sealing off the overland escape route. At the port, a T-54 roared onto the dock. Spotting ships desperately fleeing the inner harbor, the tank fired and sank one small ship. Other troops moved out from the city to link up with the rapidly approaching regiment from the 3rd Division advancing along the eastern side of Route 1. By 9:30 A.M., this mixed force had overwhelmed all remaining ARVN resistance and secured the Ninh Chu port. With both ports now in Communist hands and Route 1 cut off, the noose around Nghi's command was rapidly tightening.

As the fighting progressed, Nguyen Huu An moved his forward-headquarters element closer to the battle area. From his position on Route 1, he could see the planes taking off and bombing his troops. With Phan Rang captured, he moved to eliminate the last vestiges of South Vietnamese resistance by ordering the 325th Division to send a combined tank/infantry spearhead from Phan Rang to capture Thanh Son. The division commander in turn ordered the two infantry battalions still struggling down Route 1 to get to Phan Rang immediately.

By 8:45 A.M., a battalion-sized task force made up of infantry and tanks began pushing along Route 11 toward Thanh Son. Standing between Phan Rang and the airbase was Tran Van Nhut's 5th Regiment. Just before the North Vietnamese ran into Nhut's troops, the column divided into two elements; one drove straight into the 5th Regiment, while the other swung around to attack the airbase. The recently formed Communist local-force battalion, coordinating its assault with the main armor thrust, began attacking Nhut's 4th Regiment on Route 11. At the same time, the reinforced 25th Regiment launched its attack on the northern side of the airbase. Using explosives, the infantry cut through eleven rows of barbed wire and charged the airfield. Three North Vietnamese prongs were now converging on the embattled Thanh Son airbase.

On the ARVN side, earlier that morning, Nghi had ordered Nhut to move his headquarters closer to the III Corps Forward Command to facilitate coordination. After completing this move, Nhut left to inspect his units, while Nghi and Sang remained on the airbase monitoring the air strikes. Then at 9:00 A.M., an SA-7 missile fired from a hilltop near the airfield hit a helicopter gunship. Shortly afterwards, several other planes taking off were also hit by anti-aircraft fire. At the same time, the 4th Regiment reported it was engaging enemy forces. According to Sang, "At this point, Lieutenant General Nghi still had confidence in 4th Regiment's ability to protect the airfield and 5th Regiment's ability to stop enemy forces from surging through Gate Number 1 of the airbase."[3] That confidence was misplaced. Nhut's analysis of his troops' morale was correct. Although the 4th easily stopped the local-forces unit, Nhut's hodgepodge 5th Regiment, after a short firefight, broke and ran at the sight of the PAVN armor. Shortly thereafter, Nhut informed Nghi that his 5th Regiment had fled. The tanks soon captured the airbase's main gate. On the other side of Thanh Son, the Rangers were also under heavy artillery and infantry attack. Colonel Biet radioed Nghi that his defenses were collapsing. The 25th Regiment had brushed aside the Rangers guarding the northern gate and captured the bomb-storage area. The Communist soldiers then began moving toward the center of the airfield.

Colonel Luong ordered his reconnaissance company to retake the bomb-storage area, but the vastly outnumbered paratroopers were unable to accomplish their mission. The base defenses continued to crumble, and, soon, camouflaged PAVN soldiers were spotted running on the tarmac. With no other troops available, Luong's deputy brigade commander, Lieutenant Colonel Tran Van Son, led the brigade headquarters company in a mad charge to prevent the enemy from capturing the control tower. Fighting desperately, the paratroopers engaged the PAVN troops, but then a burst of automatic fire hit Lieutenant Colonel Son in the stomach. He died on the spot. The remaining paratroopers were quickly overwhelmed. By 9:30 A.M., PAVN troops from the 101st Regiment, 325th Division, and the 25th Regiment had linked up at the airbase control tower. South Vietnamese resistance had been crushed, and PAVN now controlled Thanh Son.

With no other alternative, Lieutenant General Nghi ordered all elements to retreat toward Ca Na, a rocky peninsula nineteen miles south of Phan Rang. Here Route 1 ran right along the shoreline, and it provided an excellent defensive position. A group of soldiers and civilians soon moved toward the main gate of Thanh Son airbase, but found it blocked by PAVN tanks. Luong ordered his engineers to cut a hole in the fence, and the three officers, Nghi, Sang, and Luong, along with James Lewis and a large group of military and civilians, escaped. Using his own communications, Lewis had managed to inform CIA officers at the U.S. Embassy that Thanh Son was falling. Outside, the group linked up with the portion of the 11th Airborne Battalion that was still near the airbase. Moving slowly because of the civilians in their midst, by noon the group had traveled about three miles and reached a sugar-cane field located between Thanh Son and Phan Rang near Route 11, where they rested in a large irrigation ditch.

Learning of the impending collapse of the Phan Rang front, Airborne Division commander Brigadier General Le Quang Luong, now based in Saigon, sent an O-1 observation plane and twenty-five helicopters to help rescue his soldiers. That afternoon, Colonel Luong's communications team established contact with the orbiting plane. The rescue team requested permission to land the helicopters at a nearby field. Nghi, fearing for the safety of the civilians if they panicked and rushed the helicopters, denied the request. He ordered Colonel Luong to tell the helicopter commander to try again in the morning, when their group would have moved further south. A reluctant Luong passed the order to the circling airplane.

Nghi decided to wait until night to continue moving south, hoping the group would remain undetected. However, the civilians were moving around searching for food, and this alerted the North Vietnamese to the group's presence. Around midnight, Luong ordered an Airborne company to break through the PAVN troops guarding Route 11. Launching a quick attack, the Airborne swept aside a few troops and made it across the road. However, other PAVN soldiers nearby began firing heavily into the underbrush and wounded the 11th Airborne commander. In the darkness and the confusion of the gunfight, Nghi, Sang, and Lewis were separated from the Airborne. While Luong and the Airborne continued heading south, the other three men and a portion of the group returned to the ditch. By 2:00 A.M., troops from the 3rd Division had the ditch surrounded, and an officer soon called on the South Vietnamese to give up. Seeing no alternative, they surrendered. Nghi was the highest-ranking officer ever captured on the battlefields of South Vietnam. Phan Rang, designed as a major ARVN blocking position, had been destroyed. The road south to Saigon and ultimate victory now lay open for the North Vietnamese.

As for the other South Vietnamese who had tried valiantly to hold the Phan Rang line, Lieutenant Colonel Le Van But had escaped with Sang's group. He eventually made it back to Saigon by walking along Route 1. He later jokingly told the author, "I was bombed by my own Air Force the entire way home." At the last minute, just as Thanh Son was being overrun, Colonel Le Van Thao radioed one of his A-37s, which landed and picked him up. They flew to Tan Son Nhut with what remained of Thao's wing. Of the seventy-two A-37s that he had had in early March, only a third of them escaped on 16 April, after more than a month of virtually non-stop fighting. No other unit of the Vietnamese Air Force in the spring of 1975 fought with as much courage or aggression as Thao's 92nd Tactical Air Wing.

Nguyen Van Tu, commander of the 31st Ranger Battalion, escaped on foot with some of his men. They made their way to the sea, where they found fishing vessels that took them to Vung Tau. From there they went by bus to Saigon. Brigadier General Tran Van Nhut escaped by helicopter to a Vietnamese Navy ship offshore. He then radioed JGS headquarters and provided the ARVN command the first news of the disaster at Phan Rang. Colonel Nguyen Thu Luong, although he had crossed Route 11 and was moving south, was ordered the next day by Lieutenant General Toan to return and rescue Nghi and Sang. Luong was captured several days later. The portion of the 11th Airborne Battalion that punched through the ring around the sugar-cane field eventually turned east to find ships. Upon arrival at the coast, however, they were quickly spotted by PAVN troops. Called upon to surrender, they answered with rifle and machine-gun fire. After being pounded with mortars on the exposed beach, they capitulated. The commander of the 3rd Airborne Battalion, Captain La Qui Trang, and his one company out alone on Route 1 retreated to a nearby mountaintop, where they were rescued several days later by helicopters. The rest of his battalion shed their uniforms and moved on foot back to Saigon. Almost 80 percent of the battalion returned safely. Generals Nghi and Sang, along with James Lewis, were quickly taken to Nha Trang, then Danang, and then flown to North Vietnam. Lewis was released in December 1975 after having suffered terrible torture. He returned to active duty, and was killed in the bombing of the U.S. Embassy in Lebanon in 1982. Nghi was released in 1987, but has refused to discuss the events at Phan Rang.

As for Brigadier General Pham Ngoc Sang, he was not released until 1992. His courage inspired his men to stand their ground in the chaotic days of early April. One of his senior staff wrote to him many years later: "I sometimes proudly tell my friends that I was fortunate to serve under a commander such as you—someone who did not, as other commanders and their units did, flee even before the enemy arrived. I must thank you for giving me that source of pride. If it had not been for you, perhaps I would not have been imprisoned, my life might have been easier, and my children might have been more successful in life, but for my entire life I would have carried with me the feeling that I had not lived up to my responsibilities. If we had acted as others did, then we would not have the peace of mind that we enjoy now."[4]

On the Northern side, there was only one notable fatality. The 673rd Air Defense Division commander was killed when his vehicle was accidentally ambushed by local Communist guerrillas. PAVN dodged another major calamity when Nguyen Huu An narrowly escaped death on 16 April. As he later recounted: "This is a funny story, the kind that turns your hair gray. In the afternoon, after we captured Phan Rang and Thanh Son, I visited the [ARVN] 3rd Corps Forward Headquarters [at Thanh Son]. There I selected a new jeep equipped with command radios that I could use to go back to inspect Second Element, 2nd Corps, which was still back at Nha Trang. Hearing about my plans, the deputy commander of Military Region

6 asked if he could hitch a ride with me. At about 10:00 that night it was raining and the road was slick, so we were afraid to drive too fast. The jeep with three of my bodyguards was driving ahead of us, and I was driving a [jeep] with another bodyguard sitting in the back seat. Just after leaving the city, I heard shots, 'Bang, bang.' I thought to myself, 'Those damn kids are shooting off their weapons again, just for the fun of it!' Suddenly I noticed that my vehicle was leaning to one side and I realized we had just been ambushed. I turned off my headlights and drove blindly another mile, and then stopped. When I got out I saw that two of my tires were flat. . . . After an hour the driver of the lead vehicle noticed that I was not behind him and turned back to look for me. We all worked together to repair the vehicle and did not get to Nha Trang until 2:00 A.M."[5]

The fighting left Phan Rang in ruins. As PAVN Major General Le Quang Hoa, the Coastal Column's political officer, put it: "On the morning of 17 April, Le Trong Tan and I entered Phan Rang city. The streets still reeked with the odor of gunpowder. Tanks, armored personnel carriers, military trucks, and artillery pieces, large and small, were lying upended or abandoned everywhere we looked. Many fires still burned that we had not yet had a chance to extinguish. We saw groups of [enemy] soldiers on the streets, all of them acting shocked and stunned. I have had many opportunities to talk to defeated troops, but this time I saw something different in these troops. The difference was that they had suffered an internal collapse, a collapse of their morale and their spirit."[6]

Not only was Hoa was right about ARVN morale, but just as important, a significant number of irreplaceable South Vietnamese units were destroyed in this battle. The 6th Air Division was shattered, the two newly reconstituted 2nd Division regiments were smashed, the 31st Ranger Group was eliminated, and the bulk of the 2nd Airborne Brigade was crushed. On the PAVN side, the 3rd Division and the 25th Regiment had taken the brunt of the casualties, leaving the main 2nd Corps units largely intact.

Still, Giap was taking no chances. He sent a cable congratulating the Coastal Column on its victory, but he urged it to immediately advance. Giap wanted Le Trong Tan's forces to rapidly capture Binh Thuan and Binh Tuy provinces in order to prevent ARVN forces from organizing new blocking positions, and then to assist in the attack on Xuan Loc.

To complete that new mission, Nguyen Huu An ordered all elements to strengthen themselves with newly captured weapons, ammunition, and equipment and prepare to depart. On 17 April, after turning control of Phan

Rang over to MR-6, the 2nd Corps organized a new advance unit of First Element as follows: "5th Armored Battalion, with the soldiers of . . . 18th Regiment riding on the armored vehicles; 15th Battalion of 284th Anti-Aircraft Regiment; one 85-mm gun platoon . . . and one engineer company. . . . The march formation of 325th Division was also reorganized. 18th Regiment moved up to lead the division's formation and, alongside other forces, attack and liberate Phan Thiet and Binh Thuan province. 101st Regiment moved back to the rear of the Division's formation."[7]

After two years of preparations, the North Vietnamese had vehicles and men to spare. The 325th Division simply moved a fresh spearhead—the 18th Regiment and the 5th Armored Battalion—forward to replace the tired units of the 101st Regiment and the 4th Tank Battalion, which had led the charge that took Phan Rang. The 3rd Division was reinforced by another thousand new recruits, who had departed from Haiphong on 16 April and landed three days later at Cam Ranh Bay. Major General An also attached to the division a battery of 130-mm guns and a tank company, and gave it a new mission: while the 2nd Corps would proceed to Saigon, the 3rd Division would move independently and liberate Phuoc Tuy province and the port city of Vung Tau.

For the new First Element, the movement to Phan Thiet along Route 1 would not be easy. Unlike the road march from Danang, the corps would now have to fight its way through areas still under South Vietnamese control. The First Element would have to destroy RF blocking positions, repair destroyed bridges, and fight off air raids. At the same time, it had "to strike back at counterattacks by the enemy Navy and guard against the possibility the enemy might launch an attack from the sea to cut our troop column in two."[8] In addition, the section of the highway at the Ca Na Bay ran right along the seacoast, where the corps would be vulnerable to naval gunfire. But Le Trong Tan could not allow the South Vietnamese to slow him down. His orders were to be in an assembly area near Xuan Loc by 25 April. It is 190 miles from Phan Rang to Xuan Loc, and Tan had nine days to get there.

An placed the 203rd Tank Brigade commander in control of the lead element. To facilitate control, the "brigade command post advanced just to the rear of the lead armored battalion. . . . As the advance guard of 2nd Corps, at this time the 203rd Brigade was responsible for commanding all attached units and performed the role of a combined-arms force commander. To ensure that the road was cleared and the corps could advance quickly, the brigade commander ordered the lead armored units to engage and drive right on through any light enemy resistance encountered along the route. Only if the enemy force was powerful should the armored units stop to organize a strong, certain attack."[9]

At 6:00 P.M. on 17 April the new First Element of the 2nd Corps moved out. It immediately came under attack by South Vietnamese forces. As the corps history notes: "The enemy detected our movement down Route 1 toward Saigon. They attacked our column with aircraft and naval gunfire, destroying a number of vehicles, killing, and wounding a number of cadre and soldiers. . . . On the night of 17 April, in spite of repeated attacks by enemy aircraft and warships, and enemy mines, roadblocks, and destroyed bridges, 5th Armored Battalion, supported by local armed forces and civilians, liberated a string of district capitals . . . and crushed and scattered many outposts along the battalion's route of advance."[10]

At Ca Na Bay, Route 1 winds its way down from the mountains and runs along the sea. Here was a natural chokepoint that the South Vietnamese Navy and Air Force could use to halt the PAVN armor. Unfortunately, the Navy's main ships did not have the armament to provide effective naval gunfire, especially without observers to adjust the rounds. Plus, the Navy's priority was to rescue escaping civilian and military personnel. One LST, the *Vung Tau* (HQ-503), was sent on 17 April to Ca Na Bay to pick up some 2nd Division soldiers who had escaped from Phan Rang. Unable to beach his ship because of the rocky shoreline, the captain of the *Vung Tau*, Nguyen Van Loc, paid some local fishermen to shuttle the men to his ship. Just after the rescue was completed, Communist gunners spotted the *Vung Tau*. A number of artillery rounds hit it, severely wounding the captain and heavily damaging his ship.[11] The cutter *Ngo Quyen* (HQ-17) moved in to fire back, but artillery shells soon bracketed HQ-17, and it retreated.

On 18 April, units of the 2nd Corps fought several intense battles in the Ca Na Bay section of Route 1. When Second Element reached the area, a number of South Vietnamese Navy ships appeared offshore and began shelling Route 1 where it ran along the seashore. The *Chi Linh* (HQ-11)—one of the smaller Patrol Escort ships, built thirty years before and equipped with only one three-inch gun—spotted the Communist tanks driving down Route 1 near the district seat. Despite being hopelessly outgunned, the HQ-11's captain, Lieutenant Commander Phan Dinh San, crept in close. The ship fired over one hundred rounds onto the road trying to stop the advancing column. To make his gunfire more effective, San maneuvered his ship even closer to the beach. As the *Chi Linh* moved in, PAVN struck back. The 2nd Corps ordered the 164th Artillery Brigade to deploy 130-mm and 122-mm guns in a direct-fire mode. Soon, the HQ-11 was under heavy fire. The captain later wrote: "Enemy tanks fiercely returned fire toward HQ-11; about 3:45 P.M., a shell directly hit the starboard of HQ-11 near the stern, damaging the crew quarters. A shell fragment killed Chief Petty Officer Nguyen Van Bang when he climbed up the mid-deck via a panel to install an alternate antenna cable. His head was blown away and his heavy body dropped into the crew quarters."[12] The damage to his ship forced San to retreat.

With no senior ARVN commander or staff officer coordinating the various ground, naval, and air elements, these scattershot attempts to slow the PAVN advance were hopeless. Even if the South Vietnamese Navy had massed all the ships it had in the area, the combined firepower was minimal. The former U.S. Coast Guard cutters were armed with only one five-inch gun, and the smaller Patrol Escort ships had only one three-inch gun. Even if Hoang Co Minh had sent the four cutters under his command to Ca Na Bay on the morning of 18 April, the firepower of the four cutters combined barely equaled that of a single U.S. destroyer. Moreover, the lead PAVN unit, the 5th Armored Battalion, had already passed through the chokepoint. As for air attack, the Air Force was not capable of flying a significant number of strike missions against the advancing Coastal Column. The PAVN forces were too far away, and the VNAF was heavily occupied hitting Communist forces near Saigon. Moreover, the closest VNAF base, Bien Hoa, was currently under sporadic artillery bombardment.

Undoubtedly Nghi had positioned himself at Thanh Son to boost troop morale in the Phan Rang area, but his headquarters staff and communications should have been in the rear at Phan Thiet. When Nghi and his staff were overrun, and with Phan Thiet under heavy pressure, the next closest major headquarters was III Corps in Bien Hoa, two hundred miles away. There was no South Vietnamese command-and-control organization higher than a district headquarters in the area between Phan Rang and Phan Thiet. The III Corps staff was strained to the limit by the pressures of Communist attacks at Xuan Loc, in the Tay Ninh/Cu Chi area, and on Route 4 south of Saigon. With little coherent information on enemy activities along Route 1, III Corps headquarters failed to coordinate RVNAF defenses in this area. A few brave ship captains, local RF/PF units, and VNAF planes tried to fight, but without a coordinated effort their attempts were useless. The JGS should have taken the reins and synchronized the

South Vietnamese forces, but by this time it was completely demoralized. As a result, by noon on 18 April, the entire First Element had arrived in an assembly area only nine miles from Phan Thiet. It immediately began preparations to attack the provincial capital.

The Binh Thuan province chief, Colonel Ngo Tan Nghia, was one of South Vietnam's better provincial leaders. In March, he had stayed at his post, rallied his Regional and Popular Forces, and fought back against Communist forces attempting to seize Binh Thuan. In early April, implementing President Thieu's orders to hold the remaining land, Lieutenant General Toan had reinforced Nghia's provincial RF battalions with the survivors of the 24th Ranger Group who had walked out of Quang Duc province back on March 21. Later he sent the 6th Regiment, 2nd Division, plus an M-113 troop from the 23rd Division. In addition to these forces, Nghia could call on occasional Air Force and Navy fire support. As with Brigadier General Sang at Phan Rang, Nghia's leadership was the reason the South Vietnamese still held Phan Thiet.

Despite his efforts, however, Nghia's defenses were slowly being compressed. The city was under constant rocket attack, most of the civilian population had fled, and the PAVN armor was rapidly advancing down Route 1. Following Tran Van Tra's previous orders, MR-6 forces had already encircled the city. The 812th Regiment, augmented by a local-force sapper battalion and province guerrillas, had captured the district town of Thien Giao on 9 April, dealing a serious blow to Phan Thiet's northern defenses. Simultaneously, two Communist local-force battalions attacked and slowly pushed back RF units guarding the outlying villages on the western approaches to the provincial capital. Thus, when the 203rd Tank Brigade arrived at the assembly area on 18 April, its commander found an embattled city ripe for "liberation." He met with the local Party leadership, and they worked out a plan to capture Phan Thiet using the same tactics that had been so successful at Phan Rang. PAVN would send the First Element, in coordination with local forces and the 812th Regiment, straight down Route 1 and into Phan Thiet.

At 5:00 P.M., the PAVN armor began moving. In the lead was an advance guard—standard Soviet armor doctrine—of one tank and six APCs. After crossing a bridge over a river north of the city that ARVN had hoped to use as a defensive line, the 5th Armored Battalion, with infantry and local guides riding on the vehicles, punched through. The ARVN forces had no air support and only limited anti-tank weapons. The results were the same as at Phan Rang. Half an hour later, the lead tanks entered the city and quickly captured the town center and the province headquarters. By 10:30 P.M., Phan Thiet had fallen. The Rangers and most of the RF, seeing they were hopelessly outgunned, retreated to the beaches. The 6th Regiment put up almost no resistance. In despair over the destruction of his regiments at Phan Rang, Tran Van Nhut had earlier ordered his men to flee rather than fight when the main Communist attack hit. In his defense, he was trying to save the lives of his men rather than sacrifice them in what he believed was a hopeless cause. As he later wrote: "I was certain that Phan Thiet would be the next city to fall, so I privately instructed [the 6th Regiment commander] to assemble a number of civilian fishing boats to use when evacuation became necessary. I told him to sail to Vung Tau when the time came."[13]

Under intense pressure to continue toward Saigon as fast as possible, the 2nd Corps turned over city administration to local forces and departed that night. The local Communists were not particularly eager to press their advantage, and Nghia, who had escaped to a VNN ship, coordinated the rescue of three thousand of his men from the beaches south of the city. A South Vietnamese RF officer later described the scene: "On the morning of 19 April, although the Communists were in control of Phan Thiet, the area of the ship docks ... and the airfield were still in ARVN hands. The beach was covered with soldiers from every branch of service: airborne, rangers, and 2nd Division troops still stuck after retreating from the battle of Phan Rang, and provincial RF and PF units. ... In the end, thanks to their discipline and patience, all the soldiers present along the beach ... were rescued. At that time the tide was falling, so the large ships had to anchor more than [half a mile] off the coast. However, using LCM landing craft, all the units, even a troop of APCs from the 8th Cavalry Squadron operating in Phan Thiet, were picked up and taken south. ... The Navy ships docked safely at Vung Tau at 3:00 A.M. ... 20 April 1975."[14]

Meanwhile, the Coastal Column continued rolling south. Trying to stop the advancing PAVN, on the night of 19 April ARVN troops blew up a major bridge on Route 1. It made no difference. Within forty-five minutes, PAVN engineers had improvised a ford to enable vehicles to cross. By 20 April the column had arrived at Rung La, a village only twelve miles from the besieged Xuan Loc.

With the arrival of the 2nd Corps at Rung La, all South Vietnamese positions along the central coast, from Quang Tri to Ham Tan, had fallen to the

PAVN armor. By 3:00 A.M. on 24 April, the entire 2nd Corps was gathered in the assembly area near Xuan Loc. For Nguyen Huu An, it was a incredible accomplishment, one of which he was justifiably proud: "The corps had moved through three different enemy military regions, including eleven provinces and eighteen cities and towns. We had covered an average of sixty miles per day, fighting as we advanced. We had fought five infantry battles in coordination with local forces; three division-sized combined-arms battles. We had . . . crushed the long-range defense line protecting Saigon, defeated the enemy's 'withdrawal and consolidation' tactics, and cleared Route 1 from Hue all the way down to the gates of Saigon. The entire corps arrived at the assembly area exactly at the time specified in the General Staff's time schedule."[15]

Another arm of General Van Tien Dung's mighty army had arrived to face the beleaguered ARVN forces defending Saigon.

17

"I WILL KNOCK THEM DOWN!"

ARVN HOLDS AT XUAN LOC

Le Duan sensed the death throes of the South Vietnamese state in the anarchy that engulfed Danang. On 29 March he sent the message to Pham Hung telling him to "act with great timeliness, determination, and boldness," giving Tran Van Tra the opportunity he had dreamed about. In fact, it was a characteristic Le Duan message: more strategic guidance and high-level thinking than precise details or, in this case, an actual authorization to attack. Nonetheless, Tra had taken full advantage of Le Duan's ambiguity, and now, while the Coastal Column was barreling down Route 1, the 4th Corps was assembling in the dense brush and banana plantations of Long Khanh province.

What made Xuan Loc the focal point for the PAVN attack was its strategic location. The city, situated thirty-seven miles northeast of Saigon, controlled Dau Giay, the vital junction of Routes 1 and 20, two of the three main paved highways that linked Saigon with the eastern part of the country. With the destruction of I and II Corps, Xuan Loc had suddenly become a critical node on the improvised defensive line the desperate South Vietnamese were trying to form around Saigon. Most observers realized that whatever slim chance ARVN had of defending the capital from the encircling enemy was predicated on holding Xuan Loc. If ARVN could make a stand there, a chance remained that it could regroup its battered forces and save the country from defeat. Because of its importance, Xuan Loc would soon become the site of the fiercest battle of the 1975 offensive.

After the meeting with Tra on 2 April, Hoang Cam and the others returned to the 4th Corps headquarters located near the La Nga Bridge on Route 20, scene of the 18 March battle. On 4 April, Cam ordered the 7th Division, which was near Dalat, to immediately head south to Xuan Loc. Given Tra's pressure to move rapidly, and with only five days before the opening barrage, Cam decided on the simplest of tactical plans: a frontal assault on the provincial capital. The strategy was to "use a portion of the corps infantry forces, together with all the corps's tanks and artillery, to launch a direct attack on the Province Military Headquarters and 18th Division. If the enemy collapsed, we would be able to quickly capture Xuan Loc. 7th Division was assigned the mission of mounting the main attack, striking from the east to seize the 18th Division's headquarters. 341st Division would be responsible for the secondary attack, striking from the north to take the Long Khanh Province Headquarters and other targets in the city."[1]

A frontal assault was an odd choice for Cam, since he had just witnessed the failure of the same tactical plan at Chon Thanh. He wrote: "It was obvious that we held a position of strength [at Chon Thanh], but our forces were not employed properly in this attack. Of particular importance was that we had underestimated our enemy and that our preparations for battle had been too cursory. This kind of mistake in the future could cause us to fail to accomplish our mission or [lead] to our paying too high a price for the accomplishment of the mission."[2] He felt the same way about Xuan Loc: that it was too late to attack the city, since the South Vietnamese had prepared their defenses. He was also concerned about the condition of the 7th Division, which had been worn down by continuous fighting. Yet for some unexplained reason he did not deviate from his plan for a frontal assault. Perhaps he hoped the ARVN soldiers were so badly shaken that they would flee at the first sound of gunfire.

Although the 7th was too far away to conduct any reconnaissance of the area, the 341st was close by, and it made a complete analysis of its attack area. The first step was for the commanders to meet with local Party officials. They discussed the terrain, and possible scenarios they might encounter during the offensive. They agreed that local guerrillas would act as guides for the assault units. According to the 341st Division history, after the conference "the cadre group was guided by our reconnaissance cells right up to the perimeter wire surrounding the city. Local armed forces selected teams to guide division and regimental reconnaissance personnel into the various military positions within the city. . . . Division Chief of Reconnaissance Le Anh Thien walked right up to the residence of the enemy Province Chief headquarters. . . . The reconnaissance forces laid out the locations of the attack targets [and] the specific points where the enemy perimeter would be breached, and determined the layout of perimeter wires, fences, and obstacles. . . . On 5 April our cadre reconnaissance group made its final reconnaissance through the enemy perimeter wire. The enemy continued normal activities within the city, proving that he still knew nothing about our operations. The enemy did not suspect that for almost a week our reconnaissance soldiers had been concealing themselves on the ground making observations and marking our targets."[3]

After conducting its reconnaissance of the northwestern approaches to Xuan Loc and the city environs, on 6 April the 341st Division commanders met to discuss the attack plan and forward it to the 4th Corps for approval. The corps agreed, and the following missions were assigned: The 266th Regiment would attack targets within the city while the 270th Regiment would strike Kiem Tan and Thi Mountain, which housed an artillery battalion, a communications center, and the ARVN 2nd Battalion, 43rd Regiment. The 273rd Regiment remained with the 9th Division. The 6th Division's two regiments, the 33rd and the 274th, would circle south of the city and attack the Dau Giay road junction and several key points along Route 1 west of Xuan Loc.

While the 7th Division was assigned the primary role in the assault, it had to travel one hundred miles from Lam Dong province. It did not arrive at its assembly area until the night of 7 April. Its orders were to destroy the 48th Regiment and liberate the intersection of Routes 1 and 2 at the village of Tan Phong south of Xuan Loc. As the 7th's staff began planning, suddenly their orders changed. The division was to liberate the city first and only then focus on destroying the 48th. With less than one day to develop a new attack plan, the 7th decided that "the 165th Regiment would lead the primary attack against the 18th Division's rear base and command post in the northeastern part of the city [and the 52nd's base camp].... The 209th Regiment would liberate Route 1 from Suoi Cat [a small village about five miles east of Xuan Loc] to the Tan Phong intersection, attack up from the south into the city, and stand ready to attack enemy... reinforcements. The 141st Regiment would serve as a reserve force."[4]

The 4th Corps shifted its headquarters to a position northeast of Xuan Loc, coordinated artillery fire for all elements, and established supply routes to its three main assault units. It also sent a forward headquarters under Deputy Corps Commander Bui Cat Vu to Chua Chan Mountain east of the city to oversee the attack. H-hour was set for 5:30 A.M. on 9 April. If the PAVN assault on Xuan Loc produced another precipitous ARVN retreat, nothing would stand between the 4th Corps and Saigon except the 1st Airborne Brigade. There would be chaos, trapping thousands of Americans and their South Vietnamese allies, employees, and friends in a defenseless city.

However, Brigadier General Le Minh Dao, commander of the ARVN 18th Division, was waiting for the North Vietnamese assault. After the attacks at Dinh Quan on 18 March, Dao sensed an imminent attack on Xuan Loc. His suspicions had been initially raised in February when a Regional Force outpost on Chua Chan Mountain surprised and killed a 4th Corps artillery survey team. His intuition was reinforced after the battles

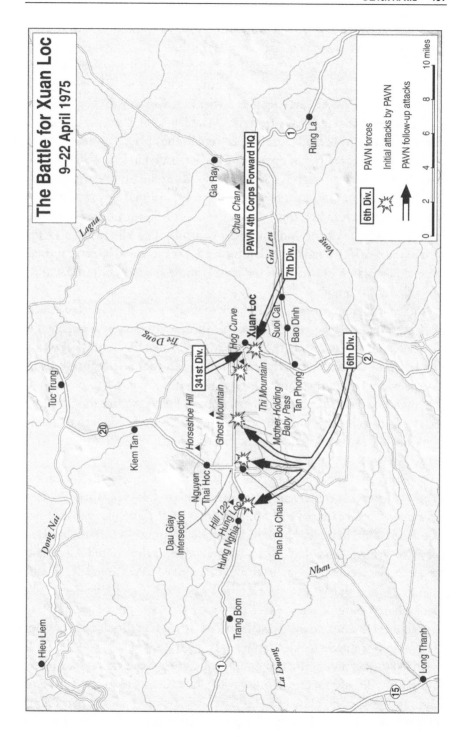

The Battle for Xuan Loc
9–22 April 1975

on Route 20 in late March in which his troops captured several POWs. Interrogating the prisoners, Dao was astonished to see how young they were. Apparently PAVN was scraping the bottom of the manpower barrel in North Vietnam. Many of the captured soldiers were barely sixteen years old, but they were carrying new Soviet Bloc weapons and equipment. When they revealed they were from the 341st Division, Dao had confirmation that three PAVN main-force units were in the area.

In early April, Dao began organizing his defenses. First, he closely examined the terrain around the city. Xuan Loc sits amidst numerous banana and rubber plantations at the base of the southern end of the Annamite Mountains, which march from China toward the South China Sea, forming the backbone of the Indochinese peninsula. The hilly terrain to the west of the city is covered by thick forest and is crisscrossed by several small rivers and streams. To the east, the land is more open, but dominated by Chua Chan Mountain.

While Dao had more than a full week to prepare for the expected attack, his forces were stretched thin. Two of his three regiments were outside the city: the 52nd was guarding the Route 20 area, while the 48th was seventy miles away in Tay Ninh. In early April, he had only the 43rd Regiment, rear-base personnel, his armor, and the division reconnaissance company holding Xuan Loc. Four Regional Force battalions helped secure the northern section of the city and the area around the province headquarters. However, this left Dao's rear wide open, the area south of the city—the exact place the PAVN 7th Division intended to strike.

Dao knew he would need his full division to halt the North Vietnamese attack, whenever it came, and he saw his chance on 3 April when Lieutenant General Toan came to visit him. During a briefing on his preparations, Dao asked Toan to return the 48th Regiment. Toan was reluctant, but Dao persisted, telling Toan that if III Corps expected him to hold Xuan Loc, he needed to secure his rear. To convince Toan, he told a small lie: that he intended to use the 48th to clear Route 1 east from Tan Phong and retake Chua Chan Mountain. Toan agreed to return the 48th, but he ordered Dao to send one battalion to the coastal city of Ham Tan to provide security for the hordes of refugees pouring in from II Corps.

The 48th Regiment returned on 5 April. On 7 April, Dao sent it to clear Route 1 but did not send it all the way to Chua Chan. Leaving the 3rd Battalion in the area, he pulled the 1st Battalion back to hold the Tan Phong intersection south of the city, along with two troops of the 5th Cavalry

Squadron, his organic armored unit. This was his reserve. Meanwhile, Dao was well aware of the disasters in I and II Corps, when entire units collapsed as soldiers deserted to rescue their wives and children. He moved as many of his soldiers' families and the local civilians as he could back to Long Binh, the huge logistics facility near Bien Hoa. Any remaining civilians would stay in bunkers near the province chief's headquarters.

More important, Dao moved his soldiers to the outskirts of the city, thinking the Communist troops would concentrate their opening artillery barrage on the city center. He armed his reconnaissance company with .50-caliber machine guns and stationed it in the high school on the northwestern edge of town. Dao also created three separate command posts: The first was his house in the city; the second was at Tan Phong; and the third was in a nearby orchard. As his soldiers dug in, it dawned on him that the enemy would undoubtedly employ the same routes of advance they had used when they attacked Xuan Loc during the 1968 Tet Offensive, with modifications based on the current situation. This was a correct appraisal.

Therefore, Dao laid a trap for them. Using his artillery, he created what he called the "meat grinder."[5] Dao's artillery chief pre-registered all his artillery, comprising thirty-six guns (twenty-four 105-mms and twelve 155-mms), onto likely avenues of approach. He ordered a bulldozer to dig revetments to protect the guns, and bunkers to pull the guns back into after they fired. Dao also expanded the existing system of bunkers and trenches for the city defenders. He wanted to render the PAVN counter-battery fire ineffective. His efforts ultimately were very successful. He later remarked, "Their artillery could never find us."

Moreover, because ARVN stockpiles of fuel and ammunition, especially artillery shells, were low, beginning in February, Dao had implemented two programs. First, he began secretly stockpiling artillery ammunition (in direct violation of JGS regulations) by reducing his daily artillery expenditure by 20 percent. Second, he formed a long-range reconnaissance platoon in each of his line battalions to assist in finding the enemy. He used the platoons to sweep the areas around Xuan Loc. On 6 April, one platoon ambushed and wiped out an enemy reconnaissance team on Ghost Mountain, the major high point northwest of Xuan Loc. Dao's troops then occupied other hills to prevent the Communists from using them as observation posts.

At noon on 6 April, Dao was informed that the 82nd Ranger Battalion had just been rescued after a harrowing escape through Communist territory. Lieutenant General Nguyen Van Toan ordered the 82nd Rangers ferried by helicopter to Xuan Loc, where Dao gave them food and ammunition, stationed them at the local airfield, and put them under the nominal control of the 43rd Regiment. Toan told Dao that the 82nd would be sent to Saigon for reconstitution the next morning. Little did the Rangers know they had walked out of the frying pan and into the proverbial fire.

As night fell on 8 April, Dao's forces were arrayed in the following manner: The 52nd Regiment and one troop of APCs from the 5th Cavalry were defending Route 20 and the vital Dau Giay road intersection. One battalion was stationed south of Dau Giay at the small hamlet of Phan Boi Chau. The northernmost element was a company on top of Horseshoe Hill, a small hill on the eastern side of Route 20 near Ghost Mountain. The 2nd Battalion, 43rd Regiment, defended Thi Mountain, the high ground on the western side of Xuan Loc. This left a worrisome gap in the lines between the 52nd and the city, which Dao could cover only by artillery. The division's reconnaissance company held the high school on the northwestern approach to the city, with two Regional Force battalions on their right flank. Two other RF units occupied positions inside the city. The 1st and 3rd Battalions of the 43rd Regiment were on the eastern approaches to Xuan Loc. The 1st Battalion, 48th Regiment, and the other two troops of the 5th Cavalry were in reserve, while the 2nd Battalion was detached for guard duty at Ham Tan. The 3rd Battalion was positioned astride Route 1 leading east out of the city. The 82nd Rangers were holding the Xuan Loc airfield.

During the morning hours of 9 April the PAVN attack elements moved into position. The 6th Division crossed Route 2 south of Xuan Loc undetected and moved rapidly through the rubber plantations north toward Route 1. The 7th and 341st Divisions moved up close to the ARVN perimeter wire. By 5:00 A.M. all elements had reported to the 4th Corps that they were in their assigned assault positions. The PAVN artillery completed preparations and waited for the order to commence firing. In the 341st's sector, right before the scheduled opening barrage, artillery observers noticed that the overnight fog had not adequately lifted, and they requested a ten-minute postponement. The 4th Corps approved the delay. At 5:40 A.M., the 4th Corps radioed the signal, and with an ear-shattering roar, the corps and divisional artillery opened fire simultaneously. The battle for Xuan Loc had begun.

One of the first artillery shells landed directly on Brigadier General Dao's home. It was a small two-story house that sat across the road from the province chief's residence, near the Catholic church in the middle of Xuan Loc. The round crashed through the roof and exploded in the bedroom, a testimony to the incredible accuracy of the North Vietnamese artillerymen. Fortunately, Dao was not at home. For an hour the PAVN batteries rained artillery shells, mortars, and rockets on the city. They hammered the city center and pounded many buildings into rubble. However, despite their prior reconnaissance, the Communists had failed to spot the movement of the ARVN forces to the outskirts. Most of the shells struck civilian targets in the town, leaving Dao's troops sitting unscathed in their bunkers and trenches. Two thousand rounds poured onto the exposed city. Then, at 6:40 A.M., two red flares flashed into the early-morning sky. The signal for the infantry and tanks to advance had been given, and the cadres and peasant soldiers of the 341st and 7th Divisions began to close with the waiting South Vietnamese troops.

In the eastern sector, the 165th Regiment led the onslaught. Four tanks joined it, with another four assigned to the 209th Regiment. Believing the South Vietnamese troops would run as soon as the artillery barrage lifted, the North Vietnamese soldiers confidently pressed forward. Instead, the men of the ARVN 18th Division held fast. The eastern side of the town was fairly open ground, and Dao had prepared for a combined tank and infantry attack by constructing strong defensive works. The assault elements of the 7th would have to move uphill across open fields, penetrate eight barbed-wire barriers, navigate several minefields, and scale an earthen berm before finally reaching the trench lines held by ARVN soldiers.

At a signal, the concealed ARVN infantry started pouring artillery and automatic-weapons fire onto the exposed North Vietnamese. The 165th's first infantry attack quickly bogged down. The lead T-54 hit an anti-tank mine, which blew off its left track and left it sitting helpless. As dawn broke, VNAF jets began making air strikes against the exposed PAVN troops.

Despite the heavy fire, the North Vietnamese mounted a second charge. As the tanks pressed forward, the soldiers of the 43rd Regiment had another surprise waiting for them: 2.75-inch rockets, normally used by helicopter gunships, mounted on bipods and fired using simple electrical batteries. Between the air strikes and the rockets, the RVNAF knocked out two enemy tanks and stopped the attack. The PAVN 209th Regiment, assigned to clear Route 1 from the east into town, ran into the 82nd Ranger Battalion at the airfield. The 82nd fought two battalions of the 209th to a standstill and destroyed two more tanks.

Hoang Cam's main assault force was pinned down. The attacks had been halted not only by air strikes and artillery, but by determined infantry. Dao had assigned every single soldier in the division to a defensive position. As he later explained, "All my men fought. Even the rear staff officers and base camp personnel dug defensive positions. Plus, many of the invalids, men who were to be demobilized or had been previously wounded, were given weapons and defensive positions. These men also fought well and killed many of the enemy soldiers."

The 341st Division on the western side of Xuan Loc initially fared better. With less open terrain and having spent time reconnoitering routes into the city, the 266th Regiment quickly breached the five barbed-wire-fence lines. Its targets were the high school, the marketplace, and the Catholic church. The division commander personally accompanied the 266th during the attack. However, ARVN artillery soon began hitting the PAVN soldiers, while a C-119 gunship laid a stream of tracers along the breach. As the enemy troops came into range, the reconnaissance company in the high school ripped apart the inexperienced soldiers with heavy machine-gun fire. The green troops of the 266th tried to open a second breach point to the east and ran straight into the two RF units, who also held their ground. Finally, after suffering extremely heavy casualties, elements of the 266th managed to bypass the high school and infiltrate about three hundred yards into the town, where they occupied positions near the market square, the church, and the province sector headquarters. Despite the PAVN penetrations, from Dao's perspective, his reconnaissance company had stopped an entire regiment.

The 341st Division's history claims that by 7:40 A.M. it had captured several positions in the city—including the parking lot near the church, the province chief's house, and the marketplace in the city center—but it admits that ARVN still held most of the city. Further out to the west, the PAVN 270th Regiment had hit Thi Mountain, but it was also driven back, leaving dozens of dead on the battlefield.

Wasting no time, at 11:00 A.M., Dao launched a counterattack outside of the city. He used his reserve force—the 1st Battalion, 48th Regiment, and the armor from the 5th Cavalry—to attempt to encircle the enemy soldiers who had penetrated into the city. The 270th Regiment immediately launched an attack to halt Dao's maneuver, and succeeded in preventing the 266th from being surrounded. Still, the 266th's situation was precarious. While some soldiers of the 266th managed to cling to a few buildings, at the end of the first day, the 341st Division had taken very heavy casualties, close to six hundred men dead and wounded.

Of the three PAVN divisions, the 6th was the most successful because it faced the least opposition. The 274th Regiment attacked and occupied the colorfully named Mother Holding Baby Pass, thus blocking Route 1 between Xuan Loc and the Dau Giay intersection. It struck precisely where Dao had no troops, and in doing so, it cut Dao off from his 52nd Regiment. The 33rd Regiment, meanwhile, attacked the hamlets of Hung Nghia and Hung Loc on Route 1 on the western side of Dau Giay. They grabbed Hung Loc but were repulsed by Popular Forces at Hung Nghia. An attack on the Dau Giay intersection was defeated by the 1st Battalion, 52nd Regiment dug-in nearby at the Phan Boi Chau hamlet. However, the 52nd was now cut off from both Xuan Loc and Saigon.

By afternoon the battlefield was so calm Dao became worried that the enemy was massing for another attack. This time he was wrong. The North Vietnamese had taken close to seven hundred dead and wounded while the South Vietnamese had suffered only fifty casualties. The stiff resistance rocked the Communists. According to the *History of the People's Army*, "Enemy aircraft taking off from Bien Hoa . . . pounded Xuan Loc with bombs. The battle became a hard, vicious struggle. Our units suffered a high number of casualties . . . our artillery ammunition was seriously depleted. More than half our tanks were knocked out."[6]

Throughout the night, the North Vietnamese struggled to resupply their troops in town and on the outskirts. The 4th Corps believed that it held half the city and had cut Route 1 from the Dau Giay intersection to the Mother Holding Baby Pass, but it acknowledged that the 7th Division had failed to take its objectives.

Also that night, the forward units reported back to the 4th Corps headquarters that while they had suffered losses, the first day had gone well. Hoang Cam decided to stick with the same tactics the next day: frontal assault. However, he was worried: "That night, Bui Cat Vu sent me a cable . . . asking my approval to commit his reserve force to the battle. I thought it was a bit early to commit the reserve, but I approved his request."[7]

With Cam's permission, the 7th Division would commit its reserve, the 141st Regiment plus an anti-aircraft battalion in a direct-fire role. The

165th Regiment and more tanks would also resume their attack, as would the 209th. The 341st Division would move the 270th Regiment into Xuan Loc to support the battered battalions from its sister regiment holed up on the edge of the town. The corps and division artillery would fire another opening barrage early in the morning to support the ground attack.

At 5:27 A.M. on 10 April the Communist batteries opened fire, pouring one thousand rounds into the smoking city. The 7th Division forces launched repeated onslaughts against the ARVN fortifications east of the city but could not make any headway against the 82nd Rangers or the dug-in 43rd Regiment. On the western side of the city, the 270th launched five assaults against the Regional Forces near the marketplace. Each time it was thrown back. Hand-to-hand fighting broke out at one point, as "a savage battle using hand grenades and bayonets ensued."[8] Four more T-54s were destroyed. South Vietnamese artillery, supported by effective air strikes, continued to inflict heavy casualties.

As the afternoon wore on, Dao counterattacked again. Seeing that the two regiments of the 341st were pinned down inside the city, Dao moved to attack from both inside and outside the city. This second counterattack was too much for the teenaged soldiers of the 341st. Under continual fire and taking heavy casualties after two days of fierce battle, many frightened PAVN soldiers lost their will to fight and began hiding in cellars and collapsed buildings. According to General Cao Van Vien, "They did not know the terrain and were afraid of the fighting and of the artillery. After penetrating the city, they hid in the sewers and did not fire any of their seventy-round basic ammunition load."[9]

One by one ARVN forces cleared the buildings PAVN had captured the day before. By nightfall on 10 April, Xuan Loc was totally in South Vietnamese hands, but the northern part of town was a smoldering ruin. An American journalist, Philip Caputo, wrote: "Almost every building has been damaged, and the town center reduced to rubble. The streets are pocked with 130-millimeter shells that come whistling in from the green, brooding hills to the north. What once were houses are now heaps of pulverized stone and charred timbers. The market, its tin-roofed stalls twisted into weird shapes, looks like a junk yard, and the bus station, where the initial fighting took place, is recognizable as such only by the blackened skeletons of a few buses. Even the Catholic Church steeple has not escaped. Like the ruin of some ancient tower, it looks over the wreckage, over the flames, and over corpses, bloated and rotting in the sun, of North Vietnamese soldiers that lay here and there in the odd positions of death. 'It looks like a city from the Second World War,' said one South Vietnamese soldier."[10]

The evening provided no respite for the tired ARVN soldiers, as Communist artillery fire blasted away the entire night. PAVN fired another two thousand rounds into the city during the night. The 18th Division responded with counter-battery fire, trying to disrupt the PAVN concentrations. The 341st Division history noted: "The enemy bombarded our artillery positions while simultaneously bombarding the routes from our rear bases into the city. C-130 gun-ships [sic] fired streams of 20-mm shells into our positions. The enemy hoped to lay down a curtain of fire to block our efforts to re-supply our forces with ammunition and evacuate our wounded."[11]

Despite the heavy casualties, the PAVN commanders would not relent. On the morning of the third day, they resumed their attacks. The 4th Corps ordered the 341st Division to shift its attack to hit the 43rd Regiment and link up with the 7th Division. The 7th was also ordered to resume its assault.

At 5:30 A.M. on 11 April, the PAVN artillery fired a thirty-minute barrage on the 43rd's positions. The results were the same. The dogged ARVN defenders threw back the attack columns of both divisions. ARVN counterattacks stopped any penetrations and reclaimed lost ground. By the end of the day, PAVN had again not taken the city, and North Vietnamese casualties were extremely heavy and growing. Cam wrote, "This was the most ferocious battle I had ever been involved in! My personal assessment was that, after three days of battle, even after committing our reserves, the situation had not improved and we had suffered significant casualties." In a footnote, Cam provides figures, which match those in the *History of the People's Army*: "During the first three days of the battle 7th Division suffered 300 casualties and the 341st Division suffered 1,200 casualties.... Virtually all of our 85-mm and 57-mm artillery pieces had been destroyed."[12] Meanwhile, the ARVN 18th Division had suffered only one hundred dead and wounded. Dao's thorough preparation, the effective air strikes and artillery fire, and his stalwart leadership were the most important factors in defeating the PAVN attacks in the first few days.

The South Vietnamese Joint General Staff realized the critical importance of Xuan Loc. It was not only an essential defensive position, but also potentially a crucial morale builder. If ARVN could inflict a significant defeat on PAVN at Xuan Loc, the military crisis might be averted. Lieutenant General Toan's battle plan for the defense of Saigon was to use his mobility to concentrate forces at points under assault and destroy enemy formations. On 11 April Toan recalled the 3rd Armored Calvary Brigade from Tay Ninh and sent it to reopen Route 1 from the village of Hung Nghia to the Dau Giay intersection. At the same time, the battalion guarding Ham Tan was rushed back by helicopter to Xuan Loc.

The 3rd Armored reached Hung Nghia on 11 April and immediately ran into a 6th Division roadblock on Route 1 east of the village. Brigadier General Khoi deployed his forces so that one of his task forces made the main attack along Route 1, while he maneuvered a second task force to the north. Khoi's units, however, were unable to break through.

More important, on the morning of 11 April, Toan began moving the 1st Airborne Brigade, commanded by Lieutenant Colonel Nguyen Van Dinh, to reinforce the 18th Division. The 1st Airborne was one of the last units in the ARVN strategic reserve. For two days, Toan used virtually every available transport helicopter left in the fleet to move three battalions of Airborne infantry and an artillery battalion into an area near Tan Phong. It was the last major helicopter assault of the war. One South Vietnamese source notes: "Every helicopter in VNAF's 3rd and 4th Air Divisions, a total of one hundred Huey's, moved more than two thousand Airborne troops . . . into the battle. Airborne artillery platoons were transported by Chinook helicopter to the Airborne Headquarters, which was located adjacent to the 18th Division Headquarters. Two airborne battalions were landed on top of enemy troops to recapture Route 1."[13] Civilians and wounded soldiers were sent out on the empty helicopters.

Dao also made an internal move to bolster his defenses. Although cut off and under artillery fire, the 52nd Regiment still held a line running from south of the Dau Giay intersection at Phan Boi Chau hamlet, moving north up Route 20 to its furthermost position on Horseshoe Hill. Other than the 1st Battalion at Phan Boi Chau, none of the other elements had faced any infantry attacks. However, the 1st Battalion was under constant pressure from the enemy. The hamlet consisted of brick houses in the middle of a rubber plantation and was an easy target for artillery. Round after round poured in on the ARVN defenders. When the artillery let up, the infantry would attack. The 1st Battalion repulsed many attacks, but it was taking heavy casualties to accomplish its mission.

Despite this pressure on the 1st Battalion, on the morning of 10 April, Dao ordered the 2nd Battalion, 52nd Regiment, to move from Dau Giay and reinforce Xuan Loc. After sneaking through enemy lines, the battalion broke through and joined the 43rd Regiment on the afternoon of 12 April. Also on 12 April, an Airborne battalion fought a difficult engagement south of Xuan Loc against a battalion of the 7th Division. On 13 April Dao moved the other two Airborne battalions along Route 1 to assault the 7th Division east of the city. One of the Airborne battalions attacked and punched a hole in the 7th Division's lines at the village of Bao Dinh, enabling the other battalion to move forward and surround the 8th Battalion, 209th Regiment.[14] Despite Dao's success to date, these would be his last offensive moves.

DUNG CHANGES TRA'S GRAND DESIGN

After the setbacks in the Delta and at Xuan Loc, Van Tien Dung moved to rein in Tra's grandiose attack plan. The stiff ARVN resistance proved that Dung's earlier analysis was correct. In his role as campaign commander, on 13 April Dung cabled Giap and the General Staff recommending that they now wait until the rest of the army joined them. Dung also told Giap that it was impossible for the 1st and 3rd Corps to arrive in time to attack Saigon by 15 April. There was also a supply problem, particularly of artillery and tank ammunition. Tra's old complaint about lack of supplies had now proven true. As PAVN massed its forces in the B-2 theater, there were not enough resources on hand to sustain heavy combat for this many soldiers.

The Politburo reluctantly agreed to delay the attack. Le Duan cabled Dung to begin his attack no later than the last week of April. Giap followed up with another cable, telling Dung that "The overall attack plan must guarantee that once the action begins there will be powerful, continuous attacks, one on top of the other, until complete victory. . . . Initiating attacks in the outlying areas and keep[ing] forces prepared to seize the opportunity to strike deep into the center of Saigon from many directions. . . . This is the fundamental direction, and the one most certain to win."[15] The Politburo also wholeheartedly approved Dung's recommendation that the upcoming campaign be named after Ho Chi Minh.

Seeing the number of ARVN reinforcements flung into the battle, the PAVN leadership began to reassess the situation and make new plans. Much to Tra's dismay, reports also began reaching him that the 4th Corps had been forced to retreat. After the euphoria of the first positive reports, Tra became very worried. The 4th Corps "complained about shortages of ammunition of all kinds, and especially that the [341st], 6th, and 7th

Divisions were under-strength because they had fought continuously since the fighting along Route 20 began."[16] On the afternoon of 11 April, after a discussion between Tran Van Tra, Van Tien Dung, Le Duc Tho, and others, Tra was sent to the 4th Corps headquarters to assess the situation and, if need be, to assume command. Moreover, he was carrying new tactical instructions with him.

For Tra, it must have been humiliating to see his grand design pulverized by the ARVN resistance, especially with his mentor, Le Duc Tho, and his rival, Van Tien Dung, close by. Additionally, Tra had failed to follow the General Staff's pre-attack instructions to neutralize Bien Hoa airbase before launching the Xuan Loc attack.

Shortly after Tra departed from the B-2 Front headquarters in Tay Ninh, Dung telephoned Hoang Cam and provided him an overview of the new orders. Realizing that ARVN had massed much of its remaining reserves to defend Xuan Loc, Dung and Tra recognized that Dao's position had two weaknesses. One was his dependence on the Bien Hoa airbase to provide air support, and the other was that the 52nd Regiment holding the Dau Giay intersection was isolated and outside of his main defensive network. Dung later wrote: "Once the enemy had amassed troops to . . . save Xuan Loc, we need not concentrate our forces and continue attacking them head-on. We should shift our forces to strike counterattacking enemy units in the outer perimeter . . . before they could get their feet on the ground. We should use our long-range artillery to destroy Bien Hoa airbase . . . so enemy fighter planes could not take off."[17] PAVN would now use maneuver to gain what it had failed to achieve with frontal assaults.

After Dung's phone call, the 4th Corps held a meeting on the afternoon of 11 April to review the situation. Strangely, and despite Dung's verbal instructions, Cam launched two more frontal attacks on 12 April. The first attack, which began before dawn, hit the northeastern edge of the city and lasted until 9:30 A.M. The VNAF used C-130s in a bomber role, with stacks of 750-pound bombs strapped onto wooden pallets and rolled out the rear cargo hatches. The ARVN artillery again fired with devastating effect. After the North Vietnamese troops retreated, ARVN counted 235 enemy dead. At noon the North Vietnamese mounted a second attack, again throwing the depleted units of the 341st Division against the dug-in ARVN. VNAF aircraft flew twenty sorties against the North Vietnamese, breaking up their formations even before they could reach the ARVN positions. Dao noticed that during the last attacks, after having suffered frightful casualties, troops had to be literally pushed out of their foxholes by their commanders. It was little wonder. PAVN losses were climbing toward a reported two thousand dead and wounded in only four days of fighting, while ARVN dead and wounded were only several hundred. Dao and the 18th Division had turned Xuan Loc into a blood-drenched killing ground.

However, after the battle on 12 April, as part of the new tactical plan, the 4th Corps received additional tanks, artillery pieces, and fresh troops. Tra notes that "the Corps had been reinforced [with] . . . a tank company, and a number of field artillery and anti-aircraft pieces, and had urgently brought in reinforcements and ammunition, so we still had good fighting strength."[18] That evening, the 4th Corps ordered the 341st Division to pull away from the outskirts of the city; by nightfall, the division's regiments had shifted positions. Meanwhile, the 6th Division remained in place, while units of the 7th Division attempted to hold off the advancing Airborne.

More ominous for Dao, however, was the secret arrival on 13 April of the 95B Regiment from the Central Highlands. When the 4th Corps ran into difficulty, Dung ordered the regiment south. Calling for this unit signaled his deep concerns. It would eventually have the distinction of being the only PAVN unit to be attached to all four corps during the 1975 offensive. Throwing it against the exhausted ARVN troops could easily turn the tide at Xuan Loc.

Tra arrived at 4th Corps headquarters on 13 April and met with the command staff. In analyzing the situation, Tra and the other PAVN officers "reached a clear-cut conclusion: Xuan Loc was an extremely important point on the enemy's defensive line, so they had concentrated many forces to defend it. . . . We no longer had the element of surprise. Thus, it was not to our advantage to continue to attack Xuan Loc."[19] However, "If we took and held the Dau Giay intersection . . . Xuan Loc would no longer be a key strongpoint because it lay outside the defensive line. . . . Thus, we would make two moves: One, concentrate our attack on Dau Giay from two directions. Second, we would withdraw from Xuan Loc." Tra realized that as long as the 18th had effective air support, his troops would have an extremely difficult time taking the ruined city. He planned to covertly move 130-mm artillery within range of the Bien Hoa airbase and shell it in order to paralyze the airfield.

As the North Vietnamese began pulling back from the city outskirts on the night of 12 April, Dao quickly pushed forward and reoccupied the previously taken outlying areas. The 18th Division also began replenishing its supplies. On the afternoon of 12 April, the VNAF flew in ninety tons of artillery ammunition on eight Chinooks. The next day, Dao moved in another one hundred tons of provisions, including food and small-arms ammunition.

The South Vietnamese government attempted to use the 18th's stand as a morale booster for its frightened populace and dispirited military. Badly needing a propaganda lift after the previous debacles, the government organized a press visit to the embattled provincial capital to showcase its triumph. On 13 April, a bright Sunday morning, the first Western correspondents flew into town via Chinook helicopters. They landed at the village of Tan Phong, where they received a briefing from a defiant Le Minh Dao, who vowed to "knock down" any PAVN division sent against him. The journalists walked into Xuan Loc along Route 1 and surveyed the destruction in the northern part of the city, wrecked by five days of constant combat. The 43rd Regiment's commander, Colonel Le Xuan Hieu, provided a tour of the market square, pointing out dead enemy soldiers and displaying mounds of captured weapons and a few POWs. Communist artillery rounds continued to hit sporadically, sending plumes of black smoke skywards. One newsman wrote that "Artillery barrages and savage street fighting have reduced entire blocks to piles of white ash, blackened bricks and twisted metal. . . . Xuan Loc's once-bustling central market is now a pile of rubble about two feet high."[20]

Unfortunately, the journalists' helicopter departure was a potential public-relations nightmare for the South Vietnamese. Local civilians scrambled to gain seats on the Chinooks, only to be knocked aside by a few ARVN stragglers desperate to escape the fighting. ARVN litter bearers, overrun by the anxious crowd, unceremoniously dumped several wounded men on stretchers onto the ground, while the American journalists pushed and elbowed their way onto the overloaded helicopters.[21] Given the rough return journey, the journalists' stories were surprisingly generous to the 18th Division soldiers.

While the South Vietnamese government proclaimed its success, as night fell on 12 April, the North Vietnamese were maneuvering their forces for their next move, an assault against the Dau Giay intersection. On 13 April, massive artillery attacks and large infantry assaults pushed the weakened defenders out of the hamlet of Phan Boi Chau back to the very edge of Dau Giay. That night, the ARVN 52nd Regiment commander ordered two companies of the 3rd Battalion to link up with the 1st Battalion and pull it out of Dau Giay. Moving at night through the dense brush, the 3rd Battalion successfully rescued what was left of the 1st Battalion. Only a third of the battalion remained after five days of shelling and attacks by the PAVN 33rd Regiment. Dau Giay was now undefended. Surrounded and unable to evacuate its wounded or receive supplies, the rest of the 52nd was now in an increasingly precarious position. Losing the 2nd Battalion when Dao pulled it back on 10 April had seriously weakened the regiment's defenses. Dao had felt he needed the additional troops to bolster his defenses in Xuan Loc, but moving the battalion was one of his few tactical mistakes.

With the retreat of the 1st Battalion, the 3rd Armored attempted once more to link up with the 52nd Regiment. Given the importance of opening the road, Brigadier General Khoi decided to bypass the roadblock. He sent a column comprising a Ranger battalion and an Armor troop on a flanking maneuver to the north of Hung Loc to link up with the 52nd Regiment at its location at the hamlet of Nguyen Thai Hoc on Route 20 just north of Dau Giay.

By mid-day on 14 April, Khoi's troops had successfully captured Hill 122, the high ground north of Hung Loc, scattering light PAVN resistance. However, the first of several streams halted the armor, forcing them to wait while the engineers attempted to create a crossing. This allowed the Communist forces to react to the surprise move, and they quickly counterattacked. Soon, Khoi's forces were under heavy fire from three directions. According to Khoi's commander, "The enemy swarmed forward like ants, launching human-wave attacks against three sides of the hill. . . . In this desperate situation I asked headquarters for artillery and air support. Unfortunately, all we got were a few armed helicopters that fired rockets and immediately departed. . . . The enemy attack continued to grow in intensity. I thought they would either overrun Hill 122 or surround it and cut us off completely. . . . Suddenly, they pulled back and the fighting died down. . . . We lost almost twenty casualties, the Rangers almost forty. . . . Enemy bodies were strewn across the rice-fields."[22] Khoi's attempt to bypass to the north was blocked, leaving both the 18th Division and the 52nd Regiment still cut off.

To break the siege, the South Vietnamese continued to scramble for any means to balance the Communist edge in artillery and infantry. One of Dao's tactical advantages was his effective use of radio intercepts. The JGS had deployed twenty-man teams to each division to monitor and intercept Communist radio traffic. Dao later told the author, "The enemy units would report their locations and strengths to their headquarters. Every day I evaluated these intercepts and targeted artillery on them. I also passed these targets to III Corps, who coordinated air strikes on these locations." Without B-52s, the VNAF planned instead to drop recently supplied 15,000-pound bombs called "Daisy Cutters" on high-priority targets.[23] On 14 April the first Daisy Cutter was dropped seven miles northeast of Xuan Loc on the suspected location of the 4th Corps headquarters. Seventy-five percent of the headquarters was reportedly destroyed.[24]

Early in the morning of 15 April, the opening phase of the new PAVN plan commenced. A sapper squad infiltrated the Bien Hoa airbase and blew up part of the main ammunition dump. The explosion rattled windows in Saigon, twenty miles away. Four 130-mm guns began shelling the airbase, cratering the runway and damaging several planes. Dao's lifeline, Bien Hoa airbase, was effectively shut down for half a day.

At dawn that same day, the 95B Regiment and the 33rd Regiment, 6th Division, began a coordinated north-south surprise attack against the ARVN 52nd Regiment defending Horseshoe Hill and Nguyen Thai Hoc. Numerous rounds rained down on the beleaguered defenders. After capturing the vital Dau Giay intersection, the 33rd prepared to assault Nguyen Thai Hoc, but it was forced to defend against Khoi's column, which had resumed its advance. On the northern flank, the 95B Regiment probed the lone ARVN company defending Horseshoe Hill. After beating off three assaults, the 52nd Regiment commander ordered a second company from 3rd Battalion to reinforce the ARVN unit on the hill. Just after the second company had arrived, resupplied the first company, and evacuated the wounded, the 95B launched its main assault, a frontal attack on the hill. Waves of enemy infantry moved across the open fields, only to be mowed down by the ARVN troops. Another battalion from 95B was sent along Route 20 to outflank the hill position, but it was stopped by concentrated ARVN artillery barrages.

The ARVN 3rd Battalion commander later wrote, "1st and 4th Companies on Horseshoe Hill were forced to fight off wave after wave of enemy assaults. . . . At 4:00 p.m. on 15 April one of the officers defending the hill reported 'there is nothing left around us . . . the base of the hill is covered with enemy bodies and the jungle vegetation has been completely destroyed, so that it seems as if even the slope of the hill has been changed . . . the green peak of the hill has become barren, devoid of vegetation. The thick orchards have become a vast garbage heap. Tree trunks and bodies are piled on top of each other in row after row.'"[25] In perhaps the 18th Division's finest moment, in one day of heavy fighting, two ARVN companies, supported by artillery, had stopped and severely damaged one of the finest PAVN regiments.

On the 52nd Regiment's southern flank, after halting Khoi's second effort, in mid-afternoon the PAVN 33rd Regiment resumed its attack on Nguyen Thai Hoc, where the remaining elements of the 5th Cavalry and the rest of the 52nd Regiment were positioned. Facing overwhelming force, at 6:00 P.M. the 52nd's commander, Colonel Ngo Ky Dung, ordered a night retreat back to friendly lines. Fighting virtually to the last round, the men on Horseshoe Hill pulled back to rejoin the 3rd Battalion. At 6:30 P.M. Colonel Dung led a convoy out of Nguyen Thai Hoc, while the 3rd Battalion moved separately. One ARVN officer stated, "There was nothing we could do. The communists shelled us with thousands of rounds—thousands. Then they attacked this morning with two regiments of infantry. Our casualties were not light, so we ran through the jungle to escape."[26] PAVN hit Xuan Loc with another thousand rounds of artillery that night to prevent the 18th Division and the 1st Airborne Brigade from assisting the 52nd Regiment.

Despite the valiant defense by the 18th Division, the Communists had maneuvered their light infantry through the scrub brush to outflank the ARVN troops. What had been touted as a major victory two days previously now was suddenly reversed. ARVN's failure to clear Route 1 to Xuan Loc after 9 April and to support Dau Giay with a strong force had come back to haunt it.

Lieutenant General Toan immediately pressed the 8th Regiment, 5th Division, which had been located north of Saigon, to assist the 3rd Armored in breaking through the Communist roadblock on Route 1. Commanded by Lieutenant Colonel Nguyen Ba Manh Hung, the unit took four hours to move by truck to Hung Nghia, where it joined Khoi's 3rd Armored. Khoi attached TF 322 to Hung's regiment and ordered him to clear the highway, while at the same time he pressed forward again from Hill 122. Hugging the blacktop, the ARVN soldiers fought a series of engagements against the 95B Regiment and the 6th Division at the now deserted hamlets of Hung Nghia and Hung Loc west of Dau Giay. Despite repeated attacks, ARVN could not reclaim the road junction from the dug-in PAVN troops. Hung states, "The Communists had built about ten strong-points, each held by a reinforced platoon. It was impossible to break through."[27] Several Western newsmen who ventured out to Hung Nghia to see the fighting were wounded, and the Communist shelling killed many civilians halted at the checkpoints on Route 1. After several days of fighting, the 341st Division moved in to replace 95B and the 6th Division. Meanwhile, the four North Vietnamese 130-mm guns, now augmented by a battery of 122-mm rockets, kept up a relentless barrage on Bien Hoa airfield. The shelling attacks greatly restricted the ability of the South Vietnamese Air Force to provide support to Dao and Khoi and helped to sound the death knell of Xuan Loc.

With the capture of the Dau Giay intersection and with the 18th Division surrounded, Lieutenant General Toan had no choice. At 9:00 A.M. on 20 April, Toan flew in to see Dao. His orders were blunt: Retreat immediately. Toan needed Dao's forces for the coming battle for Saigon. Once they had retreated, they would be moved by truck to Long Binh to re-equip and receive reinforcements. Dao and Toan decided that the 18th would escape along Route 2, the dirt road leading south out of Xuan Loc that had been attacked a month earlier by the 6th Division.

While Dao agreed with Toan's decision, he was worried about retreating down a road the Communists had recently attacked. The disasters in I and II Corps were foremost in his mind. To escape, the 18th would have to march twenty-five miles on foot at night along the dirt trail from Xuan Loc to an assembly area in Phuoc Tuy province, a tricky maneuver in the dark. Dao sent an officer in his helicopter to study the road and determine if there were any Communist roadblocks. The officer reported back that the road was passable and appeared to be free of Communist troops. Although local guerrillas still harassed the road, Dao believed he could easily brush them aside. His deeper concern was how to slip away from the enemy still ringing the town. If they detected his maneuver, his columns could be easily overwhelmed.

With only half a day to formulate a strategy to extricate his division from Xuan Loc, Dao decided on the following plan. First, he developed a deception plan to distract his opponent. He ordered the Airborne brigade to mount a major attack against the 7th Division units east of Xuan Loc. The Airborne, backed by a tremendous amount of artillery, fought all day on 20 April against the 7th Division elements.

Meanwhile, Dao himself would walk with his retreating troops while Colonel Ngo Ky Dung would fly overhead in Dao's helicopter to provide command and control. The first unit to leave from Tan Phong at 8:00 P.M. would be the 48th Regiment, followed by the armor, and then the remaining artillery and logistics units. When the artillery reached the former American outpost at Long Giao, it would establish a firebase, protected by the reconnaissance company, to support the retreat. Next would be the RF units and any civilians. The two battalions of the 43rd Regiment, the 2nd Battalion, 52nd Regiment, and the 82nd Rangers would be last in the column. Acting as rear guard were the 2nd Battalion, 43rd Regiment, and the Airborne brigade. During the night, the 2nd Battalion would abandon Thi Mountain and link up with the Airborne at Tan Phong intersection. These units would both move at dawn on 21 April.

In spite of the tremendous difficulties in moving an entire division, plus attached units and civilians, twenty-five miles along a dirt trail at night, Dao and the 18th Division conducted a masterly retreat. The division slipped out of Xuan Loc and escaped to Phuoc Tuy province with ease. Dao's personal leadership again made the difference. His chief of staff recalls, "Brigadier General Le Minh Dao walked with the troop columns to provide command and take immediate action in response to problems encountered along the route of march.... As a result, all forces were able to safely reach the assembly area early in the morning of 21 April."[28]

The North Vietnamese, caught off guard by the sudden move, ordered all elements to pursue the retreating South Vietnamese but were unable to catch them. However, things did not go as smoothly for Dao's rear guard. According to one former 18th Division officer:

During this withdrawal the 1st Airborne Brigade confronted the most danger and suffered the most losses because it was the last column and was assigned to cover the rear . . . on 20 April, when the order to move out was given, the brigade was still engaged in heavy fighting against communist forces at Bao Dinh, and the brigade's dead and wounded had still not been evacuated. All of them had to be left behind.... This had to be done because, for the survivors, the escape route of more than twenty-five miles through pitch-black rubber forests would be like passing through the gates of hell....

At 9:00 P.M., just as the airborne battalions reached Route 2, they encountered a memorable and emotional scene. All the Catholic families from the parishes of Bao Dinh, Bao Toan, and Bao Hoa were gathered along both sides of the road waiting to join the troops in the evacuation ... The task of covering scores of kilometers down a long-neglected jungle road, Route 2 from Tan Phong ... was not easy for a column with civilian refugees interspersed among the troops. . . . Only the 3rd Airborne Artillery Battalion, escorted by an airborne reconnaissance company, moved down the road. The brigade's combat battalions all moved through the rubber trees, covering the rear. At 4:00 A.M. on 21 April the 3rd Airborne Artillery Battalion and the airborne reconnaissance company were ambushed by two communist battalions near the Long Khanh/Phuoc Tuy province border. Almost everyone in Artillery Platoon C and in the reconnaissance platoon escorting it was killed or wounded in a human-wave attack. . . . Aside from these losses, the evacuation down Route 2 went very well.[29]

There had also been confusion between Dao and the 1st Airborne commander, Lieutenant Colonel Nguyen Van Dinh. Dao needed the 2nd Battalion to hold Thi Mountain to protect the northern shoulder of the retreat. The battalion would then slowly withdraw and link up with the Airborne at Tan Phong. Unfortunately, there was a mix-up, and Dinh moved out his Airborne and left the 2nd Battalion behind. Upon arriving at the assembly area, the 43rd Regiment commander reported that the Airborne had run into problems at the Long Khanh/Phuoc Tuy border. Dao immediately grabbed his helicopter and flew toward the Airborne positions to assist them and guide air strikes. As Dao was flying, the 43rd Regiment commander called him on the radio and told him that the 2nd Battalion was still waiting at Tan Phong. Dao switched to the battalion frequency and told the men not to use Route 2, but to cut through the jungle and bypass the PAVN positions. Major Nguyen Huu Che ordered his men to break up into small units. It took them three days to retreat through the jungle, fighting all the way. Their casualties were heavy, with over 50 percent of the battalion lost.

During the retreat from Xuan Loc, ARVN radio direction-finding teams located the 341st Division Forward Headquarters from the heavy communication traffic as the unit frantically tried to catch the retreating South Vietnamese. The VNAF decided to strike using a deadly weapon, the CBU-55, a fuel/air cluster bomb designed originally to clear minefields. As described by CIA analyst Frank Snepp, "With the help of DAO technicians, South Vietnamese pilots rigged up a special bomb rack for . . . the terrifying killing device known as the CBU-55. . . . A C-130 transport with a CBU on board took off from Tan Son Nhut, circled once over Xuan Loc to the east, and dropped its load virtually on top of the command post of the 341st Division just outside the newly-captured town. The casualties were tremendous. Over 250 PAVN troops were incinerated or died from suffocation in the post-explosion vacuum."[30] Once the Communists determined the nature of the attack, they loudly accused Saigon of "flouting all norms of morality" and denounced the officials who ordered the use of the weapon as "war criminals."[31]

The dropping of the CBU-55 was the last blow struck in the battle for Xuan Loc, although Khoi's 3rd Armored and the 8th Regiment, 5th Division, continued to fight over Hung Nghia. On 22 April, the 8th retook the town in heavy fighting and was driving for Dau Giay, but was ordered to stop once the 18th retreated. The same day, the 1st Airborne Brigade was detached from Dao's division and ordered to defend Phuoc Tuy province. On 25 April, the 3rd Armored was ordered to pull back to Bien Hoa to tighten the defensive lines around Saigon.

FINAL EFFORT ON AID

As we have seen, at an Oval Office meeting on 25 March, President Ford ordered General Frederick C. Weyand—who was then the Army chief of staff, but who had been the last commander of U.S. military operations in Vietnam in 1972 and 1973—to travel to South Vietnam and report on the situation there. On 5 April General Weyand returned and informed Ford that the situation was "very critical." If the South Vietnamese were to survive, "they needed an additional $722 million worth of supplies, primarily ammunition. That money would not enable them to recapture the ground they lost, but it would be enough to let them establish a strong defense perimeter around Saigon. If they managed to stabilize the military situation, there was still hope for a political solution to the war."[32] Ford decided to request the $722 million in military supplies in a speech on 10 April before a joint session of Congress.

That morning, after the first day of the battle at Xuan Loc, Ambassador Martin cabled Washington with news of the ARVN victories there and in the Delta. Aware that the president planned to request the new money, Martin told the White House, "You may wish to consider including in the President's speech references to . . . the fact that the ARVN is fighting . . . with extreme tenacity and courage."[33] President Ford's speechwriters added this news, and Ford told Congress that "the South Vietnamese are willing to fight. At Xuan Loc, although outnumbered, the South Vietnamese have fought valiantly and have held their ground and inflicted heavy losses."[34] Ford then asked for $722 million in military aid and $250 million in economic aid, and requested that Congress appropriate the money no later than 19 April.

Several days later, on 14 April, the Senate Foreign Relations Committee requested a meeting with the president to discuss the Indochina situation. During the session, Secretary of State Henry Kissinger presented the Xuan Loc stand as proof that the South Vietnamese were willing to fight. The senators were impervious to his arguments. Despite the stout defense of Xuan Loc, Congress was in no mood to support the South Vietnamese. In a stinging rebuke, Senator Jacob Javits (R., N.Y.) remarked, "I will give you large sums for evacuation [of American civilians], but not one nickel for military aid to Thieu."[35]

Bui Diem, the former GVN ambassador to the U.S. who had been sent by Thieu to solicit aid, was desperately working his old congressional friends, seeking any kind of assistance to help stem the PAVN tide. He too used the 18th Division's stand as a prod for American conscience. But his efforts also came up empty. Given the apparent lack of congressional support, Martin urged the White House to delay the scheduled aid vote, but Ford went ahead anyway. The result was as expected. On 17 April the Senate Armed Services Committee, reflecting an overwhelming desire to be done with Vietnam, rejected Ford's request.

On the political front in Saigon, the newly anointed Prime Minister Nguyen Ba Can worked diligently, but it was not until 14 April that he was able to cobble together a new Cabinet. Despite Can's efforts, the fall of Phan Rang and Phan Thiet irrevocably destroyed Thieu's credibility as South Vietnam's leader. The collapse of Cambodia on 17 April further contributed to the sense of doom.

Bowing to the pressure, on 21 April, Thieu resigned. In his farewell speech that night, he voiced his frustrations regarding what he saw as American perfidy. He bluntly declared that he had reluctantly accepted the Paris Accords only after President Nixon promised him that if North Vietnam attacked, the U.S. would respond militarily. He also revealed that the U.S. had threatened to cut off aid if he did not sign the accords. Since people now considered him the main obstacle to more aid or possible negotiations, in order to help his country he was stepping down in favor of Vice President Tran Van Huong. After eight tumultuous years in office, the man who had held South Vietnam together through military invasions, economic depression, and political firestorms was finally gone. Yet although he had been reviled as the obstacle to peace by anti-war activists around the globe, his departure had no impact on Hanoi's military plans.

The new president, Tran Van Huong, had had a long career on the Saigon political scene. Born in the Mekong Delta, the seventy-one-year-old former schoolteacher was afflicted with declining vision, high blood pressure, diabetes, heart problems, and a recent bout with cancer. His political philosophy was a blend of Confucian morality and peasant pragmatism. While respected for his honesty and patriotism, he had never acquired a large role within the Thieu administration. Yet despite his poor health and the grave military situation, he resisted demands to resign and turn over power to General Duong Van Minh. Whether out of respect for the RVN constitution, dislike of General Minh, or pure obstinacy, Huong vowed to continue fighting, and he ordered the military to defend the nation's capital.

The battle for the ultimate prize, Saigon, was about to begin.

18

"DO NOT COME HOME UNTIL VICTORY IS WON"

THE FALL OF SAIGON

As the 18th Division pulled out of Xuan Loc, Lieutenant General Nguyen Van Toan finalized his battle plan to protect Saigon. His goal was to defend as far forward as possible, mainly to keep the capital outside the range of the deadly 130-mm guns. Most of his troop strength was focused west, north, and east of the city, leaving the southern approaches relatively open. Realizing that he had few reserves and far too much ground to cover, Toan knew that his only recourse was to defend the main invasion routes and hope for a negotiated settlement.

After the 18th Division's retreat, Toan moved the unit into the positions held by the 3rd Armored Cavalry Brigade along Route 1 at the town of Trang Bom. The JGS transferred two Marine brigades to Toan's control: the intact 468th and the reconstituted 258th. Given the chaos at the Danang port and elsewhere, Toan was leery of Marine discipline, so he placed the Marines behind the 18th Division. The 258th held a line running from the Dong Nai River through the town of Ho Nai on Route 1, with the 468th from there south to Route 15. Marine Division Commander Major General Bui The Lan ordered his deputy, Colonel Nguyen Thanh Tri, to command the two brigades while he remained at the port of Vung Tau to reconstitute the rest of the division.

The 1st Airborne Brigade, after retreating from Xuan Loc, remained in Phuoc Tuy province to shield Vung Tau. The 1st Airborne and Phuoc Tuy RF had to defend a huge swath of territory and two major roads: Route 2 coming from Xuan Loc and Route 15 from Saigon. The brigade was placed under the command of Major General Nguyen Duy Hinh, who was in charge of the Phuoc Tuy/Vung Tau front. Hinh had only the Airborne brigade, the 14th Marine Battalion holding Vung Tau, local RF/PF, plus the remnants of his own 3rd Division and bits and pieces of various units continuing to stream in from I and II Corps.

The still intact ARVN 5th Division guarded the northern approaches to Saigon along Route 13, particularly between the Dong Nai and Saigon Rivers. On the western side of Saigon, the 25th Division had its regiments scattered along a line from Tay Ninh to Cu Chi on Route 1, along with the 32nd Ranger Group. Between the 25th and Tan Son Nhut airbase was the recently formed 9th Ranger Group, an untested unit.

South of the 25th Division was the Hau Nghia province RF/PF. Behind them on Saigon's western outskirts was another recently formed Ranger group, the 8th, along with remnants of the 7th Rangers. South of the city, the rebuilding 22nd Division, assisted by the badly under-strength 6th

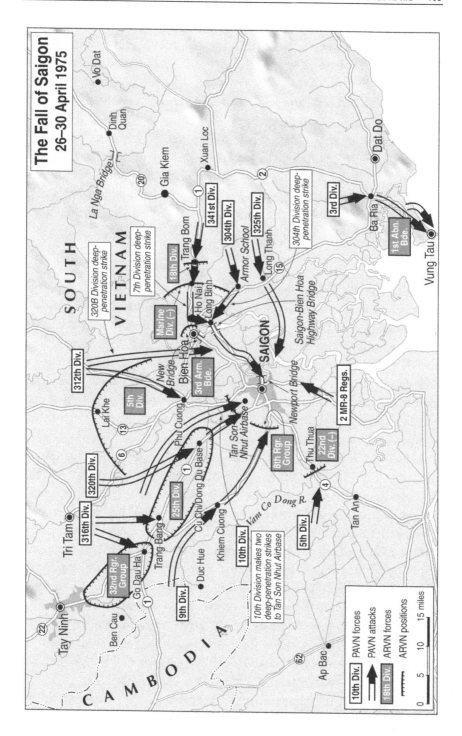

The Fall of Saigon
26–30 April 1975

Ranger Group, was ordered to hold open Route 4 from Ben Luc to My Tho. This mission was critical. If Saigon fell, ARVN had developed preliminary plans to retreat to IV Corps. It would then blow up the Ben Luc Bridge over the Vam Co Dong River to block the PAVN armor. Toan's last units, the 4th Airborne Brigade and recuperating elements of the other Airborne brigades, held defensive positions closer to the city. The 81st Airborne Rangers and a few Special Forces teams recovered from I Corps were guarding various installations. The Navy would try to interdict the canals and rivers, while the Air Force still flew from Bien Hoa and Tan Son Nhut airbases. To hold Saigon, the South Vietnamese had roughly 60,000 regular RVNAF troops, 40,000 RF plus another 20,000 Popular Force militia, and 5,000 police, totaling 125,000 men. It would not be enough.

PREPARING FOR THE HO CHI MINH CAMPAIGN

Long before PAVN forces captured Phan Rang and Phan Thiet, Dung and the campaign staff had begun developing the plan for the final assault on Saigon. Although two Politburo members, Dung and Pham Hung, were already in the south, Le Duan sent his right-hand man, Le Duc Tho, to oversee the campaign. Apparently Tho's departure from Hanoi was a dramatic occasion. He later confided to Dung that, just before he left, North Vietnam's aging President and Politburo member Ton Duc Thang told him, "Do not come home until victory is won."[1]

As Dung scrutinized the maps, he realized that his main problems in conquering Saigon were to formulate a suitable attack strategy and to select the most appropriate targets. He did not view the assault as either simple or easy, and his book describes in considerable detail how he attempted to construct the proper strategy for the final attack. Dung claims that he wanted to take Saigon with as little damage to the city and as few casualties to both sides as possible. How much he truly cared about the people of Saigon, however, is open to debate, as is whether the North Vietnamese had agreed to allow the Americans to evacuate with no interference. CIA analyst Frank Snepp recounts signal intercepts on 28 April ordering artillery to shell the heart of Saigon if the Americans were not out by the time Dung's columns arrived.[2] Whether the intercepts were a bluff designed to get the Americans out faster is unknown.

For Dung, the fundamental military problem was, "How should we attack to make the organization of this tremendous unit of enemy troops dissolve and their morale collapse?"[3] His question makes it clear that rather than focusing on killing a percentage of the South Vietnamese army, the standard PAVN practice, this time their attack would be aimed directly at the enemy's heart and brain. Dung wanted the North Vietnamese assault to be unconventional and daring, designed to cause a rapid disintegration. As Dung said, "If our style . . . was not unexpected . . . then the time would drag out . . . and the rainy season would come." He did not want to give the "political entanglements of the Americans and their protégés around the world time to . . . rescue the [Thieu] regime," an obvious slap at covert diplomatic efforts to arrange a ceasefire.[4]

After a close examination of the South Vietnamese defenses, Dung and his campaign staff chose five key objectives whose capture Dung believed would ensure the collapse of the South Vietnamese military and government. They were the Joint General Staff Headquarters, Tan Son Nhut airbase, Independence Palace, the National Police Headquarters, and the Capital Military Zone Headquarters. To achieve that collapse, Dung states, "the campaign headquarters agreed that the method of attack . . . would be to use whatever forces necessary from each direction to encircle enemy forces, isolating them and preventing them from falling back into Saigon; to wipe out and disperse the enemy . . . divisions on the outer defense perimeter. . . . This would open the way for mechanized . . . assault units to advance rapidly along the main roads and strike directly at the five chosen objectives."[5] This was the exact opposite of the strategy used to conquer Ban Me Thuot, which highlights PAVN's newfound flexibility.

To accomplish this strategy, the People's Army at the gates of Saigon had a force of five corps comprising fourteen divisions and another ten independent regiments and brigades—not counting the various B-2 Front sapper units. In addition, there were another two divisions operating nearby. While the RVNAF could barely muster 110,000 troops to defend Saigon, according to PAVN figures, "our entire combat forces totaled 270,000 troops (250,000 main force troops and 20,000 local force troops) and 180,000 strategic and campaign-level rear services troops."[6] If that is true, then together with other forces in-country during the Saigon attack, PAVN had more troops in South Vietnam—something close to 550,000—than the Americans did at the height of the U.S. commitment, around 543,000.

From this massive legion, Dung formed five attack prongs, and he assigned primary targets to each of them.[7] Striking from the west and southwest would be Group 232, consisting of the 5th, 9th, and 303rd Divisions plus the independent 16th Regiment and the 8th Division. Their mission was to defeat ARVN forces in this area, cut Route 4, and then capture the Capital Military Zone Headquarters and the National Police Headquarters. From the northwest, the 3rd Corps, consisting of the 10th, 316th, and 320th Divisions, the 273rd Tank Regiment, and the 198th Sapper Regiment, would destroy the ARVN 25th Division and capture Tan Son Nhut. From the north, the 1st Corps—the 312th and 320B Divisions and the 202nd Tank Brigade—would annihilate the ARVN 5th Division and then overrun the JGS Headquarters at Tan Son Nhut. From the east, the 4th Corps, with the 6th, 7th, and 341st Divisions, would wipe out the ARVN 18th Division, capture Bien Hoa, and then move on to Independence Palace. On the 4th Corps's left flank was the 2nd Corps, with the 3rd, 304th, and 325th Divisions and the 203rd Tank Brigade. The 304th Division would take the Armor School at Nuoc Trong, the logistics center at Long Binh, and then, in conjunction with the 4th Corps, secure Independence Palace. The 325th would cut Route 15 and then swing south of Saigon. The 3rd Division would grab Phuoc Tuy province and then move toward Vung Tau. In the Delta, the 4th Division would attack Can Tho. The 324th, 2nd, and 968th Divisions, plus local forces, would guard the newly conquered territories and the North Vietnamese supply lines.

Each corps would organize two types of forces. The first group would carry out the principle attack against the ARVN infantry divisions on the outer perimeter. After the main ARVN units were pinned down, powerful Soviet-style mechanized deep-strike units—combined-arms formations made up of an infantry regiment, armor, artillery, and air-defense units—would race into Saigon to seize the five key nerve centers, whose loss would cause an immediate South Vietnamese collapse. Armor would form the heart of each deep-strike force.

Before launching the strike forces, however, PAVN first had to grab the fourteen bridges leading into Saigon. The area around the city is crisscrossed with rivers and swamps, and Dung had limited ferry capability. What little he had he sent to Group 232, since it had to traverse the extensive marshes between the Cambodian border and the Vam Co Dong River. For Dung, seizing the bridges was almost as important as how and what to attack. Although Tran Van Tra had initially repeated the Tet '68 plan and ordered his sapper regiments and the commando cells to seize the five main objectives, on 25 April Dung reversed that order. He told the sappers to instead seize the Saigon bridges. This sudden change raised havoc with the sappers' planning. More important, timing the bridge attacks was crucial: if the sappers struck too soon, the ARVN forces would decimate them. If they waited too long, ARVN would destroy the bridges. To compensate, Dung gave each corps the authority to decide when to deploy its sappers. The timing of the sappers' attacks would be based on the rate of advance of the corps they were assigned to support.

But what if the sappers failed? If the ARVN troops retreated into the city and blew up the bridges behind them, PAVN infantry would have to leave their armored vehicles and heavy artillery behind and fight for the capital block by block, house by house. If that happened, Dung realized, "then damage, destruction, and death would be hard to avoid."[8]

As senior military commander, Dung had the responsibility of formulating the attack strategy and directing the attack. Given the dearth of Communist documentary information translated into English, most Western authors who have written about the war's end have incorrectly assumed Dung was the sole designer of the five-target/five-pronged-attack concept for Saigon. He was not, and even Dung stated that the Saigon plan was a collective labor. In fact, the final plan was a modification of the one created in early April by the General Staff's Major General Le Ngoc Hien. He based it on Giap's initial guidance, which included the deep-penetration strike concept. This initial plan was set back because of the stiff ARVN resistance at Xuan Loc. Dung also had the combined staffs to help him, and assistance from the General Staff's Central Cell in Hanoi.

Dung, though, did not mention (nor did Giap in his memoirs, written eighteen years later) that the five targets had also been key objectives in the Tet Offensive, although the 1968 plan had a total of nine primary objectives. This omission by Dung was another irritant to Tra, which he alludes to in his own postwar book. For years Tra had been wedded to the five-prong concept, which he discusses extensively in his memoir. He repeatedly dusted off elements of this 1968 plan—which in turn sprang from a top-secret plan to seize Saigon in 1965, which was aborted after the U.S. introduced large numbers of ground troops—and tried to incorporate it into his 1975 operation. Tra's account was designed to counter Dung's claim to authorship of this strategy. Tra also sought to answer his critics by demonstrating that his original 1968 attack strategy, along with his concept of attacking Saigon first in 1975, not only was sound but was the actual basis for the much-vaunted Ho Chi Minh Campaign. Ultimately, how much of the Saigon attack plan was Dung's, and how much was Le Ngoc Hien's, a variation of Tra's, or input from the Central Cell, is not known. However, in Vietnam one does not criticize Politburo members, especially in print. The result was the confiscation and banning of Tra's manuscript.

As Dung contemplated strategy, he also turned his sights to mobilizing every weapon he could muster. While the South Vietnamese had an Air Force to counter the Communists' ground superiority, Dung planned on surprising ARVN with his own air strike. On 7 April, Le Ngoc Hien cabled the General Staff that their men had captured a number of aircraft on various airfields throughout South Vietnam. The North Vietnamese Air Force quickly sent mechanics south to repair the captured equipment. Dung wanted to exploit these airplanes, and on 19 April he issued preliminary orders to the Air Defense–Air Force Command to participate in the Ho Chi Minh Campaign. The Air Force Combat Command decided to attack using the captured aircraft, mainly for the element of surprise but also because using their own Soviet-built aircraft might generate a violent American response. On 20 April, five pilots were selected and flown to Phu Cat airbase in Binh Dinh province, where captured A-37s were being restored to operational status. The People's Air Force history relates that "The entire flight immediately began conversion training from the MiG-17 to the A-37 . . . Air Defense–Air Force Headquarters approved the use of two [VNAF] air force pilots and a number of [VNAF] air force mechanics who had volunteered to assist the revolution to provide guidance to the flight in a number of technical areas and on how to utilize the aircraft."[9] On 24 and 25 April, the pilots flew successful practice flights. On 26 April the VNAF defector, F-5 pilot Nguyen Thanh Trung, was sent to help train the MiG pilots.

Dung knew that the Air Force strike would be a pinprick, but it might temporarily stun the South Vietnamese at a critical moment and contribute to the collapse of morale. His main focus, however, was on air defense. Even though the VNAF had suffered tremendous losses, it had struck hard at Communist forces during the battles for Phan Rang, Can Tho, and Xuan Loc. While Dung planned on shelling the jet airfields to disrupt South Vietnamese air operations, he also wanted the greatest air-defense shield possible. His orders to the air-defense forces were simple and direct: "Mobilize and utilize to the maximum campaign air-defense forces . . . to create a powerful air-defense umbrella over all attack sectors, at the altitudes covered by our different types of weapons and equipment, to overwhelm and suppress the operations of the enemy's air force and to gain control of the air over the battle area." Furthermore, "Air defense units should be prepared to engage U.S. aircraft if the U.S. re-intervenes."[10]

The People's Army stripped most of the air-defense shield in North Vietnam, leaving only two air-defense divisions behind to protect the homeland. Everything else was sent south. From the strategic reserve, the 375th Air Defense Division deployed to defend the newly captured cities of Hue and Danang. The 263rd Missile Regiment sent one battalion of SA-2s from Khe Sanh along the Ho Chi Minh Trail to positions on the northern approaches to Saigon. The 365th Air Defense Division, with three AAA (anti-aircraft) regiments, sent one regiment to protect Dalat, another to defend Cam Ranh, and the third, along with a missile regiment, to defend Nha Trang. The 237th AAA Regiment, equipped with radar-controlled, self-propelled ZSU-23s—a weapon that had decimated the Israeli Air Force during the early days of the October 1973 war and that had never been seen in South Vietnam—moved by train from Hanoi to the DMZ, and then continued onward by road.

The remaining air-defense units were assigned to the five corps. The 673rd Air Defense Division with three AAA regiments protected the 2nd Corps. The 71st Air Defense Brigade, consisting of one AAA regiment and six separate AAA battalions, guarded the 4th Corps. The 77th Air Defense Division (one AAA regiment, six separate AAA battalions, and one SA-7 battalion) defended the formations of Group 232. Five AAA regiments shielded the 3rd Corps. The most powerful unit, however, was the 367th Air Defense Division protecting the 1st Corps. It had its own three AAA regiments, another AAA regiment from the 377th Division, plus the en-route ZSU-23s and the SA-2s. Not counting the two air-defense divisions protecting the North Vietnamese logistics tail in the northern half of South Vietnam, the PAVN units advancing on Saigon were protected by the equivalent of five reinforced air-defense divisions. This force totaled nineteen AAA regiments, not including the organic AAA battalion assigned to each infantry division, the equivalent of another five regiments. This shield comprised almost eight hundred anti-aircraft cannon, a regiment of long-range SA-2 missiles, and large numbers of the deadly shoulder-fired SA-7 man-portable missiles. Into this air-defense buzz saw, the VNAF would fling its remaining aircraft in one last desperate attempt to halt the PAVN juggernaut, all the time dodging artillery barrages on its airfields.

Besides deployment of air defense and sappers, terrain analysis, and contingency planning for various South Vietnamese responses, the PAVN campaign staff had an enormous amount of logistics and operational coordination to accomplish in order to meet Le Duan's deadline of attacking by the end of April. Moving thousands of troops south, formulating the attack plan, presenting and gaining approval for the plan, and then directing the various units to their correct assembly area required a tremendous effort. Logistics was the primary concern.

Fortunately for Dung, the General Staff in Hanoi was handling most of the supply issues. Deputy Chief of Staff Hoang Van Thai not only monitored the southern movement of units like the 1st Corps, he also devoted special attention to furnishing all the supplies the campaign needed, especially artillery and tank shells. PAVN also pressed into service any useful piece of ARVN equipment, which in some units had risen to a sizable percentage of their artillery. The various rear-services groups worked round the clock to move vast quantities of supplies toward the distant battlefield. By mid-April the General Staff reported that 58,000 tons of supplies, including 28,000 already stockpiled at COSVN headquarters, were on hand in B-2. Yet Dung wanted more. After further requests, on 19 April the General Staff sent a cable "informing our commanders that 240 trucks belonging to Group 559 and carrying 13,000 rounds of 130-mm artillery ammunition departed on 17 April, accompanied by 40 trucks carrying tank spare parts and 150 other trucks belonging to the General Rear Services Department. All available . . . mortar ammunition had been collected from warehouses throughout North Vietnam and was on its way south."[11] What is not described is where all this material came from. If Thai had had deep concerns regarding the pre-offensive supply of artillery shells, where did PAVN suddenly get 13,000 rounds of 130-mm shells? Only the Soviets could have provided such ammunition. Regardless, the tremendous efforts of the PAVN staffs and rear-services units were successful. By 25 April all "tasks to provide material-technical support for the campaign had been completed."[12]

Supplies were one concern, but Hanoi had another major problem: guarding the newly captured territory, securing the cities, disarming large numbers of South Vietnamese soldiers and police, and protecting against sabotage by die-hard resisters. Thousands of Party and government cadres were sent south to assist in controlling the newly "liberated" areas. Many troops from the dreaded Ministry of Public Security—which during this period was operating under a more innocuous name, the Ministry of the Interior—were deployed along Route 1 to protect the road and track down ARVN holdouts.

Throughout the month of April 1975, both the South Vietnamese and the international press published numerous stories about a potential bloodbath after a Communist victory in South Vietnam. Dung later sneered at the "distorted, deceitful propaganda" put out by the American Embassy and the South Vietnamese regarding supposed "bloodbaths, reprisals, [and] hard labor camps."[13] While there was no organized slaughter, it is clear from the Communists' own historical records that there was substantial justification for the fears felt by many South Vietnamese. On 5 January 1975, the Ministry of the Interior laid out secret guidelines for dealing with South Vietnamese military and government officials during the coming attacks. "Our policy was to facilitate and clear the way for . . . soldiers and . . . governmental personnel to enter our liberated zones and join the revolution and to punish stubborn leaders (officers from the rank of captain up and . . . government officials from the district level up). The forms of punishment to be administered to those guilty of many crimes was broken down into the following categories: *For leaders, they could be killed immediately or arrested, tried, and sentenced to death, imprisonment, or re-education camps.*"[14] (Emphasis added.) On 18 April the Ministry updated its prisoner-of-war policy. Deserters or those who surrendered would be given the same "rights" as Communist soldiers. All officers "would be detained for supervision, education, and labor."[15]

On 21 April, the Campaign Command finalized the attack plan. The next day, Le Duan sent a cable to his senior officers to inform them that ARVN had detected the movement of PAVN forces toward Saigon, and had adjusted its forces to ensure that Route 4 stayed open. Le Duan was anxious and concerned. He wrote: "The opportune moment to launch the military and political general offensive against Saigon has come. We must race against time, make use of every day, to launch the offensive in time. Taking action at this moment is the surest guarantee of our total victory. Any delay will be detrimental to us, militarily and politically."[16]

Later that day, Giap sent clarifying instructions. He also told Dung that the time had come to launch the offensive. The sapper and commando teams had to take the key objectives in a timely manner, and he ordered that whichever column was in the most favorable position should race into Saigon first, regardless of the plan. Giap also believed that if the South Vietnamese forces could not hold Saigon, the GVN would attempt to retreat to Can Tho. Group 232 was given the critical mission of preventing such a retreat.

Since Le Duc Tho was the senior Politburo member present at COSVN, he responded to Le Duan's message. On 25 April he sent a ten-page cable to Hanoi discussing what had been accomplished during the last several weeks. Tho agreed that the time was ripe to launch an offensive, but he said that because of specific difficulties, they could not attack immediately. First, the recently arrived divisions were still studying the unfamiliar terrain. Second, the material sent from Hanoi on 17 April had not yet arrived, and so ammunition was in relatively short supply. Lastly, the Campaign Command's analysis of the South Vietnamese defensive strategy indicated that ARVN planned to stop the attackers at a distance from Saigon and, if that failed, to pull back into the city and blow up the bridges behind them. The campaign headquarters was studying these matters intently, and had decided to change strategy and grab the bridges using the sappers.

Furthermore, Tho disagreed with Giap's analysis that if Saigon fell, the GVN would retreat to Can Tho. He believed that GVN control of the Mekong Delta would collapse once Saigon was captured. In concluding his report, Tho told the Politburo: "You may be at ease. We are taking full advantage of every day and every hour, and within a few more days, after some basic deficiencies are overcome, we will begin the campaign as planned."[17]

On 26 April, the Politburo met in special session to hear Le Duc Tho's report. After carefully reviewing it, Le Duan rose to speak to his fellow revolutionaries. Looking around the room, Le Duan sought their views. The vote was unanimous.

Attack now.

LAUNCHING THE ATTACK

Since Lieutenant General Le Trong Tan's two corps on the eastern side of Saigon were the greatest distance from their objectives, he requested that his troops open fire first, at 5:00 P.M., 26 April. Dung approved the request, and Tan's staff quickly prepared attack plans. The 4th Corps would send the 341st Division along Route 1 to seize Trang Bom, and then move to capture the Bien Hoa airbase. The 6th Division would then surge forward and grab the III Corps headquarters and the bridges on Route 1 over the Dong Nai River. This would open the door for the 7th Division to send a deep-penetration column across the Dong Nai River and into Saigon.

The 2nd Corps also had a variety of targets. The 304th Division would attack the Armor School at Nuoc Trung on Route 15 and then turn north along that road toward the supply depots at Long Binh.

It would then cross the Dong Nai River bridge and move along the Saigon–Bien Hoa highway into the capital. The 325th Division would capture the district town of Long Thanh south of the Armor School, and then swing south of Saigon along local Route 25 and strike at the Cat Lai ferry just across the Saigon River from the Newport Bridge. The 325th would then deploy its artillery and commence shelling Tan Son Nhut airbase from the opposite side of the city. The 3rd Division would attack Phuoc Tuy province and seize the port city of Vung Tau.

At the designated hour of 5:00 P.M., 26 April, almost twenty battalions of artillery opened fire simultaneously along the eastern front, raining shells onto ARVN positions. An hour later, the 9th Regiment, 304th Division struck the Armor School and captured it. ARVN units from the school, heavily supported by air strikes, counterattacked and recaptured some ground, but they were too few to retake the school. Lieutenant General Toan quickly dispatched reinforcements, a mixed task force including a tank squadron from Khoi's 3rd Armored, the 7th Airborne Battalion, and the 82nd Border Ranger Battalion. The combined force turned back several other PAVN attacks, and inflicted heavy casualties on the 304th.

On the 304th's right flank, at 4:00 A.M. on 27 April, the 341st Division charged the ARVN 18th Division holding Trang Bom. The initial attack was repelled, but flanking attacks broke through, and at 8:30 A.M., Trang Bom fell. When the 18th Division retreated, it was ambushed and suffered heavy casualties. Le Minh Dao, newly promoted to major general, was forced to pull his badly damaged unit back to the Long Binh depot to recover. PAVN forces immediately pushed forward to engage the Marines holding the district town Ho Nai, the last town before Bien Hoa.

On the 304th's left flank, the 325th Division attacked Long Thanh, sending a tank-led infantry battalion racing into the district capital. The first assault barreled into town with little opposition, but instead of melting away at the sight of armor, the RF soldiers broke into small teams and began ambushing the PAVN troops, knocking out two T-54s and killing the commander of the lead infantry battalion. The division commander ordered his columns to retreat and resume the attack at daybreak.

In Phuoc Tuy, the 3rd Division's plan called for the 12th Regiment to strike south along Route 2, while the 141st Regiment and a tank company would sneak behind ARVN lines and assault the Phuoc Tuy province capital of Ba Ria. They would then continue south on Route 15 and grab the bridge spanning the Co May River, the gateway to Vung Tau. Once the bridge was in PAVN hands, the 2nd Regiment, also reinforced by armor, would make a deep-penetration strike to seize Vung Tau.

The 3rd Division opened fire around 6:00 P.M., 26 April. The tanks drove into Ba Ria, but the infantry was unable to keep up, allowing the South Vietnamese 1st Airborne Brigade to counterattack and drive them out. The next morning, the 141st Regiment attacked again, but the Airborne again repulsed the assault. The PAVN pressure, however, forced Major General Hinh to pull his forces back across the Co May River. Hinh ordered the bridge destroyed, which the Airborne accomplished on the afternoon of 27 April. Two Airborne battalions that were stuck on the Ba Ria side of the river had to walk across marshy salt flats to reach the other side.

The 3rd Division resumed its attack at midnight on 28 April. Throughout the night the 2nd Regiment attempted to cross the Co May, but the Airborne refused to budge. Each side poured artillery fire onto the other's positions. By dawn, the 3rd Division had managed to slip two infantry companies into a mangrove swamp on the far bank, but they were pinned down and unable to advance.

Taking casualties and stalemated at the river, the 3rd Division sent the 12th Regiment southeast to the coast, commandeered some fishing boats, and snuck across the marsh to a village about four miles south of the bridge. By noon the 12th Regiment had reached Route 15 between the bridge and Vung Tau. With the appearance of enemy soldiers in their rear, and a new attack by the 2nd Regiment, the Airborne were forced to retreat from the bridge. While pulling back they were ambushed. Despite heavy losses, they fought their way to Vung Tau.

At 1:30 A.M., 30 April, the "Yellow Star" Division resumed the attack. It drove into various sections of the Vung Tau peninsula, and by early morning had captured most of the area. Only the city center remained in ARVN hands. Some elements of the Airborne grabbed ships and attempted to flee to the Delta, and others tried to link up with the U.S. evacuation fleet stationed off the coast, while a few unlucky ones continued to hold the town. Despite some scattered die-hard resistance, Vung Tau was captured by 11:00 A.M., 30 April. The 1st Airborne Brigade, which had fought heroically at Thuong Duc, Xuan Loc, and Ba Ria/Vung Tau, was destroyed.

North of Saigon, the ARVN 5th Division was positioned astride Route 13. Its main units were dug in at three former American bases: Lai Khe, Ben Cat, and Phu Loi. To defeat the 5th Division, the PAVN plan called for the 1st Corps's 312th Division to bypass the heavily fortified bases at Lai

Khe and Ben Cat, and strike the base at Phu Loi, the one closest to Saigon. Capturing this base would cut off the 5th ARVN. Concurrently, the 320B Division would conduct a deep-penetration strike east of Route 13 along a secondary dirt road called Route 16. To enable the deep-penetration unit to easily advance, the corps engineer brigade secretly constructed a thirty-one-mile road that linked up the 320B's assembly area with Route 16.

The 312th Division opened fire at 4:30 P.M., 27 April. Two regiments moved forward to assault RF positions and seize road junctions near Phu Loi. At midnight 29 April, the 312th began its assault on Phu Loi. At the same time, the deep penetration column began advancing along the newly built road and reached Route 16. Bypassing RF positions, by dawn on 30 April, the 320B Division had reached the district seat of Tan Uyen, approximately fifteen miles northwest of Bien Hoa. With the 5th Division now bypassed, the ARVN units on Saigon's northern and eastern approaches were in great danger of being outflanked.

South and west of Saigon, Group 232 was facing major problems. In mid-April the 303rd Division had been pulled back to the newly conquered area west of the Vam Co Dong River near the Cambodian border. The 9th Division was based alongside the 303rd. To enable the two divisions to cross the river, the 303rd Division sent one regiment to the eastern side to secure a bridgehead and clear away RF positions. Fighting for three days, the PAVN troops captured two villages on the eastern bank, opening the way for the follow-on columns to cross the river without opposition.

On the night of 26 April, the 303rd was ordered to cross the Vam Co Dong River. The first rainstorm of the season, however, had turned the road to the crossing into a swampy morass. The tanks and other tracked vehicles churned up the road, making it almost impassable for wheeled vehicles, snarling traffic. A massive convoy soon stretched four miles from the Cambodian border to the river. PAVN troops press-ganged the local population into cutting bushes to place on the road so the vehicles could gain traction.

If traversing the road was difficult, crossing the river was far worse. The engineers put a half float in the middle of the river, and then built ferries to move the vehicles from one bank to the float, and then to the other side. Fortunately for Tra's troops, the VNAF did not contest the river crossing, enabling the engineers to slowly shuttle vehicles across.

By the morning of 28 April, the 303rd Division had successfully crossed over. It then moved to Route 10 and turned south to attack the Hau Nghia provincial capital, Khiem Cuong. Lieutenant General Toan had earlier reinforced the Hau Nghia RF with M-113s from the 25th Division's armor squadron, but they were of little help. The 303rd Division commander launched a tank-led attack at dawn on 29 April, and, since the defenders had no anti-tank weapons, the assault quickly penetrated into Khiem Cuong. By 11:30 A.M., the RF and the M-113s had abandoned the town and retreated toward Saigon. Hau Nghia province was overrun.

Following on the heels of the 303rd, by nightfall of 28 April, the infantry from the 9th Division had crossed the river, and by late afternoon the next day, the division's heavy equipment was also across. The 9th formed two attack columns; one regiment headed for Tan Son Nhut, while the second moved east toward Saigon.

South of Saigon, the PAVN 5th Division, still in Long An province, was ordered to cut Route 4 and block any potential retreat from Saigon into IV Corps. Moving forward, a regiment cut the road, but the ARVN 22nd Division swiftly reacted and cleared the roadblock. Massing a second time, at dawn on 28 April, the 5th Division again tried to seize the road. Savage fighting erupted as the 22nd Division cleared the road a second time. The PAVN troops retreated to a nearby village, and fired at vehicles on Route 4 to disrupt traffic.

At midnight, the 5th Division attacked for a third time, finally capturing a bridge on Route 4. Building obstacles and planting mines, the Communist troops were determined to block the only escape route out of Saigon. The 22nd Division fought all day on 29 April to clear the road, but it was unable to dislodge the dug-in enemy.

On Saigon's northwestern front, the PAVN 3rd Corps also prepared to swing into action. To prevent ARVN forces from falling back from Tay Ninh, the 316th Division would cut Route 22 and also attack the important district town of Trang Bang on Route 1. Once the 316th captured Trang Bang, the PAVN 320th Division would assault the 25th Division headquarters at Dong Du near Cu Chi. With the 25th Division pinned down, the 198th Sapper Regiment would slip past the ARVN defenses and seize two critical bridges near Tan Son Nhut: the Bong Bridge on Route 1, and the Sang Bridge on Route 15. Routes 1 and 15 are the only roads across the flat rice fields into Saigon. After these bridges were captured, the 10th Division would conduct deep-penetration attacks along both roads to grab Tan Son Nhut and the Joint General Staff Headquarters.

The 25th Division commander, Brigadier General Ly Tong Ba, had his 49th Regiment defending Tay Ninh, the 46th Regiment holding Trang Bang, the 32nd Ranger Group keeping Route 22 open, and the 50th Regiment holding Cu Chi. However, Lieutenant General Toan ordered Ba to send his armor squadron and two battalions of the 50th Regiment to bolster both Hau Nghia province and Trang Bang, depleting Ba's defense at Dong Du. Ba was furious. He had hoped to gather part of his division together at Dong Du and essentially fight a repeat of the 1972 battle of Kontum. Toan's moves had now stripped Ba of most of his combat power at Dong Du.

The 316th struck at 7:00 A.M., 28 April. Launching attacks along a twenty-mile stretch of Routes 22 and 1, the North Vietnamese troops slowly rolled up RF positions on the roads. They ignored Tay Ninh city, but fierce fighting erupted at the heavily defended town of Trang Bang, as the ARVN 46th Regiment threw back several assaults. The PAVN troops retreated and shelled the town, while continuing to overrun nearby outposts.

Then disaster struck for the South Vietnamese. Worried about his defenses at Dong Du, on the morning of 28 April, Brigadier General Ba recalled his 1st Battalion, 50th Regiment, and the armor, which he had sent out to help defend Trang Bang. What Ba did not know was that the 1st Battalion commander, Major Le Quang Ninh, was a Communist agent. Following a directive given several days before to disrupt his unit's operations, Ninh used Ba's order as his opportunity to act. While leading his men back to Dong Du, Ninh stopped and gathered his officers together. Telling them the war was over, Ninh asked them to surrender. After a short discussion, they agreed. It was a devastating blow to local South Vietnamese morale. At 3:00 P.M. the next day, after the North Vietnamese had defeated several efforts to break out of the siege ring, Trang Bang fell.

In the 320th's sector, the division engineers secretly built a bridge across the Saigon River to enable the unit to cross. By 25 April, the division was across the river and hiding in a base area northwest of Dong Du. The division's orders were clear: Dong Du must be captured so that the 10th Division could send a deep-penetration assault column along Route 1.

On 28 April, it commenced artillery fire against ARVN positions to soften up the base defenses. At 5:00 A.M., 29 April, two regiments assaulted Dong Du. Although Brigadier General Ba had few combat troops at the base, his soldiers held fast behind their defensive barriers, causing the attackers heavy casualties. The 320th Division commander committed his armor to help break the ARVN resistance, but two tanks were destroyed. Several more assaults were launched, but failed to penetrate the base. Despite the thick defenses, however, there were too few ARVN combat troops to hold such a large base. A final assault seized Dong Du at 11:00 A.M. Brigadier General Ba and several aides escaped, but they were captured later that day.

Despite stubborn resistance at various points, PAVN forces were closing in on Saigon. Early in the morning of 29 April, on orders from the Politburo, Dung launched the deep-penetration strikes. Saigon's final hours were counting down.

THE LAST EFFORTS

After Thieu's resignation, President Tran Van Huong asked Prime Minister Nguyen Ba Can to stay on to ensure government continuity. Can agreed to remain until a decision was made as to whether former General Duong Van Minh would assume power. To further assist Huong in forming a new government, it was decided that former President Thieu and former Prime Minister Tran Thien Khiem should leave the country. The U.S State Department queried several countries, but only Taiwan was willing to harbor the two men. During the night of 25 April, Ambassador Graham Martin placed Thieu and Khiem onboard his designated aircraft and had them flown out of Saigon.

However, neither move helped Huong. Under great pressure from both the Americans and the French to resign, Huong convened the National Assembly on the afternoon of 27 April to vote on a successor. After Defense Minister Tran Van Don provided a military briefing detailing the hopeless situation, Huong announced that he was stepping down, and the Assembly elected General Duong Van Minh as the new president. Minh had led the coup against President Ngo Dinh Diem in 1963, but was overthrown shortly thereafter. Although marginalized since then, he eventually emerged as a leader of the "Third Force." His main attribute was that the French claimed he was the only man with whom the North Vietnamese would discuss a possible ceasefire.

On the evening of 28 April, Minh and Huong held a ceremony to transfer power. Minh's urgent goal was to arrange a ceasefire, primarily with the Southern-based Communists, who he believed did not wish to be subservient to Hanoi. He also believed that the Northerners did not want to take over South Vietnam immediately. Minh accepted these fantasies since he maintained radio contact with the other side. Moreover, his younger brother was a PAVN senior officer, and Le Duc Tho had tried to exploit this relationship in 1963 by sending Minh's brother south to influence Minh. That effort failed.

Before the inauguration, Minh asked General Cao Van Vien to meet him to discuss the military situation. Vien politely declined, claiming he was too busy. In reality, Vien had not forgotten the carbine in his back in November 1963, and he would not help Minh. Shortly before transferring power, Huong accepted Vien's resignation as chief of the JGS. Within hours, Vien flew out on a helicopter to the U.S. fleet anchored off Vung Tau. Lieutenant General Dong Van Khuyen, Vien's deputy, left shortly thereafter. With Vien and Khuyen gone, the JGS crumbled.

Minh's acceptance speech was short. He declared he wanted to reopen negotiations with the PRG, and promised to free all political prisoners, end press restrictions, and form a government that would include all factions. With an eye on the generals, he ordered them to continue defending the remaining land. Finishing, he offered an olive branch to the PRG, asking it to agree to a ceasefire and to join him in working out a political solution based upon the Paris Accords.

Any hope that the Communists might prove amenable to a negotiated settlement with Minh was wishful thinking. Immediately after his inauguration, the COSVN Current Affairs Committee cabled its analysis to the local military commanders: "the American ploy of making Duong Van Minh the President of the puppet government is to open negotiations with us aimed at saving what is left of the Saigon government. However, in reality Duong Van Minh is no longer a representative of the Third Force but instead has become an American lackey who is being used to oppose the revolution. In the current situation, anyone, no matter who he is, who is placed at the head of the puppet government is a lackey of the Americans. We must carry out our unshakable resolve to . . . completely liberate South Vietnam, and reunify our nation."[18]

To punctuate that sentiment, Van Tien Dung's solitary air strike hit precisely at the same moment as Minh's speech. The PAVN Air Force had put five A-37s captured at Phu Cat airbase into operational status. After flying to Thanh Son airbase at Phan Rang, the planes, one piloted by the defector Nguyen Thanh Trung, departed at 4:25 P.M., 28 April. Reaching Tan Son Nhut shortly after 6:00 P.M., the A-37s dropped their bombs on the surprised South Vietnamese, damaging eleven VNAF aircraft. Several of the A-37s made a second bombing pass, and then they turned back for Thanh Son. Two planes were virtually out of fuel when they reached Phan Rang, but all landed safely. Just as Dung had hoped, the psychological impact on the South Vietnamese Air Force was devastating. Most of the VNAF in III Corps ceased functioning after the raid, and the airmen began escaping to Thailand.

Despite the bombing raid and the heavy fighting, to facilitate his efforts to form a coalition government, Minh immediately sent a letter to Ambassador Martin asking that all DAO personnel leave Vietnam within twenty-four hours. Martin complied, and Colonel Le Gro and Major General Smith began shutting down the office and destroying classified files. Soon the remaining DAO staff joined the ongoing evacuation at Tan Son Nhut.

To reconstitute the military high command, President Minh appointed former II Corps commander Lieutenant General Vinh Loc to replace Cao Van Vien. A relative of former Emperor Bao Dai, Loc had actively supported the coup against President Diem by leading armor units into Saigon. He was not a particularly competent general, and he had been sacked from II Corps after Tet '68. But with most of the JGS leadership heading for the American ships, Minh had few options. Minh gave Loc one mission: Hold for two days so that Minh could arrange a peace settlement with the other side.

Loc reached the JGS at 10:00 A.M., 29 April. After cobbling together a makeshift staff, he then phoned several generals who were still commanding their units to get a report on the situation. Unable to contact Lieutenant General Toan in III Corps, he did reach Major General Nguyen Khoa Nam, who still had IV Corps until tight control. Nam agreed to follow Loc's orders, and to prepare Can Tho as a final bastion for the GVN if Saigon fell.

Minh also brought an old friend out of retirement to help Loc. He asked Brigadier General Nguyen Huu Hanh to come to Saigon from his home in the Delta and work as an assistant to Loc. Hanh had retired as Inspector General of I Corps in early 1974. Previously he had served as commander of the 44th Special Zone in the Delta, where he earned the enmity of Colonel David Hackworth. In his book *About Face*, Hackworth rightly denigrates Hanh as corrupt and notoriously reluctant to engage the enemy. There was good reason for the latter: Hanh was secretly an agent of the revolution.[19] His presence at this juncture would soon prove critical.

As the departure of the Americans quickened, so did the PAVN attack columns. On the eastern front, Lieutenant General Tan deployed the B-2 Front sappers assigned to his command at the same time as his artillery opened fire. Tan's objective was to capture five critical bridges standing between him and Saigon to prevent ARVN troops from blowing them up. The targets for the sappers assigned to the 4th Corps were the two bridges that crossed the Dong Nai River west of Bien Hoa. The first was the New Bridge, so-called because it carried a new section of road across the Dong Nai River into Bien Hoa. The second bridge, located just south of the New Bridge, was the Ghenh Bridge, which carried both the railroad track and Route 1. For the sappers assigned to the 2nd Corps, the main objective was the bridge on the Dong Nai just west of Long Binh, plus the next two bridges on the Saigon–Bien Hoa highway. The first crosses the Chiec River, and the second is the Newport Bridge, which spans the Saigon River and is the gateway to Saigon.

On 26 April, after Lieutenant General Tan's artillery fired their opening barrages, the sappers attacked the three Dong Nai River bridges, which were guarded by the 5th Airborne Battalion. The sappers were unable to capture the Dong Nai and New Bridges, but by the early morning of 27 April, they had seized the Ghenh Bridge. The Airborne soon counterattacked and recaptured it. The equally tough sappers charged the bridges several more times, and fifty sappers died over the course of several days trying to retake the Ghenh Bridge. Although the fighting was heavy, control remained firmly in ARVN hands.

Despite the failure of the sappers to grab the bridges, after capturing Trang Bom, the 4th Corps assault column resumed its advance toward the huge military base at Bien Hoa. Only the district town of Ho Nai blocked their path. It sat on Route 1 roughly halfway between Trang Bom and Bien Hoa, and was populated by Catholic refugees from North Vietnam. The town's name was an anagram of Hanoi, and during the Tet Offensive, the population had fiercely resisted Communist attacks. This time would be no different. The South Vietnamese defenses consisted of local PF forces, an M-48 tank troop from Khoi's 3rd Armored, and the 6th Marine Battalion, led by Lieutenant Colonel Le Ba Binh. A highly respected career Marine officer, Binh had won the U.S. Silver and Bronze Stars, along with numerous Vietnamese medals. Now he was eagerly awaiting the Communist troops. As part of the 369th Brigade, which had swum out to the ships at Danang, Binh and many of his fellow Marines were enraged over the events in I Corps. They sought nothing less than revenge for the debacle at Danang.[20]

On the morning of 27 April, Le Ba Binh's wish was granted. After an extensive artillery barrage, two battalions of the 341st Division and a few tanks probed the Marine lines. Waiting until they were close, Binh ordered his artillery to fire. The exposed attackers were battered; one tank was destroyed and almost thirty soldiers were killed. The 341st units quickly pulled back.

The next day, the 341st resumed the assault. This time it used five tanks and a regiment. The ARVN M-48 tanks quickly destroyed three T-54s, while the Marine artillery pounded the infantry. Local PF troops fired from buildings. Three times the Communist troops charged the Marine lines. Each time they were thrown back. As they retreated, Binh gave them no quarter. He ordered air-burst artillery to rain shrapnel down on the retreating North Vietnamese. When it was over, dozens of bodies littered the ground.

Binh's stout defense was only one part of the tough Marine response. Each battalion along the defensive front was probed, and every North Vietnamese attack was crushed. Burning tanks and dead bodies littered the ground along the entire Marine line. The stiff resistance shocked Lieutenant General Tan, who was growing concerned about Ho Nai and his other stalled efforts at Nuoc Trong and Long Thanh. The 341st had suffered losses, and had failed to puncture the Marine lines. The 7th Division deep-penetration column was sitting in the rear, unable to advance. Given the tight timetable for entering Saigon, Tan demanded that the 341st seize Ho Nai. On 29 April, the division threw its remaining units into the battle. Closing with Binh's troops, they managed to punch through one position, but counterattacking Marines drove them out. After two more hours of fighting, Binh's unit had held for a third time. The 341st was exhausted and unable to break through. Le Ba Binh and his 6th Marines had taken a small measure of revenge for Danang

However, his joy was short-lived. After defeating the third attack, Binh received a message from his commander. His battalion and the rest of the Marine units were ordered to retreat to Bien Hoa and Long Binh. Given the heavy enemy pressure, Lieutenant General Toan wanted to pull in his lines. The night before, he had ordered his corps headquarters to retreat from Bien Hoa to Go Vap, a base closer to Saigon. Bien Hoa airbase had come under heavy shelling, putting the flight line out of operation. Nor could the corps headquarters effectively operate while under artillery bombardment. At noon on 29 April, Toan met with Brigadier General Tran Quang Khoi, Major General Le Minh Dao, and Colonel Nguyen Thanh Tri to discuss the situation. Toan ordered Dao to defend Long Binh, while Khoi would protect Bien Hoa. The two Marine brigades would leave their positions and one each would be attached to Khoi and Dao.

After giving his orders, Toan then flew out to the U.S. fleet. He claimed he was ordered to fly out and meet with U.S. Marine officers, but in reality he knew that Minh's ascension to the presidency spelled the end of an anti-Communist South Vietnam. Still, deserting his command was a surprising move by a man considered one of South Vietnam's toughest generals. With Toan's departure, and the subsequent breakdown in communications caused by the moving of the III Corps headquarters, overall South Vietnamese command and control evaporated. All units were now essentially fighting alone, with few orders or directions.

Spotting the ARVN retreat, at mid-morning on 29 April, Lieutenant General Tan ordered the 7th Division to send its deep-penetration column forward. With the Marines gone, the PAVN regulars expected no resistance. They were wrong. The Catholic militiamen were not abandoning their town to the Communists. As the lead tanks entered Ho Nai at midnight, several were hit with ant-tank rockets. Machine guns opened up on the exposed infantry. It took the PAVN regulars all night to reduce the town's defenses. An advance element of the deep-penetration column reached Bien Hoa by dawn, but was blocked by Khoi's tankers. Lieutenant General Tan decided to shift the 7th Division south to cross the river at Long Binh. Another arm of Dung's army was closing in on Saigon.

On Saigon's western front, on the night of 28 April, the 3rd Corps sent the 198th Sapper Regiment to infiltrate behind ARVN lines to capture the Bong and Sang Bridges on Route 1 and Route 15 respectively. The timing of the 198th Regiment's attack was closely tied to the 10th Division's mission: when the sappers attacked the bridges, the 10th Division would launch its deep-penetration strikes. Yet the 198th Sappers had to plan their mission with no reconnaissance of the targets, since they had just arrived from the Central Highlands. With only one day to prepare, their only terrain knowledge came from studying maps. If the bridge assaults failed, the 10th Division would be left sitting on Route 1, with its tanks and infantry exposed to air strikes and artillery. It was PAVN's riskiest maneuver in the entire Ho Chi Minh Campaign.

In fact, the sappers' lack of familiarity with the area immediately caused problems. The two sapper columns had to find detours around streams and marshes. Several times they were hit by artillery, causing the columns to split up. Only half of the original force reached the bridges by the designated assault time.

Despite the tremendous difficulties, at 3:30 A.M. on 29 April, the sappers attacked the two bridges. After several hours of heavy fighting, the sappers controlled both. At the same time, a group of COSVN sappers snuck close to Tan Son Nhut and launched a surprise rocket attack. At 4:00 A.M., volleys of rockets flashed into the sky and landed on Tan Son Nhut. One of the first rounds killed two American Marine guards, and several others hit the DAO compound. Numerous rockets hit the runways, destroying one American C-130. Soon debris and craters were clogging the tarmac, and air operations were momentarily shut down.

With the capture of the bridges, the 10th Division launched its two deep-penetration strikes. The column on Route 1 comprised the 24th Infantry Regiment, sixteen T-54s and ten K-63 armored personnel carriers, over forty trucks carrying infantry, engineers, and other specialty troops, eight anti-aircraft guns, and an artillery battalion. To surprise the South Vietnamese defenders, the column was using as its lead element five ARVN tanks captured at Cheo Reo. The second column, attacking along Route 15 to the Sang Bridge, consisted of the 28th Infantry Regiment, eleven T-54s, and twelve K-63s, plus an anti-aircraft and artillery battalion and support troops. The 10th Division had massed the most powerful attack force ever assembled by the People's Army, a tremendous one-two punch designed to knock the South Vietnamese out of the war.

As the attack at Dong Du commenced, the 10th Division ordered the captured ARVN tanks to advance down Route 1. They soon entered the district town of Cu Chi next to Dong Du. Exactly as expected, RF troops holding the town thought these were friendly vehicles, and ran out of their bunkers to greet them. The soldiers were met with cannon fire and machine-gun bullets. The RF scattered, and the captured tanks resumed the advance. Arriving at the Bong Bridge, they stopped to help defend it. Shortly thereafter, the ARVN 25th Division's M-113 unit, retreating from Hau Nghia province, approached the bridge. The captured tanks opened fire and destroyed numerous M-113s.

With the way clear, the 24th Regiment roared down Route 1. Passing the Bong Bridge, the column fought its way through ARVN defenses at the town of Hoc Mon and several other positions. When the column reached ARVN's main training center at Quang Trung, the South Vietnamese dragged trucks onto Route 1 to block the road, while the guard force opened fire from blockhouses and other buildings. PAVN engineers used a tank to tow the trucks off the road, and the column commander detached some armor and infantry to attack the base while the rest of the column resumed the advance. By 5:00 P.M., the lead elements had reached the Ba Queo intersection near the airbase.

The easy part was now over. The ARVN 3rd Airborne Battalion, which was only partially reconstituted after the Phan Rang debacle, awaited the PAVN troops at the Ba Queo intersection. Hiding until the lead element was close, the Airborne troops opened fire. After losing three K-63 personnel carriers and over twenty soldiers, the North Vietnamese were forced to halt. Heavy fighting continued until dark, but the 24th Regiment was unable to punch through.

The column attacking on Route 15 departed at 6:00 A.M., 29 April. The 28th Regiment's new orders were to assault straight down Route 15, enter the airbase, and capture the JGS Headquarters. It was a thirty-one-mile journey to Tan Son Nhut. As the column advanced, artillery fire forced it to split up. Despite mass confusion, elements continued moving forward. An infantry battalion and the lead tanks fought their way past several towns and fortified ARVN positions. By noon they had reached the Sang Bridge, only eight miles from Tan Son Nhut. With no ARVN defenders on the northern side of the airbase, the attackers' way was clear. Then a minor miracle happened. As the third tank began crossing, the bridge suddenly collapsed. For the Americans still at the airbase, it was the luckiest event of the evacuation. If the 28th Regiment had entered the base while they were still there, numerous U.S. citizens would have been taken prisoner.

After the Sang Bridge collapsed, the 28th Regiment was ordered to turn around and follow Route 8 to Cu Chi, turn onto Route 1, and then back onto Route 15 to resume its mission. By 6:00 P.M. on 29 April the lead elements had passed the Quang Trung Training Center, but they stopped because they were unsure of the right road to Tan Son Nhut. The PAVN commander sent out four armored vehicles to search ahead. RF troops ambushed the element and destroyed it. At 9:00 P.M., with vehicles strung out along Route 1 and with continuing strong ARVN resistance, both strike elements were ordered to halt for the night to resupply. The new assault would commence at 7:15 A.M. on 30 April.

Defending the airbase was the 3rd Task Force of the 81st Airborne Rangers under the command of Major Pham Chau Tai. (The rest of the 81st was defending the Bien Hoa airbase.) On 26 April, Tai and his soldiers were given the mission of guarding the JGS Headquarters. The remnants of the *Loi Ho* ("Thunder Tigers") who had escaped from Pleiku joined Tai's resilient soldiers. Tai placed his own soldiers and the *Loi Ho* troops in the tall buildings surrounding the main gate into Tan Son Nhut. His Airborne Rangers had plenty of anti-tank rockets and 90-mm recoilless rifles mounted atop the buildings.

On that last night of the Republic of Vietnam, with scenes of chaos at the American Embassy as helicopters lifted people out, the 81st Airborne Rangers, the *Loi Ho*, and the Airborne at Tan Son Nhut held their positions. Although some senior officers had fled, and large chunks of the Navy had departed that night to prevent their ships from falling into Communist hands, most of the Army and Marines were still in their bunkers, guns pointing forward. In an exchange that night, typical of many others among the RVNAF, Tai called the 81st commander, Colonel Phan Van Huan, for instructions. Even with the PAVN armor close by and expected to attack at first light, Huan's reply to Tai was straightforward: "The generals may have run, but . . . we cannot simply abandon our homeland to the Communists, so no matter what happens, the 81st Airborne Ranger Group will stay and fight."[21] The 81st would soon prove that Colonel Huan was a man of his word.

At 7:15 A.M., Major General Vu Lang, commander of the PAVN 3rd Corps, gave the order to open fire. The tanks and infantry of the 24th Regiment bypassed Ba Queo and moved toward the Bay Hien intersection, the key road junction less than a mile from the airbase's main gate. The Airborne and the *Loi Ho* were waiting for them. As the first two PAVN tanks rumbled down the street leading to the airbase's main gate, a round from a 90-mm recoilless rifle fired by a *Loi Ho* officer destroyed the first tank. A shell from an ARVN M-48 tank hit the second T-54. With two tanks burning, the North Vietnamese infantry pushed forward to clear the buildings. The Airborne fought them house to house, but by 8:45 A.M., the Communists' superior numbers had forced the ARVN troops from Bay Hien.

Reaching the main gate of the airbase, the 10th Division commander ordered an infantry battalion and three tanks to seize it. Charging forward, they ran into the waiting 81st Airborne. Hidden in nearby bunkers and buildings, firing anti-tank rockets and machine guns, the 81st troops destroyed the three lead tanks in rapid fashion and mowed down the infantry. Several times the PAVN troops assaulted the gate, and each time they were thrown back. Snipers began picking off PAVN soldiers, killing over twenty. With three tanks burning in the middle of the street, the local commander brought up an 85-mm anti-aircraft gun to provide direct-fire support to knock out the ARVN heavy weapons. The 81st destroyed it before it even had a chance to set up.

Stalled at the main gate, the 10th Division ordered another infantry battalion and eight more tanks into the assault. As they came down Route 1 to Bay Hien, a VNAF air strike from Can Tho, probably the last of the war, knocked out two tanks. Reaching the gate of Tan Son Nhut at 10:00 A.M., the surviving tanks moved forward. Without much time to discern the ARVN firing positions, the tanks drove straight down the street toward their burning counterparts. As they approached the gate, the 81st Airborne ambushed them. Two more tanks were soon hit and burning. A third tank tried a flanking movement down a side street. Roving 81st Airborne soldiers, screaming "Remember Phuoc Long," hit it with an anti-tank rocket. Six PAVN tanks now lay immobile and burning, and dozens of dead Communist soldiers lay strewn from Bay Hien to the main gate.

On the southeastern front, the 2nd Corps was again pushing forward. At Long Thanh, when the 325th Division was unable to advance against the local RF defending their homes, the division commander committed his reserve. Fighting house to house, by 4:30 P.M., 27 April, his troops held Long Thanh. 2nd Corps Commander Major General Nguyen Huu An ordered the division to cross over Route 15 and follow Local Route 25 to the district town of Nhon Trach. There it would build an artillery position to shell Tan Son Nhut, continue onward to capture the main ammunition staging area at Thanh Tuy Ha, and then move to the Cat Lai ferry near the junction of the Saigon and Dong Nai Rivers. Given the marshy terrain, the 325th commander organized his own deep-penetration column to move swiftly along the road. Placing the 46th Regiment in front with his four remaining tanks, followed by the 101st Regiment, the division commander intended to barrel straight down the road to Nhon Trach.

Departing in the morning of 28 April, the division fought its way through some strong-points, and by late afternoon, the 46th Regiment had captured Nhon Trach. Major General An ordered his 130-mm artillery to move forward. However, they had to fight their way past some RF bunkers, and they lost a dozen men killed. Finally, in the early morning of 29 April, the 130-mm artillery was in position. At 4:30 A.M., shortly after the sappers fired the rockets onto Tan Son Nhut, the 130s opened up. A total of three hundred rounds hit the airbase. The exploding rounds forced the Americans to cancel the use of C-130s to evacuate personnel. From now on, only helicopters could be used.

At dawn, the 46th Regiment resumed the advance. It attacked the ammunition dump at Thanh Tuy Ha. After an all-day battle, the 46th Regiment finally took the fort. That night, the 325th Division advanced to the river and prepared to cross the next morning. The third arm of Van Tien Dung's army had now reached the outskirts of Saigon.

As the PAVN units closed in, it was critical for them to prevent ARVN from blowing up the bridges. While Dung's main strategy of pinning down the ARVN forces on the outskirts had turned out well, the sappers had been only partially successful, having failed to grab the bridges on the eastern side of Saigon. Here is when the Communists' old agent, Brigadier General Nguyen Huu Hanh, suddenly proved invaluable. On the afternoon of 29 April, Hanh "ordered all units that they were not to destroy any bridges. If any unit wanted to destroy a bridge, it first had to receive permission from the JGS."[22] Further, in the early hours of 30 April, a series of orders were issued to the 18th Division and to the two Marine brigades. Although Khoi states there was no change in his orders to hold Bien Hoa, Dao's 18th Division was told to retreat from Long Binh and take up new positions on the west bank of the Dong Nai River, while the Marines were ordered to return to their main base just east of Saigon. The Airborne troops guarding the Dong Nai River bridges also retreated around midnight on 29 April. These orders completely destabilized South Vietnamese defenses along Saigon's eastern side. Who gave these orders remains unknown, although Dao claims it was Lieutenant General Vinh Loc. The author suspects the culprit was Nguyen Huu Hanh, but to the author's knowledge, Hanh has never claimed credit for this. Regardless, with the Dong Nai River bridge at Long Binh now undefended, the sappers grabbed it.

During the night, President Minh had moved to Independence Palace. He planned on inaugurating his new Cabinet, and arranging for peace negotiations with the Communists. However, by early morning 30 April, Minh knew that his last peace overtures had been rejected. Gathering his staff at 8:30 A.M., Minh believed that his only hope of preventing the destruction of Saigon was to surrender to the PRG, trusting that the North Vietnamese would allow the Southerners to assume power. Minh made a tape recording ordering ARVN forces to cease fire and await the arrival of the PRG forces. Lieutenant General Loc, upon arriving at the Palace, decided the situation was hopeless and fled to the Navy docks, catching one of the last ships. Following Minh's lead, Brigadier General Hanh issued a similar order in the name of the JGS. He then personally took Minh's announcement to the Saigon radio station and told the personnel there to play it repeatedly. As ARVN troops across the area heard this broadcast, they began to melt away.

At Tan Son Nhut, as burning PAVN tanks blocked the main gate, Major Tai became aware of Minh's broadcast ordering all ARVN forces to cease fire and await the PRG forces. Leaving the gate area, Tai returned to find a deserted JGS Headquarters. Walking into the building, he placed a call to Minh. Brigadier General Hanh answered the phone. When Tai asked to speak to Minh, Hanh handed the phone to the president. After introducing himself, Tai asked Minh for instructions. Minh told him to prepare to surrender, and that enemy tanks were approaching the Palace.

In a response that is as famous among South Vietnamese expatriates as Brigadier General Anthony McAuliffe's legendary retort of "Nuts!" during World War II is among Americans, Tai told Minh, "If Viet Cong tanks are entering Independence Palace we will come down there to rescue you, sir!"[23] Astonished at Tai's reckless courage, Minh essentially told him no, and hung up.

Despite his audacious proposal, Tai realized he had no choice. Calling his commanders together, he told them that the battle was over, and ordered them to pull back from the gates. Most of his men were outraged, and some continued fighting until they ran out of ammunition. Nonetheless, with the burning tanks having been pulled away from the gate, the PAVN tanks and infantry poured into Tan Son Nhut. By 11:30, it was over.

The two 10th Division deep-penetration columns had conducted a fast-paced assault over thirty miles, fighting part of the way, but it had been costly. Of the twenty-six North Vietnamese armored vehicles that began the assault with the 24th Infantry, half were destroyed at the gates of Tan Son Nhut.

On the eastern front, with ARVN units retreating, Lieutenant General Tan told Nguyen Huu An to cross into Saigon, seize Independence Palace, and end the war. With the way now clear, An gave the order to launch the 2nd Corps deep-penetration column. It consisted of the 203rd Tank Brigade, the 66th Regiment, 304th Division, an artillery battalion, and an AAA battalion, with the 18th Regiment, 325th Division, in reserve. Rumbling north on Route 15, at 4:00 A.M., 30 April, a massive line of four hundred vehicles reached Long Binh. Linking up with the COSVN sappers who had just grabbed the Dong Nai River bridge, the 203rd commander explained that his infantry was well behind the lead tanks, and he was uncertain how to get into Saigon. Since the sapper commander lived in Saigon, he offered to lead the tanks into the city and to have his sappers mount the tanks and serve as infantry. The 203rd commander accepted his offer, and at 6:00 A.M., the first tanks began crossing the bridge. It was twelve miles from the bridge to Independence Palace.

As the column pushed down the highway, the first serious resistance was at the Thu Duc Officers' School. Heavy fire erupted on the lead vehicles. The battalion commander dispatched several tanks to deal with the situation; one was destroyed before the ARVN defenses were silenced. When An reached the Thu Duc school, he chastised the lead battalion commander for not bypassing the school. Resuming the assault, another sapper group finally captured the Chiec River bridge, but lost over fifty men seizing it. Other sapper elements tried to capture the Newport Bridge, but the 12th Airborne Battalion, 4th Airborne Brigade, repulsed them.

The 12th Airborne had prepared for the PAVN assault. It had blocked the road with dirt-filled barrels, slowing down the advancing troops, and now its artillery fire began hitting the column. Even so, the lead tank battalion and some sappers reached the Newport Bridge around 9:00 A.M. ARVN tanks immediately opened fire, destroying the lead T-54 and killing the PAVN tank battalion commander. Pinned down and unable to advance, the deep-penetration column backed up behind the lead tank. Nguyen Huu An tried maneuvering his engineers and infantry across the bridge, but the Airborne kept up a heavy rain of shells. Several ARVN tanks were hit after An ordered his artillery into a direct-fire mode to clear out the enemy armor.

Fighting continued for an hour, with the 12th Airborne dug in on one side, and the PAVN 203rd on the other. Suddenly the Airborne gave way, as the battalion commander heard Minh's address on the radio. Although the Airborne had wired the bridge with almost four thousand pounds of explosives, luckily for Nguyen Huu An, upon hearing Minh's order, the 12th Battalion deputy commander tossed the electric detonator into the river.

By 10:30, the column had crossed the Newport Bridge and entered Saigon. The lead T-54 destroyed a couple of M-113s at another small bridge.

As it continued into the city, it was hit by an anti-tank rocket fired from the second story of a building and lay burning in the street. The next tank in line fired a round into the building and kept moving. Finally arriving at Independence Palace, this tank got lost and circled around the building. The next tank, #843, reached the main gate. Attempting to break into the grounds, it got its gun barrel stuck in the iron gate. The next tank, #390, pushed past its stuck comrade and raced onto the palace grounds around 11:30 A.M. The 4th Company, 4th Tank Battalion, 203rd Tank Brigade, was the first unit inside the grounds of Independence Palace. Sappers and tank crewmen leaped off the tanks. Some raced to the palace to replace the South Vietnamese flag with the revolution's flag. Others marched upstairs to the conference room where Minh and his Cabinet were waiting for them. The long war was finally over.

AFTERMATH

The joyful reactions of Communist officers and senior political figures celebrating the defeat of South Vietnam has been widely publicized, while almost nothing has been written about the reactions of our allies. The rapid collapse of South Vietnam, combined with the fierce fighting of the final days, left most officers and men in complete shock. Total RVNAF casualties in the battle for Saigon are unknown, but were certainly not light. The fighting during the last days destroyed many units; very few did not sustain heavy losses.

For example, the 82nd Border Ranger Battalion, which had walked out of Quang Duc back in March only to end up in the hell of Xuan Loc, was pressed into the fight at Nuoc Trong. Out of the 410 men who began walking from Quang Duc, only sixty men and four officers survived those battles to retreat across the New Bridge on the morning of 30 April. Shortly thereafter, they ran into a Communist ambush, and the remainder of the unit was wiped out. Only Major Vuong Mong Long and a handful of men escaped death. The 25th Division and the two newly formed Ranger groups were destroyed. The 5th Division, cut off from Saigon, surrendered en masse.

On that fateful morning, many poignant scenes played out across Saigon. Brigadier General Tran Quang Khoi was moving his 3rd Brigade back across the New Bridge in a valiant attempt to rescue Saigon when he heard Minh's initial ceasefire order over the radio. His troops were perilously close to a head-on collision with the PAVN 1st Corps deep-penetration column, which was about three miles away on Route 13. Upon hearing the broadcast, Khoi halted his unit and gave the men permission to disband. He got in a car and drove to his home in the lower Delta.

Major General Le Minh Dao's 18th Division, which had fought so gallantly at Xuan Loc, was struggling to organize a defense along the Saigon–Bien Hoa highway when Dao learned of the news. He also disbanded his unit, donned civilian clothes, and tried to escape to IV Corps, although most of IV Corps surrendered or disbanded throughout the day.

Colonel Nguyen Thanh Tri's Marines were gathered at their main base several miles from the New Bridge when he heard Minh's surrender broadcast. Tri also disbanded his unit, and then he went to a relative's house nearby.

Colonel Phan Van Huan and the men of the 81st Airborne Rangers played out perhaps the most moving scene. Huan had been ordered to move his men across the New Bridge on 29 April and set up positions near Thu Duc. After crossing the bridge, he unsuccessfully attempted to contact various headquarters. On the morning of 30 April, his men learned of the surrender order. Gathering them together, Huan gave a short speech: "We were born in South Vietnam, and it was our duty to defend the South. Now we have been defeated, and, bitterly, we must follow the order issued by President Minh to turn in our weapons to the Viet Cong. My brothers, we . . . have fought side by side for many long years. At this historic moment, we must demonstrate that we are a disciplined unit. . . . [We will] march toward Saigon in order to contact a [PAVN] unit to turn in our weapons. I want you all to remember that you are not guilty of any crime, because you are following my orders. I am prepared to accept the guilt and I will lead the way. If the enemy shoots at us, I will be the first man hit."[24]

Shouldering their weapons, lining up four abreast in a column stretching almost half a mile long, the two thousand men of ARVN's most elite unit began marching along the highway toward Saigon. As promised, Colonel Huan was in the first row. Civilians lined the road to watch them. Many offered drinks to the men. Soon Huan saw ARVN soldiers walking from Saigon, clad only in their underwear and carrying their personal documents. When Huan asked them why they were dressed like that, they replied that the Communists had forced them to take off their clothes, turn in their weapons, and walk home.

Soon a Communist officer and troops met Huan on the highway. Huan told the officer his men were prepared to turn over their weapons, but they would not undress. If ordered to do so, they would refuse, and a firefight would break out. The Communist officer relented, and the soldiers of the 81st stacked their arms and dispersed. It was the final unit in Saigon to lay down its weapons.

While the U.S. Embassy had made much of intelligence rumors that, after victory, the North Vietnamese would engage in wholesale slaughter, there were no mass killings of the sort perpetrated in Hue in 1968. Retribution, though, was still heavy. Reports of executions abound. The 32nd Ranger Group, attempting to retreat from Tay Ninh on 29 April, was blocked on Route 1 by the 316th Division. One battalion, the 38th Rangers, refused to surrender, and fought until the end. According to Ranger sources, the battalion commander, Major Tran Dinh Tu, was promptly executed. In a well-publicized example, Colonel Ho Ngoc Can, the province chief of Chuong Thien and Soldier of the Year in 1972, also refused to surrender. He fought until he ran out of ammunition. He was also executed shortly thereafter. Numerous police officers and police chiefs, particularly in the villages, were shot to death by vengeful partisans.

While the total number of executions remains unknown, revenge killings were not the Communists' main plan. There is no doubt, as seen in the 5 January document from Hanoi's Ministry of the Interior (Public Security), that the Communists planned to incarcerate large numbers of RVNAF officers. The prison system soon known as the Bamboo Gulag sprouted up across the countryside. Hundreds of thousands of military and civilian prisoners worked hard labor in the jungle with little food, medicine, or clothing. The death toll was in the thousands. Many officers holding the rank of major or higher were not released until 1987. Included in this group were Colonel Tri of the Marines and Colonel Huan of the 81st Airborne. The more recalcitrant were severely punished, especially those whose units fought until the end. Khoi, Dao, and two other generals were not released until 1992, seventeen years after the war's end. They were the last four general officers held.

Most Western journalists portrayed RVNAF officers as deserting their men in droves. In reality, very few regular Army or Marine officers commanding troops during the final days left their soldiers. While some younger officers deserted, most mid- and upper-level commanders stayed with their men. For example, not one Ranger-group or battalion commander deserted his men. Of the senior officers who escaped at the end, Lieutenant Generals Truong and Thi, for example, were no longer commanding units. Most of the senior officers who left the country early held staff positions. Unfortunately, Lieutenant General Toan and some others did desert, leaving an indelible stain on South Vietnam's image.

Some chose a path other than escape or prison. The commanders of the ARVN 5th and 7th Divisions committed suicide, as did two corps commanders—Major General Nam in IV Corps, and Major General Phu. Nam's deputy, Brigadier General Le Van Hung, also killed himself. Many lower-ranking officers and enlisted soldiers did as well.

Despite the popular conception that the final battle for Saigon was an easy affair, the generals of the People's Army disagree. In a commentary after the war, the commander of the 10th Division, Senior Colonel Ho De, acknowledged the heavy fighting that the 24th Regiment's deep-penetration column faced. He admitted that the column lost 185 men dead and wounded, and that "The entire division (including attached units) suffered more than 400 casualties. These numbers demonstrate that the attack to liberate Saigon was not conducted down a 'red carpet' laid out for us by the enemy, as many people mistakenly believe."[25]

That misperception was widespread after the war. Since Saigon was captured with little damage, many Vietnamese light-heartedly remarked that PAVN had taken Saigon "without breaking a light bulb." In perhaps the most telling comment about the cost of the final battle, Major General Hoang Dan, deputy commander of the PAVN 2nd Corps, stated: "Back then, I told people, 'If anyone says that we attacked and captured Saigon without breaking a single light, I will give him a shovel and have him dig the graves of our dead.' During our attack on Saigon, our 2nd Corps lost more than 400 men, so I wonder how people can write such things."[26] In fact, Communist troop casualties for the last few days of fighting were high. According to a post-war study of the last stages of the war, "our main force units lost more than 6,000 men killed and wounded and almost 100 of our military vehicles were destroyed, including 33 tanks and armored personnel carriers."[27]

Frankly, the cost to both sides would have been much higher if Duong Van Minh had not essentially declared Saigon an open city, and then formally surrendered after the tanks reached Independence Palace. South Vietnamese units were still putting up stiff resistance in many places, but without high-level command and control, they were simply delaying the inevitable. Even if Lieutenant General Toan had stayed until the end, or if President Thieu had appointed Lieutenant General Truong to command the final battle, PAVN commanders were prepared to send infantry into the city and fight for it block by block. If that had occurred, Saigon would have been destroyed. While many South Vietnamese despise Minh for surrendering, at best the RVNAF had twenty-four of organized resistance left. Retreating to IV Corps was not a particularly viable option.

As has been shown, the impact of U.S. congressional restraints on aid devastated America's ally. Claims that the White House started asking for reduced budgetary amounts disregard the rationale for that reduction: RVNAF expenses were expected to lessen dramatically because of the ceasefire. But the ceasefire never materialized, and Congress cut the funds anyway in maddening tandem with the escalating combat. A second argument—that some aid monies remained unspent at the end—is oblivious to the budgetary and supply process. And both contentions ignore the wider ramifications: that each side rightly interpreted the aid reductions and congressional mandates preventing the re-introduction of airpower as America shedding itself of South Vietnam. Simply put, congressional actions crushed South Vietnamese morale and emboldened the North Vietnamese. The weakening of South Vietnam that resulted from these actions was one of two primary factors in Hanoi's decision to resume offensive operations. The other was Hanoi's conclusion that it had a small window in which to act, before the U.S. and the GVN recovered from their "internal contradictions." Congress, relentlessly pressured by anti-war crusaders, cut aid and eliminated American military action at precisely the moment the Politburo viewed as its last, best chance to win the long war. These two actions must be considered among America's worst foreign-policy fiascos of the twentieth century.

Assertions that Hanoi received substantially less aid than Saigon are also disingenuous. U.S. intelligence possessed few facts about the size and true costs of Soviet Bloc and Chinese exports to North Vietnam, and thus its studies on this aspect were pure guesswork. Even if we did know the precise amounts, the costs of the two military systems are not comparable. The RVNAF was a much more expensive military to maintain. Personnel costs (salaries, health care, family housing, food, training, etc.) were far higher on the South Vietnamese side. The Communists' weapons (rifles, ammunition, tanks, etc.) were mass-manufactured by government entities, not by private firms concerned about their profit margins. Soviet Bloc weaponry was also simpler to maintain, another reason aid monies to North Vietnam could go much further. American material (helicopters, trucks, airplanes, gear) reflected the disparity between American and Soviet/Chinese military doctrine, which dramatically affected weapon costs. We built the RVNAF in our image, which meant greater reliance on firepower and machines than manpower. Lastly, the South Vietnamese had to guard everywhere, all the time, while the Communists could maintain relatively smaller forces that they could mass at will.

What is also clear is that the Communists, soon after the signing of the Paris Peace Accords, quickly and secretly moved to break them. Over two years, the North Vietnamese massed an army in the South in complete contradiction of a solemn agreement. Yet aside from the massive ceasefire violation, from a purely military perspective, the strike at Ban Me Thuot must be considered among the most brilliant strategic choices of the war. Moreover, while ARVN lines were repeatedly broken by armor thrusts, it was PAVN staff work at the strategic level, and effective command and control at the unit level, that placed Communist units at the correct location to turn the tide of battle. Despite many personal rivalries and animosities between individual Communist generals, the PAVN senior command structure functioned well.

The 1975 offensive highlighted the two main South Vietnamese military vulnerabilities. The first was Thieu's design of a weak Joint General Staff and independent corps, which prevented a coordinated response to a countrywide assault. Without strong military leadership and centralized planning at the JGS level to oversee the country's defenses, Thieu's decisions were compounded by poor oversight at key spots such as II Corps. Yet even with a better organizational structure, the South Vietnamese could not defend everywhere. Because of the country's geographical features—not because of a lack of RVNAF willingness to fight—U.S. airpower was needed to stem a major offensive.

The second problem, then, was the RVNAF's lack of reserves and the lack of adequate firepower to stem an initial and massive assault. After the Paris Accords, with the GVN's main reserve units pinned down in I Corps, the threat of U.S. air and naval firepower was South Vietnam's reserve. When Congress eliminated that threat, the South Vietnamese moved too slowly to activate new reserves. Even if they had, though, there was no money to purchase new weapons, and fuel reductions and lack of spare parts had decimated the VNAF's airlift capability. The South Vietnamese would have been unable to move large reserve units even if they had possessed them.

In the final analysis, there is nothing unambiguous about the Vietnam War. The post-war deliberations over American strategy have not provided flawless answers to difficult political/military questions, or remedies for the consequences of intense passions. Many U.S. decisions can be questioned, as can the choices made by President Thieu. Second-guessing is the fate of those who govern. While South Vietnam's government and armed forces were flawed, they were not the despotic police state and tin-pot military demonized by the Left around the world. One lesson Americans should understand from the defeat of South Vietnam is that multiple domestic and international concerns greatly shaped our policy towards that distant land. Nevertheless, we have not come to terms with the rancorous discourse over Vietnam that so deeply shook our country. Perhaps the question that remains most contentious is whether or not our domestic deliberations obstructed the effective conduct of foreign policy and, hence, decisively harmed the national interest.

Possibly only in America do moral and humanitarian philosophies both underpin and constrict our country's actions. America's greatness is not strictly evidenced by our industrial output or military strength, but by our underlying values. Pragmatism will never be our sole guide. We entered the war for many reasons, but one was to help the South Vietnamese people preserve their freedom. Those who claim the war was unwinnable and defeat was a result of historical conditions arising from de-colonization and a relentless urge for Vietnamese unity blithely ignore another reality: many Vietnamese did not want to be subjected to the deprivations of Communism. Why is their desire for freedom not seen as valid, their viewpoint dismissed? That millions of people fled in terror before the Communist advance, and then escaped in droves after the war, reveals the depth of their aspirations, a desire America tried to develop and protect. We should not be ashamed of that impulse.

The South Vietnamese were far from the incompetent bunglers so often depicted. Many of them demonstrated incredible courage, even in hopeless situations such as the battles of Tan Son Nhut, Ho Nai, and many others. By 1973, the South Vietnamese military, despite numerous internal and economic issues, had developed into a fighting force quite capable of defeating the North Vietnamese. If it had been adequately supplied, and with steady American post-ceasefire support, the outcome of the war might have been vastly different. Unfortunately, history does not offer "do-overs," only perspective.

NOTES

INTRODUCTION

1. Unfortunately, South Vietnamese documentation for the final years of the war remains mostly inaccessible to Western researchers. While materials from the First Republic of President Ngo Dinh Diem are fairly open, Communist officials often refuse access for the later years. Only recently have the Communists officially published some South Vietnamese documents.

2. Interview with Tran Tien San, former commander, 86th Ranger Battalion, 5 August 2006, Westminster, Calif.

3. "Le Duc Tho article marks 1975 victory," *FBIS Asia and Pacific*, 9 May 1986, K3-4.

4. A book by Colonel General Hoang Minh Thao about the Ban Me Thuot campaign was published in English in 1979, but it was a hackneyed propaganda screed typical of that era. Several years later, he wrote (in Vietnamese) a more readable memoir, but it remained unknown in the West, although an excellent chapter on Ban Me Thuot was translated and published by the Joint Publication Research Service (JPRS). Colonel General Tran Van Tra's book on the B-2 Front came out in 1982. His work, also translated into English by the JPRS, was in direct response to Dung's book. However, its criticism, though muted, of Dung and some Politburo decisions soon caused the authorities to ban its publication. The fourth book, by Senior General Hoang Van Thai, was also translated into English by the JPRS. Thai's book was written in part to address Tra's criticism. His is the best of the four.

5. The author thanks Merle Pribbenow, Robert Destatte, and Ron Ward for the following discussion, which is based upon a lengthy series of email exchanges on this subject.

6. *The People's Army of Vietnam: The First 55 Years* [*Quan Doi Nhan Dan Viet Nam: 55 Nam*] (Hanoi: People's Army Publishing House, 1999), 195.

CHAPTER 1

1. Nixon's "Peace with Honor" speech, 23 January 1973.

2. Henry A. Kissinger, *Ending the Vietnam War A History of America's Involvement in and Extrication from the Vietnam War* (New York: Simon & Schuster, 2003), 436–437.

3. Richard M. Nixon, *No More Vietnams* (New York: Arbor House, 1985), 169.

4. Kissinger, *Ending the Vietnam War*, 440.

5. Ibid., 459–460.

6. "Meeting with Secretary Richardson and the Joint Chiefs of Staff on Recognition for Returning Prisoners of War," 15 February 1973, National Archives and Records Administration (NARA), Gerald R. Ford Library, National Security Advisor Files, Box 1.

7. Richard Nixon, *RN: The Memoirs of Richard Nixon* (New York: Simon & Schuster, 1978), 757.

8. R. W. Apple, Jr., "President Warns Hanoi Not to Move Equipment South," *New York Times*, 16 March 1973, 1

9. Kissinger, *Ending the Vietnam War*, 468–469.

10. Interview with Hoang Duc Nha, 4 June 2009, Falls Church, Va.

11. Interview with Nguyen Xuan Tam, 18 October 2008, Springfield, Va.

12. According to the lunar calendar, Thieu was born at the hour, day, month, and year of Ty (the Rat), a rare four-fold confluence that in Vietnamese astrology is considered an extraordinarily good omen. As to whether Thieu used astrologers, former CIA Station Chief Ted Shackley claims that Thieu set the date for Operation Lam Son 719 with his astrologer. See Ted Shackley, with Richard A. Finney, *Spymaster: My Life in the CIA* (Dulles, Va.: Potomac Books, 2005), 244. When the author asked Hoang Duc Nha about this particular incident, he denied it.

13. Kissinger, *Ending the Vietnam War*, 223.

14. Arnold Isaacs, *Without Honor: Defeat in Vietnam and Cambodia* (New York: Vintage Books, 1983), 101–105.

15. "Hanoi Battles Economic Crimes," Saigon Embassy Airgram A-75, April 1974, Central Policy Files, Record Group (RG) 59, P-Reel 1974, Box 40C, Document P740040-1491, NARA, College Park, Md.

16. Odd Arne Westad, Chen Jian, Stein Tonnesson, and Nguyen Vu Tung and James G. Hershberg, *77 Conversations between Chinese and Foreign Leaders on the Wars in Indochina, 1964–1977* (Washington, D.C.: Cold War International History Project, The Woodrow Wilson Center, 1998),Working Paper #22, 172.

17. "Aide-Memoir," 2 April 1973, NARA, Nixon Library, National Security Council (NSC) Files, Country Files, Vietnam, Box 943, Folder 3.

18. Memo from Brent Scowcroft to General John Dunn, "Meeting with Vietnamese at San Clemente," 4 April 1973, Nixon Library, NSC Country Files, Vietnam, Box 943, Folder 1.

19. Memo, "The President's Meeting with President Nguyen Van Thieu of the RVN," 2 April 1973, Nixon Library, HAK Office Files, Vietnam Country Files, Box 103.

20. "Thieu Vows Never to Ask for Troops," *New York Times,* 6 April 1973, 1, 4.

21. Paul Quinn-Judge, "Inside Saigon: Eye-Witness Report," *Commonweal,* 26 September 1975, 430. Judge, a reporter who was also part of the Quaker American Friends Service Committee, then lists numerous well-known "Third Force" members who turned out to be Communists.

22. Kissinger, *Ending the Vietnam War,* 459–460.

23. Ibid., 352–353.

24. Ibid., 493.

CHAPTER 2

1. Vo Nguyen Giap, *The General Headquarters in the Spring of Brilliant Victory* (Hanoi: The Gioi Publishers, 2002), 33. It is uncertain whether Giap is referring to Vietnamese, or to Chinese Premier Zhou Enlai, who recommended that exact course in a meeting with Le Duan. Giap then devotes several pages to GVN ceasefire violations while never acknowledging Communist actions. In fact, he blatantly states that the North Vietnamese "needed to avail ourselves of the temporary suspension of enemy strikes to increase transport operations to the South," because the enemy could "cause us difficulties by requesting the stationing of international control posts at important communication junctions on the [Ho Chi Minh Trail]." Giap, *General Headquarters,* 34–35.

2. Ibid., 37.

3. Ibid., 40.

4. Lieutenant General Le Huu Duc, "Developing the Plan to Liberate South Vietnam in Two Years [Xay Dung Ke Hoach Giai Phong Mien Nam Trong Hai Nam]," *People's Army* [*Quan Doi Nhan Dan*], 9 March 2005. Duc was the chief of the General Staff's Combat Operations Department during the 1975 offensive.

5. MR-8 was the upper Delta, while MR-9 was the lower Delta. MR-9 was commanded by then Senior Colonel Le Duc Anh, who later became president of Vietnam from 1992 to 1997. His recent memoirs also parrot this story.

6. Tran Van Tra, *History of the Bulwark B-2 Theatre*, vol. 5: *Concluding the 30-Years War* (Arlington, Va.: Joint Publications Research Service Report, JPRS-SEA-82783, 2 February 1983), 33.

7. Giap, *General Headquarters*, 51–53.

8. Ibid.

9. "Chuong Thien Province—Struggle for Control in the Central Delta," Saigon Airgram #107, 9 August 1973, NARA, RG 59, Subject Numeric Files, 1970–1973, Box 2808. See also "The Lull in Chuong Thien," Amembassy Saigon to SecState, Cable #5276, 5 April 1973, NARA, RG 59, Central Foreign Policy Files, 1973–1974. http://aad.archives.gov/aad/series-list.jsp?cat=WR28. Unless noted, all subsequent cables are from this group.

10. Le Duc Anh, "The Final Phase of the War," *Vietnam Net*, 4 May 2006.

11. Ibid.

12. Tra, *Bulwark B-2 Theatre*, 57.

13. Giap, *General Headquarters*, 64.

14. Ibid.

15. Ibid., 69–70. Despite the post-war bitterness between Giap and Le Duan, Giap does not disparage the former General Secretary in his book.

16. James M. Markham, "Vietcong Order Indicates Support for Battle Step-Up," *New York Times*, 21 October 1973, 3, quoting the Communist document.

17. Le Duan, *Letters to the South* [*Thu Vao Nam*] (Hanoi: Su That Publishing House, 1985), 345–346.

18. "Meeting with Ambassador Graham Martin, 12 July 1973," NARA, Nixon Library, NSC Files, Vietnam, Box 165, May–September 1973, Folder 2.

19. Interview with Cao Van Vien, 11 November 2001, Reston, Va.

20. DAO Monthly Intelligence Survey and Threat Analysis (MISTA), September 1973, 1, 23.

21. Backchannel message from Martin to Kissinger, Martin #574, 5 January 1974, Declassified Documents Reference System (DDRS), Document, #2305, Gale Publishing, 1996.

CHAPTER 3

1. Letter from Major General John Murray to Colonel William Le Gro, 3 September 1976. Martin claimed in a cable to Kissinger that he had discussed the situation with Thieu, and that Thieu asked him not to discuss the aid cuts with the JGS or report their talk back to Washington for fear of a leak. Murray believes Martin lied.

2. Ibid.

3. Backchannel from Scowcroft to Martin, White House #31452, 29 December 1973.

4. "To Washington, the Struggle in Vietnam Has Become 'Their War,'" *New York Times*, 27 January 1974, 24.

5. William E. Le Gro, *Vietnam from Cease-Fire to Capitulation* (Washington, D.C.: Center for Military History, 1981), 87, quoting the Murray cable. Hoang Van Thai claims that in late September 1974, a spy sent the General Staff a copy of Murray's briefing slides. See Hoang Van Thai, *The Decisive Years: Memoirs of Senior General Hoang Van Thai* (Arlington, Va.: Joint Publications Research Service Report, JPRS-SEA-87-084, 23 June 1987), 65. Chapter 6 of this book discusses the spy's probable identity. Nguyen Tien Hung reprints the slides in his book. See Nguyen Tien Hung and Jerrold L. Schecter, *The Palace File* (New York: Harper and Row, 1986), 449–451.

6. Vien interview, 11 November 2001, Reston, Va.

7. Quotes taken from Thieu's 6 June speech at the Thu Duc academy.

8. Backchannel from Major General Murray to Major General Guthrie, 2 August 1974. According to the DAO, the VNAF lost seventy-five aircraft and helicopters from January 1973 to April 1974. None were replaced.

9. Backchannel from Major General Murray to Brigadier General Hoefling, 11 August 1974.

10. Letter from Murray to Le Gro, 3 September 1976.

11. "Communist Guidance on the 'New Phase' of the Revolution in South Vietnam,'" *Vietnam Documents and Research Notes* #117, U.S. Embassy, Saigon, April 1974, 2.

12. DAO MISTA, March 1974, quoting the Nghi statements. According to the DAO, these remarks had a direct impact on morale among the Southern-born Communists. They interpreted the explanations as sacrificing their interests for Northern reconstruction, and several high-ranking cadres quickly defected.

13. *The Diplomatic Struggle as Part of the People's National Democratic Revolution (1945–1954)*, vol. 2 [*Dau Tranh Ngoai Giao Trong Cach Mang Dan*

Toc Dan Chu Nhan Dan (1945–1954), Tap Hai] (Hanoi: Ministry of Foreign Affairs, 1976), 228. Dong's remarks came from a speech reviewing the Geneva Accords.

14. Giap, *General Headquarters*, 75.

15. During the 21st Plenum, the Politburo authorized the formation of the 1st Corps (called the "Determined to Win" Corps), which came into existence on 23 October 1973. The 2nd Corps was formed on 17 May 1974 by a General Staff directive stemming from the same earlier Politburo decision.

16. Thai, *Decisive Years*, 38.

17. Ibid., 39.

18. Ibid., 51.

CHAPTER 4

1. Tran Quang Khoi, "Fighting to the Finish: The Role of South Vietnam's III Armor Brigade and III Corps Assault Force in the War's Final Days," *Armor* (March/April 1996), 14.

2. Tra, *Bulwark B-2 Theatre*, 76.

3. Ibid., 84. The 6th Division had only two regiments, hence the minus designation.

4. Hoang Cam served as a battalion commander during the battle of Dien Bien Phu in 1954. In late December 1964, he was sent south to join the B-2 Front. He arrived in South Vietnam in the spring of 1965, and was eventually assigned as the first commander of the 9th Division when it was created on 2 September 1965, the first Communist division formed in South Vietnam. Cam assumed command of the 4th Corps when it was created in July 1974.

5. Interview with Major General Le Minh Dao, 7 April 2001, East Hartford, Conn. On 23 April 1975, President Tran Van Huong promoted him to major general for his valor at the Xuan Loc battle.

6. DAO, *RVNAF Final Assessment, Jan Thru Apr FY 75* (Washington, D.C.: Department. of the Army, 1975), 5–19.

7. "On Nixon's Resignation of the Presidency of the United States, and a Number of Urgent Party Tasks," Politburo Resolution No. 236-NQ/TW, 13 August 1974, *Collected Party Documents*, vol. 35, *1974* [*Van Kien Dang, Toan, Tap 35, 1974*] (National Political Publishing House, Hanoi, 2004), 116–123.

8. "FY 75 Defense Assistance to Vietnam," Amembassy Saigon to SecState, #10622, 13 August 1974.

9. Ford letter to Thieu, 10 August 1974, as seen in Hung, *Palace File*, 240.

10. Murray memo on Gayler debriefing, 1, 9.

11. "Military Operations in MR3," Bien Hoa to Saigon, #541, 21 October 1974.

12. Major General Homer Smith, "End of Tour Report," 30 May 1975, 5–6.

13. General Cao Van Vien, "Memorandum for the President of the Republic of Vietnam," backchannel from Murray to Hunt, 16 August 1974, 3.

14. Thieu letter to Ford, 19 September 1974, DDRS, #2825, 1992.

15. "Memorandum of Conversation," 12 September 1974, NARA, Ford Library, NSC Files, Bi-Partisan Congressional Leadership, Box 5.

16. "Memorandum of Conversation," 13 September 1974, DDRS, #593, 1993.

17. Thai, *Decisive Years*, 55.

18. *Review of the Resistance War against the Americans to Save the Nation: Victory and Lessons (Internal Distribution Only)* [*Tong Ket Cuoc Khang Chien Chong My Cuu Nuoc: Thang Loi va Bai Hoc (Luu Hanh Noi Bo)*] (Hanoi: National Political Publishing House, 1995), 95.

19. Thai, *Decisive Years*, 57.

20. Merle Pribbenow, "North Vietnam's Final Offensive: Strategic Endgame Nonpareil," *Parameters*, no. 4 (Winter/Spring 2000), 63.

21. "Secret Documents of the CPV on Completing the Liberation of the South, Part 1," *Vietnam Social Sciences*, vol. 2, no. 46 (1995), 110–118.

CHAPTER 5

1. The original 324th Division was disbanded in early 1967, and the regiments became independent. In February 1969, the division was reconstituted, and allied intelligence designated it the 324B Division. However, PAVN did not use this designation for the 324th. The "B" is used when a division "clones" itself. A group of core cadres from the original division remains behind to train a new one, while the original unit sets off for the battlefield. In this case, the 324th was disbanded in early 1967 and then reformed using most of the old divisional elements. Therefore, the author has decided not to use the 324B designation.

2. Nguyen Duy Hinh, *Vietnamization and the Cease-Fire* (Washington, D.C.: Center for Military History, 1984), 179.

3. *History of the 2nd Corps (1974–1994)* [*Lich Su Quan Doan 2 (1974–1994)*] (Hanoi: People's Army Publishing House, 1994), 94.

4. Hoang Dan, *Things Accumulated during Two Wars* [*Nhung Dieu Dong Lai Qua Hai Cuoc Chien Tranh*] (Hanoi: People's Army Publishing House, 2005), 237

5. Thai, *Decisive Years*, 63, 66. To be precise, while Thuong Duc was the main battle that convinced the General Staff, it was the culmination of all the battles that raged throughout I and II Corps in the summer and fall of 1974 that helped form this conclusion.

6. Lieutenant General Ngo Quang Truong, "Significant Events in I Corps from the Ceasefire January 28, 1973, until the Withdrawal from Danang March 30, 1975," 6 November 1975, General Research Corporation, *Interviews and Debriefings of Refugees from Southeast Asia*, vol. 1, 24–25. Hereafter *Interviews*.

7. Isaacs, *Without Honor*, 329.

8. "Cable from the COSVN Party Current Affairs Committee to the Politburo Reporting on the Results of COSVN's 13th Party Plenum," *Historical Chronicle of the Cochin China Party Committee and the Central Office for South Vietnam, 1954–1975* [*Lich Su Bien Nien Xu Uy Nam Bo Va Trung Uong Cuc Mien Nam (1954–1975)*] (Hanoi: National Political Publishing House, 2002), 1027.

9. Tra, *Bulwark B-2 Theatre*, 102.

10. Giap, *General Headquarters*, 131.

11. Tra, *Bulwark B-2 Theatre*, 107.

12. Ibid., 106.

13. Ibid., 112.

14. Dam Huu Phuoc, "Phuoc Long: The Wound That Never Heals," *Airborne Ranger*, no. 3 (2001), 30.

15. Le Gro, *Cease-Fire to Capitulation*, 137.

16. "US Reaction to North Vietnamese Offensive," Amembassy Saigon to SecState, #267, 8 January 1975.

17. The WSAG was composed of the national security advisor, the deputy secretaries of state and defense, the chairman of the JCS, and the director of the CIA.

18. Meeting, Washington Special Actions Group, 7 January 1975, 3, 12.

19. "DAO Saigon Monthly Assessment," 3 January 1975, 3.

20. "Supplemental Aid Request for Vietnam and Cambodia," Ford Library, NSC Files, MEMCONs, Box 8.

21. "President Ford—After Six Months in Office," *Chicago Tribune*, 9 February 1975, B1–B3.

CHAPTER 6

1. Murray memo on Gayler debriefing.

2. Maynard Parker, "Vietnam: The War That Won't End," *Foreign Affairs,* vol. 53 (January 1975), 352.

3. Vien, *Final Collapse,* 56.

4. Pham Ba Hoa, *A Few Lines of Reminiscence: A Memoir* [*Doi Dong Ghi Nho: Hoi Ky*] (Houston, Tex.: Ngay Nay, 1994), 231.

5. Philip McCombs, "Thieu: 'I Won't Give Up,'" *Washington Post,* 29 January 1975, 1, 18.

6. Letter from Thieu to Ford, 25 January 1975, Ford Library, NSC Files, East Asian and Pacific Affairs, Box 12.

7. "Meeting with President Thieu," Amembassy Saigon to SecState, #11475, 31 August 1974.

8. James Markham, "Political Foes Bid Thieu Step Down," *New York Times,* 10 February 1975, 11, quoting the speech.

9. "Three-year aid program for South Vietnam," 4 March 1975, Ford Library, NSC files, MEMCONs, Box 9.

10. MEMCON, 5 March 1975, Ford Library, NSC Files, East Asian and Pacific Affairs, Box 12.

11. Kissinger, *Ending the Vietnam War,* 510.

12. Giap, *General Headquarters,* 150.

13. Frank Snepp, *Decent Interval: An Insider's Account of Saigon's Indecent End, Told by the CIA's Chief Strategy Analyst in Vietnam* (New York: Random House, 1977), 135.

14. In discussions with General Vien and several of his staff members, they resolutely deny that this man had the access he claimed. They do not recall him specifically, but they claim internal security procedures would have prevented such an intelligence coup. At this point, it is impossible to ascertain the truth, but the author has chosen Hanoi's version of how it obtained such vital intelligence.

15. Thanh Xuan, "Intelligence Warrior H3 Inside the Joint General Staff," *Quan Doi Nhan Dan,* 25 April 2005.

16. Ibid.

17. Vo Chi Cong, *On the Road of Revolution (A Memoir)* [*Tren Nhung Chang Duong Cach Mang (Hoi Ky)*] (Hanoi: National Political Publishing House,

2001), 262. Cong was the political officer of the B-1 Front during much of the war. Afterwards he became a Politburo member and, subsequently, president of Vietnam.

18. "Secret Documents of the CPV on Completing the Liberation of the South, Part 2," *Vietnam Social Sciences*, vol. 3, no. 47 (1995), 108–117.

19. Van Tien Dung, *Our Great Spring Victory: An Account of the Liberation of South Vietnam*, trans. John Spragens Jr. (Hanoi: The Gioi Publishers, 2000), 30.

20. "Comrade Le Duc Tho Discusses a Number of Issues Related to Reviewing the War and Writing Military History," *Military History Magazine* [*Tap Chi Lich Su Quan Su*], Military Institute of Vietnam, vol. 3, no. 27 (1988), 5–6. The author thanks Dr. Nguyen Lien Hang for a copy of this article.

21. For a full discussion of the Giap–Le Duan–Dung clash over the Tet Offensive, see Merle Pribbenow, "General Vo Nguyen Giap and the Mysterious Evolution of the Plan for the 1968 Tet Offensive," *Journal of Vietnamese Studies*, vol. 3, no. 2 (Summer 2008).

22. Colonel General Hoang Minh Thao, "Ex-Central Highlands Commander Recounts Buon Ma Thuot Battle," *Quan Doi Nhan Dan* (March 1982), translated in JPRS SEA-80692, 13–14.

23. Giap, *General Headquarters*, 154.

24. Thien's real name was Phan Dinh Dinh, and he was Le Duc Tho's brother.

25. Dang Vu Hiep in cooperation with Le Hai Trieu and Ngo Vinh Binh, *Highland Memories* [*Ky Uc Tay Nguyen*] (Hanoi: People's Army Publishing House, 2000), 286.

26. Le Gro diary, January 1975, 9. According the NSA historian Robert Hanyok, "SIGINT indicated that the 316th was being regenerated in North Vietnam. All communications serving the division ceased on 11 February, although references to it receiving supplies continued into March." See Robert Hanyok, *Spartans in Darkness: American SIGINT and the Indochina War, 1945–1975* (Washington, D.C.: National Security Agency, Center for Cryptologic History, 2002), 448, note 71.

27. *Victory in Vietnam: The Official History of the People's Army of Vietnam, 1945–1975*, trans. Merle L. Pribbenow (Lawrence: University of Kansas Press, 2002), 363.

28. Thao, "Ex-Central Highlands Commander," 18–20.

29. Lieutenant General Dam Van Nguy with Le Minh Huy and Duong Duy Ngu, *The Farther You Travel* [*Di Mot Ngay Dang*] (Hanoi: People's Army Publishing House, 1994), 183–184. The title is half of a folk saying, "The farther you travel, the more you learn."

30. Hiep, *Highland Memories*, 296.

31. Nguy, *The Farther You Travel*, 185.

32. Beginning in mid-1972, Brigadier General Phan Dinh Niem, one of the best ARVN division commanders, had rebuilt the 22nd from a unit decimated in the 1972 offensive into one of ARVN's top outfits. The 22nd's traditional enemy was the 3rd (*Sao Vang* [Yellow Star]) Division, and since the end of 1972, the 22nd Division had repeatedly trounced the 3rd Division. Given the large territory it had to cover, the 22nd, like the 1st Division, was a heavy division, with four regiments instead of the usual three. The four regiments were the 40th, 41st, 42nd, and 47th.

33. Nguyen Tu, "Region II Commander Talks to Chinh Luan Correspondent about the Battle of Wits in the Central Highlands," *Chinh Luan*, 18 February 1975.

34. Hoang Ngoc Lung, *Intelligence* (Washington, D.C.: Center for Military History, 1984), 222.

35. Nguyen Khai, *March in the Central Highlands: A Report [Thang Ba O Tay Nguyen: Ky Su]* (Hanoi: People's Army Publishing House, 1976), 156. Khai was a North Vietnamese journalist who accompanied PAVN forces during the Central Highlands campaign. He later published a book that included many ARVN documents. In mid-April 1975, Phu and several other senior officers were arrested and charged with dereliction of duty for losing I and II Corps. Each was required to write a statement outlining his actions. Khai reprinted Phu's, including Thieu's handwritten comments. When Phu discussed sending reinforcements to Ban Me Thuot after the assault, Thieu wrote: "Prior to the Tet New Year he knew the situation at Ban Me Thuot was serious and planned to move the 23rd Division back. Why didn't he carry out this plan, leaving us unable to send in reinforcements in time when the enemy attacked?"

36. *968th Division [Su Doan 968]* (Quang Tri: The 968th Division and the Quang Tri Province Bureau, 1990), 150.

CHAPTER 7

1. The 3rd Troop, 8th Cavalry, was scattered throughout Ban Me Thuot guarding various important locations. When the Communists attacked, it was quickly overwhelmed. The commander of the unit was Captain Le Trung Tanh, Brigadier General Tuong's younger brother.

2. Thai, *Decisive Years*, 87.

3. General Cao Van Vien, "Instructions from the President of the Republic of Vietnam on Present War Policies" (n.d.), reproduced in Khai's *March in the Central Highlands*, 89–90.

4. Hiep, *Highland Memories*, 302.

5. *The Lowlands Division (Central Highlands Corps)*, vol. 3 [*Su Doan Dong Bang (Binh Doan Tay Nguyen)*, Tap Ba] (Hanoi: People's Army Publishing House, 1984), 259. Hereafter *320th Division*.

6. *Ban Me Thuot: A Historic Battle* [*Buon Ma Thuot: Tran Danh Lich Su*] (Ban Me Thuot: Darlac Province Party Historical Research Subcommittee, 1990), 46. The book provides the name of the unfortunate officer, Second Lieutenant Bui Ngoc Tham. While participating in the attack against the 53rd Regiment base camp about ten days later, he was blinded in both eyes.

7. Polgar was born in Hungary, departing that country in 1938 for America. He served in the U.S. Army in military intelligence during World War II, eventually joining the CIA when the agency was born in 1947. He progressed up the ranks, and in 1970 received his first major assignment—CIA station chief in Buenos Aires. In July 1971 he helped foil a hijacking there by an American and his Guatemalan girlfriend. For his actions, he received the State Department's Award for Valor. Polgar, a short, balding man with a penetrating intellect, was assigned as Saigon station chief in late 1972.

8. See for example, Kim Willenson, *The Bad War: An Oral History of the Vietnam War* (New York: NAL Penguin, 1987), 289.

9. Hanyok, *Spartans in Darkness*, 432.

10. Interview with Tom Glenn, 25 February 2008, Columbia, Md. See also Hanyok, *Spartans in Darkness*, 433.

11. Vu Van Mao, "The Battlefield Exploits of Military Intelligence Personnel: The Central Highlands Campaign [Chien Cong cua Nhung Nguoi Linh Quan Bao: Chien Dich Tay Nguyen]," *People's Army* [*Quan Doi Nhan Dan*], #12153, 20 March 1995, and #12154, 21 March 1995.

12. Dung, *Great Spring Victory*, 52–53.

13. Interview with Colonel Le Cau, 8 June 2002, Philadelphia, Pa. Colonel Cau graduated from the Dalat Military Academy in 1963, and spent the next twelve years defending his country, rising in rank from second lieutenant to colonel. He was wounded three times in battle and earned several of South Vietnam's highest medals, along with America's Silver and Bronze Stars.

14. *The Yellow Star Division* [*Su Doan Sao Vang*] (Hanoi: People's Army Publishing House, 1984), 324, 330. Hereafter *3rd Division*.

15. Ibid., 327.

16. Moncrieff J. Spear, "The Communist Offensive in Region Two" (n.d.), 2, Folder 1, Box 1, Moncrieff J. Spear Collection, The Vietnam Archive, Texas Tech University.

17. Dung, *Great Spring Victory*, 64.

18. *316th Division*, vol. 2 [*Su Doan 316*, Tap II] (Hanoi: People's Army Publishing House, 1986), 276.

19. *10th Division: Central Highlands Corps* [*Su Doan 10: Binh Doan Tay Nguyen*] (Hanoi: People's Army Publishing House, 1987), 92–95.

20. Dung, *Great Spring Victory*, 70.

21. *History of the 198th Sapper Group* [*Lich Su Doan Dac Cong 198*] (Hanoi?: Sapper Command, 1991), 54.

22. *10th Division*, 100.

23. Hiep, *Highland Memories*, 310–311.

24. Pham Huan, *The Withdrawal from the Central Highlands, 1975* [*Cuoc Triet Thoai Cao Nguyen, 1975*] (San Jose, Calif.: Self-published, 1987), 50. Pham Huan was a veteran journalist and military officer engaged in writing Phu's biography while also serving as a member of his staff. Huan was also a member of the editorial staff of *Dieu Hau* [*The Hawk*], an ARVN newspaper published in Saigon. He had served in 1973 as a press officer of the Four-Party and the Two-Party Joint Military Commissions. He also served from 1972 to 1975 as chairman of the Vietnam War Correspondents Association. Phu allowed Huan to stay constantly by his side during the climactic days of March 1975. Huan kept a diary of the events in II Corps, and after leaving Vietnam in 1987, he published his diary. His work is an invaluable asset in understanding the sequence of events in II Corps.

25. Nguyen Trong Luat, "Looking Back at the Battle for Ban Me Thuot [Nhin Lai Tran Danh Ban Me Thuot]," *World Today* [*The Gioi Ngay Nay*], issue 140 (March and April 1997), 48–59.

26. Huan, *Withdrawal from the Central Highlands*, 65.

27. Major General Hoang Minh Thao, *The Victorious Tay Nguyen Campaign* (Hanoi: Foreign Language Publishing House, 1979), 111. This is Thao's official history of the campaign, published before his memoir.

CHAPTER 8

1. Hung, *Palace File*, 267–268. Hung's information came from post-war interviews with Thieu, and is the only published explanation by the president regarding his decisions.

2. There has been speculation in South Vietnamese circles that Thieu ordered the withdrawal to create a crisis that he hoped would spur the U.S. Congress to grant more aid, or even persuade the Americans to re-enter the war. Another theory proclaims that Thieu knew the war was over, and deliberately disorganized ARVN to prevent large-scale battles that would cost thousands of lives. The author believes neither theory has any substance.

3. Interview of General Cao Van Vien by Neil Sheehan, 26 June 1973, Box 80, Papers of Neil Sheehan, Manuscript Division, Library of Congress, Washington, D.C. The author thanks Dr. Larry Berman for alerting him to the Sheehan collection.

4. Stephen T. Hosmer, Konrad Kellen, and Brian M. Jenkins, *The Fall of South Vietnam: Statements by Vietnamese Military and Civilian Leaders* (RAND R-2208-OSD [HIST], December 1978), 180.

5. Moncrieff Spear, "Comments on the Collapse of the Republic of Vietnam" (n.d.), Folder 01, Box 01, Moncrieff J. Spear Collection, The Vietnam Archive, Texas Tech University.

6. Vien, *Final Collapse*, 84.

7. General Cao Van Vien, "His Observations of Events Leading to the Collapse of the Republic of Vietnam," *Interviews*, vol. 1, 6.

8. Thomas Ahern, *The CIA and the Generals: Covert Support to Military Government in South Vietnam* (Washington, D.C.: Central Intelligence Agency, n.d.), 160, fn. 9.

9. Interview with Nguyen Quang Vinh, 7 October 2010, Dallas, Tex.

10. Hosmer et al., *Fall of South Vietnam*, 184. Phu told Pham Huan the same thing. Huan, *Withdrawal*, 150.

11. Edward Haley, *Congress and the Fall of South Vietnam and Cambodia* (East Brunswick, N.J.: Fairleigh Dickinson Press, 1982), 68.

12. "Aid for Vietnam," SecState to AmConsul Jerusalem, #055010, 12 March 1975.

13. Letter from Martin to Thieu, 14 March 1975, DDRS #3097, 1995.

14. Backchannel message from Lehmann to Martin, Martin #671, DDRS #3335, 1995.

15. Robert Martens, "Interview with Wolfgang J. Lehmann," The Association for Diplomatic Studies and Training Foreign Affairs Oral History Project, 9 May 1989, 12.

16. Snepp writes: "a CIA agent on Phu's staff alerted his local American case officer that a total abandonment of the Highlands was imminent." Snepp, *Decent Interval*, 196. In a post-war interview, Ly states: "I told the CIA peo-

ple . . . that we were withdrawing." Larry Engelmann, *Tears before the Rain: An Oral History of the Fall of South Vietnam* (New York: Oxford University Press, 1990), 229. Ly's status as a CIA source is revealed officially in Ahern's *The CIA and the Generals*, 157–158.

17. Telephone interview with Ngo Le Tinh, 18 June 2007, Katy, Tex.

18. Bao Chan, "The Spy without a Secret Code Number [Nguoi Tinh Bao Khong Mang Bi So]," *Lao Dong*, 27 April 2006. The article describes how the commander of the 247th RF Battalion, a graduate of the Dalat Military Academy and a former officer of the 23rd Division, had been a Communist agent since 1955.

19. Thai, *Decisive Years*, 92.

20. Cable #3, Dung to Giap, 11 March 1975, Dung, *Great Spring Victory*, 78–79.

21. Cable #1 from Giap to Dung, 11 March 1975, *Great Spring Victory, 1975: Party Documents [Dai Thang Mua Xuan, 1975: Van Kien Dang]* (Hanoi: National Political Publishing House, 2005), 110–113. The author thanks Ron Ward for obtaining a copy of this critical primary source collection.

22. Giap, *General Headquarters*, 185.

23. Dung, *Great Spring Victory*, 83–84.

24. Cable from the Central Military Affairs Committee to Dung, 13 March 1975, *A Number of Guidance Documents for the Spring 1975 General Offensive and Uprising and the Ho Chi Minh Campaign [Mot So Van Kien Chi Dao: Tong Tien Cong Va Noi Day Mua Xuan Nam 1975]* (Hanoi: People's Army Publishing House, 2005), 205.

25. Cable #5, from Dung to the Politburo, 14 March 1975, *Great Spring Victory, 1975*, 128–129.

26. Cable #11, from Giap to Dung, 15 March 1975, *Great Spring Victory, 1975*, 146–147.

27. Dung, *Great Spring Victory*, 104. As can be imagined, Dung's reprimand had an impact. According to the 320th Division history, Tuan was a "mature, calm, unflappable officer"; Tuan's staff had "never seen the commander as nervous and excited as he was on this occasion." *320th Division*, 275.

CHAPTER 9

1. Colonel Le Khac Ly, "The Collapse of II Corps and the Final Days in MR-2," *Interviews*, vol. 1, 110.

2. Interview with Earl Thieme, 2 March 2008. The author thanks Mr. Thieme for a copy of both his original message to Spear, dated 15 March, and

his 27 March 1975 written description of the events in Pleiku during the withdrawal. There is some dispute over the sequence of events. The CIA representative claims he told Thieme about the evacuation after speaking to Ly, rather than Thieme's hearing it from Phu. See Ahern, *CIA and the Generals*, 158–159. In Ly's interviews after the war, he neglects to mention that Phu also told the Americans to depart, making it seem that only he had done so.

3. Since Tat spent thirteen years in a Communist prison, he never spoke about his role in the retreat until now. In an interview with the author, Tat wished to correct several statements. First, General Vien wrote in his book that when Phu requested permission at Cam Ranh Bay to promote Tat, Vien said he did not know him. Tat says that he knew Vien well, and charitably excuses Vien's error as "bad memory." Ly would later accuse Tat of corruption and cronyism with Phu, and laid much of the blame for the botched retreat on Tat. Dong would also chastise Tat for his actions on 7B. Tat denies the corruption charges, stating that he had avoided corrupt activities for years and left the Special Forces because he no longer wanted to work for the notoriously corrupt Special Forces commander, Brigadier General Doan Van Quang. He strongly disagrees with Dong about Cheo Reo, claiming that Dong was under Phu's command, not his. Tat says that Phu told Dong to hold open Cheo Reo, while it was Tat's job to get the Rangers to Tuy Hoa. He is aware of the stories about him, but he had refrained from speaking publicly as he did not want to speak ill of anyone. When South Vietnam surrendered on 30 April 1975, he refused to depart, saying he hated America for deserting his country. Prison changed his mind, and he now lives quietly in Virginia. Author interview, 18 October 2008.

4. Ha Mai Viet, *Steel and Blood: Armor in the Vietnam War* (Annapolis: Naval Institute Press, 2008), 245.

5. "Attack on Retreating Enemy Force at Cheo Reo (Central Highlands), 17–25 March 1975 [Tran Tien Cong Dich Rut Chay Tai Cheo Reo (Tay Nguyen), 17–25–3–1975]," in *Battles of Vietnamese Artillery during the Wars of Liberation and to Defend the Fatherland*, vol. II [*Nhung Tran Danh Cua Phao Binh Vietnam Trong Cac Cuoc Chien Tranh Giai Phong Va Bao Ve To Quoc*, Tap II] (Hanoi?: Artillery Command, 1990), 157.

6. The 320th Division established a network of observation posts to monitor enemy forces in the My Thach–Cheo Reo area, and a radio station to relay messages. But the northernmost 320th lookout was twenty-five miles south of the Route 7B turnoff, too far for any observers to have seen the convoy. Dung

and other PAVN commentators are unclear about the origins of the convoy report.

7. Edmund W. Sprague, "Report on Phu Bon Province and Convoy," 24 March 1975, Folder 1, Box 1, Moncrieff J. Spear Collection, The Vietnam Archive, Texas Tech. Sprague was a former Special Forces sergeant who spent many years working with the Montagnards. He was the only American in Cheo Reo during this time. Sprague's report is a devastating condemnation of South Vietnamese military and police behavior in the town. He also provided a detailed interview in 1977 to Gerald Hickey. See Gerald Cannon Hickey, *Free in the Forest: Ethnohistory of the Vietnamese Central Highlands* (New Haven and London: Yale University Press, 1982), 289. Sprague's timeline of events differs somewhat from Vietnamese accounts, mainly regarding units arriving and departing.

8. Tat grudgingly admits the depredations of his troops, but explains that his Ranger units were about two-thirds Montagnard and about one-third Vietnamese. The officers and sergeants were mostly Vietnamese. He states that the Vietnamese Ranger troops were generally the dregs—deserters who had been caught and shipped to the Highlands or convicts released from jail. Morale was bad, and drug use, mostly pot smoking, was rampant.

9. Nguyen Tu, "At 8:00 P.M. Sunday Night, Kontum-Pleiku Tragically Evacuated, Leaving behind Columns of Smoke and Areas in Flames," *Chinh Luan*, 18 March 1975.

10. Email to the author from Vu Dinh Hieu, former assistant G-3 (operations officer), 22nd Rangers, 24 September 2007. Hieu learned this from Major Nguyen Thanh Van, the commander of the almost stranded battalion. Tat claims that Le Khac Ly was supposed to send trucks to pick up his men, but failed to do so. Tat speculates that instead of driving to Kontum, the truck drivers gathered their families and departed for Cheo Reo.

11. Nguyen Tu, "A Bloody Road for Refugees," reprinted in *The Saigon Post*, 24 March 1975, 1, 2. *The Saigon Post* was an English-language newspaper owned by Ambassador Bui Diem. Tu noted that the Rangers fought all night to allow the refugees to escape through the jungle. Influential people in Saigon begged the VNAF to rescue Tu, and he and a number of other people were picked up on 18 March near Cheo Reo and flown to Tuy Hoa.

12. According to Dong, Ly handed him a note from Phu informing Dong that he was now in charge, and that it was his responsibility to get all heavy equipment back to Nha Trang. Ly then departed in a helicopter. Viet, *Steel and*

Blood, 248. Pham Huan says Phu also spoke directly to Dong on the radio, and issued essentially the same order. Huan, *Withdrawal from the Central Highlands*, 153. Huan also claims that Tat was told to move on foot with the troops. All other accounts, including one by a Ranger officer who was in Tat's command vehicle, say Phu definitely ordered Tat into a helicopter. In his various accounts, Ly barely mentions the transfer of command to Dong.

13. "320th Infantry Division's Pursuit Attack against Enemy Forces on Route 7 at Cheo Reo from 17 to 19 March 1975," in *A Number of Battles Fought by Units of the Central Highlands Corps*, vol. III [*Mot So Tran Danh cua cac Don Vi thuoc Binh Doan Tay Nguyen*, Tap III] (Hanoi: People's Army Publishing House, 1995), 164.

14. Hiep, *Highland Memories*, 324.

15. Cable from the Central Military Affairs Committee to Dung, 17 March 1975, *Number of Guidance Documents*, 208.

16. Thai, *Decisive Years*, 99.

17. *Historical Chronicle of the Central Office for South Vietnam*, 1061–1070.

18. Giap, *General Headquarters*, 210.

19. Dung, *Great Spring Victory*, 124–125.

20. Hiep, *Highland Memories,* 326.

21. Cable #38B, from Giap to Dung, *Great Spring Victory, 1975*, 166–167.

22. "Appraisal of Situation in South Vietnam," National Intelligence Bulletin, 17 March 1975.

23. Backchannel from Lehmann to Scowcroft, Martin #673, 17 March 1975, DDRS, #2312, 1993.

24. "Approach to Thieu," SecState to Amembassy Saigon, #062480, 20 March 1975, in *U.S. Policy in the Vietnam War, Part II: 1969–1975*, ed. Dr. John Prados (Washington, D.C.: The National Security Archive, 1992), no. 01333. Hereafter, *U.S. Policy* and the document number.

25. "Approach to Thieu," Amembassy Saigon to SecState, #3225, 20 March 1975. *U.S. Policy*, no. 01334.

26. "Situation in South Vietnam," backchannel message from Smith to Gayler, #122-75, 23 March 1975.

27. Letter from Ford to Thieu, 22 March 1975.

28. *Under One Flag: The National Liberation Front of South Vietnam* [*Chung Mot Bong Co: Mat Tran Dan Toc Giai Phong Mien Nam Viet Nam*] (Ho Chi Minh City: National Political Publishing House, 1993), 820. In a 2007 article describing his intelligence accomplishments, De attributes to himself the statements recorded in the Memcon made by Buu and several delegates. He

claims that in his "briefing" to Ford he made the military situation seem even worse than it was, and convinced the Americans not to send troops back to Vietnam. However, while the article is accurate in many aspects, De is not recorded in the Memcon as speaking. Manh Viet, "Meeting with a 'Viet Cong' Who Once Had a Face-to-Face Meeting with the U.S. President at the Pentagon [Gap Nguoi 'Viet Cong' Tung Doi Dien Tong Thong My Tan Lau Nam Goc]," *Tien Phong*, 14 February 2007.

29. Memcon, 25 March 1975, DDRS #52, 1993.

30. Lam had written a letter to Vice President Rockefeller, and Can to Speaker Albert, in late January, pleading South Vietnam's case. In addition, on 12 January 1975 twelve Lower House deputies sent an open letter to the U.S. House, and on 4 February forty-one Vietnamese senators sent an open letter to the U.S. Senate begging for aid. It is unknown whether there was any response.

31. "Letter to President Ford from Speaker Can and Senate President Lam," Amembassy Saigon to SecState, #3472, 25 March 1975.

32. Hung, *Palace File*, 282–285.

33. Huan, *Withdrawal from the Central Highlands*, 158.

34. Nguyen Tu, "The Evacuation: Hundreds of People Stuck in Cung Son Turn Their Sun-Burned Faces toward the Sea," *Chinh Luan*, 25 March 1975. After being flown to Tuy Hoa, Tu shuttled back and forth to the stalled convoy.

35. "Phu Yen Convoy Reaches Highway 1," Amembassy Saigon to SecState, #3513, 26 March 1975.

36. North Vietnamese histories assert that in the campaign from Ban Me Thuot to Cheo Reo and along Routes 7B and 21, they lost "868 killed, 2,373 wounded, six captured, and 40 missing," for a total of 3,887 casualties. *1975 Central Highlands Campaign [Chien Dich Tay Nguyen 1975]* (Hanoi?: Military History Sub-Institute of the High-Level Military Studies Institute), 56. It is often impossible to determine the accuracy of the Communists' casualty figures, since they tend not to list losses by unit or by battle. One only gets a total, and one is expected to either accept it or not. The author has decided to include these figures, but he cautions future historians regarding their validity.

CHAPTER 10

1. Dinh Phong, "Journalist Tran Bach Dang—A Few Things That I Know about Him [Nha Bao Tran Bach Dang—Doi Dieu Toi Biet Ve Anh]," *Vietnamese Journalists Association Magazine*, 28 May 2007.

2. *The Lam River Division* [*Su Doan Song Lam*] (Hanoi: People's Army Publishing House, 1984), 36. The 341st Division was created in late 1972 from various units of MR-4, the region north of the DMZ. It was composed of three infantry regiments, the 266th, 270th, and 273rd, and was conducting troop training in Quang Binh province when Giap summoned the division commander. Hereafter *341st Division*.

3. "Cable from Pham Hung to the COSVN Current Affairs Committee," *Great Spring Victory, 1975*, 72.

4. Tra, *Bulwark B-2 Theatre*, 96–97.

5. Ibid., 145.

6. The 4th Corps was initially called Group 301. While all Western histories, including some Communist ones, claim that Major General Le Duc Anh commanded Group 232, both Tra, *Bulwark B-2 Theatre*, 146, and Giap, *General Headquarters*, 192, state that Major General Nguyen Minh Chau was the initial military commander.

7. To the author, Lieutenant General Toan strongly denied being corrupt, although he did laughingly admit to a "weakness for the ladies." In answering the corruption charges, Toan challenged that if he was so corrupt in Vietnam, why did he live so poorly in the United States? When other senior Vietnamese officers were queried about Toan's statement, most remarked that like the vast majority of corrupt officers, Toan had all his money in Vietnam.

8. Le Gro, *Cease-Fire to Capitulation*, 55.

9. Lieutenant General Nguyen Van Toan, "Significant Events in III Corps during the Period of My Command from 10 January 1975 to 28 April 1975," *Interviews*, vol. 1, 146.

10. DAO MISTA, "February Threat Assessment," 10 March 1975, 8–9.

11. Colonel General Hoang Cam and Nhat Tien, *The Ten-Thousand-Day Journey: A Memoir* [*Chang Duong Muoi Nghin Ngay: Hoi Ky*] (Hanoi: People's Army Publishing House, 1995), 401.

12. The 9th Division changed regimental designations so often, even PAVN historians have a hard time keeping them straight. In the official history for the 1975 time frame, they simply refer to them as the 1st, 2nd, and 3rd Regiments.

13. *9th Division* [*Su Doan 9*] (Hanoi: People's Army Publishing House, 1990), 274.

14. *The 303rd Division* [*Su Doan 303rd*] (Hanoi: People's Army Publishing House, 1989), 71.

15. Ibid., 73.

16. Ibid., 75.

17. On 21 April 1974, Senior Colonel Le Duc Anh was promoted two ranks to the grade of lieutenant general. The probable rationale for this rare move is that Hanoi wanted Anh to become the deputy commander of the B-2 Front, rewarding him for his earlier disobedience. In a bit of regional bias, they promoted him over both Major Generals Nguyen Minh Chau and Dong Van Cong, his counterparts at the B-2 Front, and the only true southerners in a command position. Tran Van Tra was from central Vietnam.

18. *7th Division: A Record [Su Doan 7: Ky Su]* (Hanoi: People's Army Publishing House, 1986), 271.

19. Telephone interview with Nguyen Huu Che, 22 August 2001, Warren, Mich.

20. *341st Division*, 43.

21. *303rd Division*, 86. After the attack on Phuoc Long, the original 271st Regiment of the 303rd Division cloned a 271B Regiment, which reported directly to COSVN.

22. Letter to the author from Vuong Mong Long, 25 March 2002, Seattle, Wash.

23. DAO Weekly Report for 8–14 March 1975, 20.

24. DAO Weekly Report for 15–21 March 1975, 35.

25. Nguyen Phan, "From a Bitter Time [Tu Mot Thoi Cay Dang]," *Brown Beret [Mu Nau]* (1994), 133. Phan was the operations officer of the 30th Ranger Battalion during the siege of Chon Thanh.

26. Cam, *A Memoir*, 436.

27. Tra, *Bulwark B-2 Theatre*, 152.

28. Ibid., 149.

29. Dung, *Great Spring Victory*, 203.

30. *4th Corps*, 144. The quotation is from a cable sent at 9:30 A.M. on 19 March by 2nd Forward Headquarters, 301st (the 4th Corps cover designation), to "R" (COSVN cover designation). Given that the message was from Bui Cat Vu's light HQ, and not the main HQ where Hoang Cam was located, and that Hoang Cam does not mention the message in his memoir but does discuss this strategy when he meets later with Tra, the author suspects it was Bui Cat Vu's novel, indeed brilliant, idea to strike south on Route 20.

31. Cam, *A Memoir*, 460.

32. "Documents," *Vietnam Social Sciences*, vol. 1–2 (1989), 149, quoting the Le Duan cable.

33. Tra, *Bulwark B-2 Theatre*, 154.

CHAPTER 11

1. Nguyen Thanh Tri, "Unforgettable Days [Ngay Thang Khong The Nao Quen]," *Song Than* [*Tidal Wave*], 2003, 37.

2. This is what Truong stated at the time. After the war he told RAND Corporation interviewers that even if the Airborne had not been withdrawn, "he would have required two additional divisions" to hold against the PAVN troops already in I Corps. Hosmer et al., *Fall of South Vietnam*, 224.

3. Many analysts erroneously believed then that the 341st first appeared in MR-1 in mid-March 1975, a mistake often continued to this day.

4. Nguyen Huu An, as told to Nguyen Tu Duong, *New Battlefield* [*Chien Truong Moi*] (Hanoi: People's Army Publishing House, 2002), 199.

5. Giap, *General Headquarters*, 166.

6. Ibid., 243.

7. An, *New Battlefield*, 195.

8. Lieutenant General Le Tu Dong, as told to Anh Trang, "Major Events during the Fighting in Tri-Thien-Hue," in *Central Vietnam Wins Total Victory: The 1975 Great Spring Victory (Through the Memoirs of Participants)* [*Mien Trung Toan Thang: Dai Thang Mua Xuan 1975 (Qua Nhung Trang Hoi Uc)*] (Hanoi: Encyclopedia Publishing House, 2005), 93. Dong was the commander of the B-4 Front.

9. Ngo Quang Truong, "Why I Abandoned I Corps," *Doi* [*Life*], October 1982, n.p.

10. Vien, *Final Collapse*, 57.

11. Snepp, *Decent Interval*, 156. Snepp's account of this order seems to mix up the February conversation, which the author believes did take place, with Truong's March meetings at the Palace.

12. Two close aides to Thieu, who wish to remain anonymous, deny that the president harbored any suspicions of Truong. Truong's Navy commander, Ho Van Ky Thoai, supports the contention that Truong and Thieu got along. Other well-placed ARVN sources strongly disagree.

13. Hung, *Palace File*, 269. Hung says no, but Truong's chief of staff claimed in a RAND interview that the enclave plan was designed to buy time for an eventual counterattack, possibly with American help. That was precisely Thieu's concept. While Truong could have thought of this himself, one suspects he heard it from Thieu.

14. Ho Van Ky Thoai, *Valor in Defeat: A Sailor's Journey* [*Can Truong Trong Chien B i: Hanh Trinh Cua Mot Thuy Thu*] (Centerville, Va.: Self-published, 2007), 187.

15. An, *New Battlefield*, 203.

16. From the Central Military Affairs Committee to B-4 Front and the 2nd Corps, in *A Number of Guidance Documents*, 17 March 1975, 210.

17. Xuan Thieu, *North of the Hai Van Pass, Spring 1975: A Report* [*Bac Hai Van, Xuan 1975: Ky Su*] (Hanoi: People's Army Publishing House, 1977), 140–141.

18. Ibid.

19. Thi, *The Twenty-Five-Year Century*, 344.

20. Truong, "Why I Abandoned I Corps," *Doi* [*Life*].

21. Vien, *Final Collapse*, 102.

22. "President Thieu addresses nation on war situation," Amembassy Saigon to SecState, #3187, 20 March 1975.

23. From J-3, JGS, to I Corps, cable #9428, 20 March 1975, reprinted in Thieu, *North of the Hai Van Pass*, 159.

24. From I Corps to President Thieu, cable #32, 20 March 1975, reprinted in Thieu, *North of the Hai Van Pass*, 160.

25. From J-3, JGS, to I Corps, cable #9564, 21 March 1975, reprinted in Thieu, *North of the Hai Van Pass*, 160.

26. These figures come from both U.S. Embassy and DAO reporting.

27. *Battles of Vietnamese Artillery during the Wars of Liberation and to Defend the Fatherland*, vol. II [*Nhung Tran Danh Cua Phao Binh Vietnam Trong Cac Cuoc Chien Tranh Giai Phong Va Bao Ve To Quoc*, Tap II] (Hanoi?: Artillery Command, 1990), 174.

28. Backchannel from Lehmann to Scowcroft, Martin #674, 18 March 1975.

29. "Approach to Thieu," Amembassy Saigon to SecState, #3225, 20 March 1975, *U.S. Policy*, no. 01334.

30. Interview with Do Duc Chien, 3 November 2003, Easton, Pa.

31. Thieu, *North of the Hai Van Pass*, 184–185.

32. *2nd Corps*, 171.

33. Ibid.

34. An, *New Battlefield*, 213.

35. From J-3, JGS, to I Corps, cable #9582, 22 March 1975, reprinted in Thieu, *North of the Hai Van Pass*, 204.

36. "USSAG Daily Situation Report," #75-083A, 24 March 1975, Record Group 342, Records of U.S. Air Force Commands, Activities, and Organiza-

tions, Series: Mixed Files Relating to Various U.S. Air Force Combat Operations and Other Activities in the Vietnam War Era, 1961–1977, Box 400, NARA, College Park, Md.

37. Cable #38B, from Giap to Dung, 22 March 1975, in *Great Spring Victory, 1975*, 166–167.

CHAPTER 12

1. Thieu, *North of the Hai Van Pass*, 164.

2. Ibid., 218.

3. Tri, "Unforgettable Days," 8.

4. Books that discuss the fall of Tam Ky claim that a single PT-76 tank drove into the city center, prompting ARVN to flee. The 2nd Division history states that it was two Chinese-made K-63 armored personnel carriers. *2nd Division*, vol. 1 [*Su Doan 2*, Tap 1] (Danang: Danang Publishing House, 1989), 273.

5. Both Martin and the DAO resurrected the LST issue in mid-October 1974. See "Additional LSTs for VNN," Amembassy Saigon to SecState, #13322, 17 October 1974. Kissinger at the 24 March 1975 State Department meeting asked Assistant Secretary of State Philip Habib what happened to the LSTs "he had approved in January." Habib replied that Kissinger had approved them, but only on the back burner. Kissinger said no, he meant other items were to be on the back burner, not the LSTs. What bureaucratic foul-up occurred remains unknown.

6. Vien, *Final Collapse*, 114–115.

7. "Vietnam Aid—The Painful Options," Report of Senator Sam Nunn to the Committee on Armed Services, U.S. Senate, 12 February 1974, 4.

8. For a more detailed discussion of the evaluation, see Snepp, *Decent Interval*, 160–162.

9. "Should Congress Increase Aid to Vietnam?" *Congressional Quarterly*, 15 February 1975, 343.

10. Bill Williamson, "America and the Debate over Aid to South Vietnam, January to April 1975," dissertation, University of North Texas (1996), 40.

11. "Meeting at noon, March 24, on Indochina."

12. Memcon, 25 March 1975, DDRS #152, 1997.

13. Letter from Ford to Thieu, 25 March 1975, DDRS #298, 1994.

14. State Department Press Release #172 for 26 March 1975, dated 14 April 1975, 462.

15. "Comrade Le Duan's Comments in a Politburo Meeting Held 24 March 1975, after Our Victory at Ban Me Thuot," *A Number of Guidance Documents*, 24 March 1975, 214.

16. Giap, *General Headquarters*, 221.

17. DAO, "RVNAF Final Assessment, Jan Thru Apr FY75," 15 June 1975, 7-4. HQ stands for *Hai quan*, the Vietnamese word for Navy, assuming one has the correct tone mark.

18. At the author's request, Colonel Tri asked both the 8th Marine Battalion commander, Lieutenant Colonel Nguyen Dang Hoa, and the 468th Brigade commander, Colonel Ngo Van Dinh, why the 8th did not occupy Vinh Phong. Hoa claims he never received any orders to occupy the mountain, while Dinh states he does not recall much about the events at the Hai Van Pass. Tri speculates that either the order came too late to the 468th Brigade headquarters, or I Corps headquarters canceled the order once it realized that the Navy could not complete a bridge across the inlet's mouth. Tri suspects that Truong also wanted to begin shifting the Marines to defend Danang.

19. Pham Van Tien, "147th Brigade: From a Tactical Withdrawal in 1975 [Lu Doan 147: Tu Mot Cuoc Di Tan Chien Thuat 1975]," *Song Than* (1999), 234. Major Tien was the commander of the Marine 5th Battalion.

20. *The Hue-Danang Offensive Campaign (Spring 1975) [Chien Dich Hue-Danang (Xuan 1975)]* (Hanoi: Military History Institute of Vietnam, 1991), 37.

21. Tran Van Nhut, *The Unfinished War: The Memoirs of General Tran Van Nhut* (Garden Grove, Calif.: Self-published, 2001), 280.

22. Thoai claims that Truong told him after the war that Truong sent them to the island "because of the situation in Danang, which was packed with evacuees. . . . He felt that it would be difficult for the 2nd Division to fight effectively if it was placed in this situation." Thoai, *Valor in Defeat*, 274, fn. 9.

23. Le Thuong, *2nd Infantry Division: The Final Phase of the War, a Memoir [Su Doan 2 Bo Binh: Giai Doan Cuoi Cung cua Cuoc Chien, Hoi Ky]* (Los Angeles: Self-published, 2001), 182.

24. Ibid., 183.

25. Captain Pham Manh Khue, "A Day-by-Day Account of the Evacuation of MR-1, MR-2, and MR-3 by Naval Ships," 4 November 1975, *Interviews*, vol. 2, 160.

26. "Memorandum No. 013-TT/CD/M, from President Thieu to the Military Region Commanders, Military Service Commanders, Commander of the Capital Special Zone, Division Commanders, Province Chiefs, and Com-

mander of the National Police," 24 March 1975, reprinted in Khai, *March in the Central Highlands*, 154.

27. "President Thieu to the Commanders of Military Regions I, II, III, and IV and of the Capital Special Zone," Cable #015-TT/CD, 25 March 1975, reprinted in Khai, *March in the Central Highlands*, 155.

28. "President Thieu Directs Cabinet Reshuffle," Amembassy Saigon to SecState, #3471, 25 March 1975.

29. "President Thieu's Order of the Day," BBC Summary of World Broadcasts, Far Eastern, 27 March 1975.

30. "Thieu addresses the nation on war situation," Amembassy Saigon to SecState, #3567, 26 March 1975.

31. "Refugee Evacuation from Danang," Amembassy Saigon to SecState, #3697, 28 March 1975.

32. "Refugee Evacuation from Danang," Amembassy Saigon to SecState, #3734, 28 March 1975.

33. "Memcon, Ford, Rockefeller, Kissinger, Scowcroft," 28 March 1975, *U.S. Policy*, Part II, #1552.

34. "Memcon, Kissinger, Scowcroft, Sonnenfeldt, Hyland," 29 March 1975, *U.S. Policy*, Part II, #1554.

35. Diary of Major General Nguyen Duy Hinh, 27 March 1975, 36.

36. An, *New Battlefield*, 220.

37. *Hue-Danang Campaign*, 46. PAVN provided loss statistics for the I Corps campaign in this book, but they are so ridiculously low the author declined to include them.

38. Charles Timmes, "Military Operations after the Cease-Fire Agreement, Part II," *Military Review* (September 1976), 27.

39. Truong, "Significant Events in I Corps," *Interviews*, vol. 1, 26.

40. Dr. Oscar Fitzgerald, "Interview with Commodore Ho Van Ky Thoai," 20 September 1975, Operational Archives, Naval Historical Center, 40. The author thanks Dr. Edward Marolda at the Naval Archives for obtaining this interview.

CHAPTER 13

1. Huan, *Withdrawal*, 208.

2. "General Pham Van Phu Announces at the Ca Pass: II Corps will fight to the death on the line it now holds, Martial Law declared throughout MR-2," *Chinh Luan*, 1 April 1975, 2.

3. Giap, *General Headquarters*, 247.

4. Cable #75, from Le Duc Tho to Van Tien Dung, 25 March 1975, *Great Spring Victory, 1975*, 177.

5. Dung, *Great Spring Victory*, 135–136.

6. Ibid., 137.

7. *320th Division*, 306–307.

8. Giap, *General Headquarters*, 276.

9. Thai, *Decisive Years*, 116.

10. *10th Division*, 116.

11. Along Route 21 were three major ARVN training centers: the Duc My Ranger Center, the nearby Artillery Center, and the Lam Son Infantry Center. Also located in the Nha Trang area were the Dong De NCO Academy and the Naval Training Center.

12. Interview with Tran Cong Hanh, 31 July 2002, Maple Grove, Minn.

13. Letter from Le Qui Dau, 7 February 2004, Akron, Ohio.

14. *10th Division*, 120.

15. Huan, *Withdrawal*, 215.

16. "GVN attempts to block PAVN forces directed against Nha Trang city, and current military activities in GVN MR-2," CIA Intelligence Cable, 31 March 1975, 4–5.

17. Truong, "Why I Abandoned I Corps," *Doi* [*Life*], 23.

18. "RVN Gen Pham Van Phu Comments on Situation in MR II," *FBIS Asia and Pacific*, 31 March 1975, L21.

19. Interview with Nguyen Van Dai, commander, Duc My Ranger Center, 12 March 2003, Beaverton, Ore. Dai notes that the column maintained good discipline until it reached Cam Ranh, where his men began experiencing problems due to the local disorder. By the time they reached Phan Rang, half the trainees and cadres had melted away.

20. Huan, *Withdrawal*, 224.

21. Dr. Oscar Fitzgerald, "Interview with Commodore Hoang Co Minh," 8 September 1975, Operational Archives, Naval History Division, 100–102. Minh is very vague about the events off Qui Nhon. His interview was not as detailed as others done at the same time with senior VNN officers; plus, he was somewhat anti-American. In the early 1980s, Minh helped form the National Front for the Liberation of South Vietnam, an émigré group dedicated to fostering a guerrilla war to overthrow the Communist government. He was killed in 1987 in Laos while attempting to lead a group of two hundred men into South Vietnam to instigate a rebellion.

22. *3rd Division*, 346.

23. Huan, *Withdrawal*, 222.

24. Nguyen Thieu, "41st Regiment, 22nd Division," 10. Manuscript written for the author.

25. *Binh Dinh: History of the Thirty-Year People's War (1945–1975)* [*Binh Dinh: Lich Su Chien Tranh Nhan Dan 30 Nam (1945–1975)*] (Binh Dinh: Binh Dinh Province Military Headquarters, 1992), 461–462.

26. Interview with Do Kiem, 29 August 2002, Mandeville, La.

27. Le Quang Oanh, "22nd Division's Withdrawal from Binh Dinh," *KBC* #13 (June 1995), 44.

28. Le Gro, *Cease-Fire to Capitulation*, 171–172, quoting Smith's cable.

29. *3rd Division*, 356.

30. Major General Bui Cong Ai, "Attack on the City of Tuy Hoa by 320th Division, 1 April 1975," in *A Number of Battles in the Resistance War against the French and the Americans, 1945–1975*, vol. I [*Mot So Tran Danh Trong Cuoc Khang Chien Chong Phap, Chong My, 1945–1975*, Tap I] (Hanoi: Military History Institute of Vietnam, 1991), 186–187. Major General Ai was the 2nd Corps chief of staff in 1975.

31. *10th Division*, 121.

32. Huan, *Withdrawal*, 238.

33. Isaacs, *Without Honor*, 381. For a more detailed description of the evacuation of the American consulate from Nha Trang, see Snepp, *Decent Interval*, 263–272, and George R. Dunham and David A. Quinlan, *U.S. Marines in Vietnam: The Bitter End, 1973–1975* (Washington, D.C.: U.S. Marine Corps, 1990), 131–132.

34. Lu Van Thanh, *The Inviting Call of Wandering Souls: Memoir of an ARVN Liaison Officer to the United States Forces in Vietnam* (Jefferson, N.C.: McFarland & Co., 1997), 39, 43.

35. Tran Thi Minh Canh, *The Book of Canh: Memoirs of a Vietnamese Woman, Physician, CIA Informant, People's Salvation Army Commander-in-Chief, and Prisoner of War* (Milford, Conn.: Self-published, 1996), 71–72.

36. Ibid., 73–75.

37. Khai, *March in the Central Highlands*, 160, quoting from Phu's personal report.

38. Huan, *Withdrawal*, 243.

39. The separate accounts from Pham Huan and Phu's main aide, Lieutenant Colonel Nguyen Quang Vinh, substantially agree about Phu's unsuccessful

suicide attempt on the hill outside of Phan Thiet. Huan, *Withdrawal*, 244, and Nguyen Quang Vinh, "Significant Events Concerning Military Region 2 from the Fall of Ban Me Thuot until the Death of General Phu," *Interviews*, vol. 3, 101. Phu then returned to Saigon, where two days later he fell gravely ill. Vien ordered him taken to the Cong Hoa Hospital for treatment. After two weeks, Phu was placed under house arrest with a handful of other senior generals, including Lieutenant General Lam Quang Thi, who shared a trailer with Phu at the JGS compound. Thi notes that Phu was severely depressed. Both were released on 25 April 1975.

40. Thai, *Decisive Years*, 117.

41. George W. Schwarz Jr., *April Fools: An American Remembers South Viet-Nam's Final Days* (Baltimore: AmErica House, 2001), 165. Schwarz was an employee of Alaska Barge and Transport, a shipping company contracted by the MSC. The description of the evacuation is drawn from Schwarz's excellent account of the horrible events at Cam Ranh Bay. The deserters and refugees who boarded the *Greenville Victory* at Cam Ranh would later commandeer the ship when it arrived at Phu Quoc Island to offload. A Korean LST, the *Boo Heung Pioneer* (LST-117), also was picking up refugees that night, but from small boats that sailed out to her.

42. *10th Division*, 123. While its history claims the division captured Cam Ranh on 3 April, George Schwarz's account notes that the ships were still loading refugees on 4 April until a PAVN unit appeared on the docks and fired at them. The American ships managed to escape without any damage.

CHAPTER 14

1. Giap, *General Headquarters*, 262–263. This slogan became fixed in PAVN mythology as instrumental in achieving victory. In essence, it became the Communists' formula for the rest of the 1975 offensive, and many of their post-war writings refer to it.

2. "Documents," *Vietnam Social Sciences*, 1–2 (1989), 150–151.

3. Giap, *General Headquarters*, 264.

4. *The Determined-to-Win Corps [Binh Doan Quyet Thang]* (Hanoi: People's Army Publishing House, 1988), 53. Hereafter *1st Corps*.

5. *Victory in Vietnam*, 347–348.

6. Ibid.

7. Ibid.

8. Major General Tran Tho, "In the General Offensive and Uprising of 1975: Some Successful Lessons of the Rear Services Task," *Quan Doi Nhan Dan* (October 1976), translated in JPRS #68570, 46–50.

9. Ibid.

10. While the Communists had vastly improved the transportation corridors south through the sweat of thousands of laborers—some of them unreturned ARVN prisoners—in their post-war writings they rarely mention the assistance of friendly countries. Giap's memoirs, however, include several comments that reveal such aid. "With help provided by Fidel and our Cuban allies, who had purchased and sent to us a number of specialized construction vehicles from Japan and who had paid to have our technical cadre sent to Japan to study how to use this equipment, our engineer groups and assault youth units set to work building roads," he writes. "Many new road sections were being built, and on a number of these projects picks and shovels were replaced by the construction machinery purchased for us by Cuba." Giap, *General Headquarters*, 174, 187.

11. Pham Cuong, "In the General Offensive and Uprising of 1975: Some Experiences in Assuring the Mobility of the Military Engineer Forces," *Quan Doi Nhan Dan* (December 1976), translated in JPRS #69017, 51.

12. Senior Colonel Pham Nien, "Signal Armed Forces," *Tap Chi Quan Doi Nhan Dan* (April 1976), translated in JPRS #67798, 50–51.

13. *History of the People's Navy of Vietnam [Lich Su Hai Quan Nhan Dan Viet Nam]* (Hanoi: People's Army Publishing House, 1985), 285.

14. *The 202nd Brigade [Lu Doan 202]* (Hanoi: 1st Corps, 1984), 88.

15. *35th Anniversary of the Ho Chi Minh Trail at Sea and of the Formation of the Navy's 125th Brigade [35 Nam Duong Ho Chi Minh Tren Bien va Thanh Lap Lu Doan 125 Hai]* (Hanoi: Political Department of the Navy, People's Army Publishing House, 1996), 40.

16. *History of the People's Air Force (1955–1977) [Lich Su Khong Quan Nhan Dan Viet Nam (1955–1977)]* (Hanoi: People's Army Publishing House, 1993), 301.

17. *1st Corps*, 89–90.

18. An, *New Battlefield*, 227.

19. Thai, *Decisive Years*, 118.

20. Ibid.

21. Giap, *General Headquarters*, 283.

22. *2nd Corps*, 216.

23. Giap, *General Headquarters*, 285.

24. *History of the Annamite Mountain Troops on the Ho Chi Minh Trail* [*Lich Su Bo Doi Truong Son Duong Ho Chi Minh*] (Hanoi: People's Army Publishing House, 1994), 333.

25. An, *New Battlefield*, 228–229.

26. *10th Division*, 128.

27. Ibid.

28. Ibid., 129–130.

29. An, *New Battlefield*, 229–230.

30. Giap, *General Headquarters*, 286. There is a photo of Giap's order in the book. Giap used a standard form to write the message, and its printed security regulations are interesting: "Secret Outgoing Cable. Deliver personally [by hand]. Do not leave unattended. Do not ask about or reply to this message over the telephone or in clear [unencrypted] radio messages. Do not copy for the file. Do not disseminate to unauthorized personnel. All copies must be returned to the Cryptographic section."

31. *2nd Corps*, 217

32. Senior Colonel Pham Te (pen name: Truong Son), *The Most Feverish Years on the Ho Chi Minh Trail* [*Nhung Nam Thang Soi Dong Nhat Tren Duong Ho Chi Minh*] (Ho Chi Minh City: Ho Chi Minh City Publishing House, 1994), 112–113. Senior Colonel Te was one of several deputy chiefs for political affairs of Group 559. After Ban Me Thuot fell, he served as chief of political affairs of a new Group 559 Forward Headquarters in Ban Me Thuot. He was on his way to the new forward command post when this incident occurred.

33. After the war, one of the men arrested, Senator Pham Nam Sach, admitted he was plotting Thieu's overthrow with a group that included Ky. How deeply Ky was involved is unknown. Sach was released from jail on 27 April, and he and his family were evacuated on the last day. See Everett R. Holles, "New Front Splits Vietnam Refugees," *New York Times*, 1 March 1976, 7.

34. Philip McCombs, "Ky Asks Power to Rally Troops," *Washington Post*, 29 March 1975, 1, 3.

35. Denis Warner, *Certain Victory: How Hanoi Won the War* (Kansas City, Mo.: Sheed, Andrews, and McMeel, 1978), 196.

36. Dung, *Great Spring Victory*, 185.

37. Cable from Polgar to Colby, 31 March 1975, CREST RDP80R01720R000400100014-8.

38. "Assessment of the Military Situation and Prospects for South Vietnam," Interagency Memorandum, 4 April 1975, CREST RDP80R01720R000400100006-7, 1–2.

39. Snepp, *Decent Interval*, 386.

40. DAO "March Threat Assessment," 10 April 1975, 25. This was the first time Ambassador Martin had requested to attach a statement to Le Gro's monthly intelligence summary. It was also the first time Le Gro had even let him see the MISTA before transmittal.

41. Le Gro, *Cease-Fire to Capitulation*, 171.

CHAPTER 15

1. Thanh Son airbase belonged to the 2nd Air Division, but when the 6th Air Division moved its headquarters there on 22 March from Nha Trang, the VNAF re-designated Thanh Son to the 6th. Stationed at Thanh Son was Colonel Le Van Thao's 92nd Wing, consisting of three A-37 squadrons. Also at Thanh Son but originally from the 6th Division at Pleiku was Lieutenant Colonel Le Van But's 72nd Wing, which had two Huey squadrons, along with remnants from the Phu Cat airbase and other assorted Air Force units.

2. Pham Ngoc Sang, "The Battle of Phan Rang: The Recollections of Brigadier General Pham Ngoc Sang," 10 January 2002. Sang wrote this report for the author to detail the events of the battle. He had been in the first class of South Vietnamese Air Force cadets to attend French flight training. Upon his return to Vietnam, he eventually became President Ngo Dinh Diem's personal pilot. From 1965 to 1972 he was the chief of the Military Affairs Bureau in the office of the prime minister. In 1974 he was promoted to brigadier general and assumed command of the 6th Air Division. He was captured after the fall of Thanh Son, and spent the next seventeen years in some of toughest prison camps in North Vietnam. He was held in captivity for this extended period because of his uncompromising anti-Communist stance. He was finally released in 1992 while in the hospital for severe bleeding from the colon. His wife, Nguyen Thi Bon, had held the family together and waited for him to return, despite being denied permission to visit him during his first thirteen years in captivity.

3. Letter from Nguyen Van Thiet to Pham Ngoc Sang, 1 February 2002.

4. Chris Coulthard-Clark, *The RAAF in Vietnam: Australian Air Involvement in the Vietnam War 1962–1975* (Canberra: Paul & Co Pub Consortium, 1995), 323–324.

5. While most South Vietnamese believe that Thieu ordered the defense of Phan Rang because it was near his birthplace and family gravesites, the Communists instead trumpet the charge that General Weyand "commanded" Thieu to defend this area to prove once again that he was an American "pup-

pet." In reality, it was a logical defensive position, and was part of the area Thieu intended to keep in a new, truncated South Vietnam.

6. *10th Division*, 125.

7. Interview with Le Van But, 3 March 2003, Anaheim, Calif.

8. In October 1973, the different riverine divisions in the Delta were reorganized into Task Fleet 21, which had four Task Forces (TF), 211, 212, 213, and 214. TF 213 was disbanded in 1974 because of U.S. aid cutbacks. The new Task Fleet commander was given full responsibility for naval operations in the Delta.

9. Interview with Le Van Thao, 5 September 2002, Salt Lake City, Utah. The VNAF intelligence chief, who visited Phan Rang during the final days, said this about Colonel Thao's performance: "The high spirit that prevailed among the aircrews of the 92nd Wing was largely due to the aggressiveness and courage of their Wing Commander, Colonel Le Van Thao. He would fly his A-37 at night, making radio contact with Phan Rang city, the airborne troops, and the Phan Thiet province chief, reassuring them that air support would be provided as needed." Colonel Le Minh Hoang, "Observations about the Defense of Phan Rang AB," *Interviews*, vol. 3, 107.

10. Airborne Division Commander Brigadier General Le Quang Luong was surprised at this order to swap brigades, and he flew to Phan Rang to meet with Generals Nghi and Sang. He believed it was a mistake to pull the 3rd Brigade out of Phan Rang. A highly decorated combat veteran who had led an Airborne brigade at An Loc, Luong was promoted to division deputy commander during the recapture of Quang Tri and then division commander in December 1972. After the war Luong wrote an article highly critical of Thieu's piecemealing out of each brigade during the final two months.

11. Colonel Nguyen Thu Luong, "The Battle of Phan Rang (April 1975)." Luong wrote a lengthy paper describing the actions of his unit at Phan Rang, and the author thanks him for sharing it.

12. Giap, *General Headquarters*, 263.

13. Cam, *A Memoir*, 405. Cam notes that during Tra's visit "discussions and exchanges became rather heated." Cam then rhetorically asks, "Why could not we wait for the General Staff's Main Force units to arrive to support the attack and ensure victory?" Obviously, Cam was on Dung's side on this question.

14. It is not clear whether at this meeting the 19 March request to allow the 7th Division to continue attacking south on Route 20 was discussed. Tra never specifically mentions the appeal, but he does spend several paragraphs explaining his rationale for declining to approve the early attack on Xuan

Loc. Mainly, he states, it was the lack of artillery ammunition and the need to expand the captured area on Route 20 north toward Dalat. Tra, *Bulwark B-2 Theatre*, 156. Cam says he thought about bringing the subject up, but decided against it. He believed that as a subordinate receiving new orders from his superior, it would have been improper to question his boss on a matter already long decided. Cam, *A Memoir*, 406.

15. Tra, *Bulwark B-2 Theatre*, 154–155.

16. Giap, *General Headquarters*, 266–267.

17. Tra, *Bulwark B-2 Theatre*, 156.

18. Another aspect of the plan was the defection of Lieutenant Nguyen Thanh Trung, an F-5E pilot stationed at Bien Hoa airbase. Trung was given orders to defect when possible, since he was needed to train the PAVN Air Force pilots on captured aircraft. Spotting an opportunity, on 8 April, Trung volunteered to replace another pilot who had failed to appear for a mission to attack PAVN forces near Nha Trang. Taking off in his F-5E, he instead swung over Saigon and dropped his payload on Independence Palace. After his bombing run, he flew to Phuoc Binh airbase in Phuoc Long province. Trung's real name was Dinh Thanh Trung. For an interesting Communist version of Trung's defection, see Ho Dinh Nhuong, "The Invisible Star of the Milky Way," *Vietnam Courier*, January 1976, 16–18.

19. Dung, *Great Spring Victory*, 201.

20. Tra, *Bulwark B-2 Theatre*, 156.

21. Giap, *General Headquarters*, 279–280.

22. "Documents," 152, and Le Duan, *Letters to the South*, 404–405.

23. Edward Metzner, *Reeducation in Postwar Vietnam: Personal Postscripts to Peace* (College Station: Texas A&M University Press, 2001), 48. Metzner is quoting Colonel Huynh Van Chinh, with whom he had once worked as an advisor. According to the DAO, ARVN anticipated the attacks along Route 4 and temporarily adjusted the corps boundary so that Long An was now part of IV Corps.

24. "South Vietnamese Officer Jubilant over Delta Fight," *New York Times*, 14 April 1975, 18. Thanh was promoted to colonel for his regiment's exploits. He surrendered to Communist forces on 30 April 1975. According to South Vietnamese sources, he was killed after an attempt to escape from prison in September 1976.

25. Dinh Hung Cuong, "The Last Battle [Tran Danh Cuoi Cung]," *KBC* #25 (1998), 36. Major Cuong was the Thu Thua district chief until he was wounded in action on 13 April 1975.

26. Mach Van Truong, "21st Infantry Division at Can Tho on the Day the Nation Was Lost [Su Doan 21 Bo Binh Tai Can Tho Vao Ngay Tan Mat Nuoc]," *The Gioi* [*The World*], #394 (18 April 2003), 16. Colonel Truong was promoted to brigadier general as a result of the impressive defeat of the 4th Division outside Can Tho.

27. *Military Region 9: 30 Years of Resistance (1945–1975)* [*Quan Khu 9: 30 Nam Khang Chien (1945–1975)*] (Hanoi: People's Army Publishing House, 1996), 631–634.

28. DAO Weekly Wrap-up South Vietnam, 5–11 April 1975, 23.

29. *3rd Division*, 364.

30. Truong Duong, *The Life of a Soldier* [*Doi Chien Binh*] (Westminster, Calif.: Tu Quynh, 1998), 191. Duong, a former Airborne major, interviewed Major Nguyen Van Thanh, 11th Airborne commander, for these details.

31. "Tran Van Don issues appeal," *FBIS Asia and Pacific*, 15 April 1975, L9.

CHAPTER 16

1. *History of the Armor Branch, People's Army of Vietnam 1959–1975* [*Lich Su Binh Chung Thiet Giap, Quan Doi Nhan Dan Viet Nam 1959–1975*] (Hanoi: People's Army Publishing House, 1982), 263.

2. *2nd Corps*, 244.

3. Pham Ngoc Sang, "The Battle of Phan Rang," 11.

4. Letter from Thiet to Sang, 1 February 2002.

5. An, *New Battlefield*, 286.

6. Le Quang Hoa, *Steps along the Road of Resistance to the Americans: A Memoir* [*Nhung Chang Duong Chong My: Hoi Ky*] (People's Army Publishing House, Hanoi, 1982), 228. Nothing was done to restore the city and Thanh Son after the war. According to an ARVN officer who lived in Nha Trang in 1975 and who was later imprisoned nearby, in 1979 he saw "Phan Rang airbase with its empty hangars, heaps of aircraft remains here and there, and the runway covered with holes. Phan Rang [the city] . . . was apparently savaged by the enemy after the so-called normalization of both South and North. . . . My father told me that by the end of 1977 different kinds of government trucks, full of communist cadre and economic agents, would swoop into town . . . for three or four days . . . making lists of items in the shops . . . then they moved everything out." Thanh, *The Inviting Call of Wandering Souls*, 135.

7. *2nd Corps*, 251.

8. Ibid., 252.

9. *History of the Armor Branch*, 265.

10. *2nd Corps*, 252.

11. Letter to the author from Nguyen Van Loc, 12 February 2002, San Jose, Calif. Loc was hit in the head by a shell fragment, but he managed to escape Vietnam with his ship after the surrender. He later developed Parkinson's disease, perhaps caused by the brain injury he incurred in Ca Na Bay. He passed away in 2005.

12. Letter to the author from Phan Dinh San, 21 April 2003, Santa Ana, Calif.

13. Nhut, *The Unfinished War*, 296.

14. Muong Giang, "Regional Force and Popular Force Troops during the Final Days, April 1975, in Binh Thuan [Nguoi Linh Dia Phuong Quang va Nghia Quan Trong Nhung Ngay Hap Hoi Thang 4-75 tai Binh Thuan]," *Doan Ket*, #168 (January 2004), 58.

15. An, *New Battlefield*, 242.

CHAPTER 17

1. *4th Corps*, 153.

2. Cam, *A Memoir*, 402.

3. *341st Division*, 58–59.

4. *7th Division*, 290.

5. Interview with Le Minh Dao, 7 April 2001, East Hartford, Conn.

6. *Victory in Vietnam*, 407.

7. Cam, *A Memoir*, 451.

8. *341st Division*, 70–71.

9. Vien, *The Final Collapse*, 132.

10. Phillip Caputo, "S. Viets take Skeleton of City," *Chicago Tribune*, 14 April 1975, 3.

11. *341st Division*, 63.

12. Cam, *A Memoir*, 411, fn. 9.

13. Ho Dinh, "The Xuan Loc Front," 8 May 2001, 2.

14. The 341st Division's history confirms that the Airborne attack surrounded a battalion of the 7th Division. The history is quite clear that the 341st was ordered to mount an attack to relieve the besieged battalion. *341st Division*, 73. The 7th's history barely mentions this episode, with only one section describing the 8th Battalion's defense against the Airborne attack. *7th Division*, 298.

15. Dung, *Great Spring Victory*, 176.

16. Tra, *Bulwark B-2 Theatre*, 170. The 4th Corps's history provides many reasons for its failure to take the city, conceding that "These were lessons for us on the road to the maturation of 4th Corps as a military unit." *4th Corps*, 158–159.

17. Dung, *Great Spring Victory*, 167.

18. Tra, *Bulwark B-2 Theatre*, 170.

19. Ibid., 171.

20. Nicholas C. Proffitt, "Escape from Xuan Loc," *Newsweek*, 18 April 1975, 22.

21. For the best description of the journalists' trip, see David Butler, *The Fall of Saigon* (New York: Simon and Schuster, 1985), 244–250. For six excellent pictures taken that day (although the description of events is completely wrong), see Dirck Halstead, "White Christmas—The Fall of Saigon," http://digitaljournalist.org/issue0005/ch1.htm.

22. Letter to the author from Pham Van Ban, 14 October 2001.

23. In 1969, U.S. Air Force C-130s began dropping the 15,000-pound bombs in a program called "Commando Vault" to make instant helicopter landing zones for follow-on Army troops. The U.S. offered to arm the Daisy Cutters for the VNAF to drop. The South Vietnamese accepted, and USAF C-130s flew them to Tan Son Nhut, where they were reloaded aboard VNAF C-130s.

24. "VNAF Sorties for 1–19 April in MR-3 and MR-4; BDA for 'Daisy Cutter' Strikes," CIA Intelligence Cable, 22 April 1975, 3–4. The CIA cable states the JGS reported that the VNAF flew 665 sorties in defense of Xuan Loc.

25. Phan Tan My (pseudonym Y. Yen), "The Battle for Horseshoe Hill," *Saigon Post*, n.d., 3.

26. Fox Butterfield, "A Captain Tells of Flight from Xuan Loc," *New York Times*, 17 April 1975, 20.

27. Telephone interview with Nguyen Ba Manh Hung, 19 July 2001, Garden Grove, Calif.

28. Hua Yen Len, "The Line of Steel," 6.

29. Ho Dinh, "The Xuan Loc Front," 10.

30. Snepp, *Decent Interval*, 416. On 23 April, Agence France-Presse first reported the weapon's use. See "South Vietnam Uses 'Asphyxiation' Bombs against Communist Forces," *FBIS Asia and Pacific*, 23 April 1975, L9. Giap claims he learned of the bombing from this article, and then sent a cable to the B-2 Front recommending they attack Tan Son Nhut and other airbases to shut down the VNAF. Giap, *General Headquarters*, 322. However, who ordered the dropping of the CBU-55, the location and number of bomb(s), and the combat result remain

a mystery. According to General Cao Van Vien, only one CBU-55 was ever used. He reports that it was dropped with high accuracy by the C-130 squadron commander, Lieutenant Colonel Mac Huu Loc, on the Forward Headquarters of the 341st Division. Most ARVN and Communist sources, however, refer to bombs. Colonel Hoang Dinh Tho, G-3 of III Corps, described the blast location as along Route 20 south of Kiem Tan. This is partially confirmed by a *Nhan Dan* broadcast of 25 April, which described the area as "between the provincial capitals of Bien Hoa and Xuan Loc." See "War Crimes Committee, Lawyers Group Assail[s] use of CBU-55," *FBIS Asia and Pacific*, 26 April 1975, L8–9. Nguyen Van Toan also claims two bombs were dropped, and that the decision was his. He indicates that after the Communists bitterly complained about the use of the weapon, the Americans refused to provide any more fuses for the CBUs. Although most ARVN sources agree that the CBU-55 was used against the 341st, typically, the division history neglects to mention this incident. Casualty reports have also varied widely, from several hundred to over one thousand. The author believes only one bomb was dropped, and accepts the much lower casualty figure.

31. "Foreign Ministry, Nhan Dan, condemn use of Asphyxiation Bomb," *FBIS Asia and Pacific*, 24 April 1975, K1.

32. Gerald Ford, *A Time to Heal: The Autobiography of Gerald R. Ford* (New York: Harper & Row, 1979), 253.

33. Backchannel from Martin to Scowcroft, #691, 10 April 1975.

34. *Public Papers of the Presidents of the United States: Gerard R. Ford, 1975*, Book I, 470.

35. Ford, *A Time to Heal*, 255. For the original minutes of this meeting, see DDRS, 1993, #0598.

CHAPTER 18

1. Dung, *Great Spring Victory*, 172.

2. Snepp, *Decent Interval*, 478, 500. USSAG reports indicate that Group 232 gave the order.

3. Dung, *Great Spring Victory*, 204.

4. Ibid., 206.

5. Ibid., 211.

6. *Victory in Vietnam*, 410.

7. While Dung describes only five assault directions, actually there was a sixth. Two MR-8 regiments, the 24th and 88th, reinforced with the 271B Regiment, and two Long An local-force battalions moved in from the south.

8. Dung, *Great Spring Victory*, 209.

9. *History of the People's Air Force*, 303.

10. *History of the Art of Utilizing Air Defense in Combat Campaigns (1945–1975)* [*Lich Su Nghe Thuat Su Dung Phong Khong Trong Chien Dich 1945–1975*] (Hanoi: People's Army Publishing House, Hanoi, 1996), 158.

11. Thai, *Decisive Years*, 126.

12. Ibid., 137.

13. Dung, *Great Spring Victory*, 203

14. *Anti-Reactionary Forces: Chronology of Events (1954–1975)* [*Luc Luong Chong Phan Dong Lich Su Bien Nien (1954–1975)*] (Hanoi: Public Security Publishing House, 1997), 316–317.

15. Ibid.

16. "Documents," 155, from the 22 April 1975 cable.

17. Thai, *Decisive Years*, 136.

18. "Cable from the COSVN Party Current Affairs Committee on Duong Van Minh's Inauguration as President of the Saigon Puppet Government," 28 April 1975, *Historical Chronicle of the Central Office for South Vietnam*, 1087.

19. Pham Cuong, "The Former Saigon Army General Who Did Not Know How to Shoot," *Vietnam Net*, 25 April 2005. Cuong then quotes the head of COSVN's Military Proselytizing section: "Nguyen Huu Hanh was one of the great success stories of COSVN's Military Proselytizing operations."

20. Interview with Le Ba Binh, 8 July 2003, Reston, Va.

21. Tran Ngoc, "The Final Battle of ARVN's 81st Airborne Ranger Group," *Doan Ket*, #168 (January 2004), 65.

22. *Under One Flag*, 810.

23. Ngoc, "The Final Battle of ARVN's 81st Airborne Ranger Group," 66.

24. Phan Van Huan et al., "81st Airborne Ranger Group and the Days of April 1975 [LD81/BCND va Nhung Ngay Thang Tu 1975]," *Airborne Ranger* 3 (2001), 13.

25. Ho De, "The Road into the City Was Not Covered with a Red Carpet," *Quan Doi Nhan Dan*, 29 April 2006.

26. Hoang Nhat Linh, "Our Victory Was Quick because Our Predictions Were Accurate," *Nhan Dan*, 28 April 2003.

27. *History of the Resistance War against the Americans to Save the Nation, 1954–1975*, vol. VIII: *Total Victory* [*Lich Su Khang Chien Chong My, Cuu Nuoc 1954–1975*, Tap VIII: *Toan Thang*] (Hanoi: National Political Publishing House, 2008), 452. The official PAVN military history lists 1,447 killed. *Victory in Vietnam*, 421.

SELECTED BIBLIOGRAPHY

1. AMERICAN SOURCES

1.1 Archival and Primary Source Documents

Central Intelligence Agency. "Assessment of the Current Military Situation in South Vietnam." 9 August 1974.

———. "Communist Military and Economic Aid to North Vietnam, 1970–1974." 1 January 1975.

———. "Imports of Military Equipment and Materials by North Vietnam." 10 January 1975.

———. "Likelihood of a Major NVA Offensive in South Vietnam before the End of the Current Dry Season (31 May 1974)." 18 December 1973.

———. National Intelligence Estimate (NIE) 53/14.3-73: "Short-Term Prospects for Vietnam." 12 October 1973.

———. NIE 53/14.3-2-73: "Short-Term Prospects for Vietnam." 8 November 1973.

———. NIE 53/14.3-1-74: "The Likelihood of a Major North Vietnamese Offensive against South Vietnam." 23 May 1974.

———. NIE 53/14.3-2-74: "Short-Term Prospects for Vietnam." 12 December 1974.

———. NIE 53/14.3-3-75: "Assessment of the Situation in South Vietnam." 27 March 1975.

———. "South Vietnam: A Net Military Assessment." 2 April 1974.

Defense Attaché Saigon. "RVNAF Final Assessment, Jan thru Apr FY75." 15 June 1975.

———. "Monthly Intelligence Survey and Threat Analysis (MISTA)." April 1973–March 1975.

———. "Weekly Wrap-up of South Vietnam." 4 March–11 April 1975.

Foreign Broadcasting Information Service. *Daily Report: Asia and Pacific.* January 1973–Current.

General Research Corp. "Interviews and Debriefings of Refugees from Southeast Asia." McLean, Va. U.S. Army Center for Military History, vols. I, II, III, and IV. 1975. Joint Publication Research Service. *Vietnam.* January 1973–December 1990.

Murray, John, Major General, U.S. Army (Ret). Personal papers provided to the author by MG Murray, including backchannel messages, diary of events, and assorted articles.

National Archives and Record Administration. Record Group 59, General Records of the Dept. of State, The Office of Vietnam Affairs, Vietnam Working Group, Subject Files 1963–1975, Boxes 21–27.

———. Record Group 59, General Records of the Dept. of State, Central Foreign Policy Files, 1973–1975, "Access to Archival Databases," http://aad. archives.gov/aad/index.jsp.

———. Record Group 59, General Records of the Dept. of State, Central Foreign Policy Files, Subject Numeric Files 1970–1973.

———. Record Group 342, Records of U.S. Air Force Commands, Activities, and Organizations, Series: Mixed Files Relating to Various U.S. Air Force Combat Operations and Other Activities in the Vietnam War Era, 1961–1977, Box 400, March and April 1975.

———. Record Group 472, Records of U.S. Forces in S.E. Asia, Records of the Defense Attaché Office, Saigon, Records Relating to the Fall of Saigon, Boxes 1–4.

———. Record Group 472, Office of the Special Assistant to the Ambassador for Field Operations.

Nixon, Richard M. Richard M. Nixon Presidential Library, College Park, Md.

Smith, Homer, Major General, U.S. Army (Ret.). "End of Tour Report." 30 May 1975.

———. Memorandum for General Kerwin: "What happened to the RVNAF." 11 August 1975.

———. "The Final Forty-Five Days in Vietnam." U.S. Army Center for Military History, Washington, D.C. 22 May 1975.

———. "They Did Not Lose Their Will to Fight." U.S. Army Center for Military History, Washington, D.C. 15 July 1975.

Texas Tech University, Archive of the Vietnam Conflict, Lubbock, Tex. Pike, Douglas. Indochina Collection, Unit I, Assessment and Strategy; Unit II, Military Operations; and Unit IV, Political Settlement.

The Association for Diplomatic Studies and Training Foreign Affairs, Oral History Project. Library of Congress, Washington, D.C. Interview with Wolfgang Lehmann. http://memory.loc.gov/ammem/collections/diplomacy/.

U.S. Embassy, Saigon. "Communist Guidance on 'New Phase of the Revolution' in South Vietnam." *Vietnam Documents and Research Notes* #117. April 1974.

———. "COSVN Directive 03." *Vietnam Documents and Research Notes* #115. September 1973.

U.S. Navy Historical Center. "Transcripts: Interviews and Debriefings of VNN Officers." Operational Archives Branch, Washington Naval Yard. 1975.

Weyand, Fred C., General. "Vietnam Assessment Report, 4 April 1975."

1.2 BOOKS

Ahern, Thomas L. *CIA and the Generals: Covert Support to Military Government in South Vietnam*. Washington, D.C.: Central Intelligence Agency, n.d.

Butler, David. *The Fall of Saigon*. New York: Simon and Schuster, 1985.

Dawson, Alan. *55 Days: The Fall of South Vietnam*. Englewood Cliffs, N.J.: Prentice-Hall, 1977.

Dunham, George R., and David A. Quinlan. *U.S. Marines in Vietnam: The Bitter End, 1973–1975*. Washington, D.C.: U.S. Marine Corps, 1990.

Engelmann, Larry. *Tears before the Rain: An Oral History of the Fall of South Vietnam*. New York: Oxford University Press, 1990.

Haley, P. Edward. *Congress and the Fall of South Vietnam and Cambodia*. Madison: Fairleigh Dickinson University Press, 1982.

Hanyok, Robert J. *Spartans in Darkness: American SIGINT and the Indochina War, 1945–1975*. National Security Agency: Center for Cryptologic History, 2002.

Hickey, Gerald Cannon. *Free in the Forest: Ethnohistory of the Vietnamese Central Highlands*. New Haven and London: Yale University Press, 1982.

Hosmer, Stephen T., Konrad Kellen, and Brian M. Jenkins. *The Fall of South Vietnam: Statements by Vietnamese Military and Civilian Leaders*. New York: Crane, Russak, 1980.

Isaacs, Arnold R. *Without Honor: Defeat in Vietnam and Cambodia*. New York: Vintage Books, 1983.

Kissinger, Henry. *Ending the Vietnam War: A History of America's Involvement in and Extraction from the Vietnam War.* New York: Simon & Schuster, 2003.

———. *Crisis: The Anatomy of Two Major Foreign Policy Crises.* New York: Simon & Schuster, 2000.

Le Gro, William E. *Vietnam from Cease-Fire to Capitulation.* Washington, D.C.: U.S. Army Center for Military History, 1981.

McNamara, Francis Terry, with Adrian Hill. *Escape with Honor: My Last Hours in Vietnam.* Washington, D.C.: Brassey's, 1997.

Metzner, Edward P. *Reeducation in Postwar Vietnam: Personal Postscripts to Peace.* College Station: Texas A&M University Press, 2001.

Momyer, William W. *The Vietnamese Air Force, 1951–1975: An Analysis of its Role in Combat.* Washington, D.C.: USAF Southeast Asia Monograph series, vol. III, monograph 4, Office of Air Force History, 1985.

Nguyen Tien Hung and Jerrold Schecter. *The Palace File.* New York: Harper & Row, 1986.

Nixon, Richard M. *RN: The Memoirs of Richard Nixon.* New York: Simon and Schuster, 1978.

———. *No More Vietnams.* New York: Arbor House, 1985.

Schwarz, George W., Jr., *April Fools: An American Remembers South Vietnam's Final Days.* Baltimore: AmErica House, 2001.

Snepp, Frank. *Decent Interval: An Insider's Account of Saigon's Indecent End, Told by the CIA's Chief Strategy Analyst in Vietnam.* New York: Random House, 1977.

Willenson, Kim. *The Bad War: An Oral History of the Vietnam War.* New York: NAL Penguin, 1987.

1.3 Articles, Papers, and Dissertations

Parker, Maynard. "Vietnam: The War That Won't End," *Foreign Affairs* 53 (January 1975): 351–374.

Pribbenow, Merle L. "North Vietnam's Final Offensive: Strategic Endgame Nonpareil." *Parameters* 29, no. 4 (Winter 1999–2000): 58–71.

Quinn-Judge, Paul. "Inside Saigon: Eye-Witness Report." *Commonweal,* 26 (September 1975): 429–432.

Timmes, Charles J., Major General, U.S. Army (Ret.). "Military Operations after the Cease-Fire Agreement, Part 1." *Military Review* (August 1976): 63–75.

———. "Military Operations after the Cease-Fire Agreement, Part 2." *Military Review* (September 1976): 21–29.

Tonnesson, Stein, and Nguyen Vu Tung and James G. Hershberg. *77 Conversations between Chinese and Foreign Leaders on the Wars in Indochina, 1964–1977*. Working Paper #22. Washington, D.C.: Cold War International History Project, 1998.

Williamson, Bill Alan. "America and the Debate over Aid to South Vietnam: January–April 1975." Thesis, University of North Texas, 1996.

2. NORTH VIETNAMESE SOURCES

2.1 Unit Histories and Other Books Published in Vietnamese

"320th Infantry Division's Pursuit Attack against Enemy Forces on Route 7 at Cheo Reo from 17 to 19 March 1975." In *Mot So Tran Danh Cua Cac Don Vi thuoc Binh Doan Tay Nguyen*, Tap III [*A Number of Battles Fought by Units of the Central Highlands Corps*, vol. III]. Hanoi: People's Army Publishing House, 1995.

35 Nam Duong Ho Chi Minh Tren Bien va Thanh Lap Lu Doan 125 Hai Quan [*35th Anniversary of the Ho Chi Minh Trail at Sea and of the Formation of the Navy's 125th Brigade*]. Hanoi: People's Army Publishing House, 1996.

"Attack on Retreating Enemy Force at Cheo Reo (Central Highlands), 17–25 March 1975." In *Nhung Tran Danh Cua Phao Binh Vietnam Trong Cac Cuoc Chien Tranh Giai Phong va Bao Ve To Quoc*, Tap II [*Battles of Vietnamese Artillery during the Wars of Liberation and to Defend the Fatherland*, vol. II]. Hanoi?: Artillery Command, 1990.

"Attack on the City of Tuy Hoa by 320th Division, 1 April 1975." In *Mot So Tran Danh Trong Cuoc Khang Chien Chong Phap, Chong My, 1945–1975*, Tap I [*A Number of Battles in the Resistance War against the French and the Americans, 1945–1975*, vol. I]. Hanoi: Military History Institute of Vietnam, 1991.

Binh Doan Cuu Long [*The Mekong Group*]. Hanoi: People's Army Publishing House, 1989. History of the 4th Corps.

Binh Doan Quyet Thang [*The Determined-To-Win Corps*]. Hanoi: People's Army Publishing House, 1988. History of the 1st Corps.

Buon Ma Thuot: Tran Danh Lich Su [*Ban Me Thuot: A Historic Battle*]. Darlac: Darlac Province Party Historical Research Subcommittee, 1990.

Chi Dan Duong Bo Viet Nam (Mat—Luu Hanh Noi Bo) [*Guide to Vietnam's Roads (Secret—Internal Distribution Only)*]. Dalat: Transportation Department of the General Rear Services Department, 1980.

Chien Dich Hue-Danang (Xuan 1975) [*The Hue-Danang Offensive Campaign (Spring 1975)*]. Hanoi: Military History Institute of Vietnam, 1991.

Chien Dich Tay Nguyen 1975 [*1975 Central Highlands Campaign*]. Hanoi?: Military History Sub-Institute of the High-Level Military Studies Institute, 1981.

Chien Dich Tien Cong Tay Nguyen, Xuan 1975 [*Central Highlands Offensive Campaign, Spring 1975*]. Hanoi: Military History Institute of Vietnam, 1991.

Chung Mot Bong Co: Ve Mat Tran Dan Toc Giai Phong Mien Nam Viet Nam) [*Under One Flag: The National Liberation Front of South Vietnam*]. Ho Chi Minh City: National Political Publishing House, 1993.

Dai Thang Mua Xuan, 1975: Van Kien Dang [*Vietnam Communist Party: Great Spring Victory 1975: Collected Party Documents*]. Hanoi: National Political Publishing House, 2005.

Le Duan. *Thu Vao Nam* [*Letters to the South*]. Hanoi: Su That Publishing House, 1985.

Lich Su Bien Nien Xu Uy Nam Bo Va Trung Uong Cuc Mien Nam (1954–1975) [*Historical Chronicle of the Cochin China Party Committee and the Central Office for South Vietnam, 1954–1975*]. Hanoi: National Political Publishing House, 2002.

Lich Su Binh Chung Thiet Giap, Quan Doi Nhan Dan Viet Nam 1959–1975 [*History of the Armor Branch, People's Army of Vietnam 1959–1975*]. Hanoi: People's Army Publishing House, 1982.

Lich Su Bo Doi Truong Son Duong Ho Chi Minh [*History of the Annamite Mountain Troops on the Ho Chi Minh Trail*]. Hanoi: People's Army Publishing House, 1994.

Lich Su Hai Quan Nhan Dan Viet Nam [*History of the People's Navy of Vietnam*]. Hanoi: People's Army Publishing House, 1985.

Lich Su Khong Quan Nhan Dan Viet Nam (1955–1977) [*History of the People's Air Force (1955–1975)*]. Hanoi: People's Army Publishing House, 1993.

Lich Su Nghe Thuat Su Dung Phong Khong Trong Chien Dich (1945–1975) [*History of the Art of Utilizing Air Defense in Combat Campaigns (1945–1975)*]. Hanoi: People's Army Publishing House, 1996.

Lich Su Quan Chung Phong Khong, Tap III [*History of the Air Defense Service, vol. III*]. Hanoi: People's Army Publishing House, 1994.

Lich Su Quan Doan 2 (1974–1994) [*History of the 2nd Corps (1974–1994)*]. Hanoi: People's Army Publishing House, 1994.

Lich Su Saigon-Cho Lon-Gia Dinh Khang Chien (1945–1975) [*History of the Resistance War in Saigon-Cho Lon-Gia Dinh (1945–1975)*]. Ho Chi Minh City: Ho Chi Minh City Publishing House, 1994.

Lich Su Su Doan 5 [*History of the 5th Division*]. Hanoi: People's Army Publishing House, 1995.

Lu Doan 202 [*The 202nd Brigade*]. Hanoi: 1st Corps Publishing House, 1984.

Luc Luong Chong Phan Dong: Lich Su Bien Nien (1954–1975) [*Anti-Reactionary Forces: Chronology of Events (1954–1975)*]. Hanoi: Public Security Publishing House, 1997.

Mien Dong Nam Bo Khang Chien (1945–1975), Tap VIII [*The Resistance War in Eastern Cochin China (1945–1975)*, vol. VIII]. Hanoi: People's Army Publishing House, 1993.

Mien Trung Toan Thang: Dai Thang Mua Xuan 1975 (Qua Nhung Trang Hoi Uc) [*Central Vietnam Wins Total Victory: The 1975 Great Spring Victory (Through the Memoirs of Participants)*]. Hanoi: Encyclopedia Publishing House, 2005.

Mot So Van Kien Chi Dao: Tong Tien Cong Va Noi Day Mua Xuan Nam 1975, Chien Dich Ho Chi Minh [*A Number of Guidance Documents for the Spring 1975 General Offensive and Uprising and the Ho Chi Minh Campaign*]. Hanoi: People's Army Publishing House, 2005.

Phao Binh Nhan Dan Vietnam, Tap II [*People's Artillery of Vietnam:* vol. II]. Hanoi: Artillery Command, 1986.

Quan Khu 8: Ba Muoi Nam Khang Chien (1945–1975) [*Military Region 8: 30 Years of Resistance (1945–1975)*]. Hanoi: People's Army Publishing House, 1998.

Quan Khu 9: 30 Nam Khang Chien (1945–1975) [*Military Region 9: 30 Years of Resistance (1945–1975)*]. Hanoi: People's Army Publishing House, 1996.

Su Doan 2, Tap I [*2nd Division*, vol. 1]. Danang: Danang Publishing House, 1989.

Su Doan 7: Ky Su [*7th Division: A Record*]. Hanoi: People's Army Publishing House, 1986.

Su Doan 9 [*9th Division*]. Hanoi: People's Army Publishing House, 1990.

Su Doan 10: Binh Doan Tay Nguyen [*10th Division: Central Highlands Corps*]. Hanoi: People's Army Publishing House, 1987.

Su Doan 303 [*The 303rd Division*]. Hanoi: People's Army Publishing House, 1989.

Su Doan 304, Tap II [*304th Division*, vol. II]. Hanoi: People's Army Publishing House, 1990.

Su Doan 316, Tap II [*316th Division*, vol. II]. Hanoi: People's Army Publishing House, 1986.

Su Doan 324 [*324th Division*]. Hanoi: People's Army Publishing House, 1992.

Su Doan 325, Tap II [*325th Division*, vol. II]. Hanoi: People's Army Publishing House, 1986.

Su Doan 968 [*968th Division*]. Quang Tri: The 968th Division and the Quang Tri Province Information Bureau, 1990.

Su Doan Dong Bang (Binh Doan Tay Nguyen), Tap Ba [*The Lowlands Division (Central Highlands Corps)*, vol. three]. Hanoi: People's Army Publishing House, 1984. History of the 320th Division.

Su Doan Sao Vang [*The "Yellow Star" Division*]. Hanoi: People's Army Publishing House, 1984. History of the 3rd Division.

Su Doan Song Lam [*The Lam River Division*]. Hanoi: People's Army Publishing House, 1984. History of the 341st Division.

Van Kien Dang, Toan Tap, Tap 34, 1973 [*Collected Party Documents*, vol. 34, 1973]. Hanoi: National Political Publishing House, 2004.

Van Kien Dang, Toan Tap, Tap 35, 1974 [*Collected Party Documents*, vol. 35, 1974]. Hanoi: National Political Publishing House, 2004.

Van Kien Dang, Toan Tap, Tap 36, 1975 [*Collected Party Documents*, vol. 36, 1975]. Hanoi: National Political Publishing House, 2004.

Ve Dai Thang Mua Xuan Nam 1975 Qua Tai Lieu Cua Chinh Quyen Sai Gon [*The 1975 Great Spring Victory through Sai Gon Government Documents*]. Hanoi: National Political Publishing House, 2010.

2.2 Memoirs Published in Vietnamese

Bui Tin, *Hoa Xuyen Tuyet* [*Flowers through the Snow*] (Irvine, Calif.: Human Rights Publishing House, 1991).

Dam Van Nguy, with Le Minh Huy and Duong Duy Ngu. *Di Mot Ngay Dang* [*The Farther You Travel*]. Hanoi: People's Army Publishing House, 1994.

Dang Vu Hiep, in cooperation with Le Hai Trieu and Ngo Vinh Binh. *Ky Uc Tay Nguyen* [*Highland Memories*]. Hanoi: People's Army Publishing House, 2000.

Hoang Cam, as told to Nhat Tien. *Chang Duong Muoi Nghin Ngay* [*The Ten-Thousand Day Journey*]. 2nd ed. Hanoi: People's Army Publishing House, 2001.

Hoang Dan. *Nhung Dieu Dong Lai Qua Hai Cuoc Chien Tranh* [*Things Accumulated during Two Wars*]. Hanoi: People's Army Publishing House, 2005.

Hoang Minh Thao. *Chien Dau O Tay Nguyen* [*Fighting in the Central Highlands*]. 2nd ed. Hanoi: People's Army Publishing House, 2004.

Le Quang Hoa. *Nhung Chang Duong Chong My: Hoi Ky* [*Steps along the Road of Resistance to the Americans: A Memoir*]. Hanoi: People's Army Publishing House, 1982.

Nam Ha. *Mat Tran Dong Bac Saigon: Ky Su* [*The Front Northeast of Saigon: A Report*]. Ho Chi Minh City: Van Hoc Publishing House, 1978.

Nguyen Huu An, as told to Nguyen Tu Duong. *Chien Truong Moi* [*New Battlefield*]. Hanoi: People's Army Publishing House, 2002 (Second Printing).

Nguyen Khai. *Thang Ba O Tay Nguyen: Ky Su* [*March in the Central Highlands: A Report*]. Hanoi: People's Army Publishing House, 1976.

Truong Son [Pham Te, Senior Colonel]. *Nhung Nam Thang Soi Dong Nhat Tren Duong Ho Chi Minh* [*The Most Feverish Years on the Ho Chi Minh Trail*]. Ho Chi Minh City: Ho Chi Minh City Publishing House, 1994.

Vo Chi Cong. *Tren Nhung Chang Duong Cach Mang (Hoi Ky)* [*On the Road of Revolution (A Memoir)*]. Hanoi: National Political Publishing House 2001.

Xuan Thieu. *Bac Hai Van, Xuan 1975: Ky Su* [*North of the Hai Van Pass, Spring 1975: A Report*]. Hanoi: People's Army Publishing House, 1977.

2.3 Articles Published in Vietnamese

Bao Chan. "The Spy without a Secret Code Number." *Nguoi Lao Dong* (27 April 2006).

Ho De. "The Road into the City Was Not Covered with a Red Carpet." *Quan Doi Nhan Dan* (29 April 2006).

Hung Tan. "Blocking Attack in the Cheo Reo Valley." *Quan Doi Nhan Dan* (23 March 2007).

Huynh Chanh. "The General Staff and the 1975 Central Highlands Campaign." *Quan Doi Nhan Dan* (24 March 2006).

Le Duc Anh. "The Final Phase of the War." http://www.vietnamnet.vn/psks/2006/04/565983/. Accessed on 4 May 2006.

Le Duc Tho. "Comrade Le Duc Tho Discusses a Number of Issues Related to Reviewing the War and Writing Military History." *Tap Chi Lich Su Quan Su* 3, no. 27 (1988): 4–9.

Le Huu Duc. "Developing the Plan to Liberate South Vietnam in Two Years." *Quan Doi Nhan Dan* (12–15 March 2005).

Manh Viet. "Meeting with a 'Viet Cong' Who Once Had a Face-to-Face Meeting with the U.S. President at the Pentagon." *Tien Phong* (14 February 2007).

Thanh Do. "Regarding the First Tank to Reach Independence Palace: We Still Must Give Tank 843 This Honor!" *Nhan Dan* (2 May 2003).

Thanh Xuan. "Intelligence Warrior H3 Inside the Puppet Joint General Staff." *Quan Doi Nhan Dan* (27 July 2006).

Vu Van Mao. "The Battlefield Exploits of Military Intelligence Personnel: The Central Highlands Campaign." *Quan Doi Nhan Dan* (20–21 March 1995).

2.4 Books and Articles Published in English

Dao Van Xuan, Colonel. "In the Spring 1975 General Offensive and Uprising—Tank-Armored Troops in Strategic Group Offensives." *Tap Chi Quan Doi Nhan Dan*, June 1976. Translated in JPRS SEA-67912.

Ho Ding Nhuong. "The Invisible Star of the Milky Way—True Story of Pilot Nguyen Thanh Trung." *Vietnam Courier* (January 1976), 16–18.

Hoang Minh Thao, Major General. *The Victorious Tay Nguyen Campaign.* Hanoi: Foreign Language Publishing House, 1979.

———. "Ex-Central Highlands Commander Recounts Buon Me Thuot Battle." Translated in JPRS SEA-80692.

Hoang Van Huan. *A Drop in the Ocean.* Beijing: Foreign Languages Press, 1988.

Hoang Van Thai. *The Decisive Years: Memoirs of Senior General Hoang Van Thai.* Washington, D.C.: JPRS-SEA-87-084, 23 June 1987.

"Letters to the South." *Vietnam Social Sciences*, vols. 1 and 2 (1989): 129–147.

Minh Hai. "Offensive and Uprising to Liberate the Mekong Delta." *Tap Chi Quan Doi Nhan Dan*, April 1976. Translated in JPRS SEA-67798, Erratum in 67909.

Pham Cuong. "In the General Offensive and Uprising of 1975: Some Experiences in Assuring the Mobility of the Military Engineer Forces," *Quan Doi Nhan Dan* (December 1976). Translated in JPRS SEA-69017.

Pham Xuan The. "That Was How the Saigon Cabinet Surrendered." *Vietnam Social Sciences* 2, no. 24 (1990): 107–115.

"Secret CPV Politburo Documents on the Liberation of the South, Part 1." *Vietnam Social Sciences* 2, no. 46 (1995): 110–120.

"Secret CPV Politburo Documents on the Liberation of the South, Part 2." *Vietnam Social Sciences* 3, no. 47 (1995): 108–117.

Tran Tho. "In the General Offensive and Uprising of 1975: Some Successful Lessons of the Rear Services Task." *Quan Doi Nhan Dan* (October 1976). Translated in JPRS SEA-68570.

Tran Van Tra. *Vietnam: History of the Bulwark B-2 Theatre.* Vol. 5, *Concluding the 30-Year War.* Washington, D.C.: JPRS-SEA-82-783.

Van Tien Dung. *Our Great Spring Victory: An Account of the Liberation of South Vietnam*. Translated by John Spragens Jr. Hanoi: The Gioi Publishers, 2000.

Victory in Vietnam: The Official History of the People's Army of Vietnam, 1945– 1975. Translated by Merle L. Pribbenow. Lawrence: University of Kansas Press, 2002.

Vo Nguyen Giap and Van Tien Dung. *How We Won the War*. Philadelphia: Recon Press, 1976.

———. *The General Headquarters in the Spring of Decisive Victory (Memoirs)*. Hanoi: The Gioi Publishers, 2002.

3. SOUTH VIETNAMESE SOURCES

3.1 Books Published in Vietnamese

Diep My Linh. *Hai Quan Viet Nam Cong Hoa Ra Khoi, 1975* [*The South Vietnamese Navy Sails, 1975*]. Texas: Self-published, 1990. History of the VNN efforts to evacuate military and civilian personnel from I and II Corps.

Ha Mai Viet. *Thep Va Mau: Thiet Giap Trong Chien Tranh Viet Nam* [*Steel and Blood: Armor in the Vietnam War*]. Sugarland, Tex.: Self-published, 2005. A senior officer of the 25th Division interviews various ARVN officers on their recollections of the final days.

Ho Van Ky Thoai. *Can Truong Trong Chien Bai: Hanh Trinh Cua Mot Thuy Thu* [*Valor in Defeat: A Sailor's Journey*]. Centerville, Va.: Self-published, 2007. Thoai was the Navy commander in I Corps, and his book mainly details the fall of that region.

Le Thuong. *Su Doan 2 Bo Binh: Giai Doan Cuoi Cung cua Cuoc Chien, Hoi Ky* [*The 2nd Infantry Division: The Final Phase of the War, a Memoir*]. Los Angeles: Self-published, 2001. The 2nd Division chief of artillery describes the final days.

Le Van Phat. "I Was Trapped in Khanh Duong." In *Lich Su Ngan Nguoi Viet* [*History Written by Thousands*], edited by Nguyen Chu. San Jose: Doi, 1990. The 3rd Airborne Brigade commander describes the battle of the M'Drak Pass and the retreat to Phan Rang.

Ngo Van Xuan. "A Number of Events behind the Fighting on the Central Highlands Front in 1975." In *Nhung Bien Co Can Duoc Ghi Lai* [*Events That Need to Be Recorded*]. Edited by Trinh Tieu. Sacramento: Association of Former Vietnamese Political Prisoners, 1996. The commander of the

44th Regiment, 23rd Division, describes the failed counterattack at Ban Me Thuot.

Nguyen Duc Phuong. *Chien Tranh Vietnam Toan Tap: Tu Tran Dau (Ap Bac, 1963) Den Tran Cuoi Cung (Sai Gon, 1975)* [*The Vietnam War Collection: From the First Battle (Ap Bac, 1963) until the Last (Saigon, 1975)*]. Toronto: Lang Van Publishing, 2001.

Nguyen Duy Hinh. "Commander's Diary, Part 2." *Su Doan 3 Bo Binh (Phan Thu Hai va Ba)* [*3rd Infantry Division (Parts Two and Three)*]. Edited by Giao Chi. San Jose: Tin Bien, 2003. The wartime diary of the 3rd Division commander.

Pham Ba Hoa. *Doi Dong Ghi Nho* [*My Memoir*]. Garden Grove, Calif.: Self-published, 1998. The deputy chief of logistics describes the actions of the JGS and Lieutenant General Dong Van Khuyen during the final days.

Pham Huan. *Cuoc Triet Thoai Cao Nguyen 1975* [*The Withdrawal from the Central Highlands, 1975*]. San Jose: Self-published, 1987. Huan was a journalist and Army officer assigned to Major General Phu's staff to write a memoir of the general. He recorded the events of the fall of II Corps.

———. *Nhung Uat Han Trong Tran Chien Mat Ngoc, 1975* [*Bitterness and Injustice during the Loss of Our Nation, 1975*]. Garden Grove, Calif.: Self-published, 1988. Huan's broader description of the final days, including interviews with participants.

Trinh Tieu. "Why Was Ban Me Thuot Lost Even though We Knew Beforehand That the Enemy Was Going to Attack the City?" In *Nhung Bien Co Can Duoc Ghi Lai* [*Events That Need to Be Recorded*]. Edited by Trinh Tieu. Sacramento: Association of Former Vietnamese Political Prisoners, 1996. The II Corps G-2 (intelligence officer) reflects on the intelligence that led him to believe that PAVN would attack Ban Me Thuot.

Truong Duong. *Doi Chien Binh* [*The Life of a Soldier*]. Garden Grove, Calif.: Tu Quynh, 1998. An Airborne officer describes the various battles of the Airborne Division from 1972 to 1975.

3.2 Articles Published in Vietnamese

The following articles were culled from general-interest journals and from magazines of the various branches of the South Vietnamese armed forces.

Cam Ranh [pseud.]. "7th Marine Battalion and 147th Brigade: The Last Days of March on the Hue Battlefield." *Song Than* [*Tidal Wave*] (2004): 175–180. Account of the attempted evacuation of the 7th Battalion and 147th Brigade from I Corps.

Dam Huu Phuoc. "Phuoc Long: The Wound That Never Heals." *Airborne Ranger* 3 (2001): 26–31. A medical officer with the elite 81st Airborne reflects on the effort to support the beleaguered defenders in Phuoc Long province.

Dinh Hung Cuong. "The Last Battle of Thua Thu, Long An Province." *KBC* 25 (1998): 15–18. The Thua Thu district chief provides an account of the early April fighting in Long An.

Ho Dinh. "The Xuan Loc Front." *KBC* 15 (1991): 100–106. A former 18th Division officer outlines the battle in April 1975.

Le Quang Luong. "The Angels in Red Berets—Who Has Been Lost, and Who Survived." *Doi* (1982). The Airborne Division commander provides a blistering critique of Thieu and the break-up of his division.

Le Quang Oanh. "22nd Division's Withdrawal from Binh Dinh." *KBC* 13 (1992): 41–48. A staff officer describes the chaos on the Qui Nhon beaches.

Mach Van Truong. "21st Infantry Division at Can Tho on the Day the Nation Was Lost." *The Gioi* 394 (18 April 2003): 14–20. The 21st Division commander provides an excellent account of the fighting in IV Corps in April 1975.

Muong Giang. "Regional and Popular Force Troops during the Final Days in Binh Thuan Province." *KBC Hai Ngoai* 16 (April 2003): 53–59. An account by an RF officer; the last days in Phan Thiet and Ham Tan.

Ngo Quang Truong. "Why I Abandoned I Corps." *Doi* (1982). The I Corps commander provides his only public statement on what happened in the north.

Nguyen Phan. "From a Bitter Time." *Mu Nau* 1 (1994): 127–135. The S-3 (operations chief) of the 30th Ranger Battalion, 31st Ranger Group, details the tough fighting at Chon Thanh.

Nguyen Thanh Chuan. "Military Region III Rangers during the Last Days of April 1975." *Mu Nau [Brown Beret]* 1 (1994): 41–48. The III Corps Ranger commander describes the retreat from An Loc, the fighting in Chon Thanh, and the final days of the III Corps Rangers.

Nguyen Trong Luat. "Looking Back at the Battle of Ban Me Thuot, 1975." *KBC* 21 (1995): 21–34. The Darlac province chief recounts the battle of Ban Me Thuot, and his capture.

Nguyen Van Dinh. "1st Airborne Brigade during the Final Days in South Vietnam." *Vietnam Moi* 180 (29 April 2000). The 1st Airborne commander provides an excellent description of the battles in Xuan Loc, the retreat on Route 2, and the final battle for Ba Ria and Vung Tau.

Phan Van Duong. "Unforgettable Days—The 5th Marine Battalion." *Song Than* (1998): 201–205. An account of the destruction of the 5th Marines written by one of the company commanders.

Phan Van Huan. "81st Airborne Ranger Group and the Days of April 1975." *Airborne Ranger* 3 (2001): 7–16. The commander of the most elite ARVN unit describes the last efforts of his outfit, including the final march into Saigon to surrender.

Pham Van Tien. "147th Brigade: From a Tactical Withdrawal in 1975." *Song Than* (1999): 227–237. Another account of the destruction of the 147th Brigade on the Thuan An beach.

Tran Dinh Vy. "Letter to KBC 4262: Last Days in Binh Dinh Province." *KBC Hai Ngoai* 16 (April 2003): 83–85. The Binh Dinh province chief recounts the last days.

Tran Ngoc. "The Final Battle of ARVN's 81st Airborne Ranger Group on 30 April 1975." *KBC* 15 (1994): 24–35. An interview with Major Pham Chau Tai, who commanded the 3rd Task Force, which was defending Tan Son Nhut airbase and the JGS Headquarters on April 30.

Tran Tien San. "The Twenty-Fifth Hour." *Ranger* 8 (2003): 5–19. The commander of the 86th Ranger Battalion, 8th Ranger Group, describes the final attacks on his unit.

———. "The 6th Ranger Group and Its Final Days." *Ranger* 6 (2002): 76–85. An interview with the 6th Group's commander, who acted as deputy commander of the II Corps Rangers during the retreat on Route 7B.

Vu Quoc Cong. "The Last Days on the South China Sea: Tender *Vinh Long*, HQ-802." *Doan Ket* (1998): 23–40. The captain of the HQ-802 provides a graphic description of the evacuation attempts by the VNN on the beaches in I Corps.

Vuong Mong Long. "End of the Road: Memoir." *Ranger* 20 (May 2007): 87–102. Long recounts the last days of his Ranger battalion.

3.3 Manuscripts

The following papers were written by former South Vietnamese officers to recount their actions or the actions of their units during the final days of the RVN. Many were written at my request.

Hua Yen Len. "The Line of Steel at Xuan Loc (Long Khanh)." (1998.) A description of the battle of Xuan Loc by the 18th Division chief of staff.

Le Ba Binh. "The Battles Fought by 6th Battalion, 258th Marine Brigade, Marine Division, from 20 April 1975 to 30 April 1975 at Ho Nai 1, Ho Nai

2, and the Lo Than [Coal Plant] Intersection in Bien Hoa." (2003.) A detailed description by the 6th Battalion commander of the vicious fighting at Ho Nai.

Le Qui Dau. "The 21st Ranger Group." (2003.) The commander describes his attack into Ban Me Thuot, his retreat down Route 21, and the destruction of his unit.

Nguyen Thanh Tri. "Unforgettable Days—The Marine Division in 1975." (2003.) The deputy commander of the Marine Division tells what happened to the Marines.

Nguyen Thieu. "The Actions of the 41st Regiment, 22nd ARVN Division." (2004.) The commander describes the valiant fighting retreat of the 41st Regiment to the beaches at Qui Nhon.

Nguyen Thu Luong. "The Battle for Phan Rang (April 1975)." (2000.) The 2nd Airborne Brigade commander describes the final days in Phan Rang, and his eventual capture.

Nguyen Van Loc. "The Story of Naval Vessel HQ-503." (2002.) The captain of HQ-503 describes the shelling of his ship on 19 April 1975.

Pham Ngoc Sang. "The Battle of Phan Rang: The Recollections of Brigadier General Pham Ngoc Sang." (2002.) The VNAF 6th Air Division commander recounts the final battle for Phan Rang, and his eventual capture.

Phan Tan My. "The Battle for Horseshoe Hill." (1998.) The commander of the 3rd Battalion, 52nd Regiment, 18th Division, tells how his unit severely damaged an elite PAVN regiment outside Xuan Loc.

Tran Quang Khoi. "The Activities of the 3rd Armor Brigade during the Final Days of the Vietnam War in the III Corps Area." (2002.) The commander of the 3rd Armored Cavalry Brigade details the final days.

———. "A Lightning Counterattack of the ARVN 3rd Armor Brigade at Duc Hue." (2005.)

Vuong Mong Long. "The 82nd Border Ranger Battalion and the Battle of Xuan Loc." (2001.) One of most respected Ranger officers recounts his harrowing retreat from Quang Duc province, the battle for Xuan Loc, and his refusal to surrender on 30 April.

3.4 Articles and Books Published in English

Bui Diem, with David Chanoff. *In the Jaws of History.* Boston: Houghton Mifflin, 1987.

Cao Van Vien. *The Final Collapse.* Washington, D.C.: Center of Military History, U.S. Army, 1982.

Kiem Do, Captain, and Julie Kane. *Counterpart: A South Vietnamese Naval Officer's War*. Annapolis: Naval Institute Press, 1998.

Lam Quang Thi, Lieutenant General. *The 25-Year Century: A South Vietnamese General Remembers the Indochina War to the Fall of Saigon*. Denton, Tex.: University of North Texas Press, 2002.

Lu Van Thanh. *The Inviting Call of Wandering Souls: Memoir of an ARVN Liaison Officer to United States Forces in Vietnam Who Was Imprisoned in Communist Re-education Camps and Then Escaped*. Jefferson, N.C.: McFarland and Co., 1997

Tran Quang Khoi. "Fighting to the Finish: The Role of South Vietnam's III Armor Brigade and III Corps Assault Force in the War's Final Days." *Armor* (March/April 1996): 23–27.

Tran Thi Minh Canh. *The Book of Canh: Memoirs of a Vietnamese Woman, Physician, CIA Informant, People's Salvation Army Commander-in-Chief, and Prisoner of War*. Milford, Conn.: Self-published, 1996.

Tran Van Nhut. *The Unfinished War: The Memoirs of General Tran Van Nhut*. Garden Grove, Calif.: Self-published, 2001.

4. FOREIGN SOURCES

British Broadcasting Corporation. *Summary of World Broadcasts*. Part 3: The Far East. January–April 1975.

Coulthard-Clark, Chris. *The RAAF in Vietnam: Australian Air Involvement in the Vietnam War 1962–1975*. Canberra: Paul & Co Pub Consortium, 1995.

Todd, Olivier. *Cruel April: The Fall of Saigon*. Translated from the French by Stephen Becker. New York: W. W. Norton & Company, 1987.

Warner, Denis. *Certain Victory: How Hanoi Won the War*. Kansas City, Mo.: Sheed, Andrews, and McMeel, 1978.

INDEX

I Corps, 45, 49, 69–70, 87, 95, 117–
18, 120, 126, 151, 173, 176, 188,
196, 340; I Corps Forward, 93, 96,
98, 222, 265, 266, 268–69, 271, 272,
306, 315; battle for Ban Me Thuot
and, 130–31, 135; battle for Phuoc
Long and, 92–96, 107; collapse of,
320–29, *321*, 332, 338, 407, 436,
464, 466, 484, 498; defense of Hue
and, 262, 264–65, 268–71, 274, 277,
278–80, 282–84, 286, 290–91, 295;
fall of, 299–330; headquarters of,
392; initial PAVN attacks in, *267*;
inspection tour of, 284–85; refugees
in, 290; reintegration of escaped
forces, 393; resistance of South
Vietnam and, 387, 392, 393, 395,
396, 401, 441, 456; retreat from
Central Highlands and, 220–22,
227, 228, 234
II Corps, 10, 34, 49, 52, 69–70, 108,
117, 120, 241–42, 248, 260–61, 298,
396, 482, 498; attacks in I Corps
and, 271; battle for Ban Me Thuot
and, 126–39, 153–58, 165–70, 244;
battle for, 171–202; collapse of,

185–89, *187*, 314, 333, 334–36, 340–
56, 384, 407, 436, 464; evacuation
of, 319; "Great Spring Offensive"
and, 142–43, 146–48, 162;
headquarters of, 350–51; inspection
tour of, 284–85; martial law in,
332; PAVN capture of, *187*; refugees
from, 440–41, 456; remnants of,
387–88, 393, 464; retreat from
Central Highlands and, 204–34;
stolen codes in, 170, 236
III Corps, 51–52, 70, 92, 95, 117,
197, 274, 334, 353, 440, 454; III
Corps Forward, 390, 423; attacks
in, *245*; battle for Phuoc Long
and, 100–14; fall of Saigon and,
463–99; headquarters of, 430,
474, 485; Ranger Command, 257;
resumption of war and, 72–78, 81,
87; South Vietnamese resistance
in, 388, 390, 393, 402–03, 407, 410;
surrounding of Saigon and, 235–62,
359, 381
IV Corps, 34, 41–43, 50–51, 72, 74,
81, 92, 95, 104, 108, 117, 135–36,
255, 261, 407; fall of Saigon and,

466, 478, 482, 494, 496–97;
headquarters of, 404–05; merging
Regional Force units into, 393

1st Corps, 449; ARVN retreat and,
218–19; fall of Saigon and, 476–77,
494; surrounding of Saigon and,
360–61, 364–65, 366–67, 370–71
2nd Corps, 14, 300, 483; arrival at
Rung La, 432–33; battle for Hue,
268–69, 271–76, 295, 296–98; at
Ca Na Bay, 427–30; capture of
Phan Rang, 422, 427–30; engineer
units, 268; fall of Saigon and,
474–75, 491–92, 496; First Element,
428–29, 431; Second Element, 426;
surrounding of Saigon and, 361–62,
367–73
3rd Corps, 334–35, 359, 361, 368,
370–72, 449, 488; 3rd Corps
Forward Headquarters, 426
4th Corps, 75, 406, 454, 483, 520n6,
521n30, 537n16; battle for Xuan
Loc, 436–38, 442, 445, 449–51;
surrounding of Saigon and, 240,
243, 248, 250–51, 258, 368, 397,
468, 471, 474, 483

A-75 command group, 130, 364
Abzug, Bella, 112, 122, 182
"Action Committee to Save the
Nation," 377
Africa, 63, 224
Agnew, Spiro, 80
agriculture, 29, 37, 49–50, 65, 152,
173
Airborne Division, 57, 73, 93,
96–99, 117–18, 176–78, 222, 227,

268, 271, 278, 280, 283, 334, 342,
390, 457–58, 533n10; 1960s coup,
57; Airborne Headquarters, 448;
coastal cities and, 349, 352; at
Danang, 329; headquarters of,
387; at Hue, 270, 278–80, 283, 289;
II Corps and, 336–37, 339–40;
at M'Drak Pass, 390–92; at Nha
Trang, 387; at Phan Rang, 387,
395, 412–13, 417–19, 422, 424–27;
at Phan Thiet, 432–33; at Phuoc
Long, 107–8; at Qui Nhon, 343–44;
at Saigon, 408, 410–11, 464, 471,
475–76, 483, 487–92, 494–95; at
Xuan Loc, 447–49, 456–57
aircraft: A-37s, 167, 226, 248, 337,
343–44, 371–73, 391, 394, 411–13,
416, 421, 425, 470, 481–82; B-52
bombers, 223–24, 226, 312, 344,
454; C-47s, 352; C-119 gunships,
191, 444, 447, 450; C-130 cargo
planes, 101, 110, 206, 386, 391, 395,
450, 458, 486, 490, 537n23, 538n30;
Chinook helicopters, 169, 170,
192, 231, 391–92, 448, 452; EC-
47s, 408, 419–20; F-5As, 66; F-5Es,
62, 66, 250; helicopters, 7, 214,
231, 253, 391–92, 424, 488; Huey
transport helicopters, 391–92; O-1
observation plane, 424
Air Vietnam, 206–07
Albert, Carl, 113, 225
ammunition, 77–78, 96–99, 104,
107, 118, 153, 156, 192, 195, 207,
254–55, 361, 446, 458; artillery
units, 124, 132, 151, 156, 164, 166,
169, 175, 205, 234, 240, 326–27,
363, 420–21; cuts in South Vietnam

aid and, 53–70, 82–83, 118;
rationing of, 57–58, 60, 96, 144,
236; stockpiling of, 77, 441; supply
of, 48, 74, 77–78, 82–83, 88, 96,
102–03, 106, 118, 124, 161, 183,
236, 289–90, 410, 444, 450
An, Nguyen Huu, 46, 271–72, 276,
282, 291, 295–97, 326–28, 414, 419,
427–28; capture of Hue and, 303;
capture of Phan Rang and, 416–19,
420, 423, 426–27; fall of Phan Thiet
and, 433; fall of Saigon and, 489–
92; surrounding of Saigon and, 367,
368, 369–71
An, Vo, 162, 165–66, 190, 191, 195,
273
An Dien, Vietnam, 76–77
Angel's Wing area, 239
An Giang province, Vietnam, 405
Anh, Le Duc, 43–44, 95, 106–09, 249,
400, 520n6, 521n17
An Khe Pass, 132, 136–37, 151–53,
226
An Lo Bridge, 274, 303, 315
An Loc, Vietnam, 73, 103, 108–09,
160, 174, 243, 252, 256–58, 259,
405, 417, 533n10
Annamite Mountains, 264, 395, 440
An Quang Buddhists, 32, 376
anti-aircraft units, 124, 175, 246,
248, 253; at Ban Me Thuot, 131–32,
155–56, 166, 193; fall of Saigon
and, 471, 486, 489; at Phuoc Long,
106–7, 109
anti-tank units, 108, 214, 233, 258–
59, 318, 420, 431, 488
anti-war movement, 3–4, 8, 23, 28,
47, 58, 59, 112, 122, 145, 497

Arab world, 63. *See also* OPEC oil
embargo
Arc Road, 405–06
armored personnel carriers (APCs):
K-63s, 163, 226, 233, 486, 487;
M-41s, 142, 156, 158, 230, 258;
M-48s, 214, 230, 281, 372, 483, 484,
488; M-113s, 50, 142, 160, 166–68,
178–79, 189, 205, 207–8, 230, 232,
234, 317, 320, 343, 348, 372, 403,
405, 413, 431, 478, 486, 492; PT-76s,
327; T-54s, 108–10, 163, 258–59,
374, 412, 422, 443, 475, 484, 486,
488, 492
Armor School, 468, 474, 475
Army of the Republic of Vietnam
(ARVN), 1, 6–7, 10, 32, 40, 50, 68,
172, 174, 198, 241, 443; I Corps's
collapse and, 302–29; at Ban Me
Thuot, 126–39, 142–43, 147–48,
150–51, 153–58, 165–70, 189–96,
498; Central Logistics Command,
118, 408; coastal cities and, 331–56;
codes of, 236; collapse of, 491;
communication center of, 236;
conscription and, 74; corruption
in, 5, 50–52, 241, 390, 516n3,
520n7; desertions from, 74, 387,
392, 393, 473; fall of Saigon and,
463–99; fall of Tuy Hoa and, 348;
firepower of, 269, 280, 297; "Gavin
Plan" and, 217, 238; "Great Spring
Offensive" and, 151–53; at Hue,
263–98; intelligence breakdowns
in, 99, 139, 147–48, 150, 265, 268,
277; manpower of, 269, 271; in the
Mekong Delta, 402–07; Military
Transportation Command, 315;

morale of, 6, 48, 51, 63, 67, 73, 78, 83, 87, 89, 96, 99, 111, 169, 227, 304–05, 353, 393, 427, 491; at Phan Rang, 384–89, *385*, 394–95, 411–14, 415–33; at Phan Thiet, 431–32; at Phuoc Long, 100–14; reactions to attacks in II Corps, *149*; rescues of troops, 391–92, 424–25; reserve units, 117, 278; resumption of war and, 72–89; retreat from Dalat, 253–54; retreat from Gia Nghia, 252–53; retreat from Phan Rang, 389; retreat from Central Highlands, 175–82, 185–89, 203–34; retreat to Saigon, 313; siege of Saigon and, 396–407; suicides of officers and men, 319, 347, 496; supplies of ammunition, food, and fuel, 48, 57–58, 75, 77–78, 82, 101, 106, 111, 118, 124, 150, 152, 190, 207, 231–32, 296–97; surrender of, 494–95; surrounding of Saigon and, 236–62, 357–81, 383–414; at Xuan Loc, 419–34, 435–61, 436–38, 441–47, 449–59, 469. *See also specific corps, divisions, forces, and officers*
"attack from the march" tactic, 327, 416
Australia, 386–87

B-1 Front, 14, 124, 132, 218, 269, 304, 333, 335, 341, 368; map of, *16*
B-2 Front, 14, 41–42, 45, 197, 396, 398, 400–01, 449; attacks in III Corps, *245*; Ban Me Thuot and, 130–31, 136, 156; battle for coastal cities and, 332–33, 359; fall of Saigon and, 467, 472, 483;

headquarters of, 450; map of, *16*; Phuoc Long and, 101–02, 104, 106; resumption of war and, 72, 74–75, 78, 86–87; retreat from Highlands and, 216–19; surrounding of Saigon and, 239–40, 243, 251, 260–61, 363–64, 366
B-3 Front, 14, 87, 124–26, 130–33, 138, 145–47, 150, 201, 216, 261, 334, 341, 409; collapse of I Corps and, 313–14; map of, *16*
B-4 Front, 14, 98, 300; battle for Hue and, 268–69, 271, 273–77, 283, 291, 295, 302–03, 316; map of, *16*
B-5 Front, 14, *16*
Ba, Ly Tong, 479–80
Bac, Vuong Van, 83
Ba Den Mountain, 104, 108, 236
Ban Don, Vietnam, 142, 160, 169
Bang, Nguyen Van, 430
Ban Me Thuot, Vietnam, 1–9, 101, 135–39, 216, 219, 278, 332–39, 371, 519n36; attack on, 1–3, 7, 10, 126–39, 142–43, 147–48, 150–58, 157, 165–70, 172, 211, 217, 237, 239, 244, 498, 501n4, 511n1, 511n35, 512n6; friendly-fire incidents in, 167, 230; RVNAF's attempt to retake, 173, 177–78, 180, 183–84, 186, 189–96, 196–201, 204–05, 208–09, 253, 377, 379; loss of, 165–70, 181, 221, 224, 227, 249, 260, 288, 314, 364, 467, 531n32
Bao Dai, Emperor, 482
Bao Dinh, Vietnam, 449, 457
Bao Hoa, Vietnam, 457
Bao Loc, Vietnam, 253–54
Bao Toan, Vietnam, 457

Ba Queo, Vietnam, 487, 488

Ba Ra Mountain, 107

Ba Rau, Vietnam, 389, 390, 396, 409, 410, 411, 413, 419

Ba Ria, Vietnam, 359, 475–76

Ba River, 180, 188, 204, 207, 214, 226, 229, 231–32, 348

Base 82, 77, 78

Ba Thap, 389, 390, 396

Bay Hien, Vietnam, 488, 489

Ben Cat, Vietnam, 76, 476

Ben Cau, Vietnam, 243, 244, 246, 248, 249

Ben Luc, Vietnam, 466

Ben Luc Bridge, 466

Be River, 107, 108

Bien Hoa, Vietnam, 368, 390, 395, 430, 441, 445, 468, 475, 477, 483–85, 490

Bien Hoa airbase, 108, 391, 397, 400, 402, 410, 430, 450–51, 454, 456, 459, 466, 474, 488, 537–38n30

Biet, Nguyen Van, 410–11, 412, 423–24

Binh, Le Ba, 483–85

Binh, Nguyen Khac, 377

Binh, Nguyen Van, 378

Binh Dinh province, Vietnam, 117, 124, 136–37, 151–53, 159, 174, 196, 216–17, 220, 226–28, 304, 332, 335, 341, 342–47, 369, 373–74, 409, 470

Binh Duong province, Vietnam, 72, 74, 100, 224, 240, 244

Binh Khe, Vietnam, 153, 158–59, 226, 227, 228, 342

Binh Long province, Vietnam, 73, 100, 240, 257, 260

Binh Thuan province, Vietnam, 353, 388, 389, 390, 408, 427, 428, 431

Binh Thuy airfield, 406

Binh Tuy province, Vietnam, 100, 104, 239, 240, 249, 251, 253, 392, 427

Black April (*Thang Tu Den*), 2

"blooming lotus" plan, 135, 167

Bon, Nguyen Thi, 532n2

Bong Bridge, 478, 485, 486–87

Bong Mountain/Mo Tau Hill complex, 98, 266, 271, 291, 294–95, 303–04

Border Campaign (1950), 271

Bo River, 266, 274, 291, 303, 315, 317

Bu Dang, Vietnam, 101, 104, 106

Buddhists, 32, 376, 378

Bu Dop, Vietnam, 104, 106

Bu Na, Vietnam, 101, 104, 106

Bunker, Ellsworth, 47

Buon Ho, Vietnam, 160, 169

But, Le Van, 388, 391–92, 412, 421, 425, 532n1

Buu, Tran Quoc, 184, 224–25, 376, 518–19n28

Ca Du Mountain, 419, 420, 422

Ca Lui, Vietnam, 208, 210, 230

Cam, Hoang, 75, 240, 250, 261–62, 397, 436, 437, 444–45, 447, 450, 506n4, 521n30, 533n13

Cam, Tran Van, 186, 188, 205, 211, 232, 339, 348–49

Cambodia, 14, 34, 66, 74, 111, 113, 136, 186, 239, 397, 468; collapse of, 460; PAVN withdrawal from, 20–21; rice from, 50; secret U.S.

bombing raids in, 33; U.S. aid to, 112, 121, 182–83, 309–10

Cam Ranh, Vietnam, 217, 220, 231, 333, 335, 338, 340, 370–71, 408, 417, 419, 471, 529n42; battle for, 352–56; evacuation of, 529n41, 529n42; loss of, 388–91; securing of, 389–90

Cam Ranh Bay, 170, 178, 181, 192, 201, 227, 287, 308, 338, 354, 374, 384, 387, 389, 392, 394, 408, 416, 428, 516n3, 529n41

Can, Ho Ngoc, 43, 495

Can, Nguyen Ba, 174, 225, 378, 379, 418, 460, 480

Ca Na, Vietnam, 424, 428–30, 536n11

Ca Na Bay, 428–30, 536n11

Cang, Chung Tan, 344, 348, 393, 406–07

Canh, Tran Thi Minh, 351–52

Can Tho, Vietnam, 43, 50, 52, 64, 239, 387, 399, 468, 473, 474, 482, 489; battle for, 404–07, 470

Can Tho airbase, 239, 400

Ca Pass, 339, 348–49, 350

Capital Military District, 52, 393

Capital Military Zone Headquarters, 467, 468

Caputo, Philip, 446

Case, Clifford, 119

Case-Church amendment, 33

Castro, Fidel, 530n10

Catholics, 24, 231, 376, 378, 387, 457, 483, 485

Cat Lai ferry, 475, 489

Cau, Le, 151, 152–53, 158, 159, 341, 342, 344, 347, 512n13

Cau Hai Bay, 302

ceasefire, 3, 43, 66, 144, 395; ceasefire line, 98; disintegration of, 32–33; failure of, 66; in Laos, 21; violations of, 18, 23, 24, 31, 32, 40, 58, 64, 172, 503n1. *See also* Paris Peace Accords

Central Cell, 41, 46, 86, 124, 126, 197, 469; "Outline Study of a Plan to Win the War in the South," 69

Central Committee, 46, 65; 21st Plenum, 45–47; 22nd Plenum, 65

Central Highlands, 14, 69–70, 87, 100–02, 114, 118, 124, 143, 260–61, 271, 273, 282, 335, 451, 485; airfields in, 366; Central Highlands Campaign, 1–9, 126–39, 147–58, 165–70, 173–79, 186, 196, 197–200, 237, 239, 249, 260–61, 370, 389–90; retreat from, 203–34, 236, 288, 298, 304, 379

Central Logistics Command, 118, 408

Central Military Affairs Committee, 14, 38, 40, 45, 68, 102, 125, 126–27, 129–30, 198, 359; siege of Saigon and, 401; surrounding of Saigon and, 369–70

Central Military Party Committee, 198, 333, 334–35, 341

Central Office for South Vietnam (COSVN), 14, 39, 44, 72, 74, 100, 217–18, 237, 243, 244, 251, 262, 481; 271B Regiment, 252–53; 341st Division, 261; collapse of I Corps and, 314; fall of Saigon and, 472, 473–74, 486; headquarters of, 44, 406; at Phan Rang, 388; siege of Saigon and, 397, 398, 400–01, 405;

surrounding of Saigon and, 364, 380

Chau, Nguyen Minh, 240, 243

Chau, Thich Tam, 378

Che, Nguyen Huu, 250, 458

Cheo Reo, Vietnam, 146–47, 179–80, 188–89, 197–202, 204–16, 226–34, 347, 486, 516n3, 516–17n6, 517n7, 517n10, 519n36

Chicago Tribune, 113

Chiec River, 483, 492

Chien, Do Duc, 292, 294

China, 29, 31, 64, 80, 83, 85–86, 88, 102, 225, 309–11, 440, 497–98

Chinh, Huynh Van, 534n23

Chinh, Truong, 21, 37–38, 40, 42–43, 79, 127, 358

Chinh Luan, 211–12, 376

Chon Thanh, Vietnam, 243, 257–59, 410, 437

"Christmas bombing," 19, 23, 38

Chua Chan Mountain, 251, 438, 440

Chuan, Nguyen Thanh, 257–60

Chuc, Nguyen Van, 186, 229–31

Chu Cuc, Vietnam, 194

Chu Lai, Vietnam, 269, 279, 286, 304, 305, 306, 319, 320, 325, 328, 392, 393

Chuong Thien province, Vietnam, 41–42, 43, 44, 495

Chu Pao Pass, 189

Chu Pa ridgeline, 204, 205, 210, 213

Church, Frank, 119, 121, 122, 182, 183, 313

CIA. *See* U.S. Central Intelligence Agency

civilians, 286, 304; ARVN retreat and, 206–07, 209–11, 214, 216, 231–32, 233, 281; in Cung Son, 234; discontent with Thieu's government, 211–12; evacuation of, 295; in Hue, 291, 295, 302, 306–13, 314, 315, 318, 319, 320; morale of, 6, 27, 34, 73, 137, 174, 220, 222, 278, 284, 288–89, 287, 297, 323, 407, 452, 497; in Phan Rang, 387–88, 424–25; rescue of GVN civil servants, 281–82; in Saigon, 494. *See also* refugees

Clements, Warren, 55

Clifford, Clark, 58

coalition government including Communists, 18, 19, 29, 36, 38, 61, 119, 379

Coastal Column, 368, 373–74, 408–09, 414, 416, 419, 427, 430, 432, 436

Co May River, 475–76

combined-arms operations, 6, 46, 69, 74, 88, 155, 164, 372, 428, 468

communication networks, 363–64, 387; radio messages, 138–39, 146, 148, 150, 158, 214–15, 408, 419

Communist Party (Vietnam), 8–9, 13–14, 15, 21, 36–40, 46, 72

Communists: doctrine of, 36; espionage by, 225; fear of, 351; infiltration by, 61; Nixon and, 78–79; opposition and, 29; as part of potential political solution, 311; propaganda of, 10–11, 37, 38, 64; publications of, 10–11, 12; potential South Vietnamese accommodations with, 117, 311, 376; Thieu's refusal to compromise with, 18, 19, 28–29; use of psychological warfare by, 322. *See also* Democratic Republic of Vietnam

Cong, Vo Chi, 332–33
Cua Viet, Vietnam, 274, 275, 362, 365
Cuba, 530n10
Cu Chi, Vietnam, 244, 430, 464, 478, 479, 486, 487
Cu Hanh airfield, 146, 175, 189
Cung Son, Vietnam, 180, 189, 204–05, 209–10, 216, 227, 229–31, 233–34, 334
Cyprus, 84

Daisy Cutters, 454, 537n23
Dak To, battle of, 133
Dalat, Vietnam, 173, 240–41, 248–49, 252–53, 261, 288, 369, 372, 389, 436, 471, 533–34n14
Dalat Military Academy, 50, 252–53
Dan, Hoang, 97, 272–73, 327, 496
Dan, Phan Quang, 285, 307–08, 326
Danang, Vietnam, 5, 14, 60, 81, 117, 264, 315, 318, 426; assault on, 124, 126, 196, 201, 217–18, 295, 302, 304–05, 313–14, 326–29; capture of Hue and, 471; defense of, 92–95, 99, 173, 176, 268–69, 276–86, 291, 297, 304–06, 323–24, 525n18, 525n22; isolation of, 269; loss of, 3–4, 170, 262, 332, 333, 378, 379, 399, 436, 464, 484; under PAVN control, 366–70; refugees in, 276, 289–90, 304–08, 316, 324–26, 329; revenge for, 484; withdrawal to, 280–81
Dao, Le Minh, 76–78, 438, 440–54, 456–59, 475, 485, 490, 494–95
Darlac province, Vietnam, 1–9, 101, 124, 126–39, 142–47, 153–60, 163, 167–69, 184, 194, 197, 200–01, 210, 227, 376

Dau, Le Qui, 160, 166, 167–68, 337
Dau Giay, Vietnam, 249, 251, 261–62, 436, 438, 442, 445, 448, 450–56, 459
De, Dinh Van, 224–25, 518–19n28
De, Ho, 156, 228, 496
deep-penetration columns, 468–69, 474, 477, 478, 479, 484, 485, 486, 491–92, 496
Demilitarized Zone (DMZ), 18, 19, 219, 264, 266, 360, 471
Democracy Party, 28, 92, 378
Democratic Republic of Vietnam (DRV), 2–9, 54–55, 58–61, 94, 116–20, 172, 212, 225, 309, 323, 358, 440; collapse of Paris Peace Accords and, 35–52; corruption in, 28, 65; diplomatic front and, 63–70; economy of, 37–38, 40–43, 64–67, 80, 116; foreign aid to, 51, 66, 497–98; Foreign Ministry, 67; National Assembly, 65, 116, 309, 323, 480; Paris Peace Accords and, 3, 6, 8–10, 13, 18–34, 36, 39, 42–45, 64, 361, 498; resumption of war and, 71–89. *See also* Communists
desertions, 74, 138, 224, 326, 332, 384, 387, 392–93, 473, 482, 495–96, 529n41
Diem, Bui, 63, 184, 224, 376, 460, 517n11
Diem, Ngo Dinh, 25, 54, 57, 480, 482, 532n2
Diem, Nguyen Van, 98, 296, 303–6, 316
Dien Bien Phu, Vietnam, 92, 135, 136, 271, 274, 506n4
Di Linh, Vietnam, 253
Dinh, Nguyen Van, 448, 458

Dinh Quan, Vietnam, 248–52, 438

Dinh Tuong province, Vietnam, 50, 240, 243, 399, 407

DMZ. *See* Demilitarized Zone

Do, Tran Van, 184, 376, 377

Don, Tran Van, 224, 413, 417–18, 480

Dong, Du Quoc, 104, 107–08, 110, 208, 210, 214–16, 241, 516n3, 517–18n12

Dong, Le Huu, 394, 406–07

Dong, Nguyen Van, 207

Dong, Pham Van, 20–22, 37, 42–43, 67

Dong Du, Vietnam, 478, 479–80, 486

Dong Ha, Vietnam, 362, 364–65, 367, 370

Dong Nai River, 249–50, 397, 464, 474, 475, 483, 489, 490, 492

Dong Xoai, Vietnam, 101, 102, 103–04, 106–07, 360, 366

Do Son, Vietnam, 70, 85

dry-season plan (PAVN), 100, 116, 148, 236, 239–40, 252, 260; Phase One, 236, 237, 239; Phase Two, 236, 237–38, 239, 240

Duan, Le, 21, 70, 100, 103, 106–07, 123, 126–28, 183, 216–19, 237, 262, 284, 335, 436, 449, 503n1; acceleration of war and, 196–201; fall of Hue and, 313–14; fall of Saigon and, 466, 471–72, 473–74; resumption of war and, 37–46, 78–79, 85–89; siege of Saigon and, 396–97, 399, 400–02; surrounding of Saigon and, 358–59, 364, 367–68

Duc, Le Huu, 194, 339, 350, 353

Duc Co, Vietnam, 138, 146, 148, 152, 181

Duc Hue, Vietnam, 73, 74

Duc Lap, Vietnam, 87, 101, 126–33, 138, 142–43, 146, 193, 198, 252, 389

Duc My, Vietnam, 336, 337, 339–40, 349

Du Long, Vietnam, 388–89, 390, 396, 409, 411–12, 413, 421

Du Long Pass, 388–89, 390, 395–96, 409, 410, 411–12, 419, 420

Dung, Ngo Ky, 456

Dung, Van Tien, 41, 102, 181, 210, 213, 217–20, 227–28, 230, 379, 389–90, 516–17n6, 533n13; acceleration of war and, 196–202; article published by, 116; battle for Ban Me Thuot and, 127–29, 133–35; battle for Xuan Loc and, 449–59; Central Highlands Campaign and, 128–29, 133–35, 145–46, 150–51, 154–56, 159–60, 166, 175, 181, 196–201, 208, 210, 213, 216–220, 227, 230, 236–37, 253, 260–62; collapse of I Corps and, 298, 314; conquest of II Corps and, 334–35, 353; defense of Thuong Duc and, 96–97; fall of Phan Thiet and, 433; fall of Saigon and, 466–74, 479, 481–82, 485, 490; illness of, 68, 96–97; *Our Great Spring Victory*, 10, 12, 501n4; securing of I and II Corps, 396; siege of Saigon and, 332, 333–35, 398, 399, 400, 401–2; surrounding of Saigon and, 236–37, 253, 260–62, 359, 364

Eastern Annamite Road, 114. *See also* Ho Chi Minh Trail

Easter Offensive (1972), 5, 38, 49, 55, 74, 93, 99, 128, 136–38, 151–52,

174, 181, 241–42, 271, 285, 288, 295, 323–24, 375, 405, 417

engineer units (ARVN), 185–86, 188, 189, 194, 204–05, 207, 210, 212, 229–31, 302, 316, 424

engineer units (PAVN), 6, 76–77, 97, 124, 131–32, 164, 186, 195, 204, 208, 212, 226, 229–30, 233, 250, 269, 272–73, 327, 334; battle for coastal cities and, 335–36, 348, 414, 428, 433; battle for Phuoc Long and, 104, 107; battle for Xuan Loc and, 453, 487; Central Highlands Campaign and, 146–47, 156, 158, 160, 164, 192–95, 208, 226, 233; surrounding of Saigon and, 363–65, 371–74, 477–79, 486–87, 492, 530n10

espionage, North Vietnamese, 6–7, 124–25, 147, 199, 219, 225, 269, 280, 283, 408–09. See also intelligence

Europe, 61, 310

evacuations, 206, 529n41. See also refugees

"family syndrome," 170, 295, 304, 329, 375

Fenwick, Millicent, 123

Flynt, John, 122, 123

food supply, 118, 231–32, 361

Ford, Gerald, 7, 80–85, 126, 184, 221, 325–26; aid to South Vietnam and, 111–14, 119–23, 182–85, 221–22, 310–13, 459–60; assistance to refugees and, 309, 312; correspondence with Thieu, 119–20, 223, 225–26, 312; inaugural

address of, 80–81; meeting with GVN delegation, 224–25; pardon of Nixon by, 81; promises of aid to South Vietnam, 223; response to loss of Phuoc Long, 110–14. See also Ford administration

Ford administration, 11, 60, 83–84, 122; aid to South Vietnam and, 110–11, 182–85, 311; assistance to refugees and, 312

Foreign Affairs, 116

France, 30, 57, 119, 135–36, 179, 480

Fraser, Donald, 122

friendly-fire incidents, 167, 230, 250, 411

Gallup, 47

Gavin, James M., 217, 238

Gayler, Noel, 82, 116, 120, 132, 222, 223

General Staff, North Vietnam, 41, 68–69, 72, 75, 78, 96–97, 200–01, 217–19, 236–37, 238, 396; battle for Ban Me Thuot and, 127–30; battle for Hue and, 271, 273, 297; battle for Phuoc Long and, 100–104; collapse of I Corps and, 314; fall of coastal cities and, 354; fall of Saigon and, 472; siege of Saigon and, 360, 400–401, 408–9; surrounding of Saigon and, 236–38, 262, 365–69

Geneva Agreement (1954), 21, 39, 67, 72

Germany, 46, 328; East Germany, 68; West Germany, 30

Ghenh Bridge, 483

Ghost Mountain, 441–42

Gia Dinh, Vietnam, 358, 379

Gia Nghia, Vietnam, 143, 165, 252–62

Giap, Vo Nguyen, 10, 36–46, 70, 86, 95, 98, 147, 162, 172, 208, 216–20, 449; acceleration of war and, 197–201; attack on Hue and, 265, 270–74, 275, 280, 282–84, 295, 296–98; battle for Ban Me Thuot and, 126–31, 237; battle for Phuoc Long and, 100–103, 114; capture of Cam Ranh and, 356; capture of Phan Rang and, 427; Central Highlands Campaign and, 128–32, 147, 160, 162, 172, 197–201, 208, 216–20, 237; collapse of I Corps and, 314, 326–27; conquest of II Corps and, 335; fall of Saigon and, 469, 473–74; *The General Headquarters in the Spring of Brilliant Victory*, 12, 503n1, 530n10, 531n30, 537–38n30; illness of, 67–69; siege of Saigon and, 333, 381; surrounding of Saigon and, 260, 265, 358–60, 367, 368, 369–70, 373

Glenn, Tom, 148, 150

Go Dau Ha, Vietnam, 244, 247, 248, 255, 256

Go Vap, Vietnam, 484

Government of South Vietnam (GVN), 4, 120, 122, 148, 174–75, 178, 220, 244, 248, 309, 380, 482, 498; accommodations with the Communists, 376; aid to, 63–64, 66, 111–14, 119–23, 182–85, 221–22, 310–13, 459–61; assistance to refugees and, 308–09, 326; collapse of Paris Peace Accords and, 35–52; corruption in, 3, 5, 25, 27–28, 34, 49, 58, 60, 64, 79, 136, 172, 185, 377, 482; cuts in U.S. aid and, 53–70, 82–83, 111, 118, 174, 182–85, 223–24, 312, 325, 460; defense of Hue and, 281–84; delegations to the U.S., 7, 119, 174, 223–24, 518–19n28; diplomatic front and, 63–70; evacuation of civilians by, 295; fall of, 2–3, 474, 482, 493; House of Representatives, 174, 224–25, 376, 378, 519n30; morale of, 497; Paris Peace Accords and, 17–34; refugees and, 231–32, 307–08; resumption of war and, 71–89; Senate, 119, 174, 225, 378, 519n30, 531n33

Great Britain, 119

"Great Spring Offensive," 141–70, 368

Greece, 84

Group 232, 240, 243, 400, 467–68, 471, 473, 477

Group 301, 75, 520n6

Group 559, 131, 362, 363, 364–65, 369–70, 375, 472

Group A-75, 364

guerrillas, 7, 13, 37, 38, 388–89, 390, 395–96

Habib, Philip, 182, 183, 524n5

Hackworth, David, 482

Hai Lang, Vietnam, 287

Haiphong, Vietnam, 428

Hai Van Pass, 93–94, 96, 124, 264, 266–71, 277, 281, 284, 286, 289, 291, 295, 298, 300, 302, 306, 326–28, 525n18

Ham Tan, Vietnam, 368, 392–93, 432–33, 440, 442, 448

Hanh, Nguyen Huu, 482, 490, 491

Hanh, Tran Cong, 336–37, 391

Hanyok, Robert, 148

Hau Nghia province, Vietnam, 73–74, 242, 254, 255–56, 464, 477–78, 479

Hickey, Gerald, 517n7

Hien, Le Ngoc, 130, 400–401, 469, 470

Hiep, Dang Vu, 130, 133–34, 145, 216, 334

Hieu, Le Xuan, 452

Hieu, Nguyen Van, 353

Hieu, Vu Dinh, 517n10

"Highway of Death," 276

Hinh, Nguyen Duy, 6, 93, 96, 98, 268, 326, 327, 464, 476

Hoa, Le Quang, 368, 427

Hoa, Nguyen Dang, 525n18

Hoai Duc, Vietnam, 104, 240, 242, 249, 251–52

Hoa Khanh, Vietnam, 326

Hoang, Le Minh, 533n9

Hoc, Nguyen Thi, 453–55

Ho Chi Minh. See Minh, Ho Chi

Ho Chi Minh Campaign, 475–93; preparing for, 466–74

Ho Chi Minh Trail, 23, 30–31, 38, 45, 69, 129, 131, 136, 172, 362–63, 366, 374, 375, 471, 503n1

Hoc Mon, Vietnam, 487

Ho Diem, Vietnam, 387

Ho Nai, Vietnam, 464, 483, 484, 485, 499

Hong Ngu, Vietnam, 51

Horseshoe Hill, 442, 448, 454–55

Huan, Pham, 169, 177, 230, 340, 342, 350, 353, 513n24; fall of Saigon and, 495; *The Withdrawal from the Central Highlands*, 12, 517–18n12, 528–29n39

Huan, Phan Van, 108, 109–10, 488, 494–95

Hue, Vietnam, 81, 92–94, 96, 117, 126, 196, 218, 241, 300, 366, 433, 495; capture of, 60, 300, *301*, 302, 323, 471; collapse of, 313, 315–20; defense of, 263–98; isolation of, 269

Humphrey, Hubert, 224

Hung, Le Van, 43, 405, 496

Hung, Nguyen Ba Manh, 455

Hung, Pham, 217–18, 243, 260, 262, 401–02, 436; battle for Phuoc Long and, 100–04; dry-season plan and, 100–01; resumption of war and, 74, 75, 78; siege of Saigon and, 332, 400, 466; surrounding of Saigon and, 236–37, 359

Hung Loc, Vietnam, 445, 453, 455

Hung Nghia, Vietnam, 448, 455–56, 459

Huong, Tran Van, 136, 378, 460–61, 480–81

Huong Dien, Vietnam, 300, 303

Ia Drang, Vietnam, 46, 271

Independence Palace, 7, 118–19, 184, 467, 468, 490–93, 496, 534n18

India, 63

Indochina Resource Center, 58, 110

Indonesia, 63, 307, 308

Ingersoll, Robert, 221

intelligence: Monthly Intelligence Survey and Threat Analysis (MISTA), 380, 532n40; North Vietnamese, 200–01, 219,

282–83, 408–09, 509n14; signals intelligence, 116, 124, 131–32, 148, 150, 156, 170, 192, 207, 269, 327, 466; South Vietnamese, 104, 142–51, 236, 254–55, 265, 268–70, 277, 291, 404–05; South Vietnamese, breakdowns in, 99, 139, 147–48, 150, 265, 268, 277; U.S., 99, 124, 131, 188, 242–43, 249, 279, 309, 380–81, 387, 495, 497. *See also* espionage, North Vietnamese

International Commission of Control and Supervision, 308

Iron Triangle, 76, 78, 102–03, 244, 279

Isaacs, Arnold, 27, 350–51; *Without Honor*, 12

Israel, 56–57, 84, 471

Japan, 30, 63, 85, 111, 307

Javits, Jacob, 460

Joint General Staff (JGS), South Vietnam, 48–49, 55–56, 59, 116–18, 176, 179–80, 188, 207, 211, 214, 222, 342, 392, 447, 453, 505n1; assault on Danang and, 326, 327; battle for Ban Me Thuot and, 124–25, 136, 138; battle for Hue and, 269, 278–79, 289, 297, 305, 306; battle for Phuoc Long and, 101, 107; capture of Phan Rang and, 418, 420; collapse of, 481, 482, 491; conquest of II Corps and, 338; defense of Phan Thiet and, 430–31; fall of Hue and, 319; fall of Saigon and, 464, 467, 468, 490, 491; fall of the coast and, 352; "Great Spring Offensive" and, 143,

144, 150; headquarters of, 467, 468, 478, 487, 488, 491; morale of, 222, 431; Phan Rang and, 387; Qui Nhon and, 346; resumption of war and, 82–83; surrounding of Saigon and, 375; Thieu and, 117, 179, 322, 375; weakness of, 179, 322, 430–31, 498

Khai, Nguyen, 511n35

Khanh Duong, Vietnam, 196, 227–28, 335–36, 338, 342, 350, 352, 389

Khanh Hoa province, Vietnam, 153, 194, 217, 220, 227, 333, 339, 340, 348

Khe Sanh, Vietnam, 471

Khiem, Tran Thien, 50, 54, 57, 117, 120, 172, 176–77, 178, 307, 323, 376, 377, 378; defense of Hue and, 284–85; departure for Taiwan of, 480; resignation of, 379, 480

Khiem Cuong, Vietnam, 478

Khmer Rouge, 21, 50

Khoi, Tran Quang, 73–74, 77, 248, 336–37, 391, 402, 448, 453–56, 459; fall of Saigon and, 475, 483, 485, 490, 493–94, 495; rescue of Tay Ninh, 255–60

Khue, Pham Manh, 320

Khuyen, Dong Van, 57–58, 59, 60, 78, 81, 118, 179, 222–23, 345, 352, 481

Kiem, Do, 345, 348

Kiem Tan, Vietnam, 251, 438

Kien Duc, Vietnam, 226, 252

Kien Hoa province, Vietnam, 92

Kien Kien, Vietnam, 413–14, 419, 420, 421

Kien Thuong province, Vietnam, 397

Kissinger, Henry, 112, 221, 225, 460, 524n5; assistance to refugees and, 308, 324–25; on character of Hanoi's leadership, 123; correspondence with Martin, 505n1; cuts in U.S. aid to South Vietnam and, 79, 84, 110–12, 121–23, 174, 310–13, 325–26; *Ending the Vietnam War*, 12; Paris Peace Accords and, 18–24, 27, 29, 32–34, 43, 47–48, 63–64, 66

Kontum, Vietnam, 49, 87, 117–18, 124, 128–32, 136–38, 173–77, 180, 184, 186, 189, 197–98, 284, 287–88, 517n10; 1972 battle for, 163, 174, 479; "Great Spring Offensive" and, 142–43, 145, 151–53, 163; retreat from Central Highlands and, 205–09, 211, 213, 216, 231

Korean conflict, 61, 529n41

Ky, Nguyen Cao, 25, 376, 377, 378, 393–94, 531n33

labor camps, North Vietnam, 473

Lac, Hoang Van, 326

Lai Khe, Vietnam, 259, 476

Lam, Tran Van, 119, 174, 225, 378–79, 519n30

Lam Dong province, Vietnam, 239, 240, 248, 252, 253, 261–62, 438

Lam Son 719 incursion, 128, 136, 159, 271, 502n12

Lan, Bui The, 464

"Land to the Tiller" program, 55

Lang, Vu, 132, 133, 134, 334, 488

La Nga River, 248–49, 250, 261–62, 436

Laos, 14, 20, 21, 29, 34, 55, 57, 58, 66, 128, 130, 131, 159, 264, 266, 271, 364–65

Latin America, 63

Leandri, Paul, 224

Le Gro, William, 51, 76, 110, 131, 241, 242–43, 255, 264, 380–81, 482, 532n40; *Vietnam from Cease-Fire to Capitulation*, 12

Lehmann, Wolfgang, 79–80, 183–85, 206, 324; assistance to refugees and, 290, 307–08; meeting with Thieu, 220–22, 290–91

Lewis, James, 418, 424, 425–26

Loc, Mac Huu, 537–38n30

Loc, Nguyen Van, 429, 536n11

Loc, Vinh, 482, 490, 491

Local Route 22, 244, 255, 256

Local Route 25, 489

Local Route 239, 243

Local Route 429, 163, 164

Local Route 436, 180, 229, 230, 232

Local Route 450, 394

Loc Ninh, Vietnam, 72, 74, 252

Loi Ho ("Thunder Tigers"), 232, 488

Long, Vuong Mong, 253, 254, 493

Long An province, Vietnam, 239, 399, 402, 403, 406, 407, 410, 478

Long Binh, Vietnam, 410, 441, 468, 474, 475, 485, 490, 492

Long Giao, Vietnam, 457

Long Khanh province, Vietnam, 240, 242, 243, 248–49, 250, 436, 458

Long Thanh, Vietnam, 368, 475, 484, 489

Luat, Nguyen Trong, 1–2, 159, 161, 163, 165, 166–67

Lung, Ngoc, 138, 147

Luong, Le Quang, 96, 424–25, 533n10

Luong, Nguyen Thu, 395–96, 411, 412–14, 418–19, 420, 424–26

Luong, Nguyen Van, 352, 386

Luong Dien, Vietnam, 292, 294, 296, 303

Ly, Le Khac, 186, 188, 189, 204–06, 209, 211, 215–16, 234, 515–16n2, 516n3, 517–18n12, 517n10

Mai Hac De supply depot, 129, 155, 161, 163, 164, 336

Malaysia, 63

Man, Chu Huy, 333

Mang Giang Pass, 137, 152, 153

Mansfield, Mike, 113, 119

Mao Zedong, 29

Marine Division, 93, 97–98, 117, 265, 266, 268, 271, 275, 279, 281, 283–84, 525n18; collapse of I Corps and, 326; conquest of II Corps and, 338; defense of Hue and, 282, 283–84, 286–87, 288, 291, 295–96, 297, 302, 305, 306, 315–19; discipline of, 316–18, 464; evacuation of, 328; fall of Saigon and, 464, 483–85, 486, 488, 490, 494, 495; retreat from Quang Tri, 300; revenge for Danang, 484–85

Marshall Plan, 30

martial law, 332

Martin, Graham, 79, 174, 220, 241, 312, 325; becomes ambassador, 47–48; cuts in U.S. aid to South Vietnam and, 56–57, 84–85, 110–11, 113, 182–84, 459–60, 505n1; Le Gro's MISTA report and, 532n40;

LST ships and, 94–95, 524n5; surrounding of Saigon and, 380–81, 480

McAuliffe, Anthony, 491

McCloskey, Paul, 122

McCombs, Philip, 118–19

M'Drak Pass, 196, 227, 228, 334, 335–36, 350, 384, 390–91

Mekong Delta, 41–42, 44, 49–51, 57, 92–93, 95, 104, 126, 173, 298, 359, 459, 461, 533n8; battle for Phuoc Long and, 100, 102; fall of Saigon and, 468, 476, 482, 494; resumption of war and, 74, 87; South Vietnamese resistance in, 394, 398–400, 404–05, 459; surrounding of Saigon and, 236, 239–40, 247, 254–55

Mekong River, 324, 394

Michelin rubber plantation, 243

Middle East, 84, 310

Military Regions/Fronts, 14, *16*; MR-4, 131; MR-5, 124; MR-6, 104, 239–40, 249, 388, 408, 416, 426–27, 428, 431; MR-7, 75, 240, 261; MR-8, 75, 104, 239, 254, 399, 406; MR-9, 42, 43, 44, 104, 239, 406. *See also* B-1 Front; B-2 Front; B-3 Front; B-4 Front; B-5 Front

Military Sealift Command (MSC), 324, 354–55

Minh, Duong Van (Big Minh), 32, 57, 461, 480–81, 482, 485; Cabinet of, 490, 493; fall of Saigon and, 490–91, 492, 493–94; surrender of, 490–92, 493, 494, 496

Minh, Hoang Co, 340, 344–46, 350, 419, 430, 527n21

Minh, Ho Chi, 21, 37, 39, 206, 358, 449; death of, 37

Minh, Nguyen Van, 52, 125, 393

Minh, Tran Van, 379

Ministry of Public Security, North Vietnam, 472, 495

Ministry of the Interior, North Vietnam, 472–73, 495

MISTA. See Monthly Intelligence Survey and Threat Analysis

Moc Hoa, Vietnam, 397, 399–400, 402

Mom Kum Sac hills, 276, 282, 291–92, 294, 296

Montagnards, 52, 101, 129, 163, 165, 173, 177, 186, 204, 210, 211, 224, 517n7, 517n8

Monthly Intelligence Survey and Threat Analysis (MISTA), 380, 532n40

Mo Tau Hills. See Bong Mountain/ Mo Tau Hill complex

Murray, John E., 55–57, 59–62, 75, 78, 81–82, 85, 89, 94, 116, 124–25, 132, 222, 266, 300, 306, 505n1

My Chanh River, 266, 288, 291, 295, 300, 302

My Thach, Vietnam, 516–17n6

My Tho, Vietnam, 92, 254, 466

Nam, Nguyen Khoa, 255, 405, 482, 496

napalm, 232

National Council of National Reconciliation and Concord (NCNRC), 18, 19, 32, 66–67

National Liberation Front (NLF), 13, 14–15, 29, 32

National Police Headquarters, South Vietnam, 224, 467, 468

New Bridge, 483, 493–94

Newport Bridge, 475, 492

Nghi, Le Thanh, 64–65, 116

Nghi, Nguyen Vinh, 43, 50–51, 66, 390, 394–96, 408, 412–13, 430, 533n10; capture of Phan Rang and, 417–18, 420, 423–26; siege of Saigon and, 409–11

Nghia, Ngo Tan, 431, 432

Nguy, Dam Van, 133, 134–35

Nguyen Thai Hoc, Vietnam, 453, 454, 455

Nha, Hoang Duc, 25

Nha Be, Vietnam, 394

Nha Trang, Vietnam, 14, 124, 129, 169, 173, 175, 177, 186, 285, 426, 471, 532n1, 535n6; battle for Ban Me Thuot and, 189, 193–96; battle for coastal cities and, 332–33, 339–40; fall of, 349–56, 384, 386, 389; "Great Spring Offensive" and, 147, 167; refugees in, 340; retreat from Central Highlands and, 201, 204–06, 209, 214–15, 220, 227–28, 231, 233; South Vietnamese resistance and, 408–09, 418; surrounding of Saigon and, 358, 368–71

Nhon, Pham Huu, 148, 150

Nhon Trach, Vietnam, 489

Nhu, Ngo Dinh, 25

Nhut, Tran Van, 93, 95, 277, 392–93, 432; capture of Hue and, 304, 305, 306; capture of Phan Rang and, 418, 423–26; fall of Hue and, 319–20; siege of Saigon and, 410

Niem, Phan Dinh, 6, 151, 159, 227, 338, 341, 342, 345–46, 511n32

Ninh, Le Quang, 479

Ninh Chu, Vietnam, 389, 417, 422

Ninh Hoa, Vietnam, 335, 349, 354, 384, 389, 408

Ninh Thuan province, Vietnam, 353, 369, 387, 388, 389, 390, 408, 409, 418–19

Nixon, Richard M., 33, 38, 47–48, 67, 312–13; meeting with Thieu, 24, 30–32; pardon of, 81; Paris Peace Accords and, 18–24; promises of aid and military assistance to South Vietnam, 24, 30–31, 61, 119, 172, 460; resignation of, 78–79, 80, 89

Nixon administration, 11, 22, 27, 31, 56, 58, 60

NLF. *See* National Liberation Front

non-aligned countries, 63

Nong Trai, Vietnam, 192, 193, 194–95

Northrup, 62

North Vietnam. *See* Democratic Republic of Vietnam

North Vietnamese Air Force, 366; capture of Phan Rang and, 416–17; fall of Saigon and, 470, 481–82; history of, 470

North Vietnamese Army (NVA), 13

North Vietnamese military, decision-making of, 7–8, 10–11, 41, 42–46, 67–70, 72, 87–88, 100–04, 106, 123–30, 196–201, 216–20, 236–40, 243, 260, 283–84, 295, 298, 313–14, 332–35, 353, 358–61, 364, 396–99, 400–02, 449–51, 466–70, 473–74, 506n15; emboldening of by U.S. aid

cuts, 7–8, 87, 89, 497; maintenance costs of, 309, 497–98. *See also specific branches, corps, divisions, forces, and officers*

North Vietnamese Navy, 365–66, 370

NSA. *See* U.S. National Security Agency

NSC. *See* U.S. National Security Council

Nunn, Sam, 309

Nuoc Trong, Vietnam, 468, 474, 484, 493

oil and gasoline pipeline (PAVN), 30, 69, 362

OPEC oil embargo, 54, 81, 144–45

Paris Peace Accords, 2–3, 10, 72, 79, 83, 89, 102, 110, 112, 221, 225, 271, 460; collapse of, 35–52; the first test, 22; monitoring compliance with, 308; second anniversary of, 118–20; signing of, 17–34; six-point plan and, 66–67; terms of, 56, 60–61, 66, 94, 222–23, 264, 308; violations of, 6, 8–9, 18, 23–24, 31–32, 40, 58, 64, 172, 223, 266, 374, 498, 503n1. *See also* ceasefire

Parrot's Beak, 74

Pearson, James B., 62, 121, 122, 182, 183, 313

Pentagon. *See* U.S. Department of Defense

People's Anti-Corruption Movement, 376

People's Army of Vietnam (PAVN), 6–7, 13–14, 21, 51, 68–69, 72, 85, 117, 124, 135, 175, 234, 241;

acceleration of war by, 196–202; ammunition of, 78, 86, 88, 97, 99, 100, 102–03, 361, 472, 533–34n14; casualties of, 74, 77, 95–97, 102–04, 158, 1612, 164–65, 190, 195, 199, 213, 254, 269, 276, 280, 294–95, 341, 347, 359, 427, 444–48, 450, 458, 475, 476, 479–80, 496; casualties, accuracy of reporting of, 519n36, 538n30; casualties, attempt to avoid, 466; deception campaigns by, 148, 150–51, 152; defections from, 139, 142, 249, 291, 505n12; defections to, 470, 481, 534n18; "Great Spring Offensive," logistical preparations for, 23, 30–31, 38, 45, 69, 129, 131–32, 136, 172, 273–74, 360–63, 366, 503n1; morale of, 160, 218, 375, 446, 450–51, 505n12; resumption of war and, 72–89; sapper units, 207, 327, 467, 468–69, 471, 473, 483–84, 485–86, 490, 492; self-reliance (*tu tuc*) and, 360; thirtieth anniversary of founding of, 116; weaknesses of, 88, 191, 218, 254–55, 375. *See also specific branches, corps, divisions, forces, and officers*

People's Liberation Armed Forces (PLAF), 13, 14–15

Perfume River, 94, 300

Phan Boi Chau, Vietnam, *439*, 442, 448, 452

Phan Rang, Vietnam, 24, 253, 354, 356, 368–70, 373–74, 379, 381, 408, 460, 482; battle for, 384–95, *385*, 408–14, 470, 532n2, 532–33n5, 533n9, 533n10; fall of, 415–33, 487, 535n6

Phan Rang airbase, 186, 227, 342, 352, 353, 371, 386

Phan Thiet, Vietnam, 254, 353, 368, 388–90, 392, 408, 410, 428, 430, 430–32, 460, 528–29n39, 533n9

Phat, Le Van, 335–38, 349, 384, 386, 387–88, 390–91

Philippines, 307, 308, 324–25

Phoc Toy province, Vietnam, 458

Phong, Tan, 456

Phu, Nghiem Van, 394

Phu, Pham Van, 176–79, 184, 186, 188, 191–96, 384, 511n35, 513n24, 515–16n2, 516n3, 517–18n12, 528–29n39; acceleration of war and, 196–202; ARVN retreat and, 214–16, 227–28; background of, 135–36; battle for Ban Me Thuot and, 156, 159–60, 165–66, 168–70, 176, 189, 191–93, 200; Central Highlands Campaign and, 135–39, 177, 184, 194, 196–99: coastal cities and, 332, 339–40; conquest of II Corps and, 337–40; declares martial law in II Corps, 332; defense of Hue and, 285, 287; failure at Cung Son and, 233–34; fall of the coast and, 350, 351, 352–53; fall of Tuy Hoa and, 348; meeting with Thieu, 176–82; at Qui Nhon, 342–43, 344–45; retreat from Central Highlands and, 186–88, 202, 204–11, 220, 232; retreat to the sea and, 340; scapegoating of, 222; suicide attempt of, 353; suicide of, 496; surrounding of Saigon and, 241, 252–53

Phu An, Vietnam, 343

Phu Bai, Vietnam, 303–04

Phu Bai airbase, 94, 98, 271, 283, 296, 366

Phu Bon province, Vietnam, 130, 146–47, 179, 197, 200, 205

Phu Cat airbase, 227, 343–44, 470, 481–82, 532n1

Phu Loc, Vietnam, 291, 292, 296, 300, 303, 305

Phu Loi airbase, 476–77

Phung Duc airfield, 155, 161–62, 165, 167, 169, 190

Phuoc An, Vietnam, 170, 192, 194, 195, 200, 204, 389

Phuoc Binh, Vietnam, 106–07, 108

Phuoc Binh airfield, 106–07

Phuoc Long province, Vietnam, 126–28, 150, 169, 196, 236, 249, 256, 360, 366, 534n18; battle for, 100–110, 105, 136; fall of, 118, 119, 236, 237, 240–41, 489; Ford's response to loss of, 110–14; revenge for, 489

Phuoc Tuy province, Vietnam, 428, 456–57, 459, 464, 475–76

Phuong, Tran Van, 224–25

Phu Quoc Island, 529n41

Phu Tuc, Vietnam, 180, 204, 205, 207–10, 229, 230, 231

Phu Yen province, Vietnam, 179–80, 216, 217, 220, 229, 233–34, 333, 340, 342, 348–49

Plain of Jars, 271

Plain of Reeds, 239, 397

Pleiku, Vietnam, 4, 87, 118, 129–30, 132, 137–39, 173–80, 186–89, 196–201, 233, 282, 284, 287–88, 341, 488, 532n1; ARVN retreat and, 204–13, 216, 221, 227, 231, 515–

16n2; beginning of "Great Spring Offensive" and, 142–56, 165–69

Pleiku airfield, 155, 200, 201, 206–07, 209, 213

Polgar, Thomas, 148, 178, 206, 380, 512n7

Politburo, 5, 8–11, 13–14, 64–70, 99, 116, 123–24, 143, 145, 166, 284, 310, 449, 474; acceleration of war and, 196–200; ARVN retreat and, 216, 217–18, 219, 220; battle for Ban Me Thuot and, 126–28, 130, 136; battle for Hue and, 295, 298, 313–14; battle for Phuoc Long and, 100, 102, 106; collapse of Paris Peace Accords and, 8–9, 18, 36–46; emboldening of by U.S. aid cuts, 7–8, 87, 89, 497; fall of Saigon and, 466, 470, 473–74, 479; fall of the coast and, 353; Nixon and, 79; Paris Peace Accords and, 18–22, 36–37, 39, 42, 64; resumption of war and, 72, 74, 86–88; siege of Saigon and, 332–35, 396–97, 398, 400, 401–02; surrounding of Saigon and, 228, 236–37, 260, 358–61, 364, 367, 376, 380

Popular Forces (PF), 49–50, 98, 107, 153, 159, 186, 189, 205, 211, 227, 228, 242, 244, 246; defense of Hue and, 295; defense of Phan Thiet and, 430–31; fall of Hue and, 316, 319; fall of Phan Thiet and, 432; fall of Saigon and, 464, 466, 483–84; at Hung Nghia, 445; at Qui Nhon, 342; siege of Saigon and, 406

press: American, 31, 113, 118, 452; fall of Saigon and, 472–73; freedom

of, 27, 67; French, 224, 471; South
Vietnamese, 211–12, 231, 339, 376,
513n24, 517n11; visit to Xuan Loc
of, 452; Western, 27, 452, 455, 495
prisoners of war, 24, 28, 47, 99, 135,
137, 138, 146, 151, 190, 196, 440,
452, 473, 495
Provisional Revolutionary
Government (PRG), 13, 14–15,
32, 46, 89, 102, 324, 378–79, 481,
490–91

Quang, Dang Van, 172, 206
Quang, Doan Van, 516n3
Quang, Vu The, 154, 159, 165, 167,
176–77, 178
Quang Duc province, Vietnam, 52,
87, 100, 124, 130, 136, 138–39,
142–43, 145, 155–56, 159, 165, 169,
200, 226, 249, 252–54, 362, 397–98,
431, 493
Quang Nam province, Vietnam, 92–
93, 98–99, 124, 264, 268–69, 271,
281, 291, 304, 323, 369
Quang Ngai City, Vietnam, 281–82,
286, 304–05
Quang Ngai province, Vietnam, 72,
92, 93, 226, 264, 268–69, 271, 276–
77, 279, 281–82, 304–06, 319–20
Quang Tin province, Vietnam, 92,
93, 95, 264, 268, 269, 270, 277, 282,
304, 306, 320, 369
Quang Trang, Vietnam, 487
Quang Tri City, Vietnam, 264, 276,
288, 375
Quang Tri province, Vietnam, 14,
39, 92–94, 98, 117, 128, 130–31,

155, 174, 181, 212, 264, 266, 269,
271–78, 281–84, 287–88, 300, 302,
316–17, 360, 432–33, 533n10
Quang Trung Training Center, 136,
487
Qui Nhon, Vietnam, 152, 228, 320,
338, 340, 341–47, 358, 370

Rach Bap, Vietnam, 76, 102
radio messages, 138–39, 146, 148,
150, 158, 214–15, 408, 419
rainy season, 72–89, 270
Ranger Groups, 50–51, 94–96,
108–09, 117, 136, 176–77, 179,
189, 192, 194, 389, 453; battle for
coastal cities and, 332, 339–40;
battle for Phuoc Long and, 98,
104; beginning of "Great Spring
Offensive" and, 142, 146, 153, 156,
159–60, 166–70; at Ca Pass, 339;
capture of Phan Rang and, 417,
419, 422, 424, 425–26, 427; at Cung
Son, 234; defense of Hue and, 265,
268, 274, 277–78, 280–81, 282, 287–
88, 291, 294, 295–96, 297, 303, 304,
305, 306; defense of Phan Thiet
and, 430–32; desertions, 332, 495–
96; evacuation from Chon Thanh,
258–60; fall of Hue and, 315, 316,
319; fall of Phan Thiet and, 432–33;
fall of Saigon and, 464, 466, 488,
493, 494, 495; fall of Tuy Hoa and,
348–49; morale of, 517n7; at Phan
Rang, 411, 412–13; resumption of
war and, 73–74, 76; retreat from
Central Highlands and, 205, 207–
10, 212–13, 215–16, 226, 229–30,

232–34, 516n3, 517n8; retreat from
Quang Tri and, 300; siege of Saigon
and, 410–11; supplies of, 292;
surrounding of Saigon and, 247–48,
252–54, 256–59
Ranger Training Center, Duc My,
336, 337, 339–40, 349
Red Berets, 96–97, 99, 118, 227, 278,
280, 396. *See also* Airborne Division
refugees, 29, 30, 194, 211–12, 215,
223, 231–32, 275, 276, 281, 284,
295, 314, 408, 499; ARVN retreat
and, 206–07, 209–11, 214–16, 226,
229–34, 252, 281; assistance to,
323–25, 326, 388; in Cam Ranh,
529n41, 529n42; Catholic, 483, 485;
in Danang, 289, 290, 305, 306, 308,
316, 324–25, 326, 329; evacuation
from Cam Ranh, 354–55; fall of
Saigon and, 488; fall of the coast
and, 351–52, 354–55; foreign
assistance to, 306–09, 324–25, 354–
55, 386–87, 388, 476; from Hue,
284–86, 302, 306–13, 315, 316–17,
318, 320; from II Corps, 440–41,
456; in Nha Trang, 340; from
Nha Trang, 384; at Phan Rang,
387–88; from Phan Rang, 424–25;
relocation of after 1972, 49, 252;
from Vung Tau, 476
Regional Forces (RF), 43, 49–51,
94–95, 98, 118, 175, 178, 186, 189,
191–94, 196, 457; abandonment
of Du Long by, 388–89; assault on
Danang and, 327; battle for Phan
Rang and, 428; battle for Phuoc
Long and, 104, 106–07; battle for

Xuan Loc and, 440, 446; beginning
of "Great Spring Offensive" and,
142, 147, 151, 153–54, 156, 158–61,
163; capture of Hue and, 302–06;
capture of Phan Rang and, 422;
collapse of at Dalat, 253–54;
conquest of II Corps and, 338;
defense of Hue and, 266, 271,
274–75, 277–88, 282, 284, 295, 316,
319, 320; defense of Phan Thiet
and, 430–32; desertion of Phu Cat
airbase by, 343; desertions, 384,
393; fall of Phan Thiet and, 432; fall
of Saigon and, 464, 475, 477–78,
479, 486, 487, 489; fall of the coast
and, 350; fall of Tuy Hoa and, 348;
integration into ARVN regiments,
393; morale of, 227, 284, 302;
outpost on Chua Chan Mountain,
438; at Phan Rang, 388, 412; at Qui
Nhon, 342, 345; resistance at Ben
Cau, 246–47, 248; resistance at La
Nga Bridge, 251; resistance at Tri
Tam, 244, 246, 248; resistance at Vo
Dac, 252; resumption of war and,
73–74, 77; retreat from Central
Highlands and, 204–05, 210–11,
215, 226–29, 233–34; retreat from
Quang Tri and, 300; siege of Saigon
and, 399, 402–04, 405, 406, 410,
411; South Vietnamese resistance
and, 387, 389, 393; surrounding of
Saigon and, 238, 242–43, 249–50,
253, 258, 260
Re Island, 319, 392
Republic of Vietnam, constitution
of, 461

Republic of Vietnam Armed Forces (RVNAF), 1, 104, 118, 172, 255, 275, 279, 281, 284, 443; casualties of, 48, 63, 74, 77, 95, 97, 99, 108–09, 158–59, 162, 195, 234, 250, 288, 294, 305, 337, 407, 427, 445, 453, 455, 458, 475, 493; civilian casualties, attempts to avoid, 166, 394; cuts in U.S. aid and, 6–8, 52–70, 74, 77–80, 81–83, 87, 89, 111, 117, 119, 124, 144–45, 147–48, 174, 182, 223–24, 242, 265–66, 278, 323, 325, 329, 359–60, 497; at Danang, 326–29; defense of Phan Thiet, 430; desertions, 326, 332, 473, 495–96; fall of Saigon and, 466, 467, 488, 493, 497; firepower of, 268, 269, 498; low pay and, 54–55, 111, 268; maintenance costs of, 309, 497–98; mobility of, 143, 178, 192–93, 236, 242, 265–66; morale of, 6, 99, 111, 190, 197, 222–23, 227, 228, 268, 277, 278, 284, 288, 302, 304–06, 322, 324, 326, 329, 332, 334, 339, 340, 377, 387, 393, 397, 418, 423, 427, 430, 447, 452, 467, 470, 479, 497–98, 517n8; officers, fate of, 495–96; portrayal of, 3–5, 495–96; publications of, 11; retreat from Quang Tri and, 300

Riverine Task Forces, 394, 533n8

Rockefeller, Nelson, 225

Route 1, 93–95, 98, 152, 179, 181, 495; battle for coastal cities and, 335, 339, 342, 344, 347, 351, 354, 356; battle for Xuan Loc and, 436, 438, 440, 442, 444–45, 448, 452, 455, 456; capture of Phan Rang and, 416–17, 419–24, 428–33; collapse of I Corps and, 300, 303–04, 306, 317, 326–29; defense of Hue and, 265, 266, 269, 271, 275, 281–84, 286, 288, 290–98; Ho Chi Minh Campaign and, 464, 472, 474, 478–79, 485–87, 489; retreat from Central Highlands and, 212, 219, 226, 227; South Vietnamese resistance and, 384, 387, 389, 390, 392, 394–96, 408–12, 414; surrounding of Saigon and, 240, 244, 251, 255–56, 262, 360, 3 68–70

Route 2, 249, 438, 456, 458, 464

Route 4, 100, 218, 254–55, 359, 399, 401–02, 403, 406–07, 430, 466, 473, 478

Route 7, 76, 77, 220, 333

Route 7B, 179–81, 186, 188–89, 201–02, 207–10, 213, 227–29, 232, 234, 252–53, 332, 334, 339, 371

Route 8, 487

Route 9, 366

Route 10, 400, 477–78

Route 11, 253, 384, 388, 396, 410, 419, 423–25

Route 13, 257, 258, 464, 476–77, 494

Route 14, 87, 100–01, 117, 126, 129, 132, 136, 138, 142, 145, 147, 154–56, 160, 163–64, 169, 179, 189, 197, 201, 208, 210, 212–13, 216, 364, 366, 369, 371

Route 15, 249, 464, 468, 475, 476, 478, 485, 487, 489, 492

Route 16, 477

Route 19, 129, 132, 136–39, 146, 151–54, 156, 158, 178, 181, 189, 198–99, 204, 207, 212, 216–18, 220, 226–27, 341–43, 346

Route 20, 240, 248–51, 253, 261–62, 335, 436, 440, 442, 448, 450, 453–54, 521n30, 533–34n14

Route 21, 129, 132, 136, 138, 153–54, 168, 169, 175, 179, 184, 186, 189, 191–96, 200, 204, 220, 227–29, 333, 336–39, 342, 354

Route 22, 366, 478, 479

Route 25, 475

Route 429, 161

Route 450, 372

Rung La, Vietnam, 432–33

Russia. *See* Soviet Union

Sach, Pham Nam, 531n33

Sa Huynh, Vietnam, 151

Saigon, Vietnam, 7, 87, 100–01, 104, 110, 117–18, 168, 173, 175, 197, 198; battle for coastal cities and, 338, 340, 345, 347, 353; battle for Xuan Loc and, 436, 438, 442, 455, 460; bridges leading to, 468–69, 483–84; capture of Phan Rang and, 428, 430, 433; collapse of I Corps and, 305, 307, 310, 323; defense of Hue and, 264, 278–79, 286, 290, 298; fall of, 463–99, *465*; political scene of, 461; retreat from Central Highlands and, 200–01, 216–19, 227, 228; siege of, 235–62, 313–14, 332–33, 396–402, 432–33, 447, 449, 459; South Vietnamese resistance and, 384, 386, 392; surrounding of, 235–62, 357–81

Saigon–Bien Hoa highway, 475, 494

Saigon Post, 517n11

Saigon River, 76, 243, 464, 475, 479, 483, 489

San, Phan Dinh, 429

Sang, Pham Ngoc, 186, 206–07, 384, 386, 390, 394, 410–11, 431, 532n2, 533n10; at Phan Rang, 387–88, 420, 423, 424–26; release from prison, 426; rescue of Airborne Division from M'Drak Pass, 391–92

Sang Bridge, 485, 486, 487

Saudi Arabia, 63

Schlesinger, James R., 82, 324–25

Schwarz, George W., 529n41, 529n42

Scowcroft, Brent, 56–57, 220

seacraft: *American Challenger*, 324, 355; cargo ships, 94–95, 101; *Chi Linh* (HQ-11), 429–30; *Chitose Maru*, 355; *Greenville Victory*, 354–55, 529n41; Landing Craft, Mechanized (LCM), 346, 432; Landing Ships Medium (LSM), 320; Landing Ships, Tank (LST), 94–95, 222–23, 300, 306–09, 315–20, 324–25, 338, 392, 394, 429, 524n5, 529n41; LSM *Han Giang* (HQ-401), 351–52; LSM *Huong Giang* (HQ-404), 320, 328; LSM *Lam Giang* (HQ-402), 328; LSM *Ninh Giang* (HQ-403), 346; LST *Boo Heung Pioneer* (LST-117), 529n41; LST *Can Tho* (HQ-801), 316–17; LST *Danang* (HQ-501), 315, 392; LST *My Tho* (HQ-800), 394; LST *Nha Trang* (HQ-505), 319, 320; LST *Vinh Long* (HQ-802), 319–20; LST *Vung Tau* (HQ-503), 429; *Ngo Quyen* (HQ-17), 429;

Pioneer Commander, 354; *Pioneer Contender,* 324, 354; *Sgt. Andrew Miller,* 324, 354; *Tran Binh Trong* (HQ-05), 418–19; *Tran Nhat Duat* (HQ-03), 340, 418–19; U.S.S. *Durham,* 388; U.S.S. *Enterprise,* 112; Zippos, 407

Serong, Ted, 120

Shackley, Ted, 502n12

signals intelligence (SIGINT), 116, 131, 148, 150, 170, 192, 207, 269, 327, 466

Smith, Homer D., Jr., 82, 83, 222–23, 225, 324, 347, 482

Snepp, Frank, 124, 131, 148, 279, 380, 458, 466; *Decent Interval,* 12

Son, Tran Van, 424

South Korea, 58–59, 61, 307–08, 325

South Vietnam, 14, 64, 436–38, 445, 457–59; cuts in U.S. aid to, 6–8, 18–19, 30, 49, 53–66, 77–82, 87–88, 96, 111–14, 119–23, 144–45, 147–48, 150, 172, 174, 175, 182–85, 265, 306, 309–13, 323–24, 354–55, 381, 396, 459–61, 497, 499, 505n1, 514n2, 533n8; economy of, 6, 8, 29–30, 34, 48–51, 54–55, 60–61, 64–65, 87, 89, 117, 144–45, 182–85, 220, 324, 460; geography of, 7, 51, 69, 73, 87, 94, 101, 124, 147, 264, 266, 335, 389, 429, 440; morale of, 73, 89, 111, 220, 288–89, 497; street protests in, 8; surrender of, 2, 490, 491, 494, 496, 497, 516n3, 536n11; U.S. congressional delegation to, 113, 119, 121–22, 172, 174, 309. *See also* Government of Vietnam (GVN)

South Vietnamese military. *See* Republic of Vietnam Armed Forces (RVNAF); *see also* Airborne Division; Army of the Republic of Vietnam (ARVN); Marine Division; Popular Forces (PF); Ranger Groups; Regional Forces (RF); Vietnamese Air Force (VNAF); Vietnamese Navy (VNN), *and specific corps, divisions, and officers*

South Vietnam Liberation Army (SVNLA), 13, 14

Soviet Union, 6, 34, 46, 69, 80, 102, 328; aid to North Vietnam, 31, 51, 64, 83, 225, 309–11, 325–26, 472, 497–98; "attack from the march" tactic, 327, 416; training by, 46, 270, 367

Spear, Moncrieff, 175, 206, 351, 515–16n2

Sprague, Edmund W., 517n7

Srepok River, 156, 160, 163, 164

Stennis, John, 61, 113

Sung, Dang Van, 376

Sun Tzu, 238

Suoi Cat, Vietnam, 438

Tai, Pham Chau, 488, 491

Taiwan, 54, 307–08, 325, 480

Tam, Nguyen Xuan, 25–26

Tam Giang Lagoon, 300

Tam Ky, Vietnam, 95, 271, 277, 304–05, 313, 524n4

Tan, Le Trong, 70, 85, 87–88, 128, 217, 219, 272–73, 300, 416, 427–28; capture of Phan Rang and, 427; collapse of I Corps and, 314; collapse of Hue and, 313;

fall of Saigon and, 474, 483, 484, 485; siege of Saigon and, 408–09; surrounding of Saigon and, 367, 368, 369–70, 372

Tan An, Vietnam, 399, 402–03, 406

Tanh, Lam Nguon, 393

Tanh, Le Trung, 511n1

Tanh Linh, Vietnam, 104, 240, 242

Tan My, Vietnam, 94, 305, 316

Tan My port, 300, 305, 306, 316, 317

Tan Phong, Vietnam, 438, 440–41, 448, 452, 457, 458

Tan Son Nhut airbase, 386, 425, 458, 464, 466, 467, 468, 475, 478, 481–82, 486, 487–88, 489–90, 491, 499, 537–38n30

Tan Son Nhut VNAF Officers' Club, 376

Tan Thanh, Vietnam, 389

Tan Tru, Vietnam, 406–07

Tan Uyen, Vietnam, 477

Tat, Pham Duy, 142, 180, 186, 188, 205, 207, 212, 214–15, 342, 350, 516n3, 517n8, 517n10, 517–18n12

Tay Nguyen, 124, 199

Tay Ninh City, Vietnam, 102, 104, 236, 240, 242, 243–44, 247–48, 479

Tay Ninh province, Vietnam, 100–02, 104, 108, 117, 173, 236–37, 239, 240, 243–44, 247–49, 255–60, 258–59, 334, 371, 372, 418, 430, 440, 448, 450, 464, 479, 495

Te, Pham, 531n32

Tet holiday, 119, 120, 139, 144

Tet Offensive (1968), 46, 92, 93, 99, 103, 128, 129, 239, 242, 285, 323, 441, 468, 469, 482, 483

Thach Han River, 264, 266, 274, 282, 283, 287–88

Thai, Hoang Van, 41, 42, 68–69, 70, 85–88, 99, 103, 124–25, 143, 196, 200–01, 217; *The Decisive Years*, 12; fall of Saigon and, 472

Thailand, 32, 47, 482

Tham, Bui Ngoc, 512n6

Thang, Dang Cao, 394

Thang, Ton Duc, 466

Thanh, Dang Phuong, 403

Thanh, Nguyen Chi, 127

Thanh, Tran Huu, 376, 377–78

Thanh An, Vietnam, 146, 153, 159, 189, 213

Thanh Son airbase, 384, 386, 387–88, 389, 390–92, 395–96, 409, 410, 412, 417–26, 482, 532n1, 535n6

Thanh Tuy Ha, Vietnam, 489–90

Thao, Hoang Minh, 128–29, 132–33, 139, 145, 147, 156, 160–61, 163, 166–70, 189, 191, 193–95, 232, 370, 373, 419; capture of Phan Rang and, 421; *Fighting in the Central Highlands*, 501n4, 513n27; *The Victorious Tay Nguyen Campaign*, 501n4, 513n27

Thao, Le Van, 227, 371, 394–95, 419, 425, 532n1, 533n9; daring night raid by, 343–44

Thi, Lam Quang, 93, 98, 265–66, 268, 274–76, 281, 283, 287, 295–97, 302, 305–06, 315, 317–18, 528–29n39

Thieme, Earl, 206, 515–16n2

Thien, Dinh Duc, 130, 300

Thien, Le Anh, 437

Thien Giao, Vietnam, 408

Thieu, Nguyen, 226, 227, 342–43, 346, 347

Thieu, Nguyen Van, 3, 6, 92, 99, 102, 111, 224, 264, 390, 460, 496, 505n1, 511n35, 522n12, 522n13; astrology and, 26, 502n12; beginning of "Great Spring Offensive" and, 142, 144, 148, 168, 170; Cabinet of, 54, 107–08, 178, 285, 377, 379; calls for resignation of, 377–79; capture of Hue and, 278–80, 284–89, 306, 307; collapse of I Corps and, 322; collapse of Paris Peace Accords and, 36, 40, 48–50; credibility of, 460; cuts in U.S. aid to South Vietnam and, 54–55, 57–67, 81–85, 111, 118–20, 174, 182–83, 223–24, 312, 325, 460; decision-making of, 172–76, 178, 182–86, 188, 192, 198–201, 219, 325–26, 379, 393–94, 514n2; decision to reinstall Cang, 393–94; decision to truncate the country, 4, 59, 172–74, 219, 284–85, 307, 379, 418, 532–33n5; decision to withdraw from northern I Corps, 173, 176, 278–79, 286, 325–26; "defend to the death" message of, 322–23, 332, 388, 431; defense of Phan Rang and, 532–33n5; defense of Qui Nhon and, 344; departure for Taiwan of, 480; "Eight-Year Reconstruction and Development Plan," 29–30; "eyes-only" message to commanders and province chiefs, 322; fall of the coast and, 353; Ford and, 81–82, 83–85, 119–20, 223, 225–26, 312;

Joint General Staff (JGS) and, 117, 179, 322, 375; loosening of grip on power, 375–79; meeting with Lehmann, 290–91; morale of, 183; new strategy of, 176–77; Nixon and, 24, 30–32, 61, 119, 172, 460; as obstacle to political solution, 311; opposition to, 26, 32, 87, 89, 185, 323, 375–79; "Order of the Day" radio broadcast, 323; Paris Peace Accords and, 18–19, 22–28, 30–34, 118–21; Phuoc Long and, 107–08, 110; plan to retake Ban Me Thuot and, 211; poor planning by, 176–82, 311, 498, 499, 533n10; preparing for the strategic blow, 116–17, 124–25, 136, 139; prevention of coup by Ky, 393–94; resignation of, 460, 480; resumption of war and, 74–75, 79, 87, 89; retreat from Central Highlands and, 176–82, 204, 205–06, 209, 211, 219, 220–26; speeches of, 60–61, 288–89, 323–24, 379; surrounding of Saigon and, 241–42, 256, 262, 375–79; threat of coup and, 280

Thi Mountain, 438, 442, 444, 457–58

Third Force, 32, 38, 39, 87, 184, 376, 480, 481

Thi Thinh River, 76

Tho, Hoang Dinh, 537–38n30

Tho, Lam Quang, 253–54

Tho, Le Duc, 5, 18–20, 32–34, 43, 63–64, 66, 103–04, 123, 127, 198, 218–19, 237, 311, 401–02, 450, 481; collapse of I Corps and, 314; fall of Saigon and, 466, 473–74; sent south to direct final attack, 332,

333; siege of Saigon and, 396, 400; surrounding of Saigon and, 359, 364, 368

Tho, Tran Dinh, 211, 338

Thoai, Ho Van Ky, 280, 315, 329, 344, 525n22

Thong, Nguyen Huu, 347

Thong, Vu Xuan, 108, 109

Thuan, Pham Quoc, 78, 350

Thuan An, Vietnam, 305, 316, 317

Thuan An Inlet, 94, 315

Thuan An Lagoon, 303

Thuan An port, 288, 295, 300, 316, 317

Thuan Man district, 132, 138, 145, 146, 154, 160

Thua Thien province, Vietnam, 14, 92, 93, 94, 96, 98, 128, 130, 241, 264, 265, 270–72, 275–76, 282–83, 286, 288, 290, 291, 295, 300, 302, 305–06

Thu Duc, Vietnam, 494

Thu Duc Officers' School, 492

Thuong, Le, 319

Thuong Duc, Vietnam, 95–96, 97, 99, 103, 268–69, 275, 277, 281, 291, 320, 326, 476

Thurmond, Strom, 113

Thu Thua, Vietnam, 399, 402, 403, 407

Tien Phuoc, Vietnam, 95, 268, 271, 276, 277, 278

Tieu, Trinh, 138, 142–43, 147, 150, 166

Tinh, Ngo Le, 184–85, 188, 204, 229–30

Toan, Nguyen Van, 136, 148, 159, 241–43, 247–48, 388, 393, 406, 413,

431, 440, 442, 447, 455–56, 478, 520n7, 537–38n30; capture of Phan Rang and, 418, 425–26; desertion of, 496; fall of Saigon and, 409–10, 464, 466, 475, 479, 482, 484–85, 496; rape accusation against, 241; reputation for corruption, 241, 520n7; support of Thieu, 379; Tay Ninh province and, 255–59

Tra, Tran Van, 42, 44–45, 197, 216–18, 436, 450–51, 468, 521n30, 533n13, 533–34n14; battle for Ban Me Thuot and, 126–30; battle for Phuoc Long and, 100–07; changes in grand design of, 449–59; collapse of Hue and, 313; dry-season plan, 100–01, 242–43, 244, 250, 254, 255, 260; fall of Saigon and, 469–70; *History of the Bulwark B-2 Theatre*, 12, 501n4; at Phan Thiet, 431–32; resumption of war and, 72–78; siege of Saigon and, 332–34, 396–402, 407; surrounding of Saigon and, 236–39, 241, 248, 252, 257–58, 261–62; Tay Ninh and, 255–56

Trang, La Qui, 413–14, 426

Trang Bang, Vietnam, 478, 479

Trang Bom, Vietnam, 464, 474, 475

Tran Mountain, 250

Tra Noc airfield, 406

Tri, Nguyen Thanh, 265, 281, 464, 485, 525n18; assault on Danang and, 328; capture of Hue and, 302, 303, 305, 315–16; defense of Hue and, 287–88; fall of Saigon and, 494, 495; retreat from Quang Tri and, 300, 302

Trinh, Nguyen Duy, 64, 116

Tri Tam, Vietnam, 240, 242–43, 244, 246, 248, 249, 250, 255, 256

Tri Tam District Military Headquarters, 246

Trung, Dinh Thanh, 534n18

Trung, Nguyen Thanh, 481, 534n18

Truoi River, 271, 273, 276, 282, 292, 297, 300, 327

Truong, Mach Van, 405–06

Truong, Ngo Quang, 57, 92–99, 117, 135, 176, 222, 266, 268–70, 274, 280, 295–96, 495, 522n12, 522n13, 525n18, 525n22; assault on Danang and, 327–28; assistance to refugees and, 326; attempted resignation of, 289; capture of Hue and, 302, 304, 305, 306, 315, 316, 319, 323, 496–97; conquest of II Corps and, 338; defense of Hue and, 277–80, 281–82, 284–87, 288–91, 297–98; Tet Offensive (1968) and, 285–86

Truong Mit, Vietnam, 256

Tu, Nguyen, 137–38, 211–12, 231, 376, 517n11

Tu, Nguyen Van, 411–12, 419, 425

Tu, Tran Dinh, 495

Tuan, Kim, 201, 210, 233, 348

Tu Hien, Vietnam, 315, 318–19, 320

Tu Hien Inlet, 302, 305, 306, 316–18

Tu Na Pass, 207, 209–10, 213–14, 215, 230

Tuong, Le Trung, 142, 159, 165, 168, 169, 170, 192–93, 194

Turkey, 59, 84

Tuyen Duc province, Vietnam, 224, 239, 240, 252, 253, 260

Tuy Hoa, Vietnam, 173, 179–80, 188, 201, 205, 222, 229, 231–34, 332–34,

339, 342, 347–49, 350, 358, 371, 516n3

U Minh Forest, 44, 405

United States, 2, 4, 30, 64, 241, 459, 460, 480, 481; aid to Cambodia, 112, 121, 182; aid to North Vietnam considered, 24, 66; aid to South Vietnam, 6, 7–8, 18–19, 30, 33, 49, 53–66, 77–83, 87–88, 96, 111–14, 119–23, 144–45, 147–48, 150, 172, 174, 175, 182–85, 225, 265, 306, 309–13, 323–24, 354–55, 381, 396, 459–61, 497, 499, 505n1, 514n2, 533n8; assistance to refugees, 290, 306–07, 308, 324, 354–55, 388, 476; departure of personnel during retreat from Central Highlands, 206; economy of, 8, 58–59, 81, 84, 85, 111, 113, 183, 121, 310; energy crisis in, 81, 121; fall of Saigon and, 481, 483, 485, 487; foreign-aid policies of, 58–59, 61, 84, 111–14, 182–85, 310, 499; intelligence cutbacks, 99, 132; lack of response to fall of Phuoc Long, 236; moral obligation to assist South Vietnam and Cambodia, 310, 313, 325, 499; Paris Peace Accords and, 18–34, 43, 47–48, 63–64, 66; reputation of, 310; surrounding of Saigon and, 359, 380–81; values of, 499; White House Congressional Liaison Office, 313. See also specific government branches, departments, and agencies

U.S. Air Force, 23, 33, 62, 175, 537n23

U.S. Army, 55, 60, 82

U.S. Central Intelligence Agency (CIA), 124, 131–32, 148, 177–78, 188, 206, 220, 279, 309, 329, 338, 380–81, 418, 424, 466, 515–16n2
U.S. Coast Guard, 430
U.S. Congress, 7–8, 11, 19, 21, 23, 31–33, 54–60, 81, 459–60; aid to Cambodia and, 309–10; aid to South Vietnam and, 58–63, 64, 67, 79–80, 83–84, 111–14, 119–23, 172, 174, 182–85, 224, 225–26, 309–13, 323–24, 325, 329, 497, 498, 499, 514n2; assistance to refugees and, 308–09, 324, 325; delegation to South Vietnam, 113, 119, 121–22, 172, 174, 309; FY74 budget, 59; FY76 Defense Appropriations Bill, 310; GVN delegation to, 224–25. *See also* U.S. House of Representatives; U.S. Senate
U.S. Consulate, 43, 350–51
U.S. Defense Attaché Office (DAO), 51, 55–56, 60–62, 82–83, 111, 118, 222, 248, 255, 380–81, 393, 404, 407, 482, 486, 524n5
U.S. Department of Defense, 56–59, 62, 63, 111, 148, 183–84, 306, 308–09; Defense Intelligence Agency (DIA), 220, 380
U.S. Embassy: in Cambodia, 325; in Indonesia, 308; in Lebanon, 426; in South Korea, 308; in South Vietnam, 28, 47, 60, 79, 82, 234, 290, 325, 424, 473, 488, 495; in Taiwan, 308
U.S. House of Representatives, 61, 80, 113, 121, 182, 225–26; House

Democratic Caucus, 182, 309; House Foreign Affairs Committee, 182
U.S. Marines, 485
U.S. media, 19, 31, 113, 118, 452
U.S. military, 33, 56–57, 69, 88, 172; aid to South Vietnam and, 175, 223–24, 226, 329, 375, 381, 396; assistance to refugees and, 324–25, 476; Easter Offensive (1972) and, 375; evacuation fleet, 476; failure to aid South Vietnam, 498; "Gavin Plan," 217, 238; men killed in Vietnam, 33, 310; men missing in action (MIAs) in Vietnam, 21–22, 66; operational methods of, 143, 193, 241, 497–98; Pacific Command, 62, 222; potential response to attacks, 18, 22–23, 31–33, 61, 88, 112, 125–26, 223, 226, 280, 312; prisoners of war, 47; surrounding of Saigon and, 359; troop levels in Vietnam, 467, 469; in Vietnam, 47, 79, 86, 280, 310, 469, 498–99; withdrawal from Vietnam, 24, 36, 39, 48, 49, 56, 79, 242. *See also specific branches*
U.S. National Security Agency, 148
U.S. National Security Council, 110–12, 116–17, 120, 124, 143, 144, 279, 322
U.S. Navy, 112, 175, 290, 481, 485; assistance to refugees, 388, 324–25; U.S.S. *Enterprise*, 112
U.S. Secret Service, 225
U.S. Senate, 61, 83–84, 182–83, 309–10, 313; Senate Armed Services

Committee, 55, 58, 61, 460; Senate Foreign Relations Committee, 182, 310, 460

USSR. *See* Soviet Union

U.S. State Department, 94–95, 111–12, 182, 184, 220, 290, 306, 480, 524n5; aid to South Vietnam and, 311; assistance to refugees and, 306–08; surrounding of Saigon and, 380

Vam Co Dong (Eastern Vam Co) River, 73, 74, 240, 243, 247, 400, 402, 406, 466, 468, 477

Vam Co Tay (Western Vam Co) River, 402, 406–07

Van, Nguyen Thanh, 517n10

Vien, Cao Van, 48, 57–60, 63, 107, 117, 120, 125–26, 136, 211, 224, 233, 388, 393, 446, 482, 509n14, 516n3, 537–38n30; battle for coastal cities and, 353; beginning of "Great Spring Offensive" and, 143–44, 147; capture of Hue and, 274, 279, 286–87, 289, 297, 307; capture of Phan Rang and, 418; fall of Saigon and, 481; *The Final Collapse*, 12; refusal to take part in 1963 coup, 57; resumption of war and, 78, 82–83; support of Thieu, 379; surrounding of Saigon and, 377; Thieu's decision-making and, 172, 174, 176–77, 179, 183–84, 188

Vientiane, Laos, 57

Viet Cong (VC), 13, 14, 27, 494. *See also* Communists

Viet Minh, 24

Vietnam Communist Party, 14

Vietnamese Air Force (VNAF), 50, 62, 94, 96–99, 146, 186, 193–94, 201, 227, 232, 268, 399, 406, 429, 448, 456, 532n1, 533n9, 537–38n30; abandonment of Thanh Son airbase, 387; airlift capability of, 143, 178, 193, 236, 498; battle for Phuoc Long and, 106, 108, 110; battle for Xuan Loc and, 452, 454, 458; beginning of "Great Spring Offensive" and, 148, 160, 164, 166; capture of Phan Rang and, 418–19; Daisy Cutters, 454, 537n23; defector from, 470, 481, 534n18; defense of Hue and, 280, 289; defense of Phan Thiet and, 430–31; desertions from, 482; fall of Saigon and, 466, 470, 477, 482, 489; French training of, 532n2; headquarters of, 384, 386; morale of, 482; at Phan Rang, 387–88; at Qui Nhon, 343–44; resumption of war and, 73, 74, 83; retreat from Central Highlands and, 206–07, 209, 215, 216, 226–32; retreat from Quang Tri and, 300; siege of Saigon and, 400, 409; surrounding of Saigon and, 236, 248, 250, 260; Tan Son Nhut VNAF Officers' Club, 376

Vietnamese National Army, 25, 93

Vietnamese Navy (VNN), 50, 83, 94, 268, 280, 286, 319–20, 329, 342, 393–94, 428–30; assault on Danang and, 328; defense of Phan Thiet, 430–31; fall of Hue and, 305, 315, 317–18; fall of Phan Thiet and, 432; fall of Saigon and, 488, 491; fall of the coast and, 351–52; fall of Tuy

Hoa and, 348; Navy Operations Center, 348; at Qui Nhon, 344–45; rescues by, *293, 301*, 305, 315, 316–20, *321*, 328–29, 340, 342, 344–46, 351–52, 360, 429, 432; retreat to the sea and, 340–41; riverine forces, 50, 83, 268, 394, 404, 407, 466, 533n8; withdrawal from Cam Ranh, 356

Vietnamese Red Cross, 276

Vietnamese Special Forces, 135, 232

Vietnamization, 5, 60, 122

Vinh, Nguyen Quang, 178, 528–29n39

Vinh City, Vietnam, 360, 365

Vinh Phong Mountain, 305, 315, 525n18

Vo Dac, Vietnam, 251–52

"Volunteer Army" forces, 14

Vu, Bui Cat, 250, 397, 438, 445, 521n30

Vung Tau, Vietnam, 359, 368, 392, 428, 432, 464, 468, 475–76, 481

Vy, Le Nguyen, 257

War Powers Resolution, 33, 325

"Warrior H3," 125

Washington Post, 118

Washington Special Actions Group (WSAG), 110–12, 307

Watergate scandal, 23, 33, 79, 80–81

Waxman, Henry, 311

weapons, 66; 37-mm anti-aircraft guns, 416; 85-mm guns, 246, 428, 489; 105-mm howitzers, 213, 250, 273, 346, 393; 120-mm mortars, 233; 122-mm rockets, 402, 430; 130-mm guns, 244, 259, 327, 400, 428, 430, 456, 464, 490; air-defense guns, 151; B-40 rockets, 346, 404, 413; B-41 rockets, 404; CBU-55 bombs, 458–59, 537–38n30; Daisy Cutters, 454, 537n23; howitzers, 336; M-72 anti-tank rockets, 108–09, 163; machine guns, 488; SA-2 missiles, 471; SA-7 missiles, 106, 193, 248, 394, 420, 471; ZSU-23s, 471. *See also* ammunition

Western White House, San Clemente, California, 24

Weyand, Frederick C., 225, 312, 325, 381, 459, 532–33n5

World Airways, 324, 326

World War II, 55, 61, 137, 315, 328, 447, 491, 512n7

Xuan Loc, Vietnam, 242, 248–49, 251–52, 254, 261, 347, 369, 392, 394–95, 397, 402, 410, 537–38n30; airfield, 442; battle for, 419–61, *439*, 470, 494, 533–34n14; Catholic church in, 443–44, 446; evacuation from, 457; fall of, 476, 493; journalists' visit to, 452; as killing ground, 451; resistance at, 469; retreat from, 458, 464; in South Vietnamese hands, 446

Yom Kippur War, 56–57, 471

Zhou Enlai, 503n1